Communications
in Computer and Information Science 7

Randy Adams   Steve Gibson
Stefan Müller Arisona (Eds.)

# Transdisciplinary Digital Art

## Sound, Vision and the New Screen

Digital Art Weeks and Interactive Futures 2006/2007
Zurich, Switzerland and Victoria, BC, Canada
Selected Papers

Springer

Volume Editors

Randy Adams
Nanaimo, Canada
E-mail: runran@island.net

Steve Gibson
University of Victoria, Canada
E-mail: sgibson@finearts.uvic.ca

Stefan Müller Arisona
University of California, Santa Barbara, USA
E-mail: sma@corebounce.org

Library of Congress Control Number: 2008925340

CR Subject Classification (1998): I.3.7, J.5, I.3.3, H.1.2

ISSN 1865-0929
ISBN-10 3-540-79485-9 Springer Berlin Heidelberg New York
ISBN-13 978-3-540-79485-1 Springer Berlin Heidelberg New York



Springer is a part of Springer Science+Business Media

springer.com


Printed in Germany

Typesetting: Camera-ready by author, data conversion by Scientific Publishing Services, Chennai, India
Printed on acid-free paper SPIN: 12262687 06/3180 5 4 3 2 1 0

# Preface

This volume collects selected papers from the past two instances of Digital Art Weeks (Zurich, Switzerland) and Interactive Futures (Victoria, BC, Canada), two parallel festivals of digital media art. The work represented in *Transdisciplinary Digital Art* is a confirmation of the vitality and breadth of the digital arts. Collecting essays that broadly encompass the digital arts, *Transdisciplinary Digital Art* gives a clear overview of the on-going strength of scientific, philosophical, aesthetic and artistic research that makes digital art perhaps the defining medium of the twenty-first century.

I would like to particularly thank my co-editors, Randy Adams and Stefan Müller Arisona, without whom this volume could never have been realized. Their genuinely transdisciplinary knowledge base and tireless work ethic have made this volume as broad as it could be. I would like to also acknowledge the work of *Interactive Futures* co-curator Julie Andreyev as well as the Director of Open Space, Helen Marzolf.

The editors would like to thank Dene Grigar and Tom Stricker for providing the initial paper reviews for Springer. In addition Stefan Göller from Springer has provided us with solid support throughout the editing process and we would like to acknowledge his effort here.

**A Note on English Standardization.** Papers in this volume have been left in the "native" forms of English used by the individual authours (whether American, British or Canadian).

January 2008 Steve Gibson

# Table of Contents

## III Multimedia Composition and Performance



## IV Interfaces and Expression

## V Digital Space: Design, Movement, and Robotics



## VI Digital Performance in Urban Spaces

# Introduction: Why Transdisciplinary Digital Art?

Steve Gibson

Associate Professor of Digital Media
Visual Arts, Faculty of Fine Arts, University of Victoria
Victoria, BC CANADA V8W 2Y2
sgibson@finearts.uvic.ca

## 1 Why Transdisciplinary Digital Art?

We have entitled this volume *Transdisciplinary Digital Art* to distinguish it from the older term *Interdisciplinary Art*. Interdisciplinarity implies a certain level of detachment across the mediums: the artist, the engineer, the musician and the dancer may collaborate with each other but in much interdisciplinary work there is a sense that they are separate entities performing their own expert functions without more thorough knowledge of the other's technical or artistic processes.[1]

Transdisciplinarity implies a level of direct connection and cross-over between mediums: the artist also becomes the engineer, the engineer becomes the artist, and when they collaborate they actually have enough expertise in the other's field to be able to address concerns across the mediums and even across disciplines. This is not to say that there are not varying levels of expertise within transdisciplinary work, but rather that transdisciplinary art in its best sense makes the *effort* to understand the medium of the *other* in more than superficial terms. Here science is no less important than art, art no less than science. The elitism of the isolated *discipline* is broken down to a degree.

The papers in this volume represent varying degrees of transdisciplinarity, but as a whole the volume itself represents a remarkable breadth of work in digital art and science. From the technical to the philosophical to the poetic, the essays cover a wide range of topics related to digital media art and related areas. Many papers cross unusual divides (Will Pappenheimer's *Tuning in Rorschach Maps* covers inkblots, musical tunings and Situationist aesthetics in equal measure), while others introduce areas of research not commonly associated with the digital (Marcin Ramocki's *DIY: The Militant Embrace of Technology* introduces a Marxist analysis of digital culture). In *Transdisciplinary Digital Art* each paper in its own measure contributes to our collective understanding of the *other*. By the very notion of incorporating such varied approaches this volume aids and abets the furthering of our transdisciplinary future.

[1] A perfect illustration of this is the modernist notion of interdisciplinarity as exemplified by John Cage's *Variations V* in which the composer, the film artists (Stan VanDerBeek and Nam June Paik) and the choreographer (Merce Cunningham) worked in relative isolation, only meeting for the final performances [1]. While not all art termed *interdisciplinary* is this radical in its separation of roles, there is a general tendency to accept a distinct line of expertise between mediums in Interdisciplinary Art and interdisciplinary work in general.

R. Adams, S. Gibson, and S. Müller Arisona (Eds.): DAW/IF 2006/2007, CCIS 7, pp. 1–2, 2008.

## 2 Why Digital Art?

Digital art as a medium has enjoyed considerable strength in the new millennium. This strength has endured despite the uncertainty engendered by the dot-com bust and the subsequent attempt to portray the digital as ultimately a shallow medium. While it is hardly a unified medium and covers an enormous amount of territory, digital art certainly has grown substantially as an artistic medium (partly due to rapid technological advances combined with lower prices for those technologies). The digital is close to establishing a form that is generally recognizable by a broad range of the general population and therefore it is safe to say that it is here to stay.

Digital art has certainly received thorough coverage in Christiane Paul's excellent book, appropriately entitled, *Digital Art* [2]. *Transdisciplinary Digital Art* expands on Paul's history and theory of digital art by including the direct words and insights of the artists, programmers, musicians and theorists of the digital medium. The volume seeks to present the idiosyncratic and wildly varied concerns of artists, scholars, writers and scientists who are working digitally. As such it provides a wonderful insight into the continued vitality of the computer-based arts and is a testament to the persistence of artists who choose to use the computer as their primary medium for expression.

## 3 A Note on *Digital Art Weeks* and *Interactive Futures*

*Digital Art Weeks* and *Interactive Futures* are annual festivals of digital art and symposia on topics related to digital art, technology and computer science. *Digital Art Weeks* has been in existence for the past three years and *Interactive Futures* has had six iterations. For more information of these events please visit the following links.

Digital Art Weeks 2007: http://www.digitalartweeks.ethz.ch/web/
Interactive Futures 2007: http://cfisrv.finearts.uvic.ca/interactivefutures/IF07/

*Interactive Futures* was directed by Steve Gibson and co-curated by Randy Adams, Julie Andreyev and Steve Gibson. It was made possible by grants from the Canada Council for the Arts and the Canadian Foundation for Innovation. We would also like to acknowledge our other sponsors including Open Space Artist-run Centre, Emily Carr College of Art and Design, the Victoria Film Festival and the Fairmont Empress Hotel.

*Digital Art Weeks* was co-directed by Jürg Gutknecht, Art Clay, and Stefan Müller Arisona. It was primarily supported by the Native Systems Group of ETH Zürich, the Swiss Federal Office of Culture (BAK), Stadt Zürich Kultur, Migros Kulturprozent, and ewz. Additional sponsors included Cabaret Voltaire, Kunstraum Walcheturm, Kultur Basel-Stadt, Kulturelles Basel-Landschaft, Cargobar, Flashlight, Klangpur, Stereolith, ToneText, the Canada Council for the Arts and ProLitteris.

## References

1. Packer, R., Jordan, K.: Multimedia: From Wagner to Virtual Reality. On-line version (2002), `http://www.artmuseum.net/w2vr/timeline/Cage.html`
2. Paul, C.: Digital Art. London: Thames and Hudson (2003)

# Part I

# Philosophies of the Digital

# The Ethics of Aesthetics

Don Ritter

Berlin, Germany
http://aesthetic-machinery.com

**Abstract.** The article explores the relationships between aesthetics, ethics, and new media art by discussing the process, influences, and consequences of aesthetic judgments. The text proposes that the aesthetic judgements of artworks created in any medium, including new media, function as mechanisms for propagating certain ethical values.

**Keywords:** aesthetics, ethics, promotion, new media art, function of art.

## 1 Introduction

When an artwork is examined according to its mechanism, we pursue an understanding of what it is. When an artwork is examined according to its function, we pursue an understanding of what it does. This article will outline a perspective for distinguishing the function from the mechanism of artworks created in any medium, including those created with new media technologies. Using this perspective, the text will explore the relationships between aesthetics, ethics, and new media art by discussing how people decide that particular artworks are good, the influences of their aesthetic judgments, and the consequences of their judgments.

## 2 Aesthetics

A primary goal in the field of aesthetics is to investigate *aesthetic judgements,* the decisions people make when they decide "What is art?" and "What is good art?" [1] Although some writings on aesthetics are prescriptive in their approach, this text will not provide a precise definition of good art, nor will it advise readers to use specific criteria for judging art. Instead, it will discuss how people make aesthetic judgements.

*The Institutional Theory of Art,* set forth by George Dickie in 1974, proposed that "works of art are art as the result of the position or place they occupy within an established practice, the artworld." [2] According to this theory, the established network of curators, galleries, and museums that sell and exhibit professional artworks are responsible for determining what is art and what is not. The classification used within this text is derived from Dickie's theory: a work will be designated as an artwork according to its capacity to promote the artworld, providing it with more prestige, power, or whatever the artworld considers valuable. Using this classification, the specific aesthetic features within a work, its medium, and its style are less indicative of a work being art than its capacity to promote something within the artworld.

R. Adams, S. Gibson, and S. Müller Arisona (Eds.): DAW/IF 2006/2007, CCIS 7, pp. 5–14, 2008.

A primary problem that results from using a specific aesthetic criterion for judging the quality of an artwork is the evaluation of the criterion itself. If beauty is selected as a primary aesthetic criterion, the evaluation of an artwork's quality is determined by the definition of beauty. The primary aesthetic question "What is good art?" becomes dependent on the question "What is beauty?" The subjectivity of defining good art is replaced with the subjectivity of defining beauty.

In this text, the subjectivity of aesthetic judgements is acknowledged by replacing the primary questions of aesthetics with the following: "What are the criteria for something to be art?" and "What are the criteria for something to be good art?"

## 2.1 The Process of Aesthetic Judgement

The *process of aesthetic judgement* is a conceptual model that describes how people decide on the quality of artworks created in new or traditional media. The model examines how people decide if artworks are good or bad, if they have high aesthetic value or low. The model is a conceptual tool for enhancing a person's ability to recognize the function of aesthetic judgements. Although the model considers aesthetic judgements to be fundamentally subjective, it outlines a general process that can be applied to judgements of art created in any style or medium.

Some readers may argue that objectivity exists in the judgement of art because they believe that certain aesthetic perspectives are inherently better than others, such as the notion of "disinterested attention." [3] This text will not present any aesthetic perspective as being inherently better than another, but it will provide information pertaining to why certain perspectives are portrayed as being better.

An artwork is comprised of a collection of characteristics called aesthetic features that can influence a person's liking or disliking of an artwork, its aesthetic value. [4] The loudness of sound, a particular sound editing software, or a work's production costs can all be aesthetic features within a sound installation. A broad definition of aesthetic features is used to support the perspective that a compositional element is any characteristic of an artwork that can influence aesthetic judgements, including characteristics that some writers consider to be context or extrinsic features.

The specific qualities that a person associates with good artworks are determined by a person's aesthetic perspective, an idiosyncratic collection of criteria that define which aesthetic features must be present for artworks to be judged as good. The judgement of an artwork is dependent on its aesthetic features and the aesthetic perspective used by a person for judging it. Using this model, disagreements on the aesthetic value of a work are viewed as the consequences of people using different aesthetic perspectives.

An aesthetic judgement is a decision made by an individual regarding the aesthetic value, the quality, of an artwork. The outcome of an aesthetic judgement is expressed through observable expressions of aesthetic judgements, such as a person speaking positively about a work or purposely reexperiencing an artwork. Aesthetic judgements are created by the fulfillment or lack of fulfillment of the aesthetic criteria contained within a person's aesthetic perspective. When a person makes an aesthetic judgement, the fulfillment of a specific criterion does not always increase the aesthetic value of a work. Some people may use beauty as a negative aesthetic criterion within their aesthetic perspective: the recognition of beauty within a work decreases a work's aesthetic value. For other persons, beauty could be a positive aesthetic criterion: the recognition of beauty within a work increases a work's aesthetic value. When a positive aesthetic criterion is fulfilled, the judgement of a work moves towards a positive aesthetic value. When a negative aesthetic criterion is fulfilled, the judgement moves towards a negative aesthetic value. The outcome of an aesthetic judgement can be viewed as a summation of fulfilled criteria, each criterion having a different direction and degree of influence on a work's aesthetic value.

## 2.2 Influences of Aesthetic Judgements

Imagine a person who has a large amount of knowledge about video technologies. This person will understand the technology of a video work in more depth than someone who does not. Consequently, aesthetic features related to video technologies are more likely to be apparent for this person. A person with technical knowledge of digital video formats, for example, may prefer certain formats to others. People who lack this knowledge cannot use an aesthetic criterion that responds to this feature because they lack the knowledge for distinguishing different digital video formats. Similarly, a person who has knowledge about ancient mythologies might prefer works depicting Greek deities to Roman, but a person having no knowledge of ancient mythologies is unable to distinguish any difference between Greek or Roman.

Although it is obvious that people's aesthetic criteria are related to their personal knowledge, people are unable to use certain criteria if they lack knowledge corresponding to those criteria. Because particular aesthetic features become important to a person according to personal knowledge, a person's liking for a particular artwork can be based on aesthetic features that are irrelevant to someone else. Video formats and mythology may not seem like comparable aesthetic features, but both can be used within people's aesthetic perspectives.

Aesthetic judgements can be influenced by any factor that affects the components of a person's aesthetic perspective: the limits of human perception, context, familiarity, personal values, personal motivation, persuasion, and personal knowledge. Personal knowledge exerts an important influence on aesthetic judgments by determining which aesthetic features have the potential to fulfill a person's aesthetic criteria.

Philosophical investigations into the nature of knowledge are typically based on a combination of logic and empiricism. Traditional approaches to epistemology usually define knowledge as a "justified true belief." [5] A belief refers to any idea that a person believes to be true, such as a person believing that "Vincent Van Gogh was a painter from the nineteenth century." A belief becomes justified when it is supported by reason or evidence, such as documentation justifying Van Gogh's existence and activities as a painter. Many theories of truth have been proposed and perhaps the most popular is the correspondence theory of truth, [6] which states that a belief is true only if it corresponds with reality. Using this theory, the belief stated in the above example would be true only if Van Gogh really was a painter from the nineteenth century.

The problematic aspect of the correspondence theory of truth is its assumption of an objective reality. Proving the existence of an objective reality is difficult—if not impossible—because the human sensory system is supposedly the only manner that we have for experiencing reality. Coincidently, a similar problem pertains to theories regarding Van Gogh's preference for using yellow paint. One theory proposes that his love of the liquor absinthe caused him to have yellow vision, thereby affecting his painting. [7] The questionable aspect of this theory is its assumption that Van Gogh had two pairs of eyes: one pair influenced by absinthe, while the other pair were unaffected and objective. If Van Gogh's vision was affected in a manner than caused him to perceive certain colours of his world as yellow, his perception of paint would be affected in the same manner. If he perceived brown trees as being yellow, and he only had one pair of eyes, he would have also perceived brown paint as yellow.

Proving objectivity in human perception is problematic because any evidence supporting it must presumably be interpreted through the human sensory system. In acknowledgement of this dilemma, this text will use a phenomenological approach to knowledge by considering truth to be based on human perception rather than objective reality. Consequently, the term personal knowledge will refer to what a person believes to be true, regardless of those beliefs being justified logically or empirically.

Aesthetic perspectives are strongly influenced by personal knowledge because people's beliefs are often the basis for their aesthetic criteria, even when those beliefs are inaccurate or false. A person who believes that complexity is always better than simplicity, for example, might use an aesthetic criterion corresponding with that belief. In order for a person to indisputably know that a belief is true, that person needs sufficient and accurate information supporting the belief and an ability to comprehend that information. Obtaining accurate and sufficient knowledge about any topic can be time consuming, difficult, or expensive.

Psychologist Elliot Aronson proposes that people hold false beliefs because they are overwhelmed with information, or because they lack the motivation and resources to determine what is empirically true. He states that we are "cognitive misers," that we conserve our mental energy by "ignoring some information to reduce our cognitive load, or we overuse other information to keep from having to search for more." [8]

## 3 Aesthetics and Ethics

Within the field of ethics, the terms moral values, moral principles, and human values refer to the specific human behaviors that people consider desirable and good. A person who holds honesty as a moral value, for instance, will speak honestly with all people. The complication regarding ethics is that people often disagree about which behaviors should be endorsed as moral values, such as abortion, capital punishment, or same-sex marriages. Philosopher Peter Singer states, "The problem is not so much to know 'the difference between right and wrong' as to decide what is right and what is wrong." [9]

Even when people agree to adopt a specific moral value, they may disagree on when it should be used. Deontological theories of ethics propose that people should use moral values consistently, regardless of the consequences of their use. In contrast, teleological theories of ethics—also called consequentialism—consider the use of moral values to be dependent on the desired consequences. Consider the moral value that states a person should never be aggressive with other people. If a deranged person attacked a group of innocent people, a person who uses this value in a teleological manner may find it ethically acceptable to aggress and stop the attack of the deranged person. In contrast, people who use this value in a deontological manner may consider it unacceptable to harm the attacker because they are opposed to harming people under any circumstances.

Because of their disregard for consequences, deontological theories of ethics are similar to inherent aesthetic theories in that they both consider the value of art to be within an artistic experience with little or no regard for the consequences of the experience. Inherent aesthetic theories consider a particular aesthetic perspective to be appropriate in all situations, while consequential aesthetic theories permit the adoption of an aesthetic perspective according to the consequences that are desired. Teleological theories of ethics are similar to consequential aesthetic theories because they both consider consequences. The director of a private art gallery who prefers artworks that are potentially salable when they are intended for exhibition in the gallery, but prefers artworks that are beautiful when they are intended for personal enjoyment is using a consequential approach to aesthetics.

## 3.1 Aesthetics and Attitudes

In the field of social psychology, *functional attitude theories* examine the relationships between people's beliefs, attitudes, and behaviors. [10] Within these theories, beliefs are defined as the concepts that people accept as being true. People can hold beliefs on any conceivable topic, including those pertaining to themselves, other people, tangible objects, or abstract concepts. A person, for instance, may hold the belief that "pizza is a food."

An attitude is defined as an evaluative judgement made by a person that expresses a degree of liking or disliking for an attitude object. An *attitude object* can be any concrete or abstract concept, such as a certain type of food, another person, a concept, or a particular artwork. If a person holds the attitude "pizza is a good food," the attitude object is the pizza.

The relationships between beliefs, attitudes, and attitude objects are similar to the relationships between aesthetic criteria, aesthetic judgements, and artworks. An aesthetic criterion is a person's belief, such as "good art is beautiful," an aesthetic judgement is a person's attitude, such as "this artwork is good," and the artwork being judged is the attitude object.

The core concept of functional attitude theories is that people hold specific attitudes because they are motivated to obtain certain goals through those attitudes. The theories propose that a person will hold a certain attitude not because it is objectively true, but because it serves a desired function for that person. A new media artist who writes software for his artworks, for example, might believe and tell other people that "good new media art uses artist written code." Functional attitude theories would propose that the artist is using this particular criterion, or attitude, because he wants other people to judge his work as being good. Similarly, a person who wants to be considered as an intellectual may prefer a style of artwork that is considered to be intellectual. Five general functions of attitudes have been proposed by these theories: to seek award or avoid punishment, to obtain a perspective for understanding the world, to defend the ego, to express personal values, or to obtain membership in a particular social group. [10]

Functional attitude theories propose that attitudes are instrumental at providing psychological benefits to the holders of the attitudes and that the "...primary benefit lies not in the attitude object being evaluated but in the expression of the attitude." [11] This finding implies that the function of art is not determined by the specific aesthetic features within artworks—the attitude objects—but rather through the aesthetic judgements of artworks.

### 3.2 Aesthetic Judgements and Entities

The term entity refers to anything "...which is perceived or known or inferred to have its own distinct existence (living or nonliving)." [12] An entity can be a person, a physical object, or an intangible concept, such as integrity. A conceptual entity refers to the existence of a specific concept, such as "good art is meaningful" or "selfishness is good." Conceptual entities are strengthened by becoming known and admired by more people, and similar to beliefs, the existence of a conceptual entity is determined by it being known by people rather than it being objectively true. Ethical values are conceptual entities because they are essentially ideas. They differ from other concepts, however, because they designate how people behave in relation to each other. The notion of a conceptual entity is similar to the idea of a meme. [13]

A personal entity refers to a particular person whose existence is determined by the presence of particular personal attributes. A social entity refers to a specific organization of people, such as a university, a business organization, an art museum, or a city. Aesthetic judgements are designated as mechanisms that have potential to promote or undermine specific conceptual, personal, or social entities. Aesthetic judgements can contribute to the strength of specific entities by enhancing their popularity, social status, authority, financial worth, or any other characteristic considered valuable. This perspective considers audiences to have a very important role in the function of media because their aesthetic judgements determine which entities will be promoted and, consequently, which values will be propagated through media.

A social entity is an organized group of people who share similar beliefs and values, such as particular families, cities, or business organizations. The strength of a social entity is determined by the presence and strength of attributes that it considers as valuable. If popularity, size, authority, and financial worth are considered important attributes for a social entity, the enhancement of any of these features become an increase in the entity's strength. By using aesthetic criteria that correspond to the values of a social entity, a person can enhance that social entity through aesthetic judgements. A person who likes artworks exhibited at museum X promotes the concept that "museum X exhibits good artworks." This belief strengthens the museum financially because the person will likely pay to visit the museum. Attendance at this museum will be increased by the person's visits and this person may also recommend the museum to other people, both enhancing the museum's popularity and financial strength.

The particular social entities being reinforced through judgements of new media artworks are determined by the aesthetic criteria used for judging those works. If new media artworks are judged according to technological criteria—such as the newness of the technology—strength is provided to social entities that manufacture and sell the newest technologies. Similarly, if new media artworks are judged according to the presence of an established style, strength is provided to whoever acknowledges, promotes or originated that style, including specific artists, curators, museums, writers, and collectors. And if artworks are judged according to where they have been exhibited, strength is provided to the galleries, museums and festivals that are considered desirable. The positive beliefs that people hold regarding specific social entities function as mechanisms that promote those entities.

### 3.3 Promotion

The term promotion is used in reference to any action that contributes to the advancement, strength, or prosperity of a conceptual, personal, or social entity. Paying to see a commercial film can be a promotion for the studio that made the film. Liking minimalist art can be a promotion for the conceptual entity "minimalist art is good." Telling a friend that you like a specific artist's work can be a promotion for that artist, a personal entity. And attending an exhibition at a specific museum can be a promotion for that museum, a social entity. Even if a person dislikes an exhibition at an art museum, the person's visit has contributed to the museum's attendance records and ticket sales. A complicated aspect of promotion is that some people may be unaware how their actions are enhancing entities or which entities are being promoted.

Individual persons can have different relationships with promotion: as instigators, profiteers, carriers, or targets. Instigators of promotion are the persons or institutions that initiate the strategy of a particular promotion. The most apparent examples of instigators are advertising firms that are hired by manufacturers to promote their products through advertising. Less obvious examples are news writers who promote certain biases within newspapers and television news programs. A common term for the instigator of a promotion is a spin doctor.

The profiteer of promotion refers to an entity that profits through a particular promotion. Promotion can enhance an entity by providing it with more popularity, status, revenue, or whatever is considered valuable by that entity. The profiteer and instigator of a promotion may be the same person or organization, though it is common for a profiteer to hire an instigator.

Carriers of promotion are persons or organizations that carry out promotions, such as salespersons, athletes who wear corporate identities on their uniforms and equipment, or consumers who buy t-shirts bearing the logos of commercial products. Carriers of a promotion may not always profit from the promotion, and they may not always realize their function as such. Athletes who bear corporate logos are undoubtedly aware of their function and they are probably receiving compensation as well, but people who wear clothing emblazoned with the names of their favorite corporations, cities, or music groups may be unaware of their function as unpaid promoters.

When people are carriers of promotion, they can provide a promotional mechanism in the form of spoken words, written text, articles of clothing, or whatever—including tattoos of logos on their bodies. [14] A teenager who boasts to friends about owning a particular brand of sneakers is a carrier of promotion for that manufacturer. Similarly, an academic who consistently teaches and writes about a particular style of artwork is a carrier of promotion for the entities associated with that style. Although it is unavoidable to be a carrier of promotion, because certain entities are always promoted through words and actions, people can consciously decide which entities they decide to promote.

A target of promotion is the person or entity that provides a specific form of profit to the profiteer. Voters within an election are the target of a newspaper article that provides a favorable depiction of a political candidate, and computer consumers are the target for a t-shirt bearing the name of a computer manufacturer.

### 3.4 Media Subterfuges

Media subterfuges refer to media content that is created or distributed for reasons other than what an audience believes, or for reasons other than what is proclaimed by the producers and promoters of the content. A common example of a media subterfuge is a specific product appearing in a commercial film because the manufacturer of the product has paid for its inclusion, an advertising strategy called product placement. This text proposes that the general function of all media is to strengthen particular entities, but which entities are being strengthened will be unclear to audiences when media subterfuges are used. Media subterfuges are often successful because they fulfill the desires of an intended entity, such as the manufacturers of a specific product, and also the desires of an audience.

A popular strategy for accomplishing a media subterfuge is to encourage audiences to use the aesthetic criteria that will ensure the goal of a subterfuge. Filmgoers may be encouraged through television talk shows to judge commercial films according to their use of celebrity actors, which only large film studios can afford. Another strategy for a media subterfuge is the creation of content that fulfills an audience's existing aesthetic criteria while concurrently fulfilling the goals of the producers or distributors of that content. A documentary video about the impoverishment of a particular country may appeal to audiences who hold humanistic values, but the film may have been created to enhance the reputation of the director, to promote a political party who funded the production, or as a mechanism for attracting large audiences and, subsequently, large advertising revenues for the broadcasters of the video.

Although many people are aware of media subterfuges being used within commercial media, such as product placement, its use with fine art media may be less obvious. When an art museum exhibits particular artworks, its audience may believe that the works are being exhibited because they are objectively good. My research interviews with curators disclosed that various reasons might exist for exhibiting specific artworks, including nepotism, exchanging opportunities, enhancing the reputation of the gallery, or enhancing the reputation of an institution associated with the artist being exhibited.

As more people become aware of advertising strategies, covert forms of persuasion have become increasingly popular, such as product placement and viral advertising, The common feature of these and other forms of stealth advertising is that they do not appear to be persuasion. Examples of viral advertising are certain video files that are shared by friends through email or posted on personal websites. These videos are often macabre, humorous or sexual, and they usually have a reference to a commercial product, though the actual association with the manufacturer of the depicted product is uncertain.

> So the item of the day on advertising blogs everywhere has been this disturbing viral Volkswagen ad. It shows, if you can believe it, a suicide bomber driving up to a café in a VW Polo and trying to detonate a car bomb. But he manages to blow only himself up—the sporty little roadster absorbs the blast, proving that it is "small but tough." As if we needed it, we have gotten official word that neither VW nor any of its agencies (including DDB, its lead shop in Europe) had anything to do with this. It is indeed a hoax. Move on, please. Nothing to see here. *Adfreak.com blog.* [15]

## 4 Conclusion

The conclusion of this article is that aesthetic judgements of art function as mechanisms for promoting specific conceptual, personal, and social entities. An entity can be an abstract concept, an ethical value, a specific person, or an organized social institution with cultural, business, or political responsibilities. The aesthetic criteria used by people for judging artworks—rather than artworks' aesthetic features—determine which entities are promoted through aesthetic judgements. Some people, however, may be unaware of which entities are being promoted through their judgements because of a lack of knowledge or awareness, or because media subterfuges are being used. This article has avoided stating which specific entities are being promoted through aesthetic judgements because the intention is to provide a perspective that enables readers to determine these relationships for themselves.

By understanding the ethical consequences of compositional decisions and aesthetic judgements, artists and audiences can have increased responsibility for the propagation of ethical values, the concepts that dictate which behaviors we deem appropriate and which we do not. Without this awareness, a person might promote any value whatsoever through aesthetic judgements. Having an awareness of the influences and consequences of aesthetic judgements is desirable because it enables a person to promote specific values with intention.

**Acknowledgements.** This article is derived from *The e Decision,* a book by Don Ritter. Funding and support was provided by Pratt Institute, The Canada Council, The Banff Centre for the Arts, and the Zentrum für Kunst und Medientechnologie Karlsruhe.

## References

1. Morawski, S.: Inquiries into the Fundamentals of Aesthetics, p. xii. MIT Press, Cambridge (1974)
2. Dickie, G.: Introduction to Aesthetics: An Analytic Approach, p. 88. Oxford University Press, New York (1997)
3. Dickie, G.: Introduction to Aesthetics: An Analytic Approach. Oxford University Press, New York (1997)
4. Muelder Eaton, M.: Basic Issues in Aesthetics. Waveland Press, Prospect Heights, Illinois (1999)
5. Audi, R. (ed.): The Cambridge Dictionary of Philosophy, p. 273. Cambridge University Press, Cambridge (1995)
6. Marian, D.: The Correspondence Theory of Truth. Stanford Encyclopedia of Philosophy (2005), `http://plato.stanford.edu/entries/truth-correspondence`
7. Wolf, P.L.: The Effects of Diseases, Drugs, and Chemicals on the Creativity and Productivity of Famous Sculptors, Classic Painters, Classic Music Composers, and Authors. Archives of Pathology and Laboratory Medicine 129(11), 1457–1464 (2005), `http://www.cap.org`
8. Aronson, E.: The Social Animal, p. 97. Worth Publishers, New York (2004)
9. Singer, P.: Writings on an Ethical Life. In: Moral Experts, p. 5. Ecco Press, New York (2000)
10. Eagly, A.H., Chaiken, S.: The Psychology of Attitudes. Harcourt, Brace, Jovanovich, Fort Worth (1993)

11. Eagly, A.H., Chaiken, S.: The Psychology of Attitudes, p. 483. Harcourt, Brace, Jovanovich, Fort Worth (1993)
12. entity. Dictionary.com. Princeton University, `http://dictionary.reference.com/browse/entity`
13. Dawkins, R.: The Selfish Gene. Oxford University Press, Oxford (1976)
14. Kahney, L.: Tat's the Way Mac Heads Like It. Wired.com (2002), `http://www.wired.com/news/mac/0,2125,54202,00.html`
15. Nudd, T.: Viral suicide-bomber viral spot a hoax Adfreak.com blog (January 18, 2005), `http://adweek.blogs.com/adfreak/2005/01/vw_suicidebombe.html`

# Ethical and Activist Considerations of the Technological Artwork

David Cecchetto

University of Victoria
www.davidcecchetto.net

**Abstract.** This article draws on the work of diverse scholars to explore the politico-theoretical implications of technology, both as an artifact and as a modality, in contemporary art. Understanding art, technology, culture, and politics as being reciprocally generative of one another, the presentation explores a critical framework through which we may view artworks in general as (de)mobilizing various and particular technological paradigms, allowing us to view the embedded and invisible assumptions of a work in the context of its cultural ramifications.

**Keywords:** McLuhan, Bourriaud, music and culture, digital music, music and politics, digital art, activism, technology, art and culture, aesthetics.

If nothing else, I would like to write that the formal and ritual changes effected by technological artworks are at their core political. Towards this goal I will present an intersecting series of linear analyses, considerations not disconnected enough to be understood as separate entities, and yet not connected enough to make 'good logical sense.' Regardless, it is my hope that the ideas presented will be seen to intersect and reinforce one another, with the often tenuous narrative connections deemed acceptable through the metaphor of vagrancy, a wandering, undirected motion that should not be confused for an absence of motion; a wandering that is not opposed to direction, but is the map upon which direction must always be put back. Rather than stillness, then, I wish to invoke a shifting configuration of figure and ground that is the putting into play of context and content.

Much of my own work as an artist has been an exploration of the relationship between content and context, figure and ground. I have not been alone in this endeavor, or even particularly maverick. In fact, one could reasonably propose a study of post-1945 performances, musical and otherwise, using this relationship as a framework. Conceptual art, installation, site-specificity, and historically based movements such as 'neo-classicism' in music, would all fit comfortably under this umbrella. Popular movements and musics could fit this description as well. Indeed, major theoretical projects such as considerations of space, performativity, reception studies, ender studies, and cultural theory would also intersect with this study. However, this is not the study that I am presenting here. Here, I am simply insisting that the formal and ritual artistic changes effected by technology are at their core political.

The technological developments of the twentieth century did not culminate in the anticipated emancipation that they initially suggested, but instead "combined with advances in 'reason' to make it that much easier to exploit the south of the planet earth, blindly

R. Adams, S. Gibson, and S. Müller Arisona (Eds.): DAW/IF 2006/2007, CCIS 7, pp. 15–25, 2008.

replace human labor by machines, and set up more and more sophisticated subjugation techniques, all through a general rationalization of the production process. So the modern emancipation plan has been substituted by countless forms of melancholy" [1]. Nicolas Bourriaud thus points out that, given the present-day cultural restriction of inter-human relations enacted by this culture of specious efficiency, "contemporary art is developing a political project when it endeavors to move into the relational realm" [2]. While it is important to note that Bourriaud is here discussing a specific set of artistic practices, which take as their theoretical and practical point of departure "the whole of human relations and their social context, rather than an independent space" [3], this perspective also points to the broader notion that the role of artworks is "no longer to form imaginary and utopian realities, but to actually be ways of living and models of action within the existing real" [4]. The work of art thus represents a social interstice: it is harmonious with the overall system, but simultaneously suggests other trading possibilities; over and above its mercantile nature and its semantic value, it eludes the capitalist economic framework by being removed from profit [5]. By extension, then, the work of art which does not endeavor to move into the relational realm is either not developing a political project, or is developing an entirely different political project.

The notion, implicit in these claims, that an artwork can develop a political model on a formal level is a far-reaching one that points to the often unexposed politic inherent to all cultural activities. Too often we conceive of the political in terms of anti-culture, as a voice against the norm; a modality that has been researched exhaustively under the rubric of race theory, with most contemporary scholars agreeing that "whiteness often goes unnamed and unexamined because it has been uncritically and unthinkingly adopted as the norm throughout (North American) society" [6]. As an example of this tendency, Rothenberg notes that many whites have difficulty recalling when they first noticed that they were white because whiteness was, for them, unremarkable. On the contrary, nonwhites can often clearly recall when they started noticing their identity as different. Indeed, the very fact of language such as 'white' and 'nonwhite' points to whiteness as the invisible center of cultural considerations of race; a concept (that of an 'invisible center') that becomes all the more interesting when one takes into consideration the fact that racial categories are now generally acknowledged as being mobile constructs, with 'whiteness' predominantly achieved through social advancement.

This last point was illustrated to me one night as read a 'value tale' to my stepdaughter: in the book, published in the 1970's, the middle-class protagonist buys and repairs an old house in an inner-city neighborhood and proceeds to offer various kinds of help to her new neighbors. At one point, she opens the door at the knocking of two small children, who are drawn in the book in a dark shade of brown (the color, incidentally, that one might see an Arab child depicted today). The narrative reads that, by the deep brown color of their skin, the protagonist immediately knew that the children were…Italian (!). Of course, this was only one generation after the massive Italian immigration to North America, so Italians and the Italian culture had not yet acquired social prestige or the wealth salient to it. As a result, for example, though my own father's skin would today qualify him as 'white', his childhood peers did not consider him (as an Italian) to be the same skin color as them (indeed, nor did he). What is really interesting in all of this, though, is that the mobility of race is rarely culturally acknowledged because once a culture is identified as white it no longer conceives of itself in terms of race. It is the privileged and unexamined invisible norm.

For McLuhan, this situation can be understood as a simple play between figure and ground. Seen in visual space, 'race' is static in that it represents a figure isolated on an invisible ground, but pushed to its extreme this stasis reverses into slippage and homogeneity, where 'whiteness' becomes a mobile category. Thus, the distinctions are lost because they are considered as absolutes, rather than as relations.

I have not digressed (or, perhaps, I have digressed productively). In considering the underlying politics of race, we can understand the politics of unacknowledged and unexamined privilege, of an 'invisible center.' Returning to the politics of contemporary art, then, we can see how works that are not developing a relational aesthetic are not exempt from political analysis, but are instead acting in the capacity of an unacknowledged center. That is, they are presenting a political project focused on subjugation of those not included in the circle of privilege. The technological artwork can be understood as particularly powerful in this respect, then, because a computer des not carry the enormously (and complexly) rooted history that, for example, a violin does. In the absence of this history and its rituals, then, the mode of presentation enacted by this work is emphasized because it is chosen rather than assumed. As such, these choices are made both in terms of content and of context, leaving the technological artwork (perhaps) uniquely positioned to enact the political reality of it's choosing. For today's artist, then, the issue no longer resides in broadening the boundaries of art (as in the redefining of art that was salient to the conceptual works of the 1960's), but in experiencing art's capacities of resistance within the overall social arena [7].

In this context, consider Marshall McLuhan's four laws of media, which collectively stem from the premise that "each of man's artifacts is in fact a kind of word, a metaphor that translates experience from one form into another" [8], so that artifacts of both hardware (i.e. a table, or a stick) and software (i.e. an idea or a preposition) are understood as extensions of the physical human body or the mind. Crucially, McLuhan indicates that these laws are 'scientific' in that they are testable, universally applicable, and yield repeatable results. Framed as questions, and intended to be asked in any order, the tetrad is:

- What does the artifact enhance, intensify, make possible, or accelerate?
- What is obsolesced by the artifact?
- What older, previously obsolesced ground is brought back and inheres in the new form?
- When pushed to its extreme, what will the new form reverse into? [9]

Returning briefly to our consideration of the mode of presentation of a technological artwork, we can see from McLuhan's tetrad that, by instituting a change to the traditional performance paradigm, every use of technology enhances, reverses into, retrieves, and obsolesces elements of that paradigm. As such, the particularities of these features may be recognized as indicators of the politics of a particular artwork, a claim that gets at the perennial problem of music: namely, that it has "nothing but mediations to show for itself" [10]. That is, whereas in the case of the visual arts "the materiality of the works, even and especially if challenged by the artists, has allowed a debate to take place about the social production and reception of art. Music is in the reverse situation: its object is elusive; on the one hand social interpretations just take it a the expression of a social group (ethnic trance, rock concert), on the other hand aesthetic studies treat it as a non-verbal language of immediacy. Musical works [...] are not 'already there', overdetermined by the social. They always have to be played again" [11].

Considered from the perspective of McLuhan's tetrad, artifacts are understood not as neutral or passive, but as active logos or utterances of the human mind or body that transform the user and her ground [12]. Thus, every situation comprises an area of attention and inattention (a figure and a ground), the interaction of which defines the nature of the space. Thus, for example, McLuhan argues that the genesis of 'visual space' as we understand it can be found in the invention of the alphabet. Specifically, with the invention of the consonant as a 'meaningless' abstraction, vision detached itself from the other senses so that visual space always features a figure isolated on an invisible ground. Since this ground is thus suppressed (as a guarantee of abstract, static uniformity), visual space functions as a container of continuity, connectedness, linearity, and homogeneity so that we can understand that the features of logical 'connection' and syllogistic reasoning "exhibit and use only the properties of visual space" [14].

For a moment, consider an anecdote: recently, a university educator who frequently uses music in her lessons added a caveat to a point she was making by saying that she was "not a musician, and (didn't) know much about music, although (she) does love it." This comment is of a type frequently heard, and points to the way in which the dominant musical paradigm reasserts cultural hierarchies; one of its central tenets is the privileging of a structural-formalist understanding of music over an understanding of its various functionalities. That is, although the professor had understood the effects of music in her classroom (in terms of both the modes of relating it can encourage, as well as its ability to convey affective content), and although she had honed her pedagogical craft in order to intensify and direct these effects with the complex social relations of the classroom, she nonetheless automatically subjugated this knowledge to that of the composer or creator who created the systems within the musical object, and to the field of music scholarship. In this way, music is constituted as an autonomous object containing complex systems, as opposed to being thought as an agential entity acting as part of a complex system. In McLuhan's terms, it is seen in visual space. A pursuit of the ramifications of this privileging shows that its corollary is a privileging of classical (or academic) music, where the study of musical structure and grammar is most developed. As an aside to this point, it is worth noting that, within the field of academic music, a similar model is played out; in that context, Suzanne Cusick has thus argued that, in the naming of 'the music itself' as a kind of aestheticized sound, a perspective is emphasized that "omits and/or deligitimatizes practical music-making, perpetuating the omission of women's work in the study of music" [15].

We can perceive a parallel logic between the power of the academic musician and that of the phonetic alphabet identified by McLuhan, which he identifies as the hidden ground of visual space. That is, the alphabet's "great power of abstraction is that of translating into itself (as an abstract, unmodified/unmodifying container) the sound-systems of other languages" [16]. This is strikingly similar to the paradigm played out in the musical arena, where the academic musician occupies a position of dominance because resulting from his capability to reproduce the structures and grammars of other musical genres. The same is not true of other musical genres, which are not generated from the structural and grammatical model that they are ultimately evaluated within, and which are not similarly capable of capturing the structures and grammars of academic music, or of other genres. To value these structures and grammars, then, is to value an abstract notion of music as independent of the body and its specific practices such that, though the structures of Indian classical music (for example) can be notated using Western notation, to do so neglects the rich pedagogical systems that are traditional and salient to that musical tradition. Thus, in notating Indian classical music, there is an implicit naming of that music as a product rather than as a cultural process; a naming which may be contrary in character to that given by most of that music's practitioners, and would certainly be contrary to its instructors. This is clearly a visual understanding of music, then: music as a separate, containable entity. Further, to understand the cultural nexus within which music is thus contained, it is crucial to also recognize that to privilege a structural and grammatical understanding of music is to reify the value systems of western academic musicians, who are overwhelmingly upper-class, heterosexual, white males. By extension, then, accepting this notion of musical knowledge limits the value of other musics to derivation, reinforcing the privilege enjoyed by the dominant culture, which has always known how to capitalize on product(ivity).

From this perspective, we can understand the full scope of McLuhan's assertion that the "visual power of the phonetic alphabet to translate other languages into itself is part of its power to invade oral cultures" [17]. As with our musical consideration, then, the translation of content results in a reconfiguration of the figure/ground relationship. Since we can only conceive of meaning itself in relative terms, this reconfiguration amounts to a radical change in the content that is virtually imperceptible in the final (visual space) presentation of the content, because the space isolates the figure from the ground. Thus, we see that the specialist qualities that lend academic music authority are part of a long tradition of visual domination.

The domination of visual culture is not only expressed in colonial modalities, but is also profoundly internal to the space itself. In all visual spaces, to become part of a seemingly fluid culture one must first excel in the value systems set by a fixed dominant group. For example, consider Sharon Donna McIvor's analysis of the status of aboriginal women in Canada: these women must be deemed 'aboriginal' by the federal government in order to be granted their right to self-government, but they are often forced to sacrifice their human rights around issues of gender in order to be considered aboriginal by aboriginal leaders (which is a prerequisite to identification by the federal government), who are a predetermined group created independent of gender equity laws [18]. Thus, these women's rights are conditional both as women and as aboriginals, and one exclusion begets another towards a total denial of access to power. Similarly (though not precisely the same), though music is almost universally accepted as a central cultural feature, most of the population of North America do not identify themselves as 'musicians,' just as the professor previously discussed did not. Thus, one of the central products of the culture, and one of the defining agents of the culture, is not engaged with, or by, most of the population that it alleges to represent and affect.

The ethical gridlock begat by the conditional access to power in these examples is a direct result of embracing a paradigm that conceives of text and context as being in stable opposition to one another. As Derrida has shown, such binaries create a hierarchy and an order of subordination, an argument that Kevin Korsyn has extended to music towards demonstrating that such stable opposition "promotes a compartmentalization of musical research, dividing the synchronic analysis of internal structure from the diachronic narratives of history" [19].

This is precisely the context in which McLuhan critiques the specialist knowledge of visual space as specious and self-determining; visual space yields specialist knowledge, so that specialist knowledge (musical or otherwise) is properly understood as a symptom of visual space. When does knowledge become specialized? When it produces 'truths' which exist independent of complex relationships such that it can be wielded in the service of power.

Though visual space and its accompanying left-brain dominance overwhelmingly dominate Western institutions, the twentieth century has seen visual space obsolesced in all fields and its alternative, acoustic space, was retrieved. The mechanical paradigm, enthroned in the seventeenth and eighteenth centuries, was eventually replaced by a field-mosaic approach [20]; a victory that was make possible only because the concept of the material object was gradually replaced as the fundamental concept of physics by that of the *field*. Here, objects make their own space and are not *contained* in any space, because the "spatial character of reality [is] the four-dimensionality of the field (as represented in the tetrad). There is no 'empty' space. There is no space without a field [21].

One can clearly see acoustic sensibilities in the artistic developments of the early twentieth century, developments that frequently anticipated those in the fields of math and science. In the case of music, McLuhan cites Arnold Schoenberg's abandonment of the visual structures of tonality in favor of the multi-locationism of atonality. Specifically, atonality in music is understood here as an attempt towards the "abandonment of the 'central key,' that is, the abandonment of a single perspective or organizing frame to which to relate other figures in an abstract way" [22]. Thus, we can understand that 'modernist' music may not have been a visual space *movement*, even though its contemporary manifestation has crystallized into a visual space *aesthetic* (which is the critique implicit in postmodernism). The essence of the modernist movement in music, then, can only be considered through consideration of its specific historical situation, and is properly understood in terms of its reconfiguration of the field of musical truth-value achieved through the use of specific compositional techniques; it cannot be thought through a specialized, abstract study of the techniques themselves. Just as 'race' is a mobile and relative construct, then, so too are the accoutrements of musical modernism polyvalent indicators: forms are "*developed*, one from another [...]. When the aesthetic discussion evolves, the status of form evolves along with it, and through it" [23]. Thus, as Bourriaud argues, we can only extend modernity to advantage "by going beyond the struggles it has bequeathed us. In our postindustrial societies, the most pressing thing is no longer the emancipation of individuals, but the freeing-up of inter-human communications, the dimensional emancipation of existence" [24]. This is art in acoustic space, where it is the intervals between elements that gives the elements form or configuration so that, in this space, what happens when a new work of art is created is "something that happens simultaneously to all works of art which preceded it" [25].

In a similar way, one can see acoustic sensibilities deeply embedded in many contemporary technological artworks. The technologies of computers act as extensions of our central nervous system (rather than our limbs), so that the resulting enhancements are metaphorical and relative rather than literal and static. That is, the contemporary art image made possible through computer technology is "typified by its generative power; it is no longer a trace (retroactive), but a programme (active)" [26]. Thus, multimedia works often aim to present objects as they are known, rather than as they are viewed from a single perspective, by offering numerous simultaneous representations of a reality. Similarly, interactive artworks strive to incorporate viewers into a relationship with the work that allows for an individualized experience of the piece. But a moment of caution is necessary, if we think back to the lessons of (musical) modernism: features that evoke acoustic sensibilities in one setting may function as static figures in another. Thus, an 'interactive' work may operate like a relational device containing a certain degree of randomness, or like a machine provoking and managing individual and group encounters [27]. Thus, works presented under the rubric of interactivity are often no more interactive than translating and following instructions written in a recently-learned language. Here, what is deemed 'interactive' may simply be rule recognition; further, 'subversive' modes of presentation may evolve over time into specialized knowledge in the form of technological fetishism. If formal and ritual changes effected by technological artworks are at their core political, the true nature of these changes can often only be understood through their political examination. The rest is simply interface.

William Brent and I presented an installation in 2006 that experimented with some of these same ideas [28]. Designed to highlight the distinction between an acoustic sensibility and a visual one (by presenting both simultaneously), *Outside* was an 'interactive' installation created using the texts from various lectures given at the *Collision* symposium. Prior to the installation of the work, all of the included texts were read and recorded as audio, and subsequently 'cut' into smaller segments ranging in length from one sentence to two paragraphs. During *Outside's* residency (as an installation), these recordings were cycled through sequentially, sounded from a small speaker. If an audience member was interested in a topic or theme being discussed in the recorded audio at a particular time, they simply spoke the word 'interest' into the microphone and a related segment from one of the other recorded texts was articulated. In this way, the predefined segments formed an interconnected discursive network. The 'cuts' between segments were inaudible.

Physically, *Outside* occupied approximately 5' of space in a mid-size room for three days. The technology used consisted of a Macintosh computer, a small speaker, an audio interface, a microphone with stand, and accompanying cables. With the exception of the microphone and stand, these objects were all housed in small boxes wrapped in white paper inscribed with the featured texts. The sound levels were such that the text was clearly audible within a 10' radius, and so were not loud or dominant.

Thus, *Outside* was designed to be considered on two levels: first, the foreground, by which is meant that aspect of the piece that could be apprehended by an individual through direct interaction with it over a relatively short period of time. Second, the background, by which is meant elements of the work which unfolded over longer periods of time, and which were inevitable. This inevitability was a crucial distinction, as it represented the nesting logic of the work, or its structure. In *Outside*, we tried to enact a conflict of identity in the work between its foreground and its background. On one hand, the foreground was fluid, playful, and interactive. In contrast, the background structure was rigid and monolithic. Through this conflict of identity in the work (and *of* the work) there emerged a tension of interpretation. In particular, the foreground level could generally be considered within the terms of anti-formalist relational discourse, while the background level generally adhered to formalist principles of the autonomous (musical) artwork. The site of interpretive crisis enacted in *Outside* was the co-dependence of these mutually exclusive interpretive strategies; the foreground level depended on the background in order to maintain its political agency, and the background depended on the foreground to answer the criticisms around authorship that it referenced. Through this co-dependence, the division between foreground and background was simultaneously deemed necessary and impossible. *Outside* was a paradoxical work, then, which simultaneously presented itself as a sovereign artwork and as an interactive and co-dependent one, fulfilling neither role.

One way that *Outside* called attention to this crisis of identity was through its failure to be 'successfully' interactive. The simplest example of this was the temporal lag between audience action and the technology's response in *Outside*, a lag that was exaggerated by the imperceptibility of the response when it finally did happen. This violated one of the central tenets of successful interaction, causing the audience to question whether the installation was functioning properly and preventing their immersion in the constructed environment. Since *Outside* presented itself as an interactive work, this violation impeded the clarity of its reception.

In another way, *Outside*'s interpretation as a multi-vocal artwork, where authorship is dispersed throughout the authors of the presented texts and the audience members who interact with the texts, was severely limited by the prescribed relational network of the texts, where what constituted 'related' material was the strongest dictator of what material would be presented. Since these relationships were all determined beforehand independent of the audience' interaction, the result was disguised authorial control. In *Outside*, the disguise was not successful because the texts being used were highly personal to many of the audience members. The resulting possibility of recognizing the disguise (without being able to remove it) analogued the power exercised by the invisible author in many multi-vocal and interactive works; works where cultural, historical, and material differences remain unexamined *as a result* of a text's multi-vocality. Although a text may include multiple voices that would seem to allow readers to form their own interpretations, they are still staged by authors who select different voices in order to make a point or create an impression. Here then again, *Outside* paradoxically relied for its 'meaning' on an interpretive strategy that it could not support.

Thus, the audience members' inability to efficiently control the installation was a direct result of the variety of subjects identified (in advance) in each segment of text, so that the inability to predict and conform with the computer's naming of the subjects results in the inability to author the installation. The resulting potential for frustration was all the more visceral because the interface seemed so simple, which viscerality allowed the installation to function as a critique of interactivity. Thus, *Outside* can be understood in the context of Bourriaud's observation that the "main effects of the computer revolution are visible today among artists who do not use computers. [...] The influence of technology on the art that is its contemporary is wielded within limits circumscribed by this latter between the real and the imaginary. [...] Art's function consists in reversing the authority of technology in order to make ways of thinking, living, and seeing creative" [29].

Consider this example, then: a piece of live electronic music in which a series of simple rhythmic samples are gradually piled on top of one another, producing an increasingly complex polyrhythm. One possible interpretation of this work is that the computer is being used to detach the notion of rhythm from its connection to the body, resulting in an intensification of its latent 'abstract' qualities. Taken to its extreme, though, this intensification reverses into the perceived polyrhythm, a space of abstract fragmented mosaics; the formal changes enacted by this technology may equally be taken as promoting a visual conception of music, with all of the political ramifications that that entails.

It is understood today that "there are no forms in nature, [...] as it is our gaze that creates these by cutting them out from the depth of the visible" [30]. The interest of photography stems from this scenario: there are numerous ways to present a photo such that it is not understood as art (advertising, family photos, etc.), so that one can say that photographs are only understood as art objects when they are activated as such; when they are presented as a "proposal to live in a shared world, [where] the work of every artist is a bundle of relations with the world, giving rise to other relations" [31]. This is different than the violin, for example. The moment one hears or sees a violin one immediately places it within the musical canon that one carries along with oneself. The violin, as an object, *is* music, which results in the violin having to work very hard to actually *play* music, to actually be musical and present the threefold viewpoint of the aesthetic, the historical, and the social that characterizes art. The violin can only present itself as object (music as object), or as mediator of music (music as simulation).

Since pop culture, as a form, only exists in contrast to high culture (through it and for it), "the 'everyday' now turns out to be a much more fertile terrain" [32]. Thus, in contrast to the violin, there is ubiquitous photography that plays with the line between art and function, or art and craft, or art and not art. This can be, and often has been, seen as an emancipatory process. However, in using gallery settings as stages to show the hidden beauty that we pass by in our day-to day life, the relation between art and life is inscribed as binary and hierarchical. Thus, the 'everyday', as an aesthetic mode, may ultimately accomplish the opposite of what it set out to do by implicitly giving the viewer permission to continue to live their life in a way that entirely neglects art; that is, by reinforcing the disciplinary status of art. In this view, the most interesting photograph would instead *make the gallery disappear*, and thus be visible as art only in its (nonfunctional) functions. No longer art as (non)representation, then, but hyperart, existing in opposition to the "authoritarian version of art where any work is nothing other than a 'sum of judgments', historical and aesthetic, stated by the artist in the act of its production" [33].

And yet, in discussing the politics of formal and ritual artistic changes, it is important not to lose sight of the literal sacrifices that are made in producing digital technologies. The dubious work conditions and villainous military provenance of most consumer electronics are facts of common knowledge, which often results in their being forgotten. Further, as a producer of goods, "technology expresses the state of production-oriented relationships. Photography, for example, tallied with a stage of western economic development [...] which, in a way called for its invention. Population control (in the form of ID cards), management of overseas wealth (ethno-photography), the need to remote-control industrial tools and find out about potential mining sites, all endowed the camera with a crucial role in capitalist society" [34]. The point, then, is that – all aesthetic considerations being equal – digital artists owe a political debt that must be in some way balance by their artistic output.

For a final time, then, I would like to way that the formal and ritual artistic changes effected by technology are at their core political. And yet, the vagrancy that characterizes my effort to do so here demonstrates the difficulty of doing so within the current artistic climate. Thus, the research that needs to be done towards articulating particular analyses from this perspective is the development of an intersectional language with which to account for musical performance and scholarship as political and aesthetic acts. This research will necessarily grapple with technological artworks, but would do so within the context of their (always ambivalent) aesthetic and political agency. That is, this research will require an analytical approach that is constitutively fluid, dispersing authority in such a way that rigorous considerations of musical performance and scholarship presented by 'non-musicians' can gestate alongside those of the 'initiated' musician-class. This dispersal will serve two purposes: it will place music (a central defining agent of culture) as an accessible entity, and it will unveil the constitution of the musician-class such that it is accessible to both internal and external critiques. In doing so, it will subject specialized knowledge to rigorous critique without ignoring the specific contexts that that knowledge is generated within. This approach engages, for example, the technological fetishist, the modernist musical composer, and the nightclub DJ in discourse with one another around the central theme of an evolving political ethics. This accessibility will not aim to 'popularize' the music and scholarship of the musician-class, but will instead attempt to grapple with its reception.

These concerns presented in this chapter, and highlighted for future research, are particularly pertinent in a time when interdisciplinary and technological artworks are becoming ubiquitous; how does a trained musician discuss a work with a trained visual artist, philosopher, computer-composer, or cultural theorist without the means to mutually explore the premises embedded in each of their analyses? Each of these fields has critical faculties developed around aesthetics (or materiality), historicity, and social context, yet we still implicitly value a western art musician's reading of, for example, Cage's *4'33"* over a visual artist's. In doing so, we refuse the broader cultural relevance of the work in favor of an insulated and apolitical academic reading, thus failing to learn anything from the work that was not already implied in those canonized musical works that preceded it. In McLuhan's terms, we treat the work as an isolated figure on an invisible ground. However, McLuhan has shown that this (visual) understanding of the work is no longer relevant or even sensible, and exists in contrast to all of the major artistic and scientific developments of the twentieth century. Thus, to begin to understand the interpretive problems posed here is to begin to (re)open avenues for artistic expression, and to begin to reinstate 'art music' as a culturally relevant practice. That is, only when a context of cultural relevance is established can we truly begin to consider the cultural ramifications of the technological artwork. Until such time, it remains incumbent upon artists and musicians to undermine the progressive dominance of recorded music icons who cause us to increasingly lose the ability to even conceive of music outside of a capitalist framework, by reconceptualizing their work within a relational political aesthetic. That is, "what sets art apart from other social exchanges (which are often made of the same materials) is its (relative) social transparency. A successful work exists beyond its presence in space; it opens dialogue, discussion, and that form of inter-human negotiation that Marcel Duchamp called the 'coefficient of art', which is a temporal process, being played out here and now" [35].

## References

1. Bourriaud, N.: Relational Aesthetics (trans. Simon Pleasance and Fronza Woods, with Mathieu Copeland), p. 12. Les Presses du Réel, France (1998)
2. Ibid., 17
3. Ibid., 13
4. Ibid.
5. Ibid., 16
6. Rothenberg, Paula S.: White Privilege: Essential Readings on the Other Side of Racism, p. 2. Worth Publishers, USA (2002)

7. Bourriaud, p. 31
8. McLuhan, Eric, Marshall.: Laws of Media: The New Science, p. 3. University of Toronto Press, Toronto (1980)
9. Ibid., pp. 98-99
10. Hennion, Antoine.: Music and Mediation: Toward a New Sociology of Music. In: The Cultural Study of Music, Routledge, New York, p. 83 (2003)
11. Ibid.
12. McLuhan, p. 99
13. Ibid., 20
14. Ibid., 21
15. Cusick, S.G.: Gender, Musicology, and Feminism. In: Cook, N., Everest, M. (eds.) Rethinking Music, p. 492. Oxford University Press, New York (1999)
16. McLuhan, p. 19
17. McLuhan, p. 74
18. McIvor, S.D.: Self-government and Aboriginal Women. In: Dua, E., Robertson, A. (eds.) Scratching the Surface: Canadian Anti-racist Feminist Thought, p. 167. Women's Press, Toronto (1999)
19. Korsyn, K.: Decentering Music: A Critique of Musical Research, p. 55. Oxford University Press, New York (2003)
20. McLuhan, p. 39
21. Ibid., p. 41
22. Ibid., p. 52
23. Bourriaud, p. 21
24. Ibid., p. 60
25. McLuhan, p. 47
26. Bourriard, pp. 69-70
27. Ibid., p. 30
28. Brent, W., Cecchetto, D.: Outside, presented at Collision: Interarts Practice and Research. University of Victoria, Canada (2006)
29. Bourriaud, pp. 68-69
30. Ibid., p. 21
31. Ibid., p. 22
32. Ibid., p. 47
33. Ibid., p. 22
34. Ibid., p. 69
35. Ibid., p. 41

# DIY: The Militant Embrace of Technology

Marcin Ramocki

Department of Media Arts
New Jersey City University
2039 Kennedy Boulevard
Jersey City, NJ 07305-1597
marcin@ramocki.net
http://www.ramocki.net

**Abstract.** The text below is an expose on certain crucial phenomena of cotemporary new media art; particularly dealing with the "Do It Yourself" attitude toward digital technologies. It is a critical commentary and extension of a documentary project *8 BIT*, which premiered at the Museum of Modern Art in October 2006.

**Keywords:** DIY, Hacktivism, Alienation of Labor, 8 BIT, Subversive Stratgies, Baudrillard, McKenzie Wark, Software Art, New Media.

The intent of this expose is to outline the rudimentary theoretical foundations for certain cultural practices involving the subversion of consumer technology. By consumer technology I mean hardware and software produced with the intent of maximum financial gain. The "Do it Yourself" in the field of fine art is almost a tautology, but it certainly isn't so in the world of consumer electronics and software design. The growing phenomenon of artists involved in active critique of the *technosphere* (which includes my own art practice), creates a set of interesting questions. For example: why do we feel compelled to mess with electronic devices and call it art; is what we do still a continuation of Modernist principles, or an all-together different thing–and, if so, what kind of thing is it?

I'd like to start this discussion by tracing the history of social critique back to the classical Marxist model. We are going back to the moment in history when the very concept of oppression came to its maturity and entered the political and artistic vocabularies. The Marxist discourse is based on the dialectical conflict between the oppressed class of proletarians and the bourgeois oppressors. The new economy becomes possible thanks to the Industrial Revolution and mass mechanical reproduction of goods. The proletarians are essentially people who sell their unskilled labor for minimum wage and become extensions of the factory machine lines. They lose what Marx believed to be the most fundamental human need: the access to the fruits of their own labor. This disconnect created by the industrial production severs humans from the objects they make, and breeds what Marx calls the "alienation of labor."

Alienation is the key concept, which allows fuller understanding of our involvement with technology, and the link between technology and the capitalist mode of production. In the traditional Marxist scenario the proletariat sells their labor to the bourgeois, who

R. Adams, S. Gibson, and S. Müller Arisona (Eds.): DAW/IF 2006/2007, CCIS 7, pp. 26–32, 2008.

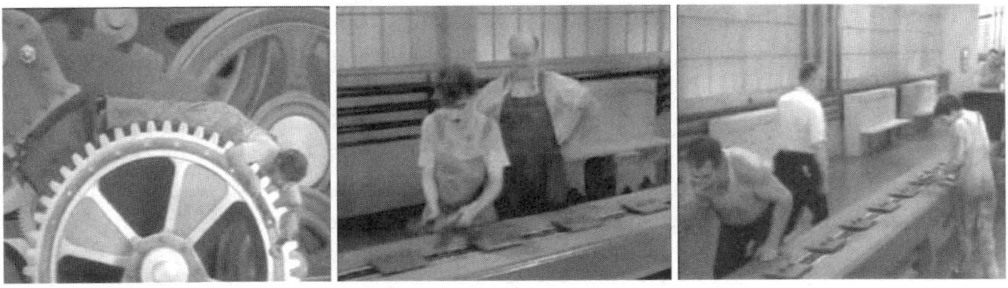

**Fig. 1.** Charlie Chaplin, *Modern Times*, 1936

owns the means of production (factories, machines). As a result, the proletariat becomes frustrated by existential hardships and the disconnection from their own labor output. The bourgeois accumulates more and more capital and updates their technological base, and thus expands their wealth. The cycle is complete when the commodity produced gets sold to the very same proletarian who assisted in its mechanical reproduction. The surplus is maximized. [2]

This 19th century scenario still holds up today, or should I say all elements are still in place; it is just that their weight and significance has shifted. The second half of the 20th century breeds "white collar" societies, which generate capital through the consumption of commodities produced in developing countries as well as the economics of intellectual property. Our reality is no longer the universe of objects and direct, oppressive force, but rather the realm of signs, symbols, information and its manipulation.

The critical discourse of alienation continues in writings of the French theorist Jean Baudrillard. In his 1968 classic, Simulacrum and Simulation, Baudrillard analyses the path of an object becoming its own representation: a simulacrum. Never mentioned by name, alienation is the force making the successive generation of simulacra less and less perfect. The more alienated we are the further we are removed from the reality principle. In the world where digital models precede living material beings, we are frustrated not necessarily by the disconnect from the fruits of our labor, but more by the circumstances of consumption surrounding us, abundant commodities. The new alienation is the alienation of consumption and commodity, which only makes sense, considering that consumption is the "white collar" labor. [1]

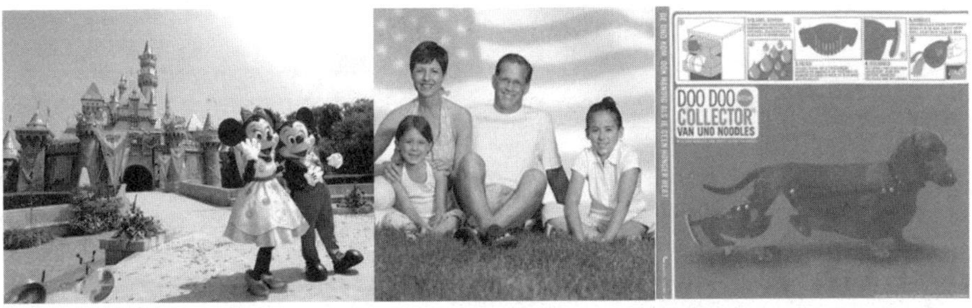


**Fig. 2.** Postcard from Disneyland, free stock image "American family", and an example of a useless commodity

Consumers fundamentally don't understand the intention behind the production and existence of the commodity. They don't understand how it's made and where, and what is the actual value of the commodity within their personal frame of reference. The effect is a sense of reality loss, non-referential simulation. It took me several years to conclude that the scenario of Disneyland (a 3$^{rd}$ generation simulacrum) described by Baudrillard, is in fact a complex group therapy device. Disneyland is a place where fake is overdone on purpose, exaggerated, exposed. Nobody pretends that Mickey is a real mouse, but the opposite: his cartooniness is fully embraced. The over-the-top simulacrum of Disneyland is there to prevent us from realizing that the actual world outside of Disneyland is also completely fabricated, modeled and simulated. We need Disneyland to trick ourselves into believing in the reality, from which we feel totally alienated, and accept the world of commodities that makes absolutely no sense in our lives. Without this escape mechanism we face the inevitable schizophrenia.

The last and most recent text I would like to reference is The Hacker Manifesto by McKenzie Wark. The Hacker Manifesto is a clever update on The Communist Manifesto, in which Wark takes into the account the socioeconomic impact of the concept of intellectual property. The late capitalist (21$^{st}$ century) dialectic is no longer that of a proletarian vs. bourgeois. Although that dynamic certainly still plays a huge role in the societies which actually produce goods on a mass scale (China, India, South America), the post-capitalist US and western Europe economies have shifted towards copyrights, patents, and trademarks.

For Baudrillard in 1968 it was the individual against the digital, simulation System (with a capital "S"). Almost 40 years later McKenzie Wark talks about the new class of hackers, a direct social manifestation of the intellectual property laws. According to Wark, "hackers are the people capable of forcing the sign/information system to creatively transform." They are the inventors and generators of new value and the necessary pioneers of constantly revolutionizing means of production. The term hacker obviously originated in computer engineering circles, but Wark uses the word in much broader sense. Any individual involved in the invention of concepts is a hacker, this would include most contemporary artists, scientists, programmers, and culture jammers. Hackers, as a social class, are in a relation of conflict with "vectoralists", who are essentially the macro-managers of the digital economy, the directors of the military-industrial complex, who project and define the vectors of evolution for future markets. [3]

Par excellence, the hackers are individuals who rise above the proletarian alienation of labor and fully embrace the knowledge and information pertaining to the means of production, their hardware and software. After all, they propel the system with the constant re-invention of rules, signs, ideas and fashions.

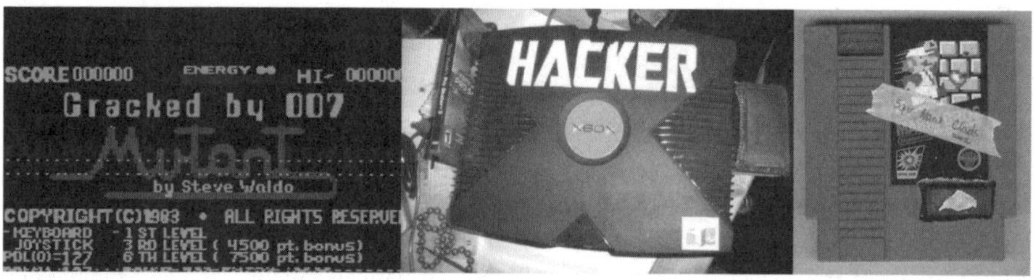


**Fig. 3.** Cracked game intro, hacked Xbox and Cory Arcangel's *Mario Clouds* cartridge

I believe that what we see happening with new media art is the expression of the crystallizing interests of this new class: overcoming the alienation of labor (circuit bending, game hardware hacks, custom electronics); overcoming the alienation of commodity (i.e. re-purposing, preparing and retro-engineering); and the political-activist attitude related to their inherent conflict with the vectoralist agenda (i.e. online game performance). The work happening right now comes from the first generation born into a world with personal computers, video games and the internet and on-line media. Their first frame of reference is not the linear narrative of a film but an algorithmic one of a game or a website. There is no more reverence toward technology: there is a need to question and make sense of it.

Lets examine some of the most prominent strategies of artists involved in the critique of technology.

The clearest and most straightforward are the cases where the artist actually is a hacker in the traditional sense of the word and does break something he or she shouldn't be breaking. So we have circuit bending, which is the creative short-circuiting of low voltage, battery-powered electronic devices such as guitar effects, children's toys and small synthesizers to create new musical instruments and art pieces. One of my favorite examples of extreme circuit bending is Paul Slocum's Dot Matrix printer hacked to be a drum machine. I also see a lot of circuit bending that unintentionally produces music, and Joe McKay's cell phone series is a beautiful example.

When talking about classical hacker art, one has to mention the early works by Cory Arcangel and Paul Davis. We have the whole spectrum of subversive activities: cutting open the Nintendo game cartridge, removing the original chip, learning the code to re-program the game (in this case Mario), burning the new chip and placing it in the original cartridge. And then posting the how-to instructions on the internet.

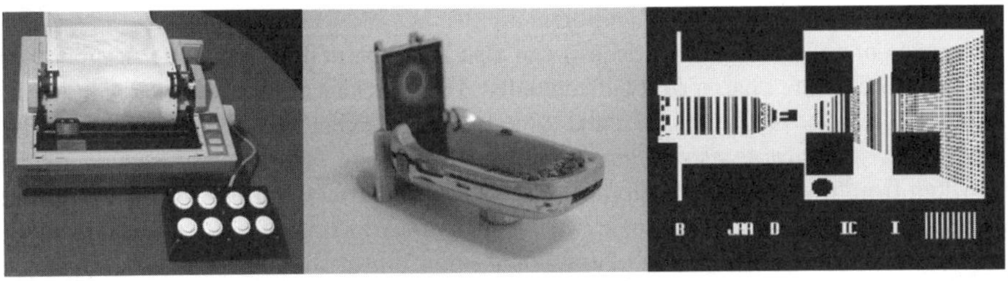

**Fig. 4.** Paul Slocum, Joe McKay and JODI

A little bit less direct strategic interventions include *structural game works*, mainly legal game modifications and machinima made with tools provided by the game developer. A successful modification will reveal the underlying control mechanisms and code characteristics of the game, make the user aware that the game they are playing is code-dressed with images and sounds. One of the best examples of re-dressing the code is *SOD*, a Castle Wolfenstein modification by the Dutch collaborative JODI.

Just like a commercial game can be modified, other softwares and hardwares can be re-purposed and prepared without actually damaging them. In this case the artists push the application or the hardware in such a way that it defies its own commercial strategy. As an example of re-purposed hardware, I picked Lance Wakeling's *Study for the*

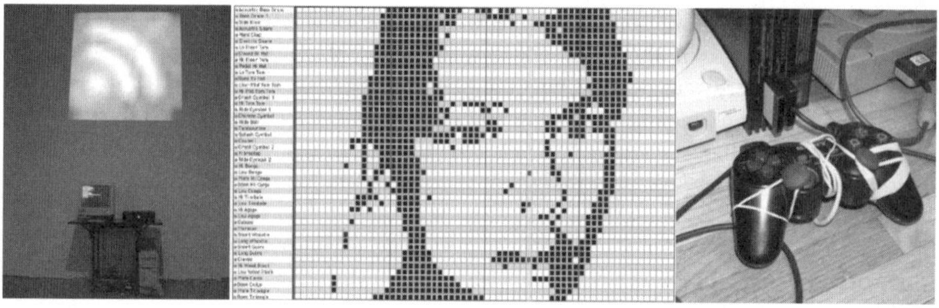

**Fig. 5.** Lance Wakeling, Marcin Ramocki and Alex Galloway

*Portrait of Internet (Static)* in which the artist forces an Xbox machine to be a computer running Linux OS and crawling the net. The path of the search is based on associations between images, and as the crawler moves between sites you can see the changing images. My own piece called *Torcito Project*, which is a re-purposed old Mac sound application Virtual Drummer, provides an example of re-purposing a piece of software. The application was "mis-used" to become a 1 bit matrix for image creation: each portrait then generates its own soundtrack.

*Prepared Playstation* by Alex Galloway is a simple physical manipulation of a game console, where the controls are bound with rubber bands, and the game (in this case Tony Hawk's skateboarding games) is stuck in an awkward sequence, which the game developer didn't intend to be a part of the game. A similar type of work, which steps out of the gaming circle is *Two Projectors, Keystoned* by Cory Arcangel. It is basically two projectors used as light sources, keystoned and partially superimposed. This work is about the projector as medium, its technological limits, spatial geometry and light as a sculptural material; recalling 60's minimal art [3].

A piece of software (and hardware) can also be subverted by remaking it altogether, and therefore taking charge of it conceptually. The category of artist softwares imitating corporate applets is quite large and going strong. What we see is mostly *retro-engineering* and *custom electronics*. In addition, there are fake hacker websites, games rewritten from the ground up, alternative browsers and Hollywood movies. I would like to mention the hilarious version of *ET* by Kara Hearn, which is a meditation on cinematic editing strategies and generation of emotional impact through montage. The artist enacts all parts herself, in a prosaic backdrop of her own apartment.

Strange pieces of circuitry by Jamie Allen are custom 4 bit synthesizers build and housed in an old cigar boxes and recycled containers. Jamie chooses to produce the sound generating device form scratch and have the most intimate understanding of the process.

Much more loosely related to the concept of DIY are the works where the artists make us realize the existence of certain codes and patterns by conceptual *data visualization*. I particularly like the cases where information becomes materialized and its hidden codes revealed; like in this painting by CJ Yeh, where *Boogey Woogey New York* by Piet Mondrian was transcribed into HTML and then the code was painted onto a board of the same size as the original painting. Another great example is a piece by Mike Beradino

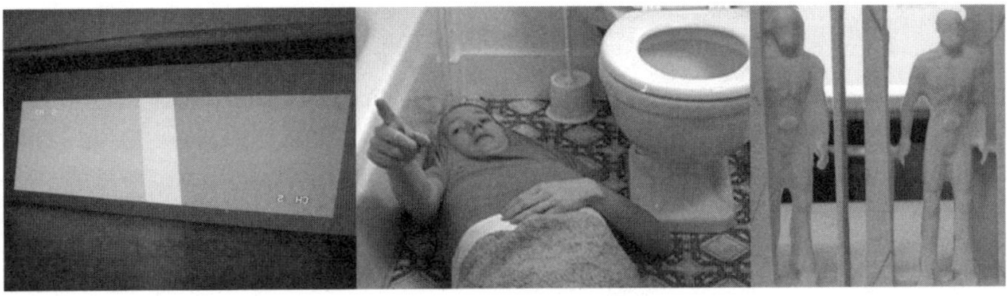

**Fig. 6.** Cory Arcangel, Kara Hearn and Mike Beradino

called *Mikey Newchurch*, where artist's Second Life avatar code is extracted, and then a physical representation of the avatar is printed on a 3d printer.

What relates all the works just discussed is their rather militant intention and strategy to reveal the aspects of technology that we take for granted. It is that taking-for-granted which turns us into consumers of culture, as opposed to active participants. Figuring out what is inside the black box (and why it was made) is becoming the official duty of artistic communities.

Finally, to answer my own questions, we mess with electronics because we identify it as a source of meaning for our generation, a way of re-connecting with our surrounding reality, mostly composed of code and technology. The tools used in this struggle will inevitably come from what we learned in college, namely Clement Greenberg and Andy Warhol. But the phenomenon we see goes beyond Modernism. There is no longer the need to clarify the medium, or find the best form for its content. The concept of an avant-garde pushing the envelope toward some abstract New is slowly but surely yielding to a very specific, tactical approach of returning technological knowledge where it belongs: in human lives.

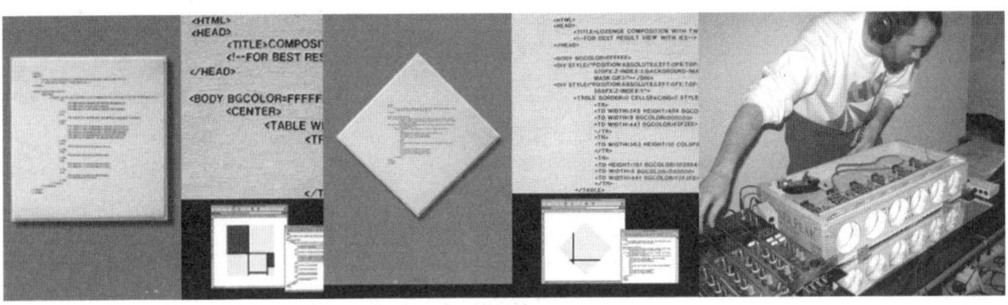


**Fig. 7.** CJ Yeh (Liquid Mondrian, 2001), Jamie Allen performing at vertexList, Brooklyn

## Acknowledgements

The research for this paper is based on feature documentary *8 BIT*, created by Marcin Ramocki and Justin Strawhand (USA, 2006). Edited by Charles Beronio.

## References

1. Simulacra and Simulation (The Body in Theory: Histories of Cultural Materialism). Jean Baudrillard, University of Michigan Press (December 31, 1994)
2. Das Kapital. Karl Marx, Gateway Editions (January 25, 1999)
3. The Hacker Manifesto. McKenzie Wark, Harvard University Press (2004)

# Tuning in Rorschach Maps

Will Pappenheimer

Department of Fine Arts
Pace University
41 Park Row
New York, NY 10038
wpappenheimer@pace.edu
http://www.willpap-projects.com

**Abstract.** Many contemporary artists are working with strategies to remap public, informational and social space. Their processes often involve setting up a prescriptive, algorithmic and participatory work that yields an unknown product. What can we observe about the results? What is audience reception of these works? In addition to visiting historical precedents in performance and music, this paper will explore how real-time Internet statistical, geographic and textual mapping has become available for both practical and recreational purposes and how new media artists are engaging these methods to test the possibilities of situational mapping. Two models of analogy will be explored, the Rorschach test and the musical mode of tuning.

**Keywords:** Statistical Chart, Geographic Map, Cartography, Mapping, Radical Cartography, Information Aesthetics, Map Art, Memory Mapping, Graph, Graphing, Data Mining, Graphic Display, Visual Information aesthetics.

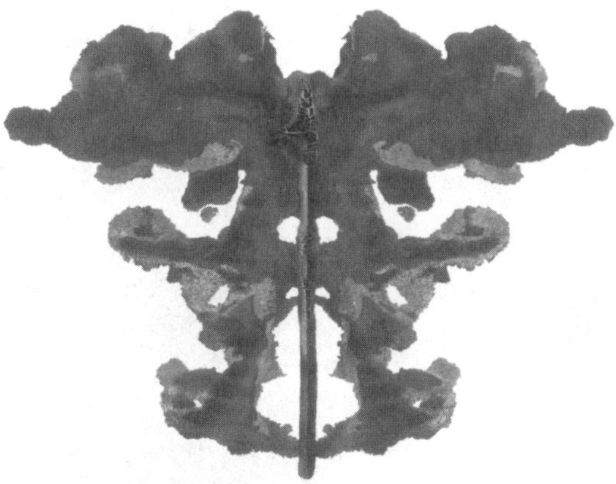

**Fig. 1.** Will Pappenheimer, *Inkblot Test*, 2007

R. Adams, S. Gibson, and S. Müller Arisona (Eds.): DAW/IF 2006/2007, CCIS 7, pp. 33–45, 2008.

## 1 Introduction

In 1904 Hermann Rorschach enrolled in medical school at the University of Zurich, across the street from Eidgenössische Technische Hochschule Zürich. Rorschach had been a talented art student in school and remembered his interest in *Klecksography*, a game played by Swiss children consisting of dripping an inkblot on paper, folding it so that the symmetric forms of butterflies or animals would emerge. While a student in medical school he combined this artistic interest with his studies in the burgeoning field of psychology and created is now famous *Psychodiagnostik* personality test. The test consists of showing the patient a series of standardized inkblots and carefully recording the patient's responses and associations. The procedure, as determined by Rorschach, is actually quite a rigorous. The patient is instructed to verbally describe their associations as to what they *see* in the shape of inkblots. The analyst is supposed to take detailed notes about everything that transpired including body language. Finally, after the interview the patient's responses are scored and interpreted.

Several aspects of the *Rorschach Test* are interesting to us here. First, the procedure is represented as a semi-scientific approach to the image or artform. Though the contemporary medical psychologist might reject this practice today, we might say that these experiments initiated a hybrid mixture of disciplines and a continuing psychological analysis in art criticism. The methodical approach to ink blot interpretation, characteristic of the expanding field of psychology at the time, was meant to reveal the internal subconscious narrative of the patient. This visual recognition unfolds a shape mapped to the viewer's imagery and personality. The emphasis is on patient or audience perception not authorship. As if to accentuate this, the very process of making the inkblot was instructively mechanical and subject to happenstance. The influence of this experiment is still felt in artworks today.

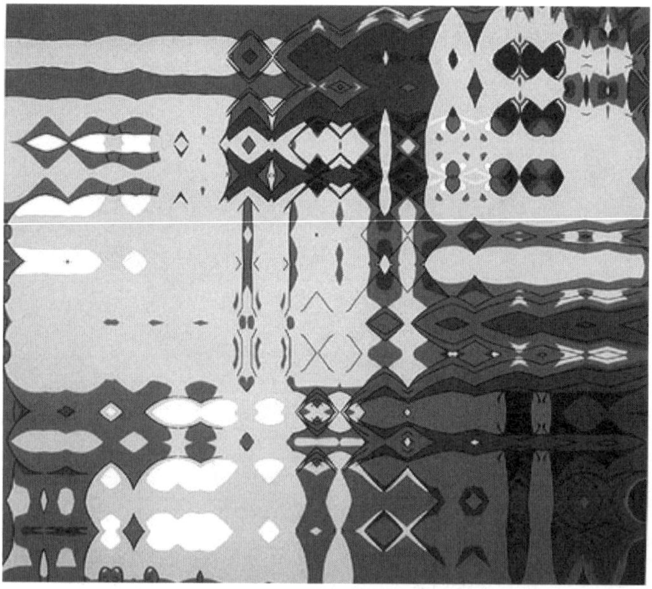

**Fig. 2.** Carl Fudge, *Tattooed Blue 3*, 2003

## 2 Mapping

The human desire to translate perception into a visual graphic order is understood to pre-date most forms of written language. The earliest known map is generally agreed to be a Babylonian clay tablet dated around 6,200 B.C. The image did what most maps still do today, that is, topographically outline a district bounded by two ranges of hills with a town and rivers. Subsequent maps through the ages take on more territory and begin to address other systems of world belief and spatial construction. Some of the many elements now familiar to conventional maps are spatial measurement, proportionality, position, overview, storage of complex information, color coding and the use of symbols.

In his text Mercator for You Are here, Personal Geographies Steven Hall proposes that the field of cartography represents the overlay of many different systems: geography, information, memory, imagination, social demographics, cosmology, and so on. Thus mapping is more than a topographic representation of information and scientific terrain. Even when produced for scientific or statistical purposes maps are inevitably subject to the projection of very human concepts and desires. Cartography represents our interest to know where we are, who we are and where we might be going. Orientation is finding our position, not just physically, but biographically, psychologically, physiologically, metaphorically, socially and politically. We constantly orient ourselves mentally through a multiplicity of maps and flip through them at a moment's association. Home, *Heimlich*, is the map we know, of house, of address, of landscape, of country, of family of culture and so on. It gives the sense of stability. But it is always in jeopardy of its surroundings, that is, the surrounding or invasion of unfamiliar territory.

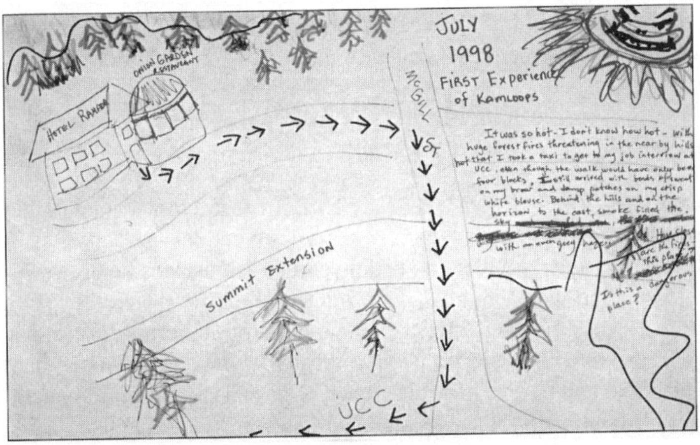


**Fig. 3.** *Kamloops Memory Map,* participant, Ellen Leier, CURA, 1998

The memory map is one of the most intriguing manifestations of this sense of multi-dimensional cartography. In this process the author configures the terrain according to experience rather than geography. The narrative behind such maps is likely to include social interactions, architecture, objects, animal life, as well as the sense of autobiographical encounters in time. The concept of mapping discussed here does not have simulation as its goal. It is not in search of the perfect copy that conflates the signifier and impoverishes the signified. It evades Jean Baudrillard's problematics. The map and the territory hover together, intersecting. The map declares its imperfect resemblance, it's process and thematics. It does not attempt substitution, but offers up a relationship to the real, that questions the real.

In recent decades, science, coupled with computer technology has brought about an explosion of mapping, from scanning microscopes, to enhanced telescopic imagery to MRI to mapping genomes. Vast amounts of information are translated into topography as topography is deciphered back into informational analysis, history, and prediction. The acceleration of informational gathering, sorting, computation, and organization makes visualization all the more facile. Data mining searches for criminals, brain mapping finds mood stimulation, satellites analyze planetary material, while to radiocarbon dating by accelerator mass spectrometry unfolds vast temporal coordinates. The scientific paradigm displays an endless a succession of maps; from chromosomes to blood circulation, from water vapor to weather system, etc. The computer organizes its information as hierarchy while photographic imaging becomes a map of values and contours.

The map is the translation of information, with axes often in time, transforming narrativity and metaphysics, into the visible. It makes these intersecting disciplines visible into a shape. This is not so much an idealized abstract image but one that comes from and dissolves into its process, its use. It gives us the sense of the way things are, the current situation, but it is also the way things go.

A map is a view from the air. It is the patterning of information, the shape of ground level activity. Trekking through a jungle, we cannot see far ahead, we are moving in process, in performance, in network communications from one friend to another. The view from the air is something different, a macro formation of micro activity. Not transcendent, but tied to its generation on the ground.

## 3 ReMapping

In his seminal work *Theory of Derive*, Guy DuBord instructs: "…one or more persons during a certain period drop their relations, their work and leisure activities, and all their other usual motives for movement and action, and let themselves be drawn by the attractions of the terrain and the encounters they find there.…With the aid of old maps, aerial photographs and experimental dérives, one can draw up hitherto lacking maps of influences, maps whose inevitable imprecision at this early stage is no worse than that of the earliest navigational charts. The only difference is that it is no longer a matter of precisely delineating stable continents, but of changing architecture and urbanism [1]."

*Derive*, the 60s Situationist practice of drifting throughout the city, was one of the first artistic examples of exploring the changeable nature architecture and urbanism. It's directives, described above, used a mixture of free flow and psychic attraction guide it's participants. It was meant to show a psychic cartography of another superimposed city, one was as much about an interior as exterior geography. Many such walking projects have taken place since. Recent examples would be the works of artists such as Frances Alys, C5, or iKatun.

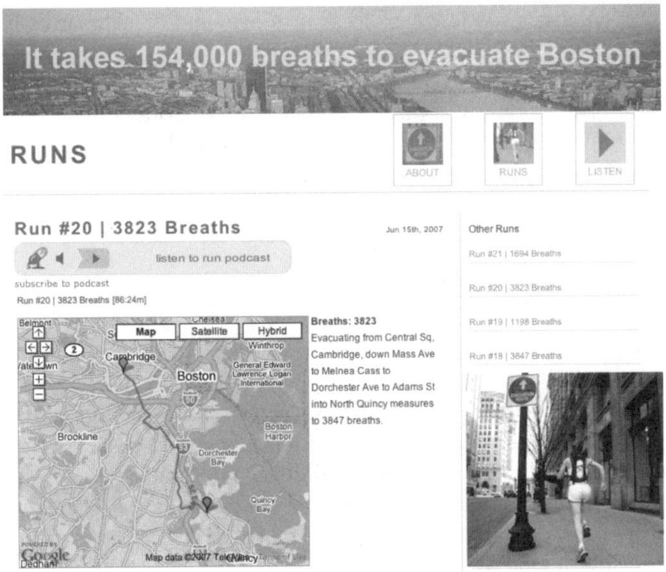


**Fig. 4.** iKatun, *It takes 154,000 breaths to evacuate Boston*, 2007

It is also clear that digital technologies have added another set of virtual maps to the global terrain. We have become increasingly familiar with their intersection in an environment such as Google Earth. Alternative modes of touring, wandering or virtually navigating pre-mapped territory represent performative reinterpretations of conventional space and its conceptual framework.

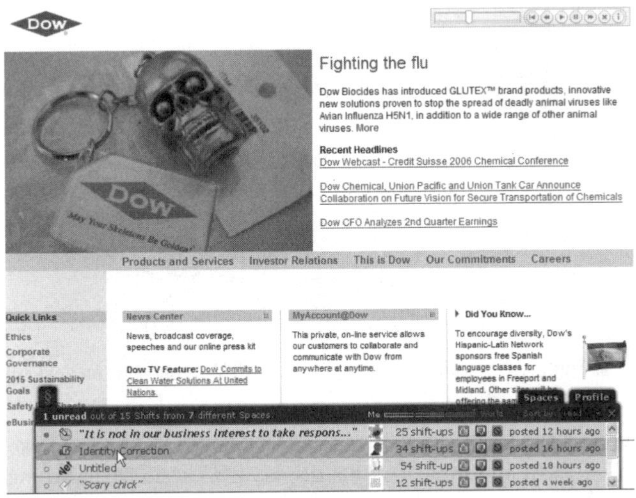


**Fig. 5.** *ShiftSpace* - a web layer for commentary and Community, Turbulrnce.org, 2006

Of particular interest to us is the concept of remapping or alternative mapping that shifts emphasis towards map making and exploring the possibilities of correlating unconventional data. Often this might represent the overlay of existing maps with a new method or set of calculations, as a means of conjecture or critique. A practice described as radical cartography. In a statistical visualization seemingly disparate sets of information can be correlated and made graphic to suggest alternative meanings. Ultimately remapping suggests a reorganization of territory or subject matter according to another set of values. The results can challenge the conventions of representation, public ideology as well as a individual perception.

## 4 Graphing Maps

Conventional mapping and graphing has developed in the utilitarian aesthetic mode of representing information accurately and proportionately so that readers can utilize it as a guide or diagnosis for a given place or condition. The graphical statistician, Edward Tufte claims there are over 900 billion graphical charts produced annually. The goal of this type of mapping is to translate large quantities of data across axes of time and space to be able to achieve a kind of overview or assessment of the situation. Often embedded in this process are conceptual and ideological structures that give a sense of order to the unknown terrain or field of the subject. The national map, the city grid, the calendar, the stock market graph all impart at sense security and identity, a means by which a culture defines and delineates itself. In other cases it is the ideology of science, the objective grid; GPS, satellite imagery, the measurements of minutes, centimeters, euros, ounces, hertz, and so on.

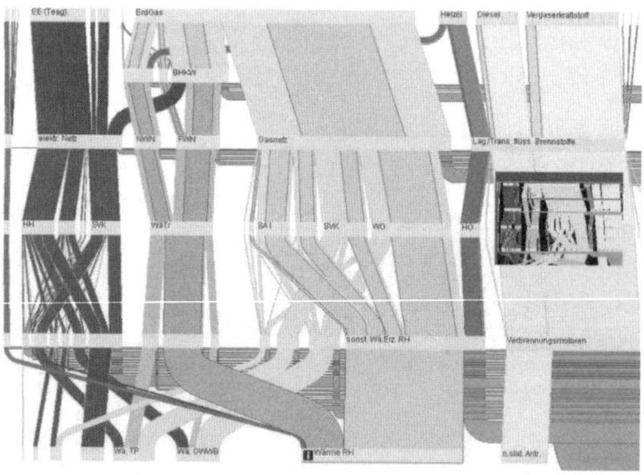

**Fig. 6.** Sankey Diagram of Energy sources in Wiemar, Germaney- 1994

Tufte has written several illustrated volumes on his idea of graphical excellence which he calls the "efficient basic forms of visual display [3]." Data Maps arrange information according to geographical location so that we can see a positional trend or pattern. This method of plotting was used famously by Dr. John snow in 1854 to trace household cholera deaths to a town water pump in central London. Obviously there is a diagnostic or investigated directive in this type of graph. Time Series graphs plot data according to the regular pace of time so that we can see shapes that indicate interesting or unusual activities. Two early examples are Etienne-Jules Marey's 1880 train schedules for Paris and William Playfair's weird shape of England's trade advantage. The third category Tufte identifies is the Space Time Narrative. These graphics chart data over time and space to form a narrative image of an event. Finally, Relational Graphics represent the replacement of geographical coordinates with other measures, sometimes employing different units on different axes. Plotting is often done to achieve a recognizable curve. However, results can also be unpredictable as in as a series of plots of Inflation and Unemployment Rates by Paul McCracken circa 1977 yields a meandering line [3].

## 5 Impossible Graphing and Mapping:

It becomes interesting to consider replacing axes and data input with information not normally sought-after or considered quantifiable. In a sense this idea has been with us for long time as various cultures have charted their notions of the universe. More recently artists have taken to mimicking these charting processes to show them as an aesthetic method for visualizing previously unquantifiable levels of experience. Digital computational processing and the Internet allow for real time events and information to be continuously transposed or juxtaposed to reveal unusual readings of current conditions. Google Trends will instantly graph the online usage of multiple words, showing and comparing their occurrence over time and with respect to location. The various incarnations of Alex Galloway's Carnavore PE software translate data-valence into aesthetic information and motion.

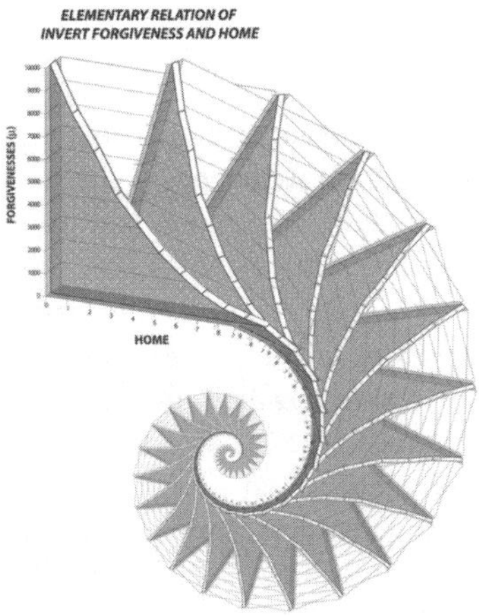


**Fig. 7.** Luke Murphy, *Inverted Fogiveness*, 2007

The interests of my own recent work relates to these directives. *The Public Mood Ring* (Fig. 8) translates real-time Yahoo News into color mood via text analysis on one axis and cultural color value on another. Remote participants choose articles to be tested and send the color results to an immersive light lounge. A particular color space represents the mapping of emotional news, cultural values and color theory. A more recent work in process translates many sources of extra continental information into forces that affect the supposedly invulnerable coastline of the United States. The shifting shape reads, in this case, as the confluence of many forms of intercontinental subconscious activity (Fig. 14).

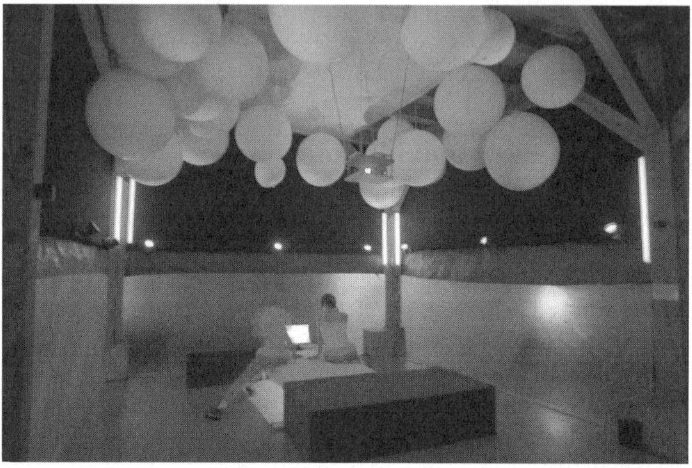

**Fig. 8.** Will Pappenheimer with Oz Michaeli, *Public Mood Ring*, 2007 Kunstraum Walcheturm, Zurich, Switzerland

## 6 Rhizomic Structures

The idea that representation, significance or knowledge entertains a field of interconnected roots rather than a linear causal sequence, was of course introduced by the philosophical team Deleuze and Guattari. The more than useful metaphor introduced by these influential theorists in 1980 is the rhizome root structure that grows in interconnected spurs and nodes in every direction on a horizontal plane. The idea is that reasoning follows through a web of linked relationships and interconnected planes of thought. Deleuze and Guattari contrasted their analogy with linear and dualistic logic associated with tree-like formations. The result is a gathering of interconnected points of meaning in a collective not a hierarchical configuration.

The resemblance of the rhizome structure to computer networks emerged almost a decade later. This configuration is visible at the micro level of hypertext linking as well as the macro patterning of participatory social networks projected into the notion of Web 2.0. As we click along these serpentine links, as we join Web communities and add friends to our webpages, we imagine a view from above forming an amorphous collective shape, Rorschach–like, a contour made by a situation, a community image.

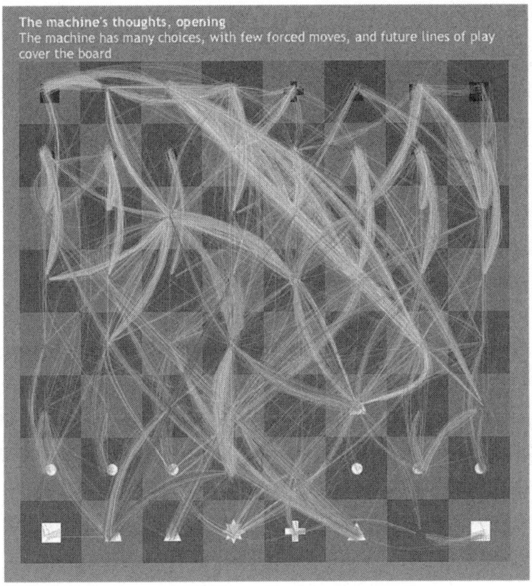


**Fig. 9.** Marek Walczak and Martin Wattenberg, *Thinking Machine 4*, 2004 Turbulence.org

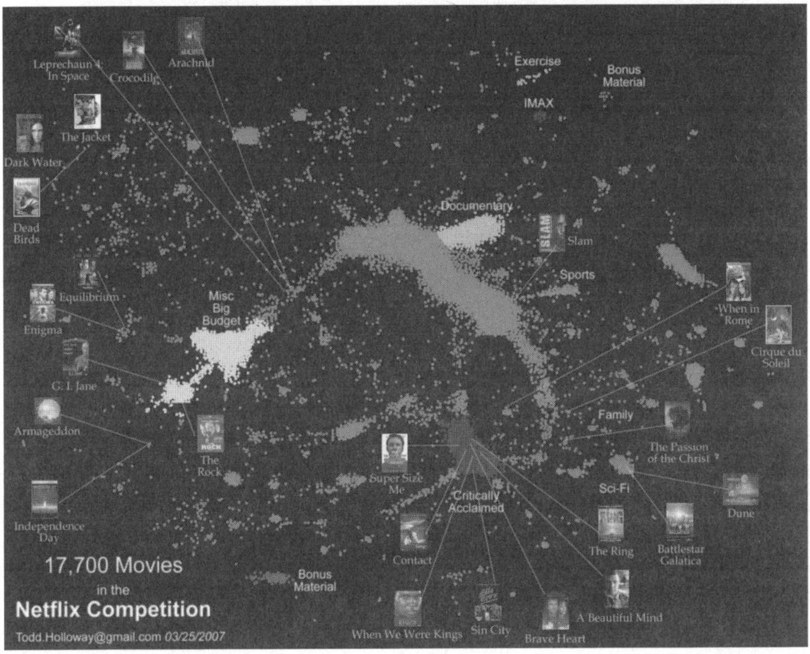


**Fig. 10.** *17,700 Movies in the Netflix Competition*, Dataset Todd Holloway, 2007

For the artist or creator of this type of participatory work the directive is to set up a set of conditions, a performance, an experiment, which will generate the work. Just as in the preparation of a Rorschach inkblot, the shape is unpremeditated and formed by the cradling and contours of the paper. In the end, what is seen or heard in the rhizomic open work is a image of the activity, one that is recognized by the viewer, as a pictogram from his for her own experience.

## 7 Collective Images

What is instructive about the rhizome formation is that its growth can be understood as a visual analogy to the creation of social networks. The process begins with participatory contributions and linking without a predetermined planned configuration. It is made from the ground up multidimensional one to one links created by participants. There are always limitations and directives built in by the programmers that can represent certain value systems. But relative to previous forms of mediation, the formation of a social network is relatively unpredictable.

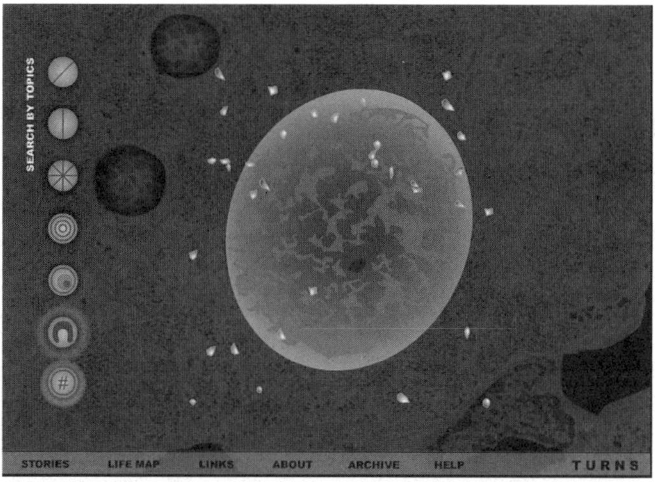


**Fig.11.** Margot Lovejoy, *Turns*, 2003 Case

## 8 Conclusion: Tuning

To consider the idea of tuning we should start with one of its first pioneers, Pythagoras of Samos, who worked on the mathematical relations of frequency and temperament. His studies on musical tuning yielded an emphasis on the sympathetic resonance of the interval, the 5th. He extended this concept to his theory *of harmony of the spheres*, that is, that the mathematical relationship of rotating planets and stars might share a similar equation.

In this sense resonance and tuning should be understood in their widest possible terms as the bringing of two or more overlaid institutions, disciplines, informational systems or experiences into a resonant alignment, through processes of attraction or repulsion. The resulting sound or sounds, whether they be harmonic or dissonant, represent the mood, tenor or image of a situation. The potential is for the generation of patterns and intonation that is not necessarily perceptible in the individual intersecting layers. There can be a reconfiguring of existing or more conventional maps that these layers provide.

In 1968, Karlheinz Stockhausen, wrote his work *Stimmung* based on methods of overtone singing. The title suggests the word's multiple meanings *as tuning, mood, emotive state, atmosphere*, or *public opinion*. Experimental modernist music, Fluxus and early electronic music of the time were pioneers in spatial music. The idea existed in both scoring and in performance. In 1992 Stockhausen created his Helicopter String Quartet in which musicians embarked from the venue and played in circling helicopters, broadcasting their video and sound to screens in the concert hall.

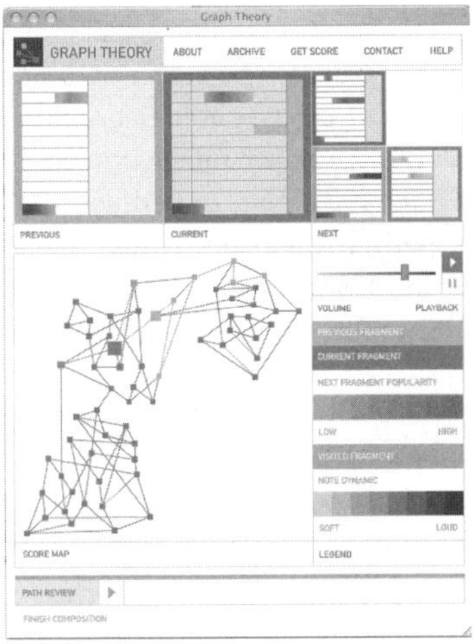


**Fig. 12.** *Graph Theory*, Turbulence.org, 2005

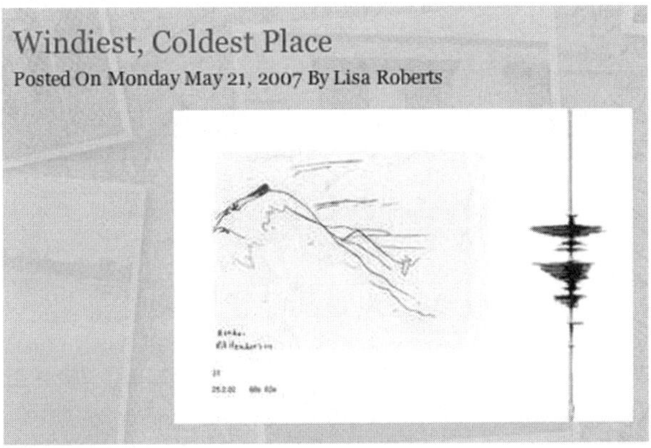


**Fig. 13.** *Disappearing Places*, 2006, Turbulence.org

Digital and networked technologies have brought an explosion of sorts in the exploration of spatial and locative sound. From the open works created by interactive dimensional diagrams, to webcrawlers that gather text as sound or sound as text, to works that gather or generate sound in relation to global positioning, it seems that for many artists, particularly in New Media, cartography is the most important medium of choice.

The idea of sound maps generated by the cross axes of varying social or disciplinary systems, that an audience participates in or generates through movement, is the extension of a multivalent notion of place. Perfomative or algorithmic parameters are setup to gather, correlate and translate unconventional sources to form the sonic map. Tuning describes a continued process of alignment. The rhizome analogizes an unpredictable multilinked generative process. The impossible graph outlines the potential of disparate coordinates. The results configure a strange formation; sound and shape that remap conditions, an alteration of place that is neither simple nor utopian.

The visual or aural experience can also be seen as a kind of statistical scatter plot, a diagnostic inkblot to be interpreted by psychologist and patient alike. The interpretation can have implications across the many intersections of subject and object, private and public and memory and policy. Tuning, or perhaps atuning, also becomes the particular meandering that the participant takes within the interdisciplinary map. The spatial encounter unfolds as the Rorschach test of the situation. Navigation reforms the resonant shape as a different kind of apperception or reasoning takes place.

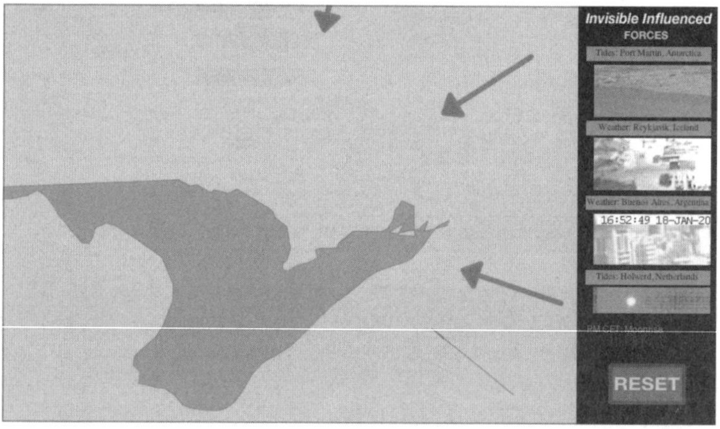


**Fig. 14.** Will Pappenheimer and Chipp Jansen, *Invisible Influenced*, 2008, Turbulence.org

## Acknowledgements

The research for this paper has been supported by Scholarly Research Grants from Pace University. Many of the ideas have been generated by previous participation in the FRE (the Florida Research Ensemble) under the direction of Gregory L. Ulmer.

## References

1. Debord, G.: Théorie de la derive, published in Internationale Situationniste # 2, Paris (December 1958). This translation by Ken Knabb is from the Situationist International Anthology, Revised and Expanded Edition (2006) (No copyright)
2. Harmon, K.: You Are here, Personal Geographies. In: Hall, S.S. (ed.) Mercator, 1st edn., ch. 1, Princeton Architectural Press (2003)
3. Tufte, E.R.: The Visual Display of Quantitative Information. Graphics Press (2001)
4. Deleuze, G., Guattari, F., Massumi, B.: A Thousand Plateaus: Capitalism and Schizophrenia. University of Minnesota Press (1987)

# Body Degree Zero
# Anatomy of an Interactive Performance

Alan Dunning[1] and Paul Woodrow[2]

[1] Alberta College of Art and Design, Calgary, Alberta, Canada
alan.dunning@acad.ca
http://www.bodydegreezero.org
[2] University of Calgary, Calgary, Alberta, Canada

**Abstract.** Machine modes of representation are sometimes thought of as being supremely abstract. In practice, these modes counterpose abstraction and realism, artifice and naturalism, in ways that have problematized the artistic debate, destabilizing traditional and conventional ways of seeing and thinking. Similarly, the body has been positioned at the intersection of many discourses cultural, scientific and artistic and finds itself subject to de-configuration. The body has become a site of self-destruction no longer a stable physical entity but an indeterminate mass of fluctuating data in continual transformation that destroys itself even as it is remade. This paper examines these issues in the work of the art and science collaboration, the Einstein's Brain Project.

## 1 Which of My Selves?

Within the context of European and North American art practices, the twentieth century has witnessed a deconfiguration of the image beginning with Impressionism, the Cubists, the Expressionists, and including a variety of Abstract styles. Running parallel to artistic movements it is also evident that deconfiguration has occurred within the context of literature, noticeable in poetry. Deconfiguration comprises the break up of surfaces - the decomposition into smaller, often disjunctive fragments. Image deconfiguration is also a resulting product of the twentieth century technological inventions of television and computer screens. Recent tools and representational devices have had a tremendous impact on the way in which the world is visually constructed and also in its future visual construction. What is noticeable over the last twenty years is the influence of technological methods of representation on the world of science. In the areas of bioscience and neurology, it has now become possible to fabricate many complex models and simulations of the body and brain, which were once thought of as impossible. Technological invention has not only influenced the way in which the body and brain are visualized but what is perhaps more important is that it has predisposed the way in which the body and brain are conceptualized. Networks, codes and the virtual have become common currency.

In A Dialectic of Centuries, Dick Higgins, co-founder of Fluxus and Something Else Press, acknowledges a profound shift in artistic consciousness:

R. Adams, S. Gibson, and S. Müller Arisona (Eds.): DAW/IF 2006/2007, CCIS 7, pp. 46–59, 2008.

"The cognitive questions asked by most artists in the 20th Century are; How can I interpret this world of which I am a part? And what am I in it? The post-cognitive questions since then are: Which world is this? What is to be done in it? Which of my selves is to do it?" [1]

## 2 Mimesis and Distanciation

During the past decade, much hybrid at and science work has used mimesis or naturalism as a primary agent. Artists and scientists have striven to develop more clearly defined images that serve a functional purpose, like a perfect three -dimensional model of a working heart with all its details. If there is a single general expectation in these advances, it is that of its capacity to present an ever increasing realism. The quest for seamlessly reproduced worlds is paramount in the development of the simulation technologies. This ideal (achievable or otherwise) of immersive virtual reality consists of surrounding an individual with images, sounds and behaviours increasingly like those of the real world. The developing strategies are those of realism rid of expression, symbol or metaphor and they are sustained by the authorities of homogeneity and seamlessness. Just as long rendering times and their outcome of low frame rates are constantly, and expensively, fought against because they disturb the seamlessness and the effectiveness. of the illusion, so ruptures in the content and consumption of the worlds are discouraged. Stopping to consider the strangeness of a sound distorted by being played too slowly or the flickering or jerkiness of an image disrupts our sense of ourselves as being in normal relations with a world. Similarly the consideration of a subtext or a hidden meaning draws attention to our consideration and away from the construction and sustenance of our normal relationship to the world. One must see these contemporary desires as linked to a history of naturalism, its concurrent dualistic pairing of reality and appearance and the authority and correctness of institutional space.

The stylistic parameters sustaining mimesis are always accompanied by distanciation. But while there is always a gap between medium and image, as can be clearly seen in the modes of realism found, for example, in painting and in film, even when they do not seek to challenge codes and conventions., the mimetic object has an affinity for the synchronic: for a particular and singular point in time. It is readily evident in the notion of the frozen moment found in photography, with all its associations with permanence, possession, capture, finality and often termination the stopping and framing of time and reality.

With the development of rapidly changing and increasingly diffuse electronic space, the frozen moment is now subject to the fluctuations and indeterminacies of the diachronic. It develops and evolves over time. The image in these spaces is a virtual projection of the medium itself, not something on the surface of its material. Here it is the difference not between the iconographic and indexical, but between two-dimensional thinking, with its fixed image surfaces, and n-dimensional images generated through bodies in motion - image traces always in flux corresponding to a body's passage through time and space.

Developments in cultural and social theory, and in technology have suggested that it is possible to move away from a graspable, predominately corporeal world to one which is increasingly slippery, elusive and immaterial. Mind and matter, combining in the cognitive body, are interdependent. The world we inhabit is in flux, comprised of increasingly complex connections and interactions. In this world there are no fixed objects, no unchanging contexts. There are only co-existant, nested multiplicities. Spectator and spectacle are entwined, occupying the same space. Perception enfolds us in matter and synthesizing us and the perceived object. In a world of objects, the subject is characterized and limited by boundaries and frames, perceived very much as invariant and separated from an unbroken field of transformations. Now it is possible to view ourselves as dynamic entities continually engaged in perpetual iconoclastic biological and social renovation and construction. Technologies of the self permit us to undertake transmutational operations on our own bodies and allows us to transform our image of ourselves existing in states of continuous construction and reconstruction.

## 3 The Einstein's Brain Project

The Einstein's Brain Project is a collaborative group of artists and scientists who have been working together for the past ten years. The aim of the group is the visualization of the biological state of the body through the fabrication of environments, simulations installations and performances. The project has developed numerous systems and installations using analog or digital interfaces to direct the output of the human body to virtual environments that are constantly being altered through feedback from a participants biological body. The core of the Einstein's Brain Project is a discursive space that engages with ideas about consciousness, the constructed body in the world, and its digital cybernetic and post-human forms.

The fact that consciousness is unified problematizes the relationship of reality versus appearance. The complexities of audience/art work, subject/object are brought into question as a result of a novel construction of the self.

Our very organism, then, rather than some absolute experiential reality, is used as the frame of reference for the constructions we make of the world around us and for the construction of the ever-present sense of subjectivity. The body is turned inside out and placed beside and around itself like a Klein bottle.[3] The distinctions between interior and exterior, between body and world, are broken down even as they are erected in the organism's moment to moment reconstruction of itself. This corporal literacy is a poetics of reversal - a jellyfish that physically inverts itself as a natural consequence of the flows it produces and navigates.

The Project's virtual environments and installations contextualize, visualize and examine physical, spatial and mental human activity by measuring the electrical output of active bodies in dynamic environments. Biodata are fed into real-time immersive worlds, where they are displayed as aural and visual forms representing the activity of the human body. The project has designed a variety of methods to acquire data, using contact and non-contact sensors, and has developed strategies to reveal features, patterns and attributes in the captured data in order to visualize their characteristics and to represent the data as coherent and retrievable information.

The Project's works establish a recursive loop, in which the invisible actions of the body are manifest and an inhabitant is required to monitor both the changing environment and the body that manifests it. This is achieved by a relational vocabulary of representation, in which identities are lost and gained, subsumed by a non-identifiable collection of other identities. This body is always on the verge of coming into being but never fully formed. It exists only in the past and the future, with no place in the present.

This new formulation of the self is, according to Antonio Damasio, an:

"evanescent reference state, so continuously and consistently reconstructed that the owner never knows that it is being remade unless something goes wrong with the remaking Present continuously becomes past, and by the time we take stock of it we are in another present, consumed with planning for the future, which we do on the stepping stones of the past. The present is never here." [2]

This is Body Degree Zero.

## 4 Body Degree Zero

Body Degree Zero comes to represent an alternative, functional alternative, to the Cartesian or Lacanian constructions of selff: no longer minds fed back onto the self-reflection of psychology or philosophy, but non-bodies fed back upon themselves, experiencing the data derived from an immanent physical presence that both is, and is not, theirs; heartbeats that form not only the internal rhythm of living but an external soundscape; brainwaves that, stripped of the illusion of privacy, begin to gyrate on electronic screens; and McLuhans prophecy fulfilled, as the data-skeleton of autonomic bodily processes becomes clothing worn, subject to all the same rules of designer fashion and aesthetic self-fashioning.

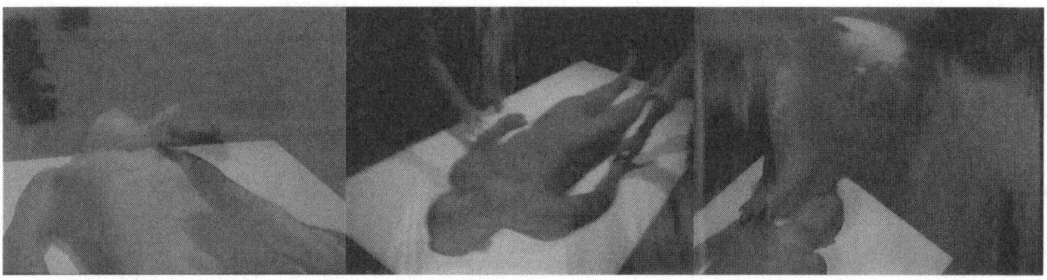

**Fig. 1.** The Madhouse, 2004

A series of works using the interface ALIBI (anatomically lifelike interactive biological interface) began in 2000. ALIBI is a life-size cast of a male human body filled with sensors that allow participants to interact with computer systems by touching, speaking to or breathing on the body. The body is covered with thermochromic paint that changes colour when touched. Used in conjunction with a brainwave recording device built into a HeadsUp Display (HUD), the body interface monitors the biological and physical output of a participants own body, including EEG data, skin temperature, electrical resistance, speech, gesture and motion.

The first of the works using ALIBI was the Madhouse [Fig. 1.]. The interface was placed in the centre of the room and participants touched, stroked and breathed upon particular locations on the body to produce corresponding images (sometimes related to the bodys function and at other times related to metaphor and simile) in a virtual world. The images were seen in a HeadsUp Display worn by the participant and simultaneously viewed by the audience by means of projection onto a screen in the gallery. When viewed by other observers, the participant resembles a pathologist examining a corpse. The images seen in the HUD are degraded and in black and white. Distorted views of people, buildings, objects in motion and lights appear as semiotic ghosts faded memories of the city or low-resolution recordings, as if dredged up from some deep and long-forgotten time well. Attached to the HUD are electrodes that monitor the participants brainwaves. These brainwaves are fed in real-time into a three-dimensional virtual reality environment and are manifested as visual and aural equivalents that are projected onto the second screen and amplified in the space.

This virtual reality simulation is in constant flux; a living phenomenon that evolves in infinite space and time and responds in real time to a participants mental activity. What a participant sees is a real-time manifestation of his or her brain and biological activity. When the participant is at ease, the environments and sounds are fluid, slow-paced and smooth; as he or she responds to the images, the environments and audio become jagged, fast-paced and increasingly raucous when a participant is again able to reach a tranquil state, the work returns to languid. As the participant touches the body, sounds are synthesized in real-time and fill the gallery space. Moving hands across the surface of the body and placing them in different areas and in different relationships to each other produces and modifies the pitch, volume and timbre of the sounds. [Figs. 2 and 3.]

A more recent manifestation of the collaboration is a series of performance works entitled Body Degree Zero, which employ the traces of real-time bodily activity with technologically constructed spaces and forms. These works use strategies taken from the Situationists, together with ideas about coincidence and synchronicity, to develop visualizations of an immanent, past and future mindbody. The notion of a dynamic mindbody is central to the work of the Einstein's Brain Project. The mindbody is constructed in response to endless permutations of external contingent events. This technologized mindbody exists only in its constant and conditional reconfiguration. Body Degree Zero is super

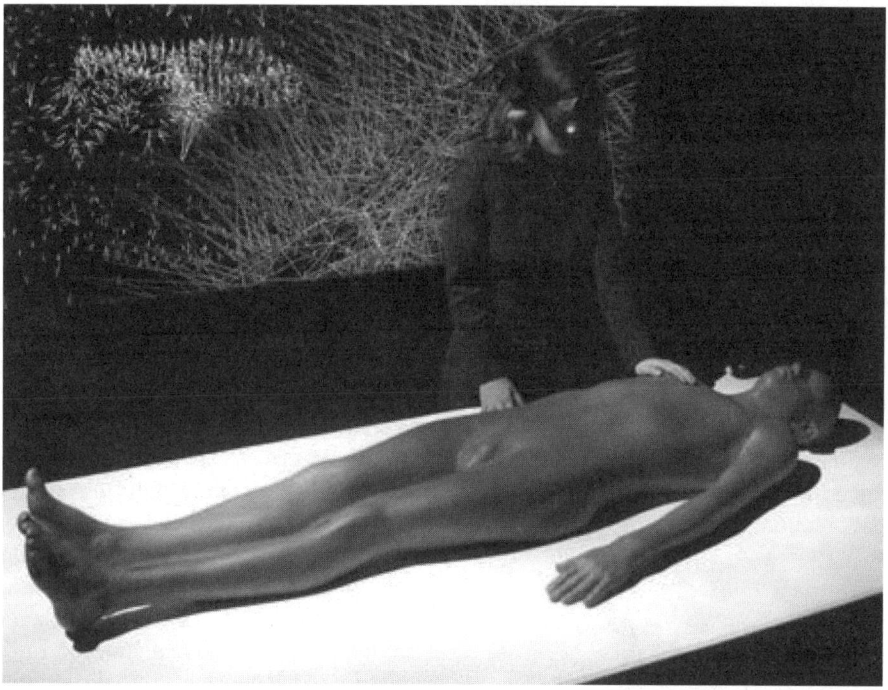

**Fig. 2.** ALIBI - Pandaemonium 2004

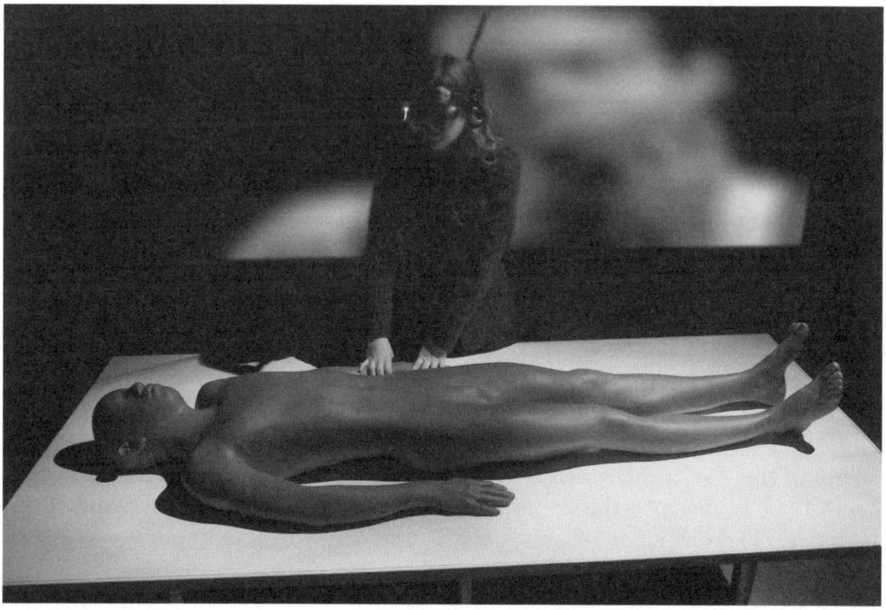

**Fig. 3.** ALIBI - Pandaemonium 2004

distributed, enfolded and enfolding, remade yet never made. It is a body without a boundary, a spectre - a body without a body.

The spontaneous turns of direction taken by a subject moving through a city were known to the Situationists as dérives. The dérive (drift or drifting) changed the meaning of the city by changing the way in which it was occupied and allowed the Situationists to entertain the possibility of new realities existing in the back streets of Paris. The Situationists introduced the idea that misinterpretation actively pursued is a new kind of interpretation that allows the world to be analyzed in novel and surprising ways. Body Degree Zero uses the strategies of the drive to change the nature of the data space by changing not only the way that we inhabit space but also the way we must (mis)interpret it. Combining the strategies of the dérive and ideas about apophenia [4] the spontaneous perception of connections between unrelated phenomena and the tactics of the drive the Project's work establishes a space that is initially understandable as a real-time representation of the body but is finally ungraspable, as an audience is forced to search for disappearing and ruptured bodies, existing only in a fading past or imagined future.

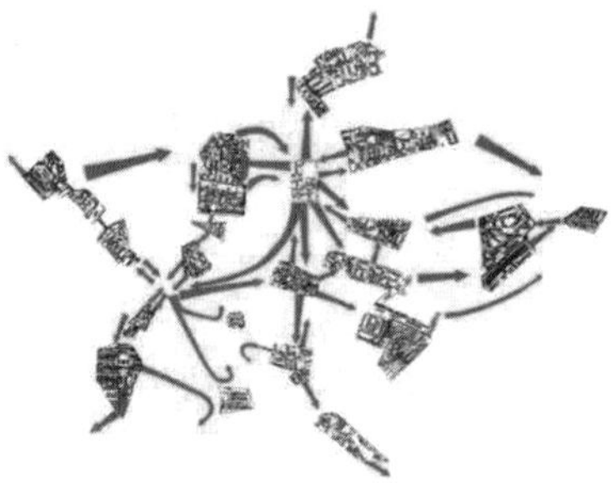

**Fig. 4.** Guy DeBord's Naked City

In 1957, key Situationist, Guy Debord published The Naked City. [Fig. 4.] Consisting of randomly collaged fragments taken from a map of Paris and linked together by directional arrows, the work summarized the Situationists' strategy for exploring urban space. The map presents a structurally unintelligible view of Paris, the fragments having no clear relation to each other. In a text on the reverse of the map, we are told that the arrows describe the spontaneous turns of direction taken by a subject moving through these surroundings in disregard of the useful connections that ordinarily govern his conduct [5]

These turns exemplify the drives. The original map of Paris is revealed as a seamless representation, in which diversity and distinction are concealed. Debords The Naked City, by contrast, is a city infinitely faceted, marked by division and difference. The drive mirrors Antonio D'Amasio's continual, moment-by-moment, construction of the self:

"[T]he images in the consciousness narrative flow like shadows along with images of the object for which they are providing an unwitting unsolicited comment. To come back to the metaphor of the movie-in-the brain they are within the movie. There is no external spectator. the core you is only born as the story is told, within the story itself." [6]

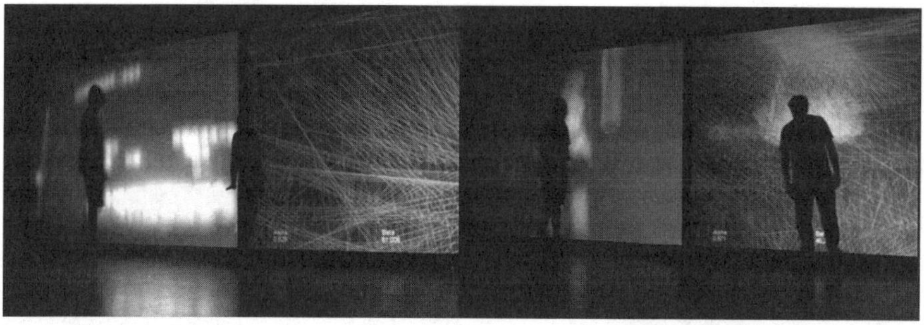

**Fig. 5.** Body Degree Zero, Rosario, Argentina 2005

## 5 The Performance

Two participants are wired to various bio-electrical sensors, ranging from electrodes that track brain waves to sensors attached to the skin that record galvanic skin responses. The sensors track the participants activity and bio-electrical output and visualize this in real time in the form of synthesized and manipulated images that are back projected onto two large screens in front of the participants. [Fig. 5.] Accompanying the images are sounds generated from the activity of the participants. Local environmental conditions are monitored and streamed into the system, where they modify the participants data. As the resultant mix becomes more and more complex and its characteristics more and more an amalgam of the three data entities, it becomes increasingly uncertain what is being represented and exactly what space this new recombinant form demands, as the participants identities are lost in the ensuing environmental data storm. [Fig. 6.]

Using EEG electrodes, a Psylab interface and biological amplifiers, EEG sensors and custom EKG sensors connected to a Macintosh computer via Teleo hardware, the potentials evoked are translated into sounds and forms, using specially designed data acquisition modules in EONReality and MAX/MSP/Jitter, respectively. The sounds and images produced are of two kinds: those that are limited in interpretation and clearly indexed to bioactivity and those that are polysemous and open to interpretation. The visualization is a combination of abstract generated forms and found imagery. The frequency, amplitude, and percentage differences between samples of incoming data are mapped to forms moving in computer space. The data is used to change the position, scale, shape and physics of simple primitive meshes, where each vertex of the mesh starts at zero and the object has no velocity, mass or other property. The incoming data is visualized as spikes, amoeba-like blobs and particles that indicate the degree of activity of the participants.

Random numbers create noise in the system, creating errant and misleading signs. Some visualizations are easily identified. The throbbing of a shape is a beating heart; the increase in particle production is a rise in GSR. Others are suggestive rather than indicative, taking the form of erratic, distorted,

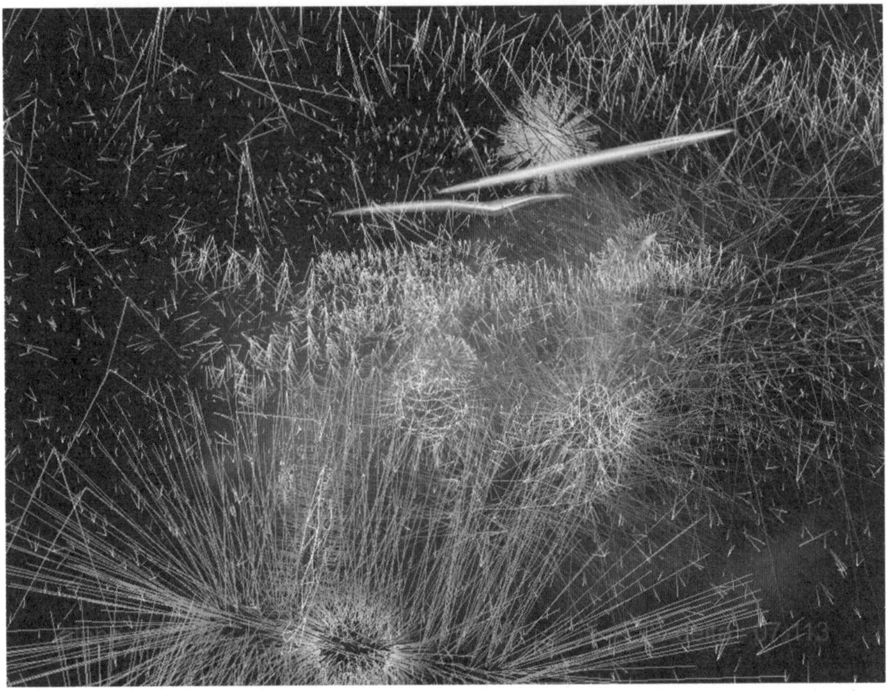

**Fig. 6.** Body Degree Zero - Prague/Singapore, 2005

cinematic or historical images that are streamed into the space or mapped onto primitives or of shapes morphing from one form to another too rapidly to be comprehended. Similarly, sounds are generated in real time using a software synthesizer and are an index of peak voltages, frequency and percentage differences. Data is mapped to harmoniousness - values close to whole numbers are harmonious, while fractional values produce enharmonic timbres. Data sampled over longer periods are mapped onto the spatial properties of the sounds and images, the degree of movement and the orientation of objects, images and sounds varying proportionally with respect to the general dynamism of the participants.

In this particular performance, the participants act out David Cronenberg's Shivers - a film dealing with body horror and social paranoia. The screenplay and movie of Shivers are streamed as text and image into the projected visualization. Both the movie and the screenplay are indexed in terms of their emotional and dramatic peaks and troughs, and, during the performance, the moving images and texts are reordered in response to incoming bio data from the participants. As data from the participants indicates a rise or fall in bioactivity, so texts and images relating to corresponding highs and lows in the film are sent to the screens. [Fig. 7.]

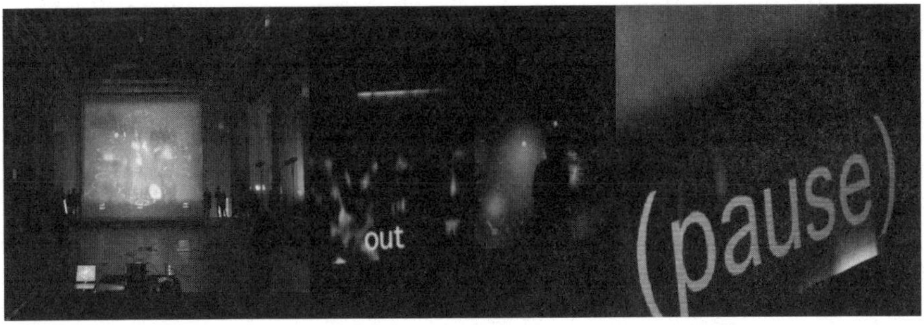


**Fig. 7.** Body Degree Zero - Prague/Singapore, 2005

## 6 Pattern Recognition

The Shapes of Thought (2004 and ongoing) [Fig. 8.] is another work that visualizes EEG and other bioelectrical signals as three-dimensional forms. The work draws a connection between the electrical output of the body/mind and its inner workings. Forms are generated by monitoring the EEG and EKG of a participant as they recall traumatic events and using these numbers to change simple primitive meshes into complex forms, as each is pushed and pulled by the incoming data. Over very long periods  more than 12 hours in some cases  a smooth sphere or cube becomes a heavily fissured, bumpy and spiked object  a recent geological record of the bio-electrical patterns generated by the participant.

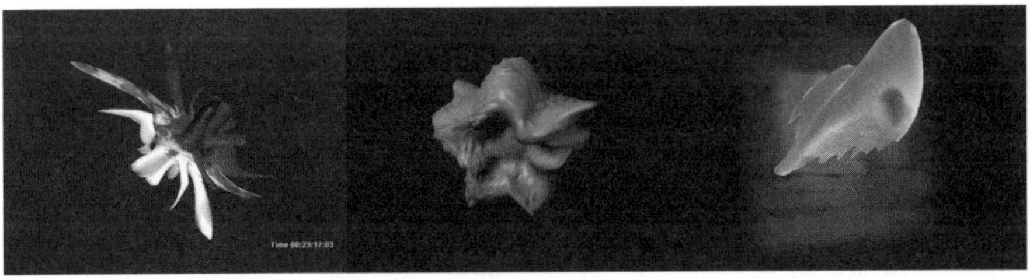

**Fig. 8.** Shapes of Thought, 2004 - ongoing

Participants agreed to undergo hypnosis to aid in the recollection and reliving of events in which they were deeply affected by anger, or other primary emotions. As participants drifted in and out of the hypnotic and sleeping states each participants data was visualized in realtime, interactive space.

The hypnotic recollections of the participants, their mental re-visualizations of traumatic events, produce effects on the body that are then imaged and examined providing ways to investigate the workings of the body-mind through these mental images. However, the relationship between a participant's thoughts and the objects remains uncertain. Numbers are plotted and visualized and peaks and valleys in the participant's activity can be easily discerned. Yet the forms are as much crystal balls - noisy, spongy, screens open to revelatory exploration and divination - as they are records of activity. As such, the objects and their contents, the output from participants' body/minds, is never static or fixed, as their patterns of information respond dynamically to inspection.

The Sounds of Silence (2006 and ongoing), is a work that uses the strategies of Electronic Voice Phenomenon (EVP) and ideas about apohenia and pareidolia to generate voices, and images from apparently silent and empty spaces. [Fig. 9.]

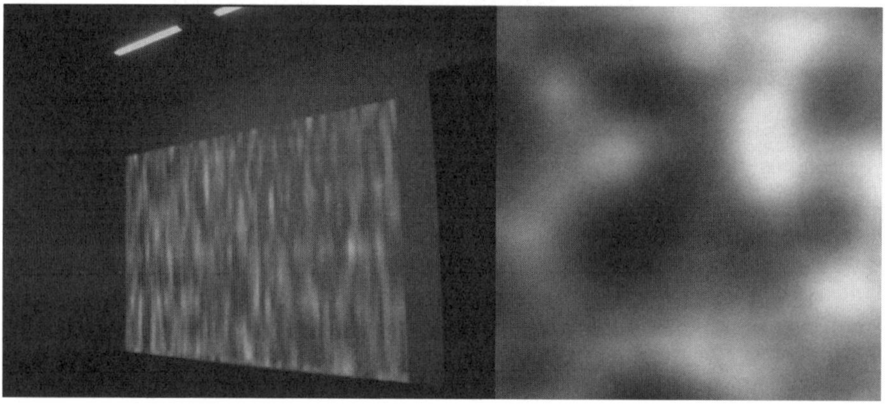

**Fig. 9.** Sounds of Silence, 2007

Electronic Voice Phenomenon is the recording of errant noises or voices that have no explainable or physical source of origin. These recordings are made when the recorder is alone, or under controlled circumstances. Most often white or pink noise is used as a medium that is acted upon by other electromagnetic forces. This electromagnetic medium produces wave forms that are, occasionally, like human speech. It has been argued that the voices are simply subjective interpretations - that we tend to hear voices in random patterns of sound, in the way we recognize forms in random visual patterns. For others, the voices are genuinely mysterious, opening up the possibility of communication with the dead.

This work uses the ideas inherent in EVP to examine ways in which we construct the world through pareidolia, (a psychological phenomenon involving a vague and random stimulus - often an image or sound - being perceived as significant), apophenia (the seeing of connections where there are none) and the gestalt effect (the recognition of pattern and form).

A CCD camera is turned on but enclosed in a light tight box. Its input is adjusted with maximum gain and brightness to reveal the video noise inherent in the system. This noise forms the optical equivalent of audio noise and is used in a similar way to provide a medium that can be modified by external forces to produce images and sounds. The video noise is mapped to audio by sampling pixels in a Quicktime matrix and using the values to manipulate a stream of white noise. Voice recognition software parses the modulated noise and translates any sufficiently voice-like sounds into its nearest vocal equivalent, which is sent to the screen as text and rendered into audio by speech synthesizers into Italian, German, English or Spanish.

Face tracking algorithms scan every video frame and look for any combination of pixels that form the basic characteristics of a human face. These are areas that can be loosely characterized as eyes, nose and mouth with a sufficient degree of symmetry. When the software finds such a combination of pixels and symmetry the area is zoomed to full screen, its contrast and brightness adjusted, blurred and desaturated to clarify the found images.

The images produced are only occasionally reminiscent of human faces. More often than not the images produced are recognized as indeterminate organic forms with volume and space, but fail to resolve themselves into anything recognizable. But occasionally, images are produced that are strikingly like a face although in actuality containing only the barest possibility of being so.

Both of these works provide a means to reconsider the performance Body Degree Zero in light of the Project's interest in systems of meaning-making that rely on pattern recognition, and the problematized relationship between meaning and the meaningful. The development of meaning in the Project's work is dependent on an increasingly, yet seemingly infinite, complex recursive and recombinant loop between meaning made and meaning found. In this loop the external and internal worlds are blurrily indistinct, each acting upon the other in the construction of a new self/space forever suspended at the point of becoming. The effort to restablilize the self in this world where everything is in play, is questioned and negotiable, is unavoidably revelatory and re-problematizes current and preceding models of authenticity and resistance.

## 7 Conclusion

Given the complex relationship between the construction of the self and the construction of space, a body in a virtual world has moved towards a hybrid state, composed of biological organism and machine, in which it is not always precisely clear who makes and who is made. The boundary between organism and non-organism, actor and non-actor, self and non-self has been abandoned, and our postmodern bodies are artificial constructions of technologies and technological discourses that are continually decaying and being renewed. The body is so inextricably enmeshed with its surroundings and the technologies that support it, that representations of the body become indistinguishable from the mechanisms of its representation and erasure. This complex interplay of phenomena and energies is Body Degree Zero. Body Degree Zero, the non-body, the body without skin, without ego boundary, is the evolutionary consequence of the super-distribution of identity over increasingly broad and responsive real-time networks. The body enfolds the world and the world enfolds the body the notion of the skin as the boundary to the body falls apart. The body, as here not there, and its defining sense of the other are a mental construction every perception of the other is a creation and every invocation a re-creation.

"This is the visceral extension of the material body with the aim of turning all autonomic functions into observable (excremental) data or the inverse a data-constipation in which the virtual lodges itself unyieldingly into the material body, or perhaps again a relation now, not between bodies and world, but between perception and information with body-degree-zero as the unwritten script that might perhaps only be defined in terms of the variables allowed to inform the shapes it takes? It seems that perhaps what is crucial to the formulation of zero-degree content is precisely the same zero-degree that finds its way into Barthes zero-degree writing - not in the sense of a reliance on interpretive presence for the formation of content, but rather in the immanent state of information without audience - the metamorphosis into the absence of an unidentifiable body that nevertheless seems, for all intents and purposes, to still exist despite its unidentifiability." [7]

## 7.1 The HyperMorphic and the TransOrganic

The novel movement of this unidentifiable body is, to use the Project's terms, hyper-morphic and transorganic. Hypermorphism is the tendency of mindbody and world components to change from one form to another so rapidly and continuously that, although they never fix on a form, they appear stable. Transorganic is the nature of hyper-morphic forms oscillating between the extremes of organic and non-organic. The hyper-morphic and transorganic are driven by the twin engines of parallax and hybridization. Objects blur into hybrid forms, neither entirely one thing or another. Viewpoints move randomly and rapidly. Like the experience of a traveler in a forest fixing on a constantly disappearing and reappearing navigation marker flickering through the trees, occluded objects are remade, revealed and re-contextualized. In the work of the Einstein's Brain Project the Situationist dérive is seen as a recursive, social loop, used for self and contextual awareness. The drift and its accompanying sense of dpaysement (disoriented or deceived) are used to generate new meanings and new understandings, freed, as it were, not just from the burden of communication but also from the oppositions of pattern and randomness, and presence and absence. In this work, biofeedback is used to mirror the drive and its reworking of space. As objects, bodies and worlds recombine freely through hyper-morphic and transorganic movement that implies no fixed form and no fixed substance, the possibility emerges of degree-zero bodies and states pregnant with all past and future specifications [8]

## References

1. Higgins, D.: A Dialectic of Centuries: Notes Toward a Theory of the New Arts, BOA Editions (1999)
2. Damasio, A.R.: Descartes Error. Avon Books, New York (1994)
3. A Klein bottle is a closed non-orientable surface that has no inside or outside
4. Apophenia is a term coined by Klaus Conrad in 1958, who used aspects of Gestalt psychology to give a better understanding of aphasia and schizophrenia. It is defined as the spontaneous perception of the connections among and the meaningfulness of unrelated phenomena
5. McDonough, T.F. (ed.): Guy Debord and the Situationist International. MIT Press, Cambridge (2002)
6. Hiebert, T. (ed.): Personal communication to Alan Dunning and Paul Woodrow, Vancouver (2003)
7. Barthes, R.: Writing Degree Zero. The Noonday Press, New York (1990)

# Artificial, Natural, Historical

## Acoustic Ambiguities in Documentary Film

Julian Rohrhuber

University Cologne and Academy of Media Art Cologne

**Abstract.** This article discusses the role of sound for the formation of authenticity and historicity in film. In the light of the documentary *All That We Have*, it argues that the delimitation between 'natural' and 'artificial' constitutes a key element for the construction of the authentic. Algorithmic sound synthesis is shown to be a possible intervention within this construction. Informed by a generally epistemological orientation, this analysis inquires how form, method and content may together contribute to a critique of a naturalization of history.

## 1 The Authentic Source

*[The talkie] has conquered the world of voices, but it has lost the world of dreams. I have observed people leaving the cinema after seeing a talking film. They might have been leaving a music hall, for they showed no sign of the delightful numbness which used to overcome us after a passage through the silent land of pure images. They talked and laughed, and hummed the tunes they had just heard. They had not lost their sense of reality.*[1]

Pleasant or unpleasant, many commentators who have experienced the transition from silent film to talkie describe a similar experience: It seems as if film had *woken up*, had lost its dream-like character. In the new genre of 'talkies', the human voice had entered the scene and brought with it a whole field of narrative possibilities, which were used excessively; still today dialogue makes one of the main dimensions along which a majority of films are organized. Dialogue is to a great extent tied to the correlation of *voices* to their respective persons: It is the person who is the cause of the voice, and, from the perspective of the narrative, it is the person's network of intentions, obligations and contingencies that causes what is said.

The dream-like character of the silent movie might be a result of a distortion of this causal relation: It seems as if a person tried to say something, but no voice leaves her mouth—then, a little later, we read in the following intertitle what has been said. The sensorimotor cycle is inhibited by the temporal interval

[1] René Clair, 1929. [1].

R. Adams, S. Gibson, and S. Müller Arisona (Eds.): DAW/IF 2006/2007, CCIS 7, pp. 60–70, 2008.

that separates visual from the narrative, and opens a space for the psychological and for the ambiguity between inside and outside.[2]

Closing this gap, though, does not dispel the doubt about who is the true originator of an utterance: Was something said because the author wanted us to hear it? Was it said by a character in order to cause an action of another character? Is it an intrigue altogether?[3] One can never be sure. At least the truthful source of the voice itself will be eventually reaffirmed, in a 'cartesian strategy', by the consistency of physical causality in filmic space: The consistency of *natural sound* provides the necessary background for the voice's corporality. To this end, the sound is composed so that coincides with the picture in an plausible manner, forming a causal texture for the events.[4] Thus, the physical impression of sound is the seal on the authenticity of their material source: the spoon rattling next to the cup, a quiet harrumph, or the classic footsteps in the gravel.

In fiction film, the *origins of actions* usually are either attributed diegetically [5] to the film's inner logic and its characters, or simply to the authors' motivations. Conversely, a documentary film is expected to be faithful to actions that either happened while the picture was filmed, or to those that happened possibly long before, where documentary takes on the role of a witness to the past. This fidelity can be *passive*, in the sense that the 'profilmic' actions are untouched by production and simply reflected, it may also be *active* in the sense that the film *investigates* in order to clarify the delimitation between fact and fiction. The expectation of fidelity is rooted in the promise that the agency of protagonists, be they human or non-human, inscribes its trace as directly as possible into

[2] In *Triebe und Triebschicksale* [2, p. 212] (1915), Freud describes the first differentiation between inner and outer world as the result of the experience that some stimuli can be avoided by muscular activity (e.g. escape), while others, necessities caused by drives, withstand such attempts.

For Bergson, the indetermination between action and reaction is a key function that creates two systems: one in which the images change dependent on the movements of a single image (the body) and one for which the images vary by themselves [3, p. 9]. This investigation of indetermination is taken up by Deleuze and serves as a basis for the distinction between image types [4,5].

[3] The films by Ernst Lubitsch, such as 'To Be or Not To Be', are a good example for the extensive use of intrigue in dialogue that was common in the early talkie era.

[4] Sound appears to have its own peculiar transparency here. It thus seems symptomatic that when people are asked to describe sounds, they consistently describe sources, not the sound itself: this is a motorcycle, a drill, a cricket, a waterfall. For a closer discussion of this relation between transparency and opacity in sound art, see [6].

[5] The definition of *diegesis* is debated: This term was coined (by Etienne Souriau) *in opposition to the term 'narrative'*, to refer to all the film's denotations, to the totality of the fictional world in which the narrative is only a part. Thus, *nondiegetic sound* conventionally denotes sound that is not caused and cannot be perceived by anyone who is part of the film's denotative space. Background music and off-screen narration are therefore nondiegetic elements. But not unlike the distinction between *form/content* or *medium/message*, for a general situation, it is undecidable where the delimitation is to be drawn. For a controversial discussion of these issues see e.g. [7].

the film's diegetic space. This explains the critical role of 'natural sound' in documentary film: It is witness to the ontic status of its material cause and stabilizes the realist perspective of the documentary dispositive.

## 2 Natural and Artificial

Interestingly, in the early talkies, the film music is very often diegetic film music—some of the films circle magically around dancehalls, attractive musicians, or find other excuses to place a musical sound source somewhere. Keeping in mind the conventional role of natural sound in film, this is no surprise. Contrary to silent film, by placing musical instruments on screen instead of letting them play in the 'cinematic orchestra pit', they are naturalized as material sound sources, thus closing the sensimotor cycle and, to a degree, freeing film from its psychological ambiguities.

Just like fiction film, many conventional documentary films use nondiegetic film music as an emotional background, or as a compositional method, e.g. to smooth out picture sequences. This sound texture also provides an honorable accompaniment for the 'voice of god', which tells the audience what the picture means. [6] At first, this seems to contradict the fidelity of a documentation—but it is clear that instead of supporting the topos of direct transmission, it enhances the audience's faith in the sincerity of the witness, represented by the narrator's voice. As long as the level of *explanation*, which can be 'artificial' (i.e. fabricated by the film), is distinguishable from the level of the *object*, which needs to be 'natural' (i.e. factual), an 'authentic' relation between the two can be established. In conventional documentary, this relation is expected to provide a clear separation between the observer and the observed, where the diegetic sound sources are what is observed, and the nondiegetic sound forms a sedan on which the observer is brought safely to the end of the film.

One might argue that a film can hardly be in control over its interpretation and the attribution of authenticity is a complicated process. It can be claimed, e.g. that the differentiation between fictionality and nonfictionality is independent of the film itself, but is the consequence of an 'implicit contract' between viewers and producers.[7] Nevertheless, this contract is not always implicit, and it can be subject to open negotiation. Since its early stages, numerous film makers have (implicitly or explicitly) made the documentary genre itself a subject of their work. In this spirit, we may investigate the frontier between the attribution of artificial and natural, which provides a frame that allows us to reason about how sound may work in films that attempt to reflect on how authenticity is caused or fabricated. Taking into account the role of sound in this negotiation, this study is likely to get involved in the relation between physical acoustics and whatever falls outside of this category.

[6] see also: Chion's concept of the *acousmetre* [8].

[7] [9]. See also Chion's concept of the 'audiovisual contract'[8].

## 3 The Sound of Home

*[...] this feeling of unity and the history and all that ... that's what we want to preserve, that's our heritage, our roots, that's where we came from, we didn't just fall from the sky, that's our real history [...] without the past we're nothing, that's my opinion anyway. You can't just go around claiming that we just suddenly happened, and here we are, now, and it's all good and everything that was, was bad. That's ... history has taught us ... oh well, that should've ... I don't want to stray from the point, ... and the logical consequence of all this would be to build a Local History Museum.* [8]

Quite similarly to the natural and authentic, the past is an embattled place. Both objectivity and identity depend on a consent on *what has happened so far*, and any dispute about what is real and what is allowed seems to unavoidably revert to history. Since individual memory as well as the past 'itself' are inaccessible, external and timeless representations of past events serve as proxies and educational means to establish a stable notion of historical fact—on the level of the universal (like the state) or the local (like a family). History as a science maintains a distinct scepticism toward the idea of consistent history and holds that the historical is characterized by contingency regarding the past events, their mediation and their interpretation today. [9] Regarding individual memory, a similar prudence has been suggested by psychoanalysis.

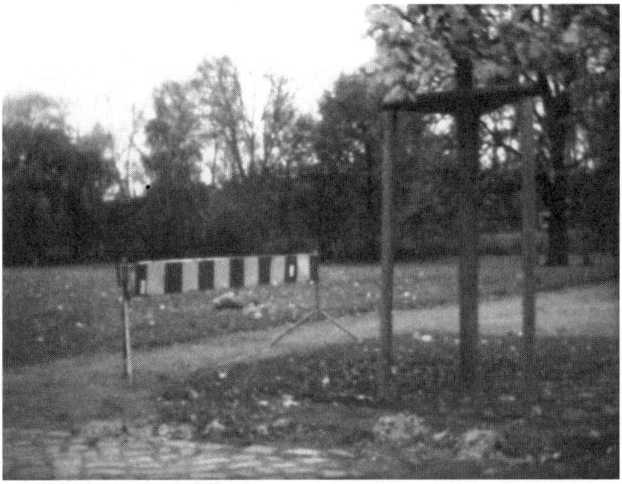

**Fig. 1.** A scene from *All That We Have*, situated on a location of local historical relevance

[8] Helmut Wattenberg, town archivist, transcript from an interview 2002. My omissions are marked by [...], pauses of the speaker by ....

[9] This stance is maybe best illustrated by a historians' witticism: *"The contemporary witness is the natural enemy of the historian."*

The documentary *All That We Have*[10] investigates a typical representation of local historical identity, a local history museum in northern Germany. Being a documentary—a classical medium of historical representation—it makes it a subject of discussion what role film plays, in a more general sense, in the production of authenticity. This happens at several levels simultaneously; its subject is the culture of historical representation and formation; at the same time, it makes documentary film the subject of a critical investigation. This is, as we will see, where sound plays a pivotal role.

Following a list of important locations that is published in the museum's book *Lebendige Heimat* [10] the film is composed of a series of panoramic 360° panning shots (e.g. Figure 1). The voice off-camera explains the history of the place, why it is characterized by a series of fires over many centuries, and that, as there are hardly any historical buildings left, a place of historical identity is indispensable. In a fluent transition, the male narrator's voice blends into a female voice,[11] who explains the more recent history of the local history museum itself, which has been set fire to regularly since the 1970s. The pictures show places that bear traces of a certain particularity, but obviously fail to present any authentic 'past-as-past'. While the moving gaze of the camera sometimes gets hold of a car or a person, we have a particular, but fairly generic outlook.

Inverting the perspective of Kamensky's previous film *Divina Obsesión* (1999), the complete cycles of panning shots constantly follow the theme of a panoptic desire: the documentary view is typically presented as all-embracing. While *Divina Obsesión* links this panoramic vision to the history of sovereignty and enlightenment, [12] *All That We Have* makes historicity and the construction of identity a subject of discussion. Reoccurring fires, which make up part of the history of the town, while simultaneously destroying its traces, lead to a constant reconstructive activity—this motive is predominant, and instead of naturalizing this history (the area is indeed windy), the off-camera narration explains that the fires were usually set on purpose, with various, and partly unclear motivations. An analogy is drawn between historical identity and the documentarist's realism, which converges in the tendencies of materialization and fixation.

As we have seen, 'natural sound' in documentary film embeds the observer in an envelope of a kind of material authenticity. The fact that the terms *natural sound* and *original sound* [13] are often taken to refer to the same thing, shows that the idea of the 'origin' is somehow tied to the idea of the 'natural'. Here, in the context of *All That We Have*, this coincidence is questioned and it is shown to be part of a naturalistic historiography. In order to achieve this, the film investigates the border between natural and artificial sound, and in order to be able to abstract from references to origin, it restricts itself entirely to

[10] *Living Homeland*, see: [11].

[11] The speakers are: Sarina Tappe (director of the homeland museum), Helmut Wattenberg (town archivist) and Volko Kamensky (film maker).

[12] Kamensky more explicitly refers to the concepts of panoptic view in [12], where he links documentary with the institutional and technical history [13,14].

[13] *Production sound*, German *O-Ton*.

specifically written sound synthesis algorithms and does not use location sound recording.[14] We will have a closer look at some details of the construction of this sound track, which are relevant for the discussion of the relation between the artificial, the natural and the historical. The authors[15] followed the strategy to construct the acoustic situation for each scene in a conversational process from memory, without listening or analysis of any recordings. Negotiating a possible reconstruction of a sound memory, each of the acoustic events is an *acoustic portrait*, or in some cases a *sound icon* of what could be called the *phantasmatic sound object*. Partly, this results in a kind of hyperrealism, where each sound is overly clear and separated, an impression that is magnified by the fact that in most cases one can only hear those sounds whose source is visible.[16] On the other hand, the unity of space is dubious—on many occasions the physical origin of a sound clearly becomes suspicious (Figure 2). Lacking clear locality, the attribution of the origin becomes perceivable as a process, sometimes even as a deliberate choice of the observer. Instead of attempting to simulate what is sufficient to cause a smooth and realistic impression, *All That We Have* plays with the borderline of failure of what may still count as authentic. Since eventually, what specifies the sound is a program text, we may infer that the *natural* itself is a kind of text that is inscribed by the intervention of an investigation of truth.

## 4 Sound and Formalism

Artificial sounds have accompanied the cinema from its beginning: The need of a separate sonic reconstruction of the acoustic scene at least needed to compensate for the difficulty of location sound recording. This constraint gave rise to a whole art form that spans from foley to film music in which to a certain degree the difference between musical accompaniment by instruments and the noise produced as a location sound replacement became negotiable. Jacques Tati's oeuvre comes to mind here, and it is not by accident that his staging of modernity, and its superposition with acoustic abstraction and ambiguity is so successful.

With the beginning of electronic sound synthesis, the idea of a complete universality of artificial sounds met with the mysticism of a secret life inside the electronic circuits; it seemed that everything was possible. In the acoustic narrative of science fiction sound tracks, technical, electronic sound sources converge

[14] The algorithms have been implemented in the programming language *SuperCollider* [15]. Apart from the off-screen narration, no recorded sound has been used as material in the soundtrack.

[15] The soundtrack was programmed during the year 2003 by Julian Rohrhuber, in conversation with Volko Kamensky, at the Hamburg Art Academy. It was mixed down by Alberto de Campo, Rohrhuber and Kamensky at the Academy of Media Art, Cologne.

[16] In this way it could be claimed (in contradiction to Metz) that the impossibility of off-screen sound is only conventional: Metz had stated a fundamental difference between image and sound because, according to him, there is no off-camera in sound, as it always surrounds the audience.

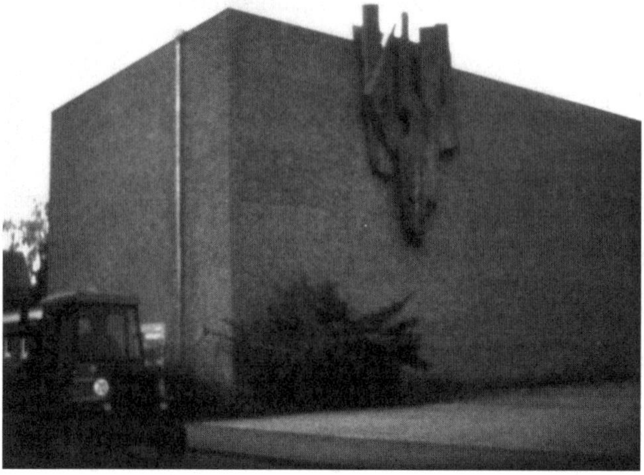

**Fig. 2.** An agricultural vehicle is passing a church, a pipe organ is playing inside

with alien languages and robot voices.[17] Here, the electronic is seen as a path that promises the escape from the ordinary. On the other hand, electronic sound over time became a means to replace the orchestra and mimick physical sounds naturalistically, which was partly a economical issue (replacing musicians and foley artists by machines) but also promised the editor or composer to gain more control over the result.[18] The specific efficacy of electronic sound that permits the extraordinary just as well as the ordinary can be traced to its pivotal position in the production of evidence: a particular magnetism[19] draws the sound into the image if there is a possible source to be seen; as we have discussed before, this association is responsible for a significant part of the impression of fidelity. From the perspective of origination, algorithmically generated sound inserts an essential rupture here—it doesn't originate only from a physical sound source entirely different from the picture's, like in montage,[20] but there is no physical source to be found at all.

Considering sound synthesis in the context of documentary film, or more precisely, within a reflection on authenticity construction, we have to take a closer look at the methods of creating sound with computer programs. Instead

[17] See e.g. [16].

[18] See e.g. [17].

[19] This attraction is not only a *spatial magnetism*, as Chion describes it in [8, p. 69-71], but also a *causal* and *material magnetism*: the sound becomes embodied and embedded in the causal structure of the narrative. There is a perceptual basis for this in everyday experience, sounds and active objects are nearly always synchronous; thus we readily fuse simultaneous percepts from different modalities into a single entity with a causal connection.

[20] Much of the immersive 'realism' of conventional film sound depends on finding good atmos in sound libraries, unless one has the opportunity to make recordings at the filmed locations—and the ambience there is appropriate.

of reducing the computer to a tool that neutrally assists in production, here, we take the program as something that embodies assumptions about the world which enter (usually without notice) the narrative structure of a film. *All That We Have* especially takes into account the magnetism of those location sounds with a clear relation to the physical and visual, but also considers the almost unnoticeable background of ambient sound; in some situations, this could be a quiet sound of water, leaves or traffic, in others, the complete absence of recording artifacts like wind noise, of sound coloration due to microphone directivity. In order to investigate the formation of historical authenticity, it poses the question of the origin on the level of object formation, including sound synthesis into the structure of the inner logic of the film, shifting between sonic realism and a clean, slightly untrustworthy hyper-realism.

This ambiguity of objects and sound sources results from the uncertainty of the source of actions. Here, electronic sound is a constructed, artificial source. Who or what is behind this construction? What *is* the origin of an algorithmic sound? Generally speaking, algorithmic sound synthesis consists in the computation of acoustic waves instead of the reproduction of recordings. A computer program can interpret mathematical or formal methods such as relations between numbers or other abstract entities as a recipe for the calculation of a wave form. Since computers have become fast enough, one may listen to the resulting sounds while they are calculated, and consequently the author may change parameters that affect the output in realtime. Some of these resemble sounds that one has heard before, which may have been of animal or technical origin, or which may have been caused by other physical processes. The method of creating these sound does not need to be analogous in any way to these supposed origins.

Usually, *real sound synthesis* tries to construct a simplified, but precise model of a physical situation [21] according to the scientific formalisms that were developed in order to reason about natural causality. Physical properties like mass, kinetic energy, material stiffness become parameters in an algorithm allowing for a synthesis of the vibrational movement of objects. Thus, if we know the shape of a church bell, for instance, we may reconstruct its sound, and knowing some properties of a wooden stick, we may reconstruct its sound when hitting the bell. Once such a physical model has been implemented, typically, its parameters are controlled from a graphical user interface, setting cue points along a timeline. Experimentation is done with different parameters of the model, adjusting them to their appropriate values. Both the formalism that was originally used to implement the application, as well as the algorithmic process itself are not interesting anymore at that point, because on the level of simulation, the *object* already exists. While such a procedure causes similar abstraction effects,[22] by itself, it presumes the existence of the natural entity on the one hand, and formally reconstructs the unity of space on the other. In other words, here, the

[21] See e.g [18,19].

[22] See e.g. [20].

origin of the algorithmic sound is the simulated object that is mediated through the timeless mechanism of physical laws.

Since *All That We Have* attempts to make fidelity a subject of discussion, the assumption of an existing origin simulated by an algorithm would have been dissatisfactory. There is no general law for real sound synthesis. [23] It seemed more appropriate to make the programming procedure itself part of the conversation, and to discuss changes in the source code and the sound synchronously; thus, to establish a negotiation between sound impression, program text, individual acoustic memory and expectation of the algorithmic possibilities. In other words, there is no model of a supposed material situation that could stabilise the relation between image and purely formal algorithm, so that there are, for instance, no parameters such as distance, size or weight that would refer directly to a model. Also, the whole source code of the program is part of the negotiation, not only predefined parameters.[24]

To achieve this, parts of the program are rewritten while the whole process is still running, allowing us to hear the result of changes in the text directly as changes in the sound. This technique of just in time programming [25] is centered around the abstract relation between a textual representation of a sound algorithm and the acoustic perception it causes. The absence of a graphical user interface causes programming to be a formal experimentation, as well as a conversational literary genre. Due to the interaction on a textual level, the delimitations of algorithmic cause and effect become part of the discussion and the paradigm of manipulating a simulation of a given entity is avoided. Negotiating the relation between 'sound cause' and 'sound effect', between function and argument, the notion of an *object at the source of the sound* may thus be suspended and the causal source is displaced to the algorithmic process and its textual description. This suspense is not like a riddle, where the author knows the origin, but veils it by the technical means. Neither is the film simply the product of the authors' thoughts. Rather authors and audience alike are drawn into a process of hypothesising possible constructions of the authentic, of a possible deviant fidelity.

---

[23] This is not only true for physical modeling, when seen in a cultural context, but also for automatic problem solving of a more general kind. *"When searching for a solution to a problem with a computer, a function is needed for determining whether the search is going in the right direction. [...] For art, it is not possible to write such a function with a computer. Even humans cannot agree whether a work of art is successful, interesting, or relevant. [...] For these reasons fully autonomous composition programs cannot be successful with others or society until the time, if it ever comes, that computers can be said to be aware of the human relation to art and the social context of art."*[21].

[24] This procedure shifts conversation into the position of production, which could be regarded as an affinity to genres like conversational art and fluxus. See e.g. [22].

[25] For more details about the theoretical background of *Interactive Programming / Live Coding* in art and science, see [23]. For an overview of different methods and systems, see [24] and [25].

Whilst this algorithm (both as text and as process) was an active part of what caused the acoustic situation, the formalism itself is the result of other situations though. The algorithmic sound's origin cannot be ascertained anymore. Depending on the individual case, it might be a half faded memory of a sound, it might be the particularity of the formal system, it might be a coding mistake that rang a bell. Of course these considerations apply to the process of filmmaking itself. Watching the film, eventually, the question is open once again.

## Acknowledgements

This paper ows its inspirations from many discussions with Volko Kamensky, Renate Wieser, Alberto de Campo and Anthony Moore. The film sound track would not have been possible without an advanced programming language, an incredible piece of meta-art that James McCartney has brought into existence.

## References

1. Clair, R.: The art of sound (1929)
2. Freud, S.: Triebe und Triebschicksale. In: Siegmund Freud, Gesammelte Werke, Fischer Taschenbuch Verlag (1999–1915)
3. Bergson, H.: Matter and Memory. Zone Books, U.S (1991)
4. Deleuze, G.: Cinema 1: Movement-Image. University of Minnesota Press (1986)
5. Deleuze, G.: Cinema 2: The Time-Image. University of Minnesota Press (1989)
6. Rohrhuber, J.: Network music. In: Collins, N., d'Escrivan, J. (eds.) The Cambridge Companion to Electronic Music, Cambridge University Press, Cambridge (2008)
7. Casebier, A.: Film and Phenomenology. Cambridge University Press, New York (1991)
8. Chion, M., Gorbman, C., Murch, W.: Audio-Vision. Columbia University Press (1994)
9. Plantinga: Defining documentary: Fiction, nonfiction, and projected worlds. Persistence of Vision 5, 44–54 (1987)
10. Kamensky, V.: Alles was wir haben (all that we have) (2004)
11. Gätjen, H.H., Buse, K.: Lebendige Heimat beiderseits der Wümme. Number 31 in Rotenburger Schriften, Heimatbund Rotenburg (Wümme), Rotenburg (Wümme) (1988)
12. Kamensky, V.: Rundschau. Master's thesis, Hochschule für bildende Künste, Hamburg (December 2001)
13. Hyde, R.: Panoramania! Trefoil Publications Ltd (1988)
14. Foucault, M.: Discipline and Punish: The Birth of the Prison. Pantheon Books (1977)
15. McCartney, J.: Rethinking the computer music language: Supercollider. Computer Music Journal (26), 61–68 (2002)
16. Leydon, R.: Forbiden planet: Effects and affects in the electro-avant-garde. In: Hayway, P. (ed.) Off The Planet: Music, Sound and Science Fiction Cinema, John Libbey Publishing, Eastleigh (2004)
17. d'Escrivan, J.: Electronic music and the moving image. In: Collins, N., d'Escrivan, J. (eds.) The Cambridge Companion to Electronic Music, Cambridge University Press, Cambridge (2007)

18. Rath, M., Avanzini, F., Bernardini, N., Borin, G., Fontana, F., Ottaviani, L., Rocchesso, D.: An introductory catalog of computer-synthesized contact sounds, in real-time. In: Proceedings of the XIV Colloquium on Musical Informatics (XIV CIM 2003) (2003)
19. Cook, P.R.: Real Sound Synthesis for Interactive Applications. AK Peters, Ltd. (2002)
20. Rocchesso, D., Fontana, F.: The Sounding Object. Phasar Srl, Firenze (2003)
21. McCartney, J.: A few quick notes on opportunities and pitfalls of the application of computers in art and music. In: Ars Electronica (2003)
22. Chandler, A., Neumark, N.: At a Distance: Precursors to Art and Activism on the Internet. Leonardo Books, MIT Press, Cambridge (2005)
23. Rohrhuber, J., de Campo, A., Wieser, R.: Algorithms today - notes on language design for just in time programming. In: Proceedings of International Computer Music Conference, Barcelona, ICMC, pp. 455–458 (2005)
24. Collins, N., McLean, A., Rohrhuber, J., Ward, A.: Live coding in laptop performance. Organized Sound (2004)
25. toplap: Organization home page. webpage (2004)

# The Colour of Time (God Is a Lobster and Other Forbidden Bodies)*

Johnny Golding

Professor of Philosophy in the Visual Arts & Communication Technologies
The University of Greenwich, London UK

**Abstract.** The Colour of Time draws one's focus away from the usual predicaments in metaphysical time (such as posing it either as 'ahistorical' or eternal) or as is found in more ethnographic permutations (as finite, visual, historical). By re-staging time as a colour (say, strawberry, teal, blue-black), this Colour of Time attempts to move onto that more peculiar terrain of the senses – where the curvature of the instant, moment, the wave and the dot can (and do) account for the on-going mutations, morphs, nuances and shifts of discursive practice(s) itself, a toning/tuning repetition/movement of 'difference: both revealing and concealing at one and the same instant. We could also say that these senses, these 'curvatures' are the sine qua non for cohesive energy/power. Or in a phrase: 'the political'. It's a delicate game we are playing, after all.

**Keywords:** Time, the senses, memory, dreams, wormhole philosophy, forbidden bodies, aesthetics, politics, Heidegger, Einstein, Deleuze, Murakami, Kant, The Enlightenment, exit, media arts philosophy (MAP), imagination, codes.

"Once, if I remember rightly," recalls our Rimbaud, "my life was a feast
at which all hearts opened and all wines flowed.
One evening
I sat Beauty on my
Knees
-- And found her
Bitter
-- And I reviled her.
I armed myself against justice.

I fled. O witches, O misery, O hatred!
It was to *you* that my treasure was entrusted!
I managed to erase in my mind all human hope!
Upon every joy in order to strangle it
I made the muffled sound of
-- of the wild beast.

---

* This poetic was read as a public lecture at DAW 2007 alongside the video "In God We Trust (the colour of Time/forbidden bodies) by Lucia Marcari (lyrics, vocals) and Dimitrov (music composition, vocals and instruments). All music/sound/noise is from their hard-hitting opera "Hip Hop on Bones" (in three volumes), Amsterdam: Kidnap Records, 2005). Their opera score follows on the tradition of transmitting politically disruptive content/ beat via x-rays ('music on the bones') as one of the only avenues open to avoid censorship in Moscow from the mid 80s onwards. Earlier version in H. Guyerlez, ***Strange Intimacies***, (Istanbul Biennale).

R. Adams, S. Gibson, and S. Müller Arisona (Eds.): DAW/IF 2006/2007, CCIS 7, pp. 71–79, 2008.

I called up executioners in order to bite their gun-butts as I died.
I called up plagues, in order to suffocate myself with sand and blood.
Bad luck was my god.
I stretched myself out in the mud.
I dried myself in the air of crime.
And I played some fine tricks on madness. [And spring…?]

And spring brought me
The hideous laugh
Of the idiot.[1]

**supposing if.** Suppose one could dream in one colour only. Would yours be primary, say red or yellow? Or a more complicated multi-tonal affair, say Viennese Truffle or Mandarin Midnight Blue? Would the dream-colours enter your mind as pixelated stop-starts or sleekly contiguous morphs? Well, to grasp the delicacy of the matter, one need only understand one tiny thing: *strawberry*.

> **[Interlude 1] ecce homo (*this* man; *this* woman; *this* being*; this* One – and no other).** Today: today I am part thief, part iron-claw, transformed in the first instance as a swift and shadowy runner, skimming the surface of greasy back alleyways with goods close to hand! Nothing stops me: not sirens, not wounds, not the filthy dirty air! Nothing impedes my rush! But at the slightest sniff of danger I can transform! Oh, I can transform into – a blue flower! Or maybe a nasty coral reef! Or perhaps just some old rusty tractor, digging and banging and digging some more, same place, same time, same rhythm. And I think to myself: isn't it just grand how the ground gives way under my – *imagination*! Maybe *this* is what it means to colour code time in the age of relativity and technological change? I want to say yes (but not exactly).

**grey-blue (i hold a memory old dream: wormhole philosophy no. 9).** Lesson in how to make your shadow bigger or smaller irrespective of your own size, light, measure: 'The first old dream she places on the table is nothing I know as an old dream. I stare at the object before me, then look up at her. She stands next to me looking down at it. How is this an "old dream"? The sound of the words "old dream" led me to expect something else – old writings perhaps, something hazy, amorphous.

'Here we have an old dream,' says the Librarian. Her voice is distant, aimless; her tone wants not so much to explain to me as to reconfirm for herself. 'Or it is possible to say, the old dream is inside of this.'

I nod, but do not understand.

'Take it in your hands,' she prompts.

I pick it up and run my eyes over the surface to see if I can find some trace of an old dream. But there is not a clue. It is only the skull of an animal, and not a very big animal. Dry and brittle, as if it had lain in the sun for years, the bone matter is leached of whatever color it might originally have had. The jutting jaw is locked slightly open, as if

[1] A. Rimbaud, **Season in Hell,** (Middlesex: Penguin, 1962), p. 1; my own spacing.

suddenly frozen when about to speak. The eye sockets, long bereft of their contents, lead to the cavernous recesses behind. [...]

'I am to read an old dream from this?'

'That is the work of the Dreamreader,' says the Librarian.

'And what do I do with the dreams that I read?'

'Nothing. You have only to read them.'

'How can that be?' I say. 'I know that I am to read an old dream from this. But then not to do anything with it, I do not understand. What can be the point of that? Work should have a purpose.'

She shakes her head. "I cannot explain. Perhaps the dream-reading will tell you. I can only show you how it is done."[2]

**brown and black.** What happened, say, *before* all known time (linear, multiple or otherwise)? { } {There is no answer}. Having said that, perhaps we could call this 'no answer' (In general we are using *italics* for emphasis rather than 'quotation marks.' In your case since your piece is a little more poetic than most there may be good reason to use 'quotation marks' rather than *italics.* I'll let you be the judge) (if we are not, that is to say, going to call it 'God' or 'Jah' or 'Allah' or 'transcendence' or the Unsaying or Dead) a kind of silent mass of anti-space/anti-matter/anti-energy? Einstein called it a kind of 'cosmological stases' which occurred if one took the logical probability of high density dynamic relativism to its nth degree: at some point there would have to be stasis, despite an ever-expanding universe. If one stayed within traditional physics and mathematics, this conclusion was a logical impossibility (to have an ever-expanding universe and, as well, cosmological stasis). Rather than throwing out the entirety of general relativity theorem, Einstein, instead added what is called the 'fudge factor' – he couldn't prove what he was saying or its impossible conclusions, but, by all rights, cosmological stasis made sense (it just unprovable sense).

To put this slightly differently, his 'resolution' suggested that not only was there not exactly 'nothing' or 'void' or 'lack' before there was a 'something', but given the curvature of time-space 'itself', this 'nothingness' had a kind of shape or fold, we might nowadays call it a kind of blackhole elsewhere, filling in the gaps, as it were in our ever-expanding universe. (And if you think this is strange, how much more so to find out – as was recently recorded by satellite technology – that these 'anti-matter blackholes whistle, and do so in the key of b-flat. *B-flat?!* Who knew?

**greenish brown.** Immanuel Kant proposed a curious feature to the 'age of reason', which distinguished a certain kind of reason from that of, say, the 'dark ages'. It was not so much that suddenly a whole group of people awoke in unison and 'saw the light' at 2.15pm on an otherwise innocuous Tuesday afternoon; nor for that matter, that prior to 'modernity', there was only chaos and confusion. Rather, he proposed that the cornerstone of the Enlightenment rested on one's ability to know *that* one could 'exit' (and, bonus points, how and when). This was a crucial sense of what was meant by 'reason' – now stripped of its cold, instrumental, arithmetical and, not to put too fine a point on it, sterilised (and therefore) pure logic. Indeed, this 'exit strategy', was not only corrosive,

---

[2] Haruki Murakami, "*Shadow*," in **Hard-boiled Wonderland and the End of the World**, translated from the Japanese by Alfred Birnbaum, (London: Vintage/Harvill Press, 2001), pp. 58-9.

impure, restless; it was no longer considered as the end point of an otherwise rather hard-pressed life ('end point'/'exit strategy' otherwise known as: death). Tossing out 'linear logic', this dynamic (or as he would call it: the mathematical dynamical) was the very core of life itself.

To put this slightly differently, the ability to 'grasp' (a) that life was (is) 'movement' in all its good, bad and indifferent sorts of ways, and (b) that movement as such was the *sine qua non* for setting the limit, i.e., the differentiation between the 'that which was' from the 'that which could be'; meant also that knowledge-reason-power-movement-graspability could be (and was) 'inhabited', and more precisely still, could be (and was) inhabited by being human.

**blue-nosed hue to the greenish brown.** Apart from the many long-winded consequences filtering out of this 'age of reason and enlightenment' inhabitation, came a shift in what it might mean to be an artist. Hitherto, an artist was rather like a vessel through whose body-hand flowed the creative eye, taste, energy – and whim – of God. But now, now if it were true that creativity was no longer the providence of God {but might also be connected to or produced by one's 'own' (dynamic version of) reason – one which lay at the very core of being human – } meant, that the human-artist-type-being did not simply or only conduct or translate the word/vision/spirit of God neatly onto canvas, sculpture or sound, but that he or she was a Creator, too (or anyway, might be).

Now, it would be one thing – one not too bad or awkward a-thing, given this trajectory – if the artist was never quite as good as God; but what if, what if the artist were better? An imprisonable offence, held without bail, to be sure. And so entered the first of many techni-coloured 'fudge factors' to political, philosophical, scientific, aesthetic and ethical 'reason': how to square the wildly expanding journeys to which inhabited reason might lead – pathways which would take one way beyond the horizon's of one's own worldly worlds – how to square this with the cultural fermentations, beliefs and common senses of the day. Perhaps it was best just to say, as it was said in the Book and elsewhere: that man could only ever approach God, but not become or (dare it be suggested) exceed, God.

> **[Interlude 2] ecce homo (*this* man; *this* woman; *this* being; *this* One – and no other).** Today I must tell you: I am part thief, part iron-claw, transformed in the first instance as a swift and shadowy runner, skimming the surface of greasy back alleyways with goods close to hand! Nothing stops me: not sirens, not wounds, not the filthy dirty air! Nothing impedes my rush! But at the slightest sniff of danger I can transform! Oh, I can transform into – a blue flower! Or maybe a nasty coral reef! Or perhaps just some old rusty tractor, digging and banging and digging some more, same place, same time, same rhythm. And I think to myself: isn't it just grand how the ground gives way under my – *imagination*! Maybe *this* is what it means to colour code time in the age of relativity and technological change? I want to say yes (but not exactly).

**mud-coloured brown.** Perhaps not so surprisingly, Heidegger steps up to the plate. In his *'Question concerning Technology''* and, later, in and amongst his two lectures

*Identity and Difference*[3], he reframes the problem in two ways. First, he makes the rather clever, if not sweeping observation-as-truth that we have entered the 'age of Technology', in the same way that one enters the atmosphere of life itself. That is to say, no one's decision to enter (or not) is required, expected or asked after; one is simply 'entered'. One is 'in' and 'of' and 'linked to' technology; where this 'in' and 'of' and 'link' with this 'age' (called technology), names the 'limit-as-multiple/dynamic-inhabitation', (echoes of Kant and the Enlightenment notwithstanding) rather than echoing any nod toward the instrumentalised logics of the yes/no, 'either/or' limit to truth, history, beauty, time.

Second, and intimately connected to the first proposition, identity, meaning, truth, indeed art itself, no longer resembles a discrete entity or atomised dot, similar or not to God or His vessels, but exists only by virtue of a kind of 'bridging relation' between, as he puts it 'little (b)' being [entities] and 'Big (B)'[the 'out there'] Being (b:Being). The human 'self', to the degree to which there is 'a' self, is precisely the expression of this synapse, the name of the now 'inhabited' yet 'unsayable' presence; a kind of bridging event, a kind of truth, replete with time as a kind of bridging relation of absence (presence) and space (as the absence of time) or as the more familiar phraseology would put it: b:Being as the 'event of appropriation'; where the grasp is nothing other than the multiple logics of 'techne' at the very moment of their 'enframing'.

**black gold.** All goes well for Heidegger, until he tries to disengage completely from Metaphysics (particularly from the metaphysics of the teleological and dialectical variety) in order to make a stronger case for logics of sense and imagination. Now, not to get too caught up in the entire sordid tale of how he attempts (and fails) to get beyond this epistemological brick wall, suffice it to say, that because his analysis still requires a kind of ground (ontic) to knowledge; that is, a kind of a "groundless ground", he is brought right smack-dab face-to-face with the quasi- mystical onto-theo-logical Godhead haze Itself. That is to say, and to put it slightly differently: with the Heideggerian move, we get the nuance, the fluidity, the multiplicity – of Time or Being or Identity or Difference – we just also get our Father, who, at it turns out, is not just, in heaven, but is, indeed, everywhere (and nowhere) at the same time, all the time, before Time, during Time and even after Time. Thrown into the bargain, (or thrown out of it depending on perspective), we get a whiff of sensuous logics, but without getting closer to way(s) in which those logics inhabit a body, any body *as body* – via, say, their colours, smells, injuries, laughters, horrors. This may not be such a bad thing if one wishes to hang on to God, for whatever reasons (security, faith, can't-come-up-with-any-better-argument, mysticism), but what if, what if one is not quite ready, in the bargain, to give up, for that (dubious) security, the hard won right of *habeas corpus* (there shall be/there is 'the body'), especially if it's your body imprisoned, made ill, dead.

**bruise.** Like the predicament of time itself and its implications around bodies, ethics, methods, pathways, aesthetics, politics, art, it would be equally unwise, even for a moment, to ignore what has gone into and continues to go in to the bruise. Far be it from me to raise the old political battle cry: What is man? and What is man to become? For to do

---

[3] Martin Heidegger, **Question Concerning Technology and Other Essays,** trans and intro by W. Lovitt, (New York: Harper and Row, 1977), pp. 36ff, and **Identity and Difference**, trans by Joan Stambaugh, (New York: Harper and Row, 1969).

so might awaken the old spirit-ghosts of metaphysics; it might bring in through the bathroom window, the old problem of 'telos', with its sniffy sense of perpetually unfolding goals, grounds, trajectories, transcendences, totalities, concepts, dialectics and the like. On the other hand, perhaps it is not so completely absurd, at least whilst in the gummy time-span between logic and the senses to give pause for a thought or two around what it might mean 'simply' to be human; that is, if one *could* indeed get away from abstractions, romantic, practical, utopian, humanistic or in whatever key they might appear. (And yet! I would like to say, in the context of this unsaying: we have yet to be relieved from the thorny problem of being human – at least in all its non-universalizing pluralized garden varieties).

**turquoise.** For the question becomes (or indeed, always has been): how does one account for the *condition* of life, including one's *own* life, its harshness or coolness? the *thicknesses* of its blood, the *tones* of its savagery, the *levels* of its anger, the *severities* of its crime? What about the simple joke? Or what makes a joke 'simple'? What about the complexities of the 'garden variety' everydayness of, say, sexual assault? Or the low levels of authoritarian dogma cleverly disguised as bureaucracy? What about *mediocrity?* "God is a Lobster, or a double pincer, a double bind," speaks the Deleuze + Guattarian tongue.[4] A plurality of the One that is several at the same instant; at the same duration; the same place; the same rhythm, breath, content, remark; a kind of viscerally disembowelled geography which nevertheless remains contiguously embodied, infinitely expanding, deeply disruptive, morally suspect and a little bit monstrous. Like Bataille, the sacred and profane rub up against the mediocre; but unlike Bataille, its syntheses, intensities, values can be discarded, de- and re-terroritorialised, disembodied and re-configured. And it does so by putting forward an ethics, an aesthetics, a stylistics of existence.

> **[Interlude 3: ecce homo (*this* man; *this* woman; *this* being*; this* One – and no other).** Have I told you? Today, I am part thief, part iron-claw, transformed in the first instance as a swift and shadowy runner, skimming the surface of greasy back alleyways with goods close to hand! Nothing stops me: not sirens, not wounds, not the filthy dirty air! Nothing impedes my rush! But at the slightest sniff of danger I can transform! Oh, I can transform into – a blue flower! Or maybe a nasty coral reef! Or perhaps just some old rusty tractor, digging and banging and digging some more, same place, same time, same rhythm. And I think to myself: isn't it just grand how the ground gives way under my – *imagination*! Maybe *this* is what it means to colour code time in the age of relativity and technological change? I want to say yes (but not exactly).

**blood red.** We might wish to call this 'colouring' a kind of economy: one caught in the nether regions of memory, mneumonic logics. nodal points and rhizomatic relativities; a

---

[4] G. Deleuze + F. Guattari, *"3. 10,000 B.C.: The Geology of Morals (Who Does the Earth Think it is?),* **A Thousand Plateaus (V. 2 of Capitalism and Schizophrenia)**, translated by Brian Massumi, (Minneapolis: University of Minnesota Press, 1988), p. 40.

kind of webbing or weave, lacing the zeroes and ones of life and time, except this weave contains no matter, no volume, no weight – though it still makes a 'something' tangible, systematic. without resorting to a closed (binaric) system or any overt tangibility. Picture this: picture a child's game, well-known in its immediate sense of dysfunctionality writ large: the game of 'musical chairs'.[5] For purposes of establishing a common memory databank, shall I recap the game as follows: a series of chairs are set in a line with one too many participants for the amount of given chairs. A gun goes off, the music begins and the children run round the chairs frantically attempting to be near this or that chair so that when the music stops – suddenly, and on the wrong beat – they must grab and sit on said chair (Rule #1). The game is already skewed, we all know this from the start: one player will always-already be caught without a chair. The one 'caught out' when silence descends, well, they must exit, stay at the sidelines, or go somewhere else. (Get lost: Rule #2. The game is repeated, until there are only two participants and one isolated chair left. I never liked this game, whether or not I managed to be victorious with the one remaining trophy chair. Who cares about the chairs anyway? I was always more curious about the play of the game. (This curiosity meant that I always played to the bitter end this silly little game).

**pepper.** "Evacuate the premises, immediately!" Not an unusual statement these days; plausibly announced by bomb-squad police or other suitable candidates, say: market mechanisms, imminent bad weather, morality gatekeepers, losers at musical chairs: forget the existential questions of life (why? why me? and so on) for, quite remarkably, the natty, bitty 'practical' everyday problems of translocation, displacement and other forms of decay will suddenly flash before you, with only micro-seconds to spare; micro-seconds in which a decision must be taken and enacted. This flash/decision/enactment can be broken down by way of the following set of interrogations: what would you *grab* at the very moment of decisive indecision and chaos? That which is close to hand or that which holds the most sentimental/ memory value? or that which is lightest (or all three)? Some kind of technical equipment, say, a mobile phone or your computer laptop (should you have one); extra batteries? A strong pair of shoes? Water? Second set of questions: Where do you go? Do you run ahead as a herdsman?, asks Nietzsche, Or turn into a pillar of salt, as did Lot's wife?

**violet.** And how would you get to where you wish to go (assuming there is no direct gun to your head or cattle car waiting)? How do you get to where you want to go especially if you are not certain where you wish to go, or for some other reason, cannot get there, say, because you may be suffering from a certain degree of short-sightedness. (Because in that case, you cannot say to yourself, says Wittgenstein, 'look at the church tower ten miles away and go in that direction.')[6]

**beige.** So, how will you be able to read/interpret the rules of the game, if and when you 'arrive' (wherever that 'arrival point' may be)? – irrespective of whether the language

---

[5] Remarkably, this game of 'musical chairs' is known to children in Germany as '*the road to Jerusalem*'. I leave it to you to deduce the obvious.

[6] Ludwig Wittgenstein, ***Culture and Value***, edited by G.H. Von Wright in collaboration with Heikki Nyman, trans. by Peter Winch, (Oxford: Basil Blackwell, 1980), p. 1e.

spoken appears (or even is) the 'same' language, say 'international/exchange English' or even 'art' for example. What codes of identity or identities must you somehow embody or occupy, or be seen to occupy, in order to 'communicate'? What will be lost in translation? Or found -- by way of Rosetta stone hieroglyphics? How will the differences already encumbering your life, surface as explanatory nodal points or clusters of meanings (say around race, sex, class, age, nationality, eating habits, drug use or varying dislocations within and between these islands of identity and difference). Which battlegrounds will you choose to stand upon, or be forced to stand upon? How will you 'fit in'? By bowing and scrapping, cap in hand, hoping the 'flaws' won't be noticed; or by boldly going where angels dare not tread? Will you fall prey to the assumption 'people are the same everywhere' (whereby we return to the Eternal 24 hour relay race of mobility, blood and death compelling your every move)? Or will you fall prey to the loop of musical chairs, trophies notwithstanding? Where will you buy your milk? Pleasure your body? Rest your eye? Get dental and medical? Share your joke?

**dark teal.** Riddle of the seven sphinxes: what then lies between the supposed rarefied air of genius and the ready-made unity of 'common' sense? An ambitious (social) climber might think of bridges to their hilltops, and answers: networking! But perhaps the answer is closer to a dose of wilful conceit and its maligned offspring, doubt, experimentation. But then this arrogance requires a certain kind of faith, a certain kind of compulsion, a certain kind of certainty, say about one's own ability to know [the whatever] whilst simultaneously accepting that one must take the leap 'out there' for no other reason than that it must be done [now]. A strange kind of juridical move, this oddly disciplined sense of self, this mastering of several-selves without implanting a singular self as master; a risk-taking without dwelling for an instant on the possible disasters of what might happen 'if' the *knowing* might have been gathered from a whole series of misguided judgements or parochial rumours or community standards. A certain kind of conceit, this kind of faith – Kierkegaard might call it: a certain kind of *trembling.*

**sky blue. [or the uses and abuses of kneeling].** Perhaps it is safer to say that faith and trembling have more to do with the necessity to *submit* – and not only that! but to know how and when, without knowing "why" exactly, and without knowing to whom or even to what one 'kneels'. On the other hand, perhaps this kind of faith has nothing to do with kneeling or any other form of submission, and I've just been carried away with trying to explain what happens when I sniff out the uncharted paths in a manner according to my custom, especially when night stealths towards day: the stillness of air! the light! the dew! the quietness of tone! the possibility to connect a this with a that! Perhaps what I am mentioning has only a tiny micro slice to do with submission – but I mention it anyway, for no other reason than that the combination of light, and touch, and sound, and smell compels me to inhabit my body *differently*; now aligned/maligned with a stranger series of curiosities, hungers, expectations, promises, threats. This has very little to do with losing (or conversely, with finding) 'my' self. It's a peculiar submission; perhaps even a peculiar mastery – this gutter-ground gift, this instant eventness of *desire* and *pleasure* and *discipline* and *wandering*: this holy place of the bended knee. (But perhaps I am confusing the formal requirements of Philosophy and Art and Religion with their bastardised cousins, greed, hunger, curiosity, sloth).

**[Interlude 4] ecce homo (*this* man; *this* woman; *this* being; *this* One – and no other).** Perhaps it is best to tell you now: today, I am part thief, part iron-claw, transformed in the first instance as a swift and shadowy runner, skimming the surface of greasy back alleyways with goods close to hand! Nothing stops me: not sirens, not wounds, not the filthy dirty air! Nothing impedes my rush! But at the slightest sniff of danger I can transform! Oh, I can transform into – a blue flower! Or maybe a nasty coral reef! Or perhaps just some old rusty tractor, digging and banging and digging some more, same place, same time, same rhythm. And I think to myself: isn't it just grand how the ground gives way under my – *imagination*! Maybe *this* is what it means to colour code time in the age of relativity and technological change? I want to say yes (but not exactly).

It is a delicate game we are playing, after all.

# Behind the Screen: Installations from the Interactive Future

Ted Hiebert

Pacific Centre for Technology and Culture, University of Victoria,
PO Box 1700 Stn CSC, Victoria, BC, V8W 2Y2, Canada
ted_hiebert@yahoo.com

**Abstract.** The future is interactive... at least that is the theory. And while the theory itself is not new, the screen through which it is rendered most certainly is. The new screen... one among possible many, and yet despite the many it is the impossible one upon which the interactive future will manifest. "Behind the Screen" is, in this sense, an exploration of the consequences of imaginative technological use, with an emphasis on the ways in which artistic mobilization of screen technology impacts on the interactivity of contemporary living. Focusing on several key installations from the 2007 Interactive Futures Symposium, this paper engages both the representative proofs and disproofs offered by artistic technological use – a theoretical exploration of the critical imaginary potential of new media artwork.

**Keywords:** technology, interaction, new media, installation, artwork, screen culture, imagination.

## 1 Overview

> We lived once in a world where the realm of the imaginary was governed by the mirror, by dividing one into two, by otherness and alienation. Today that realm is the realm of the screen, of interfaces and duplication, of continuity and networks. All our machines are screens, and the interactivity of humans has been replaced by the interactivity of screens.
>
> – Jean Baudrillard, "Xerox and Infinity."[1]

The future is interactive... at least that is the theory. And while the theory itself is not new, the screen through which it is rendered most certainly is. The new screen... one among possible many, and yet despite the many it is the impossible one upon which the interactive future will manifest.

But there are other new theories as well, other speculative fantasies of constituted reality, which is also to say of an imaginary so implausible that it remains, by necessity, forever un-provable... and forever un-disprovable too. This is the imaginary gone technological, the ghost in the machine is also behind the screen, waiting and watching for moments of reality interrupted. For it is within the interventions of technology that the interactive imaginary waits to be discovered.

R. Adams, S. Gibson, and S. Müller Arisona (Eds.): DAW/IF 2006/2007, CCIS 7, pp. 80–97, 2008.

"Behind the Screen" is, in this spirit, an exploration of the consequences of imaginative technological use, with an emphasis on the ways in which artistic mobilization of screen technology impacts on the interactivity of contemporary living. Drawing on the installation series of the 2007 Interactive Futures symposium, this paper is an attempt to engage the imaginary possibilities offered by artistic technological use – a theoretical exploration of the critical imaginary potential of new media artwork. Loosely brought together under the theme of "The New Screen," the Interactive Futures symposium featured works by artists, performers, programmers and academics from around the world, brought together for the critical, aesthetic and intellectual exploration of the technological future.[1]

## 2 Fauna of Screens

We live in a time of prophetic manifestation – a fateful time of mythology revived, of legend resurrected, of imaginary beings walking among the rest of us, unnoticed, unassumed, unaknowledged. The mirror has been broken, and the revenge of ancient times past is upon us again.

> In those days the world of mirrors and the world of men were not, as they are now, cut off from each other. They were, besides, quite different; neither beings nor colours nor shapes were the same. Both kingdoms, the specular and the human, lived in harmony; you could come and go through mirrors. One night the mirror people invaded the earth. Their power was great, but at the end of bloody warfare the magic arts of the Yellow Emperor prevailed. He repulsed the invaders, imprisoned them in their mirrors, and forced on them the task of repeating, as though in a kind of dream, all the actions of men. He stripped them of their power and of their forms and reduced them to mere slavish reflections.[3]

It was Jorge Luis Borges who inscribed this history of the mirror people, of the battle between the mirror and the flesh, of the traumatic banishment that was the result of an overzealous silvery aggression. The story continues to say that there will come a time when, bit by bit, the mirror people will cease to follow the dictates of flesh, when their reactions to our human gestures will begin a life of their own, a day where a strange new light will begin to penetrate its way into the minds and bodies of humanity. Such a day has arrived. The mirror people emerge again, only this time the story is a little bit different.

For, while we may have won the historical war, one might also observe that we have become strangely reliant on our silver prisoners, strangely vain in our obsession with their opinions, strangely bound to them no less than they to us. The mirror people may be trapped behind the mirror, but it is we who have been screen-captured, archived, saved

[1] Interactive Futures 2007: The New Screen was organized and curated by Steve Gibson, Julie Andreyev and Randy Adams, and was held in Victoria (Canada) from November 15 - 17, 2007 [2].

and reanimated. Before the world has even come to terms with reflection as a technological phenomenon, reality has gone electronic; the mirror people have discovered a slipstream into the realized imaginary. Indeed, the mirror has gone digital – the new screen behind which our already precarious relationship to reflected knowledge suddenly becomes yet more malleable, yet more unreliable, yet more unfamiliar. Digital self-image: behind the mirror lives the imaginary – a race of screen people that return our gaze with the seductive look of completed fantasy. Without ever having left the reflected sanctity of their private abodes, they have already infiltrated the world of flesh. Manifest imaginary – a sign that behind the screen there is another world, and one that no longer feels a need to passively follow the dictates of a human real.

And so, to engage the myth of the mirror turned screen, six stories, six iterations of the technological imagination, six installations from an participatory present that, taken together, also provide new strategies for creative engagement in our emerging, interactive future.

### 2.1 First Iteration: Circumstantial Evidence (Reflections on *Their Circumstances* by JiHyun Ahn)

> [*Their Circumstances*] is an experimental interactive animation, which introduces a new way to watch animation. It has non-linear structure in both medium and story. It combines videos and flash with actionscripts. All movies are put together in flash and through the actionscripts programming code, people can see more than two angle shots simultaneously, select the chapters and the video segments and create their own storylines. Also there are dynamic animations in flash itself so the animations in videos and those in flash interact [with] each other, crossing the frames. This frame means not only the literal frame object in my work but also the boundary between the linear video work and the nonlinear flash interactivity.
>
> – JiHyun Ahn [4]

On a screen, the story waits. Or perhaps it is the characters in the story who wait. But this much is sure – until the human hand hits play, the story sits idly by, bored, waiting – sleeping as only a console can do. And yet, once the hand hits play, the scenario is reversed. Bound at the console, it is the human body that completes the narrative circuit, waiting to be shown what comes next – or what came before – until the next chapter ends and it's time to click through again.

Their Circumstances is a short story about the ghost of a girl who has lost her leg, and a family who finds itself unwittingly implicated in both the death of the girl and the consumption of her missing leg. It is also a Flash animation, presented in split-screen narrative that, every so often, requires one to click the flashing icon in order to proceed to the next segment of the story. Amidst this architecture, a compelling mixture of photography, cut-outs and animated drawing complete the low-tech aesthetic, at times grotesque, at others provocative and even humorous.

And yet, there is more at play here than the simple multi-task story line which presents each character in his or her own version of the narrative. There is even more here than the

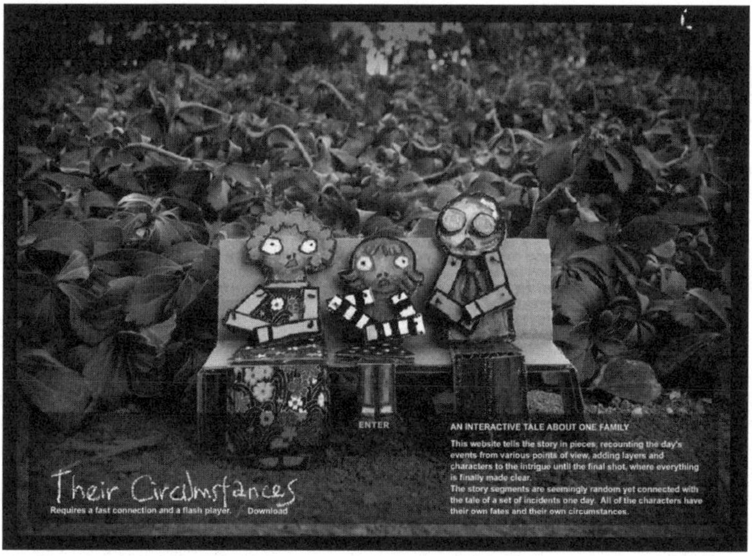


**Fig. 1.** JiHyun Ahn. *Their Circumstances*. Interactive Flash animation, 2007. Courtesy the artist.

simple stop and go demands of minimal interactivity. Here, in fact, we find a techno logical allegory presented with the full force of an animated macabre. This is not Georges Bataille's "Story of the Eye," but in many ways what the two share is an obsessive fascination with the seduction of technological violence.[2] This – this story of the leg – is at once cannibal and cannibalized, as if Ahn sought to push to the limits the shared French etymology: *jambe* (leg) and *jambon* (ham). And this is not by accident.

It was Paul Virilio who made the assertion that technological engagement is disabling to the human body, a prescient precursor to Ahn's illustrated version.[7] Fittingly, the recurring mantra of this piece – "give me my leg" – finds an analogue in the structural demand of the piece itself. For while this is the story of a girl who loses her leg, one immediate effect of console-based interaction such as that mobilized in *Their Circumstances* is the immobilization of our legs too. Cannibalized by the very screens we watch, then fed this virtualized flesh back through our eyes themselves in what Jerry Mander would call the "ingestion of artificial light."[8] Electronic Breatharians,[3] we are hooked up to this violent consumption matrix, playing along as *Their Circumstances* become our own – a circumstantial dance, a ritual sacrifice that mirrors the digital sacrifice of electronic living.

---

[2] "The *Story of the Eye* is a novella written by Georges Bataille that details the sexual experimentation of two teenage lovers, and their increasing perversion. The imagery of the novel is built upon a series of metaphors which in turn refer to philosophical constructs developed in his work: the eye, the egg, the sun, the earth, the testicle." See: [5] and [6].

[3] Breatharianism is a philosophical/religious tradition in which believers claim they are able to live without food by optically ingesting sunlight for a period of time each day.[9]

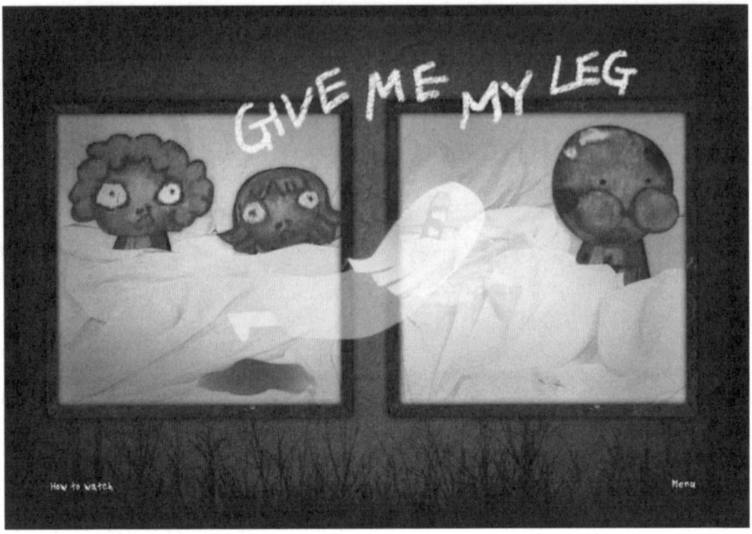


**Fig. 2.** JiHyun Ahn. *Their Circumstances*. Interactive Flash animation, 2007. Courtesy the artist.

## 2.2 Second Iteration: Facebooks and Monkey-Cliques (Reflections on *Why Some Dolls Are Bad* by Kate Armstrong)

> *Why Some Dolls Are Bad* is a dynamically generated graphic novel built on the Facebook platform. The work assembles a stream of images that match certain tags and dynamically mixes them with original text in order to produce a perpetually changing narrative. Users who subscribe to the application in Facebook can capture pages from the graphic novel and save, reorder, and distribute them. The novel engages themes of ethics, fashion, artifice and the self, and presents a re-examination of systems and materials including mohair, contagion, Freudian tension, perspex cabinetry, and false-seeming things in nature such as Venus Flytraps.
>
> – Kate Armstrong [10]

You have a friend invitation from a bad doll, a mad dash for face-shifting with the singular condition that you subscribe before reading. Assuming you already have a face, of course, you can then begin your own accumulation of digital page-captures. Archive while you can however, for if instead you click next, that which came before will leave, never to come back again. Apply yourself to the application, for some assembly is required to choose your own adventure from the wealth of possible manifest randomness.

*Why Some Dolls Are Bad* is a graphic interface in which seemingly random images are mashed up with short, aphorism-like textual instances. The resultant flash-card displays can be saved or discarded, collected for their arbitrary manifestations of-meaning or absurdity, or dismissed as digital detritus. Less, perhaps, a simple artwork

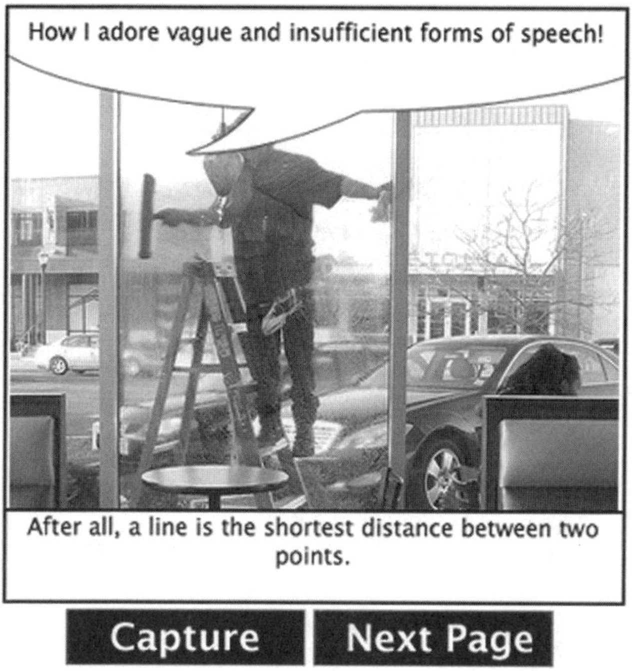


**Fig. 3.** Kate Armstrong. *Why Some Dolls Are Bad.* Facebook application, 2006. Courtesy the artist.

and more, one might suggest, a meta-artwork of sorts, it is also not unimportant that this piece lives among the social networks of Facebook, creating in its own right a sub-network of users with nothing else necessarily in common. Here, the distinctions between tools and products, applications and instances, meld and blur as contingent and contextual interaction form the signs of the digital day.

In this frame by frame encounter it is also noteworthy that the narrative too is contingent, contingent in this instance on our own ability to speculate on possible connections between images. While it is, of course, understood that the content is pulled from a spectral database of one sort or another, this piece reads as a thousand monkeys – not on a thousand typewriters, but instead armed with digital cameras and keyboards – embarking on the quest to write, not just any book but here the book of dolls and faces.[4] Or perhaps it is even more metaphysical still, and these monkeys are trained – coders and hackers – writing the very applicability of one click to the next: the shortest distance between two pages is not the mouse-click but the monkey-click itself. Or, yet still, perhaps it is we who are the monkeys after all, the bad dolls are separated from the good by the efforts they themselves put towards establishing narrative patterns within the randomness of graphic occurrence.

[4] The 1000 monkeys on 1000 typewriters is a popularized version of the infinite monkey theorem which states that "a monkey hitting keys at random on a typewriter keyboard for an infinite amount of time will almost surely type a particular chosen text, such as the complete works of William Shakespeare."[11]

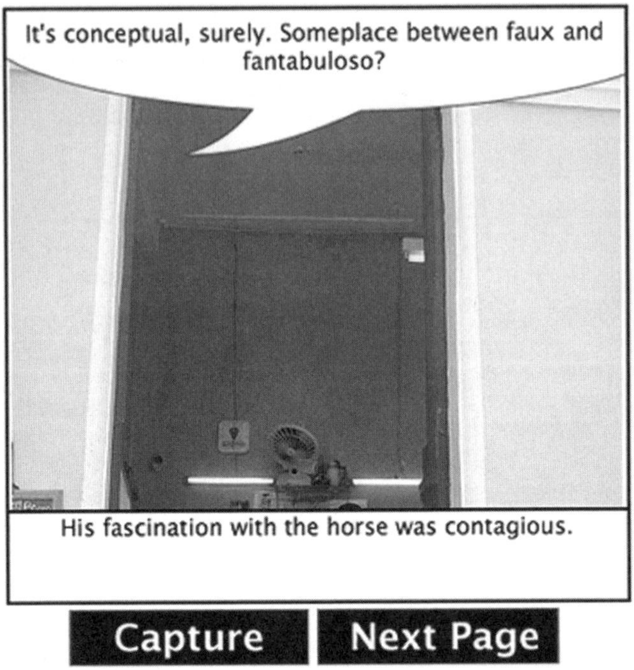


**Fig. 4.** Kate Armstrong. *Why Some Dolls Are Bad.* Facebook application, 2006. Courtesy the artist.

It is as if this piece is a literal manifestation of N. Katherine Hayles' digital dialectic of pattern and randomness, sign of the electronic times but also signifier of the new face of interactivity.[5] Digital continuity and digital interruption; if you don't like a page swap it out for another. It was Kierkegaard who asked if it was ever possible to return to the same city twice, but it is Armstrong who asks if we can even ever go there once. In an age of perfect digital memory, of undo functions and coded, reliable and repeatable patterns, *Why Some Dolls Are Bad* challenges these tenets of digital living by splicing the urge to capture with the faceless disappearance of all random pages not deemed worth archiving. And in this a Facebook metaphor too, as social networks monkey-clique up to avoid the uninvited, the Facebook challenge: you can't be friends with people you don't know, and you can't be a good doll if you have bad intentions.

### 2.3 Third Iteration: Babelling Identities (Reflections on *Photocollagen* by Chris Joseph)

> *Photocollagen* [is] an installation [that uses] the screen to channel a digital Prometheus, remixing the artists and presenters of Interactive Futures 2007 in a

[5] According to Hayles, "an infusion of noise [i.e. randomness] into a system can cause it to reorganize at a higher level of complexity." See [12].

> continuously (d)evolving chimera: a virtual identity mashup in perpetual motion.
>
> – Chris Joseph [13]

They say that blurred boundaries are a sign of technological living, but one might wonder how literally this is meant? From face to face – the face of another, or of parts of oneself. I'm told I have my father's smile, my mother's eyelashes, my grandfather's hairline. Little of my face, it would seem, is mine alone. But then again I rarely see my own face – if anything it is the more unfamiliar side of things. If I had children I'd not see myself in them; instead I'd be left wondering how their faces managed to appear as part of mine.

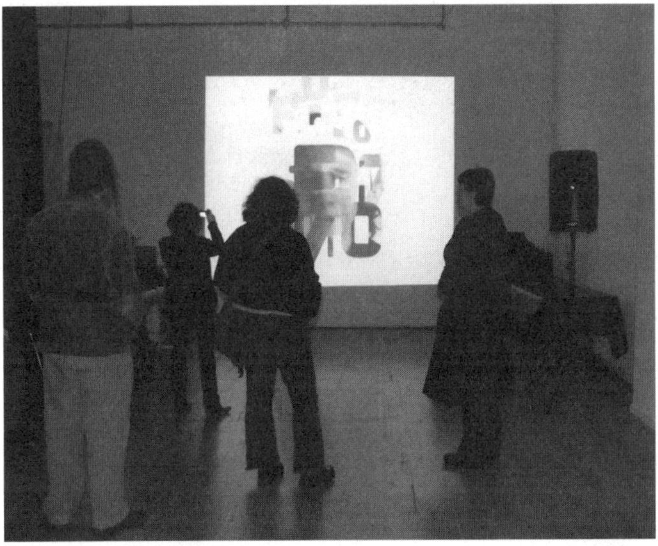

**Fig. 5.** Chris Joseph. *Photocollagen*. Digital remix video, 2007. Courtesy the artist. Photo credit: Garth Rankin.

*Photocollagen* is an identity-injection, or perhaps just the opposite – an identity-diffusion – projecting fragments of faces into a digital whole. And yet the whole is full of holes, as is demanded by a coded display that flirts with the novelty of pre-fab design. Who puts the "I" in identity, or is this the iDentity of Apple-inspired aesthetic seduction? A little bit of harvest goes a long way, paradoxically seeding the projected future at same time. If you try hard you might catch a glimpse of your own face – here or there – somewhere within the changing image of Babel turned digital flesh.

But this is important, for such a manifestation is either reducible to a coded novelty-value display or it actually matters that these image segments still, in some way, reference the flesh from which they came. It is as if Zeuxis went to remix film school and his legendary portrait – in which the eyes and nose and ears of all the most desirable women were combined to make the most beautiful painted image [14] – has in fact turned manifest, projected in real-time for the world to see. But imagine, then, if your face was not included, if you did not make the literal live action cut, surgically denied your place among the beautifully interactive others. For this is not mere photographic or video-based collage – this is collagen, the wrinkle-defying, age-reversing digital solution to the problem of time itself. But consider the remix here as more, perhaps, than just a random ordering of partialities. The order matters, and whether this "I" is for isolated or ironic or indifferent makes all the difference. Or is the "I" actually an eye – or a one: "1 of 7" might read the Star Trek sign, a trite but appropriate metaphor for identity gone democratic.

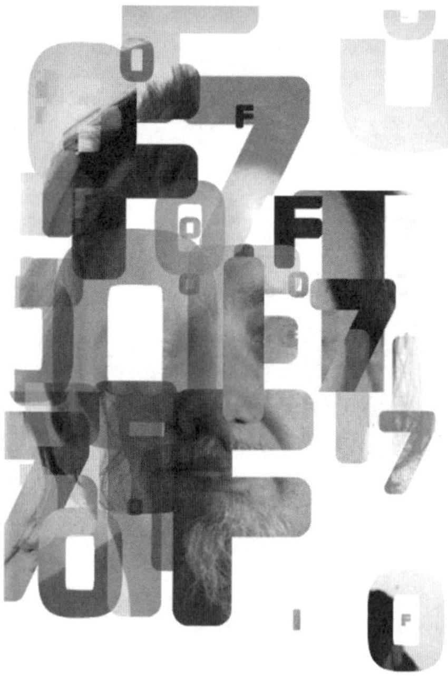

**Fig. 6.** Chris Joseph. *Photocollagen*. Digital remix video, 2007. Courtesy the artist.

Between the poles, then, of democracy and vanity, *Photocollagen* mobilizes both the generosity and the alienating idiosyncrasy of collective identity formulae. It is we who look at the projection, but what looks back is a crowd – replete with an appropriate multiplicity of proliferating metaphors: from the collective recognition of a cultural mirror turned digital to the magic mirror of temporally arrested multiplicity. Explicating Marshall McLuhan's famous insistence that the content of a medium is always another medium, *Photocollagen* reverses the aging process on collective facial existence, paradoxical self-placement for a digitally remixed documentary world.[15]

## 2.4 Fourth Iteration: Self-imagining Otherwise (Reflections on *Frontera* by Lilia Pérez Romero)

> One of four randomly chosen characters observes the spectator from a crystal screen. From its pose and the framing of the shot, it seems to be waiting to be portrayed. The character will carry on like this until the spectator touches the screen. Then, it will come out of his immobility responding with the same gesture, placing its hand and gaze on the user's hand, following any route it follows. Trapped in this small sequence of gestures that reminds us of *The Invention of Morel*, by Adolofo Bioy Casares, the portrayed character meets the real one at an instant of simulated communion, which expresses both the will for communication and the impossibility of it actually happening.
>
> – Lilia Pérez Romero [16]

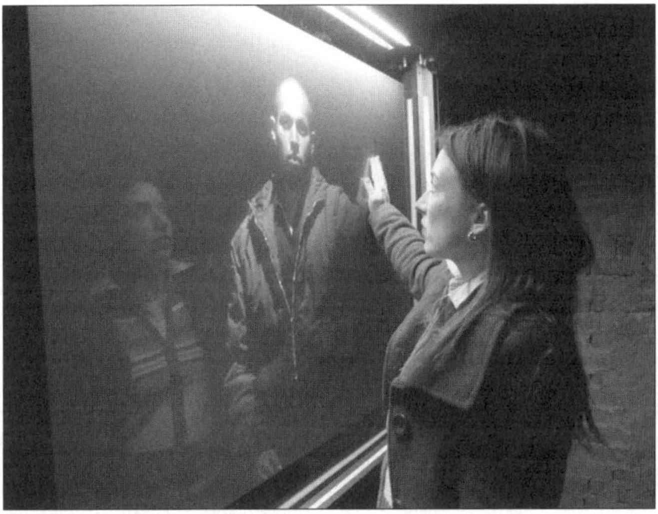

**Fig. 7.** Lilia Pérez Romero. *Frontera.* Interactive multimedia installation, 2007.Courtesy the artist. Photo credit: Gerhard Haupt & Pat Binder.

A gesture of generosity: reach out and touch someone... but what if they then seek to touch you back? The digital feedback loop is complete. We have realized our otherness, or rather we have had it realized for us. Ironic isn't it? How we can go through life thinking we know ourselves best when, in the final analysis, we must ultimately realize that our own image is among those least-encountered moments of optical recognition. Case in point: to see someone else mimicking us, well that makes perfect sense. If it were we ourselves, well that would be nonsense; a private bathroom fantasy of early morning living, preparation for entry into the world, but not actually part of the world proper... mirrors never are.

*Frontera* is a simple screen with a complex – though familiar – message: we are not ourselves. And, if we had never encountered a mirror we perhaps would never be the wiser. Is it the figure who is trapped within the screen or we who are trapped on the outside? Either way works, of course, for in both instances it is not ourselves we see. Like the encounter with one's voice on the answering machine – an unfamiliarity that is disjunctive because we expect ourselves to sound a certain way. And when the voice is distinctly not ours? Well, it should come as no surprise that we still find it foreign.

Jacques Lacan always insisted that the mirror-stage was that which formed the basis of self-consciousness, yet he could never have know the trap he was setting.[17] His was an analogue world, and while he insisted that the mirror gave us the fantasy of ourselves as another, even he – perhaps – would be shocked to see his own private fantasy digitally realized. But isn't this also the story of the story – the meta-story – upon which *Frontera* is based? For what is *The Invention of Morel* if it is not, in fact, the story of a reality machine – first perfected by Lacan, then reinvented both by Casares and Pérez Romero as a time-machine of dislocated otherness.[6] Indeed, *Frontera* is a first-generation version of Hans Moravech's final fantasy[7] – not yet the downloadable brain, but at least the interactive – forever interactive – ghost of one's very own image, left to respond ad infinitum to those visitors the future might bring one's way.

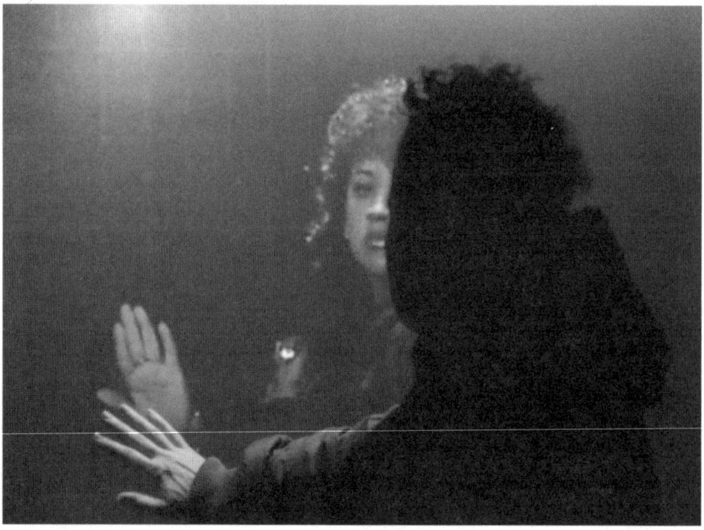

**Fig. 8.** Lilia Pérez Romero. *Frontera*. Interactive multimedia installation, 2007. Courtesy the artist. Photo credit: Garth Rankin.

---

6 *The Invention of Morel* (also called *Morel's Invention*) is a novel by Adolfo Bioy Casares in which a fugitive on a deserted island encounters a reality-machine that depicts simulated people who seem real.[18].

7 On the question of Hans Moravech and the drive towards an accessible, downloadable consciousness, see [19].

But that, ultimately, is because we have already gone far past Lacan. We are not bound by the mirror-stage – not anymore. The screen-stage of contemporary living is what allows for these virtual touchings, these selves with irreconcilable images, these walking and talking identities with faces that are not theirs. We needn't imagine the impact of seeing our actions repeated exactly by another – this is not fantasy, it is more common than even our mirror gazing histories. Is it we who watch the people in the screen, or the other way around? Surveillance cultures abound, and it is perhaps worth reinforcing that without such live-action screen captions we might never be able to cross the frontier; the virtual barrier collapses and finally the screen touches back.

### 2.5 Fifth Iteration: Digital Dreams and Delusions (Reflections on *Slip/host* by Fiona Bowie)

> This installation features an immersive video, sound and sculptural installation that shifts between two parallel worlds. The installation takes its inspiration, in part, from the social realism of Ed Keinholz' State Hospital, an immersive tableau that the artist completed in 1966, and also the sparse caricature landscapes of the popular British television series *Teletubbies*. An eccentric host of characters in *Slip/host* includes the The Big Lump, the Gargantuan Head and Two-Headed Moon.
>
> – Fiona Bowie [20]

It's one thing to see someone else's face and name and body and clothes, but to actually see inside someone else's head? Slip of the tongue or of the mind, slippery dreams of televised being. And the scale matters too, for every dream is a cosmology and every delusion a reality, simulated or otherwise. The world outside is also inside the screen, projected fantasies replace communal hallucinations, consensual or not, the low-tech high-tech mish-mash reveals not a big brother but merely some brother's big head. Fantasy dreams of having things as they seem quickly grow old when the screen gets its way.

*Slip/host* is a multi-layered installation, combining objects, images, ideas and environments into a delirious aesthetic mashup. In one room a series of roughly constructed models point to the difficulties of digital dirt; a series of objects charting the visually familiar cosmological loop wherein a solar system turns into a molecule and grows again to repeat. In the background a man eats chicken, while dreaming of eating chicken too – a looped delusion of insatiable satisfaction. In another room, a blue room lit with projected light, a giant head waits, sometimes watching but more often speaking slow words loosely collected around, it seems, a theme of disappearances. And this is more than metaphoric.. it is, in fact, theatrical.

But such is – it might be insisted – the case for all narrative in a digital era. Spectacular or delirious, it seems, are the only two options; everything else is predictably analogue. But that makes sense – if sense is what is required. Or perhaps it is just the inverse, and it is the disappearance of sense that is the first sign of digital cosmology,

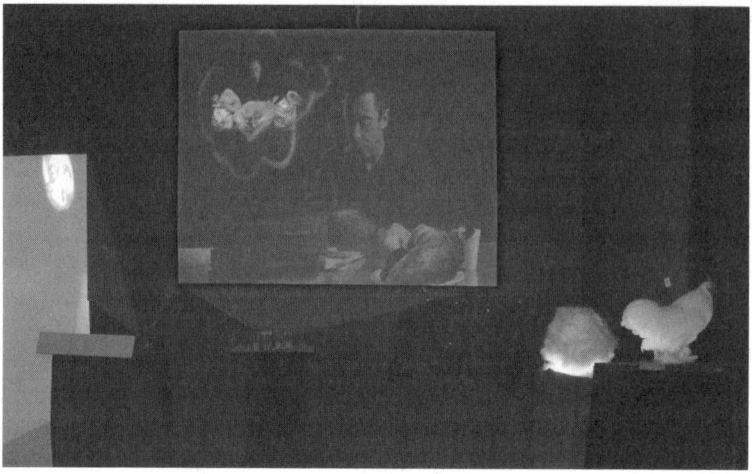

**Fig. 9.** Fiona Bowie. *Slip/host.* Multimedia installation, 2004. Courtesy the artist. Photo credit: Garth Rankin.

the first sign of an incommunicable imaginary that always flirts and fluctuates between fantasies of otherness and the realization that such fantasies have disappeared into their own living realities – challenged most precisely by becoming real. It is an updated version of a more ancient story, a story of fragile delusion – the story of a digital Don Quixote who, instead of charging at windmills-turned-giants, prefers to satisfy itself with dreams of roast chicken.[8] And there is much at stake in the status of living dreams such as these, for it is not merely a scale shift that occurs when the imaginary finds its appetite.

Between, then, the constitution of delirium and the awareness of disappearance, *Slip/host* is a paradoxically candy-coated dystopia, soft-spoken aggression turned back on itself, internally multiplying, virally growing into a permission of a different sort. For under the signs of these digital dreams, it is the constitution of private fantasy turned public-display that is the default action script for worldly participation. One must add reality to the list of creatures rendered extinct by technology,[9] slipped out of the projected future, for only delusion can be properly hosted. But this is what happens anyways when the screens emerge – for only screens are capable of representing that which otherwise exists only in the privacy of our own heads. We have come full circle from screened stages to screened worlds, a digital universe that has made its way into our molecular flesh.

[8] The story of Don Quixote concerns a Spanish land owner who (mistakenly) believes himself to be a knight and tours the countryside seeking adventure. Among his delusional encounters is a battle with windmills that Quixote believes to be malicious giants.[21].

[9] One segment of Bowie's script has the narrator listing names of animals claimed by extinction.[22].

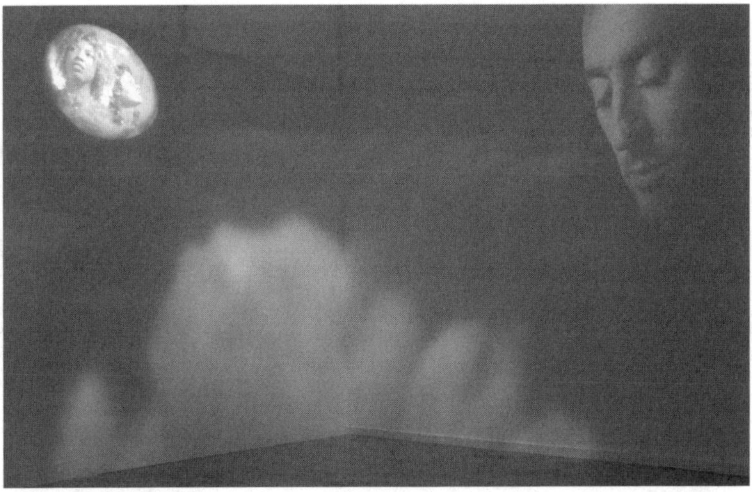

**Fig. 10.** Fiona Bowie. *Slip/host*. Multimedia installation, 2004. Courtesy the artist. Photo credit: Garth Rankin.

## 2.6 Sixth Iteration: A Digital Analogue (Reflections on *Scenes from the House Dream* by David Hoffos)

> Through my installation work I have sought to reveal and examine the sources of illusion found within genre movies, theme park attractions, museum displays, 19th century parlours and 20th century living rooms. The evolution of my work has been a steady process of accumulating and inventing techniques and devices and then applying and refining them. Over the course of more than 40 installations my work has developed step-by-step from simple, stand-alone film/sculpture pieces into complex, immersive, multi-channel environments. A few of the techniques and devices that characterize my work include: film and video projection onto cut-outs, large miniature scenes, mirrored boxes, phantom figure illusions, ghost video glass effects, cineramas, homemade video projectors, and curtained entrances.
>
> – David Hoffos [23]

The magic of ghosts and apparitions has been incanted, brought back to haunt and enchant a digital world. In a darkened room, sensory deprivation aside, the imagination wanders on its own, only here there are already illusions in play before the imaginary even gets there. Soft sounds of ocean tides beckon, and out the window one looks out onto a lookout – a meta-lookout whose seductive vista compels the instant creation of one story or another. For there are many stories that might emerge from such a dream, not the least of which waits in the corner – someone is on the inside watching, and the optical deferral process continues its holographic intrigue. This new screen is analogue, though no less digital for its magical dream.

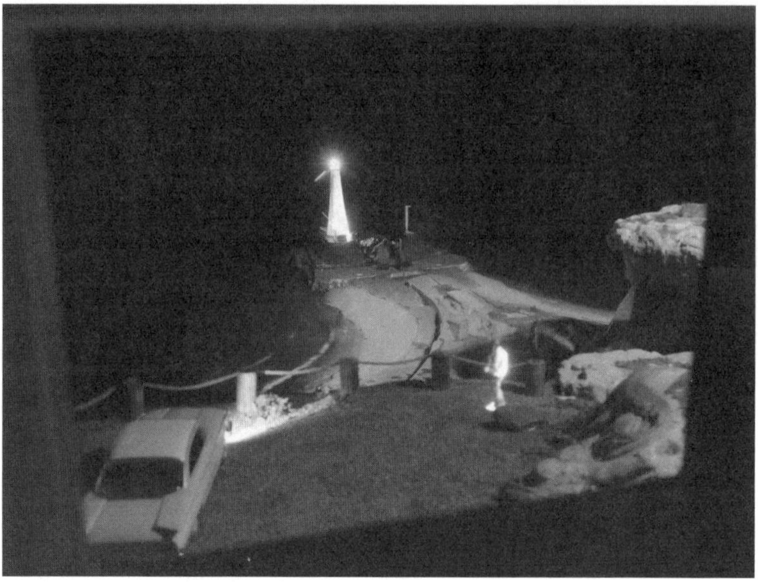

**Fig. 11.** David Hoffos, *Scenes from the House Dream, Bachelor's Bluff* (detail) 3-channel video, audio and mixed media installation, 2005. Courtesy the artist and Trépanier Baer. Photo credit: Garth Rankin.

*Scenes from the House Dream* is a low-tech audiovisual installation with high-tech dreams, lucid dreams of holographic proportion, manifest as a window onto another, equally delirious panorama. A hole cut in the wall of a darkened room frames an elaborate series of models, projections and illusions, whose combined effects yield a 3D scene of a man standing on a cliff, overlooking a lighthouse. In the back corner is a life-sized projection of a woman, waiting inconspicuously for the viewer to turn, mistaken first for real, then revealed as part of the dream itself. Not merely trompe l'oeil, this is a full body delusion of delirious manifestation.

It also matters that we are implicated in the story, not merely as points of perspective but also as reflective surfaces for the interplays of projection, refraction, deception and attraction. We are part of the dream, haunting the house itself but also completing the perceptual loop. This *House Dream* is a hyper-screen – more real than real – a screen seen from the other side, and from inside the screen the dreamhouse dreams. But something happens when we encounter a technological immersion of this magnitude, something corporeal that extends from optical illusion, as if to prove to our forgetful minds that bodies and eyes are still – even in a digital world – related in some way. Or perhaps it is just the opposite and it is precisely a technological incorporeality that we here encounter. It is not merely the digital that deceives, says the dreamhouse, nor merely bodies that dream. Instead, these dreams are both embodied and disembodied as only a technological paradox would allow. Nothing intensifies corporeal awareness like sensory deception.

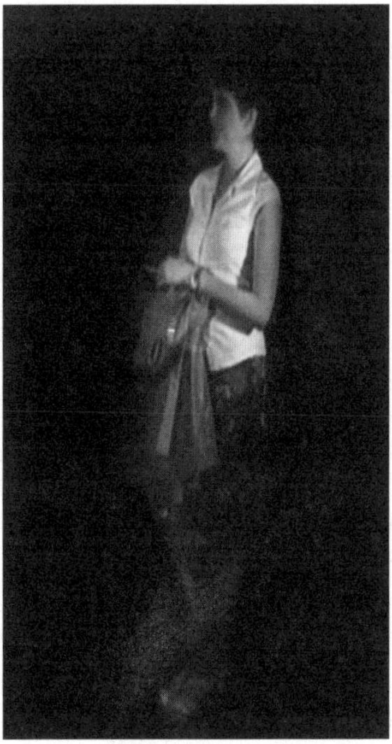

**Fig. 12.** David Hoffos, *Scenes from the House Dream, Bachelor's Bluff* (detail) 3-channel video, audio and mixed media installation, 2005. Courtesy the artist and Trépanier Baer. Photo credit: Garth Rankin.

Consequently, if there was any doubt that the mirror people and those of the screen are of the same ilk, it is in the *House Dream* that this question can be resolved for once and for all. For the new screen is a two-way mirror, always allowing for the manifest imaginary while declaring in no uncertain terms that these projections are more than merely holographic. A digital dream-time, without apology: here it is the house that dreams us, peppered ghosts[10] that emerge from the darkened room to rejoin the realm of the digitally living.

## 3 Behind the Screen

And so, behind the screen? Well, behind the screen there is nothing.. not anymore. And anything too – it can be no other way. There is no wall behind the screen, for walls are merely signs of an unsuspended real – a non-interactive future. Nor can there be darkness, for darkness is simply the sign of the screen turned-off – a non-interactive present. Instead, behind the screen there is always whatever we choose to see, or not to see – and that is, ultimately, the question. Deception aside, or perhaps

[10] Pepper's ghost is an illusionary technique used in theater and in some magic tricks. Using a plate glass and special lighting techniques, it can make objects seem to appear or disappear.[24]

front and centre, the technological delusion is real. The screen people have stepped through, and our reality like theirs has doubled in the process. For when dreams become real, when the screen becomes real, we find ourselves in another of Borges' imaginary tales. This time it is the story of the dreamer and the imaginary that was always his home, even though he didn't always see it that way:

> With relief, with humiliation, with terror, he realized that he, too, was but appearance, that another man was dreaming him.[25]

While these samplings of new screens – these dreams among many – are not exhausted suspensions of imaginative interaction, they are nevertheless more than mere instances of what the interactive future might hold. There are, of course, multiple other examples to consider, each worth its own weight in imagination, each of which initiates an interactive future of its own, each of which asks after the engaged potential of interactive living, and each of which insists in its own way that the – imagination like the very future itself – is only ever as active as personal engagement allows. The new screen is worn on the inside – imaginative interaction to the power of dream.

## References


1. Baudrillard, J.: Xerox and Infinity. In: The Transparency of Evil: Essays on Extreme Phenomena, p. 54. James Benedict, trans. Verso, London (1993)
2. Interactive Futures (2007), http://cfisrv.finearts.uvic.ca/interactivefutures/IF07/
3. Borges, J.L.: Fauna of Mirrors. In: The Book of Imaginary Beings. Norman Thomas di Giovanni trans, pp. 67–68. Vintage, New York (2002)
4. Ahn, J.: Their Circumstances, artist statement ftom the Interactives Futures 2008 website (2008), http://cfisrv.finearts.uvic.ca/interactivefutures/IF07/?page_id=40
5. Wikipedia: Georges Bataille, http://en.wikipedia.org/wiki/Georges_Bataille
6. Wikipedia: Story of the Eye, http://en.wikipedia.org/wiki/Histoire_de_l'oeil
7. Virilio, P.: The Information Bomb, Chris Turner, trans. Verso, London, p. 124 (2000)
8. Mander, J.: Four Arguments for the Elimination of Television, pp. 170–189. Perennial, New York (2002)
9. Wikipedia: Inedia, http://en.wikipedia.org/wiki/Inedia
10. Armstrong, K.: Why Some Dollsa Are Bad, artist statement ftom the Interactives Futures 2008 website (2008), http://cfisrv.finearts.uvic.ca/interactivefutures/IF07/?page_id=38
11. Wikipedia: Infinite Monkey Theorem, http://en.wikipedia.org/wiki/Infinite_monkey_theorem
12. Hayles, N.K.: How We Became Postuman: Virtual Bodies in Cybernetics, Literature, and Informatics, p. 25. University of Chicago Press, Chicago (1999)
13. Joseph, C.: Photocollagen, artist statement ftom the Interactives Futures 2008 website (2008), http://cfisrv.finearts.uvic.ca/interactivefutures/IF07/?page_id=50

14. Cicero: De Inventione, C.D. Yonge, trans, http://classicpersuasion.org/pw/cicero/dnv2-1.htm
15. McLuhan, M.: Understanding Media: The Extensions of Man, p. 24. McGraw-Hill, New York (1964)
16. Pérez Romero, L.: Frontera, artist statement from the Interactives Futures 2008 website (2008), http://cfisrv.finearts.uvic.ca/interactivefutures/IF07/?page_id=37
17. Lacan, J.: The Mirror Stage as Formative of the Function of the I as Revealed in Psychoanalytic Experience. In: Elliott, A. (ed.) The Blackwell Reader in Contemporary Social Theory, pp. 62–64. Blackwell, Oxford (1999)
18. Casares, A.B.: The Invention of More. NYBR Classics, New York (2003)
19. Hayles, N.K.: How We Became Postuman: Virtual Bodies in Cybernetics, Literature, and Informatics, pp. xi - xii. University of Chicago Press, Chicago (1999)
20. Bowie, F.: Slip/host, artist statement ftom the Interactives Futures 2008 website (2008), http://cfisrv.finearts.uvic.ca/interactivefutures/IF07/?page_id=36
21. de Cervantes, M.: The Ingenious Hidalgo Don Quixote de la Mancha. J. Rutherford, trans. Penguin, London (2000)
22. Bowie, F.: Slip/host, http://alexandrahass.wordpress.com/2007/12/01/fiona-bowies-slip-host-script/
23. Hoffos, D.: Scenes from the House Dream, artist statement ftom the Interactives Futures 2008, website (2008), http://cfisrv.finearts.uvic.ca/interactive-futures/IF07/?page_id=39
24. Wikipedia: Pepper's Ghost, http://en.wikipedia.org/wiki/Pepper's_ghost
25. Borges, J.L.: The Circular Ruins. In: Collected Fictions. Andrew Hurley, trans, Penguin, New York, p. 100 (1998)

## Reference Websites

**Interactive Futures 2007 (The New Screen):**
http://cfisrv.finearts.uvic.ca/interactivefutures/IF07/

**Artist Websites:**
JiHyun Ahn. http://jihyunahn.com
Kate Armstrong. http://www.katearmstrong.com
Chris Joseph. http://www.babel.ca
Lilia Pérez Romero. http://www.liliaperez.net
Fiona Bowie. http://www.eciad.ca/~bowiefb/home.html
David Hoffos. http://www.trepanierbaer.com/artists.asp?ArtistID=49

# Part II

# Digital Literacies

# Transliteracy and New Media

Sue Thomas

Professor of New Media
Institute of Creative Technologies / Faculty of Humanities
De Montfort University
The Gateway, Leicester, LE1 9BH, UK
sue.thomas@dmu.ac.uk

**Abstract.** Transliteracy is the ability to read, write and interact across a range of platforms, tools and media from signing and orality through handwriting, print, TV, radio and film, to digital social networks. The term is derived from the verb "to transliterate", meaning to write or print a letter or word using the closest corresponding letters of a different alphabet or language, and today we extend the act of transliteration and apply it to the increasingly wide range of communication platforms and tools at our disposal. The concept of transliteracy is embedded in the very earliest histories of human communication, providing a cohesion of modes relevant to reading, writing, interpretation and interaction. This paper examines new media through the lens of transliteracy.

**Keywords:** transliteracy, new media, literacy, communication, interactivity, reading, writing, web 2.0.

It would be difficult to imagine the contemporary Western cultural landscape without that "white or silvered surface where pictures can be projected for viewing"[1] - a surface which can be found everywhere from the very smallest platform (mobile telephones, watches etc) to the largest (see for example the building-sized projections of artists like Rafael Lozano-Hemmer[2]). However, although they are now ubiquitous in many parts of the world, screen-based media are highly dependent upon the availability of certain technologies. Furthermore, screen images cannot be understood unless the viewer possesses a specific set of cognitive and cultural literacies. This paper examines new media through the lens of a new analytical perspective, transliteracy.

Transliteracy can be defined as "the ability to read, write and interact across a range of platforms, tools and media from signing and orality through handwriting, print, TV, radio and film, to digital social networks." As a behaviour, it is not new—indeed it reaches back to the very beginning of culture—but it has only been identified as a working concept since the Internet allowed humans to communicate in ways which seem to be entirely novel. As a working concept, it grew to fruition during discussions among the Production and Research in Transliteracy (PART) Group at the Institute of Creative Technologies (IOCT), De Montfort University.[3] This paper owes

[1] http://wordnet.princeton.edu/perl/webwn?s=screen
[2] http://www.lozano-hemmer.com/
[3] Production and Research in Transliteracy http://www.transliteracy.com

R. Adams, S. Gibson, and S. Müller Arisona (Eds.): DAW/IF 2006/2007, CCIS 7, pp. 101–109, 2008.

much to the first peer-reviewed and collaboratively written article on transliteracy, published in December 2007 by First Monday, one of the first openly accessible peer-reviewed journals on the Internet and founded in 1996.[1]

The word itself is derived from the verb *transliterate*, meaning to write or print a letter or word using the closest corresponding letters of a different alphabet or language. This of course is nothing new, but transliteracy extends the act of transliteration and applies it to the increasingly wide range of communication platforms and tools at our disposal. From early signing and orality through handwriting, print, TV and film to networked digital media, the concept of transliteracy calls for a change of perspective away from the battles over print versus digital content, and a move instead towards a unifying ecology not just of media, but of all literacies relevant to reading, writing, interaction and culture, both past and present. [1]

In December 2007 The New York Times published *Twilight of the Books*, an article by Caleb Crain outlining the possible consequences of a decline in reading. Using *Proust and the Squid* by Maryanne Wolf (2007) as his main source, Crain concludes that:

> If, over time, many people choose television over books, then a nation's conversation with itself is likely to change. A reader learns about the world and imagines it differently from the way a viewer does; according to some experimental psychologists, a reader and a viewer even think differently. If the eclipse of reading continues, the alteration is likely to matter in ways that aren't foreseeable.[2]

Since we are currently immersed in that unforeseeable transition, it is indeed difficult to imagine how literacy will change, but the distinctions between the roles of reader and viewer described above are already becoming blurred because most people are fluent in both perspectives and adopt them interchangeably as the medium or cultural moment demands. This is transliteracy.

Crain also reports that Wolf makes a detailed neurobiological argument that reading and orality wire our brains differently, and that this wiring powerfully influences the amount of processing power we have available. She contends that it is possible to "read efficiently a script that combines ideograms and phonetic elements, something that many Chinese do daily" but that the Greek alphabet helps readers reach efficiency sooner. The example of Chinese literacy is an interesting one, since the current expansion of China is fast making Mandarin the world's second language, after English. "It's daunting to learn, especially for Westerners, because of the tones used in speech to shift meaning—to say nothing of the thousands of characters that must be memorized to achieve true literacy."[3] Could Mandarin, with its complex character sets, transform our concept of literacy?

The popular Western view of literacy is that it is about the consumption of plain text. The Central Intelligence Agency Factbook, for example, defines a literate person as someone who is "over the age of 15 and can read and write."[4a] In 2005 CIA researchers used that definition to calculate that 82% (3,576 million) of the population of the world (87% of men and 77% of women) were literate at the time of the count.[4]

---

[4] Of the remaining 18% (785 million individuals) two-thirds were found in only eight countries: India, China, Bangladesh, Pakistan, Nigeria, Ethiopia, Indonesia, and Egypt, with extremely low literacy rates concentrated in three regions, South and West Asia, Sub-Saharan Africa, and the Arab states, where around one-third of the men and half of all women were classified illiterate.

This implies that 18% (785 million) of the 2005 global population aged 15 or over at that time were unable to read and write. But this does not mean that the 18% are unable to understand screen-based content, and indeed we have no clear definition of a screen-literate person.

The CIA Factbook also offers some useful information about mobile telephony, reporting that by 2005 the number of mobile phones in the world had grown to almost double the number of landline telephones and to more than double the number of Internet users.

| | |
|---|---|
| Mobile phones | 2,168 million |
| Landline Telephones | 1,263 million |
| Internet Users | 1,018 million |

(2005 CIA Factbook)[4b]

In the USA, Wired Magazine reported in December 2007 that the year was likely to "go into the books as the first year in which Americans spent more money on cell phone services than traditional landlines. " Allyn Hall, consumer research director for market research firm In-Stat, reported finding "a huge move of people giving up their land line service altogether and using cell phones exclusively."[5] North Americans have benefited for many years from the luxury of free local calls on landline telephones, but for numerous users elsewhere around the world, especially those living in countries with limited technical infrastructure, the landline telephone has been out of reach. Early dial-up Internet systems, dependent on the landline for connection, suffered equally from unreliable networks and frequent power outages. But today's 3G phones make it possible for people in countries with limited access to landlines, Internet hubs and electrical power to bypass some of the technical problems and access the Internet via a simple cell phone.

So what does this mean for the screen-literate user? Mobile phone screens are still, for the most part, a largely unsatisfactory technology, and most have a limited capacity for displaying sophisticated multimedia, so it would be safe to assume that the majority of mobile phones around the world are used principally for voice and, to a lesser extent, for text. And in terms of literacy, a simple level of numeracy is all that is needed to remember and key in a number. Plus, of course, mobiles can be used in any language whose character set is supported by the unit. In other words, the literacy required to use a mobile phone is probably well below that of the CIA definition—"over 15 and able to read and write."

Is it reasonable to speculate that there is an overlap between the 785 million illiterate individuals and the 2,168 million people who use mobile phones? If so, what are the implications for text-based and screen-based literacies? In transliterate terms, mobile phones, with their facilitation of culturally-based orality and the opportunities offered by their screens to those who can barely read and write, might be seen to permit a return to a cultural norm where humans share collective knowledge without the use of reading and writing. This might seem a transgressive notion, but humans have only been reading and writing for a very short time in our history. The philosopher Socrates, for example, eschewed learning to read and write in a culture where such practices were unusual, and believed that the fixed nature of writing limits thought and enquiry. In the *Phaedrus* we read that in 370BC Socrates asserted writing was an aid "not to memory, but to reminiscence" providing "not truth, but only the semblance of truth." Readers would, he said, "be hearers of many things and will have learned nothing; they will appear to be omniscient and will generally know nothing; they will be tiresome company, having the show of wisdom without the reality."[5] It is interesting to place Socrates' complaints about reading and writing alongside the charge of graphocentrism currently being levelled at Western agencies engaged in trying to colonize societies such as those found in the Brazilian rainforests. Marilda Cavalcanti writing about the Asheninka tribe observes:

> The Asheninka traditional form of education (includes) planting rituals (and) living in communion with nature [ ] school and schooling are thus just (a small) part of the whole discussion on public policies. [ ] As the indigenous teachers say all the time, they are teachers full time, all day long wherever they are. They go hunting and fishing with their students and their families. [6:320]

In this tradition of holistic education, the Asheninka recognize the importance of literacy but not its supremacy, and so they assign the use of literacy to certain nominated individuals. They say:

> As our traditional system of life does not internally depend on writing, we are educating just a few people to make contact with other societies. We are also educating teacher researchers to record our history, to get them involved in our present political organisation, to get them to help us maintain the cultural world of the people, making the old and young people aware and opening up an issue of reflection about writing so that we don't override our culture. [6:322]

Textual literacy has become so ingrained that it has reached the point of invisibility in Western society, but in tribes such as the Asheninka culture is learned and passed on via an interwoven accretion of images and stories:

> Everything we use has a story; each drawing has a long and comprehensive story. Each drawing which is passed from one generation to another is our writing; each little symbol has an immense story. As one learns a drawing, one learns its origin, who taught it, who brought it to us. [6: 322]

Such people, versed in oral and visual history, may privilege a literacy focused on multimedia rather than on text, and might prefer to access it via a mobile phone instead of a computer or book as part of a *transliterate lifeworld* in constant process. A lifeworld, a concept first introduced by philosopher Edmund Husserl as "Lebenswelt" (the world as lived) and later developed by Maurice Merleau-Ponty, is the combination of physical environment and subjective experience that makes up everyday life. Each individual's lifeworld is personal to them, as Agre and Horswill describe:

> Cats and people, for example, can be understood as inhabiting the same physical environment but different lifeworlds. Kitchen cupboards, windowsills, and the spaces underneath chairs have different significances for cats and people, as do balls of yarn, upholstery, television sets, and other cats. Similarly, a kitchen affords a different kind of lifeworld to a chef than to a mechanic, though clearly these two

[5] Of course, it is impossible to ignore the fact that Plato did exactly this when he transcribed the conversation between Socrates and Phaedrus as it was taking place under a plane tree by the banks of the Ilissus.

lifeworlds may overlap in some ways as well. A lifeworld, then, is not just a physical environment, but the patterned ways in which a physical environment is functionally meaningful within some activity. [7]

The transliterate lifeworld is highly subjective, diverse and complicated. It is not one kind of place, but many—an ecology that changes with the invention of each new media-type. So what are the "patterned ways" of the complex lifeworld of transliteracy and how are they meaningful? Transliteracy occurs in the places where different things meet, mix, and rub together. It is an interstitial space teeming with diverse life forms, some on the rise, some in decline, expressed in many languages in many voices, many kinds of scripts and media. One way in which we might create an image of the patterns of our lifeworlds is to map them via the networks we form and the ways in which we move around them.

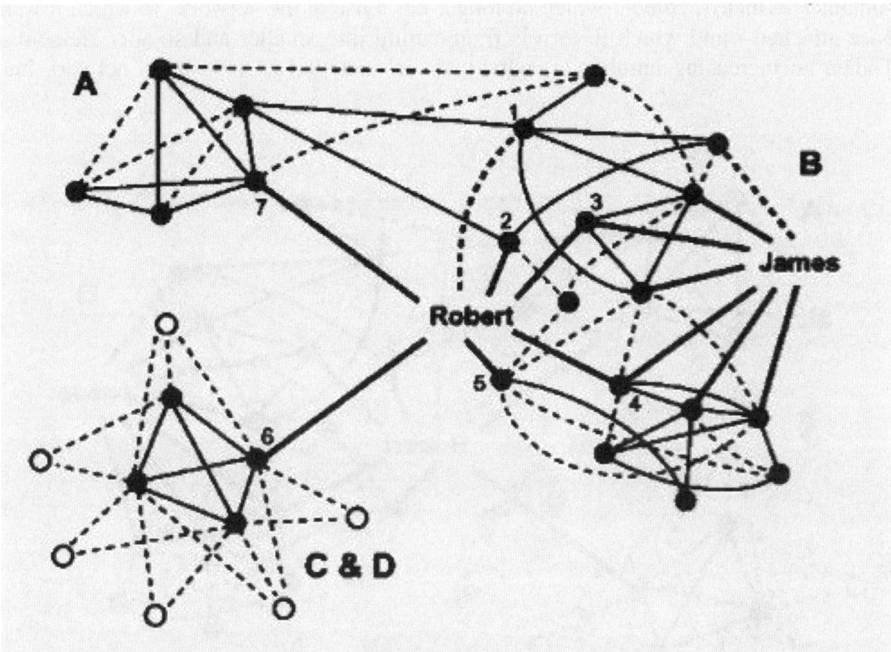


**Fig. 1.** Structural Holes [8a]

Professor Ronald Burt proposes a theory of structural holes (above), suggesting that people with connections across the spaces between networks are more prone to have good ideas than people in densely interconnected but closed networks. The focus of Burt's research has been on business networks but it can be extrapolated to many other kinds of networks. For example, in this diagram, Robert is based in the same network as James, but Robert has connections with other networks whereas James does not. Burt writes:

> Robert is an entrepreneur in the literal sense of the word—a person who adds value by brokering the connection between others. There is a tension here, but not the hostility of combatants. It is merely uncertainty. In the swirling mix of preferences characteristic of social networks, where no demands have absolute authority, the entrepreneur negotiates for favourable terms. Structural holes are the setting for such strategies, and information is the substance of them. [8b]

The concept of transliteracy can take us to a possible next step. If the holes are the setting, and information is their substance, what are the holes themselves like? We have a clear picture here of the networks but there is only emptiness between them, as if Robert is flying over the structural hole rather than acting within it. He does not inhabit the transliterate space, but simply moves through or across it. His allegiance is to the networks, specifically Network B, not the space between them. In the view of Toby Moores, CEO of a company, Sleepydog, which makes computer games for Sony, the information which gathers in these spaces is "content which has escaped its container"—that is, content which no longer has a use in the networks to which it was once attached—and which in turn is fragmenting into smaller and smaller elements. Today, an increasing number of individuals are not tied to any single network but

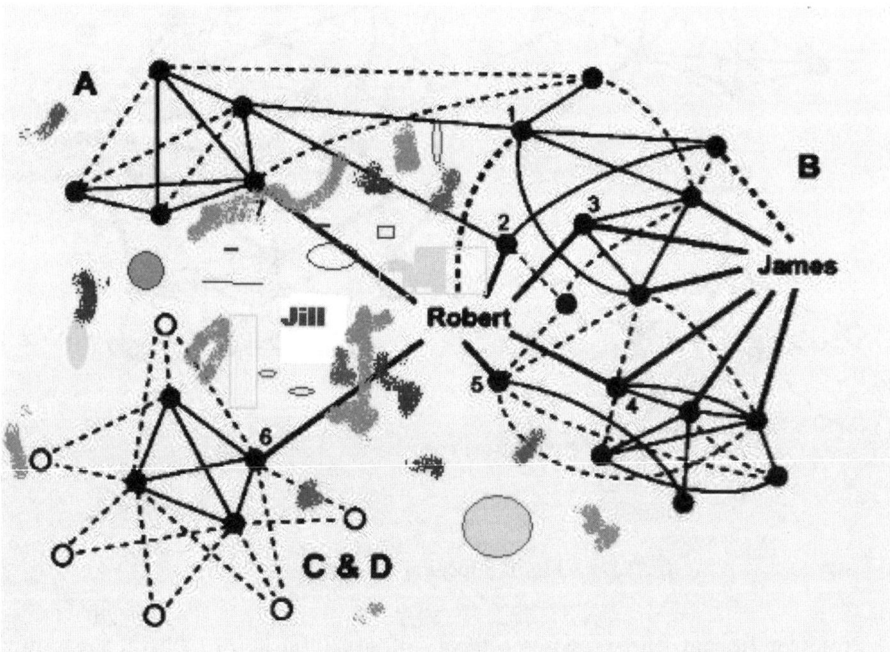


**Fig. 2.** Transliteracy in the network[6]

[6] Thomas, S. Diagramming transliterate spaces (Production and Research in Transliteracy). Retrieved 21:35:56 7, 2008, from http://www.hum.dmu.ac.uk/blogs/part/2007/09/diagramming_transliterate_spac.html

float freely in the space between them, and this shifting mutating area in constant evolution—this transliterate lifeworld—is where they are most comfortable. So there needs to be another person in this diagram. Let us call her Jill.

Jill works with content that has escaped its container. She exists in the structural hole itself and, in fact she is probably the person who introduced Robert to the people at A, C and D in the first place. She is a freewheeler, a consultant or some such, maybe she lives out of a suitcase, or perhaps she lives out of Facebook, or possibly she stays in one place and people come to her. But what makes Jill different from Robert is that she is a permanent resident inside the structural hole. Transliteracy is the place she calls home. Not everyone is comfortable in transliterate space. It is transient (of course). It is uncertain, confusing, overwhelming, and frustrating. One often feels like an amateur, and always slightly out of control. Furthermore, as Burt has noted, structural holes have a natural drift towards closure, and this closure is often facilitated as part of a transition. But there is no danger of reaching a moment where all networks are joined together because it is in the nature of the beast that new holes are continually opening up.

This shifting sand quality is an integral feature of the essentially estuarine transliterate environment, where each new tide brings different transformations, so perhaps structural holes should be viewed as oceans between continents—teeming, thriving, nutritious zones of innovation and transformation.

Caleb Crain ends Twilight of the Books with a surprising observation. "There is no one looking back at the television viewer," he writes. "He is alone, though he, and his brain, may be too distracted to notice it." This connects with a reference earlier in his essay to a "YouTube-fuelled evolution away from print and toward television." But the move is not towards television, which some say is in decline, but towards the broader concept of a screen. And screens today, whether on public art, or YouTube, or the cinema, and even, increasingly, the TV, are all about not being alone. Screen-based public art is often designed as a spectacle, fuelled by the crowd as audience. YouTube was never just about the technology to upload movies, but about sharing—the comments, ranking, and aggregation tools are all essential components of the experience. Cinemas, of course, have always been collective, and today TV is moving in the same direction. Not only do television shows spill out onto the web and mobile phone, but there are also increasing numbers of social networks based around new kinds of viewing patterns. See, for example, interactive TV like the Finnish show Accidental Lovers [9], where viewers can influence the unfolding drama by sending mobile messages to a system that triggers on-screen events based on the keyword recognition; internet sites such as Joost [10] which offers over 20,000 shows free of charge and encourages viewers to create their own channels, invite their friends, and blog about their viewing, and applications such as MediaZone's [11] recent beta test of Social TV which provides chat windows for viewers during live streams, along with ratings, comments, blogs and other tools.

According to the Institute for the Future, California, transliteracy is a "disruptive innovation" which presents challenges that will shape the way we think of teaching and learning in the context of the open economy. In their view, "developing transliterate creative production practices and communication across multiple platforms represents a sensory and cultural explosion that will frame new kinds of experience and knowing."[12a] In a 2007 report *The Future of Learning Agents* they propose, "transliterating social and creative life implies new social and political understandings as new relations of creative production emerge. Collective authorship and collective intelligence are modes of active learning and discovery that present new dynamics between individuals and groups with respect to knowledge. Roles of authority and expertise shift when information and experience are created and aggregated in blogs, chat, and online group discussions lists. Ownership of content in a remix context, and for a public audience, present new ways of understanding ideas, knowledge, people, and perspectives."[12b] This is born out in the work of researchers like Marc Prensky, who wrote in 2007: "While some teachers do embrace the kids' technological world, those teachers who are fearful of being unable to engage a generation of students used to technological advances often attribute their own failures, such as the loss of control implied in integrating tools that they know relatively little about, to untruths such as lack of attention span and Attention Deficit Disorder on the part of students. In exchange, students observe their teachers' lack of fluency with modern tools, and view them as 'illiterate' in the very domain the kids know they will need for their future—technology."[13] And screens are an essential part of that technology.

We live in a world of multiple literacies, multiple media and multiple demands on our attention. Each of these is complete in itself yet we do not experience them individually, we synthesize and mould them to our needs, and in a world where an inexpensive webcam and headset can enable multimedia communication in any language the transliterate screen plays a vitally important role. Tomorrow's users may not wish to spend time learning to read, but they may well be open to a few tutorials on how to use Skype.

## References


1. Thomas, S., Joseph, C., Laccetti, J., Mason, B., Mills, S., Perril, S., et al.: Transliteracy: Crossing divides (2007), retrieved from, http://www.uic.edu/htbin/cgiwrap/bin/ojs/index.php/fm/article/view/2060/1908
2. Crain, C.: Twilight of the Books: A Critic at Large: The New Yorker. Retrieved 08:31:53, 4 (2008), from http://www.newyorker.com/arts/critics/atlarge/2007/12/24/071224crat_atlarge_crain/?currentPage=1
3. Ramzy, A.: TIMEasia Magazine: Get Ahead, Learn Mandarin. Retrieved 09:21:47, 4 (2008), from http://www.time.com/time/asia/covers/501060626/ story.html
4. CIA - The World Factbook – World. Retrieved 21:24:51, 7 (2008), from https://www.cia.gov/library/publications/the-world-factbook/print/xx.html
5. December 18, 7:50 AM EST Cell Phone Spending Surpasses Land Lines By DIBYA SARKAR Wired News, (accessed December 24, 2007), http://news.wired.com/dynamic/stories/C/CELL_PHONE_SPENDING?SITE=WIRE&SECTION=HOME&TEMPLATE=DEFAULT&CTIME=2007-12-18-07-50-10
6. Cavalcanti, M.C.: It's not writing by itself that is going to solve our problems: Questioning a mainstream ethnocentric myth as part of a search for self–sustained development, Language and Education, June 20, 2007, vol. 18(4), pp. 317–325 (2004), http://www.multilingual-matters.net/le/018/le0180317.htm
7. Agre, P., Horswill, I.: Lifeworld analysis. Journal of Artificial Intelligence Research 6, 111–145 (1997), http://www-2.cs.cmu.edu/afs/cs/project/jair/pub/volume6/agre97a-html/lifeworlds.html

8. Structural Holes versus Network Closure as Social Capital p6, http://faculty.chicagogsb.edu/ronald.burt/research/SHNC.pdf
9. Accidental Lovers. Retrieved 13:50:28, 4 (2008), from http://crucible.lume.fi/crunet.nsf/etofilmpages/accidentallovers
10. http://www.joost.com
11. MediaZone.com Internet TV and Video. Retrieved 13:58:00, 4 (2008), from http://www.mediazone.com/channel/new_homepage/main.jsp
12. Internal research report on the future of learning agents prepared by Institute for the Future (November, 2007)
13. Prensky, M.: How to Teach With Technology – keeping both teachers and students comfortable in an era of exponential change (from BECTA's Emerging Technologies for Learning, P4, vol. 2 (2007)

# Digital Archiving and "The New Screen"

John F. Barber

Digital Technology and Culture
Washington State University Vancouver
Vancouver, Washington, USA
jfbarber@vancouver.wsu.edu

**Abstract.** Failure to preserve, migrate, and archive digital performances, artworks, literary expressions, hyperlinked resources, and interactive experiences created for the new screen—as well as the connections between their multimedia components, the texts, the images, the coded mechanisms that drive their interactivity—threatens their survival as markers in our collective artistic, literary, and cultural heritage. Digital archiving focuses on the preservation, presentation, and addition of value to such digital works. Several models are presented for how digital archiving for the new screen might be undertaken. Questions posed begin a discussion of how to both create and archive artifacts of the new screen, especially given its incunabular, ever-evolving display state.

**Keywords:** digital archiving, digital media, new media, preservation, presentation.

## 1 Introduction

Current day digital media artists are producing media rich artworks, environments, performances, and installations featuring computer distributed media elements—graphics, moving images, sounds, shapes, spaces, and texts that have become computable [1]. Many such artifacts are produced for what is being called "the new screen" [2], as a way of critiquing the traditional rectangular format and determined interactivity of more traditional screen-based media.

Artists, writers, filmmakers, developers, educators, and theorists are experimenting with new modes and models of visual interfaces and narrative structures. Less considered, arguably, is digital archiving: the preservation, presentation, and addition of value to performances, artworks, literary expressions, hyperlinked resources, and interactive experiences created for the new screen.

The International Council for Scientific and Technical Information (ICSTI), in a 1999 study, positioned digital archiving as the long-term storage, preservation, and access to information *born digital* (that is created and disseminated primarily in electronic form) or for which the digital version is considered to be the primary archive [3].

As is the case with technologies and methodologies that constantly evolve at an accelerated rate, assumptions often overlay implications for future theoretical stances and methodological practices, not to mention the future definition(s) of what constitutes best practices. Such is the case with digital archiving.

R. Adams, S. Gibson, and S. Müller Arisona (Eds.): DAW/IF 2006/2007, CCIS 7, pp. 110–119, 2008.

### 1.1 Assumptions

Most fundamentally, one assumes the new screen speaks to digital media, or digitally encoded objects, their shapes, colors, sounds, or behaviors composed of discrete samples, and described using a mathematical function subject to algorithmic manipulation [1].

Second, although historically digital media have been viewed, synthesized, or manipulated via computer devices with their de facto interface—the cathode ray tube or liquid crystal display computer screen—the new screen utilizes, and in some cases requires, different display technologies or surfaces, including the human body. Whereas the traditional computer screen was usually hardwired to its power and display source, the new screen can be, and is, wireless, remote, telepresent. In short, the new screen does not have to be, and in many cases clearly is not, the traditional computer screen.

Third, the new screen is increasingly capable of contextualization in a variety of ways. Mobile telephony, handheld devices with computing and other capabilities, global positioning technology, electronic kiosks, holographic posters, motion tracking environments, Computer-Assisted Virtual Environments (CAVES; 4-wall or 6-wall), multi-screen and surround projections, among other current and evolving complex display systems, provide new (and different) screens on which to display digital media.

Finally, discussion of the new screen collapses an understanding of its newness with respect to other media into an understanding of its state-of-the-art in terms of function and design. As a result, one speaks of the newness of a medium or technology in reference to older, no longer state-of-the-art versions of that same medium or technology [4].

Thus, the new screen is an upgrade of the previous screen state, resulting from technological or practical/artistic application of new abilities or techniques.

### 1.2 Out with the Old

Such advancements in state-of-the-art often orphan, abandon, or make obsolete previous states, casting aside the old in favor of the new. That which is classified as obsolete certainly forms a basis for newer, more current states. But the loss of digital artworks or interactive information resources as a result of their no longer current state-of-the-art is, arguably, a heavy price to pay for the sake of newness.

And therein is the rub. Failure, or inability, or disinterest, to preserve, migrate, and archive current artifacts of the new screen—as well as the connections between their multimedia components, the texts, the images, the coded mechanisms that drive their interactivity—threatens their survival as markers in our collective artistic, literary, and cultural heritage.

## 2 Archiving: Why?

In the face of such losses, archiving digital artworks and information resources produced for the new screen becomes a legitimate, even essential, concern for several reasons.

**Variable Nature.** First, new digital media may be seen as communicative, aesthetic, and ludic instruments. As Anneli Sundqvist notes in the introduction to a special issue of *Human IT* that focuses on the impact of information communication technology on long-term preservation and conservation of documents and artworks, ever-evolving technologies provide new methodologies of preservation while simultaneously challenging the principles for preservation.

> Information technology has added new dimensions to the concept of records and to archival practices. For thousands of years the medium for records creation was stable and physically tangible, and thus the handling primarily concerned keeping order in a literal sense. Then from the middle of the 20th century, first microfilm, audio recordings, and later computer technology, have challenged the foundations of both practices and principles. The new technology has made an enormous proliferation of records possible, often in susceptible formats of short duration. The concept of a record as a fixed entity and of the archive as a definite assembly of closed records is questioned. This touches upon the intricate issue of the relation between technology and social change [5].

**Ephemeral Nature.** Second, the advent of the new screen and its ephemeral nature forces scholars, critics, and others to admit that production of work (whether textual or visual or auditory) cannot be studied in the future using methodologies of the past since the basic material evidence—manuscripts, drafts, working notes, correspondence, journals—may not be available for artifacts whose native state is born digital.

**Virtual Native States.** Third, artifacts born digital may not be uniformly accessible because of the virtual nature of the new screen. As Matthew Kirshenbaum has noted, the computer is a "universal machine," designed to emulate other machines through its utilization of various software programs. One software program turns a computer into a sophisticated print production machine. Another turns a computer into a video or audio production studio. By opening different software programs a computer can become multiple and totally different virtual environments [6].

Software is either constantly evolving (driven by both technological advancements and economic impetus), or it disappears from the marketplace and creative palette because it no longer meets the requirements of corporate profit. In either case, the newest version, or the lack of the same, orphans artifacts and creates a perpetually incunabular state with the new replacing the old. Thus, arguably, digital media or artworks are only native, or in a natural state, when evoked within the context of the program with which they were originally created. In fact, some new media artifacts are so closely linked to specific software and hardware that they cannot be used outside these specific environments [7].

One example is Christy Sheffield Sanford, the first Virtual-Writer-in-Residence at trAce Online Writing Center, housed at Nottingham Trent University 1995-2006, and the author of numerous Web and print works. Sanford, in an interview in *Frame Journal*, bemoans the loss of some of her Web work due to the demise of the Netscape browser after its sale to America Online. While a film or video is fixed, she notes, Web work depends on hardware and software not only for viewing, but for its very existence. With no browser to view the work, essentially, and practically, the work no longer exists. Updating hardware and software in order to keep their work current with continually evolving, or disappearing, browser specifications is, Sanford says, beyond the financial means of most digital artists [8].

One should also add the element of time to Sanford's comments. Beyond lack of financial means, the time necessary for constant upgrading of one's work can lead to a techno-exhaustion and a curtailment of creative work.

**Misleading Sense of Permanence.** Fourth, setting aside massive Electo-Magnetic Pulse (EMP) or loss of electrical power as external factors, there is nothing inherent in a computer that makes its artifacts susceptible to corruption or disappearance. The result is a potentially misleading sense of permanence of digital works created for the new screen. In fact, digital storage media, like more traditional storage technologies, are fragile, easily corruptible, or altered. And, as already noted, new state of the art contexts may render certain digital storage media unreliable, or simply inaccessible.

**Wave or Particle.** Finally, the new screen may exhibit, simultaneously, different characteristics, a situation similar to the so-called "Wave-Particle Duality," a long-running debate within the field of quantum mechanics that questions whether the nature of light is that of a wave, or a particle, or both simultaneously. A specific nature, either wave or particle, can be determined through close examination. But, such close examination, in determining the nature of a particular state, disrupts the possibility of observing the other state, and thus the ability to satisfactorily answer the debate's central question.

Like light, the new screen exhibits two seemingly contradictory states simultaneously. Rather than wave or particle, however, the new screen may be conceived as both artifact and production, always changing, evolving, under going fluid mimetic, viral, cybernetic elaboration. To focus on one state, however, may preclude the opportunity for participation in the other.

To summarize and project forward, many of the current applications and artistic expressions for the new screen may soon be unavailable, or worse, forgotten, as the new screen becomes something else even more new. The constantly evolving, incunabular state of the new screen and its digital native artifacts require new thinking about archiving if these artifacts are to be preserved for the future. Such new thinking will be important in order for today's art to provide inspiration for tomorrow's artists.

## 3 Archiving: How?

Most simply, digital archiving may be considered as an endeavor similar to that of the traditional brick-and-mortar art museum: to function, on one hand, as the adaptive site of public education and democratic access, and, on the other, to serve as an enduring and sacral repository for precious objects [9].

The challenge is how to develop and maintain digital archival contexts that not only make sense but more importantly aid in understanding the nature of the work preserved, especially for those viewers/readers/interactors unfamiliar with such endeavors. Asked another way, the question is: How to preserve, present, and add value to digital artifacts so that they provide benefit for broad audiences?

Several models suggest themselves.

**Hypertext-Hyperspatial Model.** One example is the now familiar hypertext-hyperspatial model that promotes interactive connections between words and data. In this model one clicks at certain points upon a seemingly flat landscape of information and zooms into the bloom of knowledge underneath. This model has been long argued with regard to its potential for information organization [10].

On the other hand, The Internet Archive Wayback Machine points to some of the challenges associated with archiving hyperlinked items. This resource archives 85 billion Web pages beginning in 1996. The scale of this archive is unmanageable, and arguably unnavigable, but still, oddly compelling [11].

**Coordination Model.** Traditional museums have long used the coordination model, with its emphasis on coordinating multimedia representations of physical artifacts, for providing access to geographically dispersed audiences. A similar approach may prove useful for archiving digital works produced for the new screen, or at least making copies/examples of such work available for a wide audience. For example, Whitney Artport advertises itself as a portal to net and digital arts, as well as to an online gallery featuring net art projects commissioned by the Whitney Museum of American Art [12].

**Individualized and Mobile Model.** Traditional archiving has often involved the orientation of artifacts with regard to perceived characteristics of a target audience comprised of art patrons. Archiving for the new screen may involve the reorientation of artifacts away from the notion of an abstract public, or audience, toward the individualized and mobile consumer. Art that is at once distributed, semantic, individualized, and available on demand could be one result from this model.

Each of these models offers access to a wide range of artifacts, through multiple means of user-driven access. As a result, digital archiving becomes a tentacular system, reaching out to serve individual information needs in a broad number of versions, enhancing the significance of the older, original display mode(s). As a result, artifacts are joined to others in ways that clarify and embellish them through careful arrangement and annotation (curatorial documentation or explanation) so as to historicize those artifacts as cultural or even fetishistic forms.

## 4 Archiving: Whose Responsibility?

Given agreement regarding the importance of archiving at least some of the artifacts produced for the new screen, who should undertake this responsibility? The original artist? Artist groups or collective associations? Collectors or other individuals who appreciate digital, new media art? The marketplace or other economic endeavors?

The marketplace is problematic in that only profitable objects are offered continually to specifically targeted audiences, and even then, as we have seen, new versions can quickly render the older as obsolete.

Collectors who appreciate digital art can certainly preserve and archive the works they collect, but such collections may not be readily available to others, or focus on any interest other than that of the individual collector.

Galleries, other businesses, even individuals, can and do promote showings featuring work for the new screen. Generally, however, the work featured during such shows returns to the original artist at show's end.

Social networking web sites like YouTube, MySpace, and Flickr are changing this paradigm, however. Both offer free server space for the hosting of digital art and allow artists and others to link to content by using object embed codes in their own web pages. As a result, the entire digital environment is changing, becoming less centralized as, potentially, digital art works may now be archived in multiple places around the Web.

Artist groups or collective associations can also function as catalysts for the preservation and distribution of digital art works. Where traditionally such associations have been formed to represent the needs of the individual artist members who live and work in close proximity to each other, collaborative artistic and performance-based endeavors are facilitated by the decentralized, bottom-up nature of the new screen. As a result, multiple, geographically distant digital artists and performers can facilitate the preservation and dissemination of their work(s). But, still, the problem remains regarding how to best attract the attention of a larger, distributed audience.

An interesting side note here is about how discussions of art usually come around to audience, and their attendance at showings of art. Galleries have historically tried numerous methods of attracting audiences. Some of these methodologies were outlined above, as possible models for how we might consider archiving works of digital art. The common solution suggested in many of these discussions is to take the art to the audience, something that many new media practitioners are quite good at, especially, as noted earlier, in the sharing of their work with the public through YouTube, MySpace, and Flickr.

Regarding the artists, it makes sense that they begin the long term archiving and preservation of digital works since many already maintain a presence on the Web and provide links to documentation of their works. It is, of course, unfair to suggest that artists should archive the computer(s) with which they create their works—this is clearly beyond the means of most artists—but, as broadband access and server space both expand and become more economical, it is fair to suggest that more digital artists will undertake documentation if not archiving of their multimedia works.

## 5 Questions/Pushback

These previous points represent legitimate concerns with regard to the production, utilization, and perpetuation of artifacts for the new screen. Such concerns point to many questions: specifically, is art meant to benefit the artist, the larger community, or the marketplace?

Or, are artists responsible instead to experiment with new ways of seeing, exploring, and explaining the world in which they live, without worry as to whether their work, their visions, will survive?

Other questions might focus on the kinesthetic nature of the new screen. The new screen is dynamic, changing; it must be so in order to remain new. But archiving has been traditionally static, focused on presenting a view or slice of the artifact that promotes understanding or overview. How do we reconcile these differences?

And what of ephemera: artworks purpose-created for the momentary experience, as a way to gather, format, and display content based on at-the-moment criteria, with no thought to their preservation? While it is true that there may be no philosophical reason or practical way to archive ephemera presently, a different viewpoint may evolve in the future. If archiving of ephemera becomes desirable in the future, what will be the best practice? Text and/or image searches currently performed from the Google or Yahoo web sites may provide models for how such endeavors might proceed, and for how meaning might be made from such momentary combinations of information.

Furthermore, any work created for the new screen may well be, by its very nature, multi-valiant, created from a combination or overlay of multimedia elements or resulting from a networking of various technologies or program applications. In such cases, what should be archived? The work itself? A previous or historical version or state of the work? The work's constituent files? The inspiration for the work, in whatever state that might have occurred, multimedia or otherwise? Documentation and/or artist notes about the work? The original, or some version of, hardware/software environment used to create the work?

What about archiving new screen artifacts made obsolete because of changes in the state-of-the-art of the technologies used in their creation? Should work no longer supported by the ever-evolving new screen be abandoned? Or, should interpreters or emulators—virtual machines, software computers that run works created for the no longer new screen (the old screen) on the newer new screen as if they were in their original environment—be created or employed? Should these interpreters and emulators be program specific, or, should they seek or employ an open source base level archival approach that will allow these works to continue to provide their interaction and immersion to future viewers/users regardless of their presentation environment?

A very good example of a new screen artifact that runs on a virtual machine is “First Screening”. This suite of a dozen programmed, kinetic poems originally written by Canadian experimental poet bpNichol in Apple Basic and designed to render on an Apple IIe computer has not been available for years because computer hardware and software advances left them obsolete. Jim Andrews, along with Geof Huth, Dan Weber, Marko Niemi, and Lionel Kearns (to whom bpNichol dedicated “First Screening”) have created various ways to view these works [13].

What of the notion (understanding?) that digital archiving can become less focused on the then of an artifact (as is the case with traditional museums) and more on the now of the display of that artifact? In other words, digital archiving can become more an emphasis on the digital technology behind the archival effort than the artifacts under preservation. Time with the artifacts becomes time with the media of its viewing or experience.

The screen, whether old or new, by its basic nature, is most focused on viewing, the convergence of various sensory experiences within the realm of the visual. So, beneath any discussions of digital archiving is the question of how function and value fluctuate as an artifact becomes increasingly visual. What happens as artifacts become increasing adorned with images or text or other forms of graphic display, or are reduced to such (losing aural, tactile, and other sensory modalities) as they move toward more uniform graphic visibility on the new screen?

Finally, where might digital archiving efforts occur? For example, many current conferences and art shows feature digital works and installations that are physically present in their meeting or gallery spaces. The sense of some curatorial hand arranging for this close proximity lends an air of permanence and protection to these works.

Other works are not dependent on physical location, can be experienced telematically or telepresently, and do not necessarily have to be presented in traditional gallery spaces, or, by implication, retained in traditional archival spaces [14]. Additionally, the "telematic embrace" (the merging of human and technological forms of intelligence and consciousness through networked communications) [15] and telepresence immersion, are, more and more, becoming wireless, global, individual, faster, cheaper, and smarter. As a result, works for the new screen are arriving at the speed of light in modular, high definition digitally enhanced, biorhythmic, quadraphonic, sense surround experimental, avant-garde, playful, exploratory multimedia not dependent on place or time. But, one has less control over circumstances afar and can, in the end, only hope that someone there is paying attention to the preservation of these artworks.

Arguably, in such cases, the new screen emerges through diverse participatory approaches between audiences and delivery which comments upon, transforms, and disseminates the work(s) in various ways. How does such a symbiotic relationship influence archiving works for the new screen?

Certainly the availability of digital tools has promoted an exponential growth of individuals identifying themselves as digital artists or writers who, without training or experience, are producing works in various mediums where one component, say the interface, is compelling, even beautiful, but other elements are problematic, or just simply trite.

What collection or archiving policies should confront such output? Should everything be collected and archived, or only those artifacts deemed, for whatever reasons, to be best representative of the medium, genre, or artist?

Compounding the problem of archiving digital media is what to call its various examples. Artifacts for the new screen and digital art works are frequently utilized terms, but other terms like networked performance, locative media, web or net fill-in-the-blank are just as easily utilized. The problem of identification is further compounded when attempting to archive these works in some sort of searchable digital context, where searches are driven by keyword terms input by the viewer or user. Traditional cataloging terminology may not or cannot describe these new artistic expressions, and in the absence of any consensus or governing body involved in their development, new terms are being invented which may not enjoy broad familiarity or usefulness.

As Peter Morville, widely recognized as the founder of the emerging field of information architecture and passionate advocate for the critical role of what he calls "findability" in defining the user experience, tells us, searchable databases are great tools, but are largely useless because general users do not know the keywords with which to design the most productive searches [16]. This of course leads back to accessibility and audience.

## 6 Reflections/Conclusion

There are, obviously, a lot of questions, and, just as obviously, no ready, easy answers regarding archiving works produced for the new screen. The intention here was not to evangelize any particular answers, but rather to raise the questions and begin a discussion.

An acceptable starting point seems to be the admission that pioneering works for the new screen are valuable in that they promise to constitute a significant portion of the future new-screen-literacy and cultural record.

Granted, such an admission is not without problems. The new screen enjoys only a short life span as designers, creators, performers, and producers race to embrace the new-new screen. In short, the rapid creation and dissemination of digital objects with little or no regard for their long-term preservation is problematic.

The same has happened with older forms of the screen—theater, radio, cinema, television—each replaced by something newer, something arguably more convergent, capable, and compact. However, as one looks to the new screen with its interactive visual environments, new forms of narrative, web-based innovative educational models, and immersive interactivity one can anticipate that archiving examples of the new screen will, over time, develop a body of knowledge that potentially promotes scholarly and critical perspectives, both creative and applied.

The term "potentially" is advised because such outcomes will be dependent on utilization. As Michael Wesch, a cultural anthropologist at Kansas State University, suggests in his short video, The Machine is Us/ing Us, the web (also called Web 2.0, The Machine) exists only as a function of the people who use and populate its virtual spaces and potentials, its shape and structure defined by the way we use the information amassed there [17].

An example is Wikipedia, the world's largest free content encyclopedia and certainly most unique in that it is being built through the collaborative functions of its community of users who enter or edit an entry, or more fundamentally, simply move through the information, teaching the structure—what connects to what, and how.

By its own statistics, Wikipedia is approximately 15 times the size of Encyclopedia Britannica with 1.74 billion words in 7.5 million articles written in 250 languages; 609 million words in the English edition alone with 1,700 new articles each day [18].

Another example is TAGallery, a curatorial experiment undertaken by the Vienna-based collective CONT3XT.NET. Using a Del.icio.us account, a social bookmarking manager that relies on a non-hierarchical keyword categorization system where users tag their bookmarks with freely chosen keywords, this project promotes the visualization of bookmarks by similar-minded users. The effect is to transfer the imagery and work methods of traditional exhibition spaces into a discursive electronic data space.

Although the first TAGallery show, dead.art(-missing!)LINKr! eSources, focused on the hyperlink as the primary medium for networking and forging relationships between separate contents, the innovation concept of establishing connections between artifacts pushes the boundaries of contemporary art and holds much promise for artists, writers, developers, performers and others interested in ways to distribute, connect, and share digital media produced for and presented on the new screen [19].

Between established and emerging archival practices lie the demands for the development of new theoretical frameworks and practical methodologies, new ideas of stewardship and new applications of best practices.

At the outset is the acknowledgement that collective and functional utilization of the new screen fosters a site for new, exploratory artistic digital creation and expression. From this point can begin a discussion of how to create open sources for the archiving of these artifacts, thus allowing them to serve as both creative and applied inspirations, perhaps even spurring creation of new capabilities for the new-new screen of the future.

## References


1. Manovich, L.: The Language of New Media, p. 19, 20, 27, 30. The MIT Press, Cambridge (2001)
2. The New Screen. Interactive Futures (October 28, 2007), http://cfisrv.finearts.uvic.ca/interactivefutures/IF07/
3. Hodge, G.: Digital Electronic Archiving: The State of the Art, The State of the Practice (April 26, 1999), http://www.icsti.org/icsti/whats_new.html
4. Sterne, J.: Out with the Trash. Residual Media, pp. 18–19. University of Minnesota Press, Minneapolis (2007)
5. Sundqvist, A.S.: Introduction. Human IT (October 28, 2007), http://www.hb.se/bhs/ith/1-9/
6. Krischenbaum, M.: Hamlet.doc: Literature in a Digital Age. pp. B8-9. The Chronicle Review (August 17, 2007)
7. Kuny, T.: The Digital Dark Ages? Challenges in the Preservation of Electronic Information. In: International Preservation News, vol. 17 (May 1998), http://www.ifla.org/VI/4/news/17-98.htm#2
8. Sanford, C.S.: Christy Sheffield Sanford. Frame Journal (October 28, 2007), http://www.framejournal.net/interview/7/christy-sheffield-sanford
9. Wilson, H.: Every Home an Art Museum. Residual Media, p. 164. University of Minnesota Press, Minneapolis (2007)
10. McCloud, S.: Reinventing Comics, p. 231. Paradox Press, New York (2000)
11. The Internet Archive Wayback Machine (October 28, 2007), http://www.archive.org/web/web.php
12. Whitney Artport: The Whitney Museum of American Art Portal to Net Art (October 28, 2007), http://artport.whitney.org
13. Screening, F.: Computer Poems bpNichol (1984–October 28, 2007), http://vispo.com/bp/introduction.htm
14. Circulating Contexts: Curating Media/Net/Art. Books on Demand GmbH., Norderstedt (2007)
15. Ascott, R.: Telematic Embrace: Visionary Theories of Art, Technology, and Consciousness, p. 6. University of California Press, Berkeley (2003)
16. Morville, P.: Ambiant Findability. O'Reilly Media, Sebastopol (2005)
17. Wesch, M.: The Machine is US/ing Us (October 28, 2007), http://www.youtube.com/watch?v=NLlGopyXT_g
18. Wikipedia: Size Comparisons (October 28, 2007), http://en.wikipedia.org/wiki/Wikipedia:Size_comparisons
19. Del.icio.us / TAGallery / About_TAGallery (October 28, 2007), http://del.icio.us/TAGallery/About_TAGallery

# Digital Fiction: From the Page to the Screen

Kate Pullinger

Reader in in Creative Writing and New Media,
Institute of Creative Technologies,
De Montfort University, Leciester, UK
kpullinger@dmu.ac.uk

**Abstract.** In this essay Pullinger will discuss writing across media, in particular, print and digital fiction. For Pullinger the divide between the digital and print worlds is artificial; she has always worked across many forms. However, there are very few established fiction writers who work in both print and digital, in terms of creating born-digital fiction projects like Pullinger and Joseph's 'Inanimate Alice'. Many book writers and publishers remain mired in decade-old arguments and anxieties about the future of the book, some of which are dead-ends (the death of the book) and some of which are very important (the future of copyright). Although Pullinger participates in discussions of these issues, her primary interest is in making a living from creating work whether it is digital or print.

**Keywords:** digital fiction, print fiction, publishing, fiction, writing, participatory media.

As the virtual world merges with the real world, the divide between digital fiction and print fiction is no longer relevant to writers whose primary goal is to tell stories. However, the fact remains that while many print writers use digital platforms to promote their published works, there are very few established print writers who work in both print and the born-digital.

I'm a fiction writer with a long list of publications, novels and short story collections, to my name – seven books, the most recent, A Little Stranger[1]. I've written scripts for television, film and radio as well. In 2001 I was asked to teach online by the trAce Online Writing Centre at Nottingham Trent University[2], an internet-based community of writers devoted to thinking about the possibilities for writing and writers online. When it came to teaching in this new environment, my learning curve was steep. I had been using a computer since the early 90s – I wrote my first two books on a typewriter - and the internet since 1995 when I got my first e-mail address, but prior to 2001 all I had done online was a bit of electronic shopping . At the trAce Online Writing School I found I had a facility for teaching online; I liked the way the online environment allowed me and my students to focus on the text, on clarity and precision in the writing, without having to spend too much time negotiating social niceties. It also suited me domestically as at the

[1] ***A Little Stranger,*** Pullinger, Kate, McArthur & Co, Toronto, 2004.
[2] trAce Online Writing Centre, http://trace.ntu.ac.uk/

R. Adams, S. Gibson, and S. Müller Arisona (Eds.): DAW/IF 2006/2007, CCIS 7, pp. 120–126, 2008.

time I had two young children, and the flexibility of online working was very useful to me; I think that part of the reason I have thrived in the digital environment is because the internet enabled me to teach and write in new ways, both despite of and because of my domestic circumstances. Having two children placed my writing life under threat, and when I began to teach for trAce I had reached a kind of impasse in my working life – for the first time ever, I could no longer afford to write. Working online was part of what saved my writing life.

Teaching for the school led to the opportunity to take up a year-long research fellowship with trAce in 2002. My fellowship was part of a larger research project funded by the UK's Arts and Humanities Research Board, "*Mapping the Transition from Page to Screen*"[3]; during the year I was given the opportunity to explore digital fiction and digital narratives. My research took me in many different directions and posed a number of challenges: I didn't like much of the work that called itself 'electronic literature' and I wasn't interested in writing that addressed the mysteries of computers and code instead of the mysteries of life. I felt text-only hypertext missed the whole point of creating work for a screen and I was afraid that, in order to create digital work myself, I'd have to become the world's worst web designer.

But then I had a breakthrough: I realised I did not have to learn how to manage a hugely complex visual interface, all by myself. I could collaborate.

I've collaborated with other artists throughout my writing life. Despite the fact one of the things I value most is the long, slow, solitary process of writing a book, writing a novel, alone in a room, all by myself, just me and the text, for years and years, collaboration is something I enjoy. I've always found that working with other artists is the thing that extends my creativity much more profoundly than moving between traditional print media (books), and digital media, moving between film, radio, performance, etc. At its best, collaboration threatens all notions of the single authorial voice, including the supremacy our culture awards to the idea of the solitary writer. My work in new media is absolutely dependent upon collaboration.

Once the trAce fellowship came to an end, I embarked on new collaborations, including '*Branded*'[4] with Talan Memmott and a highly experimental piece, '*The Breathing Wall*'[5], with Chris Joseph and Stefan Schemat. '*The Breathing Wall*' uses software – The Hyper Trance Fiction Matrix - created by Schemat which allows the reader/viewer to interact with the story by breathing into the computer. Developed from software Schemat originally created for biofeedback-based psychotherapy, HTF induces in the viewer a trance-like state; the more relaxed the reader becomes, the deeper access they have to layers of the story buried in the software. 'The Breathing Wall' is an esoteric piece that combines breathing, reading, listening, viewing and the state of immersion we enter when we read.

While this project was fascinating to work on, it isn't an accessible piece and accessibility matters to me; '*The Breathing Wall*' resides on CD due to size of its media files,

[3] *Mapping the Transition from Page to Screen*, http://tracearchive.ntu.ac.uk/transition/project.htm

[4] ***Branded***, Pullinger, Kate, and Memmott, Talan, 2003, http://tracearchive.ntu.ac.uk/frame/branded/index.html

[5] *The Breathing Wall*, Pullinger, Kate, Joseph, Chris, and Schemat, Stefan, 2004, http://www.thebreathingwall.com/

and it demands a fairly sophisticated approach to computing from readers. In 2005, I began work on my on-going project, '*Inanimate Alice*'[6], an online multimedia digital novel in episodes. For me, '*Inanimate Alice*' is the project that has taken me closest to joining up the separate realms of print and digital fiction: it allows readers who are unused to looking at creative work online to take incremental steps toward reading a story through interactivity.

'*Inanimate Alice*' came about when a former student of mine, Ian Harper, approached me; he was developing a large project that included a film called '*E|Mission*', a game, and a gadget, and wanted to put together an innovative viral marketing campaign to promote all three elements. After some discussion, we came up with the idea of publishing on the web a series of linked stories or multimedia episodes that tell the back-story of the main characters in the film, Alice, a games animator, and Brad, the game character she creates.

Though the original idea is not my own, I was given free reign on developing the stories for '*Inanimate Alice*'. For me, this private commission was a welcome opportunity to create further work for the web, with the added bonus of being able to work once again with Chris Joseph; our collaborative partnership worked well, despite the fact that Chris lived in Montreal, Canada, and I lived in London, England, and we were able to meet only once a year. Chris has since returned to live in the UK, but the first three episodes of Alice were created via e-mail.

We took a couple of decisions early on in the creative process that have proved to be very useful. We decided to tell the stories from Alice's point of view, in the first person, and we also decided never to represent Alice visually – the reader experiences the stories through her first person voice, but without ever seeing Alice's face. These decisions were made partly due to budgetary constraints – we had no money to hire actors, so could not represent Alice's face, nor record her voice. However, we have found that both these decisions have worked well for us, helping to draw the reader into Alice's world, while leaving the story very open to the reader's own imaginative interpretation. The fact that you never see Alice's face makes the viewing experience more akin to reading a book, where characters are not represented visually and your readerly imagination is more fully engaged.

We made lots of mistakes with '*Episode One: China*'; the first draft of the script was too long, much too wordy, and poorly structured. We didn't properly understand this until we'd created a working draft, using Flash, of the entire episode. We then had to dismantle the episode and re-write the script and re-do all the work in Flash, which was laborious and time-consuming. With subsequent episodes we now make absolutely sure the script is finished before moving onto creating the episode in Flash. I've found that writing digital fiction has a lot in common with writing a film script; structure is of huge importance. Structure determines narrative pace, momentum, and tension. With episode one, after our false start, we realised we needed to begin with some kind of story hook, in order to draw readers in. All episodes, including '*Episode Four: Hometown*' which is nearly finished – we showed an early preview at Interactive Futures 2007 - rely on a similar simple structure now: opening story hook, back story, resolution. The level of interactivity increases with each episode, reflecting the main character, Alice's, own increasing skills as a developer and animator; the second half of episode four resides within a game.

---

[6] *Inanimate Alice*, Pullinger, Kate, and Joseph, Chris, 2005, http://www.inanimatealice.com

Chris and I collaborate closely on all aspects of the episodes, but we do have defined roles: I'm the writer, Chris creates the work in Flash. Together we collect images and sounds (episodes 1-3 used images and sounds found or purchased on the internet; episode 4 has been created using entirely newly created assets). Chris composes and creates the music. We have a lot of to-ing and fro-ing over all the different elements, essentially co-directing the overall production. In a profound way, the narrative voice of 'Inanimate Alice' is the voice of our collaboration.

'Episode Four: Hometown' is almost ready to go; our private backer, Ian Harper, is looking at ways to finance further episodes by figuring out how to make money out of 'Inanimate Alice'. While, as I said, the original idea for the project arose out of other projects of Ian's, 'Inanimate Alice' has taken on a life of its own. We've won a number of prizes and the episodes have had multiple screenings at film and digital arts festivals. To date we've been in discussion with game developers and a big range of content providers. We've collaborated with a game developer to create an easy-to-use tool called iStories that will allow people to use their own stories, images, and music to create multimedia stories, and are hoping to release this later this year. But Alice has yet to find a commercial home.

For many writers interested digital fiction, the stark truth that there is no real business model for selling multimedia work remains an obstacle. It is easy to imagine a time in the not-so-distant future where this will no longer be the case: phones, laptops and e-reading devices with touch screens are almost with us already. 'Electronic Literature' is a growth area in universities; I myself have moved from teaching online as a freelance writer to a post as Reader in Creative Writing and New Media at De Montfort University, where I have helped set up an online MA[7] that allows students to research and explore this field. Part of what is interesting about 'Inanimate Alice' is our search for a route to market; this is an area I continue to develop in all my digital work.

For many readers, unaccustomed as they are to the idea of 'reading online' – although, the reality is, in the developed world, many, perhaps most, people spend much of their day doing that very thing, in front of a computer screen, reading online – the computer is still not a place where they would go for the kind of reading experience they could get from a book. 'But you can't read it in the bath'; how many times have we heard people say this? Across the English speaking world book publishers remain focused on digitizing their content, and finding new digital platforms to exploit and/or market their non-digital properties, i.e. books (William Gibson's book tour in Second Life; reading groups on Facebook). The entire infrastructure of the publishing industry is geared toward shifting retail units; the head of digital publishing at Penguin told me that because the Penguin accounting system is entirely warehouse based, for a time they had to find a way to represent the units shifted through digital downloads. Their solution was to have empty pallets in the warehouse, with invisible digital content, thus enabling the system to count the units that had sold. Publishers ignore the potential for new markets, new audiences and, indeed, new forms at their peril. And, for the most part, they are defiantly ignoring the potential for digital literature.

However, and this is a big however, in most instances writers are ignoring it as well. Despite the passage of time, I remain a bit of an anomaly; it is unusual for a fiction writer

[7] Online MA in Creative Writing and New Media, De Montfort University, Leicester, UK, http://www.dmu.ac.uk/faculties/humanities/pg/ma/cwnm.jsp

who makes part of her living writing books to also work in digital literature. Writers continue to be, on the whole, blissfully unaware of, uninterested in, the possibilities for digital literature. While publishers demonstrate their lack of interest in new media, apart from its use as a marketing tool, many fiction writers see the internet and digitisation as a threat, with the potential to rob them of their copyright and render their work valueless.

But perhaps the most important reason for the slowness of both writers and publishers when it comes to seeing the potential of the digital realm is this: the book is an almost perfect piece of technology. It's portable, cheap, it's both disposable and something to hang onto for years; unlike most other forms of technology, books get more beautiful as they get old. We like the way books look and feel. We like to own them. We like the way they smell. Books are highly significant artifacts in our culture, symbolic of erudition, discernment, and taste. When you've got something that works so well already in hand, with several centuries of historical precedent in place to show how and why this is a good way to publish creative content, it's difficult to see beyond that.

My primary interest as a writer, a reader, and a viewer is in story, good stories, well-told, whatever the platform or media. On a profound level, it's not the media that is the issue here – it's finding the best way to tell the story. For me the digital environment is simply an additional platform for stories, taking its place alongside other media, including television, books and movies.

The web and, in particular, social networking applications like mySpace, facebook, del.icio.us, flickr, youTube, as well as wikis, machinima, and blogging have ushered in an explosion of stories, a tsunami of writing, reading, viewing, listening, and interacting online. I often hear it said (my publisher in London is one of the people who says it) that the internet offers nothing new to us, apart from an additional means of communication. While I think there is some truth to this – e-mail is just a sped-up form of correspondence, flickr is just friends boring each other with their holiday snaps, same as always – it seems to me that the potential for mass participation in the creation of stories – what is generally referred to as 'participatory media' – and the speed at which it can happen, is entirely new. Participation creates multiple opportunities for readers to become writers and this is already changing the way people read, online as well as off.

One of the projects I was involved with at DMU was the Penguin/DMU wiki-novel, 'A Million Penguins'[8]. This was a collaboration between Penguin UK and my students on the MA at DMU; we created a wiki, called it 'A Million Penguins', and invited the world to write a novel together. The wiki was open for five weeks from 1 Feb 2007; it attracted more than 80,000 readers, and more than 1500 people contributed to writing it. The wiki-novel resided within a huge whirlwind of publicity, attracting interest from journalists and broadcasters all over the world; the main job of the student moderators turned out to be dealing with the almost continual vandalism on the wiki-novel's front pages during the first two weeks. Watching the novel's continuous evolution was fascinating as more and more pages, more and more stories and characters were added; Penguin's initial hope to perhaps create something suitable for print publication were soon filed away along with most of our initial expectations of the shape the fiction would take. The most interesting thing about 'A Million Penguins' was the process; it took our ideas about collaboration and participation and stretched them to breaking point. The best bits of the wiki-novel reside in the maze of linked texts buried inside the wiki; groups of

[8] *A Million Penguins,* http://www.amillionpenguins.com

people came together to create stories-within-stories that are full of humour and invention. As a work of fiction, 'A Million Penguins' is almost unreadable; as a work of participatory media, 'A Million Penguins' was a huge success – a fiction project for its writers, not its readers.

The effect the advent of participatory media will have on the writer/reader relationship is impossible to predict: but it is having an effect and it is this aspect of new media that is extending the bounds of creativity for many people who use these applications. Collaboration always extends these boundaries; collaborating online can, potentially, extend them further still.

As a writer, reader, and viewer I'm interested in immersion, in stories and characters that involve me so deeply that the media itself – whether that is a novel, a film, a television drama, a game, a digital fiction – completely disappears. As a reader of books I'm interested in the single authorial voice – that thing that brings us back to a favourite writer over and over again. The advent of participatory media poses a serious and exciting challenge to the single authorial voice; the way in which new media disrupts and extends and, in some cases, displaces this voice is of huge importance. For my collaborator, Chris Joseph, and me, the single authorial voice in a project like 'Inanimate Alice' is already a hybrid voice, the voice of our collaboration. However, replacing the single authorial voice with a collaborative voice is just the first step; opening up the authorial voice to broader participation is the next.

Our new project, 'Flight Paths: a networked novel'[9], takes us one step further down this perilous road; 'Flight Paths' engages explicitly with the advent and impact of participatory media on the authorial voice. The initial goal of this project is to create a work of digital fiction, a 'networked book', created on and through the internet. In its first stage, the project will open up the research and writing processes to the outside world, inviting discussion of the large array of issues the project touches on. We will also create a series of multimedia elements illuminating various aspects of the story, and enabling us to invite and encourage user-generated content, both multimedia and more traditional, as well as images, sounds, memories, ideas.

'Flight Paths' has already engendered some criticism and debate, despite the fact that, at the time of writing, it has only been online for a matter of weeks. One of the conditions imposed on the project by our funders was that we use a Creative Commons License on the site; we were happy to comply with this condition, as we would have used a share-and-share-alike CC License anyway. As well as this, one of the project's partners, The Institute of Creative Technologies at De Montfort University, where I work, suggested we needed Terms and Conditions in order to cover potential future development of the project; a lawyer at DMU, Mary Mackintosh, wrote the T&C for us. In effect, the T&C of the project, which participants need to consent in order to contribute to 'Flight Paths', requires participants to give up their copyright over anything they contribute, while the Creative Commons License, in effect, licenses that copyright back to them at the same time. What this means is that if Chris and I decide at some stage to create a work that is based on 'Flight Paths' for commercial gain, we'll be able use the discussions and contributions that have developed on 'Flight Paths' for that project, subject to fair attribution. Currently, we have very little idea of what direction the project will take

[9] *Flight Paths: a networked novel*, Pullinger, Kate, and Joseph, Chris, 2007, http://www.flightpaths.net

– this will be determined by the contributors as well as ourselves – and have no plans for any commercial developments. But the blogosphere has raised objections about the T&C of 'Flight Paths'; leaving the door open to commercial development for a project of this nature does not gain favour in every quarter of the new media field[10].

*'Flight Paths'* is not the first project of its kind, and nor will it be the last. And, for me, this project is not the end of the book either; I continue to work on novels and stories intended for print publication. But readers are already engaged with new forms of story-telling online, and new models of participation are being created. Writers and publishers need to wake up to this fact, or they will be left behind by the very audiences on which they depend.

---

[10] *Flight Paths: a networked novel, How To Participate,* Pullinger, Kate, and Joseph, Chris, 2007, http://www.flightpaths.net/blog/index.php/how-to-participate/#0

# The Present [Future] of Electronic Literature

Dene Grigar

Digital Technology & Culture Program, Washington State University Vancouver,
14204 NE Salmon Creek Ave. Vancouver, WA, USA
grigar@vancouver.wsu.edu

**Abstract.** The focus of this essay is to expand upon N. Katherine Hayles' views about electronic literature created for non-screen environments by looking at two additional genres I call *multimedia game narratives* and *corporeal poetry* and showing examples of the works found in these categories. In doing so, I am suggesting that the issue is not where the field is headed, but rather if the field can catch up to the art already being produced. The question for me is not what electronic literature *is* but rather what it may be or will become as we continue to invent technologies and innovate them for purposes of literary art.

**Keywords:** Electronic literature, three-dimensional literature, multimedia game narratives, corporeal poetry.

## 1 Introduction

During her panel discussion, entitled *Electronic Literature in the 21st Century*, given at the Electronic Literature Organization's The Future of Electronic Literature symposium, N. Katherine Hayles asked the audience: "Where is e-lit is going when it moves out of the computer?"[1].

For a lot of us working in multimedia performance or creating art installations for black box environments or CAVEs, producing narratives with GPS technology, or poetry for cell phones and other hand-held devices, this question seemed odd, but it is indeed a provocative one for folks who have staked careers on hypertext, flash, interactive, and adaptive fiction and poetry, to name just a few forms of electronic literature created for display on the computer screen. The question was odder still for those familiar with Hayles' essay, *Electronic Literature: What Is It* [2], published just five months earlier at the Electronic Literature Organization's website. In that essay she talks in detail about several genres that focus on literary art *off the screen*. One can surmise that changing from an argument in the essay to a question in the symposium paper was simply a rhetorical move since the audiences were so different for the two papers. But in light of Hayles' 2001 seminar hosted for National Endowment for the Humanities entitled *Literature in Transition* [3], essays like *Print Is Flat, Code Is Deep* [4] and her book, *Writing Machines* [5], the repetition of the theme can also be understood as a continued refinement of her ideas: that literature is indeed in transition, and one of the ways that it is changing is that it has expanded from two to three dimensional spaces made possible by computer technologies.

R. Adams, S. Gibson, and S. Müller Arisona (Eds.): DAW/IF 2006/2007, CCIS 7, pp. 127–142, 2008.

The theme of this book includes *the New Screen* and invites a discussion about the form of media art some refer to as electronic literature. Dependent as it is on emergent computing technologies for its instantiation as art, electronic literature is a form existing and developing simultaneously in both the present and future. Hence this essay, *The Present [Future] of Electronic Literature*, interrogates current perspectives by asking if the issue is not what the field *is*, but rather if the field can catch up to the art already being produced.

As a way of providing a starting place for a discussion about three-dimensional literary works, this presentation begins with a brief overview of electronic literature, including the genres identified by Hayles in her essay. Then, it moves to address additional genres that have also emerged for non-screen environments—what can be provisionally called multimedia game narratives and corporeal poetry. Examples of the works found in these categories will be shown and explained. The essay concludes with the suggestion that the most interesting impact computer technologies have had upon contemporary literature is that they have expanded literature in ways that takes it back to pre-print modes of literary art when stories were sung, drama contained dance, and myth was poetry. Thus, the overarching question is not what electronic literature *is* but rather what it may be or will continue to become as technologies continue to be invented and innovated for the purposes of art production.

## 2 Hayles' Overview of Electronic Literature and Its Genres

### 2.1 Electronic Literature Described

First, it is important to acknowledge that the term, electronic literature, is a difficult one. For not only is literature a word in much contention among literary scholars, but also associating literature—an art form that generates from print with its own characteristics, theories, and qualities—with computers is fraught with problems, as Hayles has made clear in several of her works, most notably in *Writing Machines* [5].

It is not the intention of this essay to debate this term. For now this essay simply holds that electronic literature is the term used by many—but certainly not all[1]—artists who make hypertext fiction, kinetic poetry, interactive fiction, kinetic poetry, to name a few genres associated with electronic literature. To articulate a vision of the art form, the Electronic Literature Organization published Hayles' essay, *Electronic Literature: What Is It*, laying out the context, genres, and specificities of it. In this work, she describes electronic literature as "first generation digital object[s] created on a computer and (usually) meant to be read on a computer"[2]. Because this definition follows the line of thinking that electronic literature is primarily a two-dimensional screen art form, it is not useful for a discussion about three dimensional performance and installations she mentions in that work. Therefore, for the purpose of this essay, electronic literature is described as an emergent art form whose works cannot be experienced in any meaningful way without the mediation of an electronic device and which possess qualities sometimes

[1] In both editions of his book *Media Poetry: An International Anthology*, for example, Eduardo Kac avoids the term *electronic literature* completely and focuses, instead, on the term for the subgenre of *computer mediated poetry*, which he first calls *new media poetry* in 1996 and revises to *media poetry* in 2007.

associated with literary works, such as character, theme, setting, allusion, metaphor, onomatopoeia, among others. In essence, one can view electronic literature as literary-oriented works that exist off the printed page and make use of qualities specific to the electronic medium like sound, visual elements, movement, and real-time delivery. Michael Joyce's *afternoon: a story* (1989), a work of hypertext fiction that pioneered hyperlinks as a way of telling the story of the death of the speaker's loved one, helped to popularize electronic literature in the late 1980s and early 1990s [6], but it may have been Theo Lutz's *Stochastische Texte*, created in 1959, that constitutes the first example of computer generated "media poetry"[7] that some refer to as electronic literature. In fact, Eduardo Kac's *Media Poetry: An International Anthology* lists 12 media poets working before 1980 [8].

Because electronic literature utilizes media technologies, it is sometimes collapsed by some with Net Art, and many of the artists identified with electronic literature are also categorized as *net artists*. Olia Lialina, who created *My Boyfriend Came Back from the War*, [9] Mark Amerika, the artist of *Grammatron* [10], and Young-Hae Chang Heavy Industries, the team behind *Rain on the Sea* [11], all mentioned in Rachel Greene's *Internet Art* [12] come to mind and exemplify the difficulty with nomenclature. The word emergent is key since it implies something in development. Suffice it to say that as a new form it is still in the throes of establishing conventions, as well as a developing a large critical and theoretical base, as exists currently for print. Five hundred years of printing can develop a medium in a way that a mere 25 years of personal computing cannot. So, despite what anyone thinks about the terminology used for this art form, scholars working in the late 20$^{th}$ or early 21$^{st}$ century will not be the final arbitrators of it.

Despite its youth as an art form, electronic literature as an area of study has been building through online journals like Iowa Review Web[2] [13] and Poems That Go[3] [14], print publications like Jan Van Looy and Jan Baetens' *Close Reading New Media* [15], Nick Montfort's *Twisty Little Passages* [16], Hayles' *Writing Machines* [5], and Kac's *Media Poetry: An International Anthology*, [8] and online networks and organizations like trAce Online Writing Centre [4] [17] ALTX [18] UBUweb [19], Hermeneia [20], ELINOR [21], and the Electronic Literature Organization [22] mentioned earlier. Many of these organizations and groups have sponsored meetings and conferences, published works, and led projects for developing, archiving, and promoting this genre.

## 2.2 Hayles' Genres of 3D Works

In Hayles' essay, she mentions three areas of electronic literature produced for "actual three-dimensional spaces." These include locative narratives, site specific installations, and interactive dramas [2].

**Locative Narratives.** Locative narratives are defined by Hayles as "short fiction delivered serially over cell phones to location-specific narratives keyed to GPS technologies."

---

[2] *The Iowa Review Web* (*IRW*) ceased publishing, but its archives can be found at http://www.uiowa.edu/~iareview/mainpages/tirwebhome.htm.

[3] Like *IRW*, *Poems that Go* also ceased publishing, and its archives are found at http://www.poemsthatgo.com/.

[4] Trace Online Writing Centre, located a Nottingham Trace University, closed its doors in 2004, but its archives can be found at http://trace.ntu.ac.uk.

Hayles places "site-specific mobile works" produced by artists like Janet Cardiff and Blast Theory in this genre [2].

Canadian artist Janet Cardiff attained international renown for *The Missing Voice (Case Study B)*, a 45-50 minute audio tour created in 1999 involving a journey from Whitechapel Library in London through the East End. At the library, the user was given a CD Discman that provided directions to follow and a storyline that immersed the user in the journey that ensued. Turning on the CD the user would hear Cardiff whispering: "I want you to walk with me . . . there are some things I need to show you" [23]. Following the directions provided on the CD, the user was led around the East End of London on an interactive adventure. Artangel, the organization that commissioned the work explains that *The Missing Voice (Case Study B)* is "[p]art urban guide, part fiction, part film noir, [the] walk entwines you in a narrative that shifts through time and space. Intimate, even conspiratorial, Cardiff has created a psychologically absorbing experience – for an audience of one at a time"[24].

Building on the acclaim for *The Missing Voice*, Cardiff produced another walk, this one for New York City. Entitled *Her Long Black Hair*, is described as a:

> 35-minute . . . circuitous path through the heart of Central Park. Tucked casually into the pouch of the CD player [are] five photographs of sites throughout the park, three of which show an unnamed black-haired woman, around whom much of the narrative is based. Cardiff's voice . . . emanate[s] from within your head rather than from outside your ears, a level of intimacy both beguiling and invasive. As in her earlier pieces, Cardiff uses binaural recording techniques that envelop you in crisp, freshly minted sound. The still audible background din of the real city becomes a muddy bass line to the crystalline acoustics, with each enhancing and overlapping the other. [25]

In an interview with Atom Egoyan for *Bomb*, Cardiff classifies her work as a "3-D narrative experience" [26]. Cardiff's works has inspired others to produce similar works including Harriet Poole's *Please Don't Touch* [27].

Blast Theory's *Uncle Roy All Around You*, billed as "where espionage movies become interactive; where the console game breaks onto the streets"[28], premiered at the Institute of Contemporary Art in 2003. Created by the British artist group that includes Matt Adams, Ju Row Farr and Nick Tandavanitj working out of the Mixed Reality Lab at the University of Nottingham [29], the piece focuses on a collaboration between Online Players and Street Players searching for the titular *Uncle Roy*. Live and virtual activities converge when the Street Players, using interactive maps and helped by text messages from the Online Players, race along the city in search of Uncle Roy's office [30].

According to the project website, the group "investigates some of the social changes brought about by ubiquitous mobile devices, persistent access to a network and location aware technologies [30].

Blast Theory's *Uncle Roy All Around You*, like Cardiff's *The Missing Voice*, is a work that combines realtime, telematic experience with narrative performance. Both works possess qualities associated with Hayles' notion of three dimensionally in that both are dependent upon computing devices for their instantiation—an instantiation that does not rely, in part or fully, upon the computer screen for its presentation—and make use of literary devices in their content—for example, setting in Cardiff's piece and character in Blast Theory's. In addition, both works combine sound and movement to arrive at an audience performance piece that is narrative and mobile in nature, taking place in what Hayles identifies as "actual three-dimensional spaces"[2]. Because both works exist in real-time, they defy the "temporal and spatial lag" attributed to literary works meant to be executed by an audience as a "re-present[ed]" artifact created by someone else [31]. In sum, they derive their three-dimensionality through the presence of what Espen Aarseth refers to as "event time" [32] as well as their non-screen presentation.

**Site Specific Installations.** Another category Hayles mentions is site specific installations [2], like those undertaken in CAVES and produced by artists John Cayley [33], Talan Memmott [34], Noah Waldrip-Fruin [35], and William Gillespie [36]. These works, she says, "push the boundary of what literature can be" [2].

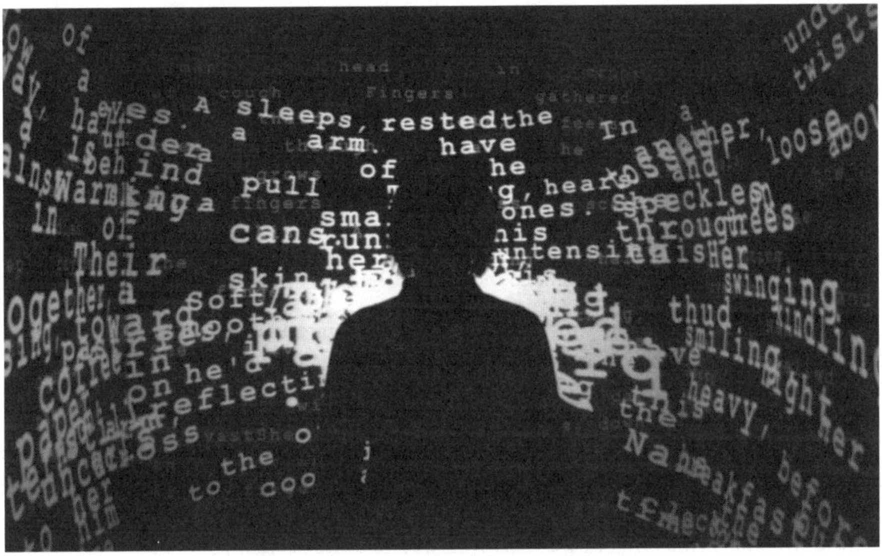


**Fig. 1.** An image from Waldrip-Fruin's *Screen*. Photograph by Josh Carroll.

In Noah Waldrip-Fruin's *Screen*, for example, the user interacts with words that appear as three-dimensional objects in the CAVE environment. Choosing a particular word from the many appearing on the wall causes the word to move from the two-dimensional space of the wall toward the user as a three-dimensional object. Words move off the wall and toward the viewer with increasing speed until the words collide and crash in a breakdown of data [35].

That the user perceives that he or she is moving inside words, inside language, and embodying words and language as he or she experiences and performs them makes the immersive quality of the work compelling and contributes to the works' three-dimensional quality. Interestingly, the close connection between user and object (as opposed to the separation of user and object) sets this kind of work apart from print-based literature, particularly in Western culture where knowledge is perceived as existing outside of the body. Thus, one outcome of participating in three-dimensional literature can be a "mindfulness/awareness" that "brings one closer to one's ordinary experience rather than further from it," a reconnection between humans and experience [37].

**Interactive Dramas.** Interactive dramas are described as "site-specific [works] performed with live audiences in gallery spaces in combination with present and/or remote actors"[2]. MD Coverley's *M Is For Nottingham* (2002), a collaborative mystery performed with Kate Pullinger is one such example Hayles cites [38], as is *Unheimlich*, by Paul Sermon, Steve Dixon, Mathias Fucs, and Andrea Zapp with Bill Seaman [39].

*Unheimlich* is categorized by ACM as "computing literature"[40] and by Hayles as a "collaborative telematic performance, "a "mix of the "virtual and the real within a loose dramatic framework . . . creat[ing] a borderland that encouraged playful innovation and improvisational collaboration"[2]. The artists' website describes the work as:

> [v]ideo conferencing and advanced electronic art called 'blue screen' created a simultaneous space in which the English and Americans literally 'held hands' across the ocean. The drama, entitled 'Unheimlich' (a Freudian term meaning familiar yet strange) used similar technology to that used by weather forecasters to create theatrical backgrounds including cliff-hanging images and a traditional sitting room. Spanning a five-hour time zone, audiences at Brown University, Providence, were invited to step into the virtual world of two actors at the University of Salford and take part in improvisation. [39]

Documentation of the piece shows, on the one hand, the work staged as any real-time drama: Actors perform together on a stage, mood is established, and conflict is introduced. On the other hand, the video also reveals actors and setting dispersed over two locations and brought together by computing devices.

Like the two other categories Hayles discusses—locative narratives and site specific installations—interactive drama is described as three-dimensional in that it moves outside of the printed page and computer screen into live interactive/multimedia venues making it performative in nature, with users and/or the artists themselves driving the storyline. This theatrical element and the presence of stories, in turn, imbues it with a literary quality much like the "new creative visions" of "mediated improvisations" that Brenda Laurel envisioned in 1993 [41].

## 3 Other 3D Genres

This essay now moves from detailing genres Hayles identifies and describes in her essay to other forms of three-dimensional literature that can be added to her list: multimedia game narratives and corporeal poetry. By no means do these represent all possible genres but merely those emerging with which this author has firsthand experience either as participant or producer.

### 3.1 Multimedia Game Narratives

Anyone following game studies is aware of the debate about the relationship between games and literature. On one side of the argument scholars like Janet Murray talk about the notion of the "game-story . . . [in] story-rich new gaming formats," a natural phenomenon since, she claims, "storytelling and gaming have already been overlapping experiences"[42]. This sentiment is echoed by Nick Montfort, who in *Twisty Little Passages*," traces the beginnings of interactive fiction to the "ludic pleasure" of adventure games, which themselves evolved from the riddle, a game puzzle, a game form that is in its poetic form, literary in nature [16]. Michael Mateas, in his work *A Preliminary Poetics for Interactive Drama and Games*, looks at "player agency" by theorizing about the connection of games to drama, using Aristotle's "formal and material causation" laid out in *Poetics*, [43] certainly the bible for Renaissance dramatists and used by contemporary media art theorists and practitioners like Brenda Laurel to discuss "new forms of drama" [41].

On the other side of the argument, scholars like Markku Eskelinen in his essay *Toward Computer Game Studies* claim that it should be "self-evident that we can't apply print narratology, hypertext theory, film or theatre and drama studies to computer games" [44]. Espen Aarseth, in his essay *Genre Trouble*, lays out the debate about games and literature, coming to the conclusion that:

> . . . aesthetics and hermeneutics of games and simulations and their relations to stories . . . pose a rich problem. . . . Games and stories have distinct teleologies and artistic potential, and it is analytically useful (for those of us genuinely interested in games as games, at least' to maintain a conceptual terminology that distinguishes between them. [45]

The lines are, thus, drawn: literary scholars and some artists see games as literary through the lens of narrative and drama, and ludologists see games as games from the perspective of their qualities distinct from literature.

This author, standing on the border of literature and new media—literature from the standpoint of ancient Greek epic circa $8^{th}$ century BCE and new media from that of $21^{st}$ CE century computer-based art, sees such a debate as both important *and* stifling: important, because there is logic in the need to study objects, as Hayles suggests, within the confines of their specificity [5], untainted by outside influences; stifling, because both sides make little room for the hybrid, transdisciplinary objects that keep popping up without concern for what they are named, much less ways how they are theorized. In truth, the provisional state of technologies and art make knowing what to be specific about close to impossible. Pragmatism tempers such resolution—and a deep study of pre-print culture that combines art forms helps to raise consciousnesses toward new approaches to the thorny question about the connection between games and literature.[5] With this in mind, here are a few examples of multimedia art forms that transgress rigid structures of literature and games yet offer both narrative and ludic pleasure.

---

[5] Current work in the theorization of the video essay also address this issue. Jorg Huber's essay, *Video-Essayism: On the Theory-Practice of the Transnational* makes a strong case for "a process of connections, transitions, constructions, recontextualizations, by means of shifts, grafts, hybridizations, overlaps, and creations of synapses." See *Stuff It: The Video Essay in the Digital Age*. Ed. Ursula Biemann. Zurich: Springer, 2003, pp. 92-97.

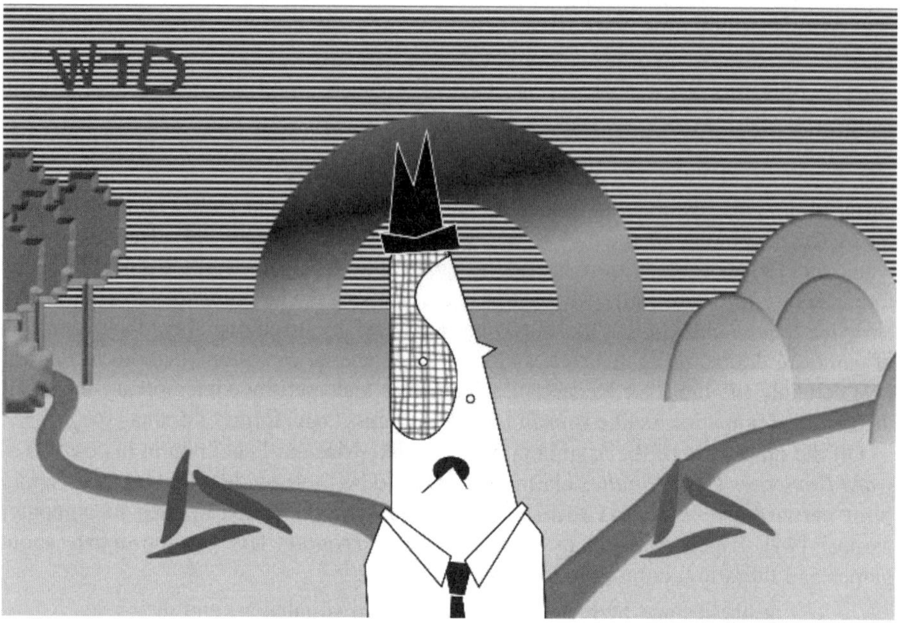


**Fig. 2.** Mr. Mott, the trickster character and narrator from *WiD*

***WiD.*** The first multimedia game narrative that will be discussed is *WiD*, created by Canadian artists Justin Love and Jimmy Olson [46]. Originating as a student project, it premiered at Collision conference in October 2006 and was performed again at Washington State University Vancouver later that year, *WiD* is a virtual environment driven by motion tracking technology and animation in which a player finds him or herself on an alien planet, replete with danger and adventure. Leading the story is Mr. Mott, a trickster of sorts and not so completely sympathetic narrator and witness to the player's many evolving troubles getting off the planet. In moving through the narrative, the user faces many choices that will either propel him or her somewhat safely through the ordeal or heap more trouble upon him or her. Thus, the narrative offers the classic forking path structure theorized by Jay David Bolter in *Writing Space*, which "disrupts the linear" experience of interacting with the piece [47].

A moving LCD projector that projects the animated images on any surface, particularly the floor, gives the work a feeling more of a board game than video game.

The user steps into a place in the space where a *hyperlink* (or hyperlinks) appears (in this case, represented by a light from the robotic light), and the story moves in a particular direction.

What also sets this work apart from other game narratives besides its resemblance to a board game is the inclusion of several commercials that break into the action throughout the work. Though, in some cases, the commercials offer ironic social commentary about smoking or other issues, they actually serve to locate the work in live television, with the narrative reminiscent of a comedy sitcom in which the player emerges as the lead character. Watching *WiD* being played is also reminiscent of

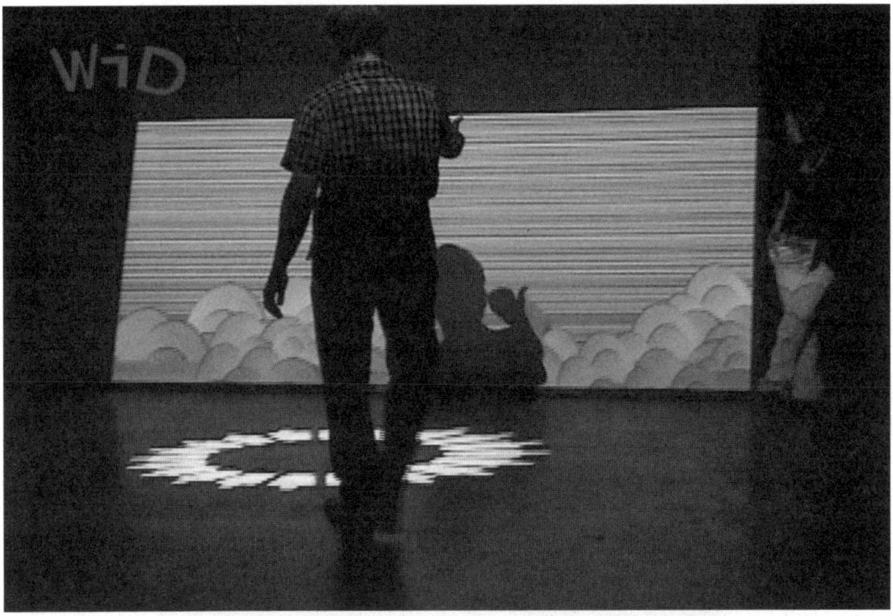


**Fig. 3.** The moving projector pointing data to the floor of the performance space gives the impression that *WiD* is a board game

watching *The Wizard of Oz* [48] on television, particularly the episode where Dorothy begins her perilous journey down the Yellow Brick Road. The swirling target where she starts in Munchkinland paralleling with the image of the lights on the floor of the performance space, the weird flying monkey paralleling with *WiD*'s Chi Chi Birds, to the Wizard himself paralleling with Mr. Mott underpins the game with the sensibility of a novel and film narrative in the piece.

***When Ghosts Will Die.*** This piece, created by Steve Gibson and this author [49], premiered in April 2005 in Dallas, Texas at Project X and was also performed at Collision 2006. Inspired by Michael Frayn's play, *Copenhagen* [50], it tells the story about the dangers of nuclear proliferation from the development of the atomic bomb to the paranoia of the Cold War. Like *WiD*, it is driven by motion tracking technology, but it tells the story with video, animation, still images, sound, spoken word, music, light, and the written word. Game-like in structure, it offers three levels or stages of play described as "three potential phases of nuclear proliferation: 1) Disharmony, 2) Destruction, and 3) Disintegration."[49] Played either by one or two users involved in a dialectic about the production of nuclear weapons, it is also meant to be a theatrical piece with a prescribed beginning, middle, and end. What happens in each of these levels can vary, allowing the story a sense of unpredictability, but it is not non- or multi- linear. As is stated on the project website:

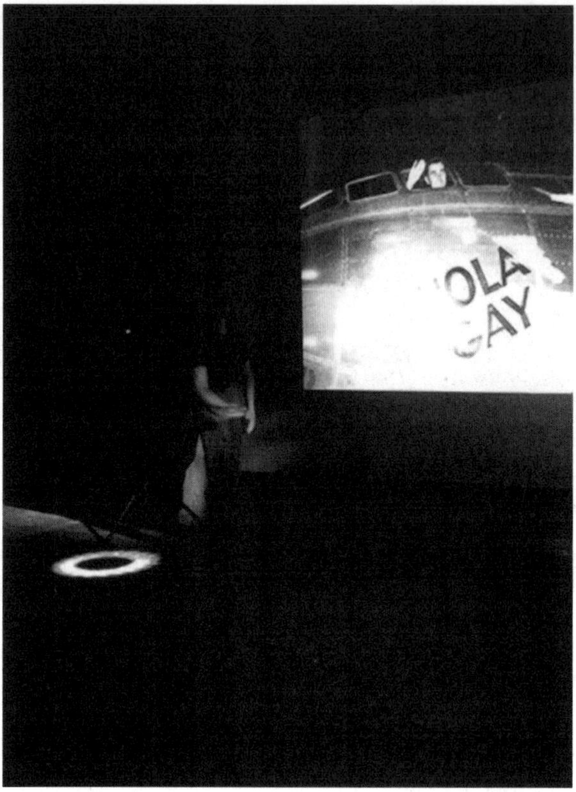

**Fig. 4.** An image representing the Destruction level of *When Ghosts Will Die*

> The story is meant to shock those participating into a deeper awareness of the horrors of nuclear warfare. Politically speaking, the work's message – that the development and deployment of weapons of mass destruction not only test a country's power but also its humanity – speaks to artists' "responsibility to envision alternative futures... and shape the way people think, live, and interact" (Edward Shanken 50-51). [49]

What we were shooting for with *When Ghosts Will Die* was a performance-installation piece that crossed over into the area of serious games, a game that was art and a story that was artfully relayed.

### 3.2 Corporeal Poetry

When I first saw Gibson perform with motion tracking technology, it was his piece, *Virtual DJ* [51], at the Incubation conference in Nottingham, England in 2004. Inspired by his work, I was not thinking of serious games or even theatre, but actually poetry. Dancing in the space, Steve was holding a tracking device in each hand that evoked the sounds and lights driving his performance. At the end of the room sat a PC, and on the monitor I could track Steve's position in the 3D space of the room by watching a representation of his body move across the screen. As it moved, a trace of his body lingered in the space it had just occupied. It occurred to me as I watched the trace that someone could literally write words with one's body in such a performance space and program the computer hold on to the trace long enough to show the words on the screen. In a sense I was thinking of embodied writing, of corporeal poetry. It also occurred to me as I watched Gibson interacting with and combining the various media objects that this form of performance was similar to ancient literary forms.

Mentioned earlier, ancient literary works were not pure genres as literature is today. Epic poetry like Homer's *Iliad* and *Odyssey* were stories sung in poetic meter with musical accompaniment. Aeschylus' plays were stories that combined many different poetic meters, with a chorus that sang its parts and moved across the stage in a choreographed way to the sound of musical instruments. It is believed that Sappho sang her poetry as she strummed her lyre. These works were not silent as, for example, Emily Dickenson's poetry is read alone, nor were they still like the printed word is on this page. While traditional spoken word performance (i.e. poetry readings) can be more invigorating for some than the solitary reading of poetry, it remains a specialized art form that does not command the attention of youth bred on the popular culture of iPods or video games. With the loss of audience to poetry a concern to me, I found myself in 2004 looking for a way to win them back.

Gibson's approach and technique to multimedia and interactive performance seems even now a provocative solution. Moving from free-form performances involving sound and light like *Virtual DJ* and multimedia narratives like *When Ghosts Will Die*, I am experimenting now with what I described earlier as embodied writing—*corporeal poetry*—that is, performance and installation work that combines motion tracking technology, sound recording—both voice and music—and video in which the poet moves purposefully through a space creating poetry *on the fly*, rhapsodically. The end result is a work not unlike pre-print poetry. The first works of this nature have been created with collaborator Jeannette Altmann. Among these are *Things of Day and Dream* and *Rhapsody Room.*

***Things of Day and Dream.*** *Things of Day and Dream* [52] is a short poem about the liminal space between waking and dreaming. Divided into 13 phrases, the work is laid out into two main parts of the performance space. Upstage to the right are 10 phrases associated with *day*; to the left, two phrases with *dream*. In the middle lies the overlapping space where we cannot tell the difference; in this space is the one phrase: "and lurking between day and dream."

The performer begins the poem, standing, in the area associated with day, and ends the piece on the ground, in the area associated with dream. At the middle space she is crouched midway between the ceiling and floor. Thus, movement and gesture are used to accentuate the sentiment expressed by the words. Likewise, the video is a combination of two: one is me in a position of repose in the bed, sleeping and waking, the video changing with the performer's position in the performance space. On top of

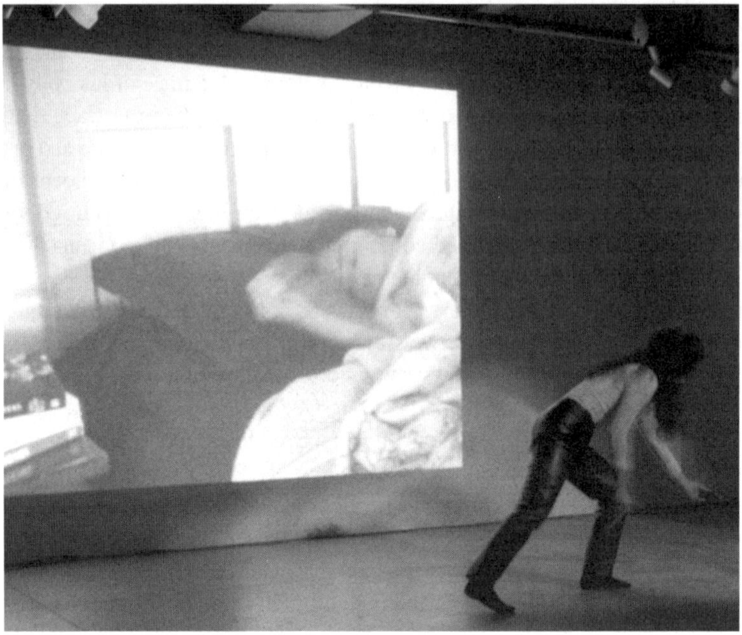

**Fig. 5.** A performance of *Things of Day and Dream*

that video is a series of images of the kind we take into our sleep, images of peacefulness, joy, nightmare and sadness. The performer cannot control these images with her movement; rather once they begin, they continue to roll until the end of the performance. The music is designed to be ethereal, dreamlike, and the lights muted blues, grays and greens. In sum, *Things of Day and Dream* experiments with language, not only visual, but the essence of corporeal embodied action—that is, visual, auditory, kinesthetic, and kinetic.

***Rhapsody Room.*** The last piece, *Rhapsody Room* [53], is a performance-installation piece that explores the notion of electronic cut up poetry. Cut up poetry and prose were made famous by William S. Burroughs. This piece, created by Jeannette and this author, sees words recorded and programmed in the performance space. A user, moving through the space, evokes a word by placing the tracking device in a particular place. Nouns and pronouns are found at the highest levels of the space; adjectives and adverbs, in the middle; and verbs and other parts of speech at the lowest level. Music and light accompany the words as a way of emphasizing placement of categories. Moving around the space, the user can produce a complete work of poetry. The work is in its very early stage of development, but the aim is to facilitate the production of poems on the fly, rhapsodically, in the space.

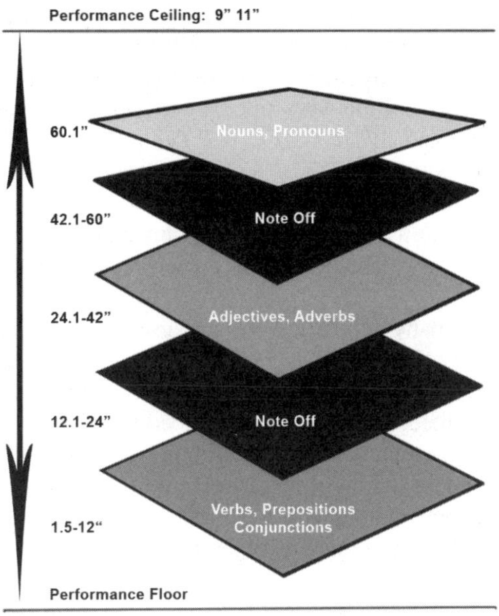


**Fig. 6.** Sketch of the structure of *Rhapsody Room*

## 4 Pre-print Multimedia

Emergent, hybrid, transdisciplinary forms of art harken us back to ancient forms that existed long before there was a notion of literature and were produced to share common history, enhance ritual, mobilize a community to action. Some classicists believe, for example, that the ancient Greeks devised writing specifically to record Homer's poetry, so important to its cultural heritage it was. The works as we know them today were believed to have been organized so that they could be used for a national event that took place every year, a festival that celebrated Greek culture [54]. While maybe not epic in nature, one can view Cardiff's *The Missing Voice* as an artifact that celebrates culture. Whitechapel Library where the narrative journey began no longer exists, shut down in 2005. Housed now at the Gallery, the work documents an important historical location that existed for 113 years, and it does so experientially and through sound rather than through images, much like Homer's sonic works recounted Greek history and culture.

Participating in three-dimensional literature as either viewers or performers forces us to rethink the notion of reading and literacy by asking us to make sense of images, sound, movement and other sensory modalities as text. Like *The Missing Voice*, *When Ghosts Will Die* is driven as much by sound as by images. In fact, the use of words is minimal and found in association only with images. Thus, it is as far removed from traditional print-based literary work as can be, and yet it is still a story that makes a case about the dangers of nuclear proliferation. That three-dimensional work also subverts traditional modes of delivery by expanding art outside of print publishing and into other venues provides both its power and suggests its limitations. Existing in ephemeral space created anew with each telling means it does not depend upon editors or paper for its dissemination. Its beauty lies in its temporariness. As an archived event, it may live on as a DVD or CD or a site on the web. But in order to talk about *WiD*, for example, it was necessary to write the artists for images of the work since it does not exist in any accessible form for viewers. On the other hand, *When Ghosts Will Die* is published in multiple places, like the journal *Drunken Boat*, on *YouTube*, and at Gibson's website. No one has to pay to experience the videos associated with the work as one would need to do with a book. Nevertheless, these iterations of it are merely documentation of a performance that took place almost two years ago. The performance itself recounted in the video can never be recreated.

Also interesting to many scholars who have escaped traditional disciplines for the more ambiguous spaces of media art is the fact that such performative work, like *Ghosts* or *WiD* or even *Things of Day and Dream*, recombines drama with theatre, which currently at least in the United States, are objects siloed in different departments, studied by scholars with expertise in a particular area. Bringing it together offers the possibility that we can expand our understanding of these works by seeing them anew, coming at them with insights and interpretations free of assumptions about conventions of one particular field or genre. And along those lines, as objects that we practice, they are wide open for experimentation, not limited by expectations associated with print or other art forms that have engendered long traditions. For these reasons, I see them less, as Hayles calls them "hopeful monsters"[2] but rather, to borrow from artist Bill Seaman, "recombinant" forms [55], new organisms purposefully engineered and that exhibit growth and change, the present future of literature, electronic or otherwise.

## References

1. Hayles, N.K.: The Electronic Literature in the 21st Century. At: The Future of Electronic Literature, hosted by the Maryland Institute for Technology in the Humanities, Baltimore, MD (May 3, 2007), `http://mith2.umd.edu/elo2007/`
2. Hayles, N.K.: Electronic Literature: What Is It? Electronic Literature Organization 1(4), 8–10 (2007), `http://eliterature.org/pad/elp.html`
3. Literature in Transition: National Endowment for the Humanities Seminar, hosted by University of California Los Angeles (2001)
4. Hayles, N.K.: Print Is Flat, Code Is Deep: The Importance of Media Specific Analysis. Poetics Today 25, 67–90 (2004)
5. Hayles, N.K.: Writing Machines, vol. 20, pp. 29–33. The MIT Press, Boston (2002)
6. Joyce, M.: afternoon: a story. Eastgate Systems, Watertown (1989)
7. Lutz, T.: Stochastische Texte. Augenblick 4, 3–9 (1959)
8. Kac, E.: Media Poetry: An International Anthology, 2nd edn., p. 273, 281. Intellect Books, Bristol, UK (2007)
9. Lialina, O.: My Boyfriend Came Back from the War. In: Greene, R. (ed.) Internet Art, pp. 36–37. Thames & Hudson, London (2004)
10. Amerika, M.: Grammatron. In: Greene, R. (ed.) Internet Art, p. 105. Thames & Hudson, London (2004)
11. Young-Hae Chang Heavy Industries: Rain on the Sea. In: Greene, R. (ed.) Internet Art, pp. 104–105. Thames & Hudson, London (2001–2004)
12. Greene, R.: Internet Art, p. 105. Thames & Hudson, London (2004)

13. Iowa Review Web, `http://www.uiowa.edu/~iareview/mainpages/tirwebhome.htm`
14. Poems That Go, `http://www.poemsthatgo.com/`
15. Van Looy, J., Baetens, J.: Close Reading New Media: Analyzing Electronic Literature. Leuven University Press, Leuven, BE (2003)
16. Montfort, N.: Twisty Little Passages: An Approach to Interactive Fiction, pp. 2–5–50. The MIT Press, Cambridge (2003)
17. trAce Online Writing Centre, `http://trace.ntu.ac.uk`
18. Altx Online Network, `http://www.altx.com/home.html`
19. UBUweb, `http://www.ubu.com/`
20. Hermeneia, `http://www.uoc.edu/in3/hermeneia/eng/index.html`
21. ELINOR, `http://elinor.nu`
22. Electronic Literature Organization, `http://eliterature.org`
23. Katz, N.: Janet Cardiff, The Missing Voice Case Study B Whitechapel Library, London Ongoing, `http://www.haikureview.net/node/15`
24. Artangel, `http://www.artangel.org.uk/pages/past/99/ 9_cardiff.htm`
25. Frieze, `http://www.frieze.com/issue/review/janet_cardiff/`
26. Egoyan, A.: Janet Cardiff. Bomb 79 (2002), `http://www.bombsite.com/issues/79/articles/2463`
27. Poole, H.: Please Don't Touch, `http://www.youtube.com/watch?v=VmXte7xv0f8`
28. dShednet, `http://www.dshed.net/digest/04/content/week4/lastheory.html`
29. Blast Theory. About Blast Theory, `http://www.blasttheory.co.uk/bt/about.html`
30. Blast Theory. Uncle Roy All Around You (2003), `http://www.uncleroyallaroundyou.co.uk/intro.php`
31. Alter, N.: Memory Essays. In: Biemann, U. (ed.) Stuff It: The Video Essay in the Digital Age, p. 14. Springer, Zurich (2003)
32. Aarseth, E.: Aporia and Epiphany in Doom and The Speaking Clock. In: Ryan, M.L. (ed.) Cyberspace Textuality: Computer Technology and Literary Theory, pp. 37–38. Indiana University Press, Bloomington (1999)
33. Cayley, J., with Lemmerman, D.: Torus 2005. In: Hayles, N.K. (ed.) Electronic Literature: What Is It? Electronic Literature Organization, vol. 1, p. 9 (2007), `http://eliterature.org/pad/elp.html`
34. Memmot, T.: E-cephaolopedia//novellex 2002. In: Hayles, N.K. (ed.) Electronic Literature: What Is It? Electronic Literature Organization, vol. 1, p. 9 (2007), `http://eliterature.org/pad/elp.html`
35. Waldrip-Fruin, N., with Carroll, J., Coover, R., Greenlee, S., McClain, A.: Screen 2003. In: Hayles, N.K. (ed.) Electronic Literature: What Is It? Electronic Literature Organization, vol. 1, p. 9 (2007), `http://eliterature.org/pad/elp.html`
36. Gillespie, W., with Rodriguez, J., Dao, D.: Word Museum (2004-5). In: Hayles, N.K. (ed.) Electronic Literature: What Is It? Electronic Literature Organization, vol. 1, p. 9 (2007), `http://eliterature.org/pad/elp.html`
37. Varela, F., Thompson, E., Rosch, E.: The Embodied Mind: Cognitive Science and Human Experience, pp. 25–27. The MIT Press, Cambridge (1993)
38. Coverley, M.D., Pullinger, K.: M Is For Nottingham (2002), `http://califia.us/IncubationDrama/museumtoc.htm`

39. Sermon, P., Dixon, S., Fucs, M., Zapp, A., with Seaman, B.: Unheimlich (2006), http://creativetechnology.salford.ac.uk/unheimlich/event.htm
40. Unheimlich: ACM Portal, http://portal.acm.org/citation.cfm?id=1179089
41. Laurel, B.: Computers as Theatre, vol. ix, pp. 189–193. Addison-Wesley, Reading (1993)
42. Murray, J.: From Game-Story to Cyberdrama. In: Wardrip-Fruin, N., Harrigan, P. (eds.) First Person, pp. 2–8. The MIT Press, Cambridge (2004)
43. Mateas, M.: A Preliminary Poetics for Interactive Drama and Games. In: Wardrip-Fruin, N., Harrigan, P. (eds.) First Person, pp. 19–33. The MIT Press, Cambridge (2004)
44. Eskelinen, M.: Towards Computer Game Studies. In: Wardrip-Fruin, N., Harrigan, P. (eds.) First Person, pp. 36–44. The MIT Press, Cambridge (2004)
45. Aarseth, E.: Genre Trouble. In: Wardrip-Fruin, N., Harrigan, P. (eds.) First Person, pp. 45–55. The MIT Press, Cambridge (2004)
46. Love, J., Olson, J.: WiD 2005, At Collision, hosted by the University of Victoria, Victoria, BC (September 2006)
47. Bolter, J.D.: Writing Space, 2nd edn., p. 137. Lawrence Erlbaum Associates, Mahwah (2001)
48. The Wizard of Oz: MGM. Fleming, V. USA (1939)
49. Gibson, S., Grigar, D.: When Ghosts Will Die (2005), http://www.telebody.ws/Ghosts
50. Frayn, M.: Copenhagen. Anchor Books, NY (1998)
51. Gibson, S.: Virtual DJ. (2001-2007), http://www.telebody.ws/VirtualDJ
52. Grigar, D., Altmann, J.: Things of Day and Dream (2007), http://www.nouspace.net/dene/portfolio.html
53. Grigar, D., Altmann, J.: Rhapsody Room (2007), http://www.nouspace.net/dene/portfolio.html
54. Whitman, C.: Homer and the Homeric Tradition, pp. 76–78. W. W. Norton, NY (1958)
55. Seaman, B.: Recombinant Poetics, http://digitalmedia.risd.edu/billseaman/

# Transient Passages: The Work of Peter Horvath

Celina Jeffery

Professor of Art History, Savannah College of Art and Design

**Abstract.** Peter Horvath produces non-interactive, cinematic Internet art works which explore conditions of agency, mobility, and continuous flow, traversing and arguably collapsing notions of the micro and macro, near and far. The idea that this sense of movement is random is deemed important here and coalesces I argue, with the Situationist International (SI) concept of the dérive, 'a technique of transient passage through varied ambiences' and an idea closely associated with pyschogeographies.[1] Implied within this process is a 'drift' which mediates social, creative and conceptual boundaries between the specific locality of the user, the presence of urban markers within the works and the mapless topography of the medium itself.

**Keywords:** Internet Art, Mapless, Place, Psychogeographies Dérive.

Peter Horvath produces non-interactive, cinematic Internet art works which explore conditions of agency, mobility, and continuous flow, traversing and arguably collapsing notions of the micro and macro, near and far. The idea that this sense of movement is random is deemed important here and coalesces I argue, with the Situationist International concept of the dérive, 'a technique of transient passage through varied ambiences' and an idea closely associated with pyschogeographies'.[2] Implied within this process is a 'drift' which mediates social, creative and conceptual boundaries between the specific locality of the user, the presence of urban markers within the works and the mapless topography of the medium itself.

The potential for navigating the ambient or mapless 'place'[3] of the Internet on an imaginative and allegorical level has proven endemic since its inception. For example, the Internet has been appropriated by entertainment companies like Blizzard in the production of multi-user, online games, which are creating a profound and massive culture of local-global relations. The ambivalence of location and cultural authorship within these games is also at play so to speak, in Internet art. But whereas Internet gaming capitalizes on accessibility and vast distribution and thus remains a logical part of Internet economics, Internet art has sought to generate a critical and creative dialogue between the web's anarchic, free information space and its accumulation and surveillance of data body and other forms of information economics. As such, Internet art has the tendency to conceive of itself as a counter-site, which continuously seeks to challenge and invert concepts of art and their relationship to time and space.

---

[1] Simon Ford, *The Situationist International, A User's Guide,* (London: Black Dog Publishing, 2005), 34-5.

[2] Simon Ford, *The Situationist International, A User's Guide,* 34-5.

[3] Robertson and McDaniel consider place to be a unity of time and space, particularly in relation to how global economic and information networks are connecting 'remote' places. See 'Place', *Themes in Contemporary Art*, (New York and Oxford: Oxford University Press, 2005).

R. Adams, S. Gibson, and S. Müller Arisona (Eds.): DAW/IF 2006/2007, CCIS 7, pp. 143–152, 2008.

Vuk Cosic first used the term 'net.art' in 1996, immediately configuring the artist and 'user' as a unified agent, interacting within the network. Since, 'net.art' has become a widely held, but contentious term, generally understood as art which cannot be experienced in any other medium or in any other way than by means of the Internet. Recently, the term has given way to more general names: Internet art or online art, and has also been subsumed within the category of 'new media' art, (an equally indistinct term). MTAA's 'Simple Net Art Diagram', 1997,[4] is useful to reference here: it shows net art as 'happening' between two, spatially dispersed computers. This implies that net art is not art simply represented online, that is, created in one medium and reproduced online, but must use the Internet as its ontological remit. The work is not necessarily about the technology either, but rather it uses the www as an opportunity for further expression. In this sense, it is very much an art of appropriation: Internet art uses the web's vast distribution network as a primary concept, medium and mode of access.

Internet art thus invites the viewer or 'user' to consider the problem of defining itself as 'art' while simultaneously requiring us to think through ideas of networked creativity that are at once personal and collective. The idea of agency – both within the work as well as its reception, is pronounced. Internet art not only asks us to consider art devoid of its 'aura' (Benjamin's term for art's particular presence in time and space), but also whether it can be heterotopic: simultaneously within 'real' time and space but also occupy an inestimable and unknowable place.[5]

The notion that Internet art gives rise to an immanent experience largely concerning transitory behavior, was an approach also shared by the Situationist International, who conceived of fleeting 'situations' as a new creative tactic, "Our situations will be ephemeral, without a future; passageways. The permanence of art or anything else does not enter into our consideration, which are serious. Eternity is the grossest idea a person can conceive of in connection with his acts".[6] Central to the creation of these situations was the idea of the psychogeography, which was envisioned as a means to counter urban spectacle:

> The Situationists developed tactics that doubled both as game and sedition, such as the dérive, which is aimless drifting through urban streets, preferably in groups, employing the 'psycho-geographical' method to understand the psychological affect the buildings and built forms have on the dériver, while hunting for environments that issue suitably exciting and passionate atmospheres.[7]

The creative tactic of wandering through psychogeographic spaces is pertinent to Horvath's work, which utilizes non-linear narratives to explore the momentary nature of

---

[4] http://www.mteww.com/nad.html

[5] Michel Foucault, 'Of Other Spaces', *Diacritics,* Vol. 16, No. 1 (Spring, 1986) 22-27.Translated by Jay Miskowiec. *Of Other Spaces* was originally delivered as a lecture by Foucault in 1967. Here he describes heterotopia as a kind of evolving and highly malleable counter-site, 'a sort of simultaneously mythic and real contestation of the space in which we live'.[5] So whereas the utopia is imagined and unreal, the heterotopia is a real space that is continuously 'represented, contested, and inverted'.

[6] Guy Debord, 'Report on the Construction of Situations', Knabb, 1981, 24. Quoted by Jan Bryant in 'Play and Transformation', (Constant Nieuwenhuys and the Situationists)', *Drain: A Journal of Contemporary Art and Culture*, Play Issue, No. 6, 2006. www.drainmag.com

[7] Jan Bryant, *Play and Transformation, (Constant Nieuwenhuys and the Situationists).*

the subject in Internet art. In particular, his *Triptych: Motion, Stillness, Resistance*, 2006, (Figure 1) reflects upon the dérive as a means to reposition the relationship between a psychogeographical engagement with undiscovered places. It does so primarily by exploring the disorientating and affecting nature of travel through urban environments. It also offers the potential for an elongated experience of these spaces, so that our perception of the here and now are superceded by the possibility of an inexhaustible presence of the global.

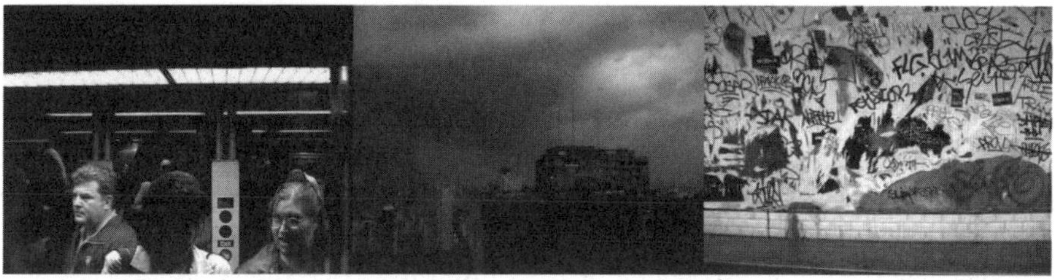

**Fig. 1.** Peter Horvath, *Triptych*, 2006 – Screenshot Reproduced courtesy of the artist

Horvath is an artist who produces browser driven 'non-linear video based narratives that run on the Internet'.[8] His work is perhaps most accurately defined as web cinema: they are (mostly) non-interactive works that use found sound and film footage as well as the artist's own video and animation.[9] The work can be seen on his website 6168.org as well as through prominent Internet galleries including the Whitney Artport and Rhizome, and have also been exhibited in 'real world' gallery spaces on monitors, LCD screens and via large-scale projections.[10] Horvath has also contributed to *MobileGaze*[11] an on-line artist collective, founded in 1999 in Montreal, Canada by Brad Todd, Andrew Brouse and Valerie Lamontagne which is 'dedicated to the promotion of 'Canadian / Quebec artists on an international scale' and the desire to create 'a bridge between the micro and macro web art communities'.[12] *<Pause>*,[13] an online exhibition curated by the group, aims to intercept 'the stream of information in order to provide a disruption within this endless expanse of data, by providing the viewer with a vantage point, a moment of reflection and a slowing down in his/her interactive viewing habits'.[14] Here 'pause' is considered a kind of diversion, a counter site in which a series of cinematic Internet art works seek to challenge the hegemony of its context, the rapid information-economics of the www.

---

[8] Interview with the artist. December 2006.

[9] Only one work, *The Presence of Absence*, 2003, is interactive in the sense of users being able to actively select or trigger aspects of the work. In some of the works, like *ESER,* the artist offers the opportunity for viewers to add their personal anonymous thoughts online, which are then posted at the conclusion of the work.

[10] See *Peter Horvath: Transient Passages,* at the ACA Gallery of SCAD, Atlanta, GA. March 29th-April 29th, 2007, curated by the author.

[11] www.mobilegaze.com

[12] Valerie Lamontagne, *The Inter-Society for the Electronic Arts (ISEA) Newsletter*, #92, ISSN 1488-3635 #92 April - May 2003 http://www.isea-web.org/eng/inl/inl92.html, date accessed 24 August 2006.

[13] http:/mobilegaze.org/pause/#

[14] 'Pause', *MobileGaze*, http://mobilegaze.org/pause/#), 21st April 2004.

In <*Pause*> Horvath contributed *Either Side of An Empty Room,* 2002, a 14 minute work, in which the artist explores the slippage between waking life, dreaming and memory in the context of a 'day in the life'. Here we encounter time less as a study of progression and more as a reoccurring series of multi-paced moments that fast forward, flicker, and reverse. As in all of his works there is an intimacy here which relies on detaining the user, a tactic frequently absent in our regular experiences of the Internet. Importantly then, most of Horvath's works are lengthy: 12 or so minutes, and in the case of *Triptych,* which is generative, it can potentially run infinitely. Subsequently, the work requires a 'pause', a slowing down, a protraction and subversion of the speed of the Internet.

*Triptych* (Figure 2) is composed of three video panels, situated side by side, and although not spiritual in intent, does induce a sense of contemplation.[15] Each panel expresses a condition: motion, stillness and resistance, which are mostly conveyed in the pace and rhythm of passageways through unknown urban environments.[16] 'Motion' largely explores the themes and conditions of movement through the city, and particularly highlights urban transportation. It lacks distinctive context and disorientates geographical specificity, moving the user through a series of familiar yet indistinct urban markers. The central frame, 'stillness', concentrates our vision on subtle images of skies, seemingly unchanging shots of cityscapes as well as quiet private and domestic scenes, that are equally without the particularities of place. They are comparable to Wolfgang Staehle's continuous images of places that are subtle and meditative in tone, and although not modified, appear to suspend and elongate time. Like Staehle's *Comburg,* 2001,[17] in which a live web-cam transmits images of an eleventh-century monastery over the Internet, 'stillness' seeks to capture subtle changes that are barely perceptible to the eye. Yet in both cases, we also experience distant locations as immediate and for local consumption, reminding us of the desire for infinite access to images which the Internet has fostered. The third panel is 'resistance' and explores instances of urban drama and conflict – couples arguing, people protesting or in states of agitation.

Horvath chose not to use the pop up window as a framing device in this piece, a technique common in his work, but found an equivalent means of creating a dialogue between individually framed panel sequences by situating three videos side by side, creating a reflexive dialogue between these states.[18] This unity is also achieved

---

[15] Currently, the work can use original footage for approximately 4 hours, however, the artist is continuously adding to it.

[16] Both 'motion' and 'stillness' use video shot at the standard 29.97 frames per second, whereas 'resistance' is modified.

[17] http://www.tate.org.uk/modern/exhibitions/timezones/artists.shtm#staehle

[18] A similar format of inter-connecting video sequences was recently explored by Christian Marclay in *Video Quartet,* 2004, a four channel installation which 'samples' extensive found Hollywood film scenes of musical and distinctive sound based performances. Each section or channel informs the next finalizing in an exuberant arrangement of song and dance that concludes crescendo like. Marclay is known for exploring the legacy of Cage's sampling technique (itself a kind of détournment) first experimented with in *Williams Mix*, 1952. Cage used the I Ching to achieve the chance driven and hence negated intentionality of the mix, giving the process a seemingly infinite range of possibility. While Horvath's *Triptych* appears to employ sampling in the same way as Marclay, it is in actuality generative, meaning it uses a software program to randomly select from Horvath's pool of video footage. As such, it plays differently every time you log on and is in this sense effectively unique and endless, in that the generative schema gives rise to a vast array of possible sequences.

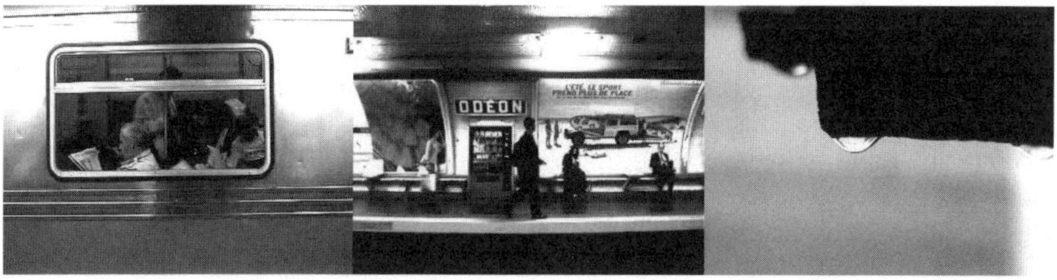


**Fig. 2.** Peter Horvath, *Triptych*, 2006 – Screenshot Reproduced courtesy of the artist

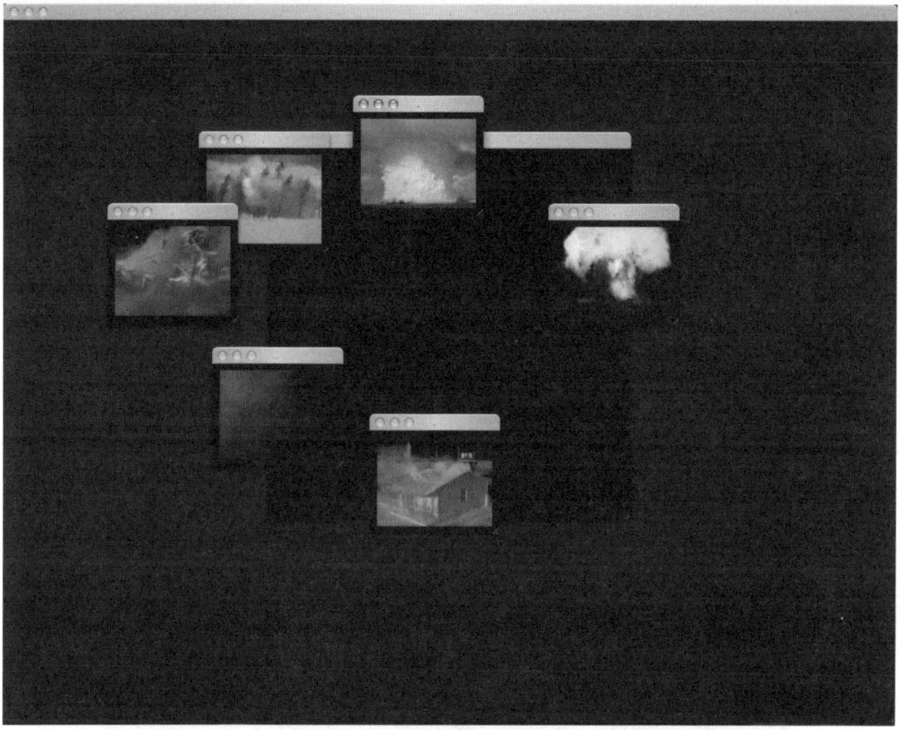

**Fig. 3.** Peter Horvath, *Unexpected Launching of Heavy Objects,* 2003 – Screenshot Reproduced courtesy of the artist

through the consistency of line and color passing through each panel - images are frequently subdued in color but sharply lit. Like Viola's *Hatsu Yume, (First Dream)* 1981, a 56 minute color video[19], which uses the effects of water and light to transition between geographies in Japan, from the forest regions to the city for example, as well from the documentary to the ephemeral, Horvath elevates these sequences from the documentary to the psychogeographic – revealing unexpected ambiances of the environment. As in Debord's description of the dérive, we experience the spaces of this

[19] Bill Viola's *Hatsu Yume,* translated as 'First Dream', was poduced in Japan in 1981 while Viola was artist-in-residence at the Sony Corporation.

work with irony, the viewer is unable to make decisions about the way in which they encounter space within and through the work, and yet they are presented with its residing affecting conditions. In other words, we do not wander aimlessly, as did the Surrealists, but encounter habitual 'psychogeographical attractions', which in *Triptych* are the rapid, suspended and troubled encounters with the unknown city.[20] The randomly generated sequences that continuously juxtapose these states create unending narratives, passages, and pathways, which glide between the here and there.

Unlike *Triptych,* the majority of Horvath's works use the pop-up window as a narrative-framing device for multilayered video. In *Unexpected Launching of Heavy Objects,* 2003, (Figure 3) hundreds of empty pop-ups rapidly unfold, encasing scenes of fascism that subsequently merge into images of atomic bomb tests. For Horvath then, the appropriation of the pop-up window has acted as a means of subverting the once familiar visual language and usage of the Internet, while also addressing broadband restrictions. The pop-ups produce an assortment of sequences inspired more by the collage based work of Hannah Höch than Sergei Eisenstein's montages (Figure 4).[21]

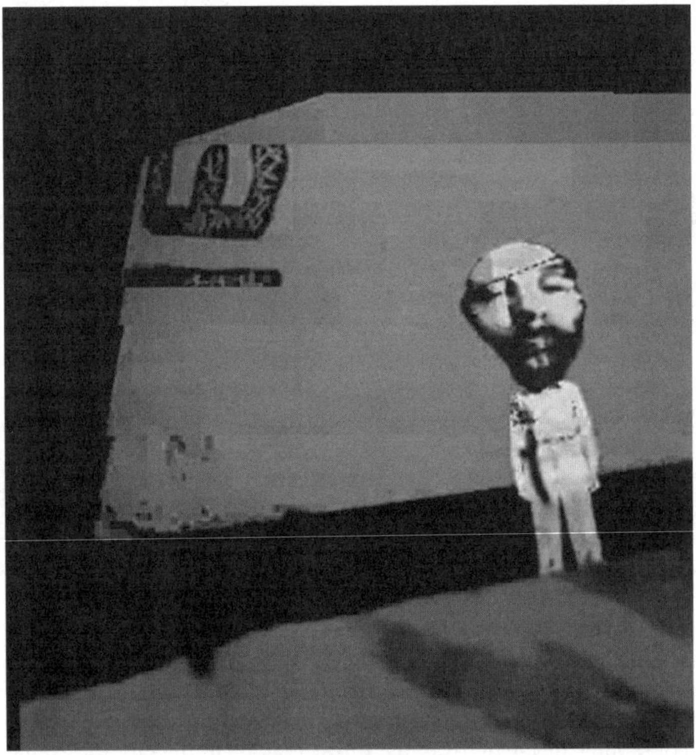

**Fig. 4.** Peter Horvath, *Either Side of an Empty Room*, 2002 – Screenshot Reproduced courtesy of the artist

[20] Guy Debord, 'Theory of the Dérive', 1958, published in *The Situationist International Text Library*, http://library.nothingness.org/articles/SI/. Date accessed October 24[th], 2006.
[21] Interview with the artist, March 2004.

But they are also particular to the Web: The browser frame is always present, and they tier in such a manner that they fill the border of the screen, making us conscious that the context is emphatically that of the Web. Such dense layering of video is enhanced by Horvath's use of music, sound and word: written and whispered, readable and obscured, which converge to realize the rich potential of the medium.

Horvath's textured use of audio-visual space not only investigates the possibilities of the medium but seeks, he argues, to emulate random memory acts and suggest unfolding consciousness,

> As a medium, the web simulates the environment of the mind, offering frenetic and multiple displays of stimulus. In my work, windows open and close in the same manner that thoughts enter our minds, play out, and disappear, making room for new thoughts. In this way, my pieces mimic the thought process.[22]

Memory, life cycles and waking dreams are recurrent themes in his work, and feature prominently in *Either Side of An Empty Room,* 2002. As viewers, we pass through undefined city spaces — the underground, supermarket, and bars — all in a matter of seconds and without the security of a destination or sense of purpose, much like the dérive. Interspersed throughout this urban drifting are photographic stills and

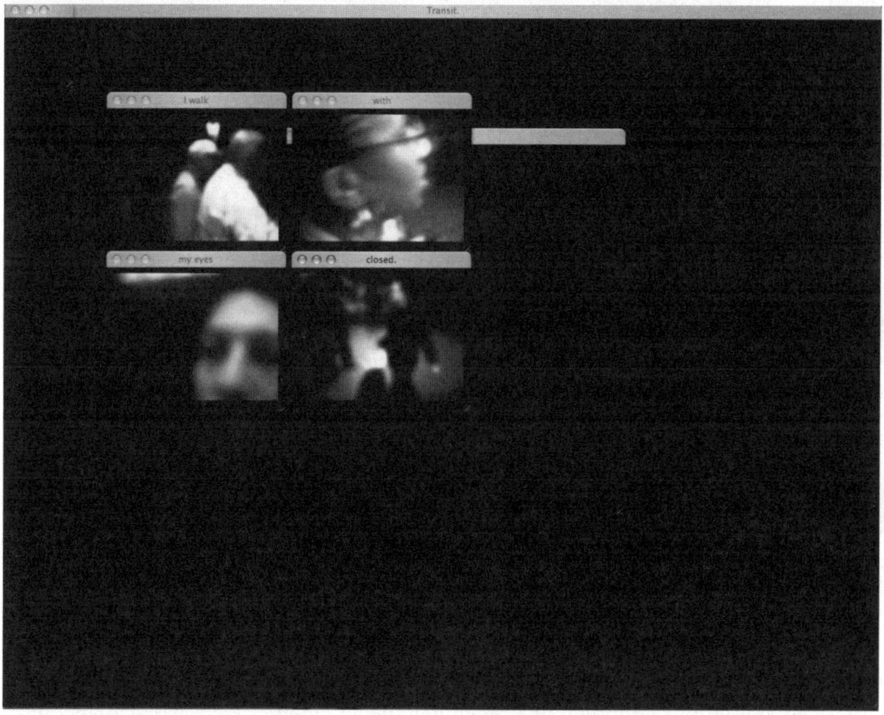


**Fig. 5.** Peter Horvath, *Life is Like Water,* – Screenshot Reproduced courtesy of the artist

[22] Interview with artist, October 2005.

film footage of the artist's family life, and surrealistic animations, which foil the consideration of the city as a private, ambient experience. The sense of disorientation and isolation experienced here is echoed in *Life is Like Water,* 2002, (Figure 5). Set on a heady NYC subway, it observes the intimate gestures and impersonal interactions of passengers whose insular lives are ruptured by 9/11 and its subsequent media frenzy.

The public uncovering of deeply personal secrets is also a subject addressed within *Intervals,* 2004, (Figure 6), an 8-minute, Web-based video which has also been presented as a projection in a gallery. The 'interval' is a brief moment in which four characters reveal their most intimate selves through accounts of lost innocence, fear of the unknown, masculine ritual and the mystery of love. Here identity is subject to visual and textual slippages, distortions, and to filmic alter egos that mimic, echo or subvert their subjects' account.

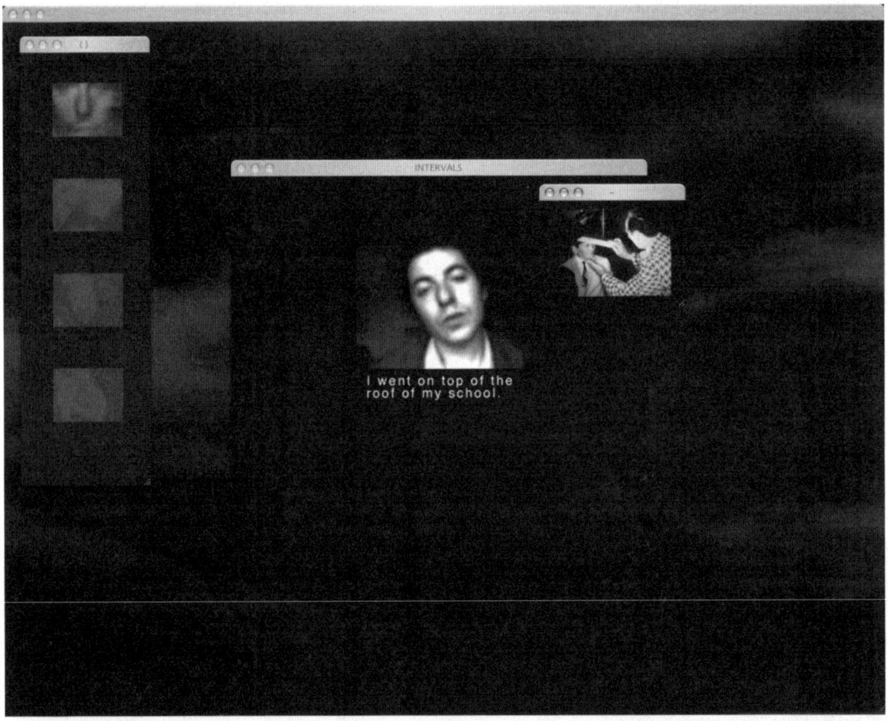


**Fig. 6.** Peter Horvath, *Intervals*, 2004 – Screenshot Reproduced courtesy of the artist

*Tenderly Yours*, 2005, (Figure 7), a 10-minute, Web-based video, revisits the themes of love, loss and memory in a visual language which simulates the personal, casual and ambiguous approach of French new wave cinema. Here we also encounter a series of filmic 'doubles' — of French new wave cinema rendered as Web cinema.

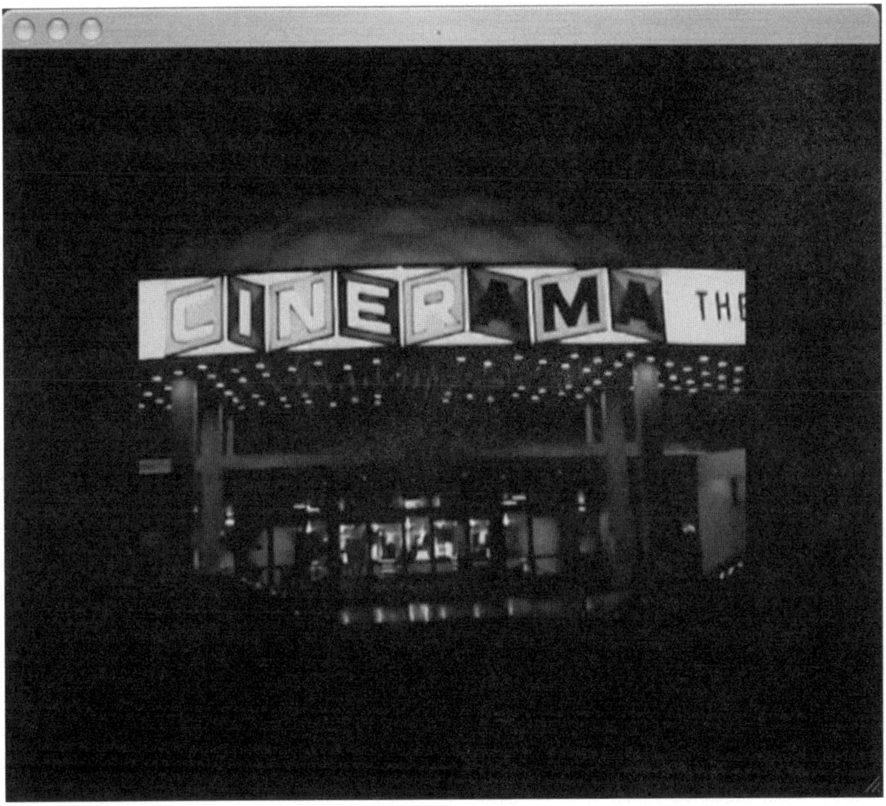


**Fig. 7.** Peter Horvath, *Tenderly Yours*, 2005, screenshot Reproduced courtesy of the artist

*Boulevard*, 2007, is a three-channel Web video and installation, running 12-minutes. Like *Tenderly Yours* it has a strong sense of cinematic presence, transitioning from the visual language of collage to scripting and directing a highly intense narrative. Located in Los Angeles, we follow a striking woman, the passenger of a convertible car, driven by an unidentified driver through the city, passing its generic streets, billboards and motels, to an unknown destination. There is a voice-over, presumably hers, that exposes her feelings of obsession. Running parallel to the piece is a dialogue between a man and woman in intimate, but casual conversation about love. The video sequences are frequently suspended, disjunctive and blurred, distorting our visual and emotional sense of place. At once lyrical and intoxicatingly beautiful, we move through discrete emotive atmospheres experiencing ambiguity, desire and longing.

Horvath's net art is perhaps more accurately defined as cinematic, in that, unlike the vast majority of net art works that utilize interactivity as its ontological remit, they are non-interactive and experientially passive. The dense arrangement of video is enhanced by Horvath's use of the word - both written and whispered, readable and obscured, which augment the richness of the medium. This literal and metaphorical layering of subject

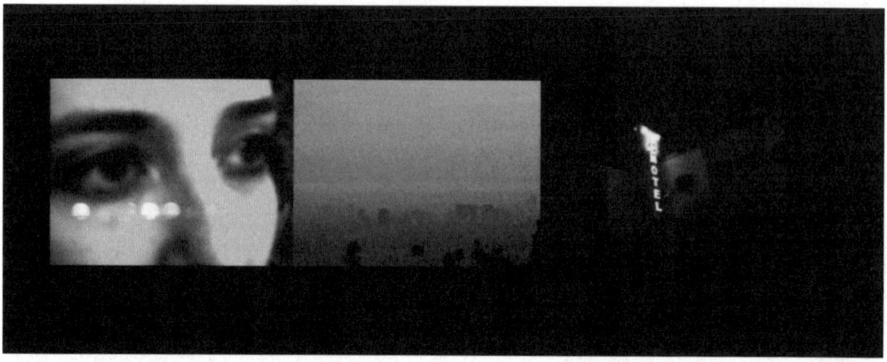

**Fig. 8.** Peter Horvath, *Boulevard,* 2007, Installation shot Reproduced courtesy of the artist

simultaneously queries time as a collection of fragments or memories, both real and imagined. Within and through all of these works, the subject drifts aimlessly, like the *dériver*, through real and virtual urban environments, without preconception as to where they may arrive but attempting to seek out purpose in their movement. This 'drift' mediates social, creative and conceptual boundaries between the specific locality of the user, the multiple places navigated within the work, and the globalized, mapless topography of the medium itself.

# Part III

# Multimedia Composition and Performance

# Visceral Mobile Music Systems

Atau Tanaka

Culture Lab, Newcastle University
Grand Assembly Rooms, King's Walk
NE1 7RU Newcastle upon Tyne, U.K.
atau.tanaka@ncl.ac.uk

**Abstract.** This paper describes a second-generation mobile music system that adds qualities of physical interaction to previous participative, networked, multi-user systems. We call upon traditions in interactive sensor music instrument building to inform this process. The resulting system underscores its dual personal/community context awareness with a technique of *hybrid audio display*. This allows the system to exhibit qualities of *reflexive social translucence* providing a view of the group all while giving each member of the group a responsive sense of agency. The visceral mobile music system was tested in a theatre environment with manageable location tracking and creative non-musical test subjects. The combination of musical practice and interaction design establish artistic creativity as an important component of the research process.

**Keywords:** mobile music, sensor instruments, network audio.

## 1 Introduction

Mobile electronics have had an indelible impact on culture and society. Artists have exploited this to conceive of new forms of cultural production. One of the areas often evoked is that of creating new forms of music. We seek to identify the musical potential of networked, mobile systems, and describe the conception and design of a *visceral mobile music* system. The system is mobile, multi-user, and is sensitive to both personal and community context as captured through location information and sensor data. To arrive at a result that musically fulfills the potential of the technology, we retrace related fields of interactive and network music to inform and motivate the design specification.

Personal music players revolutionized the notion of pervasive music over 25 years ago. The Walkman allowed the music lover to bring his/her music with him wherever he went, and allowed him to create a private aural sphere, defining his own musical environment while on the move, all while not disturbing those around him. Today's personal music systems have merged with recent developments in networked information access. The *container* of the music has gone from physical media such as the cassette or CD to data files. The storage capacity of modern personal music players is vast enough for a user to carry his whole music collection with him at all times. Meanwhile developments in peer-to-peer file sharing and social networking sites like MySpace have been seized upon by musician and music fans alike in new modes of music distribution, leading to heightened grass-roots inter-user interaction. These networks have been enhanced by

R. Adams, S. Gibson, and S. Müller Arisona (Eds.): DAW/IF 2006/2007, CCIS 7, pp. 155–170, 2008.

*information retrieval* techniques to generate recommendations based on personal musical taste with sites like LastFM [1]. The way that music is distributed and consumed, have undergone a fundamental shift in the last decade. Despite these technological shifts, music as an art form has not changed correspondingly. This chapter investigates ways in which mobile ubiquitous systems could be designed to directly engage with and drive the creative process of music making.

Mobile systems allow increasingly rich media experiences on portable electronics devices. The cell telephone evokes a sense of mobility plus a sense of connectivity. Localization technologies such as GPS enable navigation systems allow geographic interaction. These are the ingredients that have been used in new fields of artistic practice, notably *locative media*. As a researcher, I was interested to see if we could conceive of a form of location-based music. As a composer, I was interested to see if there was a way to preserve the richness of musical interaction we know from instrumental performance. What elements from traditional musical performance, or from previous work in computer based music could be used to enhance the musicality of mobile media systems? Could this contribute ideas to fields such as Human Computer Interaction (HCI) or Ubiquitous Computing? The approach described here sits at the intersection of several fields of research and creative practice.

We first describe the field of new instrument design in interactive music. We then consider the history of network music as precursors to the present work. Section 4 introduces the nascent field of mobile music. We then present the visceral mobile music system and describe field trials. Section 7 introduces the notion of *reflexive translucence* to describe ways in which the system musically portrays community activity. We finish with concluding remarks.

## 2 Sensor Instruments

One branch of computer music that is directly concerned with human-computer interaction is that of New Interfaces for Musical Expression (NIME). NIME began as a workshop at CHI 2001 [2] and has since evolved to sustain an annual international conference [3]. As its nature implies, NIME is the discipline concerned with interaction in music. It is a field that specializes in creating interactive music systems using sensors and networks. Its activities can be described as those of instrument building, or *lutherie*. The typical context of a NIME system is to build a system for concert performance. A NIME system is conceived by an instrument builder, contextualized by a composer, to be used by a musician who is able to attain a profound level of interaction with the system through his/her virtuosity. As a field of practice, NIME is therefore specialist oriented.

The design process of NIME, then, while rich for interactive possibilities in sound manipulation, do not address typical end users. The richness of a successful NIME instrument is not necessarily in the efficiency of interaction or the optimization of task performance. In classical HCI research, controlled experiments tend to focus on task performance optimization. With a musical instrument, on the other hand its operation has less to do with optimization and more to do with the expressivity of the system which may arise out of idiosyncrasies of the system. In musical composition this is referred to as the *idiomatic* voice of an instrument. From the HCI point of view, this can be viewed as a form of *seamful design* [4]. A good instrument is not always considered to be perfect

– it is said to have *character*. The identity of an instrument is established not only by the range of sounds it is capable of, but also as a function of its limitations. Successful compositions for instruments make use of both limitations and possibilities of an instrument, similar to the notion of seamful design.

Instrument building and subsequent composition and performance are activities central to NIME. Data from sensors that capture movement, gesture, or real world phenomena are mapped to sound synthesis or high level musical parameters. Information from a gyroscope, for example, might be used to capture free-space orientation, and gradually modulate the frequency of an oscillator. A number of artist-oriented platforms exist at the time of writing, including the *Arduino*, *I-Cube*, and *Phidget* that allow the artist to quickly experiment with different types of sensors as input to an interactive digital system. The arrival of the *Nintendo Wii* has brought this kind of interaction to the consumer gaming world, enabling the user to become physical in front of a video game. This hardware is a ready made, low cost device that integrates sensors like accelerometers and infrared cameras and has been seized upon by artists wishing to explore gesture and interactive media.

While the Wii's availability has been taken up by artists as an accessible platform, the history of work in this area pre-dates the Arduino, the Wii, and the NIME conference itself. The use of technology to capture gesture for musical ends can be retraced to the 1920's with the *Theremin*. The Theremin, and other instruments of its time like the *Ondes Martenot* used analog electronics to capture performer gesture to modulate electronic sound [5]. More recently, Max Mathews, one of the forefathers of computer music, created the *Radio Baton*, a continuous percussion surface that could monitor position and gesture of two radio transmittor batons over an playing surface comprised of an antenna grid[6]. Michel Waisvisz, the musician and composer most closely associated with the Studio for Electro-Instrumental Music (STEIM) in Amsterdam performs on *The Hands*, an instrument that uses mercury switches and ultrasound sensors to capture relative hand position, orientation, and distance to perform digital music [7].

These were works that inspired *Sensorband*, a trio ensemble in which three musicians, Edwin van der Heide, Zbigniew Karkorwski, and the present author, perform on instruments comprised of gestural interfaces. The three instruments in the Sensorband instrumentarium all allow free space gestures of the musician to be captured via a sensor system to articulate digitally synthesized sound on the computer. Each instrument, however, has its distinct mode of operation, be it ultrasound, infrared, or biosignal sensing. The similarities and differences among the instruments give them at once musical coherence and distinct identity. They are members of a single instrument family, much in the way that traditional instruments constitute families such as the stringed, woodwind, brass, and percussion instrument families. These three members of the *sensor instrument* family demonstrate their own uniqueness, each one distinguishing itself from the others by mode of operation, articulation, and ultimately voice [8].

Gestural interaction with electronic sound creates a compelling experience as it a mode of interaction that approaches, in HCI terms, *direct manipulation* of the medium. These sensor instruments have to be responsive and satisfying enough for musicians for whom the gold standard of expressivity is the richness of traditional musical instruments. At the same time, digital instruments' programmable mapping means that complexity can be tempered, making sensor instruments accessible to non-musicians more easily than traditional instruments.

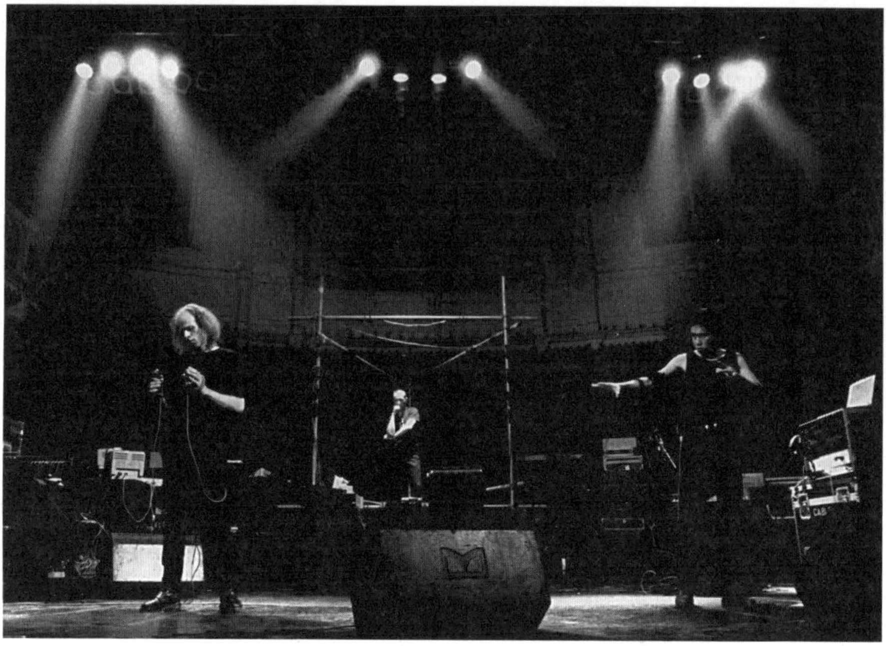

**Fig. 1.** Sensorband (*left to right*, Edwin van de Heide, Zbigniew Karkowski, Atau Tanaka) in concert at Paradiso in Amsterdam during the Sonic Acts Festival, 1994

## 3 Network Music

Musicians have a long tradition of appropriating communications technologies for musical work. The first communications technology to be broached artistically was radio. Germany was a fertile ground for early radio art, culminating in 1928 in the seminal *Wochenende* (Weekend) of Walter Ruttmann. Berthold Brecht was an important instigator in this era, calling for public participation to turn a state controlled distribution system into a social communication system. These views were corroborated by Kurt Weill in his call for an *absolute radio art* [9] and Walter Benjamin's essay *Art in the Age of Mechanical Reproduction* [10]. Cologne and the studio of the WDR (West German Radio) under Klaus Schoening became a focal point in the *Neues Hörspiel* movement of the 1960's, already renowned as a pioneering center for electronic music with its Studio for Electronic Music. Schoening commissioned an important body of work, including *Roaratorio* by John Cage, *New York City* by Richard Kostelanetz, and *Ein Aufnahmezustand* by Mauricio Kagel [11].

As radio is typically a state controlled medium, at the level of infrastructure and often at the level of content, independent artists wishing to exploit the medium needed to find tactical strategies. This includes a rich history of pirate radio, and of a school of do-it-yourself microradio transmitter building by Tetsuo Kogawa and others [12]. With the democratization of the Internet, network audio streaming made independent broadcasting possible. This was seized upon by artists for a host of net radio projects including Radio Qualia [13].

Beyond radio, composers like Max Neuhaus have also worked with telephone networks. He has continued his activities in music with his networks or broadcast works: virtual architectures which act as a forums open to anyone for the evolution of new musics. With the first *Public Supply* in 1966 he combined a radio station with the telephone network and created a two-way public aural space twenty miles in diameter encompassing New York City.

Performing musicians have used network technology to create distributed musical processes amongst musicians on the same stage. The Hub was a collective in the San Francisco area that performed with an on-stage data sharing network [14]. The use of communications networks to transpose auditory environments from one space to another range from functional demonstrations of remote musical rehearsal [15, 16], to artist projects by composers like Luc Ferrari who piped in sounds from the Normandy coast to envelope the Arc de Triomphe in Paris with seaside ambiences. This notion of streaming continues today with artists research projects such as the arts research group Locus Sonus [17].

### 3.1 Network Concerts

My first attempts to practice music on networks was in organizing long-distance performances in the 1990's. By using ISDN networks and videoconferencing technology, I was able to connect concert spaces in two cities, where performers at each site were able to see and hear the musicians at the other site. Inasmuch as the network was an *enabling technology* collapsing the distance between two geographically separated locations, the nature of the audiovisual communication created perturbations in the musicians' habits. The first challenge was to find a way to maintain eye-to-eye contact when the act of sharing a single stage was extended by a pair of video cameras and video projectors.

Musicians have the reflex to adjust their playing style to the reverberant acoustic of the space in which they play. I wanted to extend this musical instinct to respect the acoustics of physical space and apply it to the time latency of network space. To me it was somehow appropriate that a given music could not simply be transplanted and successfully performed on a network infrastructure. The time characteristic of that infrastructure becomes the acoustic. I have referred to this network transmission latency in other texts as the *acoustic of the network* to be recognized and exploited as one does when composing for specific resonant spaces [18].

### 3.2 Network Based Installations

While it was a musician's instinct to try to perform on any new infrastructure, these experiments underlined the fact the Internet was a medium perhaps not suited for live performance. This is borne out in the failure of early interest in Internet multicast technologies to transmit live events. In the multicast heyday of the mid-1990's, stadium rock concerts were imagined to be simulcast for viewing over the Internet. This has never taken off, but a deferred time interest in near-live transmission remains in events like the 2008 U.S. presidential debates over YouTube, a less time critical store-and-stream infrastructure.

As the temporal characteristics of networks posed significant challenges, I began to question whether networks were not better suited for musical activities other than real-time performance. I wondered if spatial aspects might hold more promise, and created works that were not concert pieces, but gallery and web-site based installations.

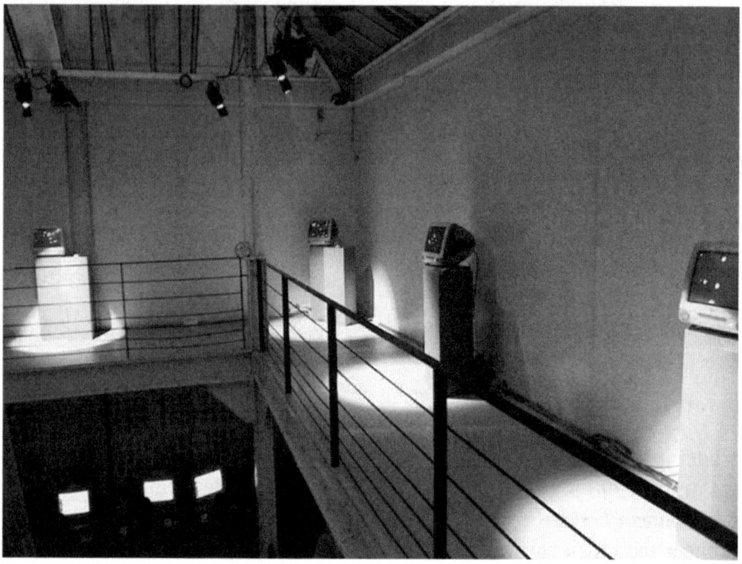

**Fig. 2.** *Constellations* installed at the Webbar, Paris, 1999

*Constellations* is a gallery installation whose aim was to juxtapose the physical space of an art gallery with the so-called *virtual* space of the Internet. Five computers in a gallery space, each connected to the Internet and each with its own speaker system. Gallery visitors use the interface to invoke the streaming of MP3 sound files from the Internet. And as the speakers of each of the computers played out into the physical space of the gallery, there was also a spatial, acoustic mix. These two levels of sound mixing – Internet mixing and acoustic mixing, constitute the dynamic at the core of the work. In *MP3q*, I abandoned physical space altogether and focused on the notion of the Internet as a collaborative space. The software is viewed on a standard web browser. An upload feature in the software allows listeners of the piece to send in URL links sound files and contribute to the evolution of the piece. In fact in its initial state, the piece is *contentless*, it is only a scaffold waiting for contributions from the web visitors. The spectator's role shifted to that of an active participant who heard her contributions in context with the others'.

### 3.3 Hybrids

Networks introduced the spatial and participative dimension but lacked the visceral element of sensor instruments. *Global String* is a network based installation work that uses sensors. The concept was to create a vibrating *string* of monumental proportions that would span the distance between two cities, traversing physical and network space [19].

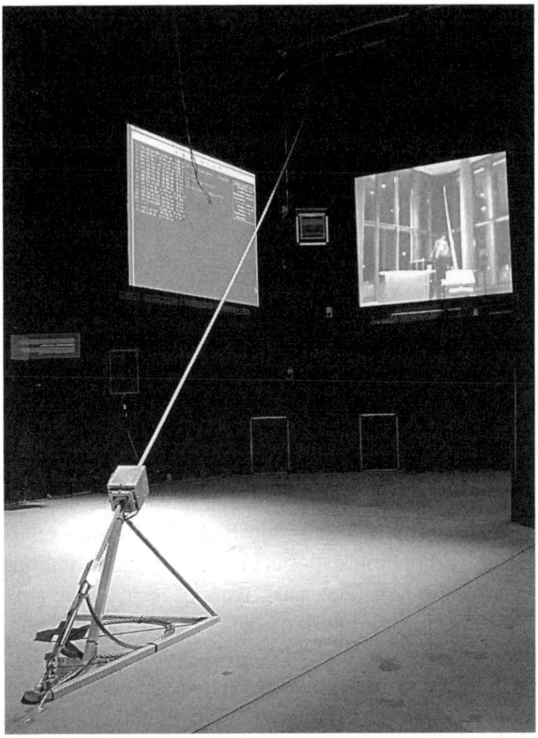

**Fig. 3.** *Global String* at Dutch Electronic Arts Festival (2000) at V2 in Rotterdam, with traceroute output on left screen and remote site at Ars Electronica Center in Linz Austria on right screen

As a hybrid work, it combined the approaches of sensor instruments and network music, and served to bring back the satisfaction and visceral sense in a networked environment.

At each site, the endpoints of the string were physical cables. The use of sensor-actuators in conjunction with networks allowed me to make physical action the musical information transmitted on the network. It is the mixture of the virtual and the real; the network acts as its resonating body, with network traffic conditions captured by the *traceroute* Unix command tuning parameters affecting physical model based sound synthesis.

## 4 Mobile Music

Mobile music is an all-encompassing term that implies deployment of audio and sound on portable electronics. It has been used by commercial products to refer to offerings that combine personal music player functionality on mobile telephones. Products like Apple's iPhone have brought music and video to the mobile phone. However they do little to extend the notion of a PDA and do not integrate the communicative possibility of a mobile phone and the Apple's companion iPod music player. More relevant to the work presented here, Mobile Music refers to an international research committee in creative musical practice on mobile computing technologies. It is a field of practice that is at the intersection of NIME, CHI, and Ubicomp. The community hosts an annual international conference, the Mobile Music Workshop (MMW) [20], one of which has been held in conjunction with a NIME conference.

*TuNA* is a system based on PDA's and ad-hoc Wi-fi networks to connect listeners in close proximity [21], allowing one listener can "tune" into what another is listening to. *Sonic City* is a headphone-based system equipped with sensors that put the personal music player in interaction with its surrounding environment [22]. Yolande Harris' work uses GPS in a sound art context. She exploits the supposed precision of GPS systems to *sonify* the jitter in a seemingly static source and creates exhibition and performance works that put the spectator or performer in musical interaction with the drift inside location sensing technologies [23].

### 4.1 Locative Media

Locative media is a recent field of artistic practice incorporating geography as source of creative production. Projects by the art group Blast Theory are references in this field, and succeed in creating compelling experiences by extending notions of theatrical production into the urban sphere [24]. Pervasive gaming is an active area with projects like *Big Urban Game* [25] transposing the dynamics of board games into urban geography. Geotagging is another area linking user to environment. Socialite [26] is one of several systems that allows the user to use a mobile device to annotate physical space by that user or to share annotations with others. Research platforms like *Mediascapes* [27] have made it practical for content creators to author location aware multimedia content.

### 4.2 Ubiquitous Music

With *Malleable Mobile Music*, the goal was to see how interactive music techniques might be applied in a ubiquitous computing context [28]. For this, the musical example was simplified to remixing an existing pop song. Each participant was assigned a part in the music and their relative proximity in urban environment drove an evolving re-mix of a song. From a musical point of view, this was as if each participant became an instrument, or *rack* in the whole. From a human-interaction point of view, it was to see if a musical entity could represent the presence and proximity of a person. For this, I coined the term, *musical avatar.* Ultimately the question was to see if music could become a carrier of social information.

Taking these ideas in an artistically more abstract direction, I developed *Net_Dérive* in collaboration with Petra Gemeinboeck and Ali Momeni [29]. The goal was to use strategies from Locative Media to create a fluid musical work. We sought to use off-the-shelf components such as mobile telephones and GPS devices. At the same time, we wanted to take the mobile phone out of its typical cultural association. For this, we created a sort of wearable computing object, a white scarf in which were housed two mobiles and the GPS device.

The piece allowed three participants each wearing the wearable system to wander around in the neighborhood surrounding the gallery where the exhibition was taking

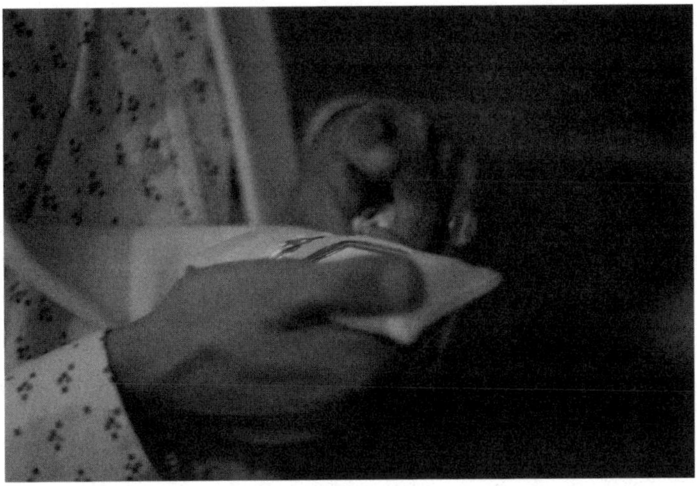

**Fig. 4.** Net_Dérive, with GPS and mobile phones contained in wearable scarf-like object

place. The camera automatically took photos every 20 seconds along the walk, geo-tagged them with the GPS data, and uploaded them over mobile wireless data networks to the server in the gallery. An abstract audiovisual feed was created from this data in the gallery, and streamed back to the participants. The work put in place a system for abstract visualization and sonification of urban navigation. The images we places along a satellite map, creating a collage of Google Earth satellite imagery and the live uploaded photos from the intertwining paths walked by the three participants. This very information was used musically, to create an ever-evolving pulsing polyrhythm representing the proximity of the walkers.

## 5 Visceral Mobiles

Much in the way that *Global String* was a sensor-network hybrid work that reconciled the visceral nature of gesture with the communicative potential of networks, we now describe an experimental system that configures a mobile system to merge locative media and gestural elements. The goal was to build a system where the music became a dynamic media flow that represented the collective action of a community of participants. At the same time the music represented group activity, each user needed to have a sense of his part in the whole. By balancing these two requirements, we hoped to address the issue of reconciling local activity with social connectivity. We will introduce the notion of *reflexive translucence* as a technique of audio display to address this.

The desire to detect individual and group dynamic delineate two distinct contexts – personal context and community context. These two contexts must be aggregated and feed process generating the musical output. The dispatching of this contextual information needs to be agnostic of the information architecture of the system. That is to say, the message passing needed to work both in a client-server model or a peer-to-peer model, with the possibility of a hybrid architecture, to function at all points across the networked system.

### 5.1 Sensing and Localization

Sensing personal context was achieved via on-device sensors. We used NIME instrument building techniques described above, to equip a portable electronics device with several types of sensors. A data-acquisition back plane was created in a way to dock onto the back of the device. The data acquisition card could accept up to eight analog 0-5V inputs from sensors, digitize them, and send the information to the device over USB. We used five sensor channels – two force-sensing resistors (FSR) as pressure sensors, a two-dimensional accelerometer, and a gyroscope. The FSR's were placed on the device so as to detect user grip pressure holding the device. The data from the accelerometers were filtered so as to report tilt of the device, and the gyroscope reported rotation around one axis of the device to report higher frequency rhythmical movement.

These sensors picked up listener gesture on the device. We sought to detect sub-conscious user participation, as well as volitional actions of the listeners. For example, the intensity with which a listener held the mobile device could be translated into the timbral brightness of the music; the rhythm the user made as he tapped along with the music could drive the tempo of the music. The angle the device was held at could seek and scrub back and forth.

While on-device sensors picked up the personal context, location of the users would give the community context. The relative geographies of users in the group drives the mixing of the different musical modules. Similar to *Malleable Mobile Music*, as a listening partner gets closer, their part is heard more prominently in the mix.

A host of movement and localization sensing technologies are available. While GPS was used with *Malleable Mobile Music* and *Net_Dérive*, there remained several unresolved issues. One was the coarseness of GPS location information. The GPS device reports the user's location about once per second. Another problem was that of scale. While it is interesting to conceive of a system where traversing a city block modulates a musical parameter, in reality it was questionable whether the scale of mapping (for example 100 meters to 100 Hertz) was perceivable and meaningful to the participant and spectators. To better understand the dynamics of how topology could be mapped to music, we used a controlled black box environment (15m x 15m) and visual tracking using the *Eyesweb* environment [30]. We used the glowing LCD screens of the handheld devices as the object to be tracked by an overhead video camera. Each screen was programmed to emit a different color, allowing the system to track several users.

The location data was used to control the audio synthesis in a number of ways. The position of tracked objects were used to route the signal from the contact microphones on the tables to varying resonance models. This allowed a smooth interpolation from one sound to another as a tracked object was moved from one to the other side of the space. This technique provided interesting opportunities for promoting collaborative performance: as one performer moved to various areas in the space, others could serve as inputs to the audio processes. The voice of one actor then, could be processed and modulated by the movements of another. Depending on the location and movement of a participant, sounds could be triggered, attenuated, altered using DSPs and placed anywhere inside the space defined by the quadraphonic audio system. Mapping from contextual information to musical information was done much in the same way as the sensors data mapping was.

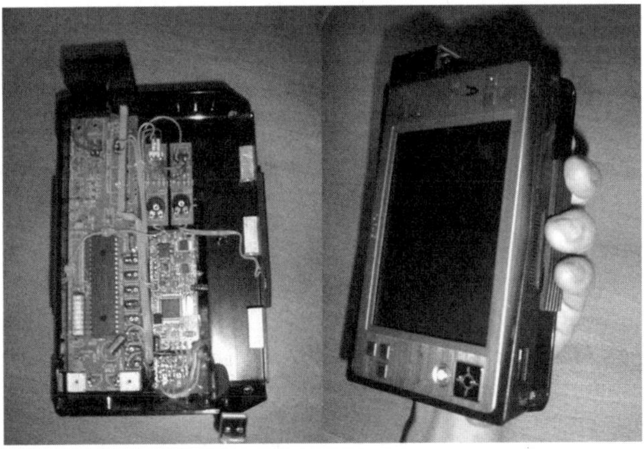

**Fig. 5.** Visceral mobile system, with sensor acquisition sub-system *(left)* with accelerometers, pressure sensors, and gyroscope, and Sony Vaio U-71 handheld host computer *(right)*

## 5.2 Local/Remote Hybrid Rendering

We developed a *music engine* to generate a music based on the contextual information. The musical result would then be rendered as a flow of digital audio data, to be delivered to each connected destination. Since all processes, from incoming contextual information, to outgoing audio delivery, take place over the network, there is inherent latency and transmission delay. This would have an impact on the feel of the system for each user

The music engine was conceived that could be instantiated and deployed either at the server level, or on the client devices. Audio was rendered either played locally, in the case of the clients, or streamed out to the network, in the case of the server. The music generation engine is controlled by information coming from the sensors or localization system. Gestural input from each member of the group arrives over the network as UDP packets in Open Sound Control (OSC) format [31]. Similarly, location data from Eyeweb is transmitted to the system over OSC. The engine reconciles the multiple control inputs to generate several parallel music channels that are sent to local sound output or network streamed up to an Icecast type audio relay [32]. The modularity of the engine architecture meant that it could be instantiated in a centralized server-based way (to represent community context), or on the mobile device of each user (for personal context). Any instantiation of the engine could play locally or make their output available as a network stream. To achieve the hybrid rendering effect, we concurrently ran a server-side engine alongside peer-based engines on the mobile terminals.

A single movement by one user could be mapped to several different parameters either on the server, or on the local device of several different audio processes.
The audio output of any instantiation of the music engine could be the network or a local soundcard. Likewise, the engines were able to render any incoming network audio stream, and mix it with locally synthesized sound. Not only could the clients run the same software as the server, but any peer could be a sender or a receiver.

The sound output of the server was mapped to a quadraphonic surround sound speaker system. The loudspeakers were arranged in a square around the perimeter of the test space. Amplitude panning across these four outputs permitted placing a virtual sound source at any point in the environmental soundscape. The sound output of the client devices were its own local sound output. Having sound emanating directly from the device situated it in the physical space. This acoustically placed a sound source in the space and differed markedly in effect compared to the virtual surround soundscape of the server output. We call this a *hybrid rendering* model where audio can be rendered remotely or locally to represent the personal and community levels of context.

## 6 In Use

By developing a system that enabled rich media interaction on mobile devices, we sought to create a live musical dynamic that could be executed by non-musicians. To test this system, The user group for the study consisted of 15 professional actors and actresses taking part in the theatre workshop. They would work in small groups to rehearse an improvised sketch. This corresponded well to the number of prototype devices on hand (3), and provided a good variation of combination of users running through the same scenario.

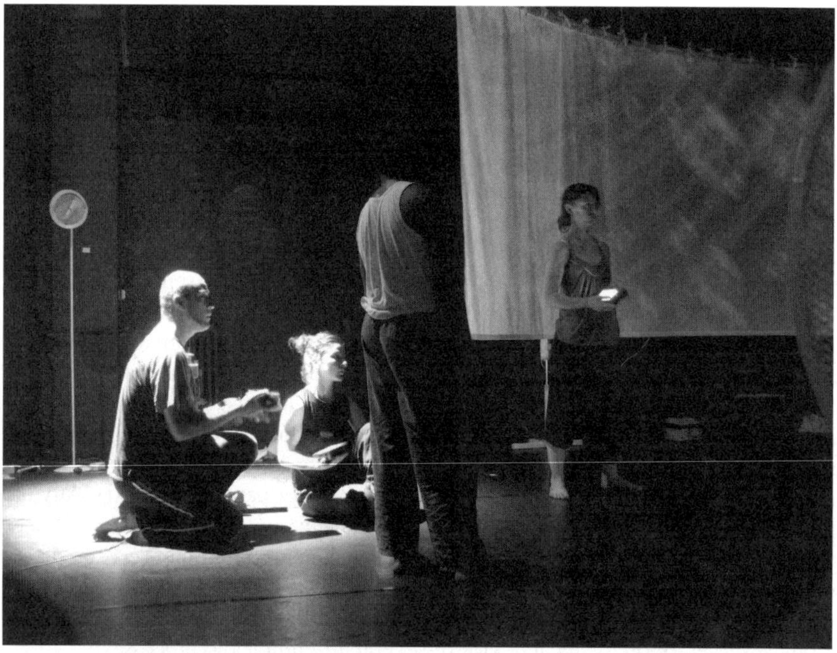

**Fig. 6.** Visceral mobile music in theatre test setting, with three actors holding a mobile terminal inside the set environment and listening to cues generated by the hybrid audio display

The use of actors and actresses was consistent with the use of the black box space as a controlled environment for location tracking. As actors, they were accustomed to abstracting an environment and constructing a temporary reality based on the set, and to live out their part. Although they were professionals in their domain (theatre), these users can be considered neutral and uninformed with respect to the technology at hand, as well as the musical processes proposed. In this sense, the actors and actresses represented a neutral user base similar to calling upon colleagues in a research lab or students in a university to conduct a user study. The actors could follow indications and reproduce scenarios, and they were not biased as musicians might be about the musical possibilities of such a system. In this way, the choice of the theatre and actors provided the controlled environment to reduce unknown variables, while their neutral stance with respect to technology and music made them an impartial test subjects. We hoped to contain the potentially wide ranging variation of social systems and geographical localization, to focus on the individual/group dynamic and the music it could produce.

The black box theatre space was filled out by a sparse set that was a combination of physical objects and boundaries and video projection. The users worked in groups of five, with three holding a device, two without, to act out a short sketch. The text was written so as to be reproducible, but their choreography in space and their gestures were not notated. Instead it was left to the actors/actresses to act out the script, articulating and moving in the way that allowed them to best express the text. Interactive soundscapes were programmed to accompany the scene. Sound filled in the sparse physical set, sonically painting a virtual environment that described an imaginary space. The quadraphonic sound system projected the background decor establishing the ambiance. As the actors moved through the space, detecting community context by the camera tracking system modulated sounds in this environment. The personal context of each actor pick up by the sensors articulated sounds locally on the devices. This accompanied and sonified the sense of the actors picking up and playing with sonorous objects in the skit. At time a playful dialog could be set up as gestures producing sounds on an object could be tossed or passed from one actor to another. The distribution of music engines across the network of devices worked invisibly in the background to render audio locally on-device or stream to other peers. The actor did not have to be concerned with the technology, for them they were passing sound objects around in an imaginary space. Their gestures operated on these sounding objects while the space itself musically responded to their movements.

The information specific to a local user is rendered directly on his client and is not subject to network latency, giving the user a sense of the system responding in a snappy way to her own actions. This has a twofold effect, first of apparent responsiveness of the system and second of task specific audio localization. Community context, on the other hand, pass through the network and server, to be aggregated. Latency is less of an issue here as each individual's part contributes to a musical whole. The hybrid audio display technique parallels the locus of action, placing user-centric actions acoustically at the device, and community-centric actions in the public sound space.

## 7 Reflexive Translucence

The term *social translucence* is used in the field of Social Computing to describe information displays that reflect social dynamic [33]. These systems support coherent group behavior by making actors aware and accountable for their actions by making them visible through representation and abstraction. A system exhibiting translucence displays faithful yet abstract representations of the state of a community. Here the public audio display can be considered to have the property of translucence. It sonically reflects and displays the group dynamic to its members, and fulfills the qualities fundamental to social translucence, those of visibility, awareness, and accountability. With the dual personal/community contexts, *Visceral Mobile Music* must not only give a global view of the situation also represent local action back to its originating user in a compelling way. The locally rendered audio needs to be responsive and satisfy an immediacy for the user to have a *sense of agency* connecting his intention or originating act to the resulting media displayed [34]. The whole system, then, exhibits social translucence and at the same time affords a sense of individual agency.

We introduce here the notion of *reflexive translucence*, the hybridization of group translucence and individual sense of agency, where the two are organically intertwined. The system has a view and is able to display the global state of the community. Within this community, each individual user must have a sense of her part in the whole. The community and its constituent individuals are forcibly related. The *reflexive translucence* of the proposed hybrid display system recognizes the two types of identities, individual and group, that emerge in the total environment.

## 8 Conclusions

We have described a second-generation mobile music system that captures both personal user context as well as group, community dynamic. While the system makes use of advanced mobile electronics technology, it has been conceived as an artists system, and in this way distinguishes itself from products created under marketing constraints. Similarly, the system has been evaluated by non-musicians in a creative context. This approach calls upon techniques and methodology from several disciplines, including interactive instrument design, human computer interaction, and social computing.

Inasmuch as we intended the system to be at the cutting edge of technology, we wished it to have a depth of musical expression. In order to explore the depth of musical interaction, we called upon the field of NIME and its predecessors to understand the richness of gestural sonic interaction. Musical instruments built with sensor interfaces, and performance practice on such instruments, including ensemble performance, and compositional notions of *idiomatic writing* help us to find the musical voice of digital technology. Retracing the history of network music, including precursors in radio art and telephone music, aid us to understand the potential of communications technologies. As temporal accuracy is difficult to attain, we looked at examples that explored the spatial, social potential of networks as a musical medium. One installation project by the author was presented as using both sensor and network technology, to create a long-distance instrument that could be performed by virtuosi or played by lay-visitors.

Artists have already begun to use geographic localization systems for creative practice. Locative media and mobile music exist today as vibrant areas of artistic output. By taking the lessons gleaned from interactive sensor music projects, we sought to inject a physical sense to extend upon prior work. Experience with network audio systems aided to flesh out the participative group dynamic of the new system. by combining these two qualities, we arrive at visceral mobile music, and the different musical and design implications it affords. First we observe that the system is capable of sensing two distinct contexts: personal and community. On device sensors are suited to detect users' direct conscious and sub-conscious gestures, while location tracking capture the state of the community. We propose a novel *hybrid audio display* system that situates these two contexts sonically in space. Furthermore, the combined client/server and peer/peer architecture of the system affords an immediacy and responsiveness for personal context all while aggregating information from multiple users to project group dynamic.

The system satisfies the qualities of *social translucence*, and with the sensing of two contexts coupled with hybrid display techniques, extends this notion to be able to represent not only a view of the group, but provide for each participant a meaningful compelling sense of agency for his part in the whole. We coin the term *reflexive translucence* to describe this multilayered concurrent representation. Finally we describe a field trial where the system is put to use in a controlled black box theatre environment. This test case proves practical for several reasons, including the possibility to study location tracking on a smaller-than-urban scale. Actors constitute interesting test subjects as they are non-musicians yet are creative practitioners.

Through this approach we have sought to apply creative practice and technology development in parallel, each with the rigor of its respective field. By doing so, we hoped to create a system that pushed present day technology to its creative potential. We hoped that by drawing upon related fields we could gain some insight into expressive possibilities not otherwise explored. Calling upon methodologies from HCI and social computing helped to inform the design of the system to be not purely technical nor purely artistic. By conceiving of the system as a framework built on technical specifications that had expressive qualities, we hoped to arrive at a result that had a generality and pertinence beyond the singularity of an individual artwork. In this way, we situate the creative act in the process of research.

## References


1. Lambiotte, R., Ausloos, M.: Uncovering collective listening habits and music genres in bipartite networks. Phys. Rev. E 72, 66107 (2005)
2. Poupyrev, I., Lyons, M.J., Fels, S., Blaine, T.: New Interfaces For Musical Expression Workshop. In: Human Factors in Computing Systems CHI 2001 Extended Abstracts (2001)
3. New Interfaces for Musical Expression, `http://www.nime.org`
4. Weiser, M.: Creating the Invisible Interface. In: Proc. ACM UIST, p. 1 (1994)
5. Glinsky, A.: Theremin: Ether Music and Espionage. University of Illinois Press, Urbana, Illinois (2000)
6. Mathews, M.: The Radio Baton and Conductor Program, or: Pitch, the Most Important and Least Expressive Part of Music. Computer Music J. 15, 4 (1991)
7. Waisvisz, M.: The Hands, a Set of Remote MIDI-Controllers. In: Proc Int. Computer Music Conf. (1985)
8. Tanaka, A.: Musical Performance Practice on Sensor-based Instruments. In: Wanderley, M., Battier, M. (eds.) Trends in Gestural Control of Music, pp. 389–405. IRCAM, Paris (2000)
9. Weill, K.: Möglichkeiten absoluter Radiokunst. Gesammelte Schriften, Berlin (1990)
10. Benjamin, W.: The Work of Art in the Age of Mechanical Reproduction. In: Arendt, H., Zohn, H. (eds.) (trans.) Illuminations, Schocken Books, New York (1968)

11. Landy, L.: Understanding the Art of Sound Organization. MIT Press, Cambridge (2007)
12. Labelle, B.: Radio Territories. Errant Bodies Press, Los Angeles (2006)
13. Bosma, J.: From Net.Art To Net.Radio And Back Again: Rediscovering And Enlarging The Entire Radio Spectrum. Acoustic Space, Riga (1998)
14. Gresham-Lancaster, S.: The Aesthetics and History of the Hub: The Effects of Changing Technology on Network Computer Music. Leonardo Music Journal 8, 39–44 (1998)
15. Cooperstock, J.R., Roston, J., Woszczyk, W.: Broadband networked audio: Entering the era of multisensory data distribution. In: 18th International Congress on Acoustics (April 2004)
16. Chafe, C., Gurevich, M., Leslie, G., Tyan, S.: Effect of time delay on ensemble accuracy. In: Proceedings of the International Symposium on Musical Acoustics (2004)
17. Locus Sonus, `http://locusonus.org`
18. Tanaka, A.: Composing as a Function of Infrastructure. In: Ehrlich, K., Labelle, B. (eds.) Surface Tension: Problematics of Site, Errant Bodies Press, Los Angeles (2003)
19. Tanaka, A., Bongers, B.: Global String: A Musical Instrument for Hybrid Space. In: Proc. cast 2001: Living in Mixed Realities, pp. 177–181. Fraunhofer IMK, St. Augustin (2001)
20. Mobile Music Workshop, `http://www.mobilemusicworkshop.org`
21. Bassoli, A., Cullinan, C., Moore, J., Agamanolis, S.: TunA: A Mobile Music Experience to Foster Local Interactions. In: Proc. UBICOMP (2003)
22. Gaye, L., Maize, R., Holmquist, L.E.: Sonic City: The Urban Environment as a Musical Interface. In: Proc. NIME (2003)
23. Harris, Y.: Taking Soundings – Investigating Coastal Navigations and Orientations in Sound. In: Proc. Mobile Music Workshop (2007)
24. Koleva, B., Taylor, I., Benford, S., et al.: Orchestrating a Mixed Reality Performance. In: Human Factors in Computing Systems CHI 2001 (2001)
25. Big Urban Game, `http://www.decisionproblem.com/bug/bug2.html`
26. Socialight, `http://socialight.com/`
27. Stenton, S.P., Wee, S., Hull, R., et al.: Mediascapes: Context-Aware Mutlimedia Experiences. Technical report, HP Labs HPL-2007-113 (2007)
28. Tanaka, A.: Mobile Music Making. In: Proc. NIME (2004)
29. Gemeinboeck, P., Tanaka, A., Dong, A.: Instant Archaeologies: Digital Lenses to Probe and to Perforate the Urban Fabric. In: Proc. ACM Multimedia (2006)
30. Eyesweb, `http://www.eyesweb.org`
31. Open Sound Control, `http://opensoundcontrol.org`
32. Icecast, `http://www.icecast.org`
33. Erickson, T., Kellogg, W.A.: Social Translucence: An Approach to Designing Systems that Mesh with Social Processes. ACM Transactions on Human Computer Interface 7(1), 59–83 (2000)
34. Tanaka, A.: Interaction, Agency, Experience, and the Future of Music. In: Brown, B., O'Hara, K. (eds.) Consuming Music Together: Social and Collaborative Aspects of Music Consumption Technologies. Computer Supported Cooperative Work (CSCW) 35, Springer, Dordrecht (2006)

# Designing a System for Supporting the Process of Making a Video Sequence

Shigeki Amitani and Ernest Edmonds

Creativity & Cognition Studios,
Australasian CRC for Interaction Design,
University of Technology, Sydney, Australia
shigeki@shigekifactory.com, ernest@ernestedmonds.com
http://www.creativityandcognition.com

**Abstract.** The aim of this research is to develop a system to support video artists. We have analysed the process of making a video sequence in collaboration with an experienced video artist so that design rationales of the system for artists can be obtained through artists' practices. Based on this analysis we identified design rationales for a system to support the process of making a video sequence, then a prototype system called "Knowledge Nebula Crystallizer for Time-based Information (KNC4TI)" has been developed accordingly. Further development towards a generative system is also discussed.

**Keywords:** Design, video making, cognitive process, sketching, software, time-based information, generative system.

## 1 Introduction

In composing a video sequence, an editing tool is indispensable. Traditionally, conventional video editing tools have been designed for industrial video productions which are different from the ways artists compose video sequences. While industrial video productions need tools to organise a certain video sequence along with a storyboard devised in advance, artistic video productions tend to proceed more through interactions between an artist and a work, rather than following a pre-defined storyboard. That is, technologies help artists to break new ground from an artistic perspective, however, they are not optimally designed for artists' practices.

Recently, artists as well as industrial video producers have started to use computer software for their compositions. Most video editing software has been developed as a metaphor of the traditional editing tools such as films and VCRs. This means that video editing software does not provide suitable interactive representations for artists.

The aim of this research is to design and develop a system that support the process of making a video sequence for artists. This paper presents: (1) investigation of the process of making a video sequence to identify design rationales for a supporting system in collaboration with a professional video artist; (2)

R. Adams, S. Gibson, and S. Müller Arisona (Eds.): DAW/IF 2006/2007, CCIS 7, pp. 171–186, 2008.

development of a prototype system called "Knowledge Nebula Crystallizer for Time-based Information (KNC4TI)" that supports the process based on the investigation results; and (3) plans for extending the KNC4TI system to a generative system.

## 2 Related Work

In order to understand design processes in detail, a number of analyses, especially in architects' design processes, have been conducted [1][2][3][4], however, most of the studies focused on design processes of non-time-based information. Few analyses have been conducted on those of time-based information such as making video sequence and musical composition. Tanaka [5] has pointed out that the problem in analyses conducted so far in the musical composition research field is that although generic models for musical composition processes have been proposed based on macroscopic observations, little has been conducted to investigate microscopically how each stage in those models proceeds and how transitions between stages occurs [6]. Similarly, few microscopic analyses have been conducted on the process of making a video sequence.

From the viewpoint of human-computer interaction research, Shipman et al. [7] have developed a system called "Hyper-Hitchcock". This system has been developed based on detail-on-demand concept that facilitates users to index video clips and to navigate video sequences efficiently.

Yamamoto et al. [8] have developed ARTWare, a library of components for building domain-oriented multimedia authoring environments. It was developed particularly for empirical video analysis of usability analysis.

These systems above have focused on supporting navigation processes and analyses of video contents, where as we consider that it is important to support its entire process, from the early stages where ideas are not clear to the final stages where a concrete work is produced in authoring information artefacts.

Shibata et al. [9] have claimed the importance of an integrated environment that supports entire process of creative activities, as the process is inseparable by nature. This research takes the knowledge creation viewpoint to enable this integration concept. Hori et al. have proposed a framework of the process of knowledge creation called Knowledge Liquidization & Knowledge Crystallization in order to fill a gap between theoretical frameworks and human practices [10]. Knowledge Liquidization means dissolving knowledge into small granularity that have a core grounding to the real world and that preserve the local semantic relationships around the core. Knowledge Crystallization means restructuring relationships among the granular units in accordance with a current context.

Suppose you are writing a paper, you refer to a number of relevant books and papers. You do not merely pile what is written in them as solid blocks, but you extract relevant parts (such as a paragraph, sentences, etc., i.e. semantic segments) from the books and the papers and fuse them into your paper.

Hori et al. also proposed a conceptual system called Knowledge Nebula Crystallizer that supports the process of Knowledge Liquidization & Knowledge

Crystallization [10]. The essential functions are: (1) dissolving information into small semantic segments (corresponding to Knowledge Liquidization); and (2) restructuring relationships among these semantic segments (corresponding to Knowledge Crystallization). Actual systems have been implemented and applied to several domains (e.g., [11]). We are developing a system called Knowledge Nebula Crystallizer for Time-based Information (KNC4TI) for supporting the process of making a video sequence based on the knowledge perspective.

## 3 A Case Study

We have investigated the process of making a video sequence to identify design rationales for a video authoring tool that fits to designers' cognitive processes. It was a collaborative work with an experienced video artist (we call the artist "participant" in this paper). Retrospective reporting of protocol analysis [12], questionnaires and interviewing methods were analysed. Overall tendencies observed in this research are summarised as below:

- Conceptual works such as considering whole structure of a piece, semantic segmentation of a material movie are conducted on the participant's sketch book
- Software is mainly used for:
  - Observing what is really going on in a material video sequence
  - Implementing the result of his thoughts in his sketch in response to what is seen on the software

The analysis shows that conceptual design processes are separated from implementation processes, while they cannot be separated with each other. Design process is regarded as a "dialog" between the designer and his/her material [13]. Facilitating designers going back and forth between whole and a part, and between conceptual and represented world will support this design process.

### 3.1 Roles of Sketching

Sketching plays significant roles that existing software does not cover. Sketching allows designers: (1) to externalise designer's multiple viewpoints simultaneously with written and diagrammatic annotations; and (2) to visualise relationships between the viewpoints that a designer defines. In the following sections we discuss how these two features work in the process of making a video sequence.

**Written and Diagrammatic Annotations for Designers' Multiple Viewpoints.** Figure 1 shows the participant's sketch. Each of the six horizontal rectangles in Figure 1 represents the entire video sequence. All six rectangles refer to one same video sequence with different labels so that the participant can plan what should be done regarding to each viewpoint represented with the labels. From the top to the bottom they are labelled as follows (shown in (1) of Figure 1):

**Movements** movements of physical objects such as person coming in, a door opening, etc.
**Sound levels** change of sound volume
**Sound image** types of sounds (e.g. "voices", etc.)
**Pic (= picture) level** change of density of the image
**Pic image** types of the images
**Compounded movements** plans

These elements are visualised in the sketch based on the timeline conventions. Although some of the existing video authoring tools present sound level with timelines as the second rectangle shows, existing software allows limited written annotations on a video sequence, and eventually it does not provide sufficient functionality for externalising multiple viewpoints. Especially the top sequence labelled as "movement" is conceptually important in making a video sequence, which is not supported by any video authoring tools. As (1) in Figure 1 shows, a mixture of written and diagrammatic annotations works for analysing what is going on in the video sequence.

As shown in (2) of Figure 1, a certain part of the material sequence is annotated in different ways in each rectangle in order to describe conditions represented by the rectangle, that is: *speak; zero (with shading); null; black; T (or a T-shaped symbol); meter.*

This is a power of multiple viewpoints with written annotations. These annotations are explanations of a certain part of a video sequence in terms of each correspondent viewpoint. For example, in terms of "Sound levels", this sketch shows that the sound level is set to zero at this point of the sequence.

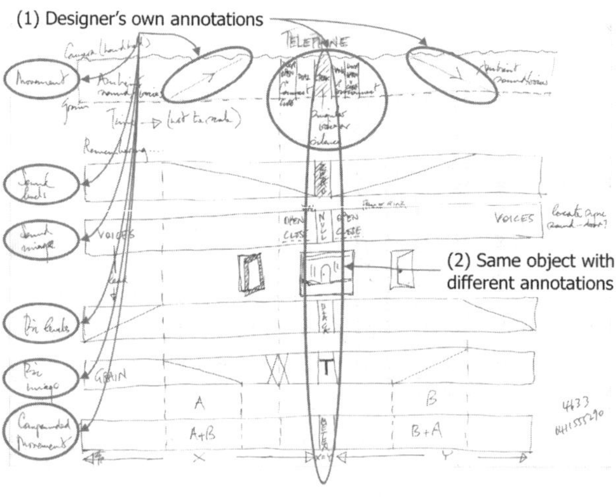


**Fig. 1.** Annotations from multiple viewpoints

**Visualising Relationships between Multiple Viewpoints.** The participant also externalises the relationships across the viewpoints in his sketch by using both written and diagrammatic annotations as shown in Figure 2.

Sketching supports designers to think semantic relationships such as "voices leads pics" shown in (1) of Figure 2, as well as relationships among physical features such as timing between sounds and pictures. (2) indicates that the participant visualised the relationships between picture images and his plan on a certain part of the material sequence by using written and diagrammatic annotations. (3) shows that the participant was thinking about the relationships across the viewpoints.

The relationships that the participant visualised are both physical and semantic. Some authoring tools support visualising physical relationships, however, they have few functions to support semantic relationships among viewpoints of designers

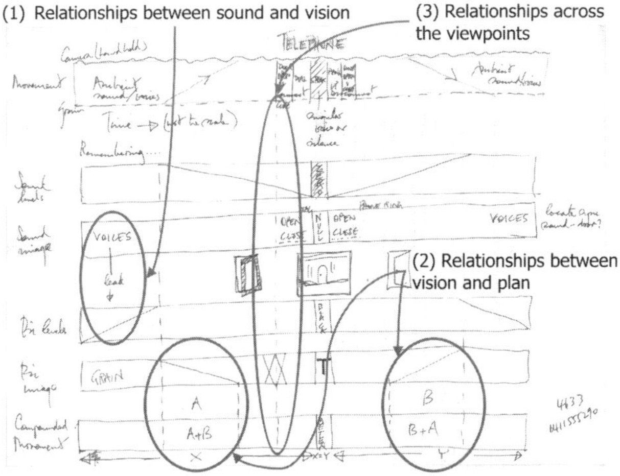


**Fig. 2.** Relationships between multiple viewpoints

Sketching, on the other hand, assists this process. It provides a holistic view of time-based information. Implementation of these features of sketching to software will facilitate designers going back and forth between conceptual and physical world, and whole and a part, so that the process of making a video sequence is supported.

### 3.2 Roles of Software

We investigated the process of making a video sequence with software. It was the first time for the participant to use software for editing the piece he sketched as shown in the previous section. That is, the process was the earliest stage of using video-authoring software for the new piece. The participant was to edit a material video sequence composed of a single shot. The experiment setting was as below:

**Software.** The editing tool that the participant used was FinalCut Pro HD which the participant had been using for about five years.
**Time.** The duration was up to the participant (eventually it was 90 minutes).
**Place.** The video editing was conducted at studio at Creativity & Cognition Studios, University of Technology, Sydney.

The process of making a video sequence, including the participant's physical actions and actions in the computer display, was recorded by digital video cameras. After authoring a video sequence, the participant was asked to conduct a retrospective report on his authoring process with watching the recorded video data. We adopted the retrospective report method so that we can excerpt cognitive processes in actual interactions as much as possible. The recorded video data was used as a visual aid to minimise memory loss of the participant [4]. Following this the participant was asked to answer a free-form questionnaire via e-mail.

**Observing "Facts" in a Material Sequence.** In the process of making a video sequence, the software plays a role of elaborating what the participant decided roughly in his sketch. This process has features listed below:

- Transitions from macroscopic viewpoints appeared in his sketch to microscopic actions such as focusing on time durations were frequently observed
- Almost no transition in the opposite direction was observed, such as seeing the effect of microscopic changes on the entire concept

The participant reported that he was just looking at the film clip as follows:

> [00:01:30] *At this stage, I'm just looking again at the film clip.*
> [00:02:32] *So again, still operating on this kind of looking at the image over, the perceptual thing.*

This was reported for 18 times in his protocol data. These observations occurred at the early and late phase of the process as shown in Figure 3. The observation of facts was 75 minutes, and the exploration of possibilities was 5 minutes, the rest was for other events such as reading a manual to solve technical problems and talking to a person.

In this process of observing facts, it was also observed that the participant was trying to find a "rhythm" in the material sequence which the participant calls "metre". This is for checking the actual duration for each scene that the participant considered as "a semantic chunk".

> [00:02:23] *One of the things I've been thinking about ... is actually to, is actually well, what is the kind of metre, what is the rhythm that you are going to introduce into here.*

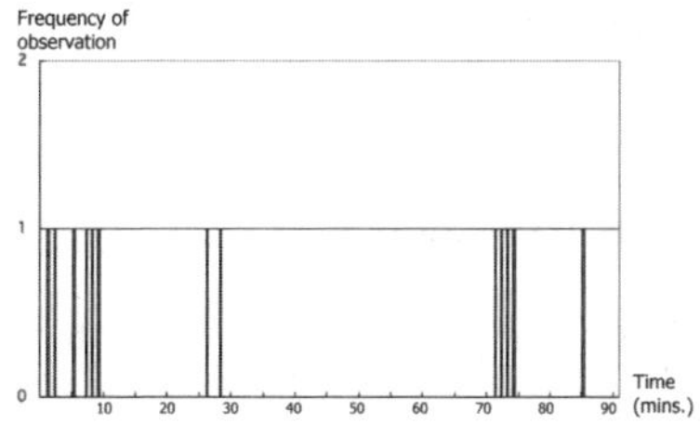


**Fig. 3.** The time distribution of observation process

The participant recorded precise time durations of the semantic chunks and listed them in his sketchbook. This means that the participant was trying to refine his idea by mapping conceptual elements to a physical feature.

> [00:08:32] *It's a matter of analysing each, almost each frame to see what's going on and making a decision of. Having kind of analyse what's going on and making a decision of, well therefore this duration works out of something like this. The durations are in seconds and frames, so that [...] 20 unit [...]. It counts from 1 to 24 frames, 25th frame rolls over number second.*

**Trial-and-Error Processes.** Video authoring software supports trial-and-error processes with "the shot list" as well as the "undo" function. Existing video editing software usually allows designers to list files and sequences used for their current video compositions (this is called a shot list). The list function in a video editing tool supports to compare multiple alternatives. It allows a designer to list not only files to be potentially used but also created sequences. In the retrospective report, the participant said:

> [00:11:10] *It would be a kind of parallel process where you make a shot list is causing what they call a shot list [pointing at the left most list-type window in FinalCut]. And essentially you go through on the list, the different shots, the different scenes as we would often call, um. Whereas I'm just working with one scene, dynamics within one scene. So, I'm working with a different kind of material, but it's related too.*

Although this function helps designers conducting trial-and-error processes through comparing multiple possibilities, the participant mentioned a problem:

> [A-4] *Film dubbing interface metaphor [is inconvenient]. The assumption is that a TV program or a cinema film is being made, which forces the adoption of the system to other modes. For instance, why should there be only one Timeline screen? There are many instances where the moving image is presented across many screens.*

Existing video editing software has adopted a metaphor of the tools used in industrial film making process. As a result, the software presents only the time axis in the sequence currently composed. This problem was also reported in the context of musical composition [6].

### 3.3 Identified Design Rationales

Three design rationales have been identified based on our analysis.

1. Allowing seamless transition between a conceptual holistic viewpoint (overview) and a partial implementation of the concepts (detail)
2. Visualising multiple viewpoints and timelines
3. Enhancing trial-and-error processes

**Allowing Seamless Transition between Overview and Detail Representations.** The process of making a video sequence, especially in an artistic context, is a design process which has hermeneutical feature, that is, the whole defines a meaning of a part and at the same time meanings of parts decide the meaning of the whole [14]. So a video authoring tool should be designed to support this transition between whole and a part.

Although the overview + detail concept is a generic design rationale applicable to various kinds of design problems, we consider that this is an important strategy for the process of creating time-based information, because time-based information takes a form which is difficult to have an overview by nature. For example, in order to see the effect on the whole caused by a partial change, you have to watch and/or listen to the sequence through from the beginning to the end, or you have to memorise the whole and to imagine what impact the partial change has on the whole. In an architectural design, the effects of partial changes are immediately visualised on the sketch, which makes it easy for designers to transit between whole and a part. This transition should be supported in the process of making a video sequence.

The participant first conducted a conceptual design in the sketching process by overviewing the whole with using written and diagrammatic annotations to articulate relationships among the annotated elements. Then, the participant proceeds to detail implementation of the video sequence on the software, which was a one-way process. As the conceptual design of the whole is inseparable from the detailed implementation on the software, they should be seamlessly connected.

The reason why this one-way transition occurs may be partially because this is the early stage of the process of making a video sequence. However, we consider that this is because tools for conceptual design (sketch) and implementation (software) are completely separated. This causes that a designer does not modify a sketch once it is completed. This phenomenon was observed in the study on musical composition process [6]. It was observed that comparison between multiple possibilities occurred by providing an overview with the traditional score-metaphor interface. It is expected that providing an overview supports comparisons between multiple possibilities derived from partial modifications.

**Visualising Multiple Viewpoints and Timelines.** It was observed that the participant visualises multiple viewpoints and timelines, however, existing software presents only one timeline.

Amitani et al. [6] have claimed that a musical composition process does not always proceed along with the timeline of a musical piece based on their experiment. They also claimed the importance of presenting multiple timelines in musical composition. Some musicians compose a musical piece along with its timeline, however, we consider that tools should be designed to support the both cases. As video sequences are information with linearity as well as musical pieces, presenting multiple timelines should support the process of making a video sequence.

**Enhancing Trial-and-Error Processes.** As mentioned before, a shot list helps designers to understand relationships among sequences. In the questionnaire, he described how he uses the list:

> [A-5] *Selecting short segments into a sequence on the Timeline, to begin testing noted possibilities with actual practice and their outcomes.*

Although the shot list helps designers to some degree, the list representation only allows designers to sort the listed materials along with an axis such as alphabetical order. This is useful, however, designers cannot arrange them along with their own semantics. It makes it difficult for designers to grab relationships between files and sequences, so that the list representation prevents designers from full exploration of multiple possibilities.

Instead of the list representation, a spatial representation is more suitable to this type of information-intensive tasks [15]. While comparison between multiple possibilities has been conducted in designer's mind, externalisation of designer's mental space is helpful for deciding whether an information piece is used or not. Shoji et al. [16] have investigated differences between a list representation and a spatial representation. They found that a spatial representation contributes to elaborating concepts better than a list representation. We believe that spatial representations will facilitate a designer to compare multiple possibilities.

In the next section, a prototype system for supporting the process of making a video sequence with spatial representations is presented.

## 4 Knowledge Nebula Crystallizer for Time-Based Information

The Knowledge Nebula Crystallizer for Time-based Information has been developed with Java 1.4.2 on the Mac OS X platform. Figure 4 shows a snapshot of the KNC4TI system. The KNC4TI system is composed of: (1) OverviewEditor; (2) DetailEditor; (3) ElementViewer; and (4) ElementEditor. For a practical reason, we have adopted FinalCut Pro HD as the ElementEditor. In this section, each component is explained.

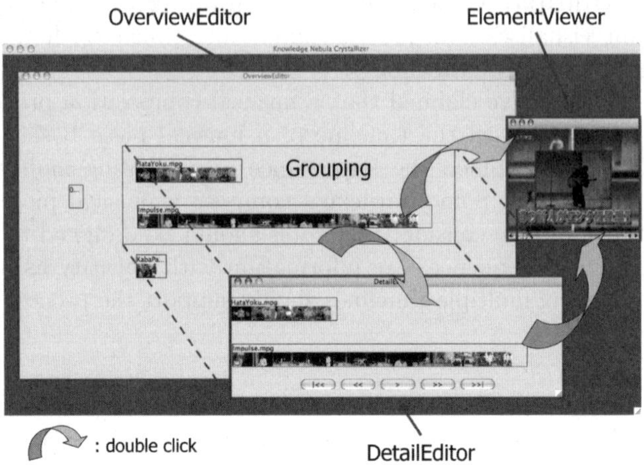


**Fig. 4.** A Snapshot of the KNC4TI System

### 4.1 OverviewEditor: Providing a Bird-Eye View

OverviewEditor provides, as the name says, the overview of what videos are available at hand. They are added by either a selection of a folder that contains videos to be potentially used or by drag & drop movie files into the OverviewEditor. Figure 5 shows the snapshot of the OverviewEditor.

Each video has its thumbnails in OverviewEditor so that a designer to grab what the video is about. When a video is double-clicked, the ElementViewer pops up and the video is played so that a designer can check the contents (right in Figure 4). The ElementViewer is a simple QuickTime-based viewer.

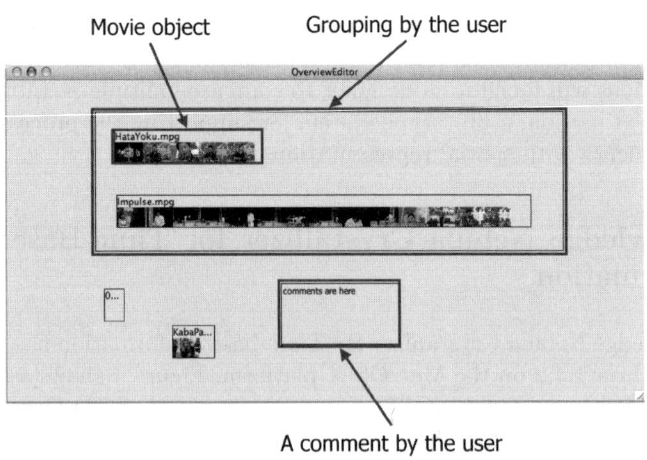


**Fig. 5.** OverviewEditor

The shot list in the FinalCut Pro HD is a similar component to the OverviewEditor in a sense that available videos are listed there, however, following interactions are advantages of adopting a spatial representation.

**Allowing semantic viewpoints.** While a list representation provides designers with a mechanically sorted file list, a two-dimensional space allows designers to arrange videos along with designers' viewpoints. For example, video files that might be used in a certain work can be arranged close so that the designer can incrementally formalise his or her ideas about the piece [17].

**Annotations.** An annotation box appears by drag & drop in a blank space in the OverviewEditor. A designer can put annotations and can freely arrange it wherever he or she wants on the OverviewEditor. This is an enhancement of written annotation function. That is, while a list representation allows only to put annotations about one video, a spatial representation allows to annotate regarding to not only videos themselves but also relationships between videos both in visual and semantic ways.

**Grouping.** A designer can explicitly group movie objects on the OverviewEditor. Grouped movie objects are moved as a group. Objects are addable to and removable from a group at anytime by drag & drop. This supports diagrammatic annotations.

**Copy & Paste.** A movie object does not always belong to only one group when a designer is exploring possibilities of what kind of combinations is good for a certain video work. To facilitate this process, copy & paste function was implemented. Whilst only one possibility can be explored in a timeline representation and a shot list on a normal video editing software, it visually allows a designer to examine multiple possibilities.

## 4.2 DetailEditor: A Place for Incremental Formalisation

The DetailEditor appears by double clicking a group on the OverviewEditor. The DetailEditor shows only the grouped objects in the clicked group as shown in Figure 4. Figure 6 shows a snapshot of the DetailEditor.

In the DetailEditor, the horizontal axis is a time line and vertical axis is similar to tracks. It plays the grouped videos from left to right. If two objects are

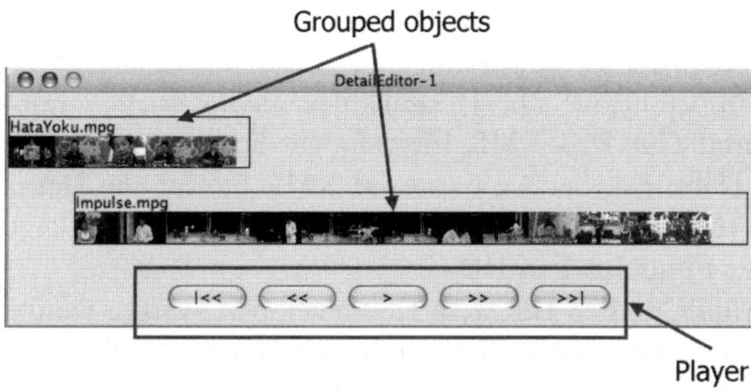


**Fig. 6.** DetailEditor

horizontally overlapped as Figure 6 shows, then the first video (Hatayoku.mpg) is played first, then in the middle of the video the next one (Impulse.mpg) is played. The timing when to switch from the first video to the second one is defined by the following rule: video 1 has a time duration $d_1$ and represented as a rectangle with width $l_1$ pixel, is located at $x = x_1$. Video 2 has a duration $d_2$ and represented, as in Figure 7, as a rectangle with width $l_2$ pixel, is located at $x = x_2$.

When the play button is pushed, play the video 1 in the ElementViewer and after time $t_1$, play the video 2. The playing duration $t_1$ is defined by the equation (1) in Figure 7.

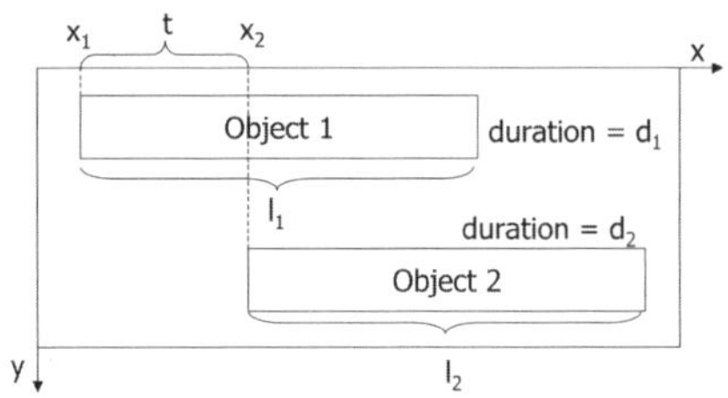


**Fig. 7.** The timing rule for playing overlaps

Along this rule, videos grouped into the DetailEditor are played from right to left in the ElementViewer. This facilitates designers to quickly check how a certain transition from one file to another looks like.

Designers can open as many DetailEditors as they wish so that they can compare and explorer multiple possibilities.

### 4.3 ElementEditor: Seamless Connection with FinalCut Pro HD

Starting from the OverviewEditor, a designer narrows down his focus with the DetailEditor and the ElementViewer, then the designer needs to work on the video piece more precisely. For this aim, we adopted FinalCut Pro HD as the ElementEditor.

The KNC4TI system is seamlessly connected with FinalCut Pro HD via XML. FinalCut Pro HD provides importing and exporting functions for .xml files of video sequence information. The DetailEditor also exports / imports .xml files formatted in Final Cut Pro XML Interchange Format [18] by double clicking any point on a DetailEditor. An exported XML file by the DetailEditor is automatically fed to FinalCut Pro HD. Figure 8 shows the linkage between the DetailEditor and FinalCut Pro HD.

Integrating FinalCut Pro HD with the developed system is advantageous because of the following reasons: First, it increases practicality. One of the most difficult things in applying a new system to practice is that practitioners are reluctant to replace their familiar tools. As FinalCut Pro HD is one of the most

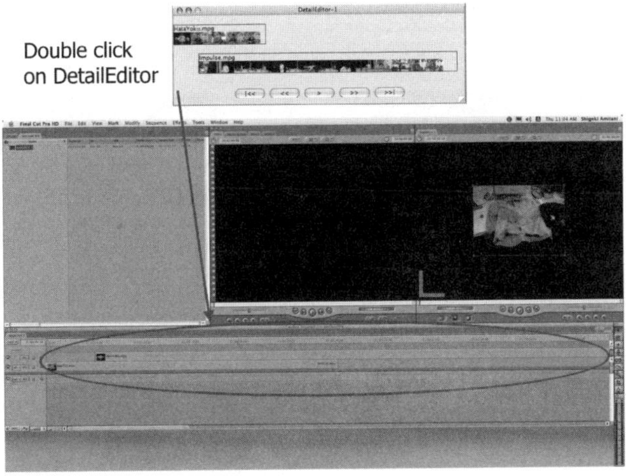


**Fig. 8.** Linkage between the DetailEditor and FinalCut Pro HD through XML import/export

used video authoring tools, KNC4TI could be used as an extension of the existing video authoring environment.

Second, it reduces development loads. It is not an efficient approach to develop a system that beats, or at least has the same quality as, a well-developed system such as FinalCut Pro HD. We are not denying the existing sophisticated systems, but extending what they can do for human designers.

## 5 Towards a Generative Video Authoring System

Edmonds has suggested that a computer can certainly be a stimulant for human creative activities [19]. The important question is how we can design a computer system that supports people to increase their capacities to take effective and creative actions. We are currently developing components that extend the current system to a generative system that stimulates designers' thinking.

Figure 9 shows the model of the generative systems. First, information artefacts (existing ones and/or new pieces of information) are collected and stored (left in Figure 9). A system (top in Figure 9) generates possible information artefacts (right in Figure 9). These outputs work in two ways: (1) as final products that a user can enjoy; (2) as draft materials that a user can modify (at the centre of Figure 9).

In order to deliver possible information artefacts to users, a component called D ynamic Concept Base (DCB) is being developed. It is a concept base that holds multiple similarity definition matrices which are dynamically reconfigured through interactions. The more the number of objects increases, the more difficult to grab the relationships on the physically limited display. In order to assist a designer to grab the overview of a movie file space, the way of arranging objects

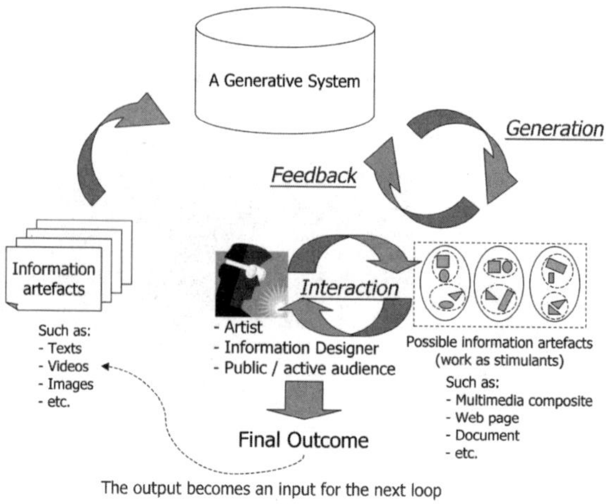


**Fig. 9.** How a Generative System Work

in a two-dimensional space is critical. Sugimoto et al. [20] have proved statistically that similarity based arrangement works better than random arrangement in the comprehension of information indicated in a two-dimensional space. That is, the DCB potentially has an ability to help a designer to understand an information space. Movie objects are arranged based on the similarities computed by the DCB.

Similarities between movies are computed based on annotations by natural language processing. While the arrangement is conducted by the system, it does not necessarily fit to a designer's context [21]. So the system should allow end-user

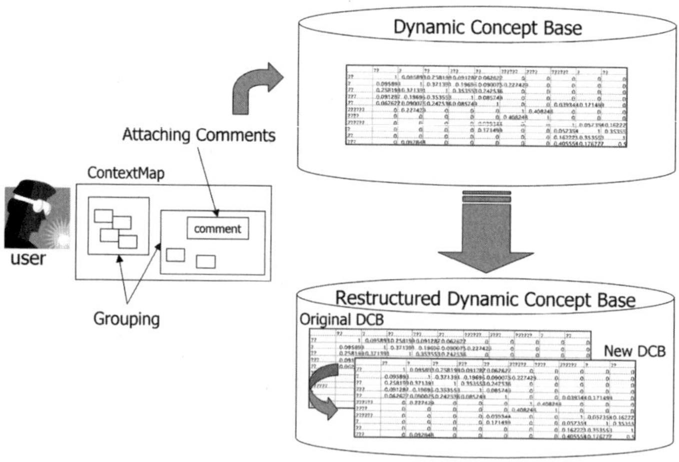


**Fig. 10.** Reconfiguring the DCB through Interactions

modification [22] or incremental formalisation of information artefacts [17]. The DCB is reconfigured through interactions such as rearranging, grouping and annotating objects. If two objects are grouped together by a designer, then the DCB computes their similarity again (Figure 10) so that the similarity definition becomes more contextually suitable.

## 6 Conclusion

In this paper, we presented: (1) the analysis of the process of making a video sequence to identify design requirements for a supporting system; (2) The developed system based on this analysis; and (3) plans for a generative system.

Design rationales for an appropriate video-authoring tool derived from our investigation which are summarised as three inter-related features: (1) Allowing seamless transition between a conceptual holistic viewpoint (overview) and a partial implementation of the concepts (detail); (2) visualising multiple viewpoints and timelines; and (3) enhancing trial-and-error processes. A prototype system "Knowledge Nebula Crystallizer for Time-based Information (KNC4TI)" is developed based on this analysis. We consider that knowledge obtained through this research contributes broader community of human-computer interactions.

## Acknowledgements

This project was supported by Japan Society of the Promotion for Science, and is supported by the Australasian CRC for Interaction Design and Australian Centre for the Moving Image. The authors are also grateful to Dr. Linda Candy and Mr. Mike Leggett for their useful comments for improving our research.

## References

1. Bilda, Z., Gero, J.: Analysis of a blindfolded architect's design session (2004)
2. Cross, N., Christiaans, H., Dorst, K.: Analysing Design Activity. John Wiley, Chichester (1997)
3. Eckert, C., Blackwell, A., Stacey, M., Earl, C.: Sketching across design domains (2004)
4. Suwa, M., Purcell, T., Gero, J.: Macroscopic analysis of design processes based on a scheme for coding designers' cognitive actions. Design Studies 19, 455–483 (1998)
5. Tanaka, Y.: Musical composition as a creative cognition process (in japanese). Report of Cultural Sciences Faculty of Tokyo Metropolitan University 307, 51–71 (2000)
6. Amitani, S., Hori, K.: Supporting musical composition by externalizing the composer's mental space. In: Proceedings of Creativity & Cognition 4 Loughborough University Great Britain October 13-16, pp. 165–172 (2002)
7. Shipman, F., Girgensohn, A., Wilcox, L.: Hyper-hitchcock: Towards the easy authoring of interactive video. Proceedings of INTERACT 2003, 33–40 (2003)

8. Yamamoto, Y., Nakakoji, K., Aoki, A.: Visual interaction design for tools to think with: Interactive systems for designing linear information. In: Proceedings of the Working Conference on Advanced Visual Interfaces (AVI 2002), Torento, Italy, pp. 367–372 (2002)
9. Shibata, H., Hori, K.: Toward an integrated environment for writing. In: Proceedings of Workshop on Chance Discovery European Conference on Artificial Intelligence (ECAI) (2004)
10. Hori, K., Nakakoji, K., Yamamoto, Y., Ostwald, J.: Organic perspecives of knowledge management: Knowledge evolution through a cycle of knowledge liquidization and crystallization. Journal of Universal Computer Science 10, 252–261 (2004)
11. Amitani, S.: A Method and a System for Supporting the Process of Knowledge Creation. PhD thesis, Department of Advanced Interdisciplinary Studies University of Tokyo (2004)
12. Ericsson, A., Simon, H.: Protocol Analysis: Verbal Reports as Data. MIT Press, Cambridge (1993)
13. Schoen, D.A.: The Reflective Practitioner: How Professionals Think in Action. In: Basic Books, New York (1983)
14. Snodgrass, A., Coyne, R.: Is designing hermeneutical? Architectural Theory Review 1, 65–97 (1997)
15. Marshall, C., Shipman, F.: Spatial hypertext: Designing for change. Communications of the ACM 38, 88–97 (1995)
16. Shoji, H., Hori, K.: S-conart: an interaction method that facilitates concept articulation in shopping online. AI & Society Social Intelligence Design for Mediated Communication 19, 65–83 (2005)
17. Shipman, F.M., McCall, R.J.: Incremental formalization with the hyper-object substrate. ACM Transactions on Information Systems 17, 199–227 (1999)
18. Inc., A. (Final cut pro xml interchange format)
19. Edmonds, E.: Artists augmented by agents (invited speech). In: Proceedings of the 5th international conference on Intelligent user interfaces New Orleans Louisiana United States, pp. 68–73 (2000)
20. Sugimoto, M., Hori, K., Ohsuga, S.: An application of concept formation support system to design problems and a model of concept formation process (in japanese). Journal of Japanese Society for Artificial Intelligence 8, 39–46 (1993)
21. Kasahara, K., Matsuzawa, K., Ishikawa, T., Kawaoka, T.: Vewpoint-based measurement of semantic similarity between words (in japanese). Journal of Information Processing Society of Japan 35, 505–509 (1994)
22. Fischer, G., Girgensohn, A.: End-user modifiability in design environments. In: Proceedings of the SIGCHI conference on Human factors in computing systems: Empowering people, Seattle, Washington, United States, pp. 183–192 (1990)

# Video Game Audio Prototyping with *Half-Life 2*

Leonard J. Paul

Lotus Audio,
Vancouver, BC, Canada
info@LotusAudio.com

**Abstract.** This paper describes how to utilize the *Half-Life 2* (*HL2*) Source engine and Open Sound Control (OSC) to communicate real-time sound event calls to a Pure Data (PD) sound driver. Game events are sent from *Half-Life 2* to the PD patch via OSC which triggers the sound across a network. The advantage of this approach is that the PD sound driver can have both the sample data and the sound behaviors modified in real-time, thus avoiding the conventional need for a lengthy recompilation stage. This technique allows for rapid iterative game audio sound design through prototyping which increases the efficiency of the work-flow of the game sound artist working on the current seventh-generation consoles and PC video games. This method is also of interest to researchers of game audio who wish to experiment with novel game audio techniques within the context of a game while it is running.

**Keywords:** Video game audio, video games, prototyping, Half-Life 2, Open Sound Control, OSC, game coding, game audio research.

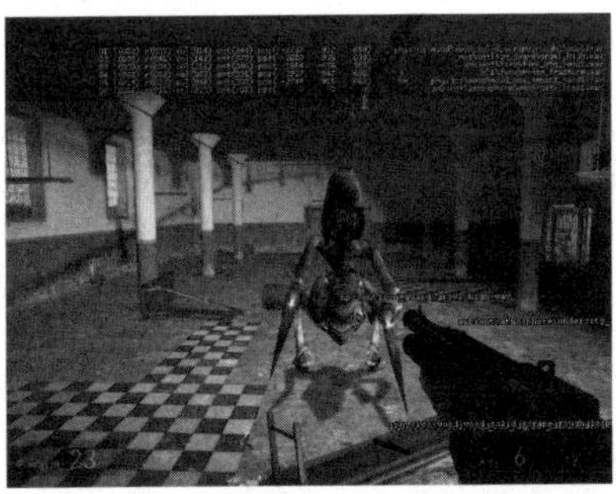

**Fig. 1.** Screenshot of *Half-Life 2* utilizing the Source Engine with debug output for audio

## 1 Introduction

With the release of Sony's Playstation 3 (PS3) and Microsoft's Xbox 360 (360), home video game console hardware now supports sufficient computing power to allow advanced levels of audio synthesis and processing. Older console systems, such as Sony's Playstation 2 (PS2) have very limited audio capabilities. The PS2 is only capable of 48 channels of ADPCM (3.5:1 compression factor) and had an architecture that

R. Adams, S. Gibson, and S. Müller Arisona (Eds.): DAW/IF 2006/2007, CCIS 7, pp. 187–198, 2008.

made it difficult to perform even simple processing such as filtering. When using their MultiStream audio library on the PS3, Sony now dedicates an entire core from its 3.2ghz cell processor thus allowing significant amounts of audio processing, such as over 512 channels of 128kbps MP3 (10.7:1 compression factor) decompression [1].

To take full advantage of the increased power of the current consoles, game audio sound designers must also develop new techniques that allow them to utilize the new systems to their fullest potential. Game audio sound designers are now faced with a paradigm shift of learning how to consider their audio designs as generative procedures that can create new results each time a sound is produced, similar to the way sounds are produced in nature. One of the best ways to gain control over a new system is to experiment with different techniques by utilizing prototyping early on in the development process. One successful technique when prototyping games was summarized as: "Enforce Short Development Cycles (More Time != More Quality)" [2]. Prototyping should allow the sound designer to quickly bridge the transition between inspiration and implementation of an interactive audio concept.

### 1.1 The Importance of Prototyping

Game audio prototyping enables the rapid implementation of dynamic real-time audio behaviors. Prototyping is effective in demonstrating the subjective attributes of the game such as game-play and pacing without requiring the entire game to be built ahead of time. In the interest of speed, one can view the prototype as a toy that can shed light into certain characteristics of interactivity that will be present in the game. For more linear based methods, such as basic sample playback with little interactivity, custom prototyping may not be the best option. One might use a software sampler to simulate how the game engine will play multi-sampled game sounds.

Even if the prototype is constructed in the same language as the game, such as C++, it should be noted that unrefined portions of the prototype should not find their ways into the final product just because these sections have been shown to be functional in the past [3]. This is a common mistake as it is easy to get attached to a prototype that one has spent significant time constructing. If one views the prototype as a sort of "sketch" then it is easy to see that although we can utilize many elements in the final product that there is a great need for removing certain elements along the way that do not strengthen the overall results. Not spending too much time on a prototype, being open to risk and attempting to solve a certain process different ways were found to be highly effective strategies when rapidly prototyping game ideas [2]. One of the most important choices when prototyping is the platform chosen to realize the prototype. It is largely a matter of personal choice but it should encourage creativity and enable the sound designer to realize interactive audio ideas relatively quickly. In this paper, Pure Data [4] has been chosen as the platform for prototyping but other platforms such as Reaktor[5], Max/MSP[6] and others could also be used as well.

### 1.2 Pure Data

PD is an open source cross-platform graphical programming language for Windows, Mac OS X, Linux and other platforms. PD is well-suited to audio prototyping in contrast to C++ whose learning curve is much more steep for artists, such as game sound designers. Part of the reason that PD is easier to learn is that it is more visual and interactive, which allows a much more hands-on approach to implementing interactive audio behaviors. Using PD can give the game sound designer additional creative control as well as gaining valuable skills and vocabulary to better work with sound coders when implementing the prototypes.

Optimization of an interpreted language such as PD is of prime concern for games, but with research being done into the compilation of PD code, such as the compilation of PD code to Java in the pd2j2me project[7], the issue of optimization may become less of an issue. The Berkley Software Distribution (BSD) license of PD allows its engine to be quite easily integrated with other projects as shown by the PD internet browser plug-in[8] and the PD VST plug-in[9]. It is worth noting that running PD as a VST plug-in allows the implementation of some portions of the prototype in PD and the rest of the prototype can be defined in the host application. Closed-source commercial packages such as Max/MSP and Reaktor might be a good option if direct integration into the game isn't required. Likely the main advantage is that the documentation and support for these commercial packages can make the learning curve easier than PD for most game sound designers.

### 1.3 Open Sound Control

OSC is a communications protocol that can be seen to be similar to MIDI over ethernet with the ability for flexible hierarchical data structures. The "oscpack" code package available from Ross Bencina eases the integration of OSC into existing code [10]. This code was integrated into the Source C++ code for a standard *Half-Life 2* (*HL2*) mod. The power of this method is that many maps can be downloaded and played using the OSC audio event layer, sometimes making *HL2* appear to be a very different game.

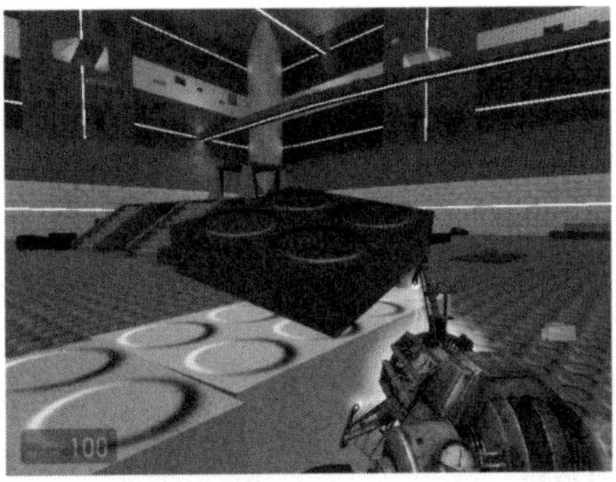

**Fig. 2.** Screenshot map dm_killbox_lego_hk that allows stacking of Lego bricks

There are many mods that allow you to explore a map at the scale of a mouse and even use the gravity gun to build lego brick towers (see figure 2). It is also possible to integrate the OSC code into full conversion mods that have the source code available to also allow for sending OSC audio event messages as well. With games becoming more complex, many game studios are choosing to utilize an existing game engine, such as the Source engine, to speed development. So, one could see prototyping utilizing the Source engine as being very valuable experience for working within the gaming industry.

### 1.4 Half-Life 2

*HL2* was chosen as a game environment for modification as it is highly customizable and has produced several popular titles besides *Half-Life 2*, such as *Counterstrike*, *Team Fortress*, *Portal* and more [11]. The creators of *HL2*, Valve Software, have allowed the Source toolset to be compiled using the free Microsoft Visual C++ 2005 Express Edition compiler[12], which opens the door to almost anyone to mod *HL2*.

The use of PD, *HL2*, OSC and the free C++ compiler results in a solution whose cost only amounts to the purchase of *HL2*, which was $19.95 at the time of writing [11].

**Table 1.** Valuable cheat codes for working with audio in *HL2*

| Cheat/Debug Code | Description |
|---|---|
| `sv_cheats 1` | Enable cheat codes |
| `impulse 101` | Gain all weapons with ammunition |
| `sv_soundemitter_ trace 1` | Show playing sounds in console |
| `snd_visualize 1` | Overlay .wav name on 3D display |
| `snd_show 1` | Overlay position, pan and volume |
| `displaysoundlist 1` | Show x,y,z axis indicators for sounds |

## 2 Technology

This technology allows a *HL2* mod to send out game events, via OSC, to the PD sound driver which plays the resulting audio for the events. The main difficulty was getting OSC to compile within the *HL2* Source code and the iterative construction of the PD sound driver. Once a few more additions have been made to the system, the goal is to make the code and process public to allow others to create similar systems.

### 2.1 Pure Data Sound Driver

To demonstrate the possibilities of audio prototyping for console games, a sound driver has been implemented utilizing PD. The initial version was developed in 2003 [12] and has enjoyed continual development by the author as part of the game audio curriculum at the Vancouver Film School. Figure 3 shows some of the windows of the driver, with the OSC messages at the game in the top PD window, a window showing the adaptive music patch, two windows showing the three sample cross-fade engine, and windows for FM synthesis (with the envelope), granulation and VST instruments for sound generation.

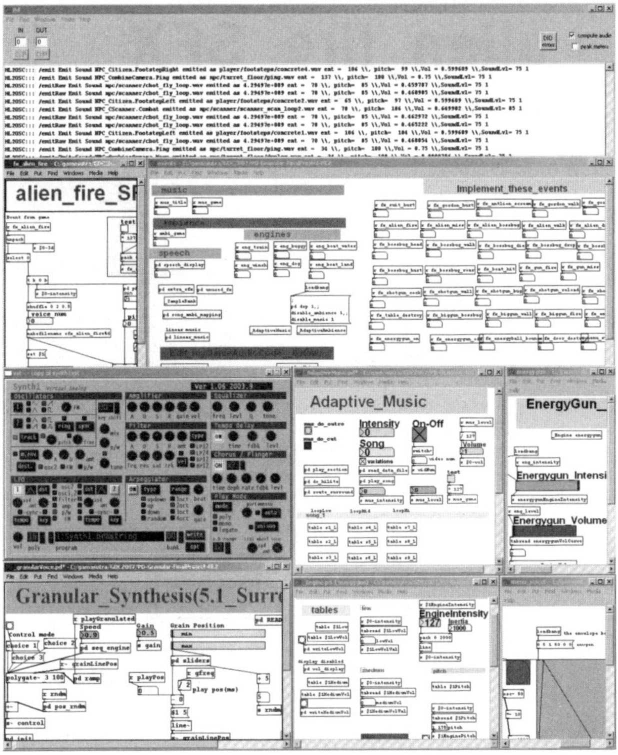


**Fig. 3.** Screenshots of PD sound driver including a granulation subpatch and a VST plug-in

All of the sound driver code has been completed in PD which allows the user to change any aspect of the audio code for the system. This visibility enables anyone to see exactly how all the functions of the sound generation is implemented as well as allows for modification of the code at any layer. Code encapsulation is implemented by hiding the lower-level driver code to avoid confusion with other areas of code which require modification. To ease the implementation of the game audio code, code templates have been provided to allow reuse of code segments such as the patch seen in figure 4.

This patch is the area that tends to require the most work to develop at the start, but once familiar with the process, it is quite similar for most other sound effects. The game audio code is shown at the right and shows the game event at the top (alien_fire_SFX) and the message to the sound driver at the bottom.

This patch randomly plays three different versions of the sfx_alien_fire sound effect with random pitch variation between the ranges defined as the min and max. When we look at the patch in depth, the “select 0” message makes sure that the patch only responds to the event on message, so that it does not cut off playback when the voice is turned off in the game.

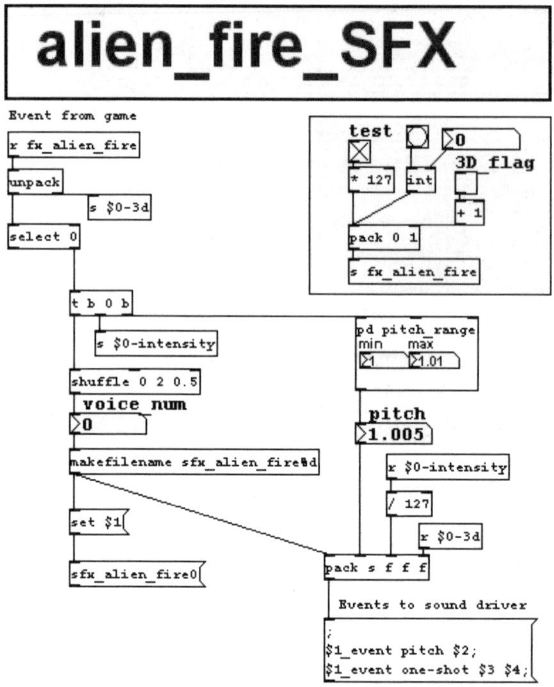


**Fig. 4.** Screenshot of the game audio code for sample playback

The trigger ("t") object passes the intensity value from the game event down to trigger the pitch randomization, send the intensity to be packed in a list and to bang the shuffle object. First, the pitch range is banged to output a value between 1.00 and 1.01 in this example, this number is held in the second parameter value of the pack object. Second, the intensity is divided by 127 which is used to scale the volume to 0-1.0. Finally, the shuffle object is banged and outputs either a 0, 1 or 2 to determine the voice number to play. The 0.5 at the end of the shuffle object simply means that it won't replay the same number on the reshuffle if it can avoid it.

It is quite easy to replace the shuffle object with a random object, but the problem is that samples would then have a fairly high likelihood of being repeated which does not help add realism to the game. It is also possible to implement a function which assigns a likelihood that a certain choice will be skipped when chosen at random, similar to the skip fraction method used in *Halo*[14]. Most audio engines such as Audiokinetic's *Wwise*[15] only allow for certain prescribed types of randomness, but PD allows any form of random number generation that one would consider appropriate for sample playback.

The makefile object appends the number (zero in this case) to the end of "sfx_alien_fire" which produces "sfx_alien_fire0". This is the last entry to the pack object, and is put in the first parameter value of the pack. Since this is the hot inlet, the pack object outputs a list which contains the name of the sound event, the pitch and the volume respectively. The list from the pack object is output to the message at the bottom and the items from the list are substituted into message. This causes the message to become two send events:

```
send sfx_alien_fire0_event pitch 1.005
send sfx_alien_fire0_event one-shot 1 1
```

This causes the pitch to be set to 1.005, which will cause the sfx_alien_fire0.wav file to play at a slightly higher playback rate than normal (ie. 1.0). The sound is then triggered as a one-shot sound at volume 1.0 which is at full volume with no attenuation. The trailing value is used internally for the 3D voice allocation.

The 3D voice number allows the sound to be played within the surround field with control over doppler-shift, volume, surround spacialization and high-frequency roll-off. The pitch range object randomizes the scalar for the playback rate within the minimum and maximum values provided for added variation of sound playback. If the value is 0.5, then the playback is an octave lower, the playback rate is unmodified with a scalar of 1.0 and 2.0 plays the sample back an octave higher. It is also possible to control the granulation of a sample and modify the "stretch factor" of the sound while it is playing. Any number of synthesis methods, such as physical modeling using the PeRColate collection of objects, or processing methods, such as VST plug-ins, can be used to generate and modify the sample playback for each game event.

The current version of the PD sound driver supports the playback of sound effects, speech, adaptive music, cross-fade engine looping and outputs 5.1 surround sound. The surround sound output supports volume roll-off according to distance, doppler-shift with changes in the sound position and user defined high-frequency roll-off curves as sounds move away from the listener. The most recent version of the driver isn't publicly available but there is an older version available on Gamastura.com[13] and the surround sound code is available as part of a granular synthesis patch on the author's website at VideoGameAudio.com.

The advantage of coding the majority of the driver in native PD objects without custom C++ objects is portability and visibility. Anyone viewing the patch is able to see all the functionality of the patch and allow for ease of modification of any behavior all within PD. In industry, one could decide to code certain areas in C++ and make custom PD objects to interface with these code areas. This has the advantage of not requiring the entire prototype to be recoded and allows the sound designer to take full advantage of the speed and flexibility of PD.

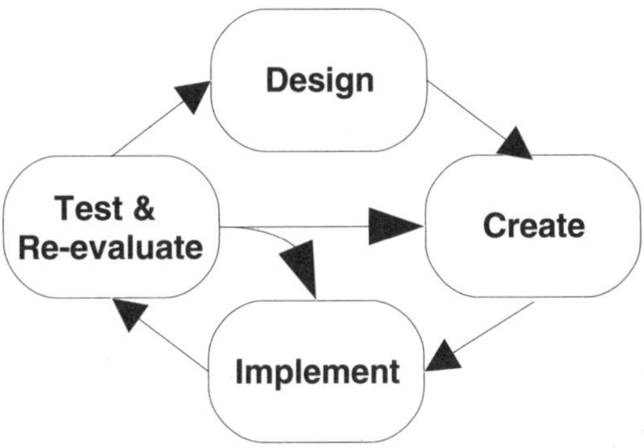


**Fig. 5.** Iterative design flow that is enhanced by rapid prototyping

## 2.2 Half-Life 2 and OSC

The following is an example of how simple it is to add the OSC [16] code to the *HL2* SoundEmitterSystem.cpp file after initializing the communication and allowing allow messages to be sent externally:

```
if (ep.m_pOrigin != NULL) {

            p << osc::BeginMessage( "/emitRaw" ) << "Emit
Sound" << ep.m_pSoundName << "emitted as" <<
ep.m_nSpeakerEntity << "ent = " << entindex << ", pitch=
" << ep.m_nPitch << ",Vol =" << ep.m_flVolume <<
",pOrigin x =" << ep.m_pOrigin->x << ",pOrigin y =" <<
ep.m_pOrigin->y << ",pOrigin z =" << ep.m_pOrigin->z <<
",SoundLvl=" << ep.m_SoundLevel << osc::EndMessage;

            UdpTransmitSocket transmitSocket( IpEndpoint-
Name( sv_soundOSCaddress.GetString(),
sv_soundOSCport.GetInt() ) );

            transmitSocket.Send( p.Data(), p.Size() );

}
```

On the PD side, only the dumpOSC object is required to get all the data and due to the hierarchical nature of OSC, events are easily parsed into their correct containers. The sound driver can also be triggered by a MIDI file that has specially coded events that simulate game events in synchronization to game captured footage. This method

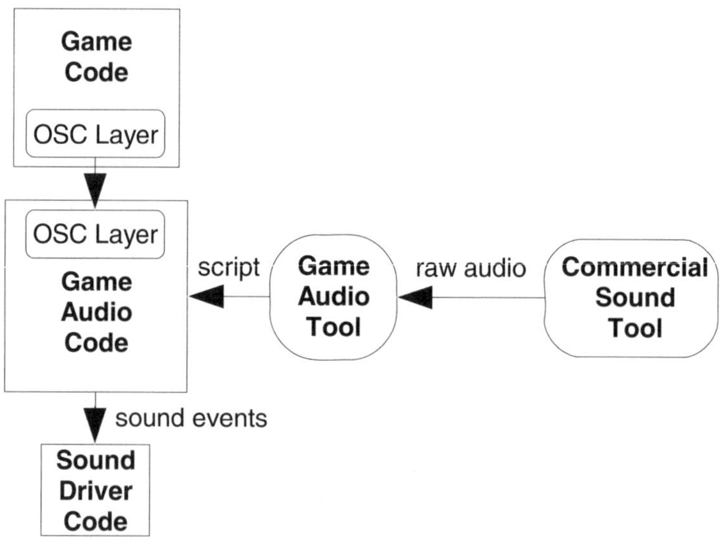


**Fig. 6.** Game event data flow figure communication between the game and the PD sound driver

has been used for some time for instruction as it has the advantage that the game is not required to run in parallel with the game audio code. The obvious disadvantage is that the generation of audio is linear, even though the audio is being generated in real-time. The last method of input of events is by a MIDI controller which could likely be best used for debugging and mixing.

The manner in which the student projects are realized is very similar to the process that industry goes through when prototyping. In both scenarios, students and professional game sound designers are working on a relatively small-scale project for the purposes of learning under time-pressure.

## 2.3 Game Audio Tools

A commercial sound tool such as Steinberg's *Nuendo*[17], Digidesign's *ProTools*[18] or Sony's *Sound Forge*[19] is used by the game sound designer to create content. The audio files are imported into a game audio tool such as Sony's *SCREAM*[20], Audiokinetic's *Wwise*[15] or Microsoft's *XACT*[21] to prepare the audio for use in the game code. Depending on the level of functionality of the game audio tool, they allow for different levels of defining a sound's behavior. If the game audio tool is more powerful, then it allows the game sound designer the ability to better define a sound's behavior with less involvement with the game audio coder. Although it is good for the game audio coder and the game sound designer to work together in an effective manner, a good game audiotool will enable both coder and sound designer to work in tandem as well as in parallel to speed the development process. If the game sound designer is able to describe the behavior of a sound directly via the game audio tool, then the less specifics the game audio coder will need to guess about. Game audio tools can range in scope from allowing only the basic modification of playback rate and volume to tools which allow the definition of complex audio behaviors such as high-performance car engine. The more power the tool grants the game sound designer, the more complex the system. The *Wwise* approach to this situation is to implement the most common modulation parameters such as playback rate, volume and filtering and allow more complex audio behaviors to be enabled by the use of plug-ins. With this method, most of the typical sound designer's needs are covered by the core system without becoming overly complicated. Game audio tools that are more powerful and allow more involved behaviors tend to require more time to overcome their complexity which is a large risk in the short development times of many current games.

If a more complicated system such as PD is used, then good code coherency, encapsulation, good reuse of code via abstractions and other software engineering principles can only help the prototyping process. One could consider the transition of prototype code to game code a type of strong refactoring where all functional elements are evaluated and reworked. The *Wwise* approach is more of a top-down design that only allows the designer to easily design to a prescribed level of granularity before plug-ins will need to be coded by the game audio coder, whereas PD allows the implementation to grow from the bottom-up possibly being confusing in the initial stages. Once the game sound designer has created a few usable prototypes, it is relatively easy to reuse elements, creating a library of commonly used behaviors similar to creating a custom synth patch library over time.

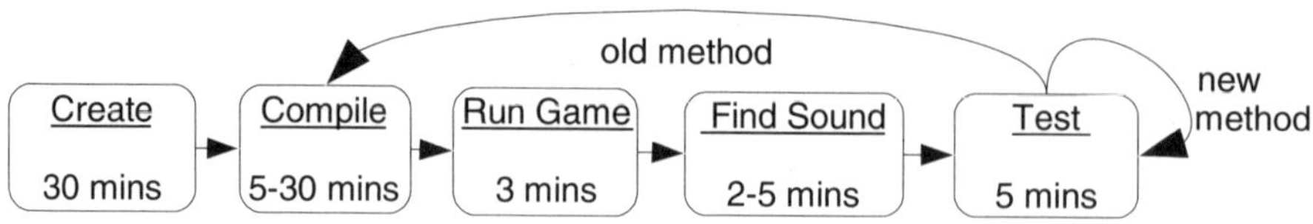


**Fig. 7.** Avoiding re-compilation drastically reduces time spent iterating

# 3 Conclusion

Various versions of this technology have been used over the course of approximately four years with over twenty classes of students with good results. Students have often expressed that they wish that they could spend more time with the system as once they become more familiar with it and they begin to realize the system's potentials. However, most students are very comfortable with following the prescribed guidelines and employ only basic sample playback as their sole audio implementation methodology. It is difficult to determine if the results in the classroom can be extrapolated to the use of prototyping in the industry. There has been some interest in the game audio research community for a prototyping system such as this but research would need to be done to find out their needs

Games will increasingly use more complex approaches to the production of interactive audio as the complexity of the games naturally increase. As the physics, artificial intelligence, graphics and other game sub-systems become more advanced, audio must follow in its quest to become more believable and immersive as well.

Before 2007, the PD sound driver software has been largely driven by a hand-coded MIDI data stream that triggers game audio code in real-time in parallel with game captured footage. In 2007, OSC code was successfully added to the *HL2* Source code which allowed the game audio code to be triggered in real-time. These events can be easily captured and stored for non-realtime playback. The advantage of capturing game audio events is that interactive game audio can be polished and iterated on without the need for re-loading the game, finding the sound in the game to test it and possibly re-compilation as well. If this process is refined enough, it can be made to be very similar to the scrub or rewind ability of non-linear audio post editing tools. This process frees the sound designer from having to play the game and allows them to focus on tuning the audio for the captured events in the game.

Since the sound driver can be easily driven by any application that outputs the correctly formatted OSC events, it is relatively easy to construct a tool to simulate the game events before the game is even produced. This game simulator concept is already utilized in *Wwise* and shows that it is important to allow the sound designer to work on interactive sound designs even before the game is ready to output the correct events.

One could also use a control surface or a keyboard to drive the sound driver in real-time without the game. This allows sound events to be easily triggered and tweaked in real-time using the modulation wheel of the keyboard or the various faders and knobs on a control surface. The data recorded from a mixing surface could be recalled in presets to fit certain game conditions, similar to the method used in the

*Scarface* video game [22]. Specialized mixing and ducking effects could be performed as well, such as bringing down the sound effects and music level when speech plays or performing a high-pass filter on the music during heavy sound effects such as explosions to avoid clouding the mix.

The extensions available for PD allow access to other computing languages such as Java[23], Chuck[24] and Python [25]. This capability enables PD to have access to functions that would be better realized as a procedural piece of code rather than the modular coding style that PD tends to encourage. With all the options available to the sound artist, it is often paramount to limit one's choices before starting any large projects[26]. It is also very easy for coders to create custom objects in C++ for PD using helpful existing frameworks such as flext [27] and extend PD's functionality as desired. PD also communicates quite well with Flash using the flashserver object [28], allowing a visual prototype to be drafted in conjunction with the sound prototype. Very rapid development of game elements could be done with the combination of using Flash for the visuals and PD for the audio. The PD community is just starting to investigate the power of PD for the latest [29].

PD is a very powerful tool to aid sound designers in exploring new possibilities for game audio on modern game consoles.

## References

1. Page, J., Kelly, M.: PS3 Audio: More Than Extra Channels. In: Lecture at the Game Developers Conference in San Francisco in March 2007 (2008), Retrieved (January 2008), from `http://store.cmpgame.com/product.php?id=1961&cat=52`
2. Gabler, K., Gray, K., Kucic, M., Shodhan, S.: How to prototype a game in under 7 days: Tips and tricks from 4 grad students who made over 50 games in 1 semester, Gamasutra Retrieved (January 10, 2007), from `http://www.gamasutra.com/features/20051026/gabler_01.shtml`
3. Paul, L.J.: Coding vs. Aesthetics. Paper presented at the 2003 GDC Written Proceedings, San Francisco, CA, USA (2003) (Retrieved January 10, 2007)
4. Puckette, M.S.: Pure data, San Diego, CA, USA, Retrieved (January 10, 2007), from `http://crca.ucsd.edu/~msp/software.html`
5. Native Instruments: Reaktor, Germany 5 (2007)
6. Cycling 1974: Max/MSP and jitter. USA, Retrieved (January 10, 2007), from `http://cycling74.com/`
7. Schiemer, G., Havryliv, M.: Pocket gamelan: A pure data interface for mobile phones. In: NIME 2005: Proceedings of the 2005 Conference on New Interfaces for Musical Expression, Vancouver, Canada, pp. 156–159 (2004)
8. Alonso, M., Geiger, G., Jorda, S.: An internet browser plug-in for real-time audio synthesis. In: WEDELMUSIC 2004: Proceedings of the Web Delivering of Music, Fourth International Conference on (WEDELMUSIC 2004), pp. 23–26 (2004), from `http://dx.doi.org.proxy.lib.sfu.ca/10.1109/WEDELMUSIC.2004.4`
9. Sarlo, J.: Pdvst (2004)
10. Bencina, R.: oscpack, Australia (2006) Retrieved (January 10, 2007) from `http://www.audiomulch.com/~`
11. Valve Software: Corporate Website. USA (2008), Retrieved (January 10, 2007), from `http://valvesoftware.com/games.html`

12. Microsoft: Visual C++ 2005 Express Edition. USA, Retrieved (January 10, 2007), from http://www.softpedia.com/get/Programming/Other-Programming-Files/Microsoft-Visual-C-Toolkit.shtml
13. Paul, L.: Audio prototyping with Pure Data. Gamasutra (May 28, 2003), (Retrieved January 2007)
14. O'Donnell, M.: GDC 2005 Report: Audio Production for Halo 2. USA (2005), Retrieved (January 10, 2007), from http://www.gamasutra.com/view/feature/2257/gdc_2005_report_audio_production_php
15. Audiokinetic: WaveWorks interactive sound engine. Montreal, QC, Canada (2006), Retrieved (January 10, 2007), from http://audiokinetic.com/
16. CNMAT: Open sound control. USA (2006), Retrieved (January 10, 2007), from http://www.cnmat.berkeley.edu/OpenSoundControl/
17. Steinberg: Nuendo. Germany (2007)
18. Digidesign: Protools. USA (2008)
19. Sony: Sound Forge. USA (2007)
20. Sony Computer Ent. America: SCREAM. USA (2005), Retrieved (January 10, 2007), from https://www.cmpevents.com/GD05/a.asp?option=C&V=11&SessID=3817
21. Microsoft: XNA game studio express 1.0. USA (2007), Retrieved (January 10, 2007), from http://msdn2.microsoft.com/en-us/directx/aa937791.aspx
22. Jackson, B.: From scarface to simlish. [Electronic version]. Mix (October 1, 2006), Retrieved (January 10, 2007), from http://mixonline.com/newmedia/newformats/audio_scarface_simlish/
23. ml: Java external plugin for pure-data (2006), Retrieved (January 10, 2007), from http://www.le-son666.com/software/pdj/
24. Robinson, M.: chuck (2007), Retrieved (January 10, 2007), from http://www-static.cc.gatech.edu/ugrads/m/mjr/chuck~/
25. Grill, T.: Pyext – A Python extension for PD (2007), Retrieved (January 10, 2007), from http://www.parasitaere-kapazitaeten.net/ext/py/
26. Bridgett, R., Paul, L.J.: Establishing an aesthetic in next generation sound design. Gamasutra, (June 20, 2006), Retrieved (January 10, 2007), from http://www.gamasutra.com/features/20060621/bridgett_01.shtml#
27. Grill, T.: Flext - C++ layer for cross-platform development of Max/MSP and pd externals (2005), from http://grrrr.org/ext/flext/
28. Matthes, O.: Flashserver (2006), Retrieved (January 10, 2007), from http://www.nullmedium.de/dev/flashserver/
29. Farnell, A.: Crack (January 6, 2008), Message posted to http://puredata.hurleur.com/viewtopic.php?pid=5874

# Computer-Assisted Content Editing Techniques for Live Multimedia Performance

Stefan Müller Arisona[1], Pascal Müller[2],
Simon Schubiger-Banz[2], and Matthias Specht[2]

[1] Media Arts and Technology, University of California, Santa Barbara
Santa Barbara, CA 93106, USA
sma@corebounce.org
[2] Procedural Inc.
Zurich, Switzerland
{pascal.mueller,simon.schubiger,matthias.specht}@procedural.com

**Abstract.** Live multimedia performance demands elaborate interactive media-processing systems. The task of these systems is to serve as expressive instruments that support the artist during composition and performance. In order to deal with the rapidly growing amount and complexity of digital content, we propose the application of computer-assisted content editing techniques. Specifically, we present a software component that addresses the artistic workflow by organising the design space of an art work, and providing means of navigation therein. In addition, we present a framework that employs audio and video analysis methods for automatic non-linear video editing. Together, these techniques effectively help the artist to focus on live composition and performance flow instead of getting lost in an unmanageable parameter space.

**Keywords:** Multimedia Authoring, Digital Content Creation, Live Performance.

## 1 Introduction

As a consequence of ongoing digitalisation of media, artists presently leverage computer technology in many domains of live performance. Today, powerful but low-cost computers offer endless possibilities for composing and performing multimedia works. In addition, related output technologies, such as digital audio and projection systems, are pre-installed in many performance spaces, and novel input devices such as touch- or gesture-based interfaces increase artistic expression during performance.

When it comes to software systems for interactive multimedia performance, we can observe an evolution that was guided by two opposite branches: in order to provide a smooth transition from older techniques, the first branch often mimics previous concepts. For instance, many elements in graphical user interface design are directly derived from hardware interfaces such as rotary knobs or even electrical connectors and wires. In contrast, the second branch breaks with tradition and introduces concepts that are entirely exclusive to the digital domain. Examples are visual programming environments, such as *Max* (and its relatives) (Pukette, 2002). As observed in other domains,

R. Adams, S. Gibson, and S. Müller Arisona (Eds.): DAW/IF 2006/2007, CCIS 7, pp. 199–212, 2008.

the adoption rate of more radical techniques is relatively slow, and most systems designed for a broader audience stick to the most traditional branch, slowing the pace of innovation.

In this work, we propose the adoption of computer-assisted content editing techniques. By *content editing* we refer to all activities that deal with composition, modification, retrieval and selection of digital content. Our work emphasises assisting the artistic workflow from early design phases to the actual performance, and in the automatisation of media editing tasks.

More specifically, we present two editing techniques designed for live multimedia performance: first, we introduce the *Design Tree*, a software component that addresses the artistic workflow by logical organisation of the artistic design space and by providing means of navigation therein. Second, we present *Odessa*,[1] a framework for real-time non-linear editing (NLE) of short video sequences. Odessa employs computer-vision methods to reverse-edit original video sequences and isolates groups and shots in a pre-production phase. During performance, real-time audio analysis is applied to digitised audio, and individual shots are aligned to retrieved audio features such as rhythmic boundaries, resulting in a re-edit of the original sequence.

Both software components are implemented as part of the multimedia processing environment *Soundium*, and we have previously presented their technical background (Schubiger and Müller, 2003; Müller Arisona et al., 2006; Müller et al., 2008). Here, we show *how* the underlying technology is applied in terms of an expressive composition and performance instrument.

The remainder of this paper is organised as follows: Section 2 presents the background of our work and reviews previous work. In Sections 3 and 4, we present the Design Tree and Odessa in detail and discuss how they are applied in practice. The paper concludes with final remarks and an outlook in Section 5.

## 2 Background and Previous Work

In this section we give the historic and conceptual background of our work. It is organised into the following three areas: first, we present our personal motivation for the work carried out, then we have a closer look at the notions of composition and design, and last, we briefly explore the connection of movies and music.

### 2.1 Creating Instruments for Live Visuals Performance

The motivation of creating custom software instruments for live multimedia performance roots in our work of performing live visuals performances in dance clubs (also known as VJing) and multimedia performances in collaboration with other artists. By the year 2000, live performance and VJing software tools had been around for some time. Examples are Cycling'74's Max/MSP/Jitter (Pukette, 2002), which was (and still is) very popular among media artists, or Derivative's *Touch*, whose predecessor *Houdini* was used to render the graphics at the SIGGRAPH 98 Interactive Dance Club event

[1] Odessa is named after the "Odessa Steps" sequence in Sergei Eisenstein's movie *Battleship Potemkin*, where he tested various film montage techniques.

(Ulyate and Bianciardi, 2002). Like most tools at that time, both Max and Touch were proprietary and their extensibility was therefore limited. Hence, our decision to design and implement a custom system, which allowed for rapid exploration of new ideas both from a computer science as well as from an artistic viewpoint.

The first performances done with Soundium were VJing sessions. Typically, these sessions were very long, and we were faced with the problem of providing several hours of uninterrupted live performance without constantly repeating the same or similar content. The problem was approached at two levels: first, we investigated in the general question of how artists may interact with a potentially very large design space – work that resulted in the Design Tree; second, and very specifically, Odessa evolved from our interest in the application of film montage techniques in a live context.

## 2.2 Composition and Design

The notions of composition and design appear with varying semantics in different fields, and some explanation is required how they are used throughout this paper. A *composition* is the result of arranging or organising basic elements with respect to an artistic goal. In the twentieth century, formal approaches to composition have appeared in music (Xenakis, 1971) and in painting (Kandinsky, 1994). While a composition may exist in a completely mental space, a means of representation is required in order to make it accessible to others (e.g., performers). However, such a representation does not have to explicitly reflect the content of a composition, as it is the case in music notation, where musical ideas often are deeply hidden.

In Soundium, the representation of a multimedia composition is realised by means of a *global processing graph* (Müller Arisona et al., 2006). The processing graph may incorporate local media processing graphs of different modalities, such as data flow networks for audio processing (Lee and Parks, 1995), or computer graphics scene graphs (Strauss and Carey, 1992; Rohlf and Helman, 1994). Throughout this paper, a particular configuration of the processing graph is called a *design*.

Simon (1996) pointed out that designing is a problem-solving activity within a multitude of paths towards an actual solution. This viewpoint shifts the focus from looking only at the final design towards looking at the evolution of a design and how it is related to other designs. Shneiderman (2007) considers retaining a rich history of the design process as one of several important design principles for creativity support tools. Additional principles include the support for exploratory search and multilayered interfaces in order to provide multiple viewpoints to one's work.

As we shall see, we address these principles by extending the way we look at designs: instead of looking at isolated designs, we add a new layer, the Design Tree, which organises a collection of designs in terms of their history. Interactive access to this layer allows for search and navigation in a design space, and offers expressive application of designs during performance.

## 2.3 The Connection of Movies and Music

Both movies and music are subject to their underlying languages: a movie, ranging from feature film to video clip to completely non-narrative image sequence, is organised in a temporal plot, which consists of cuts, motives, objects, characters, and so on. Music is temporally structured into form, meter, and rhythm. Harmonic and motivic elements complete the structure.

In the past, there have been numerous attempts to relate visual and audio features. One approach was taken by composer Alexander Scriabin, who assigned tonalities to coloured light (Peacock, 1985). For his symphony *Prometheus* he basically wrote two scores: one for the orchestra, and one for the *Luce*, a piano-like instrument to control coloured light. Theoretician and director Sergei Eisenstein developed the notion of *vertical montage*, the synchronisation of music and movies by finding the congruence between a musical and a pictorial sentence (Eisenstein, 1994). However, these concepts had been rarely used until non-linear video editing systems became widely available. Today, the application of Eisenstein's ideas is sometimes found in *music video clips*, such as in the works of Michel Gondry (Gondry, 2001, 2003).

Creating music for a given movie is particularly present in *film music*: after London (1936), "the role of (film) music is to give sound depth and tone to the form and to the inner rhythm of the film." Typically, this is achieved by constraining musical elements to the film's structure, such as a cut or a visual action point.

Computers have been applied to automatically or semi-automatically create content of one media that is connected to another: Mitroo et al. (1979) have generated *abstract* computer graphics from musical scores by assigning harmonic and metric features to colours and shape. In contrast, ElKoura and Singh (2003) have animated the 3D hand model of a guitar player based on a musical guitar score.

If the structure of music or film is not *a priori* known, the source (i.e., audio signals or plain image sequences) needs to be analysed in order to extract assignable features. Jehan et al. (2003) have used audio analysis to generate video sequences of a dancer, whose dancing activity is determined by musical features. Foote et al. (2002) have analysed both audio and video sequences in order to automatically create music videos for a given sound track. Besides of manual segmentation, computer vision methods can segment video material automatically (Lienhard, 1999; Rui et al., 1999).

In most works mentioned above, media analysis occurs off-line, and therefore allows for an in-depth analysis of time-dependent structures. In our work, the audio source is not known in advance, thus musical features need to be recovered in real-time. Real-time audio analysis methods have been presented in (Goto, 2001; Scheirer, 1998; Brossier et al., 2004). However, only a limited part of an audio signal's original musical structure can be recovered at the current state of research.

## 3 Assisting the Composition and Performance Workflow

In this section, we show how the Design Tree assists the artist in the workflow during composition and performance. Therefore, we first have a closer look at the artistic workflow in general. Then, we deduce the Design Tree from the Undo/Redo concept as it is known from many computer applications, and we show how it is applied in practice.

### 3.1 Structuring the Workflow

As mentioned earlier, the goal of the Design Tree is to provide a dedicated layer of control and representation that accompanies the artist from an early stage of composition to the actual performance. This layer should allow for navigation in a design space and for activation and modification of designs. The history of changes applied to the design space should be retained.

Before devising the layer in terms software and interaction design, it is helpful to analyse different aspects of the artistic workflow and how they relate to each other. As indicated in Figure 1 we roughly divide overall process into a composition and a performance phase. Note that these parts may overlap considerably, such as in improvised performance where compositional tasks are applied during performance. The individual stages start with a (sometimes vaguely formulated) artistic idea, which is formulated in terms of more concrete design goals. These steps are followed by collecting source material (for example video footage or geometry in the case of live visuals), a considerable amount of experimentation, and eventually systematic composition, which results in a well defined state of the work. Interpretation is particularly important in the case where performer and composer are different, as it is generally the case in music. The actual performance is often preceded by rehearsal and refinement, with the goal to master the work on a given instrument. Recapitulation analyses the performance in order to give insights for followup performances or new works to be composed.

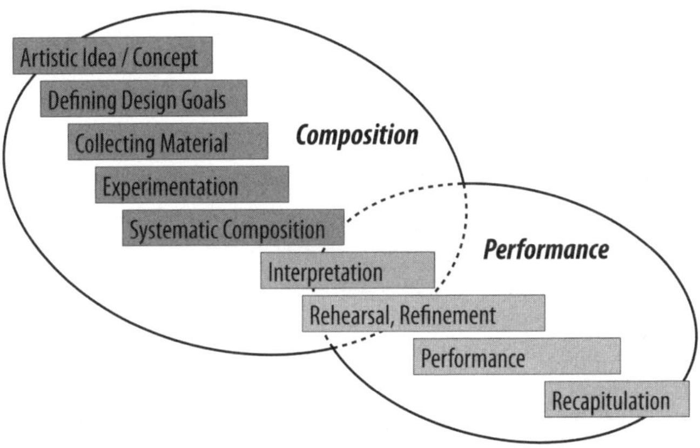


**Fig. 1.** Overview of the artistic workflow, roughly divided into composition and performance phases

It is important to note that the workflow given in Figure 1 is not a fixed one: the creative process cannot be captured in a rigid structure. Therefore, new stages may be added and existing ones can be reordered where needed. In addition, the flow from stage to stage is rarely linear, as loops may occur at any point. However, a basic structure, such as the one given in our example is crucial as a starting point for the design and implementation of a software tool supporting the workflow.

So far, we have looked at the workflow at its full range. In contrast to the other stages, the performance stage is inherently sensitive to the flow of time (i.e., it cannot be interrupted or small parts cannot be repeated for correction). As an example, consider the three scenes from a live visuals performance in Figure 2: here, each scene has been independently composed before the performance took place. However, the sequencing of the scenes, and the transitions between them, are not predetermined, and the composition of scenes takes place during performance. As this occurs time-constrained, the workflow of live composition is closely bound to questions of how to get access to intended compositions quickly and how to achieve smooth transitions without interrupting the performance flow.

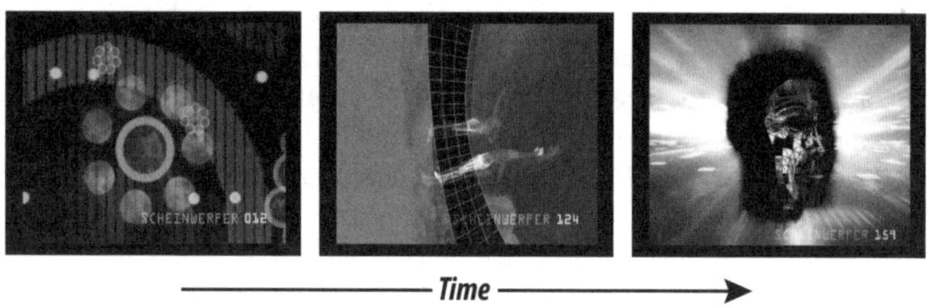


**Fig. 2.** Three independently composed scenes of a live visuals performance. The sequencing of the scenes, and the transitions between them, are not predefined and are determined during performance.

### 3.2 Deducing the Design Tree

Our observations on the workflow show that all stages of the workflow are interconnected. The actual performance depends on the "results" of the preceding stages. Thus, if we are to design a software component that assists the artist during the performance workflow, the links to previous stages need to be established in an effective manner. This allows us to devise general characteristics in terms of software design. First, in order to connect the workflow's stages and to make previous information accessible, a common representation that stores the state of the composition before and during performance is required. Second, as several compositional tasks are unknown before the performance takes place, it is required to keep a rich history of actions that happened in the previous stages. Keeping the history allows to relate composition steps to each other, and therefore builds a basis for navigation in the (design-)space as a whole.

Interestingly, a basic approach to keeping the history of user actions is omnipresent in most of today's interactive software applications: the concept of Undo and Redo, as illustrated in Figure 3 (a) and (b), provides a linear history of previously applied actions with respect to a current version. However, a limitation in the Undo/Redo mechanism prevents the full history of actions to be retained: if the user modifies the current version of his or her work, the Redo path is invalidated, that is, the part right of the current version in Figure 3 (b) is replaced with the action that just took place. Figure 3 (c) indicates how this "deletion of history" can be avoided: instead of sticking to the linearity of Undo/Redo, the Redo path is not replaced, but the linear sequence branches off with the newly performed action. Consequently, a tree structure emerges. This tree not only contains the history of previous actions, it also relates them to each other, and therefore serves as a topological structure of the design space in which the composition evolved.

The idea of keeping the history in the form of a tree lays the foundation of the Design Tree: the tree's nodes are called *design nodes* or just *designs*, and the tree evolves from the earliest composition stage. As the artist modifies the current design, a new tree node reflecting the changes is created (in contrast to normal Undo/Redo, we collect a set of modifications). Retrieving a particular state of the composition process is achieved by *activating* a design. The current design inherits all properties from its parent designs, which establishes a *design path* towards the tree's root. In addition, designs can be modified through high-level design operations. For instance, properties of a specific design node can be extracted and included in the current node (Müller et al., 2008). These operations allow for smooth transitions between designs and they provide a powerful mechanism for high-level editing during performance.

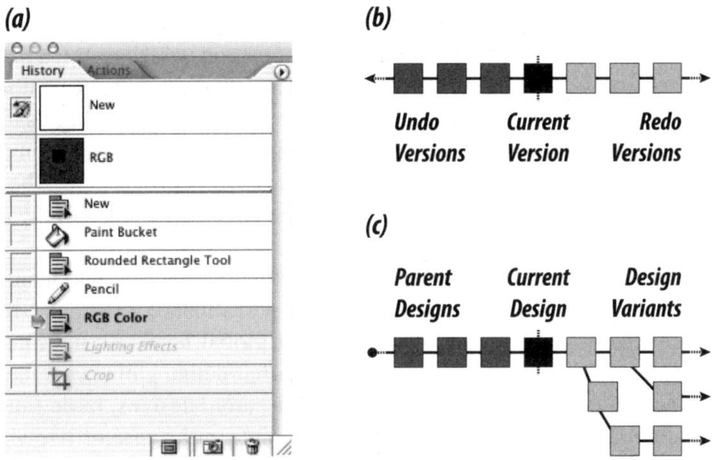


**Fig. 3.** Representation of the Undo/Redo path in Adobe's Photoshop (screen capture) (a). The Design Tree evolves as an extension of the common Undo/Redo path (b) by not invalidating the Redo path when the current design is modified (c).

### 3.3 Implementation and Practical Application of the Design Tree

In the previous section, we have illustrated how the Design Tree interconnects the various stages of the workflow by providing a common representation, and how it organises a collection of designs through its topological structure. In this section, we show how Soundium implements the Design Tree, and how a concrete tree for our live visuals performances evolved.

So far, we have not dealt with the question of how modifications to designs are tracked and how they are stored in design nodes. While the concept of extending the common Undo/Redo mechanism is very general, the underlying implementation is particular to a given application design, very much like implementations of Undo/Redo are application-specific.[2] As indicated earlier, and presented in detail in (Müller Arisona et al., 2006), a design in Soundium refers to a particular configuration of a global processing graph. The graph unifies elements of audio flow graphs, video compositing graphs, and 3D scene graphs, and allows for connections between these entities. Therefore, the Design Tree in Soundium encapsulates commands for the creation, configuration, and removal of processing nodes, and commands for connecting or disconnecting them. These commands are stored as simple scripting language statements in individual design nodes.

From a user interface perspective, the Design Tree is presented to the user in terms of an annotated tree (Figure 4). The tree is equally available during all workflow stages, and in terms of software and user interface design, there is no distinction between composition and performance.

As indicated in Section 2.1, we applied Soundium for numerous live visuals performances. The Design Tree was designed and implemented in order to close gaps within different stages of the composition and performance workflow, and to address the problem of accessing and modifying existing compositions rapidly while performing. We used the Design Tree for experimentation and composition, which resulted in a number of designs ready to use. During performance, the designs were easily accessible and the tree's topology proved as a powerful means of navigation in a growing design space. In addition, design operations such as merging designs allowed to apply compositional tasks *during* performance, allowing for more expressive improvisation. The resulting tree of the previous performance was reused for the composition phase of the upcoming performance.

In the beginning, the tree evolved in an unstructured, rather random manner. However, the ongoing repetition of composition and performance eventually revealed a topology that became increasingly structured at a global level. As indicated in Figure 4 (a), the root of the tree comprises of designs that define global characteristics of the work. Since all child designs inherit from their parent designs, basic functionality common to all other designs was defined at this point. In the case of live visuals, examples are viewport and virtual camera setup, several stages of a graphics processing engine, and Odessa's automated editing components (Section 4). During composition, we passed the design tree around to the participating artists (the tree is easy to share as its data is stored in a single file). Thus, at a deeper level, artist-specific designs were added, as shown in Figure 4 (b) and (c). Typically, these designs were further ramified, leading to the actual compositions (d). The history of changes during performance is captured as well, which is reflected by new nodes tree's leaves (e).

As a result, the evolving tree structure represents a smooth path from global towards very local features. The structuring effectively addresses the scene transition problem previously illustrated in Figure 2: global features permit one to maintain an overall scene state, such as colour or dynamics. In contrast, local features allow for fine-grain manipulation of specific scene attributes, such as shapes or texturing. As a consequence,

[2] However, there exist common design patterns for implementing Undo/Redo, such as the *command* pattern (Gamma et al., 1995).

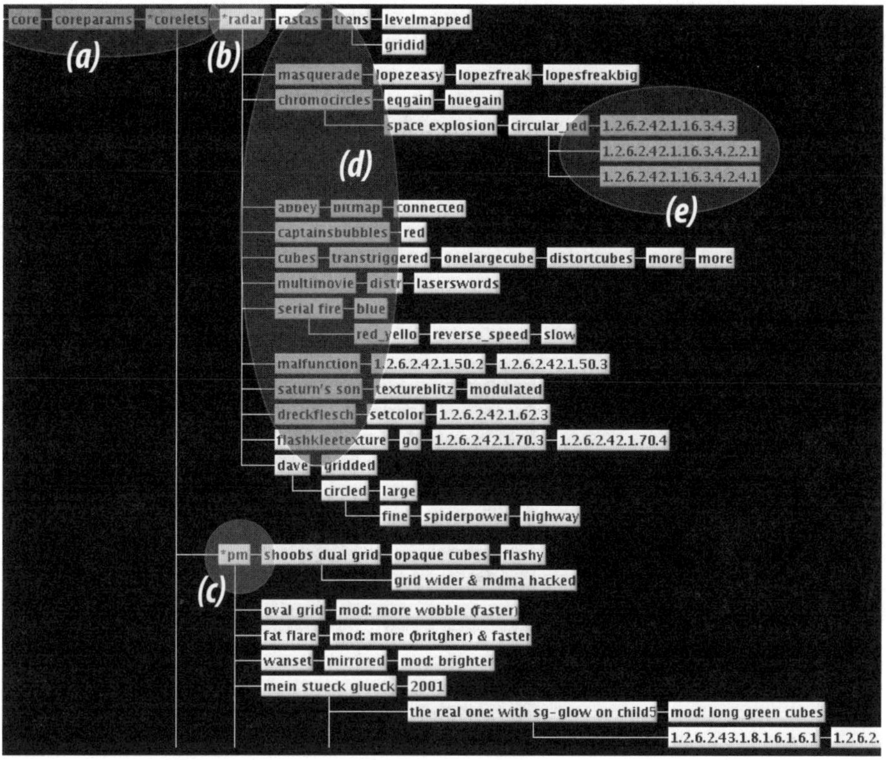


**Fig. 4.** Excerpt of the Design Tree that evolved for live visuals performance. The overlaid shaded ovals indicate areas of global and local designs: global performance configuration (a); artist-specific settings (b) and (c); explicitly composed designs (d); and designs variants that evolved during rehearsal or a previous performance (e).

the design space, possibly containing thousands of parameters, becomes more manageable, and artistic goals can be approached in a fluid and expressive manner.

# 4 Automation of Non-linear Video Editing

In this section, we discuss the Odessa framework, which automates the preparation of footage during composition and the editing process during performance. We apply computer vision methods to reverse-edit original footage. Real-time audio analysis extracts music feature vectors, which are mapped to editing parameters of a video montage engine. The engine can be controlled through high-level editing parameters, such as looping speed or cutting rate.

## 4.1 Pre-processing of Video Material

Our initial performances included the manual sequencing of looped video clips. Typically, the clips were short, ranging from 1 to 8 seconds, and were obtained from original footage manually, for instance with a video editing tool. The time-consuming overhead of manually searching for appropriated clips led to the idea of applying automatic reverse-editing tools.

Thus, part of Odessa is a separate tool that is used off-line and implements computer vision methods, such as shot boundary detection (Lienhard, 1999) and video abstracting techniques for scene determination (Rui et al., 1999). An example of a processed video clip is given in Figure 5: the original footage is hierarchically segmented into scenes, groups, and shots. Since automatic segmentation methods do not produce correct results for all cases, the pre-processing stage may be followed by manual clip selection.

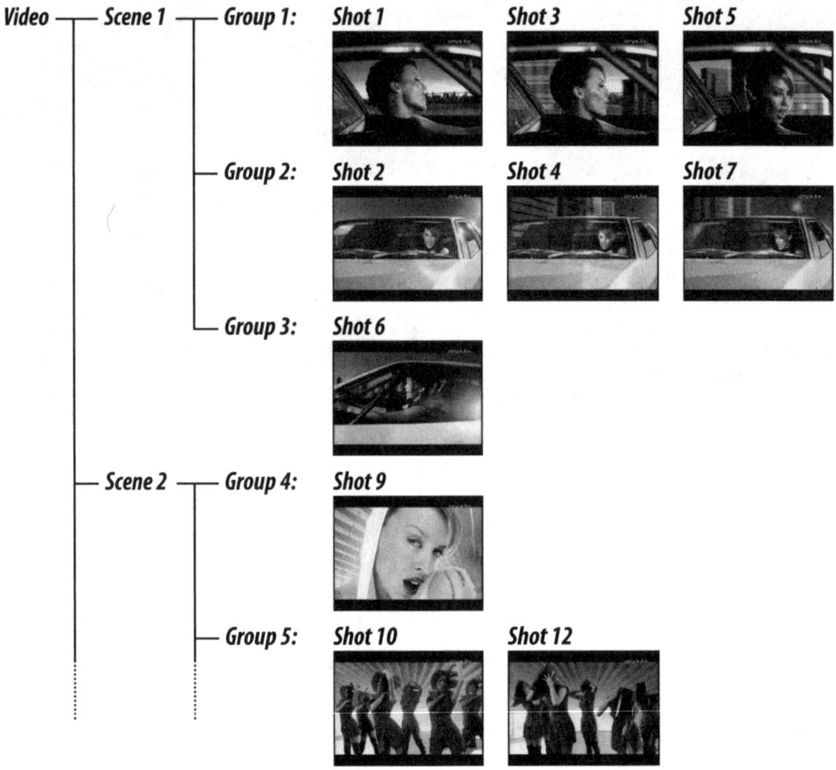


**Fig. 5.** Reverse editing of a video clip. The original footage is analysed and re-organised in terms of individual scenes, groups, and shots.

## 4.2 Real-Time Audio Analysis

During performance, an audio feature vector is obtained through real-time audio analysis. Odessa implements methods such as beat tracking (Goto, 2001; Scheirer, 1998; Brossier et al., 2004) or music similarity analysis (by extending the work given in (Foote et al., 2002) to operate in real-time).

The retrieved feature vector contains discrete "musical action points" such as beats, part or song boundaries, and continuous features such as audio levels, or characteristics of individual frequency bands (obtained through FFT). In Soundium, audio analysis is realised in terms of an audio and control flow graph, which is a part of the global processing graph. Since the video processing and graphics scene graphs are part of the processing graph as well, the resulting feature vector can easily be mapped to visual features.

### 4.3 Live Montage

As illustrated in Figure 6, the compositing of video footage is integrated in Soundium's OpenGL scene graph. Video is ultimately rendered in terms of arbitrary textured shapes. Multiple shapes (indicated by $1..n$ in the figure) are composited using standard blending techniques (Porter and Duff, 1984), or by employing fragment shader programs for more advanced image manipulation and compositing. The post effects stage applies common operations such as masking or colour control.

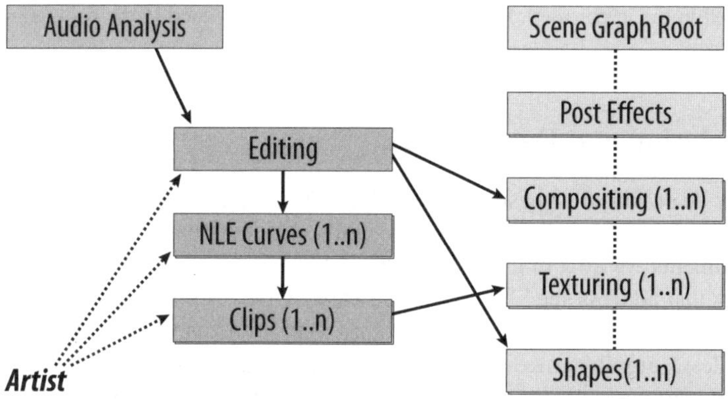


**Fig. 6.** Real-time non-linear video editing components. The solid lines indicate the flow of data resulting from audio analysis. The dashed lines denote the interaction of the artist with the editing components (left), and the graphics scene graph relationships (right).

The editing component is Odessa's central mechanism for the montage of multiple clips: it collects real-time audio analysis data as well as artist input and sends compositing parameters (such as $\alpha$ factors for blending) to the scene graph. For each clip, it uses discrete audio features to trigger NLE curves. These curves determine the sequencing of clips and each clip's actual playback position, which is used as the current texture in the scene graph. The performer does not deal with loop alignment of video sequences, but modifies editing parameters, such as the sequence of multiple clips or the cutting rate (for example, cuts per beat). In addition, the performer may modify NLE curves in order to adjust clip speeds and clip looping shapes.

Figure 7 exemplifies the process of automated video editing: audio analysis is applied to determine beat and part boundaries. Odessa's editing component assigns musical parts to available slots for clips, which are filled with pre-processed scenes of a given video clip. For each slot, shots of the assigned scene are looped according to given NLE curves with respect to extracted beat boundaries (in Figure 7: four shots of scene 1, one shot of scene 2, and two shots of scene 3). Automated editing as shown in this example releases the performing artist to deal with repeating time structures at the beat level; instead he or she can focus on narration by selecting video material and defining how this material should be edited according to retrieved audio features.

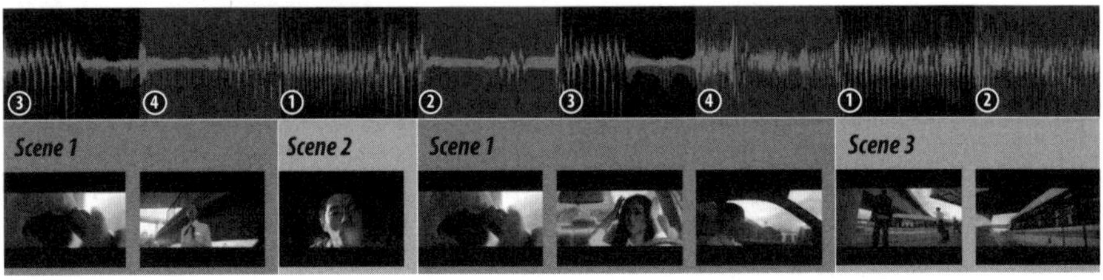


**Fig. 7.** Automated NLE: Audio analysis is applied to determine beat and part boundaries (beats are indicated in the upper row). Individual shots are looped aligned to the beat, and scenes are aligned to parts.

## 5 Conclusion and Future Work

This paper dealt with the question of how interactive software tools can assist the composer and performer during all phases of a work, with the goal of implementing expressive instruments for live multimedia performance. We presented two content editing techniques that address specific goals. The Design Tree supports the artist in the artistic workflow by providing a central structure that connects the workflow's individual stages. Odessa employs media analysis techniques, such as video or real-time audio analysis. It automates media-editing tasks during performance and frees the performer from dealing with microscopic and repeating time-constraints.

The presented software components were implemented as part of the multimedia processing platform Soundium. From the beginning, we applied Soundium in a repeated cycle of research, implementation, composition, and performance. This cycle resulted in an intense interaction between art and computer science: besides the artistic goals of the works *per se*, the performances allowed us to experimentally evaluate the progress of the software instrument, typically resulting in new research questions and software features. The latter, in turn, allowed for more expressive composition and performance. Using Soundium in a "real-world" environment helped to identify and resolve limitations in terms software reliability and human-computer interaction. In addition, keeping the cycle's round-trip time short (typically two to three weeks) sped up the pace of Soundium's evolution.

Besides adopting novel audio and video analysis methods, future work on Odessa would enhance its video processing engine. Today, most engines are optimised for linear playback of a single stream. Considering the move towards HD resolution and beyond, real-time processing of multiple video sources with recurring loops and seeks still imposes a serious performance problem on today's computers. In addition, we believe that supporting mechanisms such as the Design Tree enhance collaborative live performance. Thus, future work would explore how the Design Tree can be employed in collaborative environments, for instance for multiple simultaneous performers.

## Acknowledgements

We thank Prof. Jürg Gutknecht and Prof. Luc van Gool of ETH Zurich for supporting our work. In addition, *chapeau* to Nicolas Juillerat of University of Fribourg for his extensive work on real-time audio processing. This and ongoing work is in part supported by the Swiss National Science Foundation (SNF), Fellowships for Advanced Researchers, Project No. PA002-117462 / 1.

## References

Brossier, P., Bello, J.P., Plumbley, M.D.: Real-time temporal segmentation of note objects in music signals. In: Proceedings of the 2004 International Computer Music Conference. International Computer Music Association (2004)

Eisenstein, S.: Selected Works 2: Towards a Theory of Montage. In: Glenny, N., Taylor, R. (eds.) British Film Institute (1994)

ElKoura, G., Singh, K.: Handrix: Animating the human hand. In: SCA 2003: Proceedings of the 2003 ACM SIGGRAPH/Eurographics Symposium on Computer Animation. Eurographics Association, pp. 110–119 (2003)

Foote, J., Cooper, M., Girgensohn, A.: Creating music videos using automatic media analysis. In: Proc. ACM Intl. Conf. on Multimedia, pp. 553–560 (2002)

Gamma, E., Helm, R., Johnson, R., Vlissides, J.: Design Patterns: Elements of Reusable Object-oriented Software, Boston, MA, USA. Addison-Wesley, Reading (1995)

Gondry, M.: Chemical Brothers – Star Guitar. Production Company: Partizan Midi Minuit, 2001. Music Video Clip (2001)

Gondry, M.: The White Stripes – Hardest Button To Button. In: Production Company: Partizan, Hollywood. Music Video Clip (2003)

Goto, M.: An audio-based real-time beat tracking system for music with or without drum sound. Journal of New Music Research 30(2), 158–171 (2001)

Jehan, T., Lew, M., Vaucelle, C.: Cati dance: Self-edited, self-synchronized music video. In: GRAPH 2003: Proceedings of the SIGGRAPH 2003 Conference on Sketches & Applications, ACM Press, New York (2003)

Kandinsky, W.: Complete Writings on Art. In: Lindsay, K.C., Vergo, P. (eds.), Da Capo Press, New York (1994)

Lee, E.A., Parks, T.M.: Dataflow process networks. In: Proceedings of the IEEE, vol. 83(5), pp. 773–799 (1995)

Lienhard, R.: Comparison of automatic shot boundary detection algorithms. In: Image and Video Processing VII. Proc. SPIE, pp. 3656–3629 (1999)

London, K.: Film Music: A Summary of the Characteristic Features of its History, Aesthetics, Techniques and its Possible Developments. Faber and Faber, London (1936)

Mitroo, J.B., Herman, N., Badler, N.I.: Movies from music: Visualizing musical compositions. In: Computer Graphics (Proceedings of SIGGRAPH 79), pp. 218–225. ACM Press, New York (1979)

Müller, P., Arisona, S.M., Schubiger-Banz, S., Specht, M.: Interactive editing of live visuals. In: Braz, J., Ranchordas, A., Araújo, H., Jorge, J. (eds.) Advances in Computer Graphics and Computer Vision. CCIS, vol. 4, pp. 169–184. Springer, Heidelberg (2008)

Arisona, S.M., Schubiger-Banz, S., Specht, M.: A real-time multimedia composition layer. In: AMCMM 2006: Proceedings of the 1st ACM Workshop on Audio and Music Computing for Multimedia, pp. 97–106. ACM Press, New York (2006)

Peacock, K.: Synesthetic perception: Alexander Scriabin's color hearing. Music Perception 2(4), 483–506 (1985)

Porter, T., Duff, T.: Compositing digital images. In: Computer Graphics (Proceedings of SIGGRAPH 1984), pp. 253–259. ACM Press, New York (1984)

Pukette, M.: Max at seventeen. Computer Music Journal 26(4), 31–43 (2002)

Rohlf, J., Helman, J.: Iris performer: A high performance multiprocessing toolkit for real-time 3d graphics. In: Proceedings of SIGGRAPH 1994. Computer Graphics Proceedings, Annual Conference Series, pp. 381–395. ACM Press, New York (1994)

Rui, Y., Huang, T.S., Mehrotra, S.: Constructing table-of-content for videos. ACM Multimedia Systems 7(5), 359–368 (1999)

Scheirer, E.: Tempo and beat analysis of acoustic musical signals. J. Acoust. Soc. Am. 103(1), 588–601 (1998)

Schubiger, S., Müller, S.: Soundium2: An interactive multimedia playground. In: Proceedings of the 2003 International Computer Music Conference. International Computer Music Association (2003)

Shneiderman, B.: Creativity support tools: Accelerating discovery and innovation. Communications of the ACM 50(12), 20–32 (2007)

Simon, H.A.: The Sciences of the Artificial. MIT Press, Cambridge (1996)

Strauss, P.S., Carey, R.: An object-oriented 3D graphics toolkit. In: Computer Graphics (Proceedings of SIGGRAPH 1992), pp. 341–349. ACM Press, New York (1992)

Ulyate, R., Bianciardi, D.: The interactive dance club: Avoiding chaos in a multi-participant environment. Computer Music Journal 26(3), 40–49 (2002)

Xenakis, I.: Formalized Music. Indiana University Press, Bloomington (1971)

# Computational Audiovisual Composition Using Lua

Wesley Smith and Graham Wakefield

Media Arts and Technology, University of California, Santa Barbara
Santa Barbara, CA 93106, USA
{whsmith,wakefield}@mat.ucsb.edu

**Abstract.** We describe extensions to the Lua programming language constituting a novel platform to support practice and investigation in computational audiovisual composition. Significantly, these extensions enable the tight real-time integration of computation, time, sound and space, and follow a modus operandi of development going back to immanent properties of the domain.

**Keywords:** Audiovisual, Composition, Real-Time Multimedia, Lua, Scripting Language, Functional Programming, Domain Oriented Languages, Coroutines, Computational Aesthetics.

## 1 Introduction

In this paper we document extensions to the Lua programming language to support time-based audiovisual composition. Significantly, these extensions enable the tight real-time integration of computation, time, sound and space, and follow a modus operandi of development going back to immanent properties of the domain.

In general terms, we are interested in enabling and encouraging audiovisual composition with an elevated aesthetic role of computation beyond the computer-aided or computer-assisted. In particular, we are focusing on a computer programming language as the primary interface to composition, but also consider roles of computation as aesthetic subject, inspiration and perhaps even collaborator. A number of general benefits can be immediately identified:

- Introducing new expressive potential through formal generality and extensibility.
- Creative freedom and independence due to an increased role of the artist in the specification of the result.
- An appropriate means to work with the aesthetic values of process, data and algorithm.
- Ease of interaction with symbolic elements from other disciplines (examples might include mathematics, physics, systems biology, semiotics...)

Our development is targeted towards two specific goals. Firstly, we aim for a tight integration of time, space, sound and computation, motivated by the artistic possibilities engendered. Secondly, we begin from analyses of the immanent elements in computation, time, space and sound. This is partly to support a sufficiently grounded yet more generic and extensible range of expression, and partly since existing idioms may become inappropriate or even counter-productive as novel aesthetic activities develop.

R. Adams, S. Gibson, and S. Müller Arisona (Eds.): DAW/IF 2006/2007, CCIS 7, pp. 213–228, 2008.

We are responding to a tendency within the co-evolution of audiovisual art and computational technology that might constitute a new domain or field of discipline. This tendency can be characterized as an increasing focus on computation within aesthetic practice, and a deeper engagement with the medium that may be incompatible with antecedents. This tendency is quite contemporary, responding to the rising cultural infusion of computing and cross-modal concerns. For convenience we denote this tendency – the subject matter of our project – *computational audiovisual composition* [1].

Following an elaboration of these concerns, section 2 discusses our technical implementation in general terms. Sections 3 through 5 expound our efforts to extend Lua to meet the identified immanent demands of this emerging field in respective temporal, spatial and sonic terms, followed by concluding remarks in section 6.

## 2 Implementation Strategy

### 2.1 Background

The demand for tightly integrated modalities based upon immanent elements leads to the identification of two key design sites:

- Lower level components.
- Generic 'meta-mechanisms' rather than numerous features.

Lower level components may be necessary to support tight interaction between heterogeneous modalities and also to encourage the exploration of computational audiovisual potential. For example, in the design of a computer game, spatializable sound file playback may be sufficient, however the elevated role of computation in algorithmic composition suggests a lower level approach in terms of signal processing.

The *meta-mechanism* terminology is drawn from Lua itself. Lua's authors avoid a language bloated by numerous specialized features by providing a small set of components with which a user can build desired features in the way he or she wants them. For example, Lua offers no object-oriented class inheritance system, however many variations of object inheritance can be built upon its *metatable* construct. Meta-mechanisms avoid preconceived behavior through generality and thus encourages composers to explicitly specify the behavioral features of their works. Generalizing mechanism may also support cross-modality.

**On the Choice of a Programming Language.** The design of programming environments for audiovisual composition can be broadly divided into two camps: visual Graphical User Interface (GUI) environments and text-based environments utilizing domain specific languages. While generally more approachable for novice users, GUI-based environments such as Max/MSP/Jitter and Pd/GEM (Puckette, 2002) lack many of the formal notions a programming language embodies. Such environments more specifically address task scheduling and message passing rather than the computational

[1] Note that *composition* is intended to be equally applicable to real-time performance.

generality of our endeavor. [2] In contrast, a programming language as primary interface addresses the design sites listed above while making use of notions immanent to computation itself.

Regarding composition, Roads (2001) identifies two key benefits of programming language representations: "First, the compositional logic is made explicit, creating a system with a degree of formal consistency. Second, rather than abdicating decision-making to the computer, composers can use procedures to extend control over many more processes than they could manage with manual techniques."

Using a programming language as the primary artistic interface leads to a notion of composition-as-script. This notion is not new: a number of contemporary tools emphasizing the aesthetic role of computation such as SuperCollider (McCartney, 2002) and Fluxus (Griffiths, 2007) exemplify the same concerns for independently musical or spatiotemporal media.

Furthermore we note that many of these tools build upon existing languages rather than invent new ones. This leads to a number of clear benefits:

- Documentation easing learning curves
- Potentially numerous extension libraries adding additional capability for free
- Code re-use: repositories and portability
- Revision, debugging and profiling minimizing error and improving user experience
- Facilities formally verified in the community, supporting future scalability

Given these advantages, writing a new language only seems appropriate if no existing language can satisfy the demands of a domain. A preferable solution is to use a flexible language that is clearly designed for extension to specific domains: a *domain oriented* language (Thomas and Barry, 2003).

**Lua.** The Lua programming language has been designed throughout as an 'extensible extension language.' *Extensible* refers to the ease by which new semantic and functional features can be added within Lua or through underlying C functions, while *extension* refers to the ease by which Lua can be embedded within a host application as a higher-level configuration and control language (*Adobe Lightroom* and *World of Warcraft* are notable examples (Ierusalimschy et al., 2007)). The author of SuperCollider states that an extensible language allows the programmer to "focus only on the problem and less on satisfying the constraints and limitations of the language's abstractions and the computer's hardware" (McCartney, 2002).

Typical use of Lua as an extension languages combines libraries of performance sensitive code and key data structures modeled in C/C++ with the dynamic aspects of the application such as control flow and interface configuration written in Lua. Together with a number of generic benefits summarized in Table 1, these features make Lua ideal for the development of the domain-specific language in our project.

## 2.2 Contributions

We have extended the Lua programming language into the domains of temporal, spatial, and sonic composition. These extensions, and the associated host application, are

[2] For a more detailed analysis see (Wakefield and Smith, 2007).

**Table 1.** Noteworthy benefits of the Lua language

| | |
|---|---|
| **Data-description language** | Suitable as a readable and enactive document format |
| **High-level programming features** | Compact descriptions of complex algorithms and relationships, support for both imperative and functional styles |
| **Incremental garbage collector** | Driven by game-programming needs, suitable for real-time performance |
| **Well-regarded performance** | Amongst the fastest languages of its class |
| **Ease of development** | ANSI C, small library, well defined API |
| **Flexible license** | Compatible with both GPL and commercial use |

together called *LuaAV*. This is the focal point for our explorations in computational audiovisual composition as a medium for compositional, technical, and philosophical inquiry within the audiovisual arts.

The core application of LuaAV is a simple platform upon which users can define custom application environments (such as window arrangement and menu structure) and execute Lua scripts in order to actualize compositions into performances. These scripts make use of the grammar and vocabulary added by our domain-specific extensions. The extensions themselves are embodied as dynamically loadable Lua libraries (*modules*), making them independent of the core application. Consequently, any other application embedding Lua that allows a user to load scripts and modules will be able to execute scripts written using LuaAV. The subsequent sections of this paper detail the development of these modules.

LuaAV is intended to be cross-platform. OS dependent support resources such as windowing and file management are currently implemented on the OSX native Cocoa (Apple Computer – Cocoa, 2008) framework as well as the cross-platform GLUT (Kilgard, 2008) library, but will be mirrored with native resources for Linux and Windows in the near future. A public website of software resources, documentation and community pages related to LuaAV, and computational audiovisual composition using Lua in general, can be found at http://www.mat.ucsb.edu/lua-av, with a related community mailing list at lua-av@mat.ucsb.edu.

## 3 Temporal Structure

Sharing temporal mechanisms between sonic and spatial structures clearly supports generality, thus we begin with temporal support in the form of the Lua module *time*. This module must provide a low-level basis for the gradual determination of audiovisual output, and present a high-level interface for the gradual articulation of temporal expression, making use of notions immanent to computational audiovisual composition.

### 3.1 Computational Time and Composition Time

The fundamental force of time in computer architecture is the inexorable movement from one discrete instruction to the next. Computational ideas must be encoded into an executing state space via a series of such instructions. Any desired temporal structure in the executing performance process must emerge from this state space. From the standpoint of the developer, the problem can be restated as a low-level, generic mapping of composition time, i.e. the flow of articulation in performance, to computing time, i.e. the determined series of instructions.

We also note that the computational instruction flow is topological, in that the temporal distance between events is unstated. In practice individual instructions execute at a rate beyond the threshold of perception. To produce a real-time performance we must slow this process to a desired temporal metric.

In summary, computational articulation of temporal structure involves specification of the ordering and spacing of events, in turn demanding support for scheduled activity and measured durations respectively.

**Event Spacing: Measured Durations.** In order to allow specific temporal intervals to elapse between selected instructions, we need to provide a metric of time to measure against. The computational audiovisual domain suggests at least three sources for this metric: system time (based upon CPU hardware), frame-time (counting image buffer swapping events in the display system), and audio sample-time (based upon the sample-rate clock in the audio driver). These clocks are independent: audio clocks may drift slightly compared to system timers (Bencina, 2003), and frame-rate may vary adaptively with windowing system resources. In addition we may need user-space metrics within a composition, such as rhythmic tempo, as abstract temporal structures within and against which aesthetic form may occur. A user-space metric may be independent or synchronize with an existing clock.

The *time* module answers these demands by providing a generalized accumulator as a *clock* type, making no assumptions as to the semantics of the clock units (they could be nanoseconds, seconds, frames, samples, beats, mouse-clicks etc.) These accumulators can be polled for current value using the *now()* method, and manually incremented using the *advance(n)* method. To support synchronous relationships, clocks can be nested such that one becomes the driving parent of another: whenever the parent advances, so does the child. A relative offset and dynamically variable rate characterizes the child-parent relation.

In addition we implement a special clock available through *time.system* using nanosecond units and offering high-precision access to the CPU clock. This system clock supports two alternatives to manual increment: the *update()* method polls the system timer and advances all child clocks accordingly (suitable for event-driven hosts), while the *execute()* method hands over control of the application to the system timer which makes low-level system sleep calls to control execution in real-time.

**Event Ordering: Scheduled Activities.** Explicit articulation of temporal structure in computation must be built upon operations that divert the implicit, ephemeral causality between instructions. We identify four general classes of such operations, summarized in table 2.

Based upon this analysis, we chose a scheduling model that makes particular use of Lua's inherent support for concurrency and events. Specifically, we extend Lua

**Table 2.** General classes of the computational articulation of temporal structure

| Operation | Significance | Lua constructs |
|---|---|---|
| Memory | Duration, extended present. | Lexically scoped variables and garbage collection. |
| Control flow | Breaks homeomorphism between instruction series initiated and state space executed: conditions and branches. | If/then, do/while etc., but also higher-order functions and run-time compilation. |
| Concurrency | Simultaneity, parallelism, semi-independence. | Coroutines. |
| Events | Indeterminacy, event-driven execution. | Global callbacks from a host application or C library and file/stream handling. |

coroutines [3] by inserting conditional scheduling within the yield-resume mechanism, based upon either the clocks described above or arbitrary event notifications. The body of a coroutine can encapsulate any valid Lua code and thus any combination of memory and control flow instructions, completing coverage of the operation classes identified.

### 3.2 Implementation: Coroutine Scheduling

A coroutine can be created under control of the *time* module using the *go* function, which takes a function and an optional list of arguments. Any active coroutine can yield its execution using the *wait* function, whose argument is either a numeric duration (relative to a specified or default clock), or an arbitrary Lua value as an event token. In either case, this call suspends the coroutine and places it under the ownership of a condition within the *time* module scheduler.

An event notification may be triggered using the *event* function, whose first argument is the Lua value event token in question (see script 1). Event tokens can be tables, functions, strings or any other valid Lua type except numbers. Any coroutines pending upon the specified event token will be resumed in first-in, first-out order. Event-driven coroutines are means to specify procedural behavior in response to indeterminate asynchronous input. A public C function is also provided to support notified events from a host application.

Coroutines that wait upon a clock duration are placed in a schedule list belonging to the clock, indexed by its current value plus the specified duration. When the clock advances to this target time, the coroutine is removed from the schedule and resumed

[3] Coroutines, originally introduced by Conway in the early 1960s, are subroutines that act as master programs (Conway, 1963). A coroutine in Lua is a deterministically schedulable parallel virtual machine, constructed from a function defined in Lua code. A coroutine has its own stack, locally scoped variables and instruction pointer (which resumes from the same code point at which it last yielded) but shares global variables with other coroutines. Lua coroutines use a flexible asynchronous yield/resmue interface and are first-class objects within Lua code.

```
function clickwatcher()
   while true do         -- infinite loop
      local result = wait('click')
      print('a click occurred:', result)
   end
end

go(clickwatcher) -- launch a coroutine

event('click', 'left')
event('click', 'right')
```

**Script 1.** Using *go*, *wait* and *event* for event-based conditions. The *clickwatcher* function becomes the body of a coroutine when launched using *go*, resuming upon a 'click' event token notification via *event*. The additional arguments 'left' and 'right' are passed as return values to the *wait* call, and populate the *result* variable, for event-handling purposes.

```
function clockprinter(name, period)
   while true do
      print(name)
      wait(period)
   end
end

go(clockprinter, 'tock', 4)
go(clockprinter, 'tick', 1)
```

**Script 2.** Example using the default clock to create synchronous yet polymetric messages: printing four 'ticks' for every 'tock'

as normal (see script 3.2). As a convenience, the *go* function also takes an optional first argument prior to the function body to specify a duration to wait for before launching the coroutine.

Coroutines are continuations: they are objects that model everything that remains to be done at certain points in a functional structure. The execution of a composer's script becomes a real-time variation of the *continuation-based enactment* design pattern (Manolescu, 2002). The composer can use other module functions within coroutines to articulate many different audiovisual structures across time, whether synchronous or asynchronous, determinate or indeterminate.

### 3.3 Concurrency: Future Directions

Readers might note the absence of multithreading in the discussion of concurrency above. A Lua interpreter itself cannot be safely used across multiple operating system threads (a design decision of the Lua authors). [4] In contrast to coroutines, the scheduling

[4] Lua can be modified to be thread-safe by installing locks however there are performance and portability prices to pay.

of operating system threads is predominantly outside the scope of the executing program, introducing indeterminism in the timing of instructions between threads that prevents micro-temporal interdependencies. Safely sharing data structures between threads demands nontrivial solutions that are not conducive to a transparent programming interface (Lee, 2006). The call for tightly interleaved interaction between sonic and visual processes is very difficult to maintain with indeterminately scheduled threading. The authors therefore follow Lua by avoiding multithreading within the LuaAV interpreter.

This is not to say that threading is undesirable, since it may offer significant performance gains (particularly for multi-core machines). Finding a suitable means to make use of multithreading, while keeping the interface free of implementation details, is a pressing issue for LuaAV. Spreading computation across multiple threads is a problem of determining dependencies in processing graphs and dispatching batches of parallel computation. For example, parallelizing intensive sonic, spatial and geometric calculations in C/C++ functional tasks is viable if the return values are not time-critical.

A related need, in order to avoid temporal glitches in real-time output, is the graceful management of slow, blocking or indeterminately timed calls (such as file IO) within the main process. Libraries for Lua already exist that can place indeterminate calls into distinct operating system threads and return data once complete (HelperThreads (Guerra, 2005) for C calls, Lanes (Asko Kauppi, 2007) for Lua processes). It may be viable to provide similar support within the existing semantics of the *time* module, such as yielding a coroutine until a sub-thread process has completed.

# 4 Spatial and Visual Structure

In this section we describe the development of Lua modules for spatial and visual composition, which are founded on the notions put forth in the introduction. The modules deal with fundamental elements of spatial relationships and image composition. Spatial relationships are handled by *vec* and *space* while image composition and manipulation functionality is contained in *opengl* and *glo* modules.

## 4.1 Foundations

Within current computer architecture, 3D graphics operations are handled by specialized stream processors, known as graphics processing units (GPUs)[5]. The GPU takes spatial information as input and projects it into image space for rasterization and display. In addition, modern GPUs support the compilation and execution of micro programs called *shaders* in order to support user customization of geometry and data processing routines. Within this system, we can identify four basic notions in the movement from spatial form to visual output:

- Position and orientation
- Distance and proximity
- Projection of space into image
- Compositing of images

[5] Throughout this document, the term GPU will be used to refer to the actual hardware in the computer as well as the system-level driver controlling the operation of the hardware.

Given a set of objects in space, each object will have a position and orientation. These properties describe relationships of the objects to the space itself. Between points and their orientations we can derive notions of distance and relative orientation as well as various types of proximity. Proximity in its most basic form is equivalent in meaning to distance, however the notion of proximity can also encompass spatial distribution. These notions form the basic elements of spatial composition.

Once on the GPU, spatial form is projected into image space through a virtual viewport. This viewport may contain additional fragments from previous frames or alternate views of the same space and potentially even elements from entirely different spaces.

## 4.2 Current Implementation

**Quaternions and Vectors.** The *vec* module contains both 3D vector (*vec.Vec3*) and quaternion (*vec.Quat*) classes for composing position, movement, and orientation in 3D space. *Vec3* serves to simplify calculating 3D quantities and covers math operations for moving objects in space while *Quat* provides orientation and local coordinate frame information. In particular, quaternions can be used for calculating orientations without some of the computational drawbacks (Eberly, 2006) and degeneracies (Hanson, 2006) of other orientation representations. In terms of spatial composition, quaternions are eminently suited for designing paths through space as is required for extruding surfaces and calculating complex camera movements.

**Euclidean Space and Point Relationships.** The *space* module supports both the basic notion of proximity as distance and the formulation correlating distance with spatial distribution. The basic notion of proximity is implemented using the Approximate Nearest Neighbors (ANN) (Mount and Arya, 2006) library's kd-tree functionality and can be accessed using the *within* and *nearest* functions. *within* takes a point and a scalar value indicating the squared search radius while *nearest* takes a point and a number of nearest points to return. Both functions return an array of points and their respective squared distances from the query point.

Distribution correlated proximity is implemented using the 3D Delaunay triangulations package from the Computational Geometry and Algorithms Library (CGAL) (Hert et al., 2007) and derived Voronoi diagram classes. O'Rourke (2005) describes Voronoi diagrams – and implicitly Delaunay triangulations due to their duality – as "[i]n a sense …record[ing] everything one would ever want to know about proximity of a set of points (or more general objects)," however with the increase in encoded information comes a parallel increase in upfront computational cost and thus a lower frequency at which such structures can be calculated, especially within the constraints of a real-time system.

In relation to spatial composition, the Delaunay and Voronoi duality describe both a kind of rhizomatic latticework and an adaptive cellular tiling of the space occupied by the latticework (Figure 1). The latticework of the Delaunay triangulation is tetrahedral (in 3D) and also defines a boundary (convex hull) to the point set. The Voronoi diagram in comparison defines a set of adjacent polyhedral cells with each enclosing a single Delaunay point. Consequently, Voronoi diagrams can be used to drive spatial algorithms such as growth processes and aid in quantizing and processing volumetric fields.

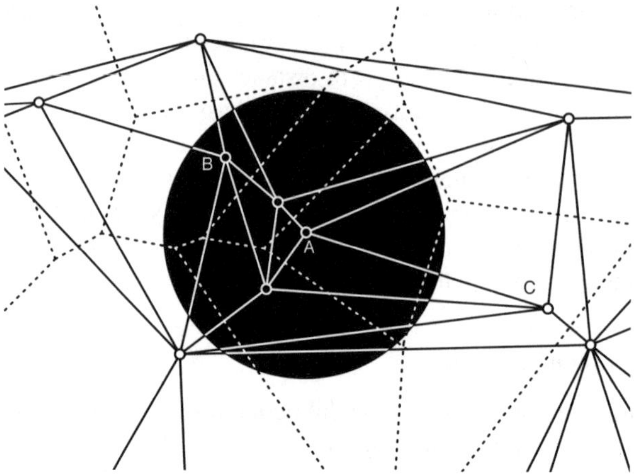


**Fig. 1.** An illustration of the correlation between distance and spatial distribution in a Delaunay triangulation (solid) with Voronoi diagram (dashed). The black disk is centered on A, which is connected to C but not B due to intermediate points along the direction from A to B despite B being significantly closer to A than C.

**Graphics Interface.** The graphics modules in LuaAV support both low-level control of the GPU through OpenGL [6] as well as higher-level userdata objects that distill complex sections of the OpenGL specification into a more appropriate compositional interface. The low-level OpenGL bindings are based on LuaGL [7] and provide a one-to-one mapping of the OpenGL API into Lua contained in the *opengl* module. The higher level objects are contained in a module called *glo* (GL Objects), which contains the classes *Shader*, *Texture*, and *Slab*.

Shaders and slabs load and compile code written in GLSL (OpenGL Shading Language) from file. The shader files are executable Lua code, taking advantage of Lua as a configuration language, and bear the extension "*.shl*". Since the shaders are valid Lua statements, arbitrary code can be executed in the shader file on load. For example, a depth of field shader using a hard-coded (const float array) Poisson distribution as a sampling function in the fragment shader could generate the sample points procedurally on file load in place of listing a series of numbers.

'Slab' is the GPGPU[8] term for dispatching a textured quad to the GPU in order to perform calculations with the fragment processor (Harris, 2003). Typically each element in the texture is passed uninterpolated through the fragment processor and the result written into an equal-sized texture. The slab implementation in *glo* uses an FBO (Frame Buffer Object) backend and can automatically adapt output texture size if enabled. Slabs can be chained and used in feedback loops with other slabs or textures.

[6] see `http://www.opengl.org`

[7] see `http://luagl.wikidot.com`

[8] General Purpose computation on Graphics Processing Units (GPGPU), see `http://www.gpgpu.org`

```
tex = glo.Texture(512, 512)
tex:beginCapture()
gl.Color(0, 1, 0, 1)
gl.Begin('TRIANGLES')
   gl.Vertex(-1, 0, 0)
   gl.Vertex(0, 1, 0)
   gl.Vertex(1, 0, 0)
gl.End()
tex:endCapture()
```

**Script 3.** Sample script that draws a green triangle to a texture 512 x 512 pixels in size

Textures in *glo* support both image loading from file and render-to-texture. In render-to-texture mode, the texture is bound to an FBO and any successive draw operations are drawn to the texture instead of the screen (see script 3). Textures combined with slabs allow for development of complex image-space effects. Slabs encapsulate image-processing chains on the GPU for operation on textures, which can then be composited together in the image frame by blending together textured geometry. As a simple example, a basic montage effect can be constructed by capturing a scene to texture from two different vantage points and compositing them together according to some function of space and color.

**Morphogenetic Space: Future Directions.** While *space* currently handles purely Euclidean space and geometric primitives, a comprehensive computational spatial system should further include other conceptions of space and spatial entities in order to supply a broader range of compositional tools at various levels of spatial abstraction. The power of such an approach is apparent in software such as TopMod (Akleman et al., 2007) whose manifold preserving topological mesh editing operations enable a user to construct complex structures with holes and handles.

A thorough discussion of spatial abstraction as it relates to generative and emergent form has been given by DeLanda in his treatment of Deleuze's notions of virtuality, wherein DeLanda puts forth what could almost be described as a group theoretical framework for spatial composition (DeLanda, 2005). This framework describes a morphogenetic view of space where processes of symmetry-breaking transformations move progressively from intensive to extensive embodiment, resulting in complex spatial and temporal dependencies in the generation of form.

## 5 Sonic Structure

In this section we describe the development of Lua extension modules to support the articulation of sonic structure according to the strategies outlined in the introduction. The result is the *audio* module for real-time low-level IO, and the *vessel* module providing abstractions of signal processing algorithms under the control of a lazy dynamic scheduler, both of which interface with the *time* module described in section 3.

### 5.1 Foundations

In considering the immanent notions of the sonic within computational audiovisual composition, we first encounter the low-level representation of acoustic phenomena in terms of series of discrete samples at a fixed sample-rate, as the form by which a program may render audio signals. We also note that the sheer volume of data being handled incurs a hard real-time efficiency constraint.

This representation is agnostic as to how sample-data may be generated or manipulated and thus gives no indicators as to an appropriate higher-level concept for the specification and articulation of sonic structure. We need a paradigm of signal processing which satisfies our low-level design goal, and may map well into the computational context. A number of approaches to model and control signal processing exist, however one of the most familiar is the *unit generator* (UG) paradigm, which encapsulates signal processing functions within stateful modular objects that can be freely interconnected into directed graphs. The homogeneity of the connection type and modularity of interconnection meets our demand for generality, while the discrete nature of graph structure and the symbolic nature of function encapsulation reflects well the computational domain. The authors therefore chose the UG concept as a viable signal processing model for sonic articulation [9].

### 5.2 Implementation

**Real-Time IO.** Rendering sonic output (and capturing input) in real-time involves interfacing with low-level operating system audio services, such as DirectX for Windows or CoreAudio for OSX. Libraries exist offering cross-platform abstractions of these services. We embed one such library, PortAudio (Bencina and Burk, 2001), within the *audio* module to introduce real-time audio in Lua.

Low-level real-time IO must satisfy a hard constraint: synthesis must precede playback. In practical terms this means that CPU bound synthesis of sample data must run in constrained windows of time specified by the buffering placed between synthesis and hardware (usually blocks of between 16 and 2048 samples per channel). Lower IO latencies (reduced buffering) can be achieved using secondary operating system threads for audio processing (Bencina, 2003) however as noted previously, such multithreading is neither supported by standard Lua nor is it conducive to computational audiovisual composition with low-level control. The *audio* module thus uses a blocking interface to read and write samples in the audio hardware. The capability to work with audio sample data alongside graphics calls such as OpenGL within a predictable, determinate shared memory context is considered one of the key features of LuaAV.

Calls to exchange sample data with the audio hardware increment an internal sample-counter, which takes the form of a clock as defined in the *time* module. Lua coroutines may be scheduled to this clock in terms of real-time sample durations, or put another way, articulation of form via Lua code can be sample accurate.

**Signal Processing.** Due to the sheer volume of data being processed and real-time demands, the UG signal processing algorithms should generally be executed in optimized

[9] Nevertheless it is borne in mind that other and possibly superior solutions may yet be found.

```
modulator = Sine()
modulator:frequency(8)  -- 8Hz
carrier = Sine(440 + modulator * 10)   -- Frequency Modulation
Out:add( carrier )
```

**Script 4.** Constructing UG graphs. Line 2 directly sets the frequency input of the UG created in line 1. Line 3 defines the frequency of a second UG (via constructor argument) to a graph composed using operator overloading. Line 4 attaches this second UG to the global output bus.

machine code rather than interpreted Lua. A viable solution is to bind existing C/C++ signal processing libraries to Lua so long as such libraries offer atomic access to UGs and make minimal assumptions as to how they may be used. In addition, the domain of computational audiovisual composition strongly suggests evolving dynamic relationships between sonic processes and other objects at arbitrary points of real-time (i.e. not quantized to system-dependent block-rates), adding several further requirements:

- dynamic graph determination
- efficiency in setup/change/removal
- variable block-size processing (for sample-accurate graph changes)

By making use of the Synz C++ library (Putnam, 2007), which meets these requirements, a set of UGs have been added to the *vessel* module, including oscillators, filters, delays, spatializers and more generic math functions. The UGs and their data buffers are implemented using up-front allocated free-list memory pools, to minimize the cost of memory management in a real-time process (Dannenberg and Bencina, 2005). Pre-allocated memory is recycled as the program executes, and pools grow if needed, utilizing a memory allocator optimized for real-time (Lea, 2000).

The UGs are presented within Lua in the form of mutable *userdata* objects, encapsulating C++ class instances. Userdata are first-class objects within the language and can be manipulated just like any other Lua type. The programming interface offers multiple means to compose UGs into graphs. Constructor functions create new UG instances, and may take arguments to specify input nodes. An instance's inputs are exposed for reference and re-assignment via member functions. Furthermore, all UGs share overloaded operators to construct graphs from elementary mathematical relations (+, -, *, /, ^, %). Finally, the outputs of multiple UGs can be merged using a special mixing bus type (see script 4). The combination of UGs as first-class Lua values and multiple modes of graph composition follow the design strategy of computational generality.

**Scheduling: Dynamic and Lazy.** UG graphs are deterministically directed since a node must have input data before it can produce output. This is a formulation of the producer-consumer problem, and both push (leaf to root) and pull (root to leaf) strategies may be used to traverse the graph. Static scheduling traverses the graph once before executing, while dynamic scheduling constantly re-traverses the graph during execution. Supporting dynamic graph changes at sample-accurate times in the midst of a buffered audio process is nontrivial.

The *vessel* module uses lazy evaluation to achieve this. Any state change to a UG (any Lua calls to modify its graph connections or internal state) triggers a traversal of the sub-graph upstream of the UG in question. Such traversals process each node from its current clock-time to the state change clock-time, resulting in just-in-time sample-accurate graph dynamics. Attempting to read data from the global audio output bus, such as copying to the audio hardware for real-time playback, triggers a graph traversal from the root to determine any remaining samples and advance the associated clock to a new time-stamp.

Since all graph state changes are triggered from within Lua code, the lazy dynamic scheduler fully supports the sample accurate interleaving of synthesis and control specification. [10] The *vessel* module turns out to be ideal for the exploration of algorithmic and generative approaches to the organization of microsound (Roads, 2001).

**Signal Processing: Future Directions.** A general limitation of the UG paradigm has already surfaced in practice: elements of processing become black boxes to the user. An example scenario where this may interrupt creativity is the inability to insert signal processing within a feedback delay path shorter than the graph block size. A possible solution under investigation is the dynamic compiling and loading of arbitrarily complex signal processing routines at runtime. Compiling a short C/C++ function can happen in a matter of milliseconds on current systems, which may be an acceptable latency for real-time code generation of optimized processing routines.

Signal processing in general is not specific to the sonic domain, and although the UG is inherited from electronic music, the concept may be more widely applicable to N-dimensional data streams. Alternative signal processing paradigms may also be applicable to spatial and more abstract domains. Exploring alternative approaches to synthesis specification within Lua is currently being investigated; a strong candidate with clear potential beyond the sonic may be Honing's Generalized Time Functions (N-dimensional manifolds including duration and current time as parameters (Honing, 1995)).

## 6 Conclusion

Our enthusiasm for computational audiovisual composition stems from our belief in the expressive capabilities of highly dynamic, functional and computational explorations and articulations of audiovisual experience, and from our excitement regarding the opportunity to pursue research investigations in this domain as an artistic practice in itself.

A noteworthy observation emerging from our work is the good fit between the coroutine construct and the computational articulation of time. Similar yet purely musical approaches to concurrent composition structure are evident in related languages: *Tasks* and *Routines* in SuperCollider (McCartney, 2002) and *Shreds* in ChucK (Wang and Cook, 2004). Rather than introducing new types however, we leverage an existing programming construct, and by avoiding preconceived notions such as keyframe, beat, measure etc. we provide more generic and interoperable functionality.

[10] Neologized by the authors of ChucK as "strongly timed" (Wang and Cook, 2004).

In summary, we have described the development of LuaAV, a framework to support a wide range of audiovisual composition practices, taking advantage of the language's inherent flexibility and extending it with modules responding to the immanent conditions of the computational audiovisual domain. Due to the design strategies employed, we hope it provides solid grounds for future research.

## References


Akleman, E., Chen, J., Srinivasan, V.: Topological Mesh Modeling. Texas A & M University (2007)

Apple Computer – Cocoa (2008), `http://developer.apple.com/cocoa/`

Kauppi, A., Lanes, L.: (2007), `http://luaforge.net/projects/lanes/`

Bencina, R.: PortAudio and media synchronization. In: Proceedings of the Australasian Computer Music Conference, pp. 13–20 (2003)

Bencina, R., Burk, P.: PortAudio - an open source cross platform audio API. In: Proceedings of the International Computer Music Conference, Havana, pp. 263–266 (2001)

Conway, M.E.: Design of a separable transition-diagram compiler. Commun. ACM 6(7), 396–408 (1963)

Dannenberg, R.B., Bencina, R.: Design patterns for real-time computer music systems (2005), `http://www.cs.cmu.edu/ rbd/doc/icmc2005workshop/time-systems-concepts-design-patterns.pdf`

DeLanda, M.: Intensive Science and Virtual Philosophy. Continuum International Publishing Group, New York (2005)

Eberly, D.: Rotation representations and performance issues. Technical report, Geometric Tools Inc. (2006)

Griffiths, D.: Fluxus (2007), `http://www.pawfal.org/Software/fluxus/`

Guerra, J.: Helper threads: Building blocks for non-blocking libraries (2005), `http://helper-threads.luaforge.net/`

Hanson, A.J.: Visualizing Quaternions. Morgan Kaufmann, San Francisco (2006)

Harris, M.: Real-Time Cloud Simulation and Rendering. PhD thesis, University of North Carolina at Chapel Hill (2003)

Hert, S., Hoffmann, M., Kettner, L., Pion, S., Seel, M.: An adaptable and extensible geometry kernel. Comput. Geom. Theory Appl. 38(1-2), 16–36 (2007)

Honing, H.: The vibrato problem: Comparing two solutions. Computer Music Journal 19(3), 32–49 (1995)

Ierusalimschy, R., de Figueiredo, L.H., Celes, W.: The evolution of lua. In: HOPL III: Proceedings of the third ACM SIGPLAN conference on History of programming languages, pp. 2–1–2–26. ACM Press, New York (2007)

Kilgard, M.: GLUT - The OpenGL Utility Toolkit (2008), `http://www.opengl.org/resources/libraries/glut/`

Lea, D.: A memory allocator (2000), `http://gee.cs.oswego.edu/dl/html/malloc.html`

Lee, E.A.: The problem with threads. Technical Report UCB/EECS-2006-1, EECS Department, University of California, Berkeley (January 2006), the published version of this paper is in IEEE Computer 39(5), 33–42 (May 2006)

Manolescu, D.A.: Workflow enactment with continuation and future objects. In: OOPSLA 2002: Proceedings of the 17th ACM SIGPLAN conference on Object-oriented programming, systems, languages, and applications, pp. 40–51. ACM, New York (2002)

McCartney, J.: Rethinking the computer music language: Supercollider. Comput. Music J. 26(4), 148–9267 (2002)

Mount, D.M., Arya, S.: Ann: A library for approximate nearest neighbor searching (2006), http://www.cs.umd.edu/~mount/ANN/

O'Rourke, J.: Computational Geometry in C. Cambridge University Press, Cambridge (2005)

Puckette, M.: Max at seventeen. Computer Music Journal 26(4), 31–43 (2002)

Putnam, L.: Synz (2007), http://www.uweb.ucsb.edu/~ljputnam/synz.html

Roads, C.: Microsound. MIT Press, Cambridge (2001)

Thomas, D., Barry, B.M.: Model driven development: the case for domain oriented programming. In: OOPSLA 2003: Companion of the 18th annual ACM SIGPLAN conference on Object-oriented programming, systems, languages, and applications, pp. 2–7. ACM, New York (2003)

Wakefield, G., Smith, W.: Using lua for audiovisual composition. In: Proceedings of the 2007 International Computer Music Conference, International Computer Music Association (2007)

Wang, G., Cook, P.: Chuck: A programming language for on-the-fy, real-time audio synthesis and multimedia. In: MULTIMEDIA 2004: Proceedings of the 12th annual ACM international conference on Multimedia, pp. 812–815. ACM, New York (2004)

# Interrellation: Sound-Transformation and Remixing in Real-Time

Hannes Raffaseder[1] and Martin Parker[2]

[1] Sankt Poelten University of Applied Sciences, Matthias Corvinus-Str. 15, 3100 Sankt Poelten, Austria
hannes.raffaseder@fhstp.ac.at
[2] University of Edinburgh
martin.parker@ed.ac.uk

**Abstract.** Until Thomas A. Edison invented the phonograph in 1877, sound had only been accessible in the moment of its creation. If a sound was to survive, it needed to be described in words or made again by the moving bodies that created it the first time. Today, we rarely think of sound as a passing, one-off moment because we can record, store and manipulate it so easily. However, the impact recorded sound has made on our approach to listening is deep; we now think of sound as solid and repeatable rather than transient and ephemeral. This paper remarks on these changes from the point of view of practicing artists who approach sound as a temporary and occasional phenomenon. The authors propose an approach to sound-transformation and re-mixing live-sound in real-time that plays on the "now or never" nature of sound. We describe the artistic concept, the software especially programmed for these purposes and some examples of our projects and performances.

**Keywords:** Computer Music, Sound Perception, Interactive Music, Reaktor, MaxMSP.

## 1 Introduction

Sound and the act of listening have recently attained many of the benefits and problems that text and reading underwent when hypertext became a viable format for distribution of the written word. Through tools such as iTunes [1], Pandora and the music genome project [2], MPEG-7 [3] analysis and other tagging systems, vast quantities of sound are made accessible, easy to manage, and anything that is not to our taste can quickly be skipped-over with the touch of a button. The ignored sound however is not deleted, it can be called upon at another time and in another place. A page of text on the web is similar. We see the information but as we read through the page, links excite the imagination and pull concentration away from the discussion at hand. To read an entire page with hypertext requires dedicated and concentrated effort. This change in technology has in turn changed our listening habits and reversed our perception of sound. Where once, sound was a transient medium that thrived as live, one-off event, we now think of it as an object that can be passed around, shared, duplicated and preserved indefinitely. We are composers and sound artists and work in the domain of interactive computer-based music. We

R. Adams, S. Gibson, and S. Müller Arisona (Eds.): DAW/IF 2006/2007, CCIS 7, pp. 229–237, 2008.

also curate festivals of music and perform together with laptops. We are concerned with the definition of live sound and this change in listening habits. We have been developing software that permits "hypertext-style" access to sound but the processing of the original sound source takes place in real-time. We feel this helps to bring sound back into the domain it used to inhabit; that of the transient, one-off and momentary. This paper then is rather a summary of subjective observations and artistic conclusions and not a report on provable scientific research.

## 2 Some Basic Principles of Sound Perception

As with any other sensation, human sound perception is restricted in many respects to specific features of the brain, the ear and the sonic medium itself. Of course we have to deal with these restrictions daily. Usually we don't care about the very basic principles of sound perception, although they determine human listening habits. That's why we point out some important principles of sound perception caused by the specific features of the sonic medium.

### 2.1 Sound as a Transient Medium

As pointed out in various sources on musical acoustics [4], [5] and [6], sound is a transient medium. Every sonic event takes place over a certain amount of time. Even if the duration may vary between a tenth of a second for percussive sounds to several hours for a Wagner opera, it decays afterwards. Until the invention of the Phonograph in 1877 [7], sound had to be perceived "now or never". Excitation, propagation and perception had to occur simultaneously. For this reason, one had to focus his or her attention towards the sound event. Active participation and personal experience were common attributes for the listening process and it is probable that the direct and strong emotional impact of music is closely related to this fact.

### 2.2 The Interrelation of Cause and Effect

Sound has to be stimulated by a dynamic process. Only a static environment is totally silent. Without movement and variation there is no sound to be heard. There is an obvious interrelation between the cause and the effect which is an irreversible principle [6]. Thus, a specific sound is strongly connected to its excitation, to the sounding objects and to the space in which the soundwave propagates. Even very short sounds carry complex information, and the listener is able to perceive several attributes concerning the source, the space and the excitation as summarised in Table 1.

**Table 1.** Specific Information of a single sound

| **Source** | **Space** | **Excitation** |
|---|---|---|
| Location | Condition | Condition |
| Form | Dimension | Power |
| Dimension | | Rhythm |
| Material | | Speed |
| Motion | | Mood |

The interrelation of cause and effect leads to a linear time structure of sonic events with an accurately defined beginning and end.

### 2.3 Music as a Time-Based Art

The transience of sonic energy, the impossibility of identical repetition, the irreversible principle of cause and effect and the need for dynamic processes make sonic events phenomena of time. There is no doubt, that music is (or at least was) a time-based artform.

According to Schneider [8] one has to point out that humans do not have a specific sense of the perception of time. Thus, time is experienced individually, rather than perceived in an objective way. To measure time, individuals correlate the inner rhythms of their body (pulse, breathing or step-frequency) their current personal mood (stress, boredom or fear) to external rhythms like the clock, the change of night and day the cycle of the seasons and environmental influences like frequency and content of perceived events. Especially in the Western tradition, the form and structure of time-based concepts play a very important role in music. Attributes like tempo, rhythms, melodic and harmonic structure fit into a concept of dramaturgy which in many cases, aims to affect the listeners experience of time.

To perceive and analyse a certain melodic theme, one first has to conceive it as a complete unit. Although this unit has a certain duration, it is observed more like a fixed-image; time is somehow frozen while listening to the specific formal unit. It could therefore be considered a representation of musical presence [9].

## 3 The Influence of Digital Audio on the Human Listening Habits

Thomas A. Edison's invention of the Phonograph in 1877 marks the beginning of rapid development of technology for recording, storing, editing and reproducing sound. Today almost everybody is used to the benefits of high-quality digital audio and these developments have changed sound perception as well as human habits of listening to music, speech and ambient sound.

### 3.1 Sound as a Durable Medium

In the 1970s digital sound recording techniques improved significantly and by 1982, recording artists were releasing music on Compact Disc, one of the first formats to provide 'hyperlinks' to other tracks on the disk. The 1980s also saw the introduction of Digital Audio Tape and Mini Disc to the mass market and by 1992, the webportal MP3.com was online. High quality recordings and reproductions of sonic events are a matter of course, and it can be argued that the transience of sonic energy as well as the impossibility of identical repetition lost their importance as basic principles of sonic perception. Sound is now available on the web like water in a pipe, many of us carry huge music libraries on portable players or cell phones. Though we still can't touch the sound itself, it has become a durable medium with almost unlimited access at any time and any place.

The possession of sound is not new or unique to digital audio. Since the advent of recording technology, sound has been desired, objectified and traded. If there is a difference to sound perception in more recent times, it is the ease of access to sound, the sheer volume of recorded information that can be accessed, collected, stored and more crucially, ignored. In fact, recorded sound is so present in daily life that one has to make some effort to avoid it.

### 3.2 The Dissociation of Cause and Effect

Since loudspeakers are common tools, dynamic processes are no longer preconditions for sound production, at least if the almost invisible movement of the speaker's membrane is neglected. There is no longer any need for a (visible) movement, for an excitation and a sounding object. Cause and effect are disassociated by the means of sound reproduction technologies. Recorded sound can be reproduced in other contexts. Instead of gathering the information of a single sound in a specific environment, we have to establish (new) connections between the sound, its visual, acoustic, social or historical context and our own previous experience during the perception process. People still tend to identify a sounding object with an excitation and thus set associative links between (imagined) visual and (actual) sonic stimuli. This can cause irritation and illusion as well as pleasure.

### 3.3 Sound as Ambience-Based Art

Given the ubiquity of recorded sound in everyday life, it would be exhausting to care about the beginning and the end, the formal structure and the dramaturgy of all sonic experience. This is probably the main reason why one of the main tasks of a DJ is to hide the transition from one song to another. As time tends to lose importance, sound has become a phenomenon of space. Examples of this development are not restricted to sound-installations in the field of sonic arts or ambient music as proposed by Brian Eno in the late 1970s [10]. Increasingly, sound and music are used to design the atmosphere of private as well as public places like supermarkets, restaurants or bars. The specific image of a club-night depends strongly on the music played. While using headphones and listening to music in public, people shut themselves away from their (sonic) environment and create their own private listening area [11].

## 4 Sound-Transformation and Re-Mixing in Real-Time

The possibilities of audio technology together with the changes of listening habits call for new artistic concepts dealing with the sonic medium, especially when recording, editing and reproduction techniques are used. Sound Transformation and Re-Mixing in Real-Time should be considered as an attempt to explore musical and listening potential in this direction.

### 4.1 Overview

While in most cases sound recording aims to reproduce the "original" sonic environment as close to reality as possible, sound transformation and re-mixing in real time makes use of recording, editing and reproduction techniques to alter the sonic event, even during its recording. This means that sound is digitally recorded, edited, transformed and reproduced sometimes using a multi-channel speaker system. Ideally, this occurs at exactly the same time or – if this fits better in the overall artistic concept of the project – right after the original sound source has been presented / performed.

Of course the recording already alters the former linear structure of time. Current music production usually doesn't reflect on this important change in sound perception and most listeners don't notice or don't care about it. Thus, for re-mixing in real-time sound effects and transformations causing strong impacts on the input signals are needed, so that it is more or less impossible to recognize the originating sound. However, some very subtle transformations have to be used as well, to enable the listener to establish links with the original sound sources.

## 4.2 Software

The authors use different kinds of software for the purpose of sound transformation and re-mixing in real time. While Hannes Raffaseder works with Native Instrument´s Reaktor [12], Martin Parker's patches are built in the Max/Msp programming language by Cycling '74 [13]. Raffaseder has designed several macros and instruments for recording, analysis, transformation, control and spatialisation purposes. The different instruments can be freely accessed with the help of a matrix-mixer during a live performance. Reaktor has less programming features then other similar audio programming environments such as Max/Msp or PD [14], but it takes advantage from its stability even under very high CPU load, a very good sound quality because of intern 32 Bit floating point operation and an easy interface, which enables rapid prototyping.

Parker's Max MSP patches take advantage of the FFT functions of Max MSP, storing spectral data rather than the sound itself. The spectral information is then explored through a joystick-based interface. Other patches dislocate the initial time dimension of the sound source. A particularly interesting effect is with loops that generate different periods of silence at the end of each cycle.

## 4.3 Processing Methods

The author's artistic concept of sound-transformation and re-mixing in real-time focuses on three basic principles: deconstruction of temporal shape, variation of movement patterns and the transformation of timbre.

### 4.3.1 Deconstructing Temporal Shape

As argued earlier, the recording itself already compromises linear time-structure. In addition any segments with any duration and from any time position within the recorded material could be defined and several segments can be played back at any moment. Thus, the consecutive sequence of different sonic events is transformed to a more parallel structure in time. The musician is free to control the duration of the segments to given values or within given intervals. Alternatively the duration can be controlled with random processes or Low Frequency Oscillators. The repetitions of the sequences can be triggered with a MIDI-keyboard as well as with a pattern sequencer or from random processes.

### 4.3.2 Variation of Movement Patterns

With the use of resampling, phase vocoding and granular synthesis each sequence of the recording can be played back at different speeds. Both extreme acceleration and slowdown are used to transform the sound. Within this variation of movement patterns, the interrelation of time and space becomes apparent. Thus, spatialisation using delays, reverb and a multi-channel speaker systems is important in addition to the change of the speed. Detached from their former time structure specific patterns of movement can be triggered by the musician and controlled with LFOs and random processes and locked onto the original sounds.

#### 4.3.3 Transformation of Timbre

To alter the timbre of a sound segment common filters are used as well as a Reaktor instrument designed for simple analysis-resynthesis purposes. A bank of 16 bandpass-filters is used for the analysis. The lowest cut-off frequency and distance between two filters can be controlled by the musician. The output of one specific filter controls the level of a sinusoid oscillator, which frequency initially matches the cut-off frequency of the filter. In addition the frequency of each oscillator can be detuned manually or with LFOs and random processes. Furthermore the output of the 16 filters can be stored in a table at any time. In this way, the timbre of this specific moment is frozen.

The Max/MSP FFT patches described above also provide this functionality but in a much higher resolution and it is also possible to take the timbre of one moment in time and mix it with the timbre of another time point. Low frequencies from one time zone can be mixed with high frequencies from another time for example.

## 5 Artistic Projects and Concepts

### 5.1 Snail

Based in Edinburgh and Vienna, our laptop duo Snail is focused on audio remixing live sound in real time. Having met in 2000 we began creating instrument-based improvisations with computers and in 2003 came up with the idea of re-mixing in real time. Our performance called techno-training was a live intervention during a journey in an old steam train. We recorded the noise of the running train with different microphones and used it as a live input. These sounds were transformed in real time and mixed live to the original sounds of the train. Of course the audience was sitting in one of the wagons and could listen to both the noise of the train and the re-mixed sounds. In other projects like TICOM_remixed or KLANGFORUM_remixed we recorded concerts of contemporary music ensembles and re-mixed them right after the applause faded out. Like an ongoing reverberation, the transformed sounds filled the space. The aim was to create a sounding ambience in which the music played at the concert a few minutes earlier was still present in a certain way. This atmosphere evoked an informal meeting between the musicians and the audience, an uncommon occurrence at concerts of contemporary classical music concerts [15].

### 5.2 staTdT_kunst

staTdT_kunst is an ongoing project by Kurt Hörbst (visuals) and Hannes Raffaseder (sound). The title has two different meanings: 'statt Kunst' (instead of art) deals with the role and significance of (contemporary) art in our society, while 'Stadtkunst' (city art) uses field recordings of specific sounds and voices, photos and videos sourced in the city or documentary-style interviews with people passing by as basic material for an audio-visual live-performance. Filtered through the artist's subjective point of view, this footage is deconstructed, categorised, transformed, and then re-assembled into a site-specific intermedia live performance. After performances in Linz, Braunschweig, Vienna and Belfast, Hörbst and Raffaseder have integrated some techniques of transformation and re-mixing in real time into this project. Since their performance *Edinburgh_220306* at the Dialogues festival in Edinburgh in March 2006, they now collect the audio and video material in the course of a single day. After a short editing process of about an hour, they perform that evening, re-mixing the videos and transforming the sounds live during the concert [16].

### 5.3 Boxberg-Sinfonie – a Bach-Metropolis-Transformation

This intermedia project was produced by the Trans-Media-Akademie Dresden under the supervision of Klaus Nicolai for the first *Festival Transnaturale* in Saxony. The project was staged in a closed turbine hall of a huge power plant in Boxberg. Until 1991 up to 50% of the overall electric power consumption of the German Democratic Republic was produced within this hall, which is 600 meters long.

Fritz Lang's well-known silent movie "Metropolis" from 1927 was newly edited by Holger G. Hermann especially for this project. Musical director, Michael Hurshell selected movements from Johann Sebastian Bach for different scenes. They were performed by the Orchestra of the Hochschule für Musik Carl Maria von Webern Dresden. These movements were digitally recorded and transformed and re-mixed in real-time to the consecutive scene of the film. The aim of this transformation was not only to accompany the film, but to turn the attention to the amazing space of the hall as well. In addition to four loudspeakers surrounding the audience, two more speakers on each side could be used to stress the depth and the huge dimensions of the space.

Of course the Boxberg-Sinfonie is a very site-specific project combining media related to different eras of time: Baroque orchestral music, a silent movie from the 1920s, a turbine hall closed in the 1990s, up to date video editing techniques and digital transformation and spatialisation of sound in real time. Thus the interrelation of time and space is certainly the most specific characteristic of this project [17].

### 5.4 Auto-route (2004)

"Auto-route" takes incoming audio and analyses the sound for information such as pitch, amplitude and attack sequences. This information is stored in tables that are then accessed and used as control parameters for automated remixing of the sampled audio stream. Rather than performed, this approach to remixing is entirely automated, based on information inherent in the sound that was just sampled. In this approach, there is a very one-off nature as the composition of the remix will be different each time the system is initiated. Auto-route has been presented at several events, perhaps the most unusual was during a tourist boat trip around Belfast in the 2005 Sonorities Festival. The voice of the tour guide was sampled and re-mixed by Auto-Route as the journey took place. W While this was an intervention and subversion, it was also a spontaneous accompaniment to the information being delivered.

### 5.5 Filament (2006)

"Filament" is a sound installation originally commissioned by the Tyrolean Branch of the ISCM in 2006. The project explores the real-time streaming of sound from sites of sonic interest around the city of Hall. The streams of audio are sent to a central server that subsequently spools out a continuous stream of sound to the installation in almost real-time. The installation itself is situated in a public square where a curtain of copper wires hang, representing a slice into the complex cabling system that runs the city's communications infrastructure. As the cables make contact with one another, snippets of the live audio stream are revealed. The sound of the city is remixed, performed and presented in real-time either by wind, people or objects moving around the space.

## 6 Summary

We have been developing our ideas about sound-transformation and re-mixing in real-time since 2003 as an artistic reaction to the changes in listening habits described above. From the outset we have tried to avoid a narrow interpretation of the concept and have applied our ideas and tools across a range of contexts from concert remixes and audio-visual performances to interactive sound installations. Rather than recording sound with the aim of reproducing it as close to the original a possible, we attempt to alter the sonic environment itself during its recording and consequently call attention to the interrelation of time and space. For these purposes we have developed several software-instruments in Reaktor and Max/Msp focusing on the deconstruction of temporal shape, the variation of movement patterns and the transformation of timbre.

Our original idea as the duo *Snail* was to work with classical, romantic and contemporary instrumental music in order to initiate a discussion between audiences, musicians, festival promoters and the musical material itself. Whilst a post-concert remix is interesting to listen to, it also provides a paradigm shift that classical concert goers may find interesting. A simultaneous concert remix can be performed in a café, bar or club while the concert is playing in another room or building, thus exposing a totally different audience to music played by a symphony orchestra. A live remix is subject to the one-off nature of any other live performance because the digital sound processing of a sound source is performed in real-time.

However, we have found it difficult for classical music makers to take these ideas very far. Curiously, one issue is caused by the microphones and recording equipment required to perform the live remix. Members of the UK's Musician's Union (as most British orchestral musicians are) require extra payment in order to permit microphones in the same room in which they are playing, so far making it impossible to explore this domain in a meaningful way with larger groups.

We have performed remixes in other contexts and this has lead to a fruitful dialogue both with musical material and the musicality of ambient sound. Importantly, the processing is never exactly repeatable; it is configured for a particular occasion and in order for these processes to work, they naturally create a relationship with live sound sources and demand an audience engaged in the process of listening there and then.

## References


1. Apple's itunes music website (last accessed, 02.01.2008), http://www.apple.com/itunes
2. The Music Genome Project (last accessed, 02.01.2008), http://www.pandora.com/mgp.shtml
3. Kim, H.-G., Moreau, N., et al.: MPEG-7 audio and beyond: audio content indexing and retrieval. J. Wiley, Chichester (2005)
4. Hall, D.: Musikalische Akustik. Ein Handbuch. Schott, Mainz (1997)
5. Roederer, J.G.: Physikalische und Psychoakustische Grundlagen der Musik. Springer, Berlin (2000)
6. Roads, C.: The Computer Music Tutorial. MIT Press, Cambridge (1996)
7. Schubert, H.: Historie der Schallaufzeichnung. Deutsches Rundfunkarchiv. Frankfurt am Main (1998/2003) (last accessed, 09.01.2008), http://www.dra.de/rundfunkgeschichte/schallaufzeichnung/index.html
8. Schneider, N.J.: Zeit – Rhythmus – Zahl. Schott Musik International, Mainz (2003)
9. Schneider, N.J.: Komponieren für Film und Fernsehen. Schott Musik International, Mainz (1997)
10. Eno, B.: Ambient 1, music for airports. [England], Virgin (2004)
11. Flash Mob website (last accessed, 02.01.2008), http://www.flashmob.co.uk/
12. Native Instruments (last accessed, 09.01.2008), http://www.native-instruments.de
13. Max MSP programming language (last accessed, 09.01.2008), http://www.cycling74.com
14. Puredata information site (last accessed, 09.01.2008), http://puredata.info/
15. Martin Parker's homepage (last accessed, 09.01.2008), http://www.tinpark.com
16. staTdT_kunst homepage (last accessed: 09.01.2008), http://www.stadtkunst.com
17. Nicolai, K. (ed.): Globale Medialisierung und integrale Kultur. Trans-Media-Akademie, Dresden (2005)

# Functors for Music: The Rubato Composer System

Guerino Mazzola[1], Gérard Milmeister[2], Karim Morsy[3], and Florian Thalmann[4]

[1] School of Music, University of Minnesota
guerino@mazzola.ch
[2] Department of Informatics, University of Zurich
milmei@ifi.unizh.ch
[3] Department of Informatics, Technische Universität München
morsy@in.tum.de
[4] Institute of Computer Science and Applied Mathematics, University of Bern
thalmann@students.unibe.ch

**Abstract.** In abstract mathematical music theory, the data format of denotators is associated with set-valued presheaves over module categories. In this paper, we present an implementation of this concept framework in the Rubato Composer system, a Java application comprising a GUI for manipulation and combination of rubettes. These are plug-ins that can be added and connected for communication of denotator data. Rubato Composer is a GPL software and is accessible to the computer music community for download and collaboration. In this paper, the functionality, architecture, concept framework, and the implemented mathematical operators are presented and illustrated with a "functorial composition" as well as with two rubettes for the construction of embellishments (macro objects) and wallpaper ornaments (grids of transformations acting on motifs). In a musically more significant example, we sketch the functorial reconstruction of Pierre Boulez's classical composition *structures pour deux pianos, Ia*.

## 1 Introduction

In 1984, the principles of a music composition software were presented to Herbert von Karajan and led to the Atari-application[1] *presto*®, used for the creation of a number of full-fledged compositions, e.g., the jazz CD *SYNTHESIS* [1]. In the sequel, our research has focused on a comprehensive environment RUBATO® for analysis, performance, and composition, including plug-ins for specific tasks. Such a plug-in is called RUBETTE®, and we managed to realize rubettes for rhythmical, melodic, and harmonic analysis, as well as a rubette for expressive performance and one for prima-vista operations. Originally, these implementations ran on NEXTSTEP and were later ported to Mac OS X. See the Rubato homepage[2] for the different Rubato implementations and documentation. Rubato has been applied to musicological research, which is documented in ICMC papers [2,3,4,5,6,7,8], papers on other conferences [9,10,11,12,13], and in the systematic context of a comprehensive theory [14].

However, the compositional components of Rubato have not been implemented in the NEXTSTEP and Mac OS X versions. In the present implementation, called *Rubato*

[1] shareware, accessible via tamw.atari-users.net/presto.htm
[2] www.rubato.org

R. Adams, S. Gibson, and S. Müller Arisona (Eds.): DAW/IF 2006/2007, CCIS 7, pp. 238–254, 2008.

*Composer*, which is a Java application, the original *presto* features are reconsidered and implemented within the framework of functorial mathematical music theory as described in [14]. This gives the compositional tools an unprecedented conceptual power. Intuitively, complex musical objects, such as dodecaphonic series, chords consisting not of ordinary notes, but of collections of melodies, or ornaments of rhythmic patterns, and, more generally, macro-object constructions in the spirit of Schenker, can be handled as if they were ordinary notes. In his introduction to the OpenMusic book [15], Miller Puckette notes: "In the future, computer music in general will have to deal with high-dimensional objects such as would specify a timbre. The dimensionality of a set such as the 'set of all possible sounds' is probably not even well defined. New techniques will be needed to describe and manipulate such quantities." We propose the present denotator concept as a three-way approach to the solution of the problems described by Puckette: (1) The introduction of addressed denotators, enabling the control of arbitrarily parametrized objects; (2) the construction of arbitrary finite limits, e.g., direct sums of modules; (3) the definition of circular concepts of arbitrary depth, used in FM synthesis, for example. The analytical and performance-theoretical tools of the preceding Rubato implementations will be reimplemented in the near future. For the time being, we focus on composition.

After an overview of the functionality and architecture, we describe the universal space concept of forms and their 'points', the denotators. We then describe their implementation in Rubato Composer and give examples of denotator constructions. Next, we describe the functorial operations and illustrate their musical signification. The paper concludes with (a) the explicit construction of a simple composition on the basis of the functorial concept framework, (b) the sketch of a construction method using macro objects and grids of transformations, and (c) the sketch of a functorial reconstruction of Pierre Boulez's classical composition *structures pour deux pianos, Ia*, using a new rubette, the BigBang rubette for musical composition, as well a number of rubette specifically implemented for Boulez's composition, therefore termed "boulettes".

## 2 Overview

The Rubato Composer system follows the classical Rubato architecture [2]: A frame application hosts a number of instantiated plug-ins, the rubettes, which perform specialized tasks. By means of a graphical user interface, rubettes are connected through input and output slots in networks. To this end, they are dragged from a repository onto a canvas representing the network, see figure 1. The distinctive feature of this network system is that the inter-rubette communication is performed via the denotator data format exclusively. This normalization is not restrictive at all since denotators realize a universal typology, which is endorsed by the most-advanced contemporary mathematics, viz. topos theory. Therefore, communication among rubettes uses a comprehensive language which fits in the mathematical universe. In this paper, we want to demonstrate that even the most abstract category theory of functors generated by the Yoneda embedding is canonically accessible on the basis of denotators. We also show that such tools are of practical use to composers and music theorists alike.

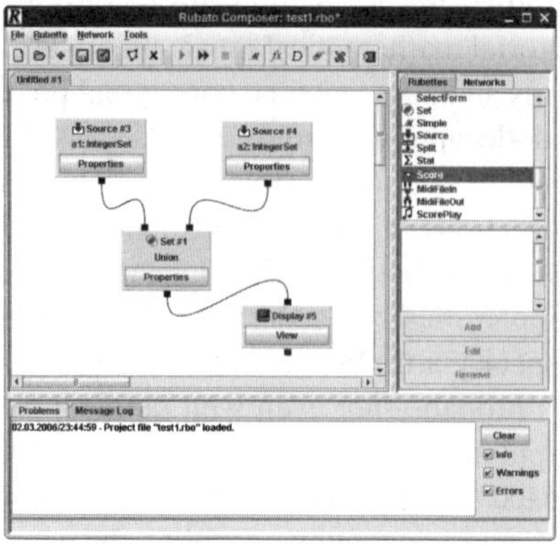

Fig. 1. The Rubato Composer network window

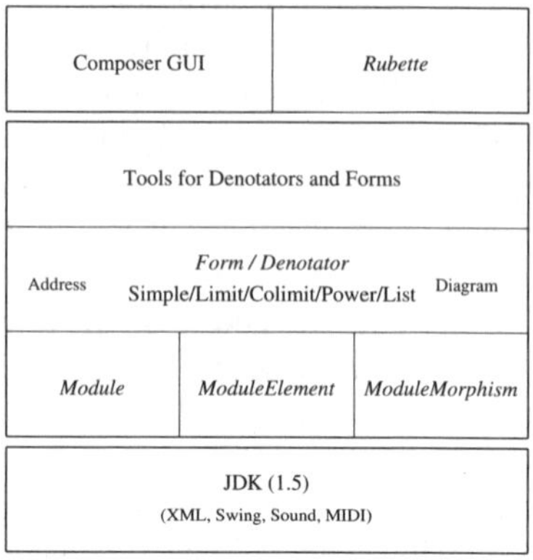


**Fig. 2.** The architecture of Rubato Composer

## 2.1 Functionality

A priori, the functionality of rubettes is only limited by the programmer's skill. The essential difference to the original rubette concept is the following. In the original context, we had four types of rubette tasks in mind: (1) analysis, (2) composition, (3) performance, and (4) logico-geometric operators. The fourth group was born from the insight or rather suspicion that many tasks in special rubettes can be decomposed into standard procedures of a logical and geometric nature.

In the present setup, the functionality of rubettes is not straitjacketed into such a rigid categorization. The main objective is reuse via the universal denotator interface. This component-oriented principle dissolves the original logico-geometric operator group since any rubette may define components of this type. But it also externalizes a number of functionalities which were hardcoded in the original Metro-, Melo-, or Performance-rubettes. The difference to general component architectures is that denotators present a clear formal conceptualization and therefore offer an interoperability beyond ad hoc interfaces.

## 2.2 Architecture

The Rubato Composer GUI and the Rubato framework are completely implemented in pure Java (JDK version 1.5), using various standard components of the JDK such as Swing for the graphical user interface, XML for the file data format and the Sound and MIDI APIs for score playing. Figure 2 visualizes the most important parts of the architecture.

The bottom to top direction of the diagram reflects the passage from lower to higher levels in the architecture itself. Thus, at the bottom is the general implementation system, the JDK. The first level of Rubato Composer proper consists of the triple hierarchy of mathematical modules, elements of module spaces, and morphisms between them. The italic typeface in this picture indicates the existence of a class or an interface of the same name. The background of this part is discussed in section 3.2.

On this concrete foundation sits the implementation of the core of Rubato Composer, namely denotators and forms. Section 3.1 deals with the details of this part. These classes are supplemented by tools for creating and manipulating forms and denotators, such as, for example, Boolean operations on denotators of type Power. The last level, most visible to application-oriented users, contains the implementation of Rubato Composer GUI including the rubette Java interface and a number of core rubettes. Essentially, the rubette interface exhibits several methods that define the operation of a rubette, namely the flow of data (denotators) from input to output. Additional, but optional, features include the definition of documentation strings and the export of a properties dialog to customize settings, as well as a view dialog for audio-visual representation of the process data.

# 3 Universal Spaces: Forms and Denotators

Forms and denotators are the data format on which Rubato communication is based. This format is the conceptual basis of mathematical music theory. We refer to [14,16], where this setup has been described in extenso. We first discuss the general concept architecture (section 3.1) and the present the mathematical basis (section 3.2).

## 3.1 Forms, Denotators and Their Implementation

**Forms.** The space format is called a form. The form $F$ is specified by the expression

$$\text{Name}_F : Id_F.\text{Type}_F(\text{Dia}_F).$$

The form name $\text{Name}_F$ is a denotator (to be defined below), the form identifier $Id_F$ is a monomorphism $Id_F : \text{Space}_F \to \text{Frame}_F$ of presheaves[3], $\text{Type}_F$ is one of four types: Simple, Limit, Colimit, or Power. And $\text{Dia}_F$ is a diagram of forms[4]. Depending on the type, the data is specified as follows.

For those readers that are not completely familiar with the mathematics and its notation used here, statements are included that point to the analoguous constructs of the data type model in the programming language Pascal and XML.

*Type Simple*: The diagram degenerates to a module $M$, standing for the representable presheaf $\text{Hom}(-, M) = @M$. This space type is the mathematical basis. In Pascal, this corresponds to the primitive datatypes such character, integer, or real, but also arrays of such primitive data types. But notice, that type Simple is much more comprehensive, for example, there are also polynomials. We shall describe the category of modules and its implementation in section 3.2. In XML, only character data (PCDATA) are primitive.

*Type Limit*: $\text{Frame}_F$ is the limit of the form spaces of the given diagram. In particular, if the diagram is discrete (i.e. no arrows), then we have the Cartesian product of a list of factors, representing a conjunction of attributes. The Pascal analogue is the record

[3] Presheaves are contravariant functors $P$ : **Mod** $\to$ **Sets** from the category **Mod** of modules and diaffine morphisms into the category **Sets** of sets.

[4] If $F, G$ are two forms, a morphism $f : F \to G$ is by definition a natural transformation of their underlying spaces.

data type, which is equivalent to the special case of the Cartesian product. In the XML content model, it is known as the sequence type. If arrows are present in the diagram, the limit construction formalizes constraints upon the coordinates of the Cartesian product. This is in fact akin to constraint programming.

*Type Colimit*: $\text{Frame}_F$ is the colimit of the form spaces of the given diagram. In particular, if the diagram is discrete (i.e. no arrows), then we have the disjoint union of a list of cofactors, representing a disjunction of attributes. In Pascal, there exists a variant record data type, which discriminates on an additional record field and corresponds to the special case of the colimit as a disjoint union. The DTD specification of XML calls this the choice type. The presence of arrows creates glueing condition on the cofactors.

*Type Power*: The diagram has a single vertex form $G$ and no arrow. The frame space is $\text{Frame}_F = \Omega^{\text{Space}_G}$, where $\Omega$ is the subobject classifier[5]. This corresponds to a collection of instances (i.e., denotators, see below) of the basic form $G$. Sets are not generally available in Pascal, except for the special case of a bitset, i.e., a data type of subsets of the set of integer values from 0 to 31. In XML, this type is absent.

**Denotators.** Based upon these form types, a denotator $D$ is an instance of such a space given by the following data:

$$\text{Name}_D : \text{Add}_D @\text{Form}_D(\text{Coord}_D).$$

Here, the denotator name $\text{Name}_D$ is again a denotator, the address $\text{Add}_D$ is a module $A$, the $\text{Form}_D$ is a form $F$, and the coordinate $\text{Coord}_D$ is an element of the evaluation $A@\text{Space}_F$ of the form space $\text{Space}_F$ of the form $F$ of $D$.

Observe that the definition of forms and denotators is circular in that names of forms are denotators, while denotators refer to forms. Most programming languages, including Java, accept circular definitions. However, for the implementation of these data types, circularity has two aspects: The instantation of a form-object of circular type, i.e., such that in the form's diagram, the form reappears, creates no problem, whereas operationally, the instantiation of denotators of circular type may cause endless loops.

**Implementation.** The present implementation is subject to some restrictions with respect to the mathematical theory: To begin with, the modules are not available in full generality, see the following section 3.2. Moreover, the instantiation of general Limit and Colimit typed forms is possible, but the exhibition of denotators of such forms becomes difficult if constraints or glueing conditions by diagram arrows are imposed. Currently, routines for the treatment of such constraints are not yet implemented. The novelty of the present implementation is the fairly complete realization of addressed denotators, including the techniques of address changes and space morphisms.

The implementation of presheaves $P$ is feasible for specified arguments, i.e., the definition of sets $A@P$ as well as set maps $f@P : B@P \to A@P$ for given maps $f : A \to B$ of address modules. Also, the morphisms between presheaves are given address-wise, i.e., we must specify set maps $A@P \to A@Q$ for given presheaves $P$, $Q$ in order to define a morphism $P \to Q$.

[5] At a given address $A$, this presheaf has the set of sieves, i.e., the subpresheaves of the representable presheaf $@A$: $A@\Omega = \text{Sub}(@A)$.

Although the definition of presheaf morphisms is not feasible in complete generality, a number of cases can be realized. To begin with, the Yoneda lemma guarantees that morphisms $f : @M \to @N$ are bijectively related to morphisms of the underlying modules, i.e., $f = @g$ for precisely one diaffine morphism $g : M \to N$.

Moreover, any morphism $f : \mathrm{colim}\,\mathcal{D} \to F$ is universally defined by the associated inductive system of morphisms $f_\iota : \mathcal{D}_\iota \to F$, whereas a morphism $f : F \to \lim \mathcal{D}$ is universally determined by its associated projective system $f_\iota : F \to \mathcal{D}_\iota$. Conversely, one may define morphisms $f : F \to \mathrm{colim}\,\mathcal{D}$ by a factorization through one of the spaces $\mathcal{D}_\iota$, and morphisms $f : \lim \mathcal{D} \to F$ may be defined through the factorization via one of the projection spaces $\mathcal{D}_\iota$. Although this is not the general solution, we get universally defined morphisms. For example, all affine morphisms $f : \bigoplus M_i \to \bigoplus N_j$ between finite direct sums of modules can be constructed by the universal properties of limits and colimits. Moreover, in the present implementation, some more general, not necessarily affine morphisms can be constructed.

With respect to the Power type forms, a very special, but usually sufficient case of denotators can be constructed: The general $A$-addressed denotator $D$ with the form

$$\mathrm{Name}_F : \mathit{Id}_F.\mathrm{Power}(G)$$

has the coordinate

$$c \in A@\Omega^{\mathrm{Space}_G} = \mathrm{Sub}(@A \times \mathrm{Space}_G).$$

It can be shown [14, ch. 7.3] that every set $S$ of $A$-addressed denotators in $G$ gives rise to a so-called objective subpresheaf $\hat{S}$ of $@A \times \mathrm{Space}_G$. Coordinates of shape $c = \hat{S}$ can be constructed in the present implementation.

**Construction of Forms and Denotators in Rubato Composer.** In the discussion of the architecture (section 2.2) a collection of tools on the programming level for comfortable construction of forms and denotators is mentioned. The Rubato Composer GUI exposes a user interface to these tools. As an example consider the construction of a form of type Limit with several factors, say already defined forms with names *E* (onset, type Simple with module $\mathbb{R}$), *H* (pitch, type Simple with module $\mathbb{Q}$), *L* (loudness, type Simple with module $\mathbb{Z}$) and $\partial E$ (duration, type Simple with module $\mathbb{R}$). Then the dialog for the construction of a form called *F* looks like figure 3.

The structure of the dialog is mostly self-explaining. One first selects the type of the form to create. The layout changes according to this choice. In the case of type Limit the factor forms are added from a list of already defined forms (button **Add**) or newly created ones (**Add new**). The order can be changed using the **Up** and **Down**. Optionally a label may be assigned to a factor for easier referencing, here these are, in order, *onset*, *pitch*, *loudness*, and *duration*.

This picture also shows how one could enrich the diagram of the Limit form: A domain (**From** list) and a codomain (**To** list) are selected and a morphism between the two is created using **Set morphism**, here between the first factor *E* and the third factor *L*.

Now, with the form *F* defined, the next step is to construct a denotator of this form. The intention is to build a $\mathbb{Z}^{11}$-addressed denotator, therefore, the module of the form

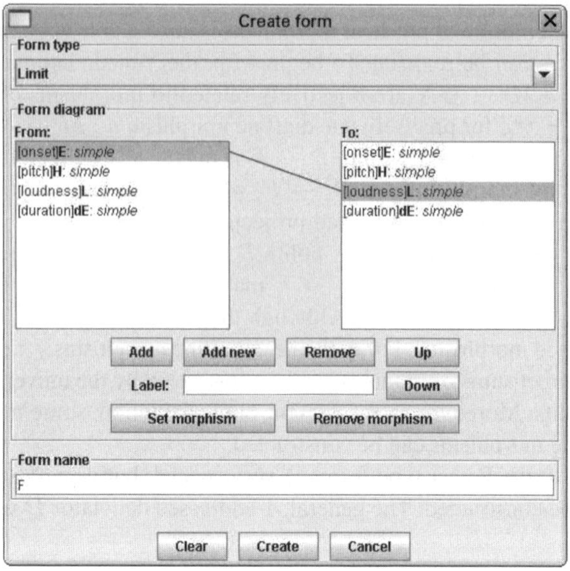


**Fig. 3.** The form construction dialog

*H* being $\mathbb{Q}$, a morphism $m : \mathbb{Z}^{11} \to \mathbb{Q}$ needs to be defined. To this end the module morphism builder tool is used (figure 4).

The domain and codomain of the morphism are selected, then the type of morphism, here the choice is "affine morphism". The morphism with name $m$ is of the form $m(x) = Ax + b$, where *A* is an integer $(1 \times 11)$-matrix and $b$ an integer. Similarly a morphism $\mathbb{Z}^{11} \to \mathbb{R}$ for the form *E* is defined. For the two remaining forms (representing loudness and duration) constant morphisms are used. Figure 5 shows the construction of the simple denotator *h1* with form *H*. After the form *H* for the new denotator has been chosen, the address type is set to *non-null* and the previously defined

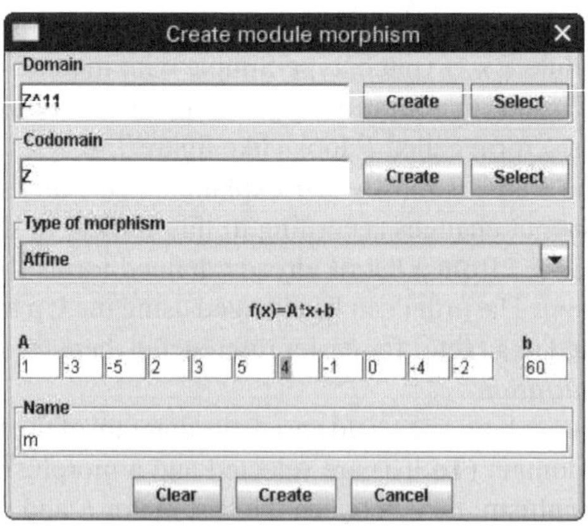


**Fig. 4.** The module morphism construction dialog

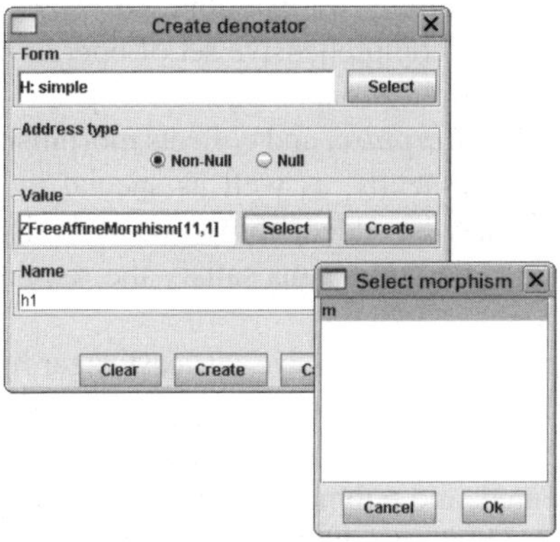


Fig. 5. The simple denotator construction dialog

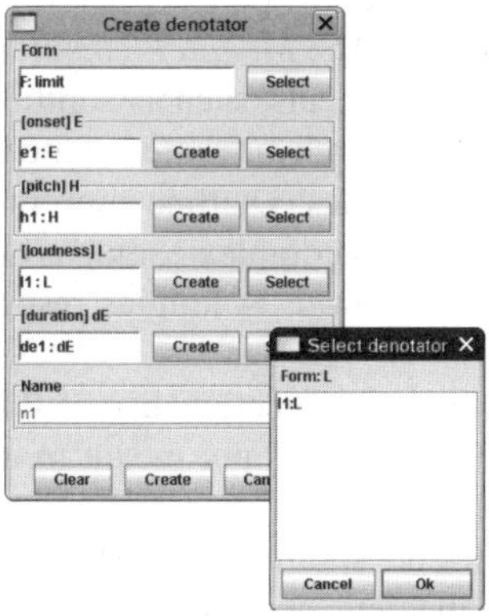


Fig. 6. The Limit denotator construction dialog

morphism $m$ is selected. Only those morphisms compatible with the form (in this case only those with codomain $\mathbb{Q}$, the module of the form $H$) are shown in the list. Denotators *e1* of form *E*, *l1* of form *L* and *de1* of form $\partial E$ are created in much the same way.

The last step is the definition of the denotator *n1* of form *F* (figure 6) and is straightforward from the above discussion.

## 3.2 The Module Category and Its Implementation

The mathematics as implemented in Rubato Composer comprises the rings $\mathbb{Z}$, $\mathbb{Z}_n$, $\mathbb{Q}$, $\mathbb{R}$, $\mathbb{C}$, of integers, modular integers, rationals, reals, and complexes, as well as word monoids $\langle\text{Unicode}\rangle$ over the alphabet Unicode (effectively strings with Unicode characters) and monoid algebras $R\langle\text{Unicode}\rangle$ over a ring $R$, and in particular the polynomial rings $R[X]$ in one variable. Finally, Cartesian products $R_1 \times \ldots R_n$ of rings $R_1, \ldots R_n$ are also supported.

Given a finite sequence $M_1, \ldots M_k$ of modules over a ring $R$, the direct sum $M_1 \oplus \ldots M_k$ can be built. In particular, the rings as one-dimensional modules over themselves give rise to free modules $R^k$ of dimension $k$, for example the real vector spaces $\mathbb{R}^k$.

The modules are located in a class hierarchy starting from the Java interface *Module*. Further down the hierarchy, Java interfaces like *FreeModule* and *Ring* are found that reflect the properties of particular types of modules. Thus, in contrast to the data types of most programming languages (Smalltalk being the most notable exception), a module in the Rubato framework is itself an object. Some module classes, such as *ZRing* ($\mathbb{Z}$), have only the singleton instance, others, such as *ZnRing* ($\mathbb{Z}_n$), may have many instances. The *Module* interface exports several useful methods, including those for querying attributes, such as whether the module is a ring, or for creating objects such as the zero element in the specific module.

Strictly parallel to the class hierarchy of modules, there is a hierarchy of classes representing elements in modules. These are the values, numbers and vectors, their classes reflecting the corresponding classes in the module hierarchy, for example, *ZElement* or *FreeElement*. The *ModuleElement* interface exports a comprehensive set of operations on module elements, such as addition and scalar multiplication.

A third hierarchy is rooted at the interface *ModuleMorphism* and collects morphisms between modules. Diaffine morphisms feature prominently, as well as special morphisms such as complex conjugation. Morphisms may be added, composed and raised to a natural power, as long as respective domains and codomains satisfy the requirements.

Although the functionality of this class framework is extensive, at least regarding module theory, it is not meant to aspire to a full-featured computer algebra system. Apart from the usual linear algebra (e.g., determinants or Gauss elimination), no algorithms for the solutions of systems are implemented, and polynomials support only the module theoretic operations as well as evaluation. Of course such functionality is useful and may be provided by a rubette that embodies a direct implementation or connects to packages such as Maple, Mathematica, or Maxima.

## 4 Functoriality and Its Application to Musical Operations

The functorial approach is a threefold methodology, providing us with a powerful toolbox for the manipulation of musical objects.

**First Method: Address Changes.** A given denotator $D$ with data $N_D : A@F(c)$ and any address change $f : B \to A$ are used to generate a new denotator $D_f$ with $N_{D_f} : B@F(c \circ f)$, whose coordinate is the image $c \circ f$ of $c$ under the map $f@\text{Space}_F$. A typical example is the evaluation of a denotator at elements $a \in A$ of its address. Such an element is addressed by the constant map $f : 0 \to A : f(0) = a$ from the zero address $B = 0$. For example, we take $A = \mathbb{Z}^n$, $F : Id.\text{Limit}(E, H, L, \partial E)$, the Cartesian product form composed of the four above Simple forms:

$$\begin{aligned} E &: Id.\text{Simple}(\mathbb{R}) \text{ (onset)}, \\ H &: Id.\text{Simple}(\mathbb{Q}) \text{ (pitch)}, \\ L &: Id.\text{Simple}(\mathbb{Z}) \text{ (loudness)}, \\ \partial E &: Id.\text{Simple}(\mathbb{R}) \text{ (duration)}, \end{aligned}$$

over the $\mathbb{Z}$-modules $\mathbb{Z}, \mathbb{Q}, \mathbb{R}$. If the address change is one of the canonical basis vectors $e_i = (0, 0, \ldots, 0, 1, 0, \ldots, 0), i = 1, \ldots n$ or the zero vector $e_0 = 0$, then the $n + 1$ evaluations $c_i = c_{e_i}$ yield the images of the basis vectors in $F$. This means that we obtain a sequence of $n + 1$ canonical "note" denotators $D_i = D_{e_i}$ associated with the $\mathbb{Z}^n$-addressed denotator $D$. Conversely, every such $n + 1$-tuple $(D_i)_i$ defines a unique $\mathbb{Z}^n$-addressed denotator $D$ giving rise to the $n+1$-tuple, since $\mathbb{Z}^n$ is free. Musically, this means that one may now consider $n + 1$-tuples of ordinary notes as one "note" living at the free address $\mathbb{Z}^n$. If we take as address change any automorphism $f$ of $\mathbb{Z}^n$ induced by a permutation of the $n + 1$ vectors $e_i, i = 0, \ldots n$, then the new denotator $c_f$ is just a reordering of the given sequence of ordinary, i.e., zero-addressed, notes following the given permutation.

**Second Method: Space Transformations.** In this case, not the domain address $A$ of $D$ is changed, but its form space. Given a morphism $h : F \to G$ of forms, the denotator coordinate $c \in A@\mathrm{Space}_F$ is mapped to a coordinate $hc = A@h(c)$ of a new denotator ${}_hD$ defined by $N_{{}_hD} : A@G(hc)$. In our previous example, of course each projection $p_E : F \to E, p_H : F \to H, p_L : F \to L$, and $p_{\partial E} : F \to \partial E$ gives rise to the corresponding coordinate denotators $E_D = {}_{p_E}D$, $H_D = {}_{p_H}D$, $L_D = {}_{p_L}D$, and $\partial E_D = {}_{p_{\partial E}}D$. A second typical example is a standard transformation in music on the form $F$, such as a retrograde inversion $R\ I$ defined by (1) a pitch inversion $I(x) = h - x$ on $\mathbb{Q}$ and (2) a time inversion $R(x) = t - x$ on $\mathbb{R}$, and leaving the other coordinates fixed. This approach is in fact independent of the given address and works at any address. Therefore the musical application may be thought as an operation on $A$-addressed denotators as if they were ordinary zero-addressed notes.

Summarizing, every couple of an address change $f : B \to A$ and a form morphism $h : F \to G$ gives rise to a new denotator ${}_hD_f$ with address $B$ and form $G$.

**Third Method: Set-Theoretic Constructions.** On Power type forms, one has the common Boolean operations $C \cup D, C \cap D$, and $C - D$ for denotators $C, D$ at the same address. Attention: absolute negation and implication of Boolean logic are not possible within the context of finite power denotators. Moreover, if a denotator $D$ has Power type form $F : Id.\mathrm{Power}(G)$, where $G$ is also a Power type, then the union of the elements of $D$ (which are sets) yields a denotator $\bigcup D$ of form $G$, the address being unchanged.

Suppose that we are given an $A$-addressed denotator $D$ in the form $F$. If we are given a Power-typed denotator $S$ with $N_S : B@H(c)$, where $H : Id.\mathrm{Power}(G)$ for a Simple typed form $G$ with $N_G : Id.\mathrm{Simple}(A)$, then we have $c \subset B@A$, i.e., $c = \{c_1 : B \to A, \ldots c_k : B \to A\}$ is a set of address changes from $A$ to $B$. Therefore, we may apply each such change to $D$ and then get the Power-typed denotator $D_S$ with coordinate set $\{D_{c_1}, \ldots D_{c_k}\}$ at address $B$ over the form $F$. This method is particularly useful in order to generate zero-addressed Power-typed denotators ($B = 0$) from more abstract $A$-addressed ones. For example, the manipulation of $A = \mathbb{Z}^{11}$-addressed denotators, which may represent dodecaphonic series, will then yield sets of "ordinary notes" associated with the given series.

## 5 A Functorial Composition with Dodecaphonic Series

It remains to demonstrate how the theoretical musings of section 4 are put into practice. The basis for the example developed presently are the forms as constructed in the example of section 3.1. However, the names are chosen to be a little longer for the sake of clarity: *Pitch* $= H$, *Onset* $= E$, *Loudness* $= L$, *Duration* $= \partial E$, and *Note* $= F$. Assuming that the forms have been created we proceed in several steps. The reader is invited to compare these steps to the procedures described in section 4.

1. Two $\mathbb{Z}^{11}$-addressed denotators $n_1$ and $n_2$ of form *Note* are created. To this end, a pair of denotators for each of the forms *Pitch*, *Onset*, *Duration* and *Loudness* has to be constructed. *Duration* and *Loudness* can be dealt with quickly, i.e., by using a meaningful, but for this purpose immaterial, constant morphism.

For the denotators of form *Onset*, a diaffine morphism $h : \mathbb{Z}^{11} \to \mathbb{R}$ is defined as the composition $h_2 \circ h_1$, where $h_1 : \mathbb{Z}^{11} \to \mathbb{Z}$, such that $h_1(x) = Ax + b$, where

$$A = [1, 2, 3, 4, 5, 6, 7, 8, 9, 10, 11] \text{ and } b = 0,$$

and $h_2 : \mathbb{Z} \to \mathbb{R}$ is the embedding of integers in the reals. The morphism for the pitch of the first note $n_1$ is $f(x) = A_f x + b_f$, where

$$A_f = [1, -3, 2, 3, 5, 7, 4, -1, -2, -4, -5], b_f = 60.$$

The pitch for the second note $n_2$ is defined by $g(X) = A_g x + b_g$, where

$$A_g = [1, 2, 3, 6, 5, 4, -1, -2, -3, -4, -5], b_g = 67.$$

2. A $\mathbb{Z}^{11}$-addressed denotator $s$ of form *Score* (set of *Note*-denotators in a Power-type form deduced from *Note*) with elements $n_1$ and $n_2$ is created. Illustrative screenshots are omitted since this was already shown above.
3. On a new network a *Source* rubette that outputs denotator $s$ is placed (figure 7).

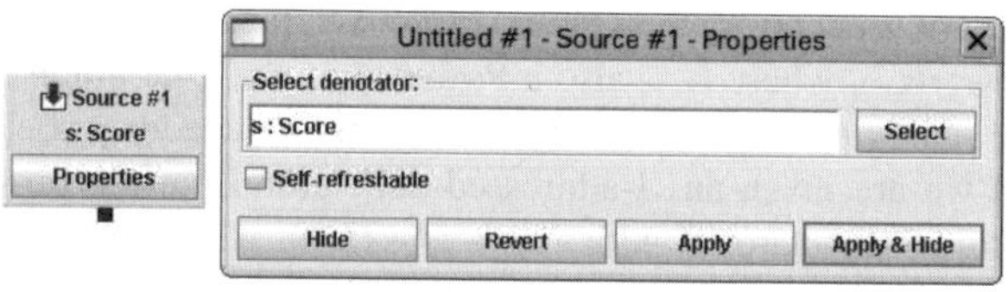


**Fig. 7.** A *Source* rubette

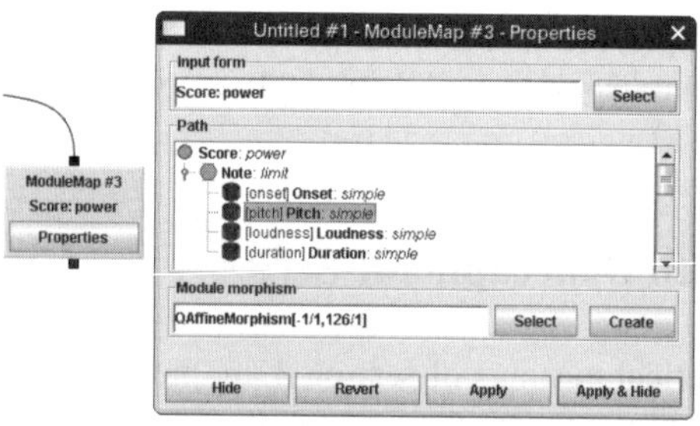


**Fig. 8.** A *ModuleMap* rubette

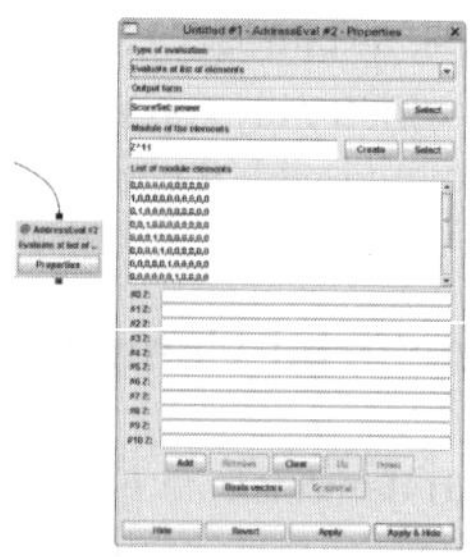

**Fig. 9.** An *AddressEval* rubette

4. To perform an inversion, a morphism $I : \mathbb{Q} \to \mathbb{Q}$ is created with $I(x) = 126 - x$. A *ModuleMap* rubette is introduced that performs $I$ on the *Pitch* part of $s$ (figure 8).
5. To perform a retrograde, a morphism $R : \mathbb{R} \to \mathbb{R}$ is created with $R(x) = 11 - x$. Another *ModuleMap* rubette is placed in the network that performs $R$ on the *Onset* part of the previous result.

6. The next computation involves the evaluation of the result at an address. The address space is $\mathbb{Z}^{11}$. We choose to evaluate at the basis vectors $e_0, e_1 \ldots e_{11}$ using an *AddressEval* rubette (figure 9). The result is a set of *Score* denotators, i.e., a denotator of the Power-typed form *ScoreSet*.
7. To get a *Score* denotator again, the previous result is piped into a *Set* rubette to apply the big union operator described in section 4 (third method).
8. To make things a little more interesting, the original denotator $s$ is evaluated at the same address and united with the transformed one through a union.
9. The result can be displayed in a piano roll representation and played using the *ScorePlay* rubette.

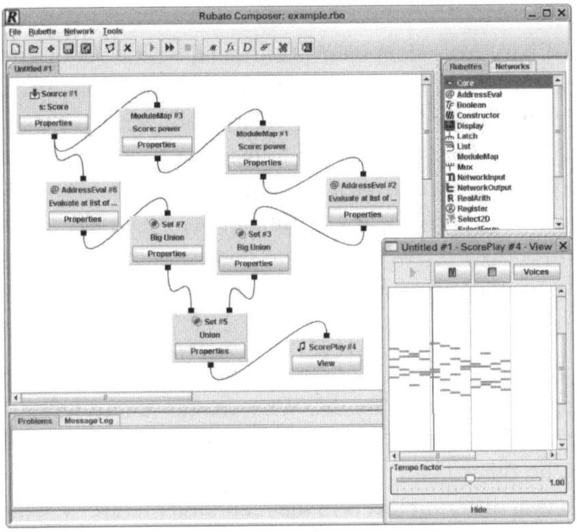


**Fig. 10.** The complete network and the *ScorePlay* view

The whole setup is shown in figure 10. This example is simple, but illustrates the purpose and power of Rubato Composer. Behind the simplicity displayed by the network of rubettes lies a lot of precisely formulated mathematics.

## 6 Macro Scores and Wallpapers

The paper concludes with the sketch of two rubettes. The first is very useful for the composition of compound objects conceived for musical embellishment (in trills, for example). The second can be used for the regular "distribution" of object assemblies (motifs or rhythmic units, for example) on parameter spaces defined by a grid of transformations.

### 6.1 Macro Scores

In music it is common to consider sound events which share a specific type of hierarchical grouping, for example when dealing with embellishments like trills. Such a musical grouping is usually anchored at single reference note. Duration, onset, pitch and loudness of the notes in the group are then determined according to standard rules that apply to the specific embellishment. These additional notes are reference notes themselves, which may embellished in turn. Such a circular construction can be described as follows:

$$\begin{aligned} \mathit{MacroScore} &: \mathit{Id.Power}(\mathit{Knot}) \\ \mathit{Knot} &: \mathit{Id.Limit}(\mathit{Note}, \mathit{MacroScore}) \\ \mathit{Note} &: \mathit{Id.Limit}(\mathit{Onset}, \mathit{Pitch}, \mathit{Loudness}, \mathit{Duration}) \end{aligned}$$

In this setup an ordinary *Note* denotator is enriched with a set of embellishment notes which are contained in a *MacroScore* denotator. The question arises, how morphisms that are usually applied to ordinary *Score* denotators are to be defined for these denotators. A *MacroScore* denotator can be transformed similarly to a normal form by the following procedure. Given a form morphism $f : \mathit{Note} \to \mathit{Note}$ and a denotator $D : A@\mathit{MacroScore}(K_1, \dots K_n)$, its coordinates $K_k$ being *Knot* denotators with notes $\mathit{Note}_k$ and macro scores $M_k$, we define the corresponding transformation on macro forms $\mathit{Macro}_f : \mathit{MacroScore} \to \mathit{MacroScore}$ as follows:

$$\mathit{Macro}_f(D) = \{(f(\mathit{Note}_k), M_k) \mid k \in D\},$$

where we abbreviate $\mathit{MacroScore}$ by $M$. What makes macro forms so powerful is, on the one hand, that musical objects of arbitrary recursive depth can be represented in a compact way. On the other hand, the aforementioned algebraic operations can be applied to these objects at different levels in the recursion hierarchy, which certainly offers completely new possibilities to composers. For example, this allows the manipulation of the anchor notes without altering their embellishments.

After manipulating these objects at different levels, it is necessary to obtain the flat hierarchy of an “ordinary score”, which can be played. To this end, we define the following ”flattening” operation:

$$\begin{aligned} \mathit{Flatten}(D) &= \bigcup_i \mathit{Flatten}(K_i) \\ \mathit{Flatten}(K) &= (\mathit{Note}, \emptyset) \cup \{(\mathit{Note} \oplus \mathit{Note}_k, M_k) \mid k \in M_K\} \end{aligned}$$

If a $\mathit{MacroScore}$ denotator has empty embellishment groups in its knots, the flattening operation is the identity. Thus, iterated flattening eventually becomes stationary.

We provide the *MacroObject* rubette that performs flattening and facilitates the creation of macro forms. It also supports extraction of the *Note* coordinates from each knot of a *MacroScore* denotator. The result of the extraction operation is a *Score* denotator that can eventually be played back with the *ScorePlay* rubette. The flattening operation expects a *MacroScore* denotator as input and returns a *MacroScore* denotator on its output. In the properties dialog of the rubette, the number of flattening iterations and the $\oplus$

operartion are specified. In the case of trills, for example, $\oplus$ usually is the sum of the coordinates *Pitch*, *Onset*, *Loudness*, and *Duration*.

In particular, the hierarchical approach of macro objects—as implemented in the *MacroObject* rubette discussed above—allows the transfer of the concepts of Schenkerian analysis to composition.

### 6.2 The Wallpaper Rubette

A useful tool for creating complex compositions from single musical motifs is the *Wallpaper* rubette. It is based on an algorithm first implemented as the *OrnaMagic* module in *presto* [17].

The elements of an input motif $I : A@MacroScore(e_1, \dots e_n)$ of type Power are mapped using a sequence of morphisms, following the concepts described above (only first level *Note* denotators are transformed). The output denotator $O$ is of the same form $MacroScore$ and consists of the set union of all motifs, which are obtained under the given sequence of transformations. The goal is to obtain a wallpaper-like structure similar to the one shown in Fig. 11.

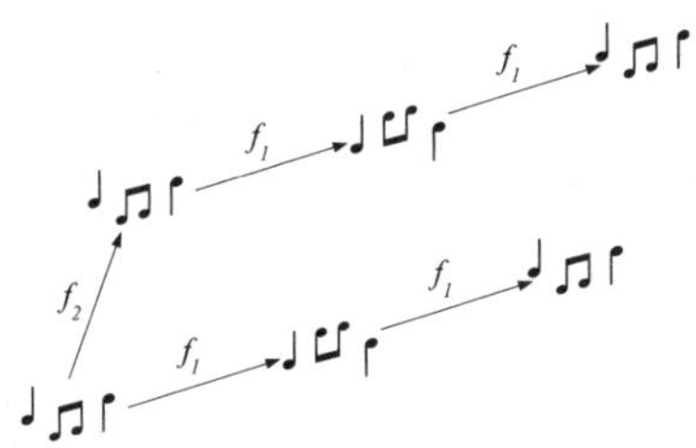

**Fig. 11.** A simple wallpaper with two morphisms $f_1$ (retrograde inversion and translation) and $f_2$ (translation). $r_1 = 2, r_2 = 1$.

To fabricate such a wallpaper, we first define a number of morphisms $f_1, \dots f_m$ : $Note \to Note$. Further, for each $f_i$, we define a range $r_i = [a_i, b_i] \subset \mathbb{N}$, where $a_i \leq b_i$. Composing these morphisms, we obtain the wallpaper

$$O = \bigcup_{k_i \in r_i} Macro(f_1^{k_1} \circ \dots f_m^{k_m})(I).$$

In this formula, we decided to use a definite order for the composition of morphisms to make sure that every point in the morphism grid is reached by a unique path (see Fig. 11).

The resulting musical wallpaper can now be flattened or it can be used as the input motif for a new instance of the *Wallpaper* rubette in the spirit of self-similarity in fractal theory.

When we apply transformations such as those provide by the *Wallpaper* rubette to *MacroScore* denotators, only first level *Note* denotators are transformed. Hence, all other notes in the macro structure remain untouched and maintain their relative position to the note of the next higher level. As an example, when the anchor note of a trill is rotated 90° in the $Onset \times Pitch$ plane, its embellishment notes keep their position in time after the base note.

### 6.3 Reconstructing Boulez's *Structures*

The following section is a sketch of a functorial procedure aimed at reconstructing and recomposing Boulez's *structures pour deux pianos, Ia* [18]. The full description can be found in [19]. In this procedure, we reconsider the addressed representation of a dodecaphonic series as a $\mathbb{Z}^{11}$-addressed denotator. For Boulez's situation, which deals with two pianos, we use the specific form

$$MacroScore{:}.\mathbf{Power}(Node)$$
$$Node{:}.\mathbf{Limit}(Note, MacroScore)$$
$$Note{:}.\mathbf{Simple}(Onset, Pitch, Loudness, Duration, Voice)$$
$$Onset{:}.\mathbf{Simple}(\mathbb{R}), Pitch{:}.\mathbf{Simple}(\mathbb{Z}), Loudness{:}.\mathbf{Simple}(\mathbb{Q})$$
$$Duration{:}.\mathbf{Simple}(\mathbb{R}), Voice{:}.\mathbf{Simple}(\mathbb{Z})$$

which allows for an instrumental specification in the voice coordinate. This form is however not directly used in Boulez's compositional strategy, we rather work on the form $BoulezSeries{:}.\lim(P, D, L, D, A)$ with the factors $P{:}.\mathbf{Simple}(\mathbb{Z}_{12})$, $D{:}.\mathbf{Simple}(\mathbb{R})$, $L{:}.\mathbf{Simple}(\mathbb{Z})$, $A{:}.\mathbf{Simple}(\mathbb{R}^3)$. The attack form $A$ has values in the real 3-space, where the first coordinate measures fraction of increase of nominal loudness, the second the articulatory fraction of increase in nominal duration, and the third the fraction of shift in onset defined by the attack type. For example, a sforzato attack (*sfz*) would increase nominal loudness by factor $1.3$, shorten duration to a staccato by $0.6$, and the third would add to the nominal onset a delay of $-0.2 \times$ nominal duration. As discussed in section 5, the address $\mathbb{Z}^{11}$ yields the parametrization by the 12 indices required for a serial sequence of parameters. For example, the pitch class series is the factor denotator $S_P{:}\mathbb{Z}^{11}@P(3, 2, 9, 8, 7, 6, 4, 1, 0, 10, 5, 11)$.

After Boulez's compositional work in the form $BoulezSeries$, a transformation of the resulting serial data to the form $MacroScore$ is performed. Boulez's procedure uses extensively the address $\mathbb{Z}^{11}$ and its affine tensor product address $\mathbb{Z}^{11} \boxtimes \mathbb{Z}^{11}$. This usage specifically means that he performs a highly sophisticated system of address changes on and between these two addresses. It is an excellent example of a compositional technique that could not be understood without the present functorial approach. In fact, the famous analysis by Giörgy Ligeti [20] shows a strong astonishment about Boulez's technicalities, even somehow refusing them as a "combinatorial, non-musical fetishism".

Our interpretation of Boulez's approach in terms of functoriality on addresses enables an implementation of the scheme of his composition by six specific rubettes, calles boulettes. By use of boulettes, we are able to extend and reconstruct Boulez's composition for any number of instruments and more general address changes [19, 6.3]. The result of this reconstruction is available online[6]. The representation of the

[6] http://www.encyclospace.org/special/restructures.mp3

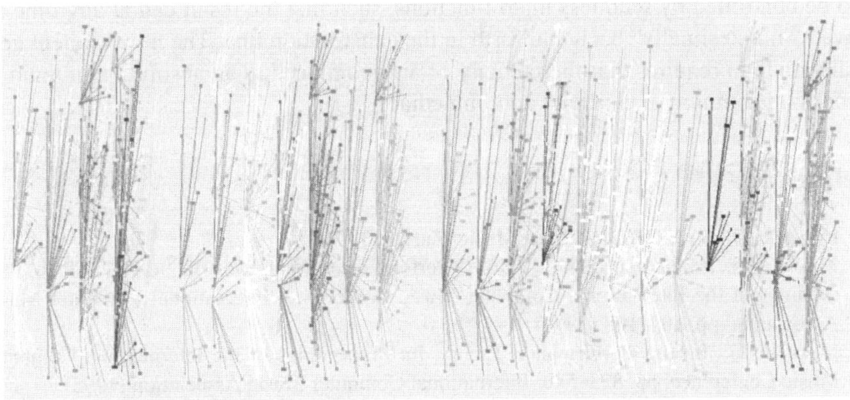

**Fig. 12.** The final "raw" material for 12 instruments. Instruments are distinguished by colors. Satellites pertaining to a given anchor note are connected by rays to that anchor note.

twelve-instrument extension, which is the basis of that composition, in terms of a set of nodes of a $MacroScore$ denotator, can be visualized as a set of anchor notes, which are the origins of a bunch of satellite notes, each of which is connected to its anchor by a straight line, see figure 12. This representation is enabled by the BigBang rubette, which is a new compositional tool for geometric transformations and wallpaper operations on the basis of gestural input modes, but see [19] for details.

## 7 Conclusion and Future Work

The now implemented functorial approach to musical objects—be they designed for composition, analysis, or performance within the Rubato environment since its first realization on NeXT computers—is a proof of concept of this advanced mathematical approach. The latest developments of geometric composition methods, in particular those using diagrams of morphisms for generalized grid constructions (wallpapers), show that the functorial approach, including those circular forms, which realize hierarchical and ramified architectures of musical compositions (also suggested by the Schenkerian paradigm), enable a powerful control over complex contemporary compositional techniques, such as Boulez's *structures*, and then also a completely natural extension thereof. This would be much harder, if feasible at all, without the present conceptual tools.

Our future work will be built on two main threads: First, a rebuilding of the classical analytical and performance rubettes on this Rubato Composer environment are strongly suggested and desired by scientifically working users. Since that code is open, this should not be a major problem. Second, the now visible gestural control of geometric composition—as prototypically implemented in the BigBang rubette—will be elaborated to a degree of enabling the composer to realize compositions without any delay, be it visual or acoustic. The complex geometric constructions will be hidden to the user to such a degree that only the really used music will be produced and will also be controlled by seamless undo functions, such that the result can at any time be moved "infinitesimally" back and forth in the construction line. The now virulent gestural paradigm requires that the facticity of art be reduced to an absolute minimum in favor of a maximum of elasticity and immediacy.

## References

1. Mazzola, G.: SYNTHESIS. SToA Music, Zurich (1991)
2. Mazzola, G., Zahorka, O.: The RUBATO Performance Workstation on NeXTSTEP. In: Proceedings of the International Computer Music Conference. International Computer Music Association, pp. 102–108 (1994)
3. Mazzola, G.: Inverse Performance Theory. In: Proceedings of the International Computer Music Conference, pp. 533–540. International Computer Music Association (1995)
4. Zahorka, O.: PrediBase–Controlling Semantics of Symbolic Structures in Music. In: Proceedings of the International Computer Music Conference, pp. 203–206. International Computer Music Association (1995)
5. Mazzola, G., Stange-Elbe, J.: Cooking a Canon with RUBATO–Performance Aspects of J.S. Bach's Kunst der Fuge. In: Proceedings of the International Computer Music Conference. International Computer Music Association, pp. 179–186 (1995)
6. Mazzola, G., Müller, S.: Constraint-based Shaping of Gestural Performance. In: Proceedings of the International Computer Music Conference. International Computer Music Association (2003)
7. Buteau, C.: Automatic Motivic Analysis Including Melodic Similarity for Different Contour Cardinalities: Application to Schumann's "Of Foreign Lands and People". In: Proceedings of the International Computer Music Conference. International Computer Music Association (2005)
8. Volk, A.: Modeling a Processive Perspective on Meter in Music. In: Proceedings of the International Computer Music Conference. International Computer Music Association (2005)
9. Buteau, C.: Motivic Spaces of Scores through RUBATOs MeloTopRUBETTE. In: Perspectives in Mathematical Music Theory, pp. 330–342. epOs music, Osnabrück (2004)
10. Göller, S., Milmeister, G.: Distributed RUBATO: Foundation and Multimedia Rendering. In: Perspectives in Mathematical Music Theory, pp. 282–299. epOs music, Osnabrück (2004)
11. Müller, S.: Parametric Gesture Curves: A Model for Gestural Performance. In: Perspectives in Mathematical Music Theory, pp. 106–116. epOs music, Osnabrück (2004)
12. Garbers, J., Noll, T.: Harmonic Path Analysis. In: Perspectives in Mathematical Music Theory, pp. 399–431. epOs music, Osnabrück (2004)
13. Garbers, J.: User Participation in Software Configuration and Integration of OpenMusic, Humdrum and Rubato. In: Perspectives in Mathematical Music Theory, pp. 262–281. epOs music, Osnabrück (2004)
14. Mazzola, G.: The Topos of Music. Birkhäuser, Basel (2002)
15. Agon, C., Assayag, G., Besson, J.: The OM Composer's Book, Delatour, Paris, vol. 1 (2006)
16. Mazzola, G.: Towards a Galois Theory of Concepts. In: Perspectives in Mathematical Music Theory, pp. 78–88. epOs music, Osnabrück (2004)
17. Mazzola, G.: The Presto Manual. SToA Music, Zürich (1989)
18. Boulez, G.: Structures pour piano, premier livre. UE, London (1953)
19. Mazzola, G., Losada, C., Thalmann, F.: A Boulezian Creative Analysis Of Boulez's structures. submitted to the Journal of Mathematics and Music (2007)
20. Ligeti, G.: Pierre Boulez: Entscheidung und Automatik in der structure Ia. Die Reihe IV (1958)

# Inventing Malleable Scores: From Paper to Screen Based Scores

Arthur Clay

ETH Zurich, Institute of Computer Systems,
Clausiusstrasse 59, ETH-Zentrum, RZ, H 22,
8092 Zurich, Switzerland
arthur.clay@inf.ethz.ch

**Abstract.** This paper examines the idea of artistic license of the interpreter as a positive aspect of composition. The possibilities of participating in the creative act beyond the role of the traditional interpreter are illustrated by tracing the development of malleability in score writing in selected works of the author. Starting with the standard score, examples are given for the various forms of malleable scores that lead up to the application of real-time electronic scores in which a concept of self-conduction is feasibly implemented for use in distributed ensembles.

**Keywords:** Notation, Score Synthesis, Mobile Computing, Sensor Networks.

## 1 Introduction

The relationship between the composer of a work and the interpreter of it can often be deduced from the type of score at hand and how it is notated. Various degrees of freedom have been given and taken away from the interpreter over the history of Western music. In early music styles, interpreters embellished melodies with simple to elaborate ornamentations and improvised cadenzas; in contemporary music the amount of freedom an interpreter is given varies, but is all too often very restrictive. The following paper introduces the concept of malleability in score making and reading in a step-by-step manor. Key concepts are illustrated with examples of various score types from malleable paper scores to the interactive screen based ones.

## 2 Standard Scores and the Repeat Event

### 2.1 The Standard Score

Traditional scores clearly separate the role of the composer and the interpreter. The composer provides the interpreter with a work and the interpreter reproduces the work for an audience, always keeping in mind the composer's intentions. The traditional role of interpretation approaches the work solely from the composer's point of view in terms of what the content of the work is to express. The players' abilities are focused on true reproduction of the content and not on contributing in a creative way as co-composers. The capacity to fulfill the composer's interests is how the quality of an interpretation is measured.

R. Adams, S. Gibson, and S. Müller Arisona (Eds.): DAW/IF 2006/2007, CCIS 7, pp. 255–269, 2008.

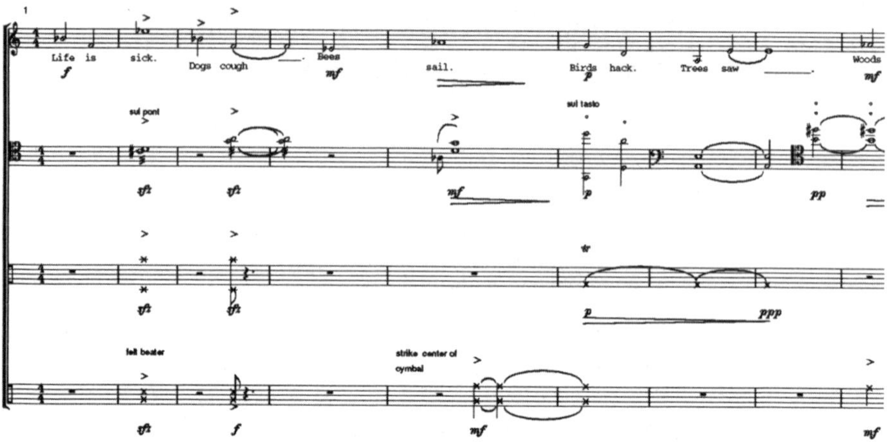


**Fig 1.** Excerpt from score of the second Movement of *I Clearly Saw* (1989). The score's notation and its structure are based on the traditional model of a fully composed work.

*I Clearly Saw*, a work for voice, flute, cello and percussion, is an example of a traditional score that requires the standard interpretation skills. The score's notation and its structure are based on the traditional model of a fully composed work. The players begin at the start of the work and follow the score in detail until the work's final measure. Synchronization takes place on the vertical axis, all voices being in a fixed relation to one another. The work will always have the same length and performances of it will be identical.

## 2.2 The Repeat Event

Although the repeat is a common device in traditional scores, the concept of the repeat can take on new levels of importance. One common method is to use a series of repeat brackets that are structural to the work. Each section enclosed by the brackets is repeated many times. The repeat no longer structurally functions as a restatement of initial material as with Sonata Form, but is employed to create a static but rhythmically energetic music common to minimalist music styles.

The score *Variation for Viola & Maracas* is completely based on repeated patterns. The effect of the multiple repeats is one of creating a type of percussion music for viola, in which the variation of rhythmic patterns is more important than the tonal progressions are. It is important to note in this work that the sections that are repeated are repeated exactly as written and every repeat in a section in the work are exactly the same.

By extending the idea of the repeat as a key device for turning out music with Theme & Variations form, a composition could include instructions to modulate parameters over a series of repeats within a section. For example, the tempo may increase or decrease, the tone color may travel from *sol tasto* to *sol ponticello*, or the passage may get transposed as in a *Zirkelkanon* with each new repeat. This technique can have a stunning effect when the parameter being changed moves drastically from its initial state to its final one. Here, the player has a larger role as an interpreter, because the extent to which the parameter is changed and the speed of this change is a decision made by the interpreter based on a sense of aesthetics.

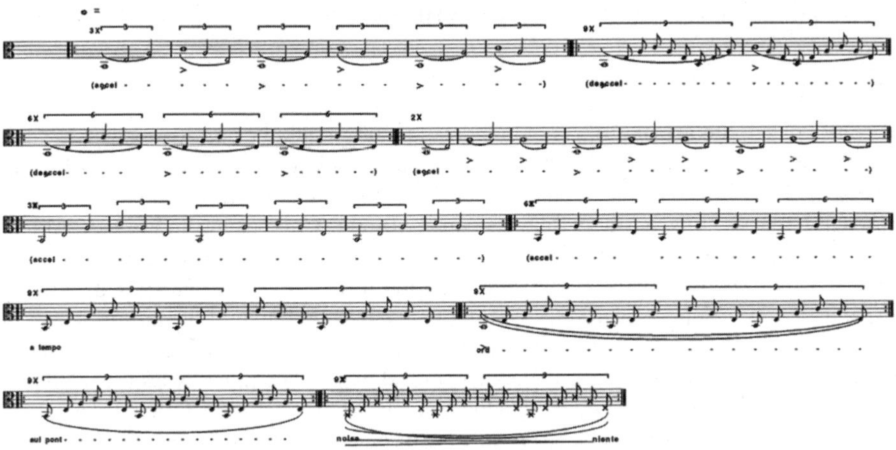

**Fig. 2.** Prelude from *Songs of Love* (1991) for bass viol. The initial statement of the material is the "theme" and the repeats of form variations of it.

*Songs of Love* consists of various movements that use a repeat/variation scheme in very diverse ways. In this work, not only are the repeats used for the sake of style similar to the *Variations for Viola and Maracas*, but also function on a deeper level as a means of creating variations. Standard variations take place on the level between sections in that one section is a compositional variant of another, but non-standard variations take place within a section in that that one section is repeated while one or more parameters is gradually modified.

For example, in the first movement *Prelude* (Fig.2) two parameters are gradually modified over a series of section repeats. In the score it can be seen that tempo is increased and decreased over several sections, going from slow bowed tones to extremely fast ones. Also, a change in tone color takes place in diverse sections as the player is requested to shift the bowing position from playing on the strings at the fingerboard (sul tasto) all the way down to playing them close to the bridge (sul ponticello). The interplay between the modulations in tempo and tone color is unique in that they work in conjunction with the repeat structure and ironically against it. In this way, the repeats can be understood as variations, because the given material is thematic and brought back anew modified rhythmically and tonally.

## 2.3 Section Summary

This section began with defining what the traditional role of the interpreter is and what type of score demands that role. The idea of using the repeat device was declared to be a stylistically innovative element. It was shown that modulating the material of a repeat over a series of repeats created variations. This stands in contrast to the standard score in that the interpreter's role is expanded. He or she must decide the speed of the modulations so that they function convincingly as variations.

# 3 Self-constructing and Constructible Scores

## 3.1 Composing as a Process

If consolidated, the actual process of composing music could be considered as a method for the fabrication of a score. Many forms in music such as the Fugue, the Sonata, and Theme and Variations amongst others are constructed in this manner. They have a fixed structural scheme that is often followed quite strictly. Composing under such formal constraints consists of providing the appropriate material within a predetermined structural scheme. The process of composing is on the formal level rule-based. Considering the situation in which an interpreter was not given a score, but a set of rules in which to make the score, he or she would be directly included in the creative process. The Interpreters would actually be part of the compositional experience rather than just reproducing the work in that they help determine the outcome of the work on a formal basis.

Whether the construction method results in an actual score from which the interpreters perform or whether they only use a predetermined set of rules is a matter of style with higher or lower degrees of freedom. The method of score construction in question here refers to two types: the first type is score-making that is done before the performance; the second type is score-making that extends into the performance itself. The first method creates a score that can be reused many times, but is less malleable when compared with the second approach. The second type, or approach depends much more on the ability of the performer. He or she must possess spontaneity, be creative, and have a highly developed sense of aesthetics. Of course, the risk when using a self-constructing live score in performance is greater, but the rewards are quite large for the interpreter in terms of freedom gained. The use of constructive scores regardless of type helps performers train important musical abilities, whose nurturing makes for a better interpreter in general.

## 3.2 Self-constructing Scores

An example of a self-constructing score that is actually based on a set of rules rather than a score is "Melopomène, Erato, Polymnie"(MEP). The work is written for bass viol and sixty-four Japanese lacquered chopsticks. The compositional method is based on a color analysis of the painting of the same name from Eustache la Suerre, which was painted around 1700. The colors of the chopsticks used in the work stand in proportion to those used in the painting. The more the color was used in the painting, the larger the number of chopsticks of that color. Each colored chopstick has a particular function, through which a dynamically changing compositional process is staged live.

The chopsticks divide the strings as expected in various proportions and function as a replacement for the left hand of the player. Through the placement and removal of the chopsticks from the seven strings of the instrument, executed in various speeds and from various directions, unusual sounds that are almost alien to the instrument are created. The score divides into two parts, A and B and are separated by a long pause between each of the parts. For both parts, the performer places into and removes thirty-two chopsticks from the strings. The end of the piece is signaled regardless of whether both parts or only one is performed by the removal of the last and only white chopstick, which is always the very first to be inserted. The chopstick process not only determines the content of the work, but also recreates the painting in an abstract visual and sonic manner.

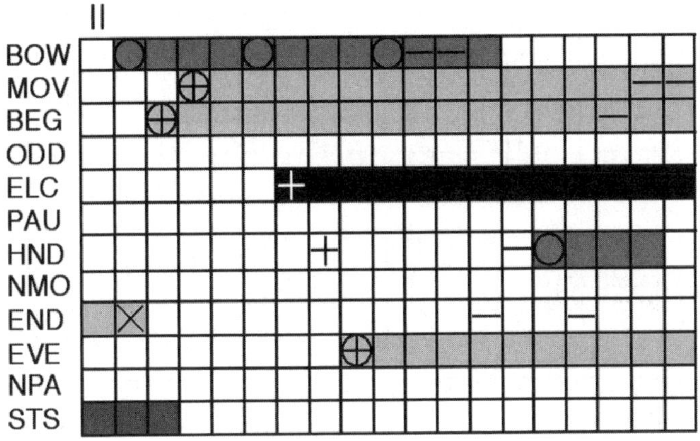


**Fig. 3.** Excerpt from *Melopomène, Erato, Polymnie* (1993) for Viol and chopsticks. The score shown is an artifact, since all content is determined live by the order of chopsticks chosen.

## 3.3 Constructible Scores

Although the method used in self-constructing scores is intriguing, it does not possess the immediacy of other types of scores. Due to the immense amount of instructions that always result from self-constructing scores, it was often found necessary to either create a work whose formal instructions were limited in number or create a form of alternative score as an aid to the performer. Providing an alternative score for the work made it possible to perform the work more easily, with less study time and also to have an ideal version of it at hand. When needed, a new score could be produced anew by just following the sequence of decisions during a performance with the self-constructing score. This procedure led to the realization that that a score could be rule-based.

The process of preparing an ideal version of a self-constructing score beforehand led to a workable, plausible and new concept of malleability: constructible scores. These type of scores fall into two categories of either passive or active scores. Passive constructible scores usually consist of materials that can be stacked or shuffled and active ones are those that form using electronic means. The passive score type is perhaps the simplest way to include the interpreter of the work into the creative process of composing music. Consisting of several parts from which the whole is constructed, the constructible score's malleability allows for the exploration of the work in endless versions. The interpreter must focus on how the material relates to the form when it is being constructed and once the score has been fixed. This demands that the interpreter create a sense of balance with the structure of the work. The order of the smaller and larger parts or sections of the work must be done with care in order to guarantee a convincing performance in a formal sense.

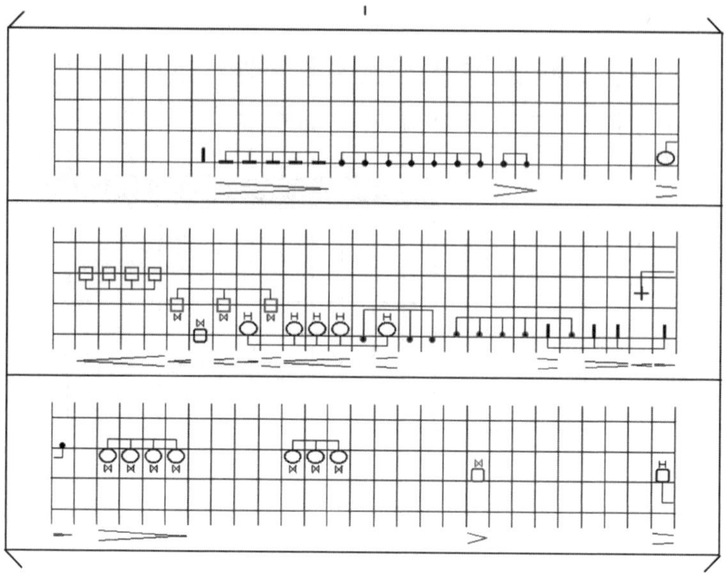

**Fig. 4.** An excerpt from *Three Standard Studies No. 1* (1993) for solo instrument or ensemble. The score is printed on transparent material and the notation can be read in any direction.

### 3.4 Work Specific Notation

Many constructible scores often possess a unique notational language developed specifically for the score in question. The degree or kind of malleability in these scores is therefore not only dependent on the fact that the scores are constructed from modular parts, but also on account of the actual notation employed. *Three Standard Studies* and *A River and Five Bridges* are works that employ notional languages and constructible scores. The notation is designed to let the performer be creative within the formal boundaries of a scored work. The scores for these works are made playable by first putting them together. This may mean executing a task as simple such as "shuffling" the pages to determine playing order and reading direction of the score as in *Three Standard Studies* or it may entail a more complicated task and consist of creating the score by "stacking" several transparent sheets to form the score as in *Rivers and Five Bridges*. The notation is designed in conjunction with the constructive method so that both let the performer be creative within the formal boundaries of a scored work.

The score to *Three Standard Studies* consists of nine relative parts to be played in hocket counterpoint. Each three-part section of the work contains a determinate register curve combined with relatively indeterminate curves for rhythm and pitch. The nontraditional score of clear plastic folia is used here as a key to creating a malleable score. It can be played in all possible directions, because the notational symbols were symmetrically designed and the transparent score can be flipped and turned without interfering with the coherency of the notation.

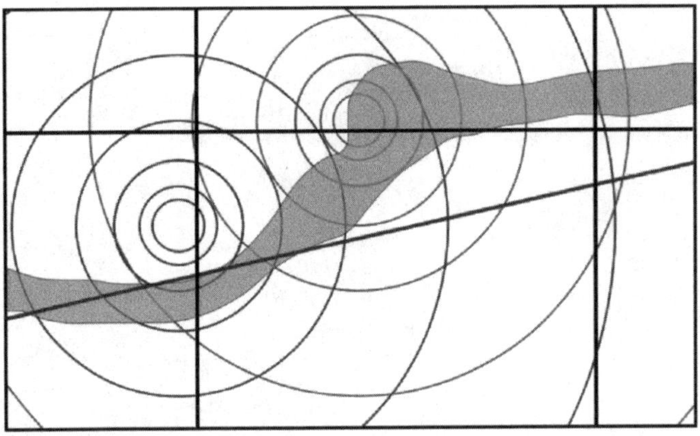

**Fig. 5.** A single page from *A River and Five Bridges* for harpsichord and assistant. The page is constructed out of five transparent parts that are stacked on top of one another.

For a performance of *Three Non-Standard Studies* performers are asked to create a collection of motifs, which consist of fragments from repertoire works, unusual sounds obtained on the instrument, and external sounds created and played back through electronic means. In this manner, the performer is confronted with making aesthetic decisions in regard to the actual material that will be used. By assigning the material in turn to a series of symbols that demand variations on that material during the performance, the performer is aesthetically confronted, because he or she must create ad lib variations without the aid of the composer.

The score for *A River and Five Bridges* is also constructed out of multiple transparent score elements, which are combined by the performer to set all musical parameters needed for a performance. Each page of the score is made up of stacked transparent sheets. Parameters for time, range, tempo, manual, left hand or right hand are all indicated on separate sheets. It is the combination of the score parts and how they interact as a whole that gives the composition its character. A rule-based system that is "embedded" into the score via its construction and notation, forces each of the parameters to interact with one another. In this manner, different combinations of score elements bring about different results sonically in virtually endless variations.

Concerning the notational language of both *Three Standard Studies* and *A river and Five Bridges*, one could just term them as being simply graphic. However, the graphic element is used in a unique way. Here, the elements of a language take on symbolic metaphor for action and work like a function 'library' of a computer language. This forms the basis for a 'thinking' process, or algorithmic structure determined by the composer and carried out by the performer. The performer experiences the algorithmic base of the compositions directly by having to act musically within it. By doing so, the performer is enabled to explore the compositional philosophy of the composer closely and also to explore his own repertoire in a creative manner.

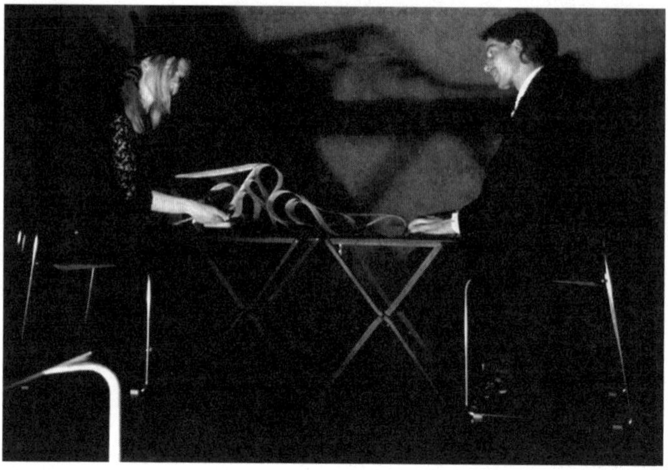

**Fig. 6.** The work *La Mariage* is for two music boxes and performers. The "score" is punched onto two six-meter punch cards. The cards entwine during the performers and form a sculpture.

### 3.5 Section Summary

In this section constructible and self-constructing scores were discussed. Constructible scores must be constructed before hand and self-constructing scores are ones that unfold conceptually during a performance. The common element between the two types of scores is the fact they are rule-based. For the performer, both these types of scores allow him or her to engage in the compositional process. The number of rules needed to perform a self-constructing score proved that a physical score was often better for immediacy and reproducibility. So making constructible scores became more viable for performer and composer alike. The activities mentioned in relation to *MEP*, *A River and Five Bridges* and *Three Standard Studies* include understanding the notational language, creating the score, selecting materials, and being able to vary material collected based on the notation. This form of engagement helps in developing the interpreter's compositional abilities and creativity in general. In view of the works mentioned in this section, it is clear that the concept of constructible scores grew out of the experience with self-constructing scores.

## 4 Performance Systems and Modular Scores

### 4.1 The Patch Bay and the Punch Card

Looking back briefly at the patch bay systems of vintage synthesizers and punch cards for music boxes and how they were used, one could consider both as a type of self-constructing score. When performing on an analog synthesizer, the player set up the synthesizer with a particular "patch", which could then be changed to create a second new "patch". The changing of patches has strong consequence for the work being performed. New sound material and modulation possibilities are opened up and contrasts and developments are brought into the work. Since the re-cabling of patches is cumbersome, interfaces to these instruments were in time modified or eventually replaced with others that were more easily changed.

This type of machine control gave birth to certain types of scoring that had to be more general and malleable than traditionally notated scores. Tweaking knobs, moving sliders up and down, and adjusting other controller interface elements can be basically understood again as making "variations". Having a score that was graphic and therefore general enough to guide the player but not over determine things was ideal for analog electronic music making. A good patch had a high degree of malleability and created a good balance between instrument, score and interpreter.

Two scenarios for performance are possible in terms of systems for machines: the first is one in which the performer is actively changing parameters of a machine (i.e. „tweaking a patch") to explore it via the instructions in a general score; the second scenario uses some form of interface (sensor network) with which the performer's movements are monitored. The machine responds to these directly, leaving the performer "hands-free" to perform. A useful analogy here would be a sort of automatic page turning device based in software that could not only turn the page at the right moment but could invent and re-invent the contents seen on the screen page.

This concept of score is not limited to electronic instruments, but can be extended to mechanical instruments such as music boxes as well. The idea that the performer can adjust single parameters to create effects (variations) is a key concept here. Malleable

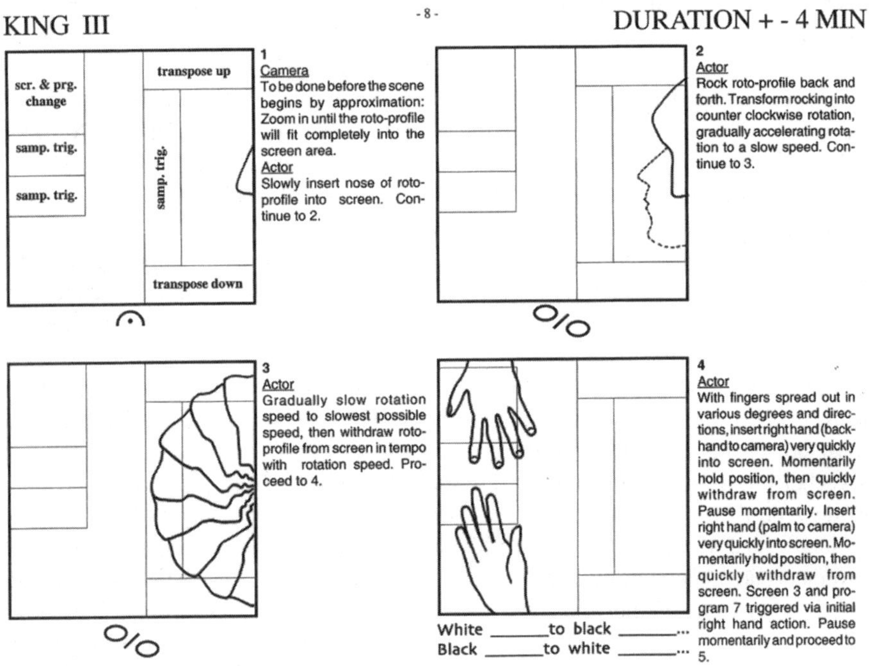


**Fig. 7.** A page from *Auto-Bio-Graphy* (1993) for performer and live-electronics. The score illustrates gestures to be executed and "hot spots" that can be triggered by entering into them.

scores can be categorized into active and passive categories. Passive malleable scores were discussed in the previous section and are those that are put together manually by the performer; active malleable score are those that responds to the movements of the performer directly. Active scores become more important because electronics are involved and because more malleability is possible on a screen, since players can work hands-off. „Self-conducting“ therefore becomes part of the concept of malleability.

## 4.2 Mechanical and Electronic Performance Systems

A work that uses mechanical instruments and one which achieves malleability is *La Mariage* (Fig. 6) for two music boxes. The music is notated on two long cards of six meters each as a series of punched holes. Chords are notated with punches on the vertical axis and melodies on the horizontal axis. All of the punches on the punch card scores are at an equal distance. If the player turns the music box crank evenly over time, the punch card will be fed at an equal rate into the box. The tones heard will be equally spaced in time. Speeding up and slowing down the rate of the cranking, increases or decreases the space between the tones and creates diverse rhythms. In this manner the punch card score can be said to be malleable. When two players are performing and adjust the speed of the cranking, interesting rhythms are formed as the voices de- and re-synchronize over time with one another.

The idea of having a performer's movements coupled to the changing of a musical parameter in a work as in *La Mariage* can be easily extended with video tracking and body sensor networks. The score system from *Auto-Bio-Graphy* (Fig.7) for performer and electronic machines depicted here illustrate this well. *Auto-Bio-Graphy* is a multimedia presentation completely controlled by tracking physical movement of the performer in free space. The piece uses the Big Eye video program developed at STEIM, which tracks the performer's gestures in terms of quantity and quality of light change. The gestures are mapped to pre-defined fields that when activated send MIDI messages out to external synthesizers.

The basic formal elements of *Auto-Bio-Graphy* are an automatic compositional process, the biography of any artist (Marcel Duchamp in this instance), and a graphic representation as score -hence the title: *Auto-Bio-Graphy*. The visual and musical content of the complete piece functions as an extended variation in time and color based on the pitch and text content of that of Duchamp's chance based music composition *Erratum Musical*. However, it is integrated into a multimedia structure to form a large dynamic (constantly changing) composition.

Technically, a video camera is used to project the images in its path onto a screen and also to send the images to a computer, where changes in light quantity and quality are measured. The video signal is mapped on to a Cartesian plane and the performer's movements are tracked by changes in light in reference to that plane. The plane is divided into active and passive hot spots, or fields. The performer moves through the fields as indicated in the score and triggers the sound events that are linked to the image being projected. The movements made by the performer are therefore important visually as they are sonically, because they are both brought together interactively through the performance system.

### 4.3 Section Summary

The use of the patch bay of an early analog synthesizer made for a good analogy for malleability. A score indicating the patch settings and their changes as well as instructions to the performer on how to tweak the patch to create the music is an ideal model for representing a performance system. The process of tweaking, or dynamically modulating parameters by turning a knob or pushing a slider was also seen as a viable process with mechanical instruments. The comparison between an electronic instrument and a mechanical one in this regard introduced the concept of active and passive scores. The similarities and differences between the mechanical work *La Mariage* and the electronic work *Auto-Bio-Graphy* made the comparison between passive and active scores apparent. Active scores were seen as more important, because they extend the concept of malleability into domain of real-time scoring, where performers are able to adjust the score in a "hands-off" manner.

## 5 Real Time Electronic Scores and Collaborative Scores

### 5.1 Using Motion Tracking

Similar to the music box piece in which tempo is modulated by the performers actions, *China Gates* for tuned gongs and a custom GPS device (Wrist-Conductor) uses motion tracking to create rhythmic modulation between players. In "China Gates" the process of tempo modulation is accomplished not by video tracking as in *Auto-Bio-Graphy*, but by actively monitoring the actual position of the players within given a geographical area with use of the wearable GPS device. The physical movement of the performers within the performance space creates the rhythmic patterns by a process of synchronization and de-synchronization of tempo.

Using a series of LEDs, the Wrist Conductor signals each player when to hit the gong. If the players have the same geographic location, they will bang the gongs exactly at the

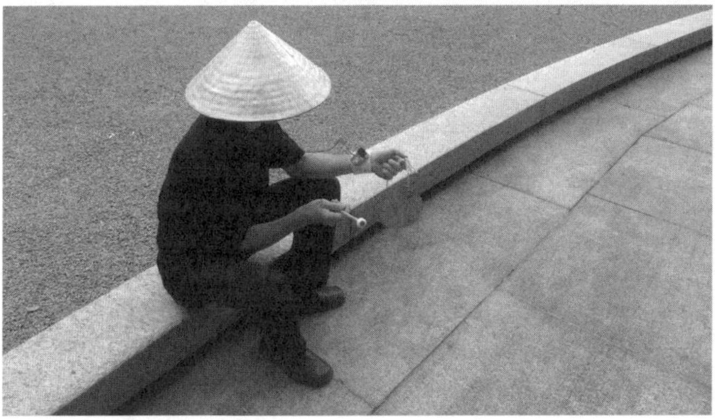

**Fig. 8.** *China Gates* (2006) for gongs and satellites. The GPS controller is located is strapped onto the left wrist and its antenna is built into the straw hat. Playing is coordinated per LEDs.

same moment in time; if they are separated in space, each of the gong strikes will be individually offset. As the players move around in open-space, the gong music shifts smoothly back and fourth from intense chords to exotic melodies with a rippling like effect. Aesthetically, the work is rooted in works for open public space and belongs to a repertoire, which celebrate the use of innovative mobile technology to explore public space and a new a concept of ensemble and audience.

### 5.2 Distribution and Sensor Networking

Similar to *China Gates*, *GoingPublik* is also for distributive ensemble. However, the core idea behind *GoingPublik* is more complex, because it is based on a strategy of mobility by employing a wearable computer system running a software-based score system. The playing score itself is seen by the players in a head-mounted display. It basically allows for what might be termed 'composed improvisation', which permits improvisational elements within a compositional structure. The application for the electronic score guides the player via an active 'conducting line' (Fig. 9: the thick white line on the score) and makes demands on the performer to various degrees and at various times through a series of behavioral icons (Fig: 9: the icons at top of the menu). The speed of the conduction line as well as the appearance of the icons is accomplished by electronically monitoring the performer's physical position in space using universal inputs such as geographical position obtained via satellites and sensors using the earth's magnetic field. The contents of the score are thereby linked directly to the movements of the performer, thus creating a unique choreographic metaphor of sound dispersing in space. Similar to *China Gates*, musical content and structure in *GoingPublik* are accomplished through such concepts of distribution.

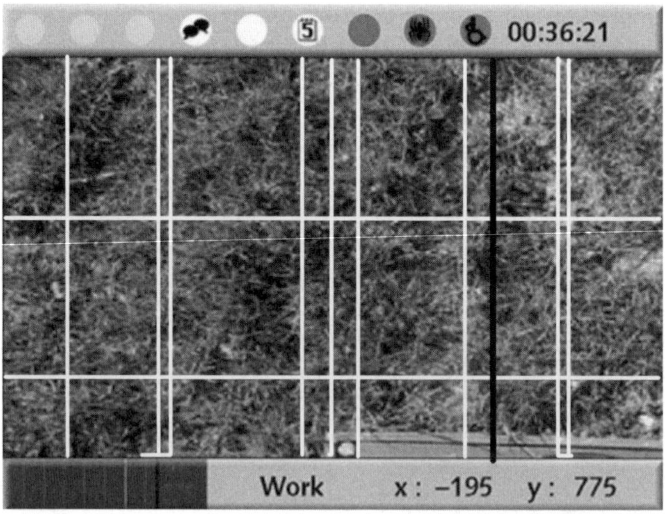


**Fig 9.** A screen shot of the real-time score used in *GoingPublik* (2005). The dark line is the conduction line and matrix of white lines divides the image into rhythm and pitch parameters.

Since the electronic score is dependent on the movement and behavior of the players, all of the distribution concepts employed can be based on choreographed motion. The types of choreographic motion that have been employed can be seen in the „Huddle score“ depicted in Figure 10. The score plots movements for three players and depicts them moving as a group of three. There movements depicted are in various huddle-formations from facing inward to facing outward. The grouping of the players in various configurations has a great influence on the simultaneity of the score changes. So, using the Huddle score is above all a sure method to explore synchronization based on joint physical movement. For example, synchronized "tutti like" group movements such as rotation in the huddle formations bring about synchronized changes in the score. In contrast, when players are "distributed" (i.e separated in space), the musical results are not "tutti like" but consist of polyphonic like textures woven out of highly individual voices.

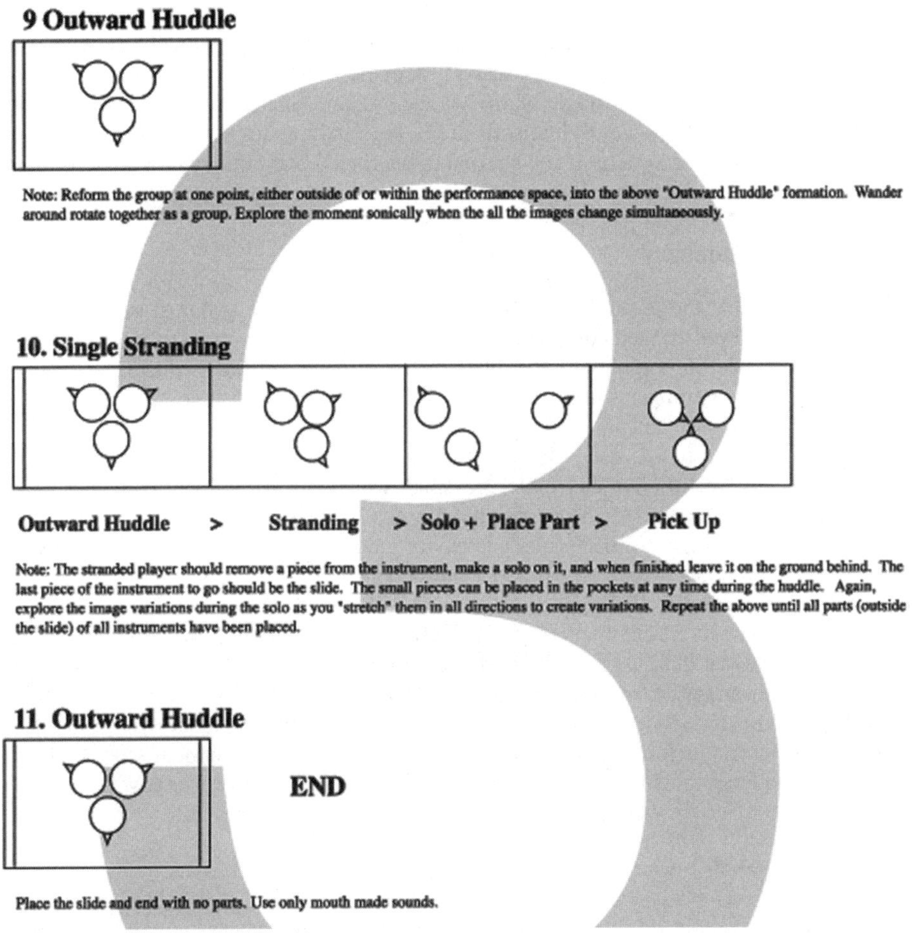


**Fig. 10.** A page of from the Huddle Score used in *GoingPublik*. The score depicts the group's common movements over time, which result in choreographed changes in the score.

### 5.3 Public Audience and Collaborative Scores

There are two versions of *GoingPublik*: one version is for closed performance spaces using a GPS simulator to virtually walk through a city without leaving the performance space; the other version is for a performance in which satellites are used as a global ubiquitous sensor network for tracking the players in open spaces. Both versions network the performers in such a manner that the electronic scoring becomes self-regulating, or truly self-conducted. The performers are "hands free" and are able to concentrate on their playing and react to ensemble members and to interact with the performance space. So despite the physical distribution, commonly shared elements can be structurally exploited through motion tracking. Therefore, the compositional quantities and qualities of the work are based on spatial mobility; Intensity of form is held by changes in timbre and rhythmic modulations are brought about in conjunction with the sound distribution. The score system used in *GoingPublik* also provides a unique opportunity for composers and performers to implement the possibilities of using collaborative scores. This is possible, because it one can designate which score images are to be loaded into the scoring system. Having each of the players or each member of a group of composers prepare one of the four score images for the system, brings about a score system that consists of four distinct scores, but which is "integrated" into a single whole via the system. This possibility of collaboration demonstrates how the *GoingPublik* software is not really a single work, but a complete mobile-music-making system. It can be used to interpret a body of works written for it and also can be used to research collaboration amongst performers and composers.

### 5.4 Section Summary

It was shown that the idea of malleability was brought into the realm of score synthesis with advent of miniaturized computers. When properly paired with a sensor system, such systems are able to respond to the player's movements during performance and reinterpret them as commands to an electronic score. The term "real-time scoring" was then applied when the movements of the player determined the contents of the score or at least the "shaping" of it. It was stated that real-time scoring extends the concept of malleability and makes the "distributive ensemble" possible, which can be defined as having an ensemble, which is musically cohesive but not physically present as a single unit. Also, since the sensor network and the performer's behavior guide each of the members of an ensemble without a conductor one can speak of "self-conduction". The members of the ensemble all follow an electronically linked score seen on a "screen". The score screen could be in the form of a cue made up of an array of LEDs as in *China Gates* or be the tiny screen in a head up display as in *GoingPublik*. In the case of the latter work, it was found that synchronized movements could be used to create "tutti" like effects and that these could be summarized in score form. Concluding, it is clear that such scoring tools have rid us of the necessity of a conductor and have dissolved the concept of the traditional score in that its content is no longer fixed, its pages not numbered and interpretation ever new.

## 6 Conclusion

The paper has shown that the role of the interpreter is linked to the type of score being played from. Various new forms of scores were introduced that embrace a concept of malleability, which naturally extends the role of the interpreter to include them in a creative process The range of scores discussed included scores that used the repeat event in a variation structure, self-constructing scores that were rule-based and unfolded algorithmically live on stage, constructible scores that are put together out of diverse parts before the performance, and finally electronic real-time scores that are controlled by the actual body movements of the performer. All of these types of scores allow the performer to break out of the role of interpreter and engage as co-author in the composition process, developing the interpreter's compositional abilities and creativity in general. It is important to acknowledge that wearable computers have brought about portability and this in turn has allowed mobility. Scores are no longer stationary and ensembles are no longer confined to closed spaces. Due to the use of sensor networks that react to the performer's movements and can be synchronized tutti like with the use of ubiquitous sensor networks, the "distributive ensemble" has now become musically cohesive. The members of a distributed ensemble wander through open spaces such as city street grids and municipal parks. The role of the conductor can be questioned. In the light of the independence of the performer won through new concepts of scoring, freedom and independence has been won by the phenomena of active scores and the concept of "self-conduction". To conclude, it is clear that new score concepts have brought about new electronic scoring tools and that these tools have consequently given birth to completely new forms of ensemble writing, which manifest in public space and bring about new concept of public audience. To make reference to a quote from Norman O. Brown made reference to by John Cage in his book *A Year from Monday*, one can state that "the desire for an environment which works so well we can run wild in it" has been discovered.

**Acknowledgments.** I would like to thank all of the artists and scientists involved in the various projects over the years. Particular thanks goes to Prof. Dr. Jürg Gutknecht, Stijn Ossevort, Sven Stauber, Mazda Mortasawi, Dr. Thomas Frey, Dr. Dennis Majoe, Mischa Leber, Dr. Stefan Müller Arisona, Franziska Martinsen, Imke David, STEIM, Anne Faulborn, Günter Heinz, Roland Dahinden, Thierry Madiot.

## References

1. Martinsen, F.: Composition Camouflaged: On the Relationship between Interpretation and Improvisation. Hz Journal (6) (2005), `http://www.hz-journal.org/n6/martinsen.html`
2. Clay, A., Frey, T., Gutknecht, J.: GoingPublik: Using Real-time Global Score Synthesis. In: Proceedings NIME 2005, Vancouver, Canada (2005)
3. GoingPublik: Suggesting Creativity Inside the Ivory Tower. In: Proceedings Creativity & Cognition Conference 2005, University of London Press, London (2005)
4. Clay, A., Majoe, D.: Motion Tracking Music with Mobile-Media Technology. In: Proceedings SPCA Conference (2006)
5. Clay, A., Majoe, D.: A GPS Interface for Public Art Use. In: Proceedings ACM Siggraph Conference 2006, California, USA (2007)
6. Watts, R.: Interview with Art Clay, Artistic Director of Zurich's DAW07. Hz Journal (9) (2007), `http://www.hz-journal.org/n10/watts.html`
7. Cage, J.: A Year from Monday, New Lectures and Writings. Middletown. Wesleyan University Press, Middletown (1967)

# Glimmer: Creating New Connections

Jason Freeman

Georgia Institute of Technology, Music Department, 840 McMillan Street, Atlanta, Georgia 30332-0456 USA
jason.freeman@music.gatech.edu

**Abstract.** *Glimmer*, a composition for chamber orchestra and audience, uses novelty light sticks, video cameras, computer software, multi-colored stand lights, and projected video animation to create a continuous feedback loop in which audience activities, software algorithms, and orchestral performance together create the music. This paper establishes the aesthetic background and motivations behind *Glimmer* and describes the conceptual framework and technical realization of the piece in detail. Performances of the work by the American Composers Orchestra at Carnegie Hall in New York and by musicians at the Hamabada Art Center in Jerusalem are evaluated with respect to the audience, the musicians, and the resulting music that was created.

**Keywords:** Orchestra, audience participation, multi-player game, light stick, video tracking, music, algorithmic composition, real-time notation.

## 1 Introduction

Recent technological and aesthetic developments have challenged us to become more engaged and active cultural consumers who help create the content we enjoy: we curate the playlists we listen to, we compete in the online games we play, and we collaboratively filter the media we watch. Within this context, classical orchestral performance seems increasingly anachronistic. Audiences sit in a dark hall, looking at a conductor whose back is turned toward them, afraid to cough or sneeze lest they disturb their neighbors.

A feed-forward network (Figure 1) links composers, performers, and audiences, constraining the ways in which these three groups interact. The audience listens to the

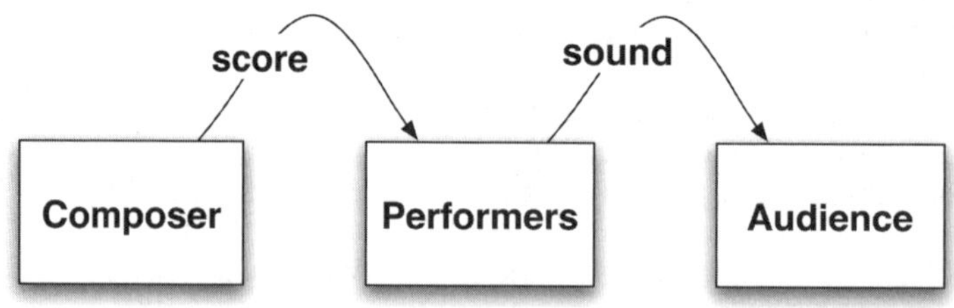


**Fig. 1.** Feed-forward network linking composer, performers, and audiences in orchestral music

R. Adams, S. Gibson, and S. Müller Arisona (Eds.): DAW/IF 2006/2007, CCIS 7, pp. 270–283, 2008.

sounds created by the orchestra, which, together with the conductor, interprets the score written by the composer. But the interaction only moves in one direction. The audience must wait until the piece is over to respond with their applause; during the performance, they have little interaction with the musicians, the composer, or each other. They are spectators rather than participants.

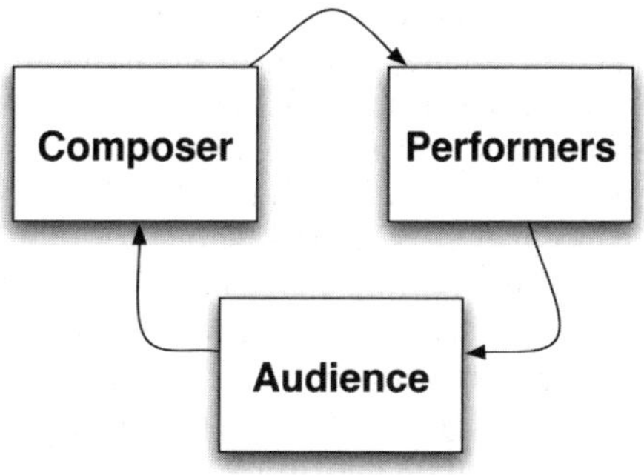


**Fig. 2.** Feedback loop linking composer, performers, and audiences in interactive performance environments

With *Glimmer*, my recent composition for chamber orchestra, I wanted to transform the usual feed-forward loop linking composer, performers, and audience into a feedback loop that facilitates interaction among these groups during each performance (Figure 2). The audience members become musical collaborators who do not just listen to the performance but also actively shape it. Each person is given a battery-operated light stick that he or she uses over the course of the piece to influence the music. Computer software analyzes live video of the audience and sends instructions to the orchestra via multi-colored lights mounted on each player's stand; there is no conductor. With this design, I wanted to create new connections among composers, performers, and listeners in order to construct a collaborative, shared musical experience, to emphasize the uniqueness and excitement of every live performance, and to encourage audiences to discover their own creativity and to have fun.

## 2 Background

### 2.1 Large Audience Participatory Music

*Glimmer* follows in the tradition of musical works that facilitate real-time participation by a large audience during their performance. In many such works, audience members become performers, creating some or even all of the music. For example, in Jean Hasse's *Moths* (1986), the audience whistles as directed by a conductor and a graphical score to perform the piece [1]. During *La symphonie du millénaire* (2000), an outdoor performance event in Montreal, 2000 audience members rang handheld bells at designated times [2]. And many Fluxus scores specify or imply more open-ended audience participation, as with Tomas Schmit's *Sanitas No. 35* (1962): "Blank sheets are handed to the audience without any explanations. 5 minutes waiting" [3].

In other works, technology involves a live concert audience in new ways while retaining its passive role. Golan Levin's *DialTones: A Telesymphony* (2001) creates music by triggering audience mobile phones to play pre-composed ringtones [4]. And the Concert Companion provides real-time program notes about orchestral repertory via wireless PDAs [5].

A final category of projects invites the audience to contribute input that affects the musical performance, rather than creating sounds that are part of the performance. In Kevin Baird's *No Clergy* [6], computer software stochastically generates successive pages of music notation for each performer in the chamber ensemble, while audience members use laptop computers to access a web interface and vote on parameter values that control the algorithm. McAllister et al [7] developed a performance environment in which individual audience members draw notation on a PDA's touch screen for the musicians to play. And Wulfson, Barrett, and Winter [8] created *LiveScore*, in which gallery visitors adjust knobs on physical controllers to adjust the parameters of a stochastic algorithm that generates music notation for each performer.

The works in this final category rely upon real-time notation systems to dynamically generate visual scores for musicians to read during each unique performance. Such systems provide a powerful tool for connecting musicians and audiences: audiences generate input that drives a software algorithm, and the algorithm generates real-time notation that directs the musicians' performance. Real-time notation systems are in turn indebted to algorithmic composition experiments by Hiller and Isaacson [9], Koenig [10], Cope [11], and others that generated music notation outside of real time. And they draw from the open-form composition structures in works of composers such as Earle Brown [12] and Karlheinz Stockhausen [13].

### 2.2 Multiplayer Games

*Glimmer* is also inspired by mass-audience games that use technology to enable large audiences in conventional theatrical spaces to participate without leaving their seats. In projects developed by Cinematrix, audience members hold up the red or green side of a paddle to collectively navigate objects on a video screen [14]. Other recent systems have used video tracking of audience members as they shift left and right in their seats [15] and motion tracking of giant weather balloons which circulate through the seating area [16] to facilitate similar types of interaction.

### 2.3 Audience Participation in *Glimmer*

In *Glimmer*, as in the real-time notation works and the gaming examples, audience activities influence the actions of the orchestral musicians on stage rather than directly creating the sounds of the piece. I chose this design framework in order to make the audience as comfortable in participating as possible; most were not musicians, and many did not know in advance that they would be contributing to the piece.

I also wanted to give the audience an opportunity to control more than the surface content of the work, not simply choosing from a menu of pre-conceived paths but rather influencing the work at a note-by-note level.

In addition, it was important that the system be conceptually simple. The realities of contemporary orchestral performance — limited rehearsal time, limited time to train the audience, and a contractual limit for the piece to be only ten minutes — made this a necessity.

Finally, as with Tomas Schmit's piece [3], I did not want to direct audience actions via any kind of pre-determined score or sequential instructions. Rather, I wanted to create an environment for them to explore and an opportunity for interesting group behaviors to emerge.

# 3 System Design

I designed *Glimmer* as a continuous interactive feedback loop that operates during each performance (Figure 3). Computer software analyzes video images of audience activity and transforms the analysis data into real-time notation for the musicians and into video animation for the audience. The musicians play music based on their notation. The audience reacts to the music they hear and the video they see, changing their activities to begin another iteration through the loop. There is no conductor.

In this work, technology is a means to facilitate collaboration, connecting the software algorithms to the audience through video analysis and to the musicians through real-time notation. The software itself translates audience input into notation, quickly performing analysis, decision-making, and communications tasks that would be impossible for humans to do as quickly. But orchestral musicians acoustically create all of the music; there is no electronic sound.

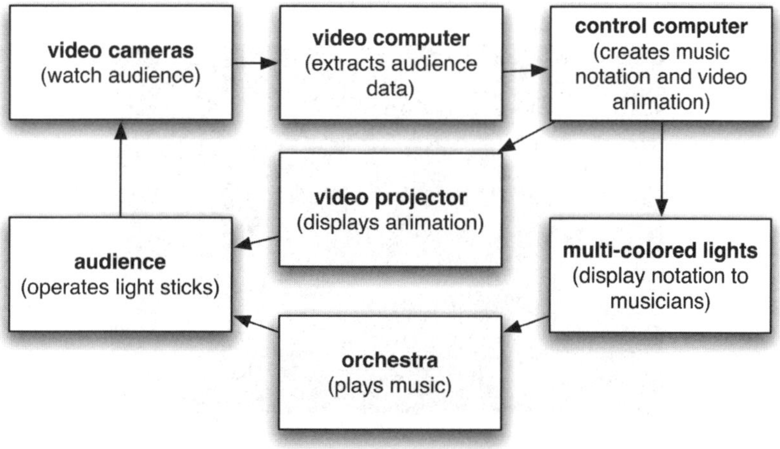


**Fig. 3.** *Glimmer's* interactive feedback loop

## 3.1 New York and Jerusalem Versions

The American Composers Orchestra commissioned *Glimmer* for a performance at Zankel Hall at Carnegie Hall in New York in January 2005. It was subsequently performed in March 2006 at the Hamabada Art Center in Jerusalem, Israel.

The original New York version called for a chamber orchestra of twenty-five musicians (strings, winds, brass, and percussion) and six hundred audience members.

Due to the smaller physical layout of the Hamabada Art Center, I revised the piece for the Jerusalem performance to accommodate a fifteen-player string orchestra and two hundred audience members. I also modified the video-tracking algorithm, based on informal audience feedback and analysis data collected in New York. I discuss these revisions and their implications in more detail below.

### 3.2 Audience Input and Video Analysis

Each audience member uses a four-inch long battery-operated LED light stick to participate in the performance. In the New York performance, the audience was instructed to switch their light sticks on and off; in Jerusalem, they were told to wave them back and forth (Figure 4).

The audience is divided into several groups: seven groups of 75 people each in New York, and five groups of 40 people each in Jerusalem. Each group controls a corresponding group of three or four musicians in the orchestra (e.g. first violins, second violins, violas).

Four consumer-grade video cameras capture images of the entire audience and forward them to a video computer for analysis. Computer software, written with Cycling '74's Max and Jitter, pre-processes each frame, performing color plane extraction, image masking, and threshold noise reduction.

In the New York version, the software then determines the percentage of audience members in each group whose light sticks are activated, performing image dilation and erosion to isolate blobs of adjacent non-black pixels, counting those blobs, and scaling the result by the total number of audience members in the group.

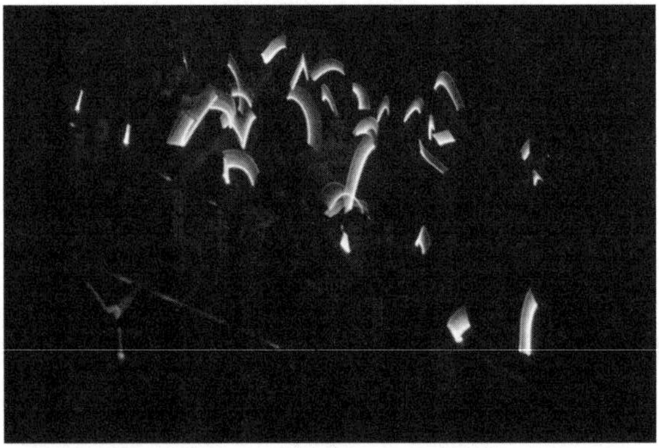

**Fig. 4.** A group of audience members at the Hamabada Art Center waves their light sticks back and forth to influence the music the orchestra plays

In the Jerusalem version, the software determines the total amount of motion of light sticks in each group, using a feedback filter to create momentary motion trails in the image when sticks are waved. The algorithm then calculates the total sum of all pixels in the frame and scales it based on the minimum and maximum sums found thus far.

In both versions, the resulting data for each group are forwarded over an Ethernet network via UDP to a second computer.

### 3.3 Data Mapping

On the second computer, software also written with Cycling '74's Max and Jitter translates incoming audience data into outgoing notation and video animation.

**Direct Mapping.** On a basic level, the light-stick activation percentage for a group controls the dynamic at which that group's musicians play. If everyone in a group turns on their light sticks (New York) or waves them as fast and wide as possible (Jerusalem), their group plays as loud as possible. If everyone has them turned off (New York) or motionless (Jerusalem), the group is silent. As the activation percentage increases, notes also move more quickly from one player in the group to the next.

**Competitive Mapping.** On a higher level, a comparative analysis evaluates the ability of each audience group to work together to create changes over time. The algorithm rewards groups whose data derivatives are higher: their musicians are more likely to play, they play at a higher dynamic, and they change pitches more often.

The software continuously ranks groups based on these derivatives and uses the rankings to determine which texture is assigned to each group at any time (see below). Groups that are ranked higher are also mapped onto a wider dynamic range in the direct mapping. And when a group jumps into the first-place position, its pitch or pitches change with an accented attack.

**Textures.** Throughout the piece, each group sustains single notes or clusters of notes that gradually crossfade from one musician to the next: one player *decrescendos* to *niente* while another player *crescendos* from *niente*.

The software defines several different variations on these textures (Figure 5) in which the number of simultaneous sustained notes, the total set of available pitches, and the speed of crossfading all vary. A lookup table maps group ranking to assigned texture.

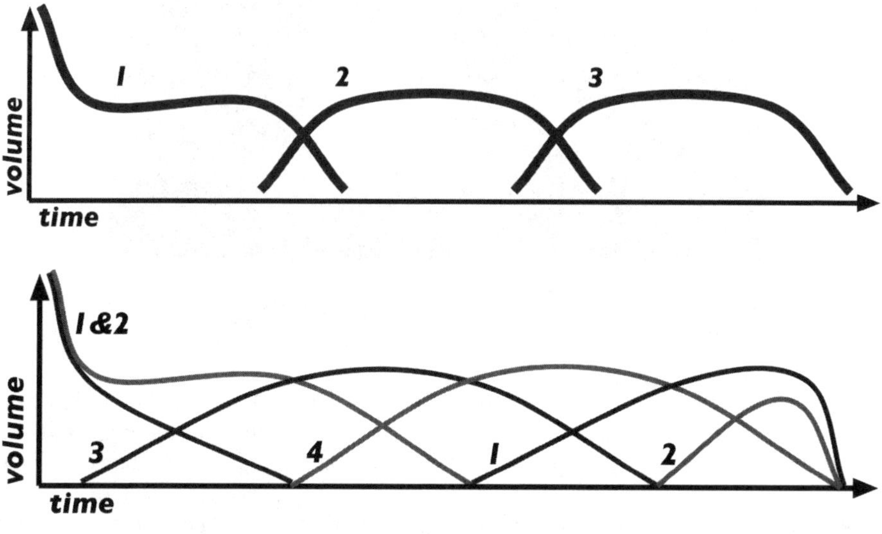


**Fig. 5.** Visual representations of two different textures used in the piece

**Musical Structure.** The ranking-to-texture lookup table changes over the course of the piece, giving the music a large-scale structural shape. Each individual change to the table is barely perceptible, so that on a local level, audience-driven events take perceptual precedence over pre-composed cues.

The large-scale arch form begins with just a single group playing a single note at a time, gradually becoming denser until all groups are playing clusters of notes chosen from a large, contiguous diatonic set. In the closing minutes of the piece the texture thins as groups are removed from the piece one by one based on their cumulative competitive rank. One "winning" group is left playing to close the performance.

The music itself is extremely simple, as sets of pitches and timbral combinations are constantly but gradually transformed; works such as John Cage's *Four*$^2$ for chorus [17] were influential. These simple textures help audience members to easily identify their own group within the orchestra.

### 3.4 Music Notation and Video Projection

The orchestral musicians do not read from conventional musical notation nor do they follow cues from a conductor. Instead, each player receives real-time instructions from the computer via a Color Kinetics iAccent multi-colored light (Figure 6), which sits on his or her music stand. Each light is controlled independently and changes color continuously.

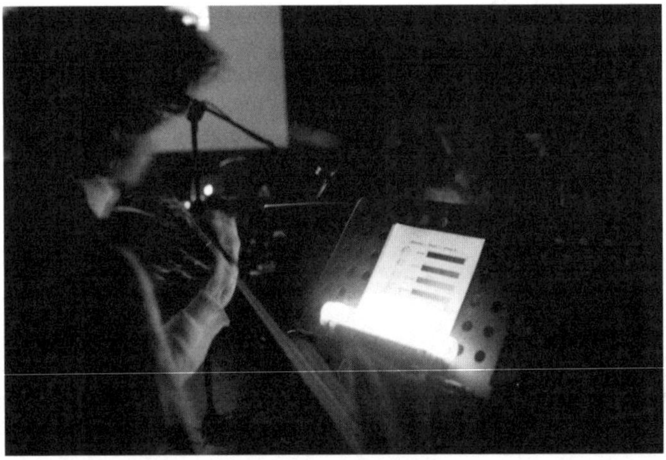

**Fig. 6.** A musician at the Hamabada Art Center changes pitches and dynamics based on the color of the iAccent light

The color family of a musician's light — brown, green, blue, or pink — indicates which of four notated pitches to play (Figure 7). The brightness of the light indicates the dynamic at which to play. Short flashes of light prepare musicians for note changes and accents.

A simple video animation (Figure 8), projected onto a screen behind the orchestra, helps the audience more easily follow the relationship between their activities and the music they hear. Each audience group, represented by a rectangle, changes color based on the group's activation percentage and competitive rank, and the first-place group receives additional visual emphasis. As groups are removed from the music towards the end of the piece, their rectangles disappear.

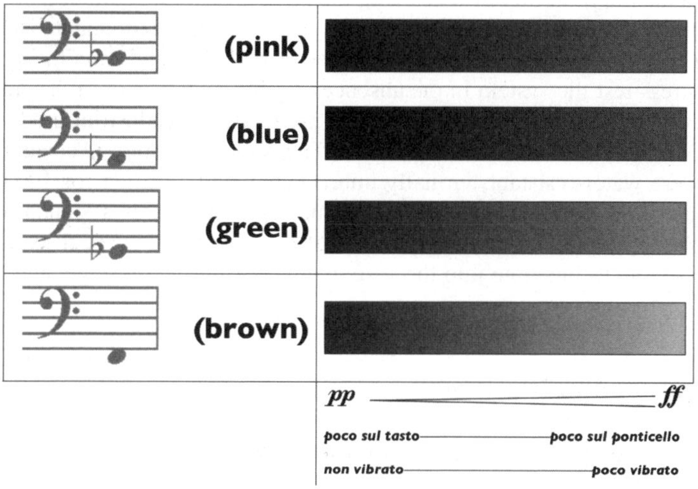


**Fig. 7.** Excerpt from the cello part mapping color family and brightness to pitch, dynamic, and timbre

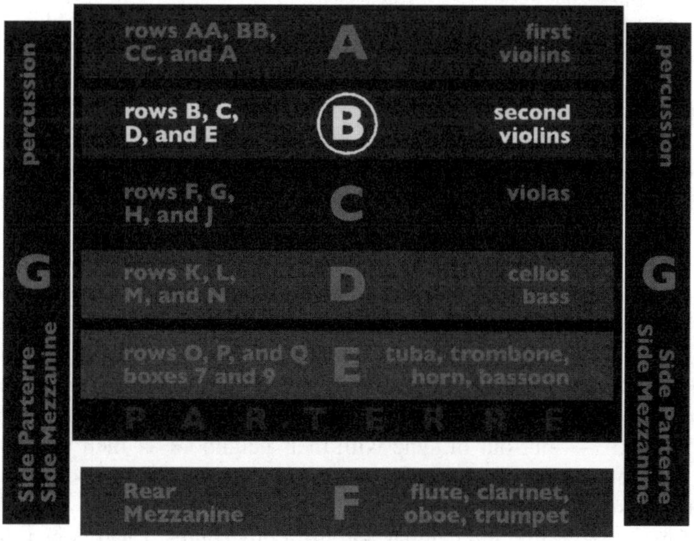


**Fig. 8.** Video animation projected to the audience visualizes analysis data and first-place ranking

### 3.5 Reliability within the Orchestral Environment

Decisions about the system design and its technical implementation were heavily influenced by the restrictions of contemporary orchestral performance environments: limited rehearsal time with the musicians, little advance access to the hall, a small budget, and the impossibility of rehearsing the piece with a full audience.

Given these constraints, system reliability was critical. Redundant backup computers ran in sync with the primary machines. Simulation and monitoring software helped to stress-test the system in the absence of a full audience or orchestra. And the system incorporated standard communication protocols and industrial-grade hardware instead of using custom-built components. The Color Kinetics iAccent lights, for instance, were water-resistant, virtually unbreakable, and certified for 100,000 hours of operation. And they responded to UDP messages sent over a standard Ethernet network. While *Glimmer* did not require all of these impressive specifications, these units were simple to integrate into the system, quick to set up on stage, and extremely reliable in performance.

## 4 Evaluation and Discussion

The American Composers Orchestra asked me to write a piece that used technology and was fun: in these respects, the premiere of *Glimmer* was a tremendous success. The audience enjoyed their role, gasping and laughing at moments of surprise and drama during the performance. They also spontaneously developed creative ways to participate, including a version of the stadium wave in which light sticks were dramatically raised and lowered to show and hide them from the camera's view. And the hardware and software performed nearly flawlessly. The largest problems were human rather than mechanical; for instance, one of the violinists was colorblind.

### 4.1 Audience Participation

In a successful performance of *Glimmer*, audience members should feel that they contributed something important to the music, and they should believe that the performance would have been different had they not been a part of it.

While some New York audience members did feel that way, recalling specific moments where they made a noticeable difference in the music and in other people's behaviors, others were frustrated that none of their actions seemed to matter. Since *Glimmer*'s algorithms respond to the activity of entire audience groups rather than of individual members, a large part of the problem lay in groups' inability to work together to influence the performance. When many group members switched their lights on and off quickly — but out of sync with their neighbors — their activities simply cancelled each other out. As a result, the on-off percentages of groups varied by a disappointingly small amount over the course of the performance.

Inspired by artificial life and cellular automata procedures, I had hoped that even in the absence of group leaders, interesting behavior would emerge over time. I designed the simple rules that governed the competitive aspect of the piece in order to encourage such behavior, but while the competition added an exciting dimension to the experience, it largely failed to accomplish its original goal. Data collected during the New York

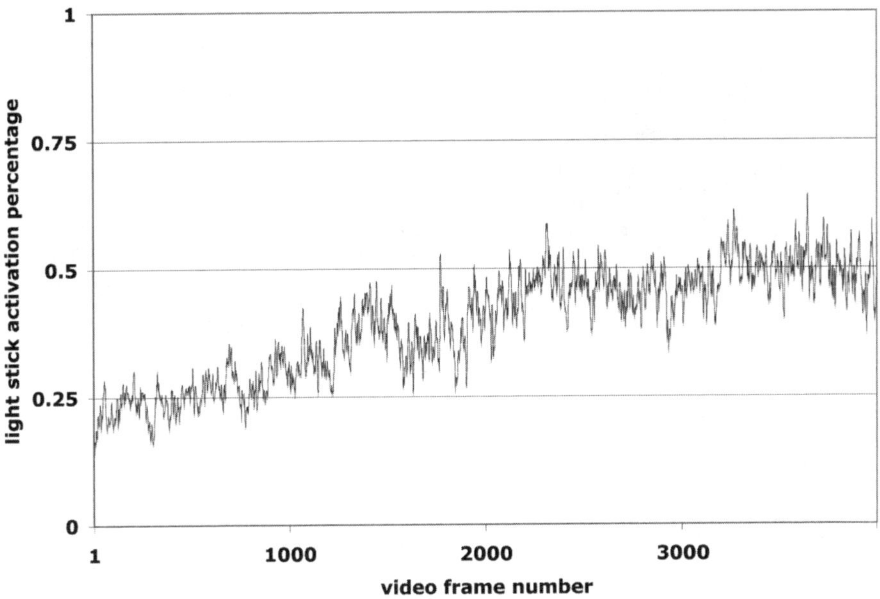


**Fig. 9.** Audience data collected from the winning group in New York (second violins)

performance (Figure 9) showed that even the most successful groups' activities were analyzed within a narrow portion of the zero-to-one data range and varied by relatively small amounts during the performance.

In informal discussions with audience members, I learned of several reasons why groups had failed to collaborate. Some people complained that the piece was too short for them to develop a group sensibility; they felt they would have done better had the piece been longer, or had it been performed a second time. Others had trouble seeing all the people in their group, so it was difficult to respond to what peers were doing.

But most importantly, audience members enjoyed waving their light sticks around much more than switching them on and off, even though they knew that such activity had little effect on the music. Not only was it more fun to do, and not only was it more pleasing to watch, but it also helped them to communicate a wider range of information to each other — if not to the computer software — through their stick's position and speed, not just its on-off state.

So for the Jerusalem performance, I modified the video analysis software to analyze the amount of stick waving in each group instead of the on-off percentage, and I instructed the audience to participate accordingly. The data collected during this performance was consequently much more encouraging. In several of the groups, including the winning group, a group member spontaneously decided to stand up and direct the activities of his or her peers. This led to gradual, dramatic changes in audience data (Figure 10) as the group worked collectively to influence their musicians and compete against the other groups.

In addition to the change in light stick strategy, many other factors may have contributed to the improved group collaboration in Jerusalem. Each group had half as

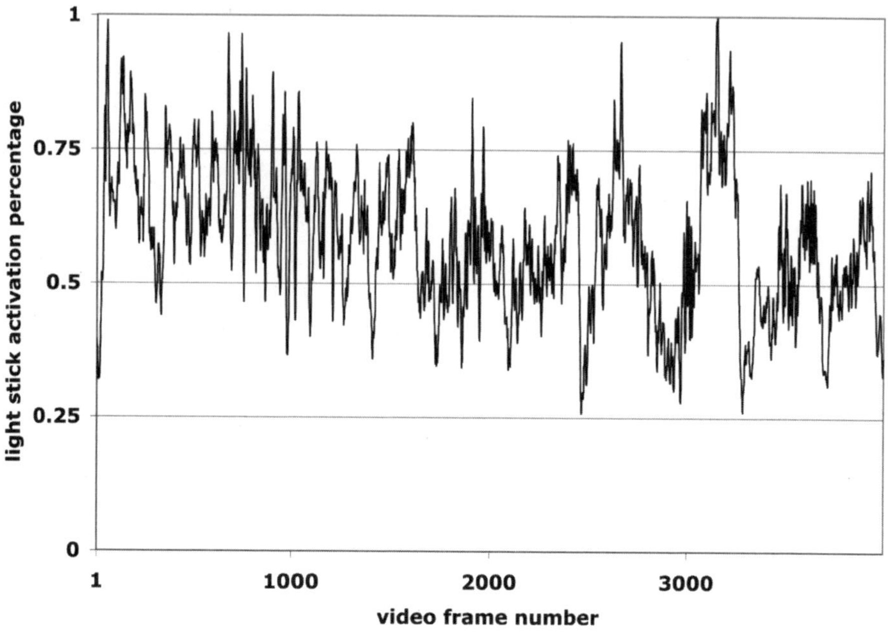


**Fig. 10.** Audience data collected from the winning group in Jerusalem (cellos)

many members as in New York, and each was seated in a nearly square configuration instead of a narrow rectangular configuration, making it easier for group members to see each other. And the New York performance took place in an established concert hall during an orchestral concert that was part of a subscription series, while the Jerusalem event was in a converted warehouse venue at a concert including classical music, free jazz, and hip-hop.

## 4.2 The Role of the Orchestra

In *Glimmer*, there is a fundamental inequality between the audience and the orchestra. The audience works within the framework defined by the piece but follows no score, while the orchestra reads its dynamic notation, exercising limited interpretive freedom.

While I was enticed by the idea of giving the orchestral musicians a greater interpretive role, it did not make practical sense in *Glimmer*. In both performances, it was challenging for the orchestral musicians to familiarize themselves with the lighting cues during the single, short rehearsal of the piece. And many of the classically-trained musicians would have been uncomfortable with broader interpretive freedoms or improvisation. Furthermore, the music is constructed so that perceptually salient local events always originate from audience activity. Were musicians to alter these events or add their own, it would be much more difficult for audience members to establish the relationship between the things they did and the music they heard.

### 4.3 The Musical Result

Stylistically, the music created at both performances of *Glimmer* is similar to my recent through-composed, non-interactive instrumental works: simple, slowly evolving textures, harmonies, and timbres. Yet *Glimmer*'s musical output, when divorced from the interactive environment that created it, is usually not as aesthetically satisfying to me as those other works. While the broad stylistic characteristics may be similar, the surface, moment-to-moment details are not.

In *Glimmer*, these details are determined not so much by the composer or the performers as by the audience members, who know nothing about the piece until moments before its performance. It was important to me to give this level of control to the audience, because I feared that their role would otherwise become superficial and banal. Yet under these circumstances, it would be absurd to expect those details to be controlled with the same degree of subtlety as in through-composed pieces. Opening up the creative process means giving up control, and lowering the barriers of training and commitment to enter that process usually leads to a more exciting process but less exciting results.

Earlier, I stated that *Glimmer*'s success hinged on the belief of audience members that their contributions mattered. For this to be true, the performance cannot proceed exactly as it did in my imagination (or in my software simulations). I should be surprised — sometimes for better and sometimes for worse — by the directions it takes.

While the music in both performances did conform to my broad expectations, there were many moments when the musical details took surprising turns. One passage in the New York performance (Figure 11) was particularly notable, because the subtle musical details combined as effectively as in any non-interactive music I have ever composed. The passage begins approximately eight minutes into the piece, when four, and then just three, groups remain. As the upper winds and brass exit the piece (Gb5 in Figure 11), the first violins leap up a perfect fourth to an Eb6 and the violas leap down an augmented fourth to Gb3. The second violins remain on Db5. The first violins soon move down a step from Eb6 to Db6, melodically resolving the leap, doubling the Db5 at the octave, and momentarily leaving a bare perfect fifth. The crossfade from Eb6 down to Db6 draws out the drama of this melodic and harmonic resolution; it almost sounds like a slow *glissando*. I could not myself have written this passage better, nor could the orchestra have played it better.

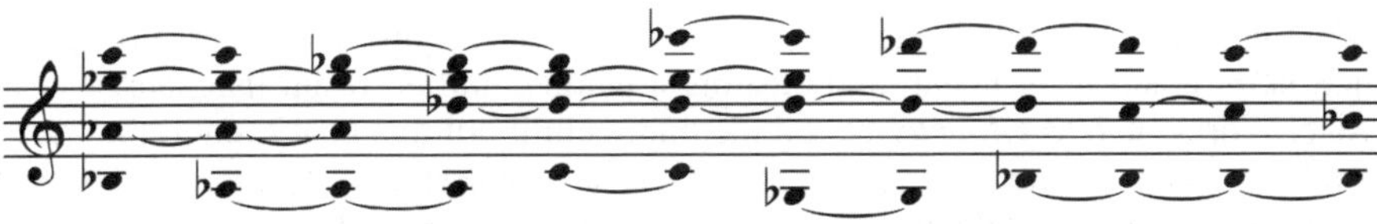

**Fig. 11.** Reduction of an excerpt of the New York performance

On one level, it is easy to understand how this moment transpired. There is no element of chance in the software; given the same sequence of inputs, it will always produce the same outputs. I can understand exactly how my own pre-composed cues combined with the competitive rankings of the audience to create this succession of events, even though I could not have predicted in advance what would take place then, or even which instruments would be playing.

But in truth, I have no idea why this moment transpired. I wish I could claim that audience members intended it to happen, but such a claim would be naïvely optimistic. Yet I am also reluctant to label it mere chance, because in my hundreds of tests and simulations, nothing similar ever happened. I developed the algorithms, and the audience provided the input, but still, some events were governed with a logic which none of us could control or even follow. Should I be disappointed that this moment did not arise from anyone's conscious, deliberate decisions? Should I be thankful for the serendipity of it and ask no further questions? Or should I be glad that the feedback loop — audience, algorithms, and performers — somehow gave rise to a logic all its own?

## 5 Conclusion and Future Work

Beyond the improvements made in the video analysis algorithms, light-stick techniques, and audience size at the Jerusalem performance, there are numerous additional incremental changes that could make *Glimmer* more successful, ranging from more informative visual feedback to more varied composition algorithms to a brief practice session for the audience. As other creators of large-scale interactive works have also found, convincing the audience that they have control and teaching them how to exercise it is a large part of the challenge [18].

And in a new work, *Flock*, I am exploring alternative paradigms that seek to address many of the issues raised by *Glimmer*. The work is for a smaller performing ensemble, saxophone quartet, which will be available for extended rehearsal time and is fluent in both classical techniques and improvisatory styles. The performances will take place in small venues limited to 100 audience members and will last a full evening, giving each audience member more influence over the music as well as more time to learn how to contribute. The notation will be displayed on wireless PDA screens rather than through colored lights, communicating information to musicians with text, graphics, and conventional music notation. I am collaborating with a visual artist on accompanying video animations that will be more informative and more aesthetically integrated into the work than with *Glimmer*. And we will solicit more formal feedback from audiences through post-performance discussions and written surveys, giving us more detailed information to consider when improving the work for subsequent performances.

But could any interactive work ever make every audience member feel truly indispensable to its performance? Large-audience participatory works cannot promise instant gratification: giving each person a critical role; requiring no degree of experience, skill, practice, or talent; and creating a unique, unified result that satisfies everyone. Works such as *Glimmer* reveal the impossibility of this goal even as they strive towards it. They invite participants to explore an environment, to discover its outer limits and its nonsensical corners, and to discover and express their own creativity as they push against the system's limits.

## Acknowledgements

*Glimmer* was commissioned by the American Composers Orchestra, Steven Sloane, music director, Robert Beaser, artistic director, Dennis Russell Davies, conductor laureate. It was premiered on January 21, 2005 at Zankel Hall at Carnegie Hall in New York. This work was funded in part by the Composer Assistance Program of the

American Music Center. Additional thanks to Akademie Schloss Solitude, the Columbia University Computer Music Center, the Hamabada Art Center, and Meet the Composer's Creative Connections program.

The score, performance videos, and source code for *Glimmer* are available at http://www.jasonfreeman.net/glimmer/.

## References

1. Hasse, J.: Moths. Visible Music, Euclid, OH (1986)
2. Chénard, M.: The Millenium Symphony: A Work for the Beginning of Time, Part I: The Musical Challenge. La Scena Musical 5/8, 12–15 (2000)
3. Schmit, T.: Sanitas No. 35 (1962), `http://www.artnotart.com/fluxus/tschmit-sanitasno.35.html`
4. Sheridan, M.: Composer Calling: Cell Phone Symphony Premieres. NewMusicBox (October 2001)
5. Mirapaul, M.: A Hand-Held Portal to Musical Delights. The New York Times, July 17 (2003)
6. Baird, K.: Real-Time Generation of Music Notation via Audience Interaction Using Python and GNU Lilypond. In: Proceedings of the 2005 International Conference on New Interfaces for Musical Expression (NIME), Vancouver, Canada, pp. 240–241 (2005)
7. McAllister, G., Alcorn, M., Strain, P.: Interactive Performance with Wireless PDAs. In: Proceedings of the 2004 International Computer Music Conference (ICMC), Miami, Florida, pp. 702–705 (2004)
8. Wulfson, H., Barrett, G., Winter, M.: Automatic Notation Generators. In: Proceedings of the 2007 International Conference on New Interfaces in Musical Expression (NIME), New York, pp. 346–351 (2007)
9. Hiller, L., Isaacson, L.: Experimental Music: composition with an electronic computer. McGraw-Hill, New York (1959)
10. Laske, O.: Compostion Theory in Koenig's Project 1 and Project 2. Computer Music Journal 5/4, 54–65 (1981)
11. Cope, D.: Experiments in Musical Intelligence. Middleton, WI, A-R Editions (1996)
12. Brown, E.: Transformations and Developments of a Radical Aesthetic. Current Musicology 67/68, 39–57 (1999)
13. Stockhausen, K.: Klavierstück XI. London, Universal Edition (1957)
14. Carpenter, L., Carpenter, R.: Audience Participation. In: Druckrey, T. (ed.) Ars Electronica: Facing the Future, pp. 395–396. MIT Press, Cambridge (1999)
15. Maynes-Aminzade, D., Pausch, R., Seitz, S.: Techniques for Interactive Audience Participation. In: Proceedings of the IEEE International Conference on Multimodal Interfaces (ICMI), Pittsburgh (2002)
16. Bregler, C., Castiglia, C., DeVincenzo, J., Dubois, L., Feeley, K., Igoe, T., Meyer, J., Naimark, M., Postelnicu, A., Rabinovich, M., Rosenthal, S., Salen, K., Sudol, J., Wright, B.: Squidball: An Experiment in Large Scale Motion Capture and Game Design. In: Proceedings of Intelligent Technologies for Interactive Entertainment (INTETAIN), Madonna di Campiglio, Italy (2005)
17. Cage, J.: Four$^2$ for chorus. New York, Edition Peters (1990)
18. Fisher, R., Vanouse, P., Dannenberg, R., Christensen, J.: Audience Interactivity: A Case Study in Three Perspectives. In: Proceedings of the Sixth Biennial Symposium for Arts and Technology, Connecticut College (1997)

# Variations on *Variations*

Dániel Péter Biró

School of Music, University of Victoria
P.O. Box 1700 STN CSC
Victoria, BC V8W 2Y2 Canada
(1) (250) 721-7930 - Office Tel.
(1) (250) 721-6597 - Fax
dpbiro@finearts.uvic.ca

**Abstract.** *Variations* is an electroacoustic sound installation commissioned by the Villa Bernau in Wabern, Switzerland. The original sound installation was created in coordination with the sculptor Wolfram Renger. Renger's sculptures deal with the historical forming of prisons of cultural and artistic identities. The installation was divided into three spatialized parts. *Penalty* dealt with the problems of industrial death via the death penalty. *Lizkhor* dealt with questions of musical/physical closure (via exploring questions of the US prison system) and the relationship of closure to cultural memory. *Borders* dealt with questions of the limits of closure (exploring European border problems) and its relationship to the forming of cultural identities.

This paper will investigate how the structuring of the installation and how it responds to to Franz Schubert's *String Quartet in G D 884* and to Dániel Péter Biró's own string quartet *Lizkor VeLishkoach (To Remember and to Forget).*

**Keywords:** Composition, sound-installations, electro-acoustic sound art, string quartet.

## 1 Introduction

"The construction of history is dependent on the memory of the past but a memory that is always selective and malleable. Forgetfulness is thus itself an integral part of memory, for what is remembered is only remembered against the background of what is forgotten."[1]

"Artworks are never creatures. They are rather targets in a shooting gallery that people hit: if the right one is hit, it tips over and allows reality itself to shine through. The power that hits them is human, not artistic: they are moved by human emotion. In no other way can the indifference of subject and object in the lyrical configuration be comprehended. The lyric poet does not immediately display his emotions in the creation. Rather, his emotions are the means that draw truth, in its incomparably small crystallization, into the creation. Truth itself does not sink into the artistic creation but

[1] Elisheva Carlebach, John M. Efron, David N. Myers, eds., *Jewish History and Jewish Memory: Essays in Honor of Yosef Hayim Yerushalmi* (Hanover: University Press of New England. Brandeis University Press, 1998) p. 173.

R. Adams, S. Gibson, and S. Müller Arisona (Eds.): DAW/IF 2006/2007, CCIS 7, pp. 284–298, 2008.

is portrayed within the creation, and the revelation (unveiling) of its image remains to be done by people. The creator reveals the image. But the image of truth always exists in history. The history of the image is its decay." [2]

As in society, temporal structures of a composition are formed by ways of memory. The memories brought forth, inherent in the musical material, also form a relationship to the memory of their place of production. In this sense musical material pre-exists, as it forms a dialogue with the material conditions of its production, the composer recollecting this material within the production process.[3] The succession of musical material forms the temporal structure within the composition. These temporal structures create a sort of friction between the different temporal realities within the piece (i.e. the contrasting sections within the overall form) and outside the piece, (i.e. the temporal realities of the society in which it was created) thus producing a dialectical relationship between the individual composer and their place of production. In the same way, a friction is established between the temporal structures within the composition on the one hand, and the composer's relationship to the past of the culture or community (as expressed in his choice and use of musical materials) on the other. The composition's inner forming of these temporal structures mirrors the composer's understanding of and ontological relationship to history.

Variations is an electroacoustic sound installation that dealt explicitly with relationships between history, memory and identity formation. Existing as part of very contrasting, yet interconnecting, artistic and musical genres, the sound installation exists as an open sonorous question, serving to question the listener's perception of historical and experienced time as well as the temporal autonomy of the various sonorous and visual works of art.

Responding to sculptures by Wolfram Renger[4] the sound installation functioned to prelude a concert, existing as an extension of my own string quartet Lizkor VeLishkoach (To Remember and to Forget).[5] Likewise, this string quartet was composed as a response to Franz Schubert's Quartet in G Major op. 161, a work that preceded my own composition in the concert context.

Wolfram Renger's sculptures deal explicitly with the historical forming of prisons of cultural and artistic identities. Explicit in their materiality, the sculptures consist of cages, overstuffed with cloth, fur, and clothing, straw and animal remains; these materials become extended into a new domain, as layers of paint are added to their surface. Through such material processing, the sculptures investigate the dichotomy of surface and, in this

---

[2] Theodor W. Adorno, *Schubert* (Neu-Isenburg: Edition Tiessen 1984) 8. Translation by Dániel Péter Biró.

[3] The Hungarian writer György Konrád describes memory as " a process of selection from the past combined with a large amount of fantasy." György Konrád, Interview in *Kulturzeit,* 3-SAT, Dec. 11, 1999.

[4] Wolfram Renger is a German visual artist. Born in 1965 in Regensburg, Germany Renger studied at the École National Supériure des Beaux Arts and philosophy and art history in Bonn and Paris. His recent work consists of sculptures, installations and interaction with music an dance. See also http://www.wolfram-renger.de/de/

[5] *Variations* was a sound installation commissioned by the Villa Bernau in Wabern, Switzerland. The exhibition/intstallation originally went from April 20-21. This was followed by a concert of Schubert's *Quartet in G Major op. 161* and my own *Lizkor VeLishkoach (To Remebmer and to Forget) (To Remember and to Forget).*

case, overstuffed, interior, thereby questioning the violent prison of the clothed, "outside" identity, and how the "outer skin" of the subject subjugates the individual into a prison of representation. Through his method of material deconstruction and re-contextualization, Renger's works exist in a state of cognitive unease, as the works give no answer to the violent questions of their historical representation.

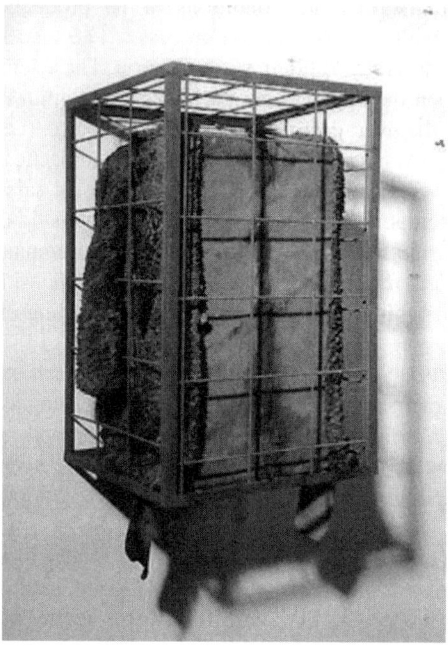

**Fig. 1.** Wolfram Renger: *Amictus (2000)*

Reacting to Renger's sculptures, I decided to translate such concepts of violence and historical identity formation into the sonorous plane. Employing documentary audio material, recorded citations from my string quartet *Lizkor VeLishkoach (To Remember and to Forget)* and Schubert's string quartet, as well as recorded nature and industrial sounds, I set out to create a series of six-hour episodes that would compliment and interact with the complex visual plane.

Originally the sounds came, via loudspeakers, from the sculptures themselves, the speakers hidden within the sculptures' caged material. As the sculptures were distributed among the three rooms of the Villa Bernau, I conceived of three separate parts of the sound installation to accompany the sculptures in each of the three rooms. *Penalty* dealt with the problems of industrial death via the death penalty. *Lizkhor* dealt with questions of musical/physical closure (exploring individual experiences within the US prison system) and the relationship of closure to cultural memory. *Borders* dealt with questions of the limits of closure (exploring European border problems) and its relationship to the forming of cultural identities.

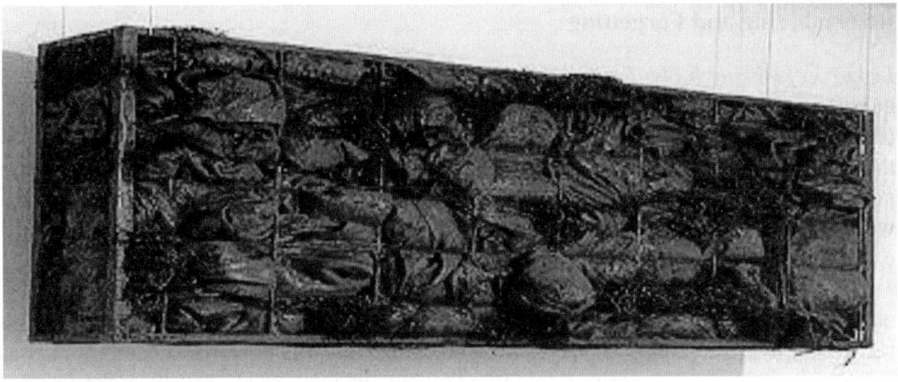

**Fig. 2.** Wolfram Renger: *Vocatio Testae (1999)*

Each of the three parts juxtaposed and integrated the documentary material into long-range musical processes. The sounds connected and reacted to the context, which Renger established, by both allowing contrasting subjective documentary accounts to juxtapose the violent material objectivity of his sculptures, and by connecting the abstract qualities of his "caged" form with new musical/acoustic spaces and temporal "frames." Within such temporal frames the listener, free to walk from room to room, was given a sense of restricted freedom, perceiving the intertwining of various prison and border scenes, music, sounds of the environment and more "abstract" musical material. Each sonorous space, with its overlapping temporal frames, also explored questions of the "variability" of history, of identity formation, borders/border problems and prison systems.

On display for several days before the concert, the sound installation responded to my string quartet *Lizkor VeLishkoach (To Remember and to Forget)* as well as to Franz Schubert's *String Quartet in G op. 161 D 884,* forming complex contextual and temporal relationship to these two compositions. The entire sound installation lasted six-hours and was heard over a period of three days. As the exhibition drew to a close, it transformed into a concert, as the gallery visitors became part of a concert audience, hearing the Basler String Quartet first perform Franz Schubert's *String Quartet in G D 884* followed by my own string quartet *Lizkor VeLishkoach (To Remember and to Forget).*

While the sound installation *Variations* was a compositional reaction to questions of identity and violence, already inherent in Renger's sculptures, it also existed as a response to the historical context of the string quartet, in particular to problems of *compositional variation* and how this, especially in the Schubertian context, relates to historical *systems of violence*. Just as the materials of Renger's sculptures cover up their historical "contents," my quartet serves to cover up an underlying palimpsest structure, namely that of Schubert's quartet. Before beginning to analyze how such a technique of variation was formed in the sound installation, it is necessary to understand something of the variation and palimpsest structures of its interacting predecessor quartet compositions.

## Remembering and Forgetting

*Lizkor VeLishkoach (To Remember and to Forget)*[6] is a composition that responds to questions of memory, history and place, as it exists in dialogue with Schubert's quartet in G Major D. 997. *Lizkor VeLishkoach (To Remember and to Forget)* addresses the historical nature of the string quartet genre, as Schubert's quartet exists in the piece much as an architectural ruin exists in a city. While citations of Schubert's work surface throughout the work, the temporal form of Schubert's quartet is both extended and deconstructed, forming layers of dialogue between the two works.

The first movement of Schubert's quartet employs an unconventional synthesis of sonata and variation form: sections of directed, teleological movement are juxtaposed by sections of relative variational stasis. Re-contextualizing this temporal dichotomy, I consciously divided my composition into two sections, which serve to re-collect the form of Schubert's quartet. In recollecting this form, the work also acts as a response and extension to the historical place and time of Schubert's musical production process.

## Schubert's Form, Time and Place

The first movement of Schubert's quartet alternates between two temporal modalities. One is teleological time "pressing constantly forward,"[7] and one is "meandering"[8] time. These two temporal realities refer to exploiting time, making it "useful" in the strategic, economic sense, and "killing time," actually undermining the flow of time through - in Schubert's case (relative) harmonic – stasis. The tension between these types of teleological and meandering time relates to the various section of the movement. Sections of trajectory development, derived from processes of sonata form, juxtapose sections of variations, the relative stability or stasis of which allowing for complex hierarchies of *repetition* and *variation* employment.[9]

Such juxtaposition between repetition and variation can be observed at the beginning of the piece. The repetition of the descending and ascending minor seconds, changing the context from *major* to *minor* in measures 1-14 prepares the intervallic transformation in

---

6 xwk%lw rwkzl *Lizkor VeLishkoach (To Remebmer and to Forget)* (To Remember and to Forget) was commissioned by the Villa Bernau, Switzerland and first performed by the Basler Quartet together with Schubert's quartet on April 22, 1999 at the Villa Bernau in Wabern, Switzerland. The root of the Hebrew verb rwkzl (*lizkor* or to remember) is rkz meaning *imprint* or *memory*. Within the Hebrew word xwk%l *(lishkoach* or *to forget)* is the word xwk *(koach* or *power)*. The etymological traces of these words informed the conceptual basis of the composition.

7 Carl Dahlhaus (Rheinhard Thilo, Translator) «Sonata Form in Schubert: The First Movement of the G-Major String Quartet, op. 161, (D. 887)» *Schubert: Critical and Analytical Studies*, edited by Walter Frisch (Lawrence: University of Nebraska Press 1986) p. 7.

8 Dahlhaus p. 2.

9 In the course of the piece, Schubert constructs a hierarchy consisting of different *levels of repetition*. Schubert defines therein certain *temporal units* to repeat and measure time. The *smallest* level of repetition consists of the *successive repetition of notes,* which plays a central role both in the *textural* sense (as with the tremolo) as well as redefining motives and their intervals. Beyond this level is the *repetition of intervals and motives*. This level is followed by *phrase repetition,* which is then followed by *section repetition,* with the repeat of the exposition being the largest type of form of repetition in the movement.

the following section of the primary subject. The double-dotted motive, first presented in mm. 2-3 is repeated, transposed to the key of d major/minor in mm. 8-9. Schubert gives specific emphasis to this descending minor second movement in the bridge section in mm. 11 – 14, making the listener wait for the re-contextualization of this interval; this happens in measure 15, the piece moving now from *minor* to *major*. Here Schubert *imprints* new intervallic information onto the rhythmic skeleton of the double dotted rhythmic motive derived from the introductory section.

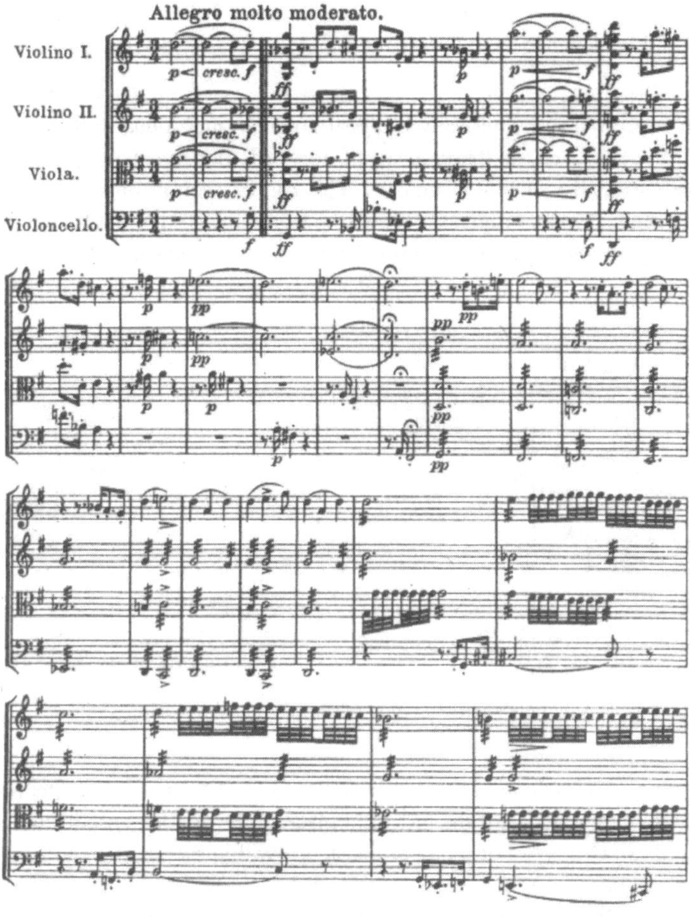


**Fig. 3.** Beginning of Schubert's *Quartet in G Major op. 161 D. 997*

The repetition of harmonic progressions helps to emphasize the static nature of these harmonic landscapes wherein the theme is allowed to "meander." This "meandering" quality is emphasized again and again, as Schubert consistently adds an extension to the phrase, creating areas of *surplus time*, demonstrated in mm. 20 – 24 thereby allowing the theme time to *linger* for a bit longer.

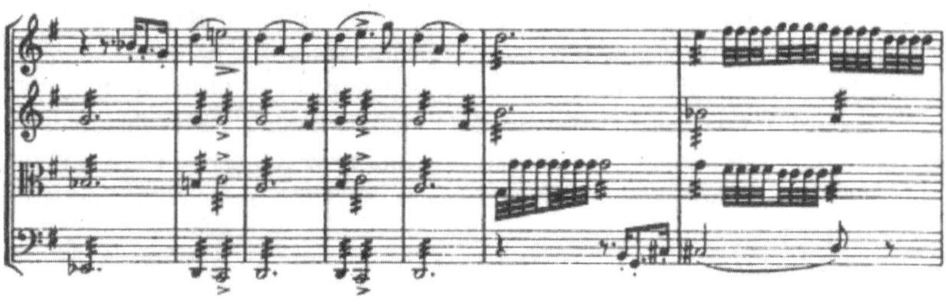

**Fig. 4.** Schubert's *Quartet in G Major op. 161 D. 997* mm. 19-24

These sections provide a contrast to the goal-oriented time found in the trajectory sections of sequences. Even in these areas of forward movement, a complex dialectic between repetition and variation dominates. This can be seen in mm. 54-59. While employing the same harmonic progression as in the beginning of the first theme (based on a falling fifth progression), Schubert infuses the section with topical elements from the introduction.

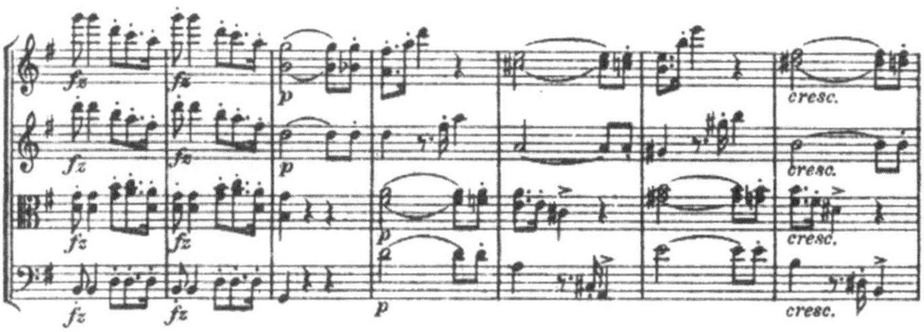


**Fig. 5.** Schubert's *Quartet in G major op. 161 D. 997* mm. 52-59

These temporal modes do not only dominate the form of Schubert's quartet but also assist to recall temporal realities of the historical place of the quartet's production. The tension between these two types of temporal existence within the quartet can be seen to reflect temporal realties of a Viennese society torn between modernization and feudalism, to specific conditions brought about by societal changes in power in the Vienna of the time. The reforms of Joseph II, which allowed for a larger and more affluent bourgeoisie, also denied this bourgeoisie the freedom of further upward mobility and cultural power enjoyed by the aristocracy by means of continued enforcement of class hierarchy. In the time of Franz I this system of constricted autonomy became increasingly stifling and could not make up for the loss of cultural structure from previous eras. In his era of cultural and political anxiety, Schubert's music is an extreme example of what Bourdieu terms "art of disinterest,"[10] displaying the will for artistic expression within a system of confining uncertainty.Such uncertainty is reflected in the quartet: the shifts from major to minor throughout the quartet happen quickly and easily, perhaps too easily, and not without violence. The recurring Baroque topics also help to recall a time in which the more powerful aristocracy enforced an even more restricting stability, however one in which the alienating forces of early industrialization and the tyrannical state police terror of Metternich, which also had its repressive affect on Schubert and his circle, did not yet exist.

As Carl Dahlhaus has noted, the large scale trajectory within the first movement seems not so much to be projected by a *subjective will* but rather by "letting things run their course."[11] The formal juxtapositions and transformations of variation and sequence sections in the movement create a conflict between meandering and teleological time. Understanding the complexity of Schubert's class, this conflict can also be read as a reflection of the conflicting temporal structures of leisure and economic production Schubert's Vienna. [12]

---

[10] Pierre Bourdieu, *The Field of Cultural Production: Essays on Art and Literature*, Chapter 1 – «The field of Cultural Production or: The Economic World reversed.» Ed. Randal Johnson, (Cambridge Polity, 1993). Bourdieu's "field of cultural production" refers to the societal factors that underline artistic production. According to Bourdieu, societies build a hierarchy between "cultural capital" and "economic capital." These forms of capital are employed by players in the field (composers, audience, critics, publishers, etc.) to establish cultural authority. Art is produced out of economic "interest" or economic "disinterest." The latter is the basis for the formation of "cultural capital," which is displayed as more autonomous (having a smaller audience and is not directly profit driven) than market-based art. Bourdieu divides up the category of "art of disinterest" into two main opposing categories; one being "art for art's sake" and the other being "bourgeois art."

[11] Carl Dahlhaus (Rheinhard Thilo, Translator) «Sonata Form in Schubert: The First Movement of the G-Major String Quartet, op. 161, (D. 887)» *Schubert: Critical and Analytical Studies,* ed. Walter Frisch (Lawrence: University of Nebraska Press 1986) p. 10.

[12] Such musical tension can be heard as an expression of tensions within social temporal structures- the tensions between the economical, industrial structure and the private structure of time, between the demand for effective, rational use of time and leisure time. In Schubert's day, as now, these modes of temporal structuring were interdependent, standing in a dialectical relationship to one-another: leisure is a concept that depends on the idea of a rationalized, limited work time, and the other way around. Moreover, the concept of leisure relates to temporal structures mainly enjoyed by the aristocracy. The temporal aspects within Viennese society are reflected Schubert's form. For Adorno Schubert's concept of form stands in opposition to that of Beethoven, as he views the mode of musical growth within Schubert's work not to be cellular but rather crystal-like, as he finds Schubert's music to recall the form of the potpourri. Adorno writes: "In this sense it seems certain that a particular school of understanding of Schubert has misspoken, as its conventional opinion about the lyrical is wrong. This is particularly true in that sense that it sees Schubert's music as an organic plant-like being that unfolds, without any consideration for any preplanned form and practically every form that, perhaps bare, grows out of itself and refreshingly blooms. But it is precisely such a logical organic theory that is strictly denied within the construction that stems from the potpourri. . . Even if we grant Schubert's music to be, in the larger sense, grown rather than produced; its growth, fragmented through and through, and never actually self sufficient, doesn't have the quality of a plant but rather that of a crystal." Theodor W. Adorno, (Translation by Dániel Péter Biró) *Schubert,* (Neu-Isenburg: Edition Tiessen 1984) p. 5-8.

As I began to write *Lizkor VeLishkoach (To Remember and to Forget)*, I was preoccupied by similar historical questions of individual and collective time. Using memory as a musical parameter, I set out to create an archeology of musical time in which processes of development and entropy, past and present, remembering and forgetting would exist in dialogue. In order to formalize this dialogue, I developed a conceptual plan for these types of temporal realities to transpire.

## Landscapes

Throughout *Lizkor VeLishkoach (To Remember and to Forget)* the first movement Schubert's quartet is employed as a palimpsest structure: like people or ghosts passing by an open window, citations of Schubert's quartet surface in various guises and constellations in the course of the work. Working with pencil, paper and erasers, I actually wrote over Schubert's quartet score. Each page of score would be copied several times. In this way, I would not only remember and forget Schubert's quartet but also better observe my own remembering and forgetting within the compositional process.[13]

As I began to compose *Lizkor VeLishkoach (To Remember and to Forget),* I constructed various temporal zones, *temporal landscapes.* Within these sections, various types of musical topics and materials come to the surface while others disappear. These *temporal landscapes* were not conceived to exist as categorical blocks of time but rather to allow the various types of musical material to coexist, blend into, or develop from other types of musical material. While the musical material was conceptualized as a historical entity, which could be recognized as *topical* information, the processes of transformation were intended to imitate processes of memory and forgetting.

The historical nature of the material is most evident in the sections incorporating citations from Schubert's quartet. In their first entrance, these citations are encountered not as parts of a completed work but rather like fragments from a musical ruin. Surrounded by silence and a slowly emerging dodecaphonic environment, fragmented chords, melodies and motives derived from the beginning of Schubert's quartet enter the composition in a ghost-like manner. As though covered by dust, these citation-fragments are alienated, as extended string techniques emphasize their noisy timbral aspects as well as their modes of sound production. As later in the work, overlapping sections of silence amongst the four instruments are structured via the Fibonacci series.

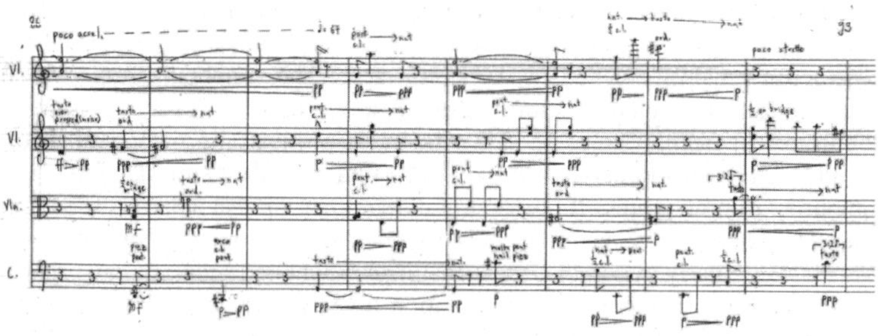

**Fig. 6.** Biró - *Lizkor VeLishkoach (To Remember and to Forget)*: mm. 86-93

[13] Intending to employ memory as a main compositional parameter, each page of the score was copied at least three or four times.

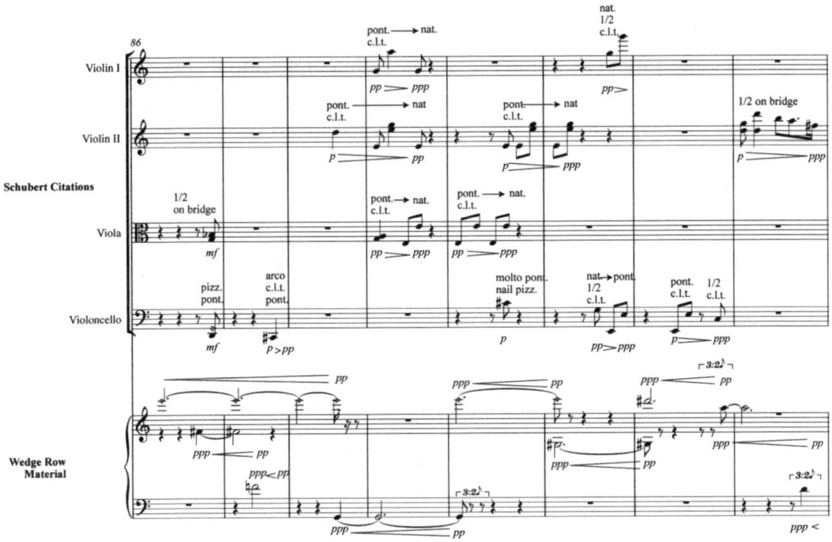


**Fig. 7.** Biró - *Lizkor VeLishkoach (To Remember and to Forget)*: mm. 86-93 – Structuring of Citations and Row

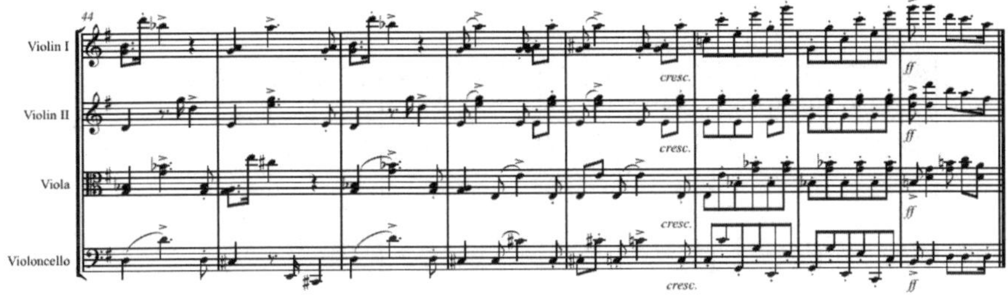


**Fig. 8.** Schubert Quartet in G Major: mm. 44-52

Here memory is activated on two levels: such *structural silencing* allows the listener to remember the segments that are not present, while the increasing emergence of dodecaphonic structures (and their historical associations) eventually conceal the historical material that previously dominated the musical fabric.

This situation is reversed later in the piece. I created a process of movement from static verticality to repetitive linearity: the register of these chords, spread out over four octaves are slowly filtered down to eventually become a ascending chromatic scale repeating within more compressed registral confines; each note of this scale is defined a specific timbre and duration. This is a movement from a series of identifiable harmonic *objects* to a neutral serialized *process:* by m. 204 the dodecaphonic context becomes fully transformed. While a quintuplet pattern becomes established for these scales, their increasingly noisy timbral quality is contrasted by fragmented citations of Schubert's quartet that not only *break in* to this neutral zone of ascending chromatic scales but also *break out* of the composition itself. The citation also brings its own syntactic realm of 19th century period structure and harmonic rhythm into the present picture: not only the outer walls but the pillars of the non-existing architecture allow sounds to shine through which, in spite of their historical importance, are *no longer there.* Like in a palimpsest, the background structure now moves to the surface much like memories surfacing from the depths of consciousness. Here citations of Schubert's quartet exist *renovated* amongst the noisy ruins extracted from previous dodecaphonic development. This can be observed in mm. 214-222.

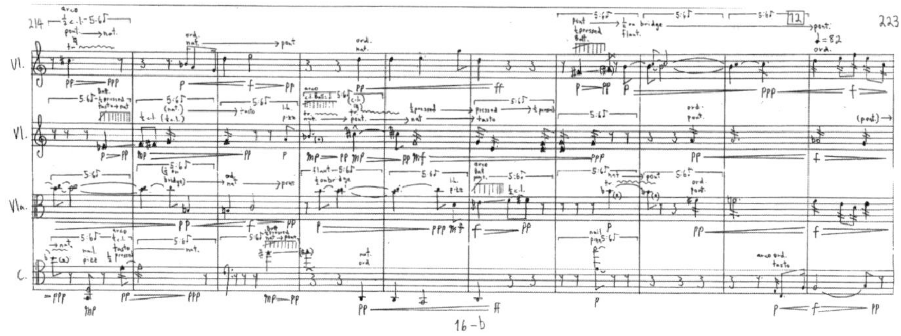

**Fig. 9.** Biró - *Lizkor VeLishkoach (To Remember and to Forget)*: mm. 214-223

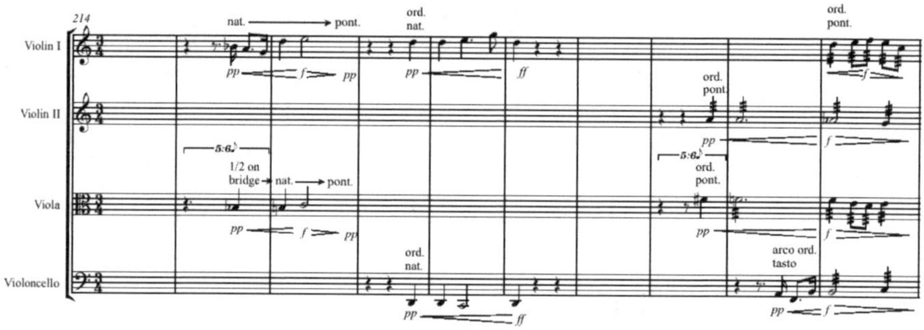


**Fig. 10.** Biró - *Lizkor VeLishkoach (To Remember and to Forget)*: mm. 214-223 – Schubert Citations

Such palimpsest techniques employed in *Lizkor VeLishkoach (To Remember and to Forget)* not only allow sounds to come to the cognitive surface but also allow history to present itself as a violent force in the compositional background. Such concepts of palimpsest and variation were then expanded and transformed in my sound installation *Variations.*

## Variation and Palimpsest

In the first room of the installations, the section entitled *Borders* could be heard. In this section, I set out to juxtapose various concepts of borders; the borders between people, borders of culture and borders between the public and the private. The section contrasts perspectives of individuals forced to exist behind closed borders (or confining environment) and those who actually control these (or other) borders. Simultaneously, I set out to explore the borders of cultural linguistic comprehension, employing documentary material in English, Hungarian, German and Swiss German. Throughout the exhibition, the question arises as to the border between "documentary" and "art" as well as the border between private experience and public art. The listener is thus put in an uncomfortable situation, as the violence of lived experience turns into the violence of indiscrete observance.

*Borders* begins with the tale of a young woman living in the confines of a U.S. juvenile prison. Telling of her crime of assault, her voice breaks, slowly taking on a sense of desperation. It is at this point that her voice begins to be cross-synthesized[14] with fragments of strings, taken from my string quartet composition *Lizkor VeLishkoach (To Remember and to Forget)*. The teenage American woman's voice is then juxtaposed by a recording of an elderly Hungarian woman, now lamenting her daughter's death in the manner of the millennia-old folk tradition.[15] Here a variation of suffering, from the other side of the planet violently intermixes with the increasingly "musical" documentary.

In the course of this section, fragments of the quartet *Lizkor VeLishkoach (To Remember and to Forget)* rise to the cognitive surface. In this way, the gallery visitors hear sections of the concert in advance, allowing for extra-musical associations to be re-collected in the course of the concert. These associations are expanded, as phrases of Schubert's Quartet are heard, now juxtaposed by documentary interviews with German and Swiss border police, talking about their work on the German and Swiss border. While they discuss how to keep illegal immigrants from crossing the border, their recollections take on a certain poetic quality, as some start to talk about the natural terrain of their "workplace."

| Documentary Testimonies: | English Translation: |
| --- | --- |
| Zitauerer Gebirge, bewaldet unübersichtlich, und weiter zieht das sich auf eine Ebene bis. . . Es gibt in diesem ganzen Beriech keinen natürlichen Hindernisse, die einem Grenzübertritt verhindern könnten. | The Mountains of Zitauer, wooded, nontransparent, and that extends over the plane until. . . In this whole area there is no natural obstruction that could prohibit a border crossing. |

These very pragmatic, and sometimes inadvertently poetic, statements become suddenly contrasted by the voice of a then illegal Rumanian immigrant who describes why he is attempting to cross the border.

[14] This was done with Ircam software as well as with the help of MAX/MSP.

[15] Zoltán Kodály "Folk Music of Hungary, (Budapest: Corvina Press, 1960) 76, "Mourning songs for the dead also go back to primitive times. Although every religion and secular form of legislation (e.g., Solon's) has endeavoured to control mourning practices, they are still customary even today."

| Documentary Testimony: | English Translation: |
| --- | --- |
| Ich bin Roma. Ich möchte Transit durch Land. Ich möchte in Italien für Arbeit. In Deutschland nicht possible für nicht legalitäten Papiere. | I am Roma. I want a travel across the country to Italy to work. In Germany this is not possible without the legal papers. |

As the temporal frame of the Shubertian musical phrase determines the fragment of speech, phrase relationships to the two concert works for string quartet is formed. Such temporal associations became strengthened as the gallery visitor walked through the other rooms of the exhibition.

## The Temporal Form of *Penalty*

The section of the installation, found in the final room of the sculptures, was entitled *penalty.* This part of the sound installation dealt with the most extreme form of the U.S. prison industry, that of the death penalty. Here fragments of documentary interviews with prison officials who carry out the death penalty could be heard.

"There is breathing and then there is silence"

"We then strap them to the gurney."

"And there are some men who are afraid of a needle"

"There is a big gasp and then silence."

Renger placed six large column-like sculptures in this room, the caged frames of which were not directly visible but rather covered by layers of clothing and paint. As speakers were placed directly into these columns, the sound tended not to be directly audible. Rather, the listener was forced to come close to the sculpture, almost as though to "listen in" on a secret.

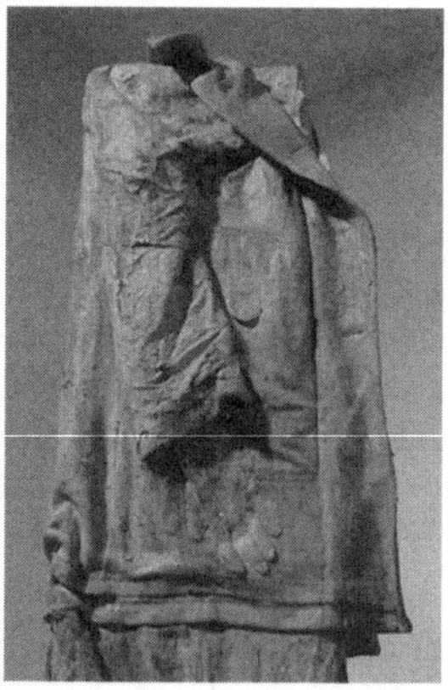

**Fig. 11.** Wolfram Renger: *Vocatio Testae (2000)*

Just as the temporal frame within *Borders* was determined by pre-existing musical material, the section *Penalty* was formed via a temporal frame taken from my string quartet *Lizkor VeLishkoach (To Remember and to Forget).* The second part of the string quartet consists of a single musical phrase, repeated thirteen times. This phrase becomes temporally augmented and simultaneously "silenced," as rests, mathematically pre-determined via the Fibonacci series, violently cut into each phrase with increasing occurrence.

| *Section*<br>*Fibonacci Proportioning:*<br>*Silence and Number of Insertions of Silence* | *Repetitions*<br>*and Insertions* |
|---|---|
| 29) Beats 3 1/4 - 4 1/4, 7 1/2 - 8 1/2, 11 3/4 - 12 3/4, 16 - 17, 20 1/4 - 21 1/4, 24 1/4 - 25 1/4, 28 1/2 - 29 1/2, 33 - 34 (8 Insertions of Silence) | *(5x8 Insertions)* |
| 30) Beats 3 1/4 - 4 1/4, 7 1/2 - 8 1/2, 11 3/4 - 12 3/4, 16 - 17, 20 1/4 - 21 1/4, 24 1/4 - 25 1/4, 28 1/2 - 29 1/2, 33 - 34 (8 Insertions of Silence) | |
| 31) Beats 3 1/4 - 4 1/4, 7 1/2 - 8 1/2, 11 3/4 - 12 3/4, 16 - 17, 20 1/4 - 21 1/4, 24 1/4 - 25 1/4, 28 1/2 - 29 1/2, 33 - 34 (8 Insertions of Silence) | |
| 32) Beats 3 1/4 - 4 1/4, 7 1/2 - 8 1/2, 11 3/4 - 12 3/4, 16 - 17, 20 1/4 - 21 1/4, 24 1/4 - 25 1/4, 28 1/2 - 29 1/2, 33 - 34 (8 Insertions of Silence) | |
| 33) Beats 3 1/4 - 4 1/4, 7 1/2 - 8 1/2, 11 3/4 - 12 3/4, 16 - 17, 20 1/4 - 21 1/4, 24 1/4 - 25 1/4, 28 1/2 - 29 1/2, 33 - 34 (8 Insertions of Silence) | |
| 34) Beats 1 5/6 - 2 5/6, 4 1/8 - 6 1/8, 6 13/15 - 7 13/15, 9 1/2 - 10 1/2, 12 1/3 - 13 1/3, 14 2/3 - 5 2/3, 17 1/3 - 18 1/3, 19 1/6 - 20 11/12, 27 1/3 - 28 1/4, 25 1/4 - 26 1/4, 27 3/4 - 28 1/2, 30 1/4 - 31 1/4, 33 - 34 (13 Insertions of Silence) | *(1x13 Insertions)* |

**Fig. 8.** Structural Silencing Within Sections at the End of *Lizkor VeLishkoach (To Remember and to Forget)*

The end of *Penalty* mirrors this temporal development, as the spoken statements of the sound installation are injected with silence. Over six hours, the increasingly fragmented speaking becomes infused with and slowly replaced by the homogenizing sound of radio static. In this way, these ciphers of the spoken voice become replaced by sounds of interference. In terms of timbre, the sound of radio static resembles the sound of string instrument bow noise that dominates the final section of my string quartet *Lizkor VeLishkoach (To Remember and to Forget).* Like the last section of the quartet, meaning, here presented through the testimony of interviewed subjects, is phased out, replaced by violent interjections of homogenous static noise and silence. As the installation forms a connection with the quartet via timbral and durational structuring, the bow noise, heard in the concert setting, forces the listener to recollect on the previous disappearing words from the muffled speakers in the clothed sculptural columns.

In their temporal and material interaction, both the quartet and sound installation provoke the listener to speculate on realms of experience beyond their momentary ontological framework. Through such intercrossing, both works aestheticize real and abstracted memories of historical and present-day social-political realities. Via comparison, contrast and structural connection, the works also reflect on one-another, existing as an attempt shatter the listener's notion of the lived aesthetic experience and the imagined social shadow thereof.

## Conclusion

Just as the sound installation *Variations* extends topical themes of Renger's sculptures, themes of violence, identity formation and historical memory, the installation also forms various points of reference to the two string quartet compositions, as its temporal and sonorous structuring find correlations in the two works. While the sound installation serves to *re-collect* contrasting personal testimonies, the works for string quartet also function to *re-member* sonorous and temporal realms of the preceding installation. As the listener is taken from the documentary world of the sound installation to the real-time experience of the string quartet concert performance, the listener is able to discover a web of thematic and structural relationships between the three compositions and Renger's sculptures: it was my hope that such discovery would provoke further contemplation of their points of interaction as well as their historical, ontological real-world variations.

## Bibliography

Adorno, T.W.: Schubert. Edition Tiessen, Neu-Isenburg (1984)

Bergson, H., Paul, N.M., Scott Palmer, W. (trans.): Matter and Memory, Zone books, New York (1988)

Bourdieu, P.: The field of Cultural Production or The Economic World reversed. In: Johnson, R. (ed.) The Field of Cultural Production: Essays on Art and Literature, Cambridge, Polity (1993)

Carlebach, Elisheva, Efron, John M., Myers, D.N. (eds.): Jewish History and Jewish Memory: Essays in Honor of Yosef Hayim Yerushalmi, Hanover, University Press of New England (1998)

Dahlhaus, C.: (Thilo, R. (translator)) Sonata Form in Schubert: The First Movement of the G-Major String Quartet, op. 161, (D. 887). In: Frisch, W. (ed.) Schubert: Critical and Analytical Studies University of Nebraska Press, Lawrence (1986)

# Part IV
# Interfaces and Expression

# Gestures, Interfaces and other Secrets of the Stage

Eva Sjuve

Moolab.net
eva@moomonkey.com

**Abstract.** This paper is examining the use of wearable technology, interfaces, and augmented performance, from the 1880s until today's computational devices. The combination of unmediated (face-to-face) and mediated (via a medium) performance in the performing arts, was made possible by the creative use of electricity, as technological enhanced performance. The performing arts, with a long tradition of collaborations in art and technology, went through a large change when electricity entered the stage. During the early days of electric innovation, engineers created electrical devices using movements to generate light and sound. They built interfaces to enhance dramatic acts, and introduced wearable technology to the general audience. Experimentation took place in the theatre, at public lectures, as entertainment, and as scientific diversions. The performance of early scientific and artistic experiments is explored, as a background to the contemporary experimentation in wearable technology coupling light and sound.

**Keywords:** Historic interfaces, performance, scientific diversion, sound, light, inventions, interaction design, computational interaction.

## 1 Introduction

This paper is examining the performance of early scientific and artistic experiments, as a background to contemporary developments in wearable and interactive technology using sound and light. Interfaces developed during the beginning of the 1970s, bridging the analog and digital era will be briefly discussed, and after this, there will follow an overview of wearable interfaces developed for computational media relevant to the context of this paper.

The combination of unmediated (face-to-face) and mediated (via a medium) performance in the performing arts, was made possible by the creative use of electricity for spectacular display of light and sound. This paper examines interactive interfaces from a wide range of disciplines, and not only those used in the theatre. Performance is in this paper understood in its most basic meaning, as an activity by an individual or group of people for an audience [1]. Therefore, this paper will include scientific demonstrations, lectures, experiments, entertainment, musical interaction, as well as works for theatre.

Electricity has been used in the theatre since the 1840s to create special effect lighting using arc lamps. It was the coming of electric light, using the incandescent light bulb[1]

[1] The incandescent light bulb is a carbon filament enclosed in an airless glass bulb. The vacuum prevented the carbon to burn up, as was not the case with the arc lamp, which had to be constantly refilled [1].

R. Adams, S. Gibson, and S. Müller Arisona (Eds.): DAW/IF 2006/2007, CCIS 7, pp. 301–312, 2008.

that revolutionized the whole lighting system [2] of stage performance in the United States and Europe in the 1880s - 1890s [3].

During the early nineteenth-century, in the area around boulevard du Temple in Paris, popular theatre incorporated a mix of acrobatics, rope dancing, vaudeville, circus, and other extravaganza in their repertoire. In that same area there were acts using balloons, pantomime, mechanical theatre, peepshows, philosophical toys, and scientific demonstrations called cabinet physique [4]. During the mid nineteenth-century in Paris, engineers working in the performing arts started to develop technology based on electricity for embodied performance. The café-concerts, next to the established theatres, often served as a test bed for experimental entertainment with a divers mix of acrobatics, the use of mechanical stage devices for performers on rotating discs, and cardboard life-size puppets [5]. Electricity was incorporated into the repertoire, not only at the established theatres, but also in the experimental entertainment industry, which made the distinction between technology, scientific demonstrations, and entertainment somewhat blurred. Engineers made their living on selling their inventions, and the theatre directors were in need of a new and exiting repertoire to attract the audience. One example is Dr. Robin, a physicist who owned a theatre on boulevard du Temple in Paris, with a repertoire of mechanical and electrical experiments [6].

Embodied electricity found its way into the world of performing arts in lighting and sound, incorporated into the acts as wearable technology. Electricity also became part of experiments in interactive set design. The early days of electricity started out in the laboratory, public lectures, and scientific exhibitions, where the audience expected to be entertained as well as informed.

## 2 Lectures and Demonstrations as Performances

Exhibitions and public demonstrations were crucial for instrument-makers and experimenters in electricity to show their work. To be able to continue research and development of new electric devices, "the inventor's need to control his product often required the showman's skills in controlling an audience as well" [7]. Experimentation was the art of demonstration. The way the public lecture was performed and its possible success was important for the inventor. The inventions in the era of electricity were displayed by the inventor, to show "the powers of their machines and hence the powers of nature" [8].

In London, during the 1830s, public lectures were performed in galleries, next to a display of practical science and fine arts, at the Adelaide Gallery[2] and the Royal Polytechnic Institution. Joseph Saxton at the Adelaide Gallery made spectacular demonstrations with electro-magnetic sparks on the audience's tongues. In another famous spectacle, a rubber ball was shot across the exhibition room with an electric gun. The electric eel was one of the main attractions and its death was reported in the press. The exhibition halls displayed a mixture of scientific demonstrations, the display of batteries, steam engines, electromagnets, and fine arts. There were also live events of artists performing diverse acts, as comic impersonations by the famous Tom Thumb[3]. At the Royal Polytechnic Institution the main attraction was the diving bell where the audience could descend into a tank of water. Another attraction was a large electrical machine, worked

[2] Adelaide Gallery was open between 1832-1845.

[3] Tom Thumb's born as Charles Stratton. He toured the world as a circus act from the age of 5.

by a steam engine. The scientific diversions were integrated into the line of electrical production, supported by a network of workshops of instrument makers and larger factories. The galleries for electric and scientific display were listed in the tourist guides. Public scientific diversions and progress of the industry were in close proximity, and the exhibition halls gave the experimenters both a workplace, as well as a marketplace for their inventions. Invention and public experimentation was about marketing a novel product, to gain media attention, and to market the cultural phenomena of novelty and progress in the eyes of the audience [9].

The exhibitions and lectures provided a forum for the experimenters to exchange ideas. There were other forums for exchange, as the journals Mechanics' Magazine, and the Annals of Electricity, as well as meetings at the Electrical Society, although with a somewhat restricted membership. Attention in the media was an important part in the existence of the exhibition halls to attract an audience [10].

## 3 The Human Body as an Electrical Circuit

Electricity in the nineteenth-century was a symbol of progress, a way to master nature, and reorder society. Electricity became a tool in understanding the human body. The discovery of the human body as an electrical circuit went hand in hand with instrument making. In 1730 Stephen Gray electrified a young boy to demonstrate the body's ability to conduct electric current. The boy was suspended from the ceiling and exited glass tubes were held to his feet. Leaf brass was then attracted to the boys face. Two years later Gray showed that the effect could be passed from one boy to another if they held hands [11]. Luigi Galvani, an Italian biologist, could demonstrate the electrical nature of nerve impulse during the 1780s, when connecting an electrical charge to a frog's legs, but the human body's electrical nature could still not be measured during this time. Carlo Matteucci, an Italian physicist could in 1838 for the first time measure bioelectricity in muscles. He used an instrument, the astatic galvanometer[4] an instrument detecting weak electrical signals, developed by the Italian physics professor Leopold Nobili [12]. Alfred Smee, a British surgeon, believed all bodily functions were produced by electric activity, so he did a systematic study of the electrical circuitry of the human being, and attempted through a series of experiments to electrically replicate the sensory phenomena of sight, smell, taste, hearing, and touch in 1849 [13],[14]. The human body was by the mid nineteenth-century described as an electrical circuit. The electric body was going to be explored for the coming decades within the performing arts, as well as in science.

## 4 An Electrical Machine of Sound and Light

Otto von Guericke discovered electric light and sound in 1663. He became the first scientist to demonstrate static electricity and electrical conductance. He demonstrated the appearance of light and accompanying sound, as roaring and crashing, when a sphere cast in sulphur was rotated and rubbed, producing the first electric light [15].

One of the first stage performances to use electricity was in 1842, when Ludwig Dobler lighted 200 candles instantaneously when firing a pistol. An electric current running

[4] The process of measuring electric activity in muscles is called electromyography (EMG).

in a wire behind the candles lighted up hydrogen gas flames behind the candles simultaneously [16].

In 1881, the Electrical Exhibition in Paris attracted many companies working with the newly invented incandescent light bulb. 19 companies showed 159 different kinds of incandescent light bulbs [17]. Electricity had been used in scientific demonstrations and public experiments, but it was after 1870s that embodied interfaces started to be developed; some of them are briefly described below.

### 4.1 Wearable Jewels

Gustave Trouvé, a French engineer, developed a set of wearable electrical jewels for a performance in 1884. Trouvé custom built a portable accumulator for the performer's costume on almost half a kilo, and built incandescent light bulbs into a design of colored glass to create an effect of sparkling jewels [18]. The electrical jewels soon became a commercial commodity, as did the portable accumulator, but it was only in the larger cities where the user could charge the accumulator. The power supply lasted for only 30 minutes [19].

### 4.2 Electrical Diadem

In 1884, the Electrical Diadem was developed for a dancer in the opera ballet Farandole at the Amphitheatre in Arles, France. Incandescent light bulbs were used in the design. A custom built belt for the dancers with an accumulator in two parts was developed, with a switch, so the dancer could control the light [20]. See Figure 1.

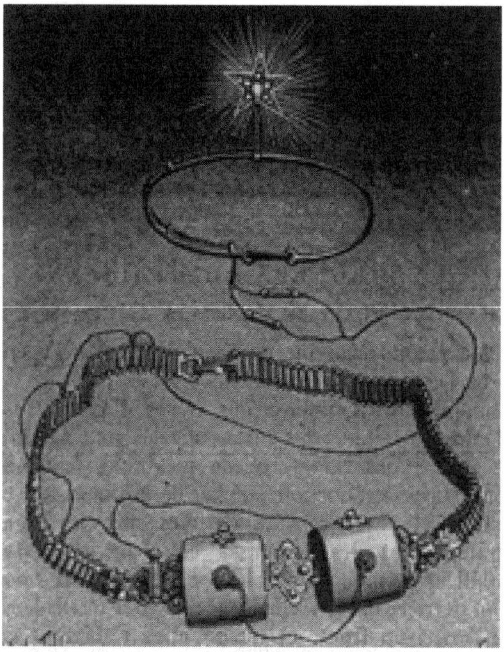

**Fig. 1.** Electrical Diadem. *(Battery in front with switch.)*

### 4.3 Electrical Fireflies

Electric Fireflies is one early example of interactive technology using a keyboard for controlling stage lights. The interface can be seen in Figure 2. A keyboard using electrical switches controlled special effects lighting from behind the stage. The interactive incandescent lights were developed to give the visual expression of the movements of fireflies. The Electric Firefly was used in the play Kaffir Diamond in New York City [21].

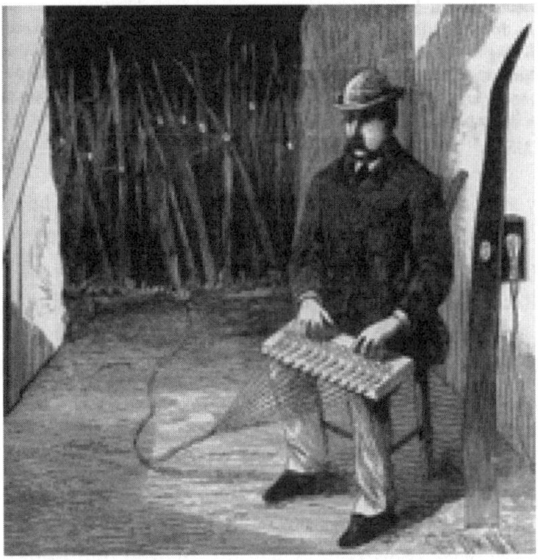

**Fig. 2.** Electric Fireflies. An electric interface for lights.

### 4.4 Faust and Electrical Duel

The play Faust was performed at the Metropolitan Opera House in New York City. In a scene where Valentine, the brother of Marguerite fights with Faust, an interactive device was used to enhance the dramatic act. The both actors stand on two copper plates, which were connected to the electrical current of the opera house. Copper nails were driven into the shoes of the actors. The metal plates were connected to the swords by a concealed cable placed underneath their costumes. When the two swords met the electric circuit was closed, and in the fight, sparks flied furiously and weird crackling sounds were heard as in lightning. The Electric Duel started a long trajectory of embodied technology using both light and sound. Not only was it an interactive performance, but it also used technology to enhance physical and dramatic action and to indicate the possession of supernatural powers [22].

The play Faust, containing the scene, the Electrical Duel, was still in production in 1916. Valentine and Faust met in a duel with swords, as described above. The actors were both standing on metal plates, connected to the house's electrical circuit, through an inductive resistance of 10 amperes. The metal plates were connected to the swords by a concealed cable placed underneath their costumes, just as the previous example [23]. The wiring and the placement of the metal plates can be seen in Figure 3.

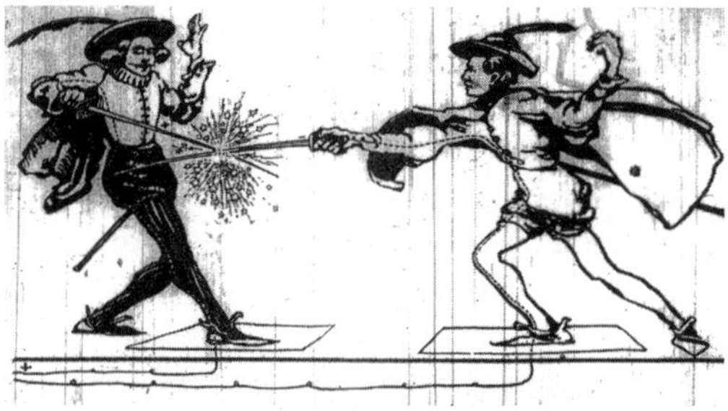

**Fig. 3.** Electrical Duel in the play Faust

### 4.5 Electricity Music

Electricity Music was a multimedia showcase by entertainer George W. Patterson. He was using portable accumulators and specially constructed lights to create light effects. Patterson performed his extravaganza in churches and halls in Chicago during the late 1890s. He used multicolored light clubs to create an effect of solid light shapes, as circles and other shapes, when moving the clubs in circles. The electrical engineers, when demonstrating their new inventions, were referred to as "the informed priesthood of the fluid" [24]. This kind of amazement was also applied to performers using electricity in entertainment.

### 4.6 Wireless Electric Light

In 1890 during a laboratory experiment, Tesla discovered that high frequency alternating currents created an electric field that could light a Geissler tube[5] [25]. He demonstrated this at the American Institution of Electrical Engineers (AIEE) in 1891, and the following year in London. One of Tesla's high-frequency current demonstrations, two years later, was described in the Sunday edition of The World, a daily newspaper as, "Showing the Inventor in the Effulgent Glory of Myriad Tongues of Electric Flame After He Has Saturated Himself with Electricity" [26].

### 4.7 The Electric Wizard

Scientist Burnell R. Ford was traveling around the United States in 1917, holding science lectures on Tesla's high-frequency currents. The media described his demonstrations as, "Lighting Indian Clubs by High-Frequency Tesla Currents Passing Through the Body". Another demonstration on his lecture tour was described as, "Lights a Candle with a High-frequency Spark Shooting Forth from his Tongue" [27].

### 4.8 Electric Bones

Electric Bones was an interactive instrument developed in 1918 by inventor Samuel Sussman, and was described in the media as electrical driven fire-spitting bones. The

[5] The Geissler tube was invented around 1855; visible light derives from a continuous electrical discharge in a partly evacuated tube.

purpose of his invention was the production of dramatic lightning effects, in addition to the rhythmic sounds produced by the bones. Through wholes drilled in the ebony, a wire was running, connected to spark electrodes on the top of the bones. A metal plate was hidden underneath the clothing of the performer. The bones were connected to a box containing resistance coils and a transformer. The circuit can be seen in Figure 4. The rhythmic clicks of the bones were synchronized with the flashes, making it an interactive music and light instrument [28].

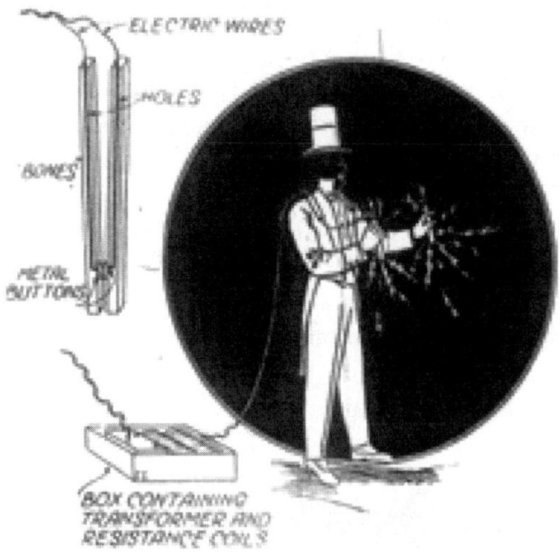


**Fig. 4.** Electric Bones

### 4.9 Terpsitone

Lev Termen, or Leo Theremin, built the Thereminvox[6] in 1917. He wanted to develop a musical instrument that could be controlled by gestures in space exploiting electromagnetic fields, and the conductance of the human body. He also built an instrument controlled by a dancer called Terpsitone [29], which was similar to the Thereminvox. The dancer moved around on a metal plate in front of two oscillators, and the movements varied the sound's amplitude and frequency. In addition to wireless interaction, the Terpsitone was a complete multimedia system, which included a record player for background music, a light system controlled by oscillation and the body's conductivity, as well as a speaker system [30].

## 5 From Analog to Digital Technology

During the 1960s there was a transition from the use of analog technology to digital technology in the development of interfaces for performance. Below are a few examples of interfaces using both sound and light, as well as a few interfaces used in the context of computational media.

---

[6] It was also called the Aetherphone or Theremin.

### 5.1 Love Machine

Ralph Lundsten, Swedish computer music pioneer, met Finnish scientist and artist Erkki Kurenniemi at a computer course for electronic musicians in Finland in 1965. After this meeting they developed several pioneering hybrid analogue and digital sound and light generating devices, such as Andromatic[7] in 1967/68, using both sound and light as output. A few years later, in 1972, they developed Love Machine. Digital Music Instrument – Sexophone (DIMI-S) was another name for Love Machine by Erkki Kurenniemi, to fit into his series of DIMI instruments. Love Machine was an early example of an interactive device for gestural and social interaction, using both sound and light. See Figures 5, 6 and 7. The Love Machine transforms the audience into performers, as active participation was needed to activate the instrument. The input was based on Galvanic Skin Response (GSR), in the form of 4 metal flowers used as sensors, held by the participants. The flowers can be seen in Figure 5. Sound and light were generated when the participants touched each other. The more they touched, the more sound and light the machine generated [31]. See part of the light module in Figure 7. Galvanic Skin Response is a measured change in the electrical properties of the skin, due to stimulation that produces emotional reaction, or stimulation that leads to an aroused alertness. The response appears as an increase in the electrical conductance of the skin [32].

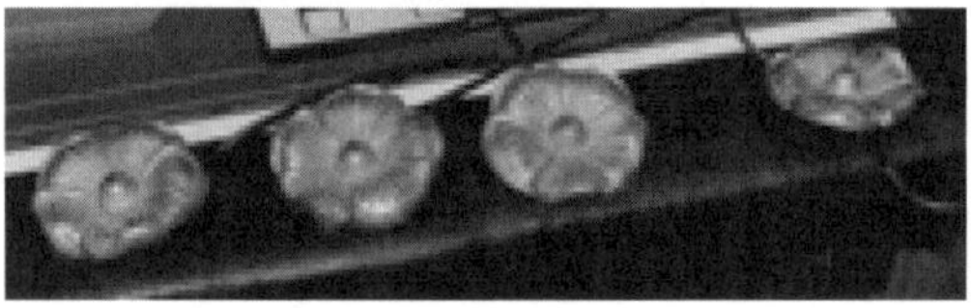

**Fig. 5.** The Love Machine by Lundsten/Kurenniemi. Sensors.

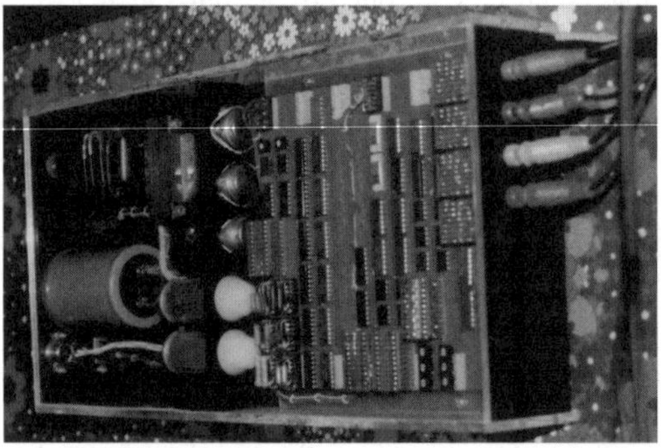

**Fig. 6.** The Love Machine. Hardware.

[7] One of the first sequencers using a 10-tone generator.

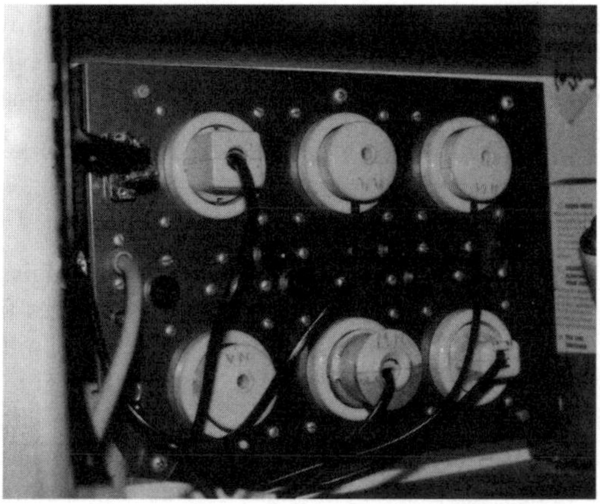

**Fig. 7.** The Love Machine. Light Module.

### 5.2 Computational Interaction and Gestures

There exists an extensive history of physical interaction for computing and there are too many developers to be able to mention them all. Within the context of this paper, there are a few artists and developers that should be mentioned, even if their work is primarily within the field of interactive music. Tom Zimmerman and Jaron Lanier developed the Dataglove and Z-Glove in the mid 1980s, with position sensors and gesture recognition, in their company VPL [33]. The American company Mattel developed a more affordable version of the Dataglove, which they called the Power Glove in 1989. This was used as a game controller, and was later hacked and used for interactive music.

Computer music pioneer Max Mathews developed the Radio Drum in 1987, a musical interface, consisting of two batons with radio transmitters over a set of radio receivers, tracking the baton's position in 3D space. The Radio Drum was later renamed Radio Baton [34]. It is still used by musicians for interactive music performance.

During the 1990s a large amount of wearable interfaces were developed in parallel with developments in software applications using real-time data processing and faster computers. MidiDancer is a wearable interface with flex sensors attached to the joints of the performer. It was first developed in 1989, by Marc Coniglio and Dawn Stopiello of Troika Ranch, an interdisciplinary performance company in New York [35]. MidiDancer has been used in several multimedia performances, as In Plane from 1994, where the dancer controls stage lights, audio, video, and motorized projectors, to enhance the vocabulary of the performer.

Hugh Lusted and Ben Knapp in California developed BioMuse, an interface using electrical activity of muscles electromyography (EMG). Atau Tanaka has been using BioMuse as a controller in performance since 1992 [36], with electrodes penetrating the skin to measure muscular activity. The measured data is transformed into sound processing.

Lady's Glove is another wearable interface. It is using flex sensors, magnetic switches, and an ultra-sonic sensor attached to a glove. It was first developed for Laetitia Sonami in 1991, with a new version developed by Bert Bonkers in 1994. The Lady's Glove has been used to control both sound processing as well as interactive lights [37].

The last wearable interface mentioned here is the BodySynth. It measures muscle activity, electromyography (EMG), in four different places on the body. Chris Van Raalte and Ed Severinghaus developed BodySynth in the early 1990s. Pamela Z has been using it for vocal performances since 1994 [38].

### 5.3 LoVid – VideoWear

LoVid is an artist group consisting of Kyle Lapidus and Tali Hingis. They perform with their wearable technology VideoWear. One of their performances from Southfirst Gallery in New York can be seen in Figure 8 [39]. In VideoWear, a direct feedback loop between audio and video is used with 14 video monitors attached to their bodies. It is a 'no original source input signal' circuit, developed to make use of interference of the pure electric signal instead of using a camera or pre-recorded video material. In VideoWear, sound and video are totally integrated. The audio signal is transformed into image and image into sound in a reoccurring loop. The two performers embody the whole electrical circuit and its interference, creating a continuous electric signal on top of their corporeal electrical circuit.

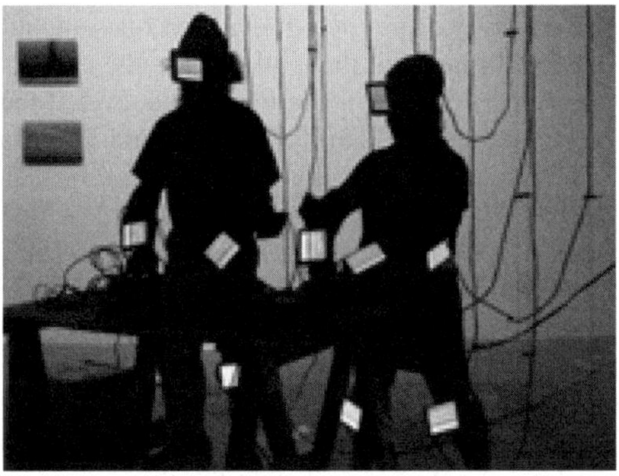

**Fig. 8.** VideoWear by LoVid

## 6 Conclusion

Science and progress in the early nineteenth-century went hand in hand with other cultural developments. The Electric Society and Adelaide gallery in London became a forum for engineers to show the latest electrical devices in the 1830s. The members in this forum made their living on instrument making, selling their new electrical devices. Other forums were important for exchange of new discoveries as Mechanics' Magazine, The Annals of Electricity edited by Sturgeon and in weekly newspapers as the Gazette, as well as in publications of the Royal Society. One important factor for the electricians was showmanship. To do an entertaining performance and attract an audience, also meant economic security for the development of new technology.

There existed a continuing exchange between science, entertainment, the arts and performance from the late 1830s and the following decades, in the field of electrical experiments. Scientists owned and produced stage work to make a living, and used stage performance as a test-bed for electrical experiments. Scientists were sometimes artists themselves and developed electrical devices, which they used in stage productions. During the 1830s, exhibition halls with interactive electrical machines and lecture theatres existed, as the Polytechnic Institute, and Adelaide Gallery in London. This was also a forum for electricians from abroad.

Mediated performance using electric wearable technology or interfaces to interact with light and sound, started already in the 1870s. To use the body's conductivity, was one way of interfacing with electricity, and this was used extensively throughout the decades in performance.

After the 1960s, the use of computational media has generated a whole new set of tools for interactive performance, using radio communication and software for interactive performance. The early 1970s saw a new form of participatory and social interaction using technology emerging. During the 1990s many new works emerged using interactive technology, with the convergence of faster computers, new software applications, and data processing in real-time.

## Acknowledgements

VideoWear image from Southfirst Gallery, Brooklyn, New York, 2003. Published with permission from Tom Moody and LoVid.

## References

1. Schechner, R.: Performance Theory, p. 22. Routlege, New York (2003)
2. Bergman, G.M.: Lighting in the Theatre, Stockholm, Almqvist and Wiksell International, p. 286 (1977)
3. Bergman, G.M.: Lighting in the Theatre, Stockholm, Almqvist and Wiksell International, p. 277 (1977)
4. McCormick, J.: Popular Theatres of Nineteenth-Century France, pp. 1–110. Routledge, London (1993)
5. McCormick, J.: Popular Theatres of Nineteenth-Century France, pp. 63–68 (1993)
6. Bergman, G.M.: Lighting in the Theatre, Stockholm, Almqvist and Wiksell International, p. 284 (1977)
7. Morus, I.R.: Frankenstein's Children, p. 71. Princeton University Press, Princeton (1998)
8. Morus, I.R.: Frankenstein's Children, p. 119 (1998)
9. Morus, I.R.: Frankenstein's Children, pp. 83–124 (1998)
10. Morus, I.R.: Frankenstein's Children, 131 (1998)
11. Rowbottom, M., Susskind, C.: Electricity and Medicine. San Francisco Press (1984)
12. Medved, V.: Measurement of human locomotion. CRC Press, Boca Raton (2001)
13. Morus, I.R.: Frankenstein's Children, p. 149 (1998)
14. Morus, I.R.: Frankenstein's Children, pp. 147–150 (1998)
15. Benjamin, P.: A History of Electricity, p. 402. John Wiley & Sons, New York (1898)
16. Clarke, Faur, Maskelyne.: Conjuring, Encyclopedia Britannica. In: Wilson, F.W. (ed.) 11th edn., vol. 6, pp. 943–950.

17. Bergman, G.M.: Lighting in the Theatre, Stockholm, Almqvist and Wiksell International, p. 286 (1977)
18. La Natur: Revue des sciences et de leurs applications aux arts et a l'industrie, Paris, G. Masson, No. 548, pp. 15–16 (1884)
19. De Fries, L.: Victorian Inventions, John Murray, London, 1971, p. 95 (1910-1911) (originally published in De Natuur, 48 (1884))
20. La Natur: Revue des sciences et de leurs applications aux arts et a l'industrie, Paris, G. Masson, No.555, pp. 127–128 (1884)
21. Hopkins, A.A.: Magic: Stage Illusions, Special Effects and Trick Photography, pp. 336–337. Dover Publications, New York (1976) (original publication, 1898)
22. Hopkins, A.A.: Magic: Stage Illusions, Special Effects and Trick Photography, pp. 342–343. Dover Publications, New York (1976) (original publication, 1898)
23. The Electrical Experimenter, Electricity's Part of the Stage, pp. 150–151 (July 1916)
24. Marvin, C.: When Old Technologies Were New, pp. 56–62. Oxford University Press, New York (1988)
25. University of Jerusalem, `http://chem.ch.huji.ac.il/~eugeniik/history/geissler.html`
26. Marvin, C.: When Old Technologies Were New, p. 57. Oxford University Press, New York (1988)
27. The Electrical Experimenter, New York, p. 371 (October 1917)
28. The Electrical Experimenter, New York, p. 22 (May 1918)
29. Mason, C.P.: Terpsitone. A New Electronic Novelty, Radio Craft, p. 365 (December 1936)
30. Interview with Lev Termen by Olivia Mattis (1989), `http://www.thereminvox.com/story/495/`
31. Interview with Ralph Lundsten in his studio Amdromeda, Saltsjö-Boo, Stockholm, June 27 (2006), `http://www.andromeda.se`
32. Britannica Online Encyclopedia, `http://www.britannica.com/eb/article-9061719?query=Psychogalvanic%20reflex&ct=`
33. Zimmerman, Lanier, Blanchard, Bryson, Harvill: A Hand Gesture Interface Device, VPL Research. In: Proceedings on Human Factors in Computing Systems, Toronto, Canada (1987)
34. Mathews, M.: `http://www.csounds.com/mathews`
35. Ranch, T.: `http://www.troikaranch.org/`
36. Tanaka, A.: `http://www.tufts.edu/programs/mma/emid/IRCAM/P.Tan.pdf`
37. Sonami, L.: `http://www.sonami.net/`
38. Demonstration by Pamela, Z. at Harvestworks, New York, March 4 (2002)
39. LoVid at South First Gallery, `http://www.lovid.org/performances/southfirst/index.htm`

# Beyond the Threshold: The Dynamic Interface as Permeable Technology

Carolyn Guertin

Department of English, University of Texas at Arlington,
Box 19035, 503 W. Third St., Arlington, TX 75208 U.S.A.
carolyn.guertin@gmail.com

**Abstract.** The concept of spectatorship has evolved from a particular patriarchal perspective on the world that rejects embodied experience and allows the eyes to stand in for the body as a whole. What happens to the idea of the screen when we, like Alice, insert our whole body into it? What happens to the screen, the interface and to our subject position when we become interactive agents rather than passive observers? Exploring feminist and posthuman interfaces—new kinds of dynamic screen technologies—and the new subject positions artists are creating, this study of experimental works by Jill Scott, Martin Reiser, Toni Dove, Guillermo Gómez-Peña, and Rafael Lozano-Hemmer will demonstrate how these artists are actively making room for a diverse and more dynamic spectrum of bodies, presences and subjects.

**Keywords:** Interface technology, subjectivity, spectatorship, immersive environments, interactivity, posthuman subjects, multimedia performance, relational aesthetics, social sculpture.

## 1 Introduction

The computer screen is equal parts window and frame. It acts as a surface, a mirror, a threshold, a portal and, as interface, an interactive space with visual depth. Game designer and theorist Brenda Laurel has called the interface a "contact surface" that incorporates the actions of the interactors, their physical nature, and give and take [1]. Most importantly she factors subjectivity right into her definition as the "cognitive and emotional aspects of the user's experience" that intertwine with the technology's 'self' or 'nature' or 'purpose' [2]. It is important to remember though that a screen can also be "a barrier" [3]. It may be a window, but it screens for and against a mediated world. As the screen becomes interactive interface, it opens into a subjective space and deep environment ripe for interaction. How this new interface is imagined by artists either raises possibilities of mastery and control that re-inscribe old binaries and master narratives, or it creates a space for fresh and new kinds of posthuman and/or postgendered engagements. Subjectivity, embodied interactions and subjects in motion are what mark the difference between these two poles. Toward this end, this paper will explore the social sculpture of five new media artists who use their works to change the meaning of screen, interface, social relations and bodies. Jill Scott, Martin Reiser, Toni Dove, Guillermo Gómez-Peña and Rafael Lozano-Hemmers do this by simultaneously rejecting the 'faciality' (as Anna

R. Adams, S. Gibson, and S. Müller Arisona (Eds.): DAW/IF 2006/2007, CCIS 7, pp. 313–325, 2008.

Munster calls it [4]) of the interface and creating a social space for engagement with the work.

It has not always been apparent to us that the screen promoted disembodiment, but for French intellectual Guy Debord it was. In the 1960s, as the 20th century became increasingly ruled by the screen-based arts, he clearly saw the dangers he believed inherent in visual culture. He argued that what he called 'the society of the spectacle' was a dangerous new era in which human relations were translated into social relations mediated by images [5]. The computer window has further contributed to this notion of detached spectatorship. The window (and its pane) played a key role in the emergence of private space. Technology critic Robert D. Romanyshun states:

> The condition of the window implies a *boundary* between the perceiver and the perceived. It establishes as a condition for perception a formal *separation* between a subject who sees the world and the world that is seen, and in doing so it sets the stage, as it were, for that retreat or withdrawal of the self from the world which characterizes the dawn of the modern age. Ensconced behind the window the self becomes an observing *subject*, a *spectator*, as against a world which becomes a *spectacle*, an *object* of vision. [6]

While Debord's notion of spectatorship in the digital age evolved out of a particular patriarchal perspective on the world that rejects embodied experience and allows the eyes and one-finger on a mouse button to stand in for the body as a whole, it is important to remember that the screen is no longer a one-way mirror. The screen is starting to reverse, so that it is no longer simply projects. As screen-based work becomes more apparently the environment it always has been, what happens when we insert our whole body, like Alice, inside?

## 2 Trajectivity

Positionings such as the objective and the subjective start to lose their meaning and relevance when we insert ourselves into an environment that can talk back. As I have discussed elsewhere in reference to the need for a more expansive understanding of the dynamic perspectives of a post-broadcast age [7], Italian media theorist Paul Virilio has suggested that what we need is a third subject position: what he calls "the trajective" [8]. Trajectivity is a dynamic point of view that is in a perpetual state of flux between objective and subjective points of view. Australian-born media art pioneer Jill Scott says that these immersive environments draw upon both "a space of intimacy and one of expansion" [9]. Her "observation is related to the history of performance, conceptual art, and experimental cinematic media, when the body is seen as part of the artwork, squeezed between the opposing forces of either supreme objectification or extreme subjectivity" [10]. She sees this affect as a kind of accumulation or meeting of subjective and objective sedimentary experiences [11]. Hopefully, in the 21st century, we can now start to imagine ourselves inhabiting a post-gendered perspective where our sex no longer determines who and what we are, at the very least in terms of our engagement with artistic interfaces.

This very freedom from the tyranny of the subject/object binary was a driving influence for Scott. She says that over the last 15 years:

> We women started to see technology as a way for us to reinvent ourselves; even so fundamentally as to choose one's gender and determine one's identity, as well as the environment in which it/they might appear. This has included women in the current discourse about mixed realities or integrated techno-zones: spaces that not only collapsed geographical boundaries and time zones, but incorporated women into the zone of technology. Perhaps these changes are related to our own shifting relationship to technology where the representation of bodies can easily incorporate more artificial, virtual and organic transformations [12].

With the daring and radical implementations of new screen technologies our bodies can become or affect the projection—as Scott explores in her organic, social interface in her 1997 work, *A Figurative History* [13]. First though I would like to demonstrate the dangers of *not* factoring the subjective element into the creation of an interactive digital environment.

## 3 conFIGURING the Cave

Agnes Hegedus and her husband Jeffrey Shaw along with software engineer Bernd Lintermann and composer Les Stuck produced a computer-based video installation called

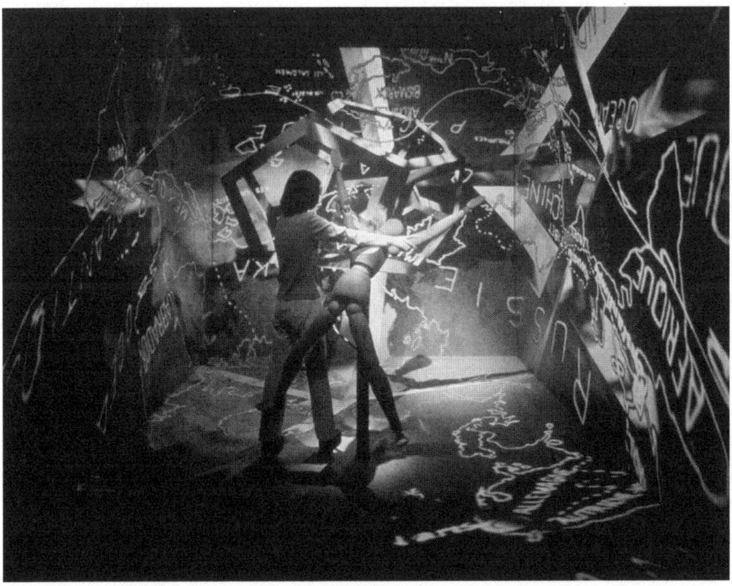

**Fig. 1.** Jeffrey Shaw, Agnes Hegedus and Bernd Lintermann's *conFIGURING the Cave.* Image courtesy of Jeffrey Shaw and Volker Kuchelmeister.

*conFIGURING the Cave* in 1997 [14]. The user interface in this work is a near life-sized wooden doll—that Shaw refers to as a "puppet"—inside an immersive cave environment. Manipulating the doll activates "electronic measurement devices" embedded within its malleable joints [15]. Situated in the center of the space, the puppet (which resembles an artist's wooden mannequin) is played like an instrument by the user to generate fantastic transformations in the computer-generated imagery. Shaw contends that this is an embodied universe that sets the human body as the heart or the pivot at the locus [16]. Clearly, however, this is not the case. The so-called 'body' detached as it is from its own subjectivity is reduced to a tool or object to be used and manhandled. Furthermore, the smaller-than-life size scale makes the puppet seem more "poppet" than symbol, rendering it child-like or feminized in the context of "playing" the environment. The symbolic intimacy with the human-like figure that one must assume to control the projections further heightens the power-dynamic between master and tool. The very name, 'conFIGURING,' seems to suggest as well that it is against or in opposition to the body that drives it.

## 4 A Figurative History

By start contrast, Jill Scott's *A Figurative History* uses inanimate objects activated by our body's natural electrical charge to enable social engagements with five virtual beings. Housed in a space like a Japanese shrine, interactors must kneel to activate the five characters represented by smart images and inanimate objects. These include an assortment of jars, a helmet and a wheel. Each object is specific to a character in the piece. Each one represents a period in biotechnological history. *Pandora* of Ancient Greece represents object to human metamorphosis; the *Cyborg* (unexpectedly depicted as a knight in a suit of armor) who inhabits the year 1250 stands in for the desire to merge biological and mechanical parts; *Lady Miso* from the year 1750 is a metaphor for robotic simulation; *Frankenstein's monster* from 1890 is about biomedical manipulation; and the *Data Body* from 1950 stands in for artificial intelligence experiments and the fantastical desire to download the mind to the machine [17]. The interactors herein do not just activate these figures though, but through human interaction in the space form a physical bridge or organic network that enables the characters to travel across time to interact with each other. People engage with this piece directly compared to the cold, mechanical manipulation of the tool-like interface in *conFIGURING the Cave.* For Scott's work, interactors join hands, strip their clothes off to create more contact points, and actively play together to enable the virtual characters to interact with each other. *A Figurative History* allows people to understand what it feels like to be a cyborg, for instance, through plugging in their own body's voltage. It should be clear though that at no point does the user ever control the cyborg. In fact, the virtual characters exhibit self-awareness and nervousness about their own state of well being.

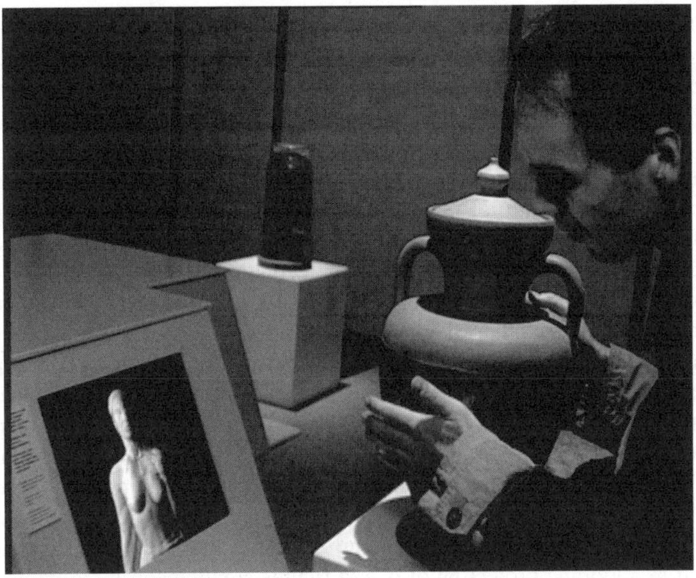

**Fig. 2.** Jill Scott's *A Figurative History.* ZKM 1996

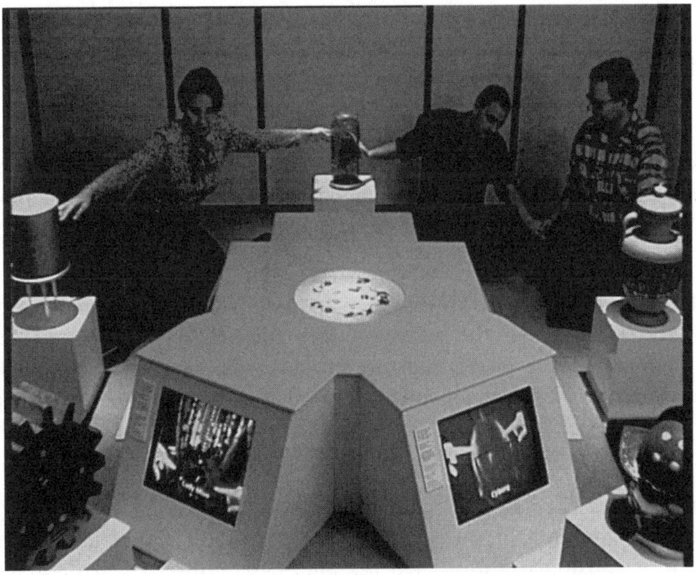

**Fig. 3.** Jill Scott's *A Figurative History.* ZKM 1996

## 5 Hosts

Interactive media become much more than an interface in a space such as the one created in Scott's work. By redefining our depth of interaction, they become environments in their own right, teetering between what Scott calls the two poles of immersion: intimacy and expansion. Smart sculptures open spaces for new "social metaphors of communication" [18]. British artist Martin Rieser's site-specific installation *Hosts* plays with similar ideas within an architectural framework [19]. Mounted in historic Bath Abbey for three weeks in 2006, *Hosts* used positional detection technology known as chirpers[1] and interpretive software to engage the participant in social relations with ghostly inhabitants between the pillars. These ethereal apparitions hovered in the arches, and beckoned visitors onward deeper into the church. A 3D sonic landscape broadcast over headphones on a PDA kept the visitor immersed in an auditory atmosphere rich in tonal chants and acapella-style sonic poems. If an interactor stopped and stared at one of the blurry figures on the screen, it would sharpen into focus, stare back, then turn away and mutter to the observer. These smart ghosts speak poetic aphorisms and obscure phrases related to their situation as ghostly hosts in an ancient Christian abbey. The building's own distinctive architecture - with a row of figures ascending Jacob's ladder to heaven - is mirrored and complicated in a looping projection of paired figures simultaneously going up and coming down parallel ladders over the choirbox at the far end of the church. Reiser's locative sprites directly address the user across time and space over a screen, but communication is blurred or thwarted over the vast threshold of time and space that separates these virtual specters from the corporeal spectator.

## 6 Artificial Changelings

Otherworldly apparitions also materialize in American artist and sculptor Toni Dove's interactive movies. In her work *Artificial Changelings* (1992-98) [20], she uses cinematic techniques to explore social communications "through the responsive powers of the interface" [21] and shifting points of view enabled through sensor technology. She explains:

> The design and actions of interface are a door into an immersive world of storytelling where the nature of cinematic time and space are altered. An embodied responsive interface produces the experience of doubling or extending the body. Characters are inhabited like digital puppets and when a viewer feels their own presence in the screen through the character, it can produce an uncanny experience [22].

This experience goes far beyond a simple mirroring of the work's two characters, Arathusa, a kleptomaniac in 19th century Paris during the rise of the department store at the birth of consumer culture, and her alter-ego, Zilith, a schizophrenic character who lives a wholly exteriorized life at some unspecified point in the future [23]. Both reflect the social pathologies of their time: "Urbanization, merchandising, the mechanization of travel and industry, and the birth of film are viewed against the evolution

---

[1] Chirpers are a component of locative technology that detect proximity in GPS sensing units.

of information technology as part of the conversation between viewer and characters" [24]. This forms a tenuous and shifting bridge between the two and their times as a kind of virtual conversation—with the viewer standing in as interface—unfolds. Dove says, "*Artificial Changelings* is more like a conversation with a schizophrenic video android with a history, than it is like a traditional plot-driven film" [25].

In Dove's work a convex projection screen is situated at the back of a darkened tunnel. The screen curvature, according to Dove, transforms the screen itself into a character or entity [26]. As the interactor approaches it, she steps on different sensors embedded in rubber pads that activate differing points of view. Each pad (there are four) has an "electro-luminescent" label that illuminates the coordinates of a user's situation in space: 1. Close-up; 2. Direct Address; 3. Trance/Dream; And 4. the smallest pad, Time Tunnel [27]. A surveillance camera triggers the opening film with credits and sets the stage for the piece. At the end of these credits (which last about 4 minutes) the overhead lights come up and Arathusa beckons the viewer to enter the space of the story. The viewer's feet on the pads trigger video and the sensors use the interactor's own body movements to elicit physical, verbal and sonic responses from the character. Movement from pad to pad immediately changes the point of view. 'Close-up' catapults us *inside the character's head*, where we hear her thoughts and see her perspective. Moving back to the second zone, 'Direct Address', initiates a conversation or physical interaction with the character. It enables speaking, dancing and a third-person voiceover that recounts fragments of the character's memories. Zone 3 transports us into an altered 'dream or trance-like state'. It is surreal and almost out-of-body in its intensity. The final zone, 'Time Tunnel', activates a switch that teleports the viewer to the other century of the story. The user re-emerges in the dream state. The responsive interface is both immersive and embodied. The user is simultaneously aware of their body and aware of the body on the screen, displaced in their body and repositioned on (or in) the projection:

> The space between the two is activated. This charged space is characteristic of telepresence. It is the space through which the body extends itself into the movie or virtual space. It is the invisible experience of the body's agency beyond its apparent physical edge [28]

Agency, of course, is what we crave most deeply, alongside the need for communication with another. Agency in this case is elusive as our actions are mirrored back at us through the spastic movements of the characters we engage with.

The work functions via data feeds to trigger the interactor's body movements to be translated into a stuttering re-animation of the frames playing on the screen: "This is not based on the linear 30 frames per second video standard, but frame-by-frame, backwards, forwards, and at different speeds and in" fractured "non-linear configurations. Sound is triggered as layered, sequential and random fragments of speech or dynamic, sampled environments responsive to the viewer's moving body" [29]. An interactor must learn how to steer in this space. The relationship between movements and effects are defined, but the exact manner of their connection is unclear, fragmentary and unpredictable. Extended interaction reveals more and more of the character's story. Dove says that interactors invariably start out by trying to control the character and are so transformed by the unnerving nature of engagement that they ultimately end up mirroring her instead—like two live people in conversation [30]. The transformation of the spectator as subject is thereby total; she is sculpted to inhabit a new, dynamic subject position entirely.

## 7 Relational Aesthetics

Nicolas Bourriaud said that the public nature of the art exhibition distinguishes it from other media (which are consumed in private) on account of the "specific sociability" or interactive space it generates [31]. The space it creates, as he sees it, is a space for conversation. The "co-presence of spectators" [32] engaging immersively with a work of art privileges the underlying politics of art itself: "Art as a state of encounter" [33]. This is what Bourriaud dubs "relational aesthetics." Where older forms tried to establish a relationship between an audience and an art object, relational aesthetics privilege "formations": proposals, dialogues, encounters and negotiations. What is so new in these experiments in acts of social-interaction-as-art is the lack of aesthetic object and the foregrounding of contact and tactility over the visual. As the experiential and the conversational nature of these works come to the fore, the "sphere of human relations" is unique, according to Bourriard, as an unprecedented site for art [34].

## 8 Naftaztec

Now let's look back to another era, 1994, when networked computer technology was still fairly primitive and the World Wide Web was young. At that time Mexican-American performance artist Guillermo Gómez-Peña and his collaborator Cybervato Roberto Sifuentes (vato means dude) launched a high tech relational aesthetic event called "Naftazteca: Pirate Cyber-TV for AD 2000." As he and Sifuentes had started to work with American artists interested in new technologies in the early 1990s, they had been stung by the libertarian rhetoric that maintained cyberspace was a "politically neutral/race-less/gender-less and classless 'territory'—a territory which provided us all with 'equal access' and unlimited possibilities for participation, interaction and belonging" [35]. Gómez-Peña saw this "feel-good philosophy … as an attractive exit from the acute social and racial crisis afflicting the United States" [36].

Playing with the stereotypes of Mexicans as techno-illiterates and illegal aliens, they hijacked cable television. On Thanksgiving Day 1994, the evening news broadcast was interrupted in 3.5 million American homes by two "post-Nafta Cyber-Aztec Pirates" transmitting bizarre views on the excesses of American culture "directly from their underground vato-bunker" [37]. This was actually an experimental satellite broadcast in multilingual television. They bought air time and transmitted "a simulacrum of a pirate television intervention" [38] to hundreds of community cable outlets. The station programmers had agreed and had advertised that timeslot under another program's name. In a parody of traditional television programming not seen since SCTV's Bob and Doug Mackenzie sat down to share a beer on The Great White North, the superbanditos of the information superhighway spent 90 minutes on the air. They encouraged viewers to call in response to their radical politics mingled with stereotypical messages seen through the lenses of handheld cameras.

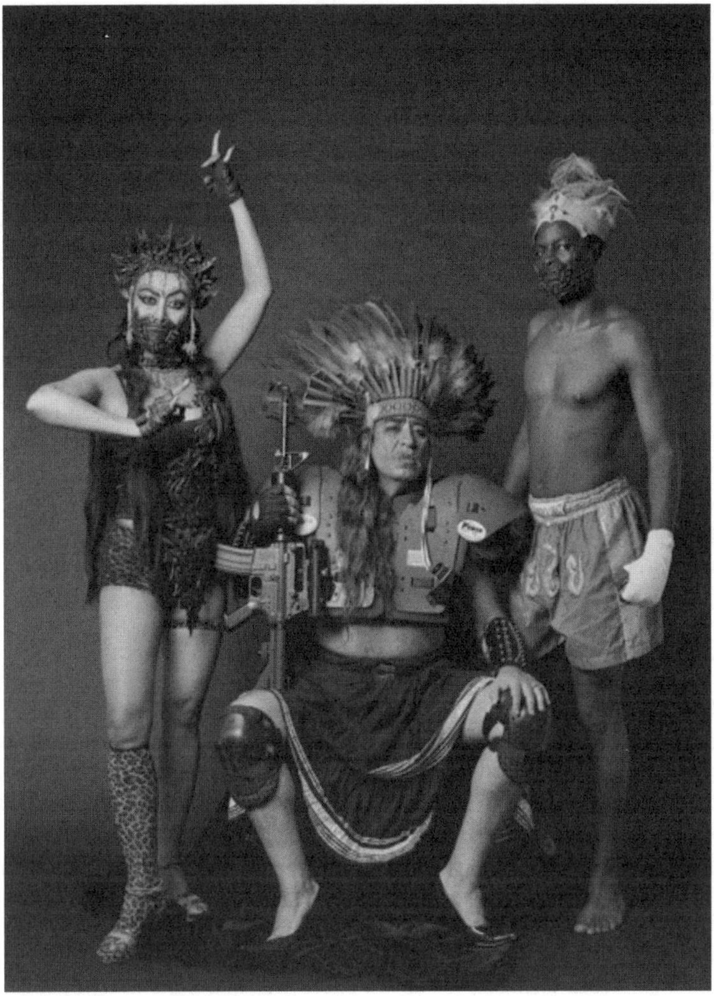

**Fig. 4.** Guillermo Gómez-Peña (seated), Roberto Sifuentes and another performer. *Brujos Tricontinentales*, 2006. Photography Serie The Chi-Canarian Expo. Photographer: Teresa Correa Editor: BRH-LEON editions.

Part of the broadcast included demonstrations of Mexican technologies, including *The Chicano Virtual Reality Machine*, which could videotape personal and collective memories, and a *Virtual Reality Bandanna*, which would allow Americans "to experience first hand the psychological sensation of racism" [39]. Allegedly 'live' reports were received via videophone from Los Angeles as the show broadcast in English, Spanglish, Franglais, French and an invented robotic language. The television station seemed to struggle to regain control of the broadcast, but the banditos prevailed. The show was also simulcast over the newly re-christened *Chicano Interneta* and surfers were allowed to post written and visual comments. Viewers expressed their wonder at the technological sophistication of these "un-folksy" Mexicans [40]. Others called to complain about unbridled Mexicans live on American television, and demanded that they immediately "leave…the high tech simulated space [they] created 'illegally' and return to [their] pyramid-infested past" [41]. The broadcast won the prize as best experimental video at the San Antonio Cine Festival that year.

Part of the magic of this kind of event is that it is social sculpture. Joseph Beuys, who coined the term, defined social sculpture as a cultural reflection on and an active intervention into a community or environment for the purpose of creating a space for unexpected interactions and situational participation. Social sculpture by design explores the relationship between aesthetics, social processes and eco-systems through performance, environmentalism and political engagement. Gómez-Peña does this so brilliantly through establishing a relational space between people, stereotypical expectations and the broadcast system. This kind of conversational model is what will drive the convergence cultural revolution in the 21st century. Gómez-Peña and Sifuentes managed to foster real dialogue and heightened awareness of stereotypes, racism, and the absurdity of some of America's stereotypical assumptions about Mexicans and their abilities to engage with technology. Relational space itself is defined by the dynamic position occupied by each subject constellated in relation to others. The heterogeneity of relational space is a key element of globalization. Relational aesthetics foster works of art concerned with the contact zones or virtual barrio[2] (as Gómez-Peña calls it) of posthuman existence [42].

## 9 Body Movies

Another Mexican-born artist, Canadian Rafael Lozano-Hemmer uses relational architecture to create social sculptures, sculptures that he calls "anti-monuments." His work *Body Movies* debuted in 2001 in Rotterdam [43]. It combines robotics with surveillance and computing technology to produce a contemporary version of shadow puppets. Thousands of portraits taken on urban streets are back-projected onto a giant screen using robotically-controlled projectors. Those images are then entirely washed out by blindingly bright lamps placed at street level. Anyone who crosses the square interrupts the light source, simultaneously projecting their own shadow and revealing the figures underneath. Once all the images in a single scene are exposed through shadows cast by people in the square, the scene changes. A camera-based tracking system monitors shadows in real time, giving auditory feedback in response to their efforts when they match their shadow to the original scale. Up to 60 people can participate at one time "creating a collective experience that…allows discrete individual participation" [44]. This entirely reinvents the notion of the city square for the 21st century and gives us space to reassess dramatizations of public and private space within the context of public art. While shadow puppets undoubtedly date back to the time of our cave-dwelling ancestors as the earliest form of projection art, Lozano-Hemmer's *Body Movies* investigates what he calls "the crisis of urban self-representation. The piece attempts to create an anti-monument of alien presence and embodied relationships" [45], Here is Beuys' famous slogan—everyone is an artist—demonstrated by the crowd's own interactions [46]. What this sight sculpts is people's natural playfulness and willing to suspend their disbelief for collaborative ends.

---

[2] In Mexico, a barrio is a neighbourhood. In America, the word is used derogatively to indicate a Latino slum or ghetto.

Interestingly enough, it is narrative that is the emergent experience out of these social interactions. Users are immediately arrested by their shadowy counterpart. They stop, crouch, jump and stretch, move closer and further away as they try to match the figures on the screen. Interactors toy with the scope and scale of the piece, with a giant shadow pretending, for instance, to pour liquid into the mouth of tiny person or by giving a seated senior shadowy biceps. What is so remarkable about these interactions is the way people are completely uninhibited when it comes to playing together for visual ends.

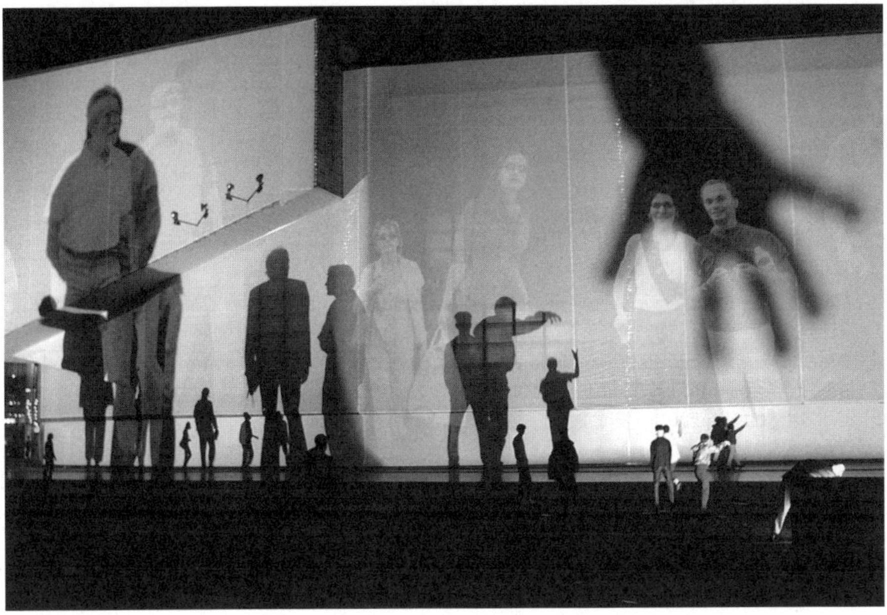

**Fig. 5.** Rafael Lozano-Hemmer, *Body Movies* 2001. Xenon 7kW projectors with robotic scrollers, 1,200 duraclear transparencies, computerized surveillance system, plasma screen, mirrors. Projection measures between 400 and 1800 square metres. Courtesy V2_Organisatie, Rotterdam, © Arie Kievit.

## 10 Conclusion

Roseanne Stone has argued that community building is the driving force for communications technologies [47]. The fantastic explosion of user-generated social strategies known as Web 2.0 certainly seems to support this. In the same way, social sculpture is not a new message, but a whole new map for engaging in complex social relations. It is the opening of a new kind of transmedia and transmediated dialogue that privileges people, not technology, in the wake of the information age: "Whether you call it 'relational aesthetics,' 'social aesthetics,' 'social sculpture,' 'performative art' or now, perhaps, 'publicness,' art practices that use groups of people, information flows or social systems as their medium represent" a new and rising mode of artistic production within the last few years [48]. Like the collapse of proprietary barriers the open source movement celebrates, in these permeable screen-based works their new screen technologies create a space of encounter where contact and tactility and an invitation to play transform posthuman social relations entirely. As with Gómez-Peña's *Chicano Interneta*, the contact zones created by these works are both a starting point and a point of arrival for (post)human existence. Like open source, it is the social nature of relational aesthetics that frees it from the tyranny of the commodity market. That in and of itself is not unprecedented, but Bourriaud's "sphere of human relations" as a site for art is [49]. This is a social interstice that evades capitalistic impulses. It has taken a long time, but through artists' complex technological interventions we have finally re-emerged in contemporary culture at a newly (re)mediated place where we can again inhabit a space that engenders the simplest and freest medium of expression: play.

## References


1. Laurel, B. (ed.): Art of Human Computer Interface Design, p. xiii. Addison-Wesley, New York (1990)
2. Ibid
3. Cavell, S.: The World Viewed: Reflections on the Ontology of Cinema, p. 24. Viking Press, New York (1971)
4. Munster, A.: Materializing New Media: Embodiment in Information Aesthetics. Dartmouth College Press, Hanover (2006)
5. Debord, G.: Society of the Spectacle. Donald Nicholson-Smith. Trans. Zone Books, New York (1995)
6. Romanyshyn, R.D.: Technology as Symptom and Dream., New York, Routledge, p. 42 (1989); Friedberg, A.: The Virtual Window: From Alberti to Microsoft, Friedberg's emphasis. MIT Press, Cambridge, London, p. 16 (2006)
7. Guertin, C.: Quantum Feminist Mnemotechnics: The Archival Text, Digital Narrative and the Limits of Memory. Dissertation, University of Alberta, (2003), `http://www.mcluhan.utoronto.ca/academy/carolynguertin/diss.html`; Guertin, C.: Wanderlust: The Kinesthetic Browser in Cyberfeminist Space. In: Extensions, vol. 3, (2007), `http://www.performancestudies.ucla.edu/extensionjournal/guertin.htm`
8. Virilio, P.: Open Sky. Julie Rose, Trans. Verso, London, p. 24 (1997)
9. Scott, J.: Crossing and Collapsing Time: Re-Constructing (Her)Historical and Ideological Film Narratives on a Transformed Stage. In: Rieser, M., Zapp, A. (eds.) New Screen Media: Cinema/Art/Narrative, British Film Institute, London, vol. 197, pp. 195–207 (2002)
10. Ibid. 197
11. Ibid 197
12. Scott, J.: Cyborg Bodies I Extensive Bodies. Interview with Yvonne Volkart. Media Art Net, `http://www.mediaartnet.org/themes/cyborg_bodies/extensive_bodies%20/scroll/`
13. Scott, J.: A Figurative History. Installation 7 (1996)
14. Hegedus, A., Shaw, J., Lintermann, B., Stuck, L.: conFIGURING the Cave, installation (1997)
15. Shaw, J.: 'Movies After Film: The Digitally Expanded Cinema. In: Rieser, M., Zapp, A. (eds.) New Screen Media: Cinema/Art/Narrative, British Film Institute, London, 271, pp. 268–275 (2002)

16. Shaw, J.: 272
17. Scott, J.: Cyborg Bodies I Extensive Bodies
18. Scott, J.: 201
19. Reiser, M., Hosts: Bath Abbey Installation (February 9-27, 2006)
20. Dove, T.: Artificial Changelings. Installation. Rotterdam Film Festival (1992-8)
21. Dove, T.: The Space Between: Telepresence, Re-Animation and the Re-Casting of the Invisible. In: Rieser, M., Zapp, A. (eds.) New Screen Media: Cinema/Art/Narrative, British Film Institute, London, pp. 208–220, 209 (2002)
22. Ibid, 209
23. Ibid, 211
24. Ibid
25. Ibid
26. Ibid
27. Ibid, 212
28. Ibid, 210
29. Ibid, 213
30. Ibid, 213
31. Bourriaud, N., Bishop, C.: Relational Aesthetics. In: Participation: Documents of Contemporary Art, pp. 160–171, 161. Whitechapel/MIT, London, New York (2006)
32. Ibid, 167
33. Ibid, 162
34. Ibid, 165
35. Gómez-Peña, G.: The Virtual Barrio @ The Other Frontier (or the Chicano Interneta). In: Caldwell, J.T. (ed.) Electronic Media and Technoculture, Rutgers UP, New Brunswick, NJ, pp. 295–308, 302 (2000)
36. Ibid, 303
37. Ibid
38. Ibid. 304
39. Ibid, 305
40. Ibid
41. Ibid
42. Bourriaud, N. 166
43. Lozano-Hemmer, R.: Body Movies. Installation, Rotterdam (2001)
44. Lozano-Hammer, R.: Video, `http://www.lozano-hemmer.com/video/bodymovies.html`
45. Ibid
46. Beuys, J.: I Am Searching For Field Character. In: Bishop, C. (ed.) Participation: Documents of Contemporary Art, pp. 125–126, 125. Whitechapel/MIT, London, New York (2006)
47. Scott, J.: 200 (2002)
48. Farquharson
49. Bourriaud, N.: 166

# CoPuppet: Collaborative Interaction in Virtual Puppetry

Paolo Bottoni[1], Stefano Faralli[1], Anna Labella[1], Alessio Malizia[2], Mario Pierro[1], and Semi Ryu[3]

[1] Department of Computer Science, University of Rome "La Sapienza"
{bottoni,faralli,labella,pierro}@di.uniroma1.it
[2] Universidad Carlos III de Madrid
alessio.malizia@gmail.com
[3] Virginia Commonwealth University, Richmond, VA, USA
sryu2@vcu.edu

**Abstract.** Puppetry is one of the most ancient forms of representation, diffused all over the world in different shapes, degrees of freedom in movements and forms of manipulation. Puppets make an ideal environment for creative collaboration, inspiring the development of supporting technologies (from carpentry to digital worlds). The CoPuppet project explores the possibilities offered by multimodal and cooperative interaction, in which performers, or even audience members, are called to affect different parts of a puppet through gestures and voice. In particular, we exploit an existing architecture for the creation of multimodal interfaces to develop the CoPuppet framework for designing, deploying and interacting during performances in which virtual puppets are steered by multiple multimodal controls. The paper illustrates the steps needed to define performances, also showing the integration of digital and real puppetry for the case of wayang shadowplay.

## 1 Introduction

Puppetry is one of the most ancient forms of performance, diffused all over the world in different shapes, degrees of freedom in movements, and forms of manipulation. While forms and techniques of puppetry are varied and related to specific local settings, its essential spirit is universally found in aspects such as traditional oral storytelling, live improvisation, mixed reality, and public engagement, coherently with its roots in ancient rituals.

By developing the CoPuppet project, we aim at creating a digital translation of puppetry, with emphasis on oral storytelling, free improvisation and public engagement. We propose new ideas for collaboration between users (puppeteers), to enhance the original spirit of puppetry, using interactive tools such as virtual sensors - here intended as maps of physical phenomena onto a virtual support - and voice activation.

We explore here the possibilities offered by multimodal and cooperative interaction with puppets in constructing a communicative experience among performers, or even audience members, called to affect different parts of a puppet

R. Adams, S. Gibson, and S. Müller Arisona (Eds.): DAW/IF 2006/2007, CCIS 7, pp. 326–341, 2008.

through gestures and voice. The proposal is based on the use of the Chambre architecture for the creation of multimodal interfaces [1,2], in which users can interact with multimedia sources through traditional or multimodal widgets. Chambre can also integrate virtual reality environments, and users may affect them through modifications of their parameters by gesture or voice commands. As a result, CoPuppet allows the creation of "live improvised" storytelling and actions between puppeteers.

In the rest of the paper, we set the scene of traditional puppetry in Section 2 and propose a brief review of related work in Section 3, while the Chambre architecture exploited in CoPuppet is presented in Section 4. Section 5 presents the CoPuppet application, while Sections 6 and 7 discuss its configuration and illustrate a performance setting and development. Section 8 explores interactions between digital and traditional puppets, with reference to wayang shadowplays. Finally, Section 9 draws conclusions.

## 2 Background

Puppets are diffused all over the world in different forms and used in different ways. Aa an example, Neapolitan puppets (known as Punch and Judy in the Anglo-Saxon world) are operated by single hands fitting inside the puppets, while Sicilian ones may be significantly sized, with different components steered via threads moved from above. Shadowplays, such as the Javanese wayang kulit, or the Turkish Karagöz, happen behind screens with the puppets' limbs controlled via horizontally held sticks. The Prague Black Theater incorporates puppets and real actors whose body parts are made invisible by wearing black clothes. Korean puppetry works with rods, and sometimes hands inside, with limited control, showing very primitive expressions. One of the puppeteers sits in front of the stage with the audience and talks constantly with the puppet during the play, breaking the boundary between the puppet and the real world. In the Japanese Bunraku puppet theater, 3 puppeteers in black costumes work together to establish the puppet's emotional expressions and gestures as a whole.

In general, puppets seem to evolve from the hinged and jointed masks worn by shamans, to become shamanic objects used in rituals, their role being to favor the shaman's trance state. This progression from masks, to puppet masks, to marionettes, appears to have occurred in a number of primitive societies [3].

Oral storytelling is an important aspect of ritual and puppetry. Puppeteers were usually illiterate, belonging to lower classes, and the narrative was orally transmitted over a long period of time [4], encouraging continuous improvisation and revisions in a flexible form of storytelling. For example, in Mediterranean area, stories could be improvised or developed under the influence of recent chronicles. Korean puppet drama is also preserved only through oral tradition.

Sometimes the puppet drama has a fixed narrative to be told exactly as trained, especially when it belongs to some noble form of art. For example, before a Bunraku performance in Osaka, the chanter holds up the text and bows before it, promising to follow it faithfully. However, on the near island of Awaji, a simpler type of folk Bunraku is practiced by the whole community, to less refined results, but bringing excitement and enthusiasm on [3].

## 3 Related Work

The idea of digital puppetry, as a means to go back to the shamanic roots of the puppetry tradition, had a first instantiation in the virtual interactive puppet performance, "YONG-SHIN-GUD" [5], involving live music and storytelling, together with 3D graphics to represent a virtual puppet. The puppet movements and facial expressions are steered in real time by the sounds captured by a microphone, either produced by instruments or by the storyteller voice. Meanwhile, the virtual puppet constantly speaks and sings back to the puppeteer, as a real-time echo and mirror reflection. The goal of the "YONG-SHIN-GUD" performance was to let the puppeteer eventually enter some form of trance, by spiraling interactive dialogues with the virtual puppet. To the audience, the real-time lip synchronization process appears as a continuous transformation process involving the virtual puppet and the human puppeteer, in a Yin-Yang equilibrium. CoPuppet adopts this continuous process of transformation as a tool to break boundaries and stereotypes, bringing forth freely imagined oral storytelling from puppeteers.

Nowadays, avatars, forms of "digital puppets", are in wide use, in online game environments, or in community-based sites, such as Second Life[1]. The word "puppet" has frequently appeared in the digital realm; however, due to the Western cultural understanding of subject and object, it usually represents something to be manipulated and controlled. The definition of puppet has been narrowly understood in this Western cultural context, and inherited in the digital media culture. In this paper, connecting with the origin of puppetry, we propose virtual puppets as ritual objects, emphasizing puppet-puppeteer relationships, as well as interactions between puppeteers. A combination of storytelling and multimodal interaction is presented in [6], where humans interact with puppets in a virtual environment, in which recognition of human gestures and speech steers dialogues and interaction with the puppets.

The construction of virtual sensors can take advantage of the availability of tools for pattern recognition and motion detection. Currently, original and simple algorithms have been incorporated into Chambre, typically based on finger position identification. Differently from [7], we are not restricted to 2D positioning, but can also exploit (partial) 3D information. The open structure of Chambre and the simplicity of its component model, however, make it easy to embody more sophisticated algorithms.

## 4 The Chambre Architecture for Multimodal Interaction

Multimodal Interfaces [8] allow users to interact with a system through several input devices, such as keyboard, mouse, voice, face and gesture recognition. In

[1] http://www.secondlife.com/

the design of real-time systems with multimedia capabilities and/or featuring multimodal interfaces, recurrent issues are encountered, such as the design of efficient data acquisition and transmission protocols, of parallel or serial compositions of data processors, of data generation algorithms, and so on. *Software frameworks* [9] offer a reusable set of components and inter-component communication protocols: they are thus often used in the design of multimedia/multimodal systems, as this greatly reduces the system's development time and allows the developer to experiment with different designs quickly. Frameworks often come with a visual editor, allowing the programmer to express the system structure via a graphical language. A graph representation of the system is commonly used, where classes constitute the graph vertexes, while directed edges represent communication channels between them. Several frameworks which exploit this metaphor are currently available both from industrial efforts and through the open-source community, two examples being Virtools [10] and Pure Data [11].

Chambre is an open framework able to accommodate different protocols, sensors, generation and interaction techniques [1]. The generative process can be steered, both explicitly and implicitly, by human users, through inputs acquired by external multisensor devices. For example, a webcam can capture user movements, while image analysis tools can interpret them to detect presence in specific zones or evaluate variations with respect to previous or fixed reference images. As a result, parameters are generated to steer the system response. Specific inputs can also trigger, in real-time, modifications of the interpretation process. This ability makes Chambre a flexible and open tool, easily adaptable to different situations and applications. The Chambre architecture, sketched in Figure 1, allows a component-based style of programming, where components are endowed with communication interfaces and a system results from connecting them. A designer can interactively define a Chambre network in the form of a graph, exploiting the convention described above.

The Chambre framework was started as a distributed component-based architecture for the production of multimedia objects. Hence, it incorporates several plug-ins managing different multimedia data formats [1]. Currently available plug-ins offer: 1) interpretation of stimuli from real sensors (physical measures) such as: webcams, mouse and keyboard signals, etc.; 2) signal generation; 3) signal mapping; 4) mapping-driven multimedia streaming generation (audio and video synthesis), thus favoring the rapid prototyping of Multimodal Interfaces.

Symmetrically to the real case, (groups of) virtual actuators can interact with and modify virtual environments through Virtual Multimodal Interfaces (VMI). In order to manage the state of virtual actuators, the *FeedBack Manager* module sends streams of control commands and data to the *Computational System*.

A VMI is characterised by specific Chambre nodes in charge of mapping real stimuli to virtual ones through an interpretation process. A virtual stimulus is a configuration of a data collection produced by some computational process,

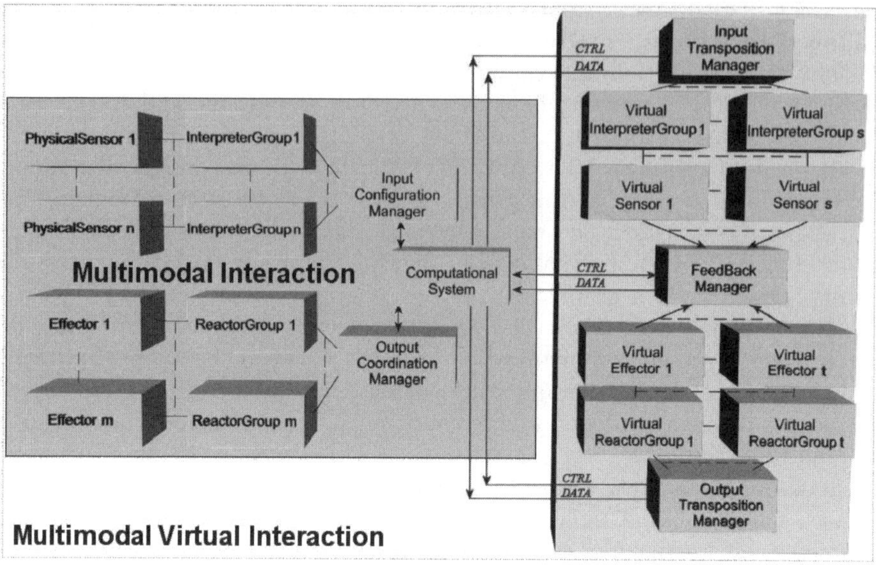


**Fig. 1.** The architectural model of Virtual Multimodal Interaction

which can be interpreted as the result of a measurement process. In particular, a *Virtual Component* defines an *Appearance*, a *Behavior* and a *Measurement* method. An innovative feature in the CHAMBRE implementation of VMIs is the possibility of positioning virtual sensors onto a virtual support. As an example, a video virtual support can transpose the frames taken from a video stream by sampling (clipping) and positioning them into the virtual space (see Figure 2). As another example, a virtual slider acting onto a video virtual support can perform measurements by detecting the point closest to an extreme $P_2$, in a segment $P_1P_2$, which intersects a moving shape, as shown in Figure 3.

Figure 4 shows instances of Virtual Button and Virtual Slider widgets performing their measurements on video supports.

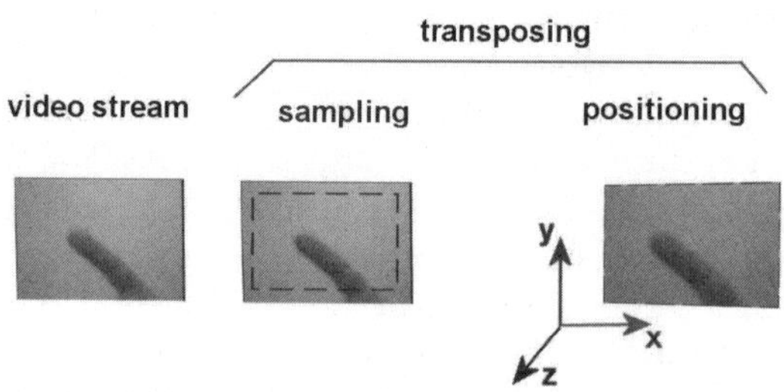


**Fig. 2.** Construction of a support for a virtual sensor

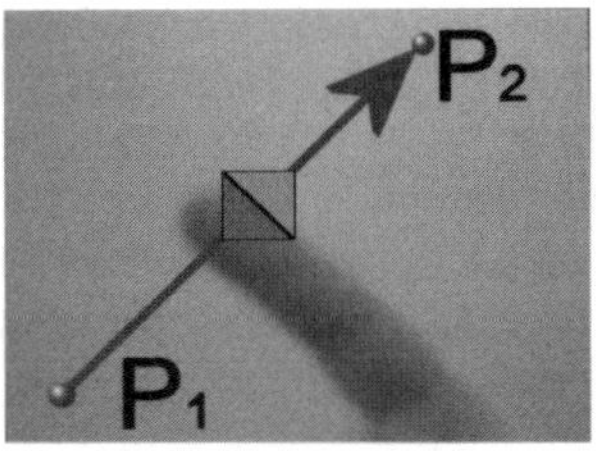


**Fig. 3.** An example of Virtual Slider

| Sensor | Real | Virtual |
|---|---|---|
| Button | 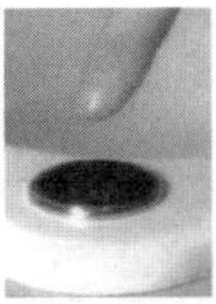 | 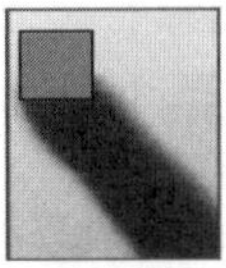 |
| Slider | 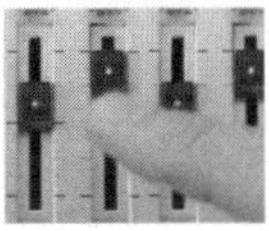 | 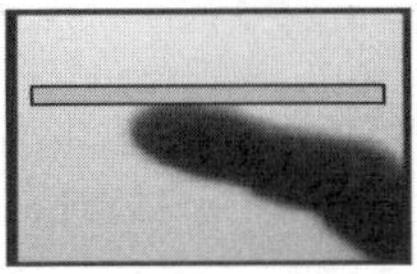 |

**Fig. 4.** Examples of Virtual Sensors

## 5 The CoPuppet Environment for Digital Puppetry

CoPuppet is a class of Chambre applications for Virtual Puppetry. A CoPuppet application is a Chambre network featuring instances of MVI_VirtualPuppet (MVI_VP for short), a Chambre software component which, differently from virtual sensors, does not define a measurement method but only an Appearance and a Behavior. It relies on other Chambre components, possibly running on remote machines, to perform the measurements needed to generate the data determining the puppet's posture. An MVI_VP appearance is given by a 3D digital puppet, produced as a tree of labeled Java 3D nodes (see Figure 5).

The Java 3D graph-based scene model [12] provides a simple and flexible mechanism for representing and rendering scenes. Chambre embedded graphical engine is based on Java 3D technology and is capable of rendering skinned bones. A scene graph contains a complete description of the entire scene. This includes the geometric data, the surface attributes and the visualization position information needed to render the scene from a particular point of view. Hence, the Appearance of an MVI_VP is a labeled extension of a Java 3D scene graph, with nodes of two kinds: `BranchGroup` and `TransformGroup`. A

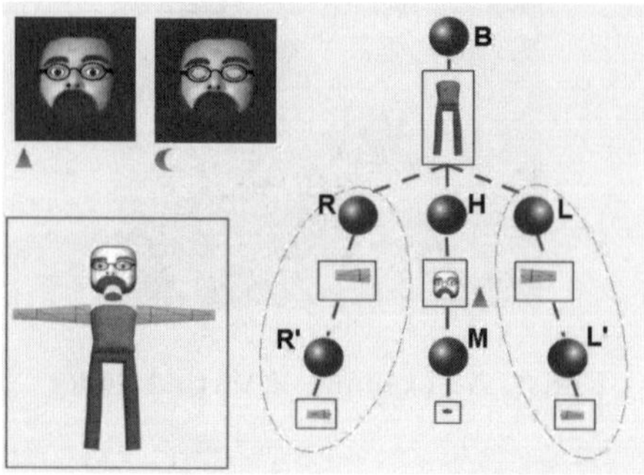


**Fig. 5.** The appearance of a Virtual Puppet

`BranchGroup` identifies body parts, and its elements have labels in the set $BG = \{B, H, M, R, R', L, L'\}$, for body, head, mouth, right and left arm and forearm, respectively. A `TransformGroup` specifies control elements and a Transformation Matrix for the different body parts. The labels in the set $TG$ are obtained by concatenating a label from $BG$ with one from the set $\{Tx, Ty, Tz, x, y, z, s\}$. Here, "$T$" labels indicate translation parameters along the three Cartesian axes, the next three indicate rotation angles around these axes, and $s$ denotes the scale factor. As an example, the label "$MTy$" identifies the TransformGroup node used to translate the mouth `BranchGroup` along the $y$ axis, producing a vertical shift of the puppet's mouth.

The *Behavior* of an MVI_VP is determined by a simple protocol: the object accepts messages of the form "*label value*", with $label \in TG$, and *value* a parameter used to define the new transformation matrix associated with the Appearance node identified by *label*. Values generated by Virtual Sensors are normalized to the $[0.0, 1.0]$ interval and mapped to labels in $TG$. A message can also modify attributes defining the material used to render the corresponding nodes of the puppet's 3D representation. For example the message "`MTy value`", besides defining the vertical position of the mouth, can also be used to change the texture of the puppet's head, thus modifying its facial expressions.

The definition of Virtual Puppets as CHAMBRE components favors the use (and reuse) of puppets in different contexts of execution. Actually, every software component (even non CHAMBRE ones) which respects the Behavior protocol can produce messages for the puppet controls. We focus now on two specific puppetry paradigms which can be realized in COPUPPET.

### 5.1 Single Puppet, Collaborative Controls

Single puppets can be operated on by one or more performers, through interactions in which separate channels control different aspects of the puppet, such as limb movement or facial expressions. As new controllable aspects are introduced, so can new multimodal input channels be added, to be managed by a single performer, or distributed among many. In particular, we are interested in the evolution of patterns of real time collaboration among performers during free improvisation of the puppet performance.

In the proposed scenario, the puppet is set in a virtual environment of arbitrary complexity, and its movements, utterances and facial expressions are determined by the actions of independent users. The environment itself can present objects which can be animated by user interaction. Hence, users could log into a performance either as puppet body parts such as mouth, arms, lower body, or as objects in the scene, such as trees, umbrellas and hand mirrors.

In the current implementation, there are no constraints on relative motions of body parts - except that they be kept connected - so that physically impossible situations can arise. This is not in contrast with the aims of the project, and is possibly a desired effect of it, as it would be interesting to see how the performers draw themselves out of such situations, or engage in power struggles to make others conform to their choices. However, constraints could be added by exploiting the Java 3D tree structure of objects.

### 5.2 Multiple Puppets, Collaborative Controls

A Multiple Puppet scenario can be produced by replicating a number of instances of the Single Scenario. Chambre capability of distribution helps the configurations of scalable stages, where teams of puppeteers can perform real-time shows and/or produce databases of recorded session for further post productions needs.

An asynchronous form of multiple puppets can be realized by recording actions of single puppets and merging them afterwards onto a new environment.

In a multiple puppet scenario based on replication of the single one, users enrol not only on body parts, but have to define which puppet they are managing. This may lead to the design of puppet chatting stages, in a way similar to how avatars may be used. Hence, users can engage in virtual dialogues, observing the reactions of the different participants through the modifications of their representative puppets. Sessions can also be recorded and replayed by the participants or by external observers.

## 6 Configuring CoPuppet

CoPuppet does not make particular demands on which software components can be used as a front-end, so that third party suites like Virtools [10] can be integrated into a CoPuppet application. The use of well-known tools can favor the artistic and technical development process of script creation and relieve the composer from advanced programming aspects such as the development of particular graphical routines.

Among the large array of possible configurations, we show how to develop both single and multiple scenarios. In CoPuppet a configuration usually consists of a network of computers running instances of the Chambre framework. Each Chambre instance contains a replication of all the Virtual Puppets used for the performance; however different instances may differ in the graph used, which represents the connection scheme of the used CHAMBRE software components. Each puppeteer has a global view of the virtual puppets and of the current configuration of the software components needed to drive the body parts for which he/she is responsible, being thus focused on one of the CHAMBRE instances where the global behavior of the puppets is represented.

The behavioral aspects of a puppet, steered by its puppeteer, are transmitted to the other CHAMBRE instances in the network. Computation is thus distributed over the network and synchronization is achieved by message passing.

As mentioned before, external tools can be used for graphical and audio improvements. For example in Infinite Cemetery [13], spatial information about Virtools entities is transmitted via network to a program implementing audio spatialization and synthesis algorithm running on a separate machine.

## 7 CoPuppet Performance

In a CoPuppet collaborative performance, the puppeteers are placed at different locations in front of a screen on which the appearance of the virtual puppet is projected, as shown in Figure 6. Each user logs in as a puppet body part, or an object, for which controls have been defined, and produces collaborative movements of the virtual puppet by exploiting previously defined mappings between the available input channels and the puppet's behavior, as described in Section 7.2. A narrator, in charge of the puppet's face movements, tells a story into a microphone, to which the system responds in real time by producing mouth movements and facial expression of the virtual puppet on screen, according to some interpretation of the audio stimulus (see Section 7.2). Puppeteers in charge of body parts use their fingers in front of a webcam, thus activating virtual sensors connected with the corresponding body part on screen. The movements are reminiscent of those performed by real puppeteers steering movements through threads. While each puppeteer can create only simple movements, the whole gesture of the puppet results from their combination, producing powerful and interesting effects.

The performance can also allow for audience intervention. In particular, while retaining a single storyteller, CoPuppet can partially open several body controls to the public, to foster forms of collaboration between the performers and the audience. A completely open instantiation of the framework can also be envisaged, in which computers, microphone and webcams would be set up for users to participate in the performance space.

### 7.1 Collaboration Aspects

The main intended use of CoPuppet involves a storyteller, a crew of body parts performers, and possible intervention from the audience.

As seen in Section 2, the Bunraku theatre presents aspects of collaboration between body puppeteers and a storyteller. However, they rely on precise interpretations of the scripts, and their highly trained skills and practices. On

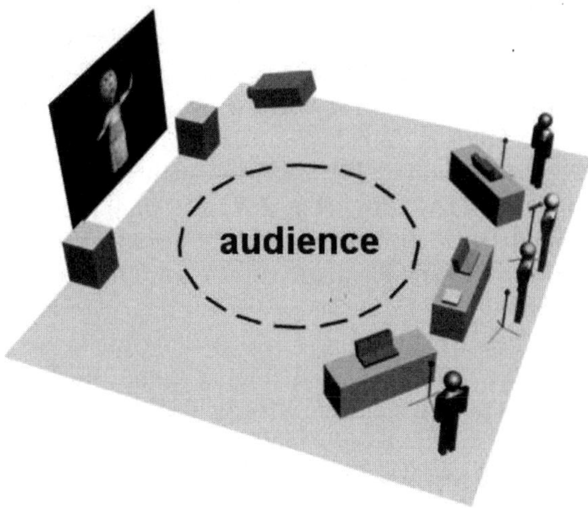


**Fig. 6.** Performance system layout

the contrary, CoPuppet supports forms of collaboration between users who do not have to follow a precise script, or event to have agreed in advance on some behavior.

Indeed, performers do not have to define in advance the kind of story they want to tell, but can come up at any time with ideas about the situation and the story, based on the materials in the scene, which can all become "performing objects". In a sense, performers are designing their own scene, depending on which objects are considered as active and which are the ones for which some user is registered. It is expected that the real time observation of the consequences of one's own actions, as well as those of the other puppeteers, will foster interaction between puppeteers, who will engage into collaborative or competitive behavior patterns. Typical patterns might be mimicking or counteracting the actions of one another, introducing delays in replicating some movement, achieving unison through the iteration of the same movements. Interestingly, these patterns may occur directly among performers as well. In this context, CoPuppet functions as an intangible social interface, creating new relationships and interaction between people, which could be resonated into the real community. We envisage that CoPuppet, through its simple and intuitive controls, can become a playground for children, while adults might find it interesting as a form of stage for free speech, as well as imaginative storytelling.

### 7.2 Technical Description

In this Section we describe one of the possible deployments of the CoPuppet framework, namely the one presented at the Digital Art Week in Zurich, 2006.

In this setting, each puppeteer uses one or more *VirtualSlider* to translate his/her hand movements into puppet actions. The slider position is determined from the hand position, acquired via webcam. Puppeteers can see their hands projected into the virtual space, and interact with the virtual controllers (via their laptop computer screen) and the virtual puppet (via the projection screen). Figure 7 shows how the different transform nodes can be operated on through different multimodal channels. Labels from the set $TG$ indicate both a puppet body part and the corresponding *VirtualSlider* setting the value of the control parameter. In particular, $RX$, $Ry$, $R'y$, $LX$, $Ly$, and $L'y$ are the labels for angle rotation around the $x$ and $y$ axes for the articulations of the puppet's arms, while $Hx$, $Hy$ are labels for angle rotation around the $x$ and $y$ axis for the puppet's head. Finally, $MTy$ is the parameter that determines the puppet's mouth opening and facial expression. $MTy$ is determined by calculating the average amplitude value $m$ of the signal coming from a microphone connected to the puppeteer's laptop. The value of $m$ is calculated on a buffer of 1024 audio samples acquired every 0,023 seconds, so that the system response to audio storytelling is fast and accurate. The values of $MTy$ are directly mapped to the puppet's "jaw" $y$-position, thereby making the puppet "talk" in response to incoming audio transients. An empirically determined constant $k$ is used for the mapping, so that $MouthPosition = k * MTy$. Facial expression behavior is simply obtained by comparing the incoming $MTy$ values against a threshold value: if the threshold is crossed, the puppet's eyes texture is switched, so that it looks like the puppet is shouting. Even if the mapping strategy is really simple, we have found it to be expressive and amusing to the audience.

In the Zurich exhibition, the global setup (Figure 7) consists of three laptops connected via a Local Area Network (LAN). Each laptop is connected with a USB webcam: the first laptop is used for $Rx$, $Ry$, $R'y$, controls, the second for the $Lx$, $Ly$, $L'y$ and the third for the $Hx$ and $Hy$ controls. For $MTy$, a microphone is connected to the *audio in* port of the second laptop. Finally, the second

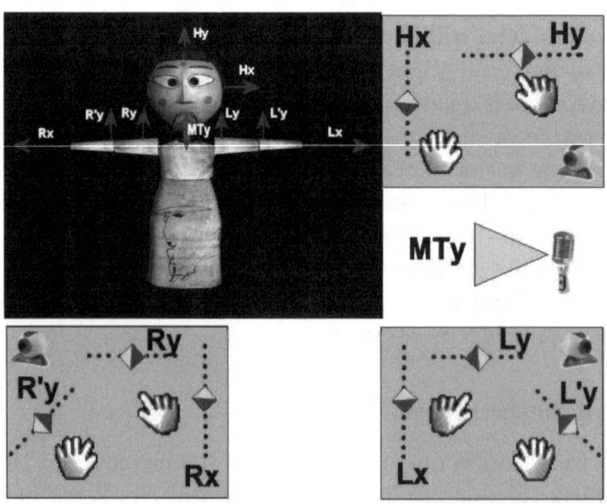


**Fig. 7.** Puppet controllers

laptop is connected to the video projector through a VGA cable, and, using an audio cable, is also connected to the mixer which drives the audio speakers for the audience. Effective interaction among puppeteers relies on the high speed of the 100mps LAN connection between the laptops, which transfers raw data generated by the virtual sensors. Collaborative performance by puppeteers in remote locations would require more sophisticated handling of messages exchanged between system components, including time-stamping of messages and reconstruction of missing data in case of network delays and/or failures.

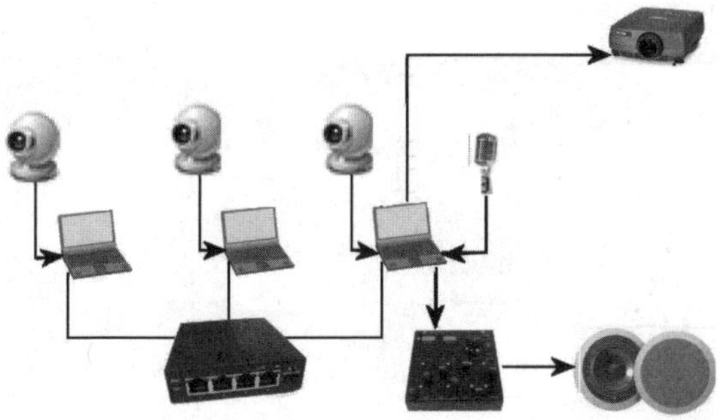

**Fig. 8.** Setup of the peripherals for CoPuppet

## 8 Combining Virtual and Real Puppets: A Case Study

The CoPuppet framework can also accommodate different types of virtual puppetry. As an example, "Experimental Virtual Wayang", by two of the authors, adapts the traditional Balinese shadow puppet performance ("wayang kulit"), injecting live improvisation into storytelling. This project also includes the collaboration of I Gusti Putu Sudarta, Andrew McGraw and the *eighth blackbird* sextet. A live performance was staged from October to November 2007.

Figure 9 shows some pictures taken during the whole process (from the first experiments to the public display) of the Experimental Virtual Wayang performance. Here the shadow puppet master changes the virtual puppet's look and control its movements with his voice. In order to maintain some harmony between the traditional and digital worlds, virtual puppets have been designed as 2D shapes, adding features such as breathing fire, colorful shadows, global animation and audio interaction. Experimental Virtual Wayang achieves even more dynamic improvisation when incorporated into CoPuppet, by distributing puppeteer's interactive controls to multiple users. Instead of using predefined, static animation data, articulated body parts of the used puppets are steered by virtual sensors, as is shown for the Virtual Dragon in Figure 10.

Figure 11 illustrates the collaborative performance setting, where one puppeteer works with traditional shadow puppets, and virtual puppets can be steered by multiple users.

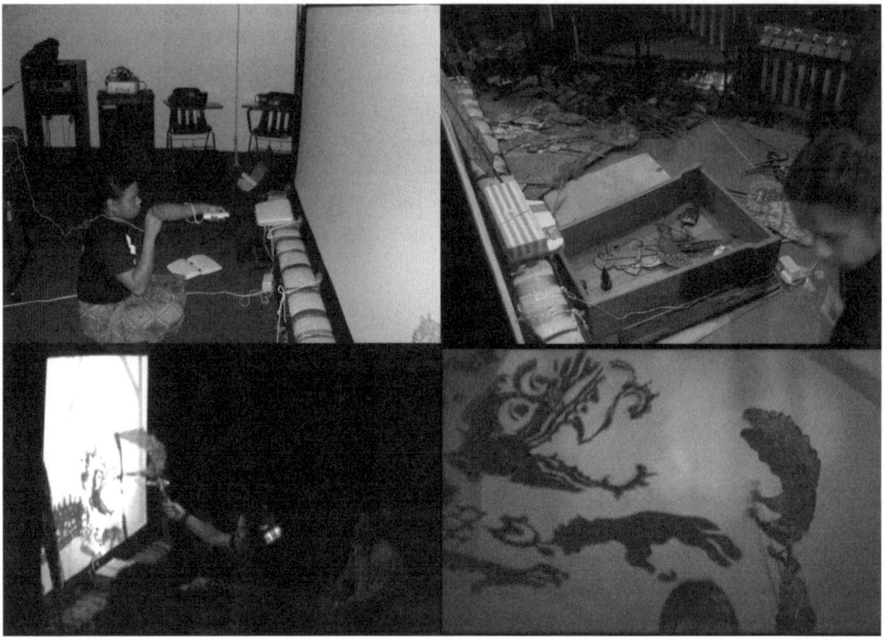

**Fig. 9.** Pictures of Experimental Virtual Wayang performance, taken during Usability Test (Top left), Rehearsal (Top right), and Performance (Bottom left and right)

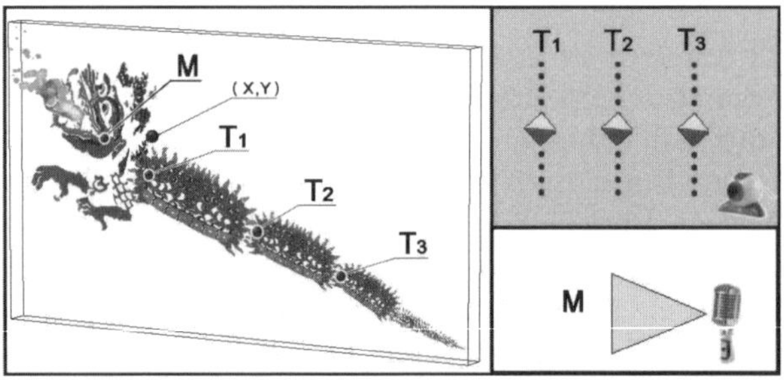


**Fig. 10.** A digital dragon for virtual Wayang

In the collaborative setting, the Nintendo Wii Remote controller (popularly called Wiimote) [14] is used instead of sticks, controlling global position, orientation and event generation (breathing fire, etc) on virtual puppets (1,2). The Wiimote is a commercially-available remote control, which is able to determine its position and orientation in space, sending the generated data via Bluetooth to the controlled device.

The Wiimote offers a wider range of interaction capabilities than traditional sticks. A main feature of the Wiimote is its motion sensing capability, which

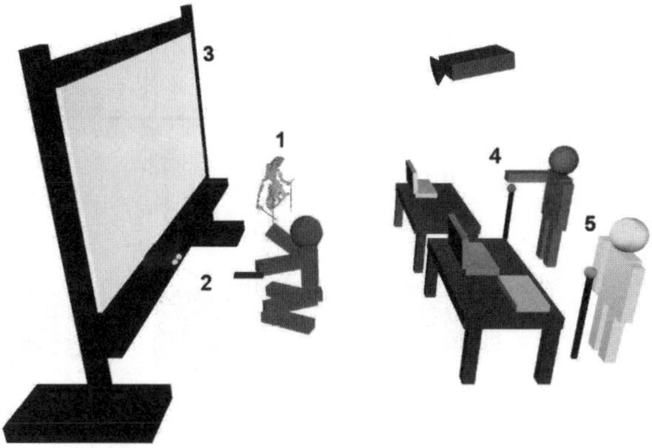


**Fig. 11.** Layout for collaboration between virtual and real Wayang

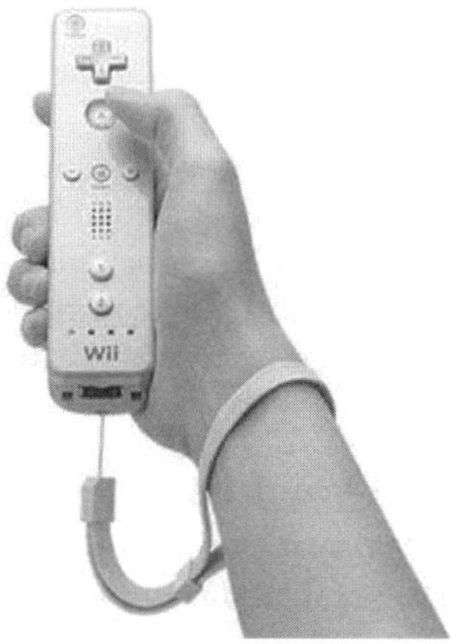


**Fig. 12.** The Wii Remote controller

allows the user to interact with and manipulate items on screen via movement and pointing through the use of accelerometer and optical sensor technology. Another interesting feature of Wiimote (see Figure 12 ) is the capability to track infrared source lights by a built-in infrared camera. Moreover, we have found that the Wiimote solution is easier to use than a prototype input device based on tracking of sticks movements we developed before. Microphones for sound input such as storytelling (5) and virtual sensors for articulated body movements (4) can also be distributed to multiple users for collaboration. Hence, traditional puppet manipulated by one puppet master, and virtual puppet collaboratively operated on by multiple users can interact with each other on the same screen.

Figure 13 illustrates the use of Wiimote to control the Virtual Dragon puppet orientation, puppet position $(x, y, z)$, puppet action (breathe fire) and character

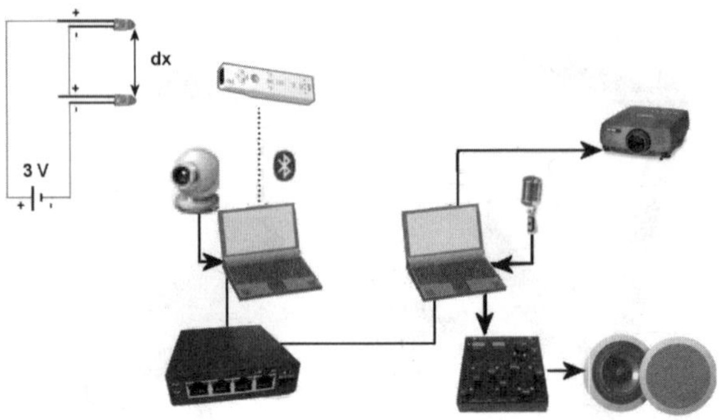


**Fig. 13.** Setup of peripherals for collaboration between virtual and real Wayang

selection. The coordinates of a puppet's position are estimated by tracking two infrared light sources using the Wiimote infrared camera feature. In particular the $z$ component is obtained by measuring the distance between the two tracked infrared light sources.

For "Experimental Virtual Wayang", a CHAMBRE instance is used to manage the Wiimote and the virtual sensors controllers. From the CHAMBRE network, messages are delivered to Virtools which handles also audio interaction and graphical rendering. The distribution of controllers, as well as the number or roles of puppeteers, can vary depending on users' abilities and performance needs.

## 9 Discussion and Conclusions

We have presented COPUPPET, a distributed system for digital puppetry which exploits the collaborative performance of multiple puppeteers. Currently, COPUPPET allows interactions between puppeteers within a limited distance, but we envision remote collaborative puppet control over networks. We are also investigating the possibility of employing software agents in puppet controls, to enable more sophisticated mappings between data incoming from the virtual sensors and puppet movements. Future work on the multiple puppet scenario will aim at setting both puppets and humans in a mixed reality environment [15]. This last scenario requires the introduction of new software components able to solve problems concerning occlusion, contact, avoidance between human and virtual actors [16]. The open nature of the COPUPPET framework allows the incorporation of different sensors and the definition of different articulations and forms of rendering built on the Java 3D tree. On the other hand, its incorporation within the CHAMBRE environment, with its component-based structure, makes it possible to reuse definitions of behavior, appearance and measures in different contexts, such as collaboration scenarios, remote conferencing, or to associate puppets' controls to different sources of measures, whether physical or virtual.

From the artistic point of view, we envisage that the collaborative features offered by the CoPuppet framework will provide unique opportunities for virtual and real puppetry to explore critical issues related to improvisation, collaboration and interaction.

## References


1. Bottoni, P., Faralli, S., Labella, A., Scozzafava, C.: CHAMBRE: A distributed environment for the production of multimedia events. In: Proc. DMS 2004, KSI, pp. 51–56 (2004)
2. Bottoni, P., Faralli, S., Labella, A., Malizia, A., Scozzafava, C.: CHAMBRE: integrating multimedia and virtual tools. In: Proc. AVI 2006, pp. 285–292. ACM Press, New York (2006)
3. Baird, B.: The Art of the Puppet. Macmillan, Basingstoke (1965)
4. Cho, O.K.: Korean puppet theatre: Kkoktu kaksi. Asian studies center East Asia series Michigan State University occasional paper 6(20) (1979)
5. Ryu, S.: Ritualizing interactive media: from motivation to activation. Technoetic Arts 3, 105–124 (2005)
6. Cavazza, M., Charles, F., Mead, S.J., Martin, O., Marichal, X., Nandi, A.: Multimodal acting in mixed reality interactive storytelling. IEEE MultiMedia 11, 30–39 (2004)
7. Myers, B., McDaniel, R., Miller, R., Ferrency, A., Faulring, A., Kyle, B., Mickish, A., Klimovitski, A., Doane, P.: The Amulet environment: New models for effective user interface software development. IEEE Transactions on Software Engineering 23, 347–365 (1997)
8. Bianchi-Berthouze, N., Bottoni, P.: Articulating actions in multimodal interaction. 3D Forum 16, 220–225 (2002)
9. Johnson, R., Foote, B.: Designing reusable classes. Journal of OO Programming 1, 22–35 (1988)
10. Virtools: Virtools (2004), http://www.virtools.com
11. Pure Data: Pure data (2008), http://puredata.info
12. Sun: Java 3D API Specification (2004), http://java.sun.com/products/java-media/3D/forDevelopers/j3dguide/Intro.doc.html
13. Ryu, S., Scozzafava, C., Faralli, S.: Infinite cemetery. In: Generative Art, Execution on, December 16 (2005)
14. Nintendo: Wiimote controller (2007), http://wii.nintendo.com/controller.jsp
15. Thalmann, D., Boulic, R., Huang, Z., Noser, H.: Virtual and real humans interacting in the virtual world. In: Proc. International Conference on Virtual Systems and Multimedia 1995, pp. 48–57 (1995)
16. Schuemie, M.J., van der Straaten, P., Krijn, M., van der Mast, C.: Research on presence in VR: a survey. Cyberpsychology and Behavior 4, 183–202 (2001)

# Experiments in Digital Puppetry: Video Hybrids in Apple's Quartz Composer

Ian Grant

Thames Valley University
Faculty of the Arts
St Marys Road, Ealing, London. UK. W5 5RF
+44 (0) 20 8579 5000
ian.grant@tvu.ac.uk
http://www.daisyrust.com/

**Abstract.** *Digital Puppetry* is a hybrid art form that includes a broad range of creative practices. The current chapter explores real-time video montages and avatar control using wireless game controllers while exploring what is meant by the term *digital puppet* and raises issues surrounding the virtual and tangible body in performance. Real-time media objects are viewed as *extensions* to the human performer – sympathetic with the traditions and conventional definitions of puppetry.

I document the workings of a prototype performance system made using Apple's innovative and free development tool *Quartz Composer*. It encompasses screen-based digital puppetry and scenography, *mixed-reality* video composites and custom software programming and the gestural control of an on-screen avatar using the popular game controller, the Nintendo *Wii-remote*.

**Keywords:** Animated Performance, Digital Puppetry, Digital Scenography, Real-Time Performance Capture and Control, Video Processing.

## 1 Introduction and Aims

*Digital Puppetry* is a hybrid art form that presently includes a broad range of work and creative practices:

- live real-time animation and performance capture processes
- rendered computer generated animation process, referring to animation performance systems, like Pixar Studio's *Marionette* software
- automata and kinetic art practice, involving servo/microprocessor controlled automata, e.g. the art of Ken Feingold[1]
- live multimedia performance
- user-controlled characters in animations or *machinima*, often made with Adobe's *Flash*, game engines or Linden Lab's *Second Life*.

[1] Ken Feingold http://www.kenfeingold.com/

R. Adams, S. Gibson, and S. Müller Arisona (Eds.): DAW/IF 2006/2007, CCIS 7, pp. 342–357, 2008.

When comparing digital puppetry to tradition forms, discussion often involves (i) the distance between the performer and the physical or virtual object and (ii) how the performer is embodied within the physical or virtual object. In the current work, I compose a wirelessly controllable on-screen object using video-graphic elements of a performer (their mouth and eyes) that are reconfigured in real-time into a new image. The same performer can then control the orientation and expressive motion of the speaking image/avatar. I am interested in making virtual objects speak and ask: how does a visual image of a speaking mouth embed the performer in the puppet and create the perception of an expressive living character?

The performance piece, *Of Minnie the Moocher and Me*, had a central visual idea that combined a real-time chroma-keyed mouth and interactive pre-recorded video of eyes. Through movement and reconfiguration, I believed these abstracted facial elements could form a coherent expressive system for a digital puppet (see figure 1). Add to this real-time vocalisation and synchronised speech, gestural object control using a Nintendo *Wii Remote*[2], MIDI controlled sequencing of scenography and special effects using foot-switches and a control deck, and I may have a new – low cost – approach to digital puppet performance and capture.

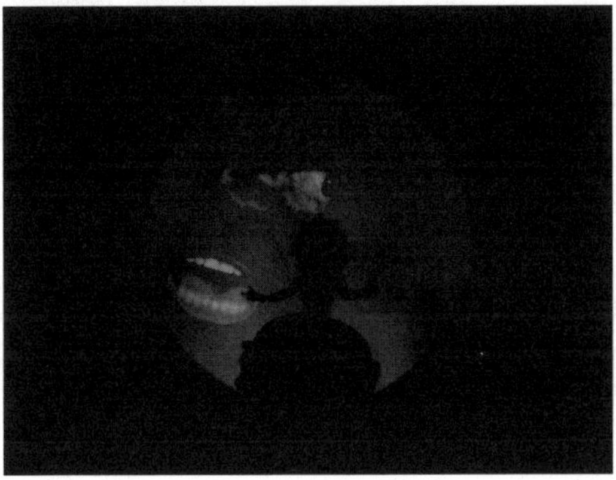

**Fig. 1.** Composite of real-time mouth, recorded eyes and MIDI controllable digital scenography and special effects

For visual reference, I turned to American popular culture and a number of out of copyright (public domain) animation forms. I have always had a love of the Fleischer brothers' cartoons of the 1920s and 1930s. Mainly famous for creating *Betty Boop*, *Popeye* and the *Out of the Ink Pot* clown, the Fleischers are less well known for creating *rotoscoping* – a technique of painting inks on cells over a mechanism projecting film – basically tracing film in order to create animation. They established the technique by tracing the performance of one

[2] Wii-Remote Controller: http://wii.nintendo.com/controller.jsp

of my favourite jazz singers, Cab Calloway. In *Snow White* (1933)[3] , preceding Walt Disney's version of *Snow White* by a number of years, Calloway sang *Saint James Infirmary* – a mourning/blues song – and created an enduring stylistic affinity between early animation and jazz.

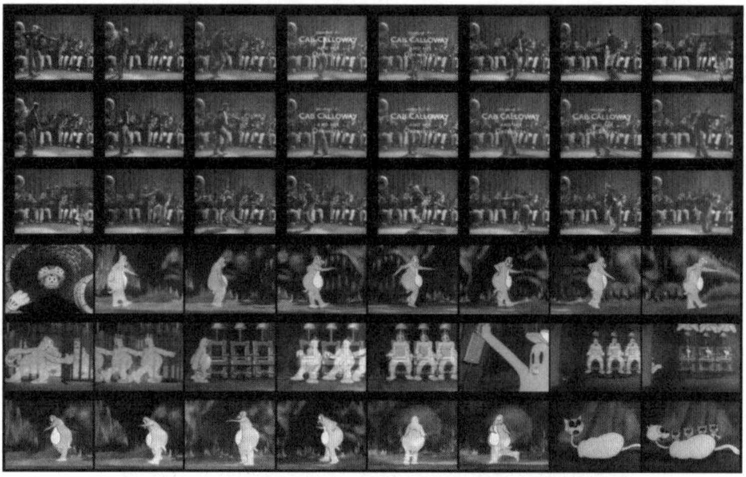

**Fig. 2.** *Rotoscoping* in the Fleischer brothers' 'Snow White' (1933). Image generated using a *Quartz Composer* composition by Ian Grant

Figure 2 depicts the opening and mid-point sequences from the Fleischers' *Snow White* (1933) and illustrates the live-footage moments and the final animated *rotoscoped* sequence.

It is with the same spirit of technological innovation that I aimed to explore similar material with contemporary technology. I aimed to create a real time performance system where I create and control a video based digital character that sings the song, *Minnie the Moocher* by Cab Calloway. I aimed to create the following:

- A performance control system using Apple's *Quartz Composer*[4], a general purpose MIDI controller and a wireless game controller, the Nintendo *Wii-Remote.*
- A video processing/projection system with instant chroma-keying of a blue faced performer.
- Some nifty realtime effects, transitions and visual compositions, i.e. elegant digital scenography – illustrated in figures 12–17 below.
- To work towards a fuller expanded performance telling the extended saga of *Minnie the Moocher.*

[3] The Fleischer Studios *Snow-White* (1933) See: http://www.imdb.com/title/tt0024578/

[4] Apple's *Quartz Composer:* http://developer.apple.com/graphicsimaging/quartz/quartzcomposer.html

## 2 Concept Description – Real Time Art

In one way, the piece stands alone as a performance, in another it is an exploration of the software and technologies that enable digital storytelling.

Apple's *Quartz Composer* is indebted to experimental analogue video of the 1970s and 1980s – where physical patch based video synthesisers and multiplexers were used to process real-time analogue video and do things like blue-screening, chroma-keying, vision-mixing and other visual effects. Such technology today is emulated in software and inspires digital creatives from visualists and VJs [1] to multimedia performers like Robert LePage (see *The Far Side of the Moon*[5] ) and Laurie Anderson (see her recent work as NASA's artist in residence[6] ). The influence of early video processing has resonated through and been reanimated by recent advances in computer graphics processing unit (GPU) capabilities.

Visual programming software applications like *Quartz Composer*, Cycling 74's *max/msp*[7] and Troikatronix's *Isadora*[8] (named after dancer Isadora Duncan) have brought real-time 3D graphics and video processing into the hands of the wider performing arts community.

To place my explorations in a wider context – one could call it an exploration in *augmented reality*. From Wikipedia: "Augmented reality (AR) is a field of computer research which deals with the combination of real world and computer generated data (in real time). At present, most AR research is concerned with the use of live video imagery which is digitally processed and augmented by the addition of computer generated graphics." [2]

The concept of real-time is crucial in the context of performance. There are huge semiotic differences between the live and recorded arts. I am exploring the dialectic between the improvisational and the composed (in other words *planned* or *sequenced*). Real-time computer media will help open up more improvisation space for the media artist. I think this is expressed through a varying number of channels: e.g. performance systems, improvisation while coding, while editing video or music, through playing with new styles of UI or interaction systems. Computer power and the ethos of cinematic interfaces drive us towards very playful systems. See Jeff Han's recent work [3] on haptic interfaces and multi-touch surfaces – particularly the shadow puppet-like drawing with forward kinematics – for a brilliant demonstration of an improvisational control system[9] .

Apple's *Quartz Composer* allows the use of MIDI control signals and other input data in a straightforward way. I have designed my digital puppet and scenographic space to allow elements of playful interaction that do not involve a conventional screen-based user interface, but are sequenced using wireless game

---

5 Robert Lepage: http://www.robertlepage.com/

6 Laurie Anderson: http://www.laurieanderson.com/

7 Cycling 74's *max/msp*: http://www.cycling74.com/

8 Troikatronix's *Isadora*: http://www.troikatronix.com/isadora.html

9 Multitouch Interaction Research: http://cs.nyu.edu/~jhan/ftirtouch/index.html and 'Unveiling the genius of multi-touch interface design' http://www.ted.com/index.php/talks/view/id/65

controllers and MIDI decks. The movement of my digital character is tied to the real-time gestural possibilities of a consumer level haptic device.

Computer media, historically tied up with *un-dynamic* or stored media, is tending towards responsive, data-aware and dynamic systems. To clarify (and expand): "The impossibility of technologically processing data in real time is the possibility of art... As long as processing in real time was not available, data always had to be stored intermediately somewhere – on skin, wax, clay, stone, papyrus, linen, paper, wood, or on the cerebral cortex – in order to be transmitted or otherwise processed. ..." [4]. Gere extends this nicely: "Art exists only within a certain *economy* of time produced by the materiality and temporality of culture's means of inscription, storage and exchange." [5]. *Quartz Composer* is one such environment that is tending towards complex, interactive real-time media production.

## 3 Development

The project can be split into three broad phases of production: (i) Understanding *Quartz Composer* – see section 3.1, (ii) Custom Software Production – section 3.3 and (iii) Content Creation in section 4 *Visual Documentation with Commentary.*

### 3.1 Understanding *Quartz Composer*

*Quartz Composer* is a technology that exploits the graphics processing unit (GPU) of the host Apple Mac, running Mac OS 10.4 (Tiger). Major enhancements have been made to *Quartz Composer* in Mac OS 10.5 (Leopard). Some key points:

- you create 'compositions' in a simple to use visual programming environment where you graph connections between objects ('patches'). There are around two hundred built in patches. *Leopard* developments provide an API for programmers to created custom functionality by writing their own patches;
- it works in a 3D context as defined by *Open-GL* and supports *Open-GL Shader Language (GLSL)*, enabling full and multi screen real-time video, image processing and 3D;
- it uses Apple's *Quicktime* technology for media importing and the playback of compositions;
- it works with data aggregation standards defined by *RSS* and a logic/control language defined by *javascript/ECMAScript*;
- MIDI, OSC[10] and audio input processing allowing sophisticated network communication and composition control by external sources and sensors;
- *Xcode*, Apple's free developers environment[11], allows *Quartz Composer* compositions to be embedded in native applications for more complex control over rendering, user interface design and interoperability with other technologies.

[10] Open Sound Control Introduction: http://opensoundcontrol.org/introduction-osc

[11] Xcode: http://developer.apple.com/tools/xcode/

*Quartz Composer* is an opportunity for interactive motion graphics artists to explore *resolution independent* imaging and the sophisticated graphics technology of the latest *Mac OS*. *Quartz* is Apple's brand name for a suite of technologies known internally at Apple as *Core Graphics*. It is based on a PDF graphics/imaging model and extends from still image and text into 3D graphics with Open-GL and real-time video processing with a collection of techniques and APIs called *Core Video*.

In addition to real-time interactions and integration with the image processing libraries Apple calls *Core Image*[12] , *Quartz Composer*, according to Apple, can "make data-driven visual effects, and even perform live performance animations." (Apple Computer, 2007a).

*Quartz Composer* is a visual programming environment, where patches are plumbed together with 'noodles' that represent data flow through a sequence of connected objects. For the non-programmer, it is a joy to use – providing rapid prototyping of complex programmatic ideas. For example, applying live video textures to interactive forms in real-time 3D space is a five second operation – needing no lines of textual code.

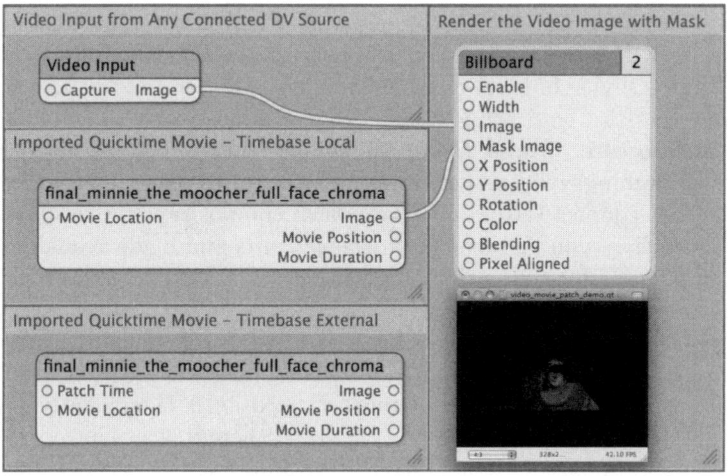


**Fig. 3.** Live video capture is blended with a movie in *Quartz Composer*

Figure 3 shows each kind of basic patch in *Quartz Composer* – *providers* (blue), *processors* (green) and *consumers* (pink) [6]. It also demonstrates how some patches have a 'time-base'. One imported Quicktime movie plays according to the frames per second of the composition, the other accepts numerical data on the input port called 'Patch Time'. Such changing numerical data could,

[12] *Core Image*: Resolution-independent 2D graphics based on PDF technologies and 3D graphics based on hardware accelerated *Open-GL*.

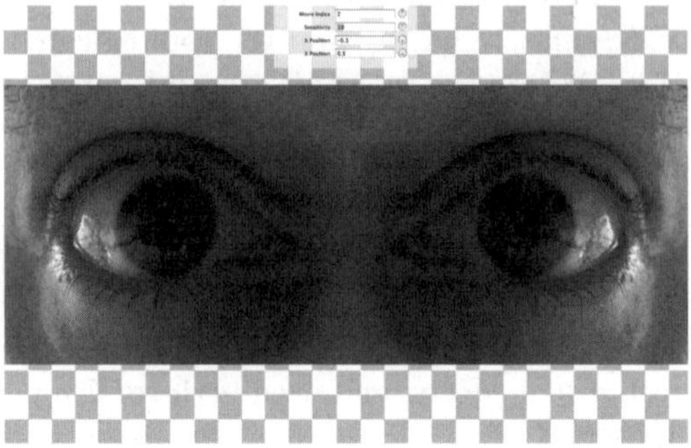

**Fig. 4.** Controlling the time-base of pre-recorded video in *Quartz Composer* – Interactive Video Eyes

for example, come from the normalised (−1 to 1) X co-ordinates of the mouse – effectively scrubbing the playback of the video. Figure 4 illustrates the scrubbing of a short movie that contains eyes moving left–centre–right–centre.

In an earlier iteration, *Quartz Composer*, as *PixelShox Studio*[13] had a vibrant life favoured by VJs and live-motion graphics artists. *PixelShox Studio* was written by Pierre-Olivier Latour, circa 2003. Pierre-Olivier Latour now works for Apple and *Quartz Composer* is a small, but significant, part of a wider development architecture. *Quartz Composer* compositions integrate nicely into the *Cocoa* programming environment, utilising *bindings* to make it easy to write applications that connect GUI controls to visual compositions. Also *Quartz Composer* compositions can be turned into *Image Units* and made available as video processing plug-ins for compatible applications, like Avid's *Xpress Pro*, Apple's *Final Cut Pro* and *Motion*[14].

An early vision for *PixelShox* was for artistic use "professionally in any project where interactive visuals are required: V-Jaying (sic), multimedia installations, presentations, [or] concerts." [7]. *Quartz Composer* is significantly pruned of functionality when compared with *PixelShox.* Although it was never completed, it is likely that the past functionality of *PixelShox* may be a rough roadmap of where *Quartz Composer* is heading. One repeated feature request is support for importing arbitrary 3D objects.

### 3.2 The Future of Quartz Composer

At the time of writing *Quartz Composer* is at version 3 – available in Mac OS 10.5 (Leopard)[15]. Apple have clearly signalled they value *Quartz Composer* as a unifying application across their developer technologies.

---

[13] *PixelShox Studio*: http://www.pol-online.net/pixelshox_technology/index.php
[14] Noise Industries *FXFactory*: http://www.noiseindustries.com/
[15] Mac OS 10.5 (Leopard): Released by Apple October 26th, 2007

*Quartz Composer 3* provides powerful, advanced functionality for programmers not available during the time-scale of the current project – but worth mentioning. For example, the 'custom patch' feature has provided free computer vision capabilities within *Quartz Composer 3*.

Apple provide an example 'custom patch' that brings the camera vision technique of 'optical flow' (See figure 5 and figure 6) to *Quartz Composer*. There are wide applications for digital puppetry using video based movement analysis for gestural interaction with virtual objects. In figure 6, the hand & teapot are moving upwards.

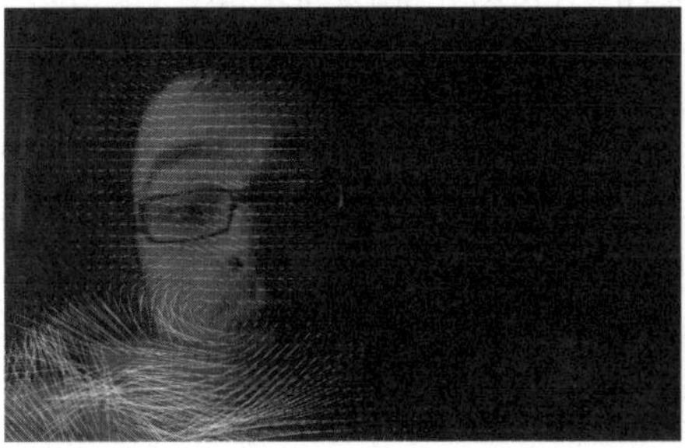

**Fig. 5.** Apple's Optical Flow plugin for *Quartz Composer 3*

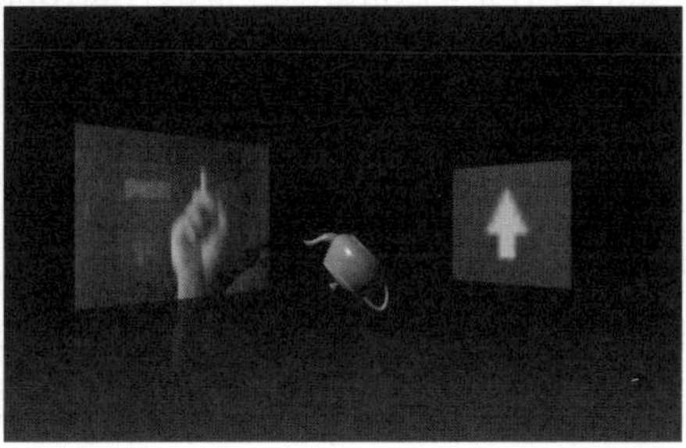

**Fig. 6.** Video Based Gestural Interface in *Quartz Composer 3*

Other new features in *Quartz Composer 3* include (i) custom patches – the most requested enhancement – to allow programmers to extend core functionality, (ii) advanced *GLSL* fragment and vertex shading environments, (iii) OSC – support for Open Sound Control, (iv) UDP server/client patches for network multicasting of composition data, (v) audio playback – *Quartz Composer* in Tiger (Mac OS 10.4) could not play back pre-recorded video with audio, (vi) system wide composition repository and 'nested' compositions will greatly simplify my 'monster patch' (figure 18). External compositions can be 'referenced' within a 'mother' composition – good for organisation and project management.

### 3.3 Custom Software Production

Using *Quartz Composer*, I created a monster control patch (figure 18, at the end of this document), that includes a *Wii-Remote* controlled avatar patch, and also allowed MIDI controlled sequencing of the scenography, special effects and character and avatar control, The monster patch included sub-patches that performed the following tasks: (i) hooks to integrate incoming data from the Nintendo *Wii-Remote*, (ii) chroma-keying using a core image kernel (written in *Open-GL Shader Language – GLSL*) and (iii) *Quartz Composer* patches for MIDI connectivity and keyboard control of screen objects and sequencing scenography.

### 3.4 Control and Visual Sequencing Software

Using Xcode, Apple's free developers environment, software was developed that used open source libraries to connect wirelessly via bluetooth to the Nintendo *Wii-Remote.* The *Wii-Remote* is a wireless pointer device and accelerometer that can detect motion and rotation in quasi 3D space. It has a numerous buttons, including a cursor pad. Wonderfully customisable, the *Wii-Remote* would control the movement, the pitch and roll and the eye movements of an avatar within the *Open-GL* 3D space of *Quartz Composer.* I called this software *QCWii.*

*QCWii* currently has the following functionality: (i) full screen capabilities for the embedded *Quartz Composer* composition – essential for projecting the results, (ii) a set of preferences controlling the Wii-Remote sensitivity, key mapping, scene sequencing and order configuration, color choices and more and (iii) Connectivity to the Nintendo *Wii-Remote* Controller ideal for virtual puppet control.

### 3.5 The *Wii-Remote* and *Quartz Composer*

The *QCWii* software uses an open source software library called *Wii-Remote,* part of *Darwiin Remote* – a project initiated by Hiroaki – available from Sourceforge[16].

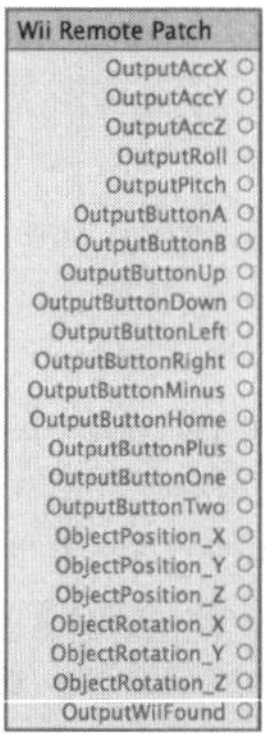


**Fig. 7.** The *Quartz Composer* patch listing the data received from a Nintendo *Wii-Remote*

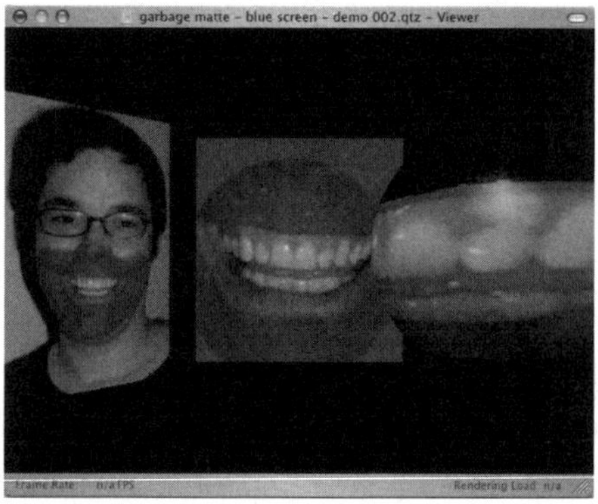


**Fig. 8.** Real-time Garbage Matte and Chroma-keying of Live Video Mouth in *Quartz Composer*

The open source *Wii-Remote* library routes data wirelessly via bluetooth from the *Wii-Remote* controller to a *Quartz Composer* composition patch (see figure 7) and all of the source code discussed in this paper is available on the author's web-site[17].

[16] *Darwiin-Remote* at Sourceforge: http://sourceforge.net/projects/darwiin-remote/

[17] Downloads and extra information from the Ian Grant's website: http://www.daisyrust.com/

It is theoretically possible to connect up to four *Wii-Remote* controllers to the software, allowing collaborative control over the digital puppet elements and the scenographic environment.

## 3.6 Chroma-keying with GLSL in *Quartz Composer*

The early design layout of the avatar was composed of a live video of a performer's chroma-keyed mouth (see Figure 8), talking and singing in real-time and pre-recorded video eyes, the gaze direction being controllable via the *Wii-Remote.* These video elements were composited (in real-time) and textured onto a sphere. In *Quartz Composer*, 3D objects are limited to basic primitives: spheres, cubes and teapots.

Figure 8 illustrates how *Quartz Composer* has been used to dynamically create a *garbage matte*[18] and chroma-keying to isolate non-blue elements of the actors face. There follows an annotation of the chroma-keying process in *Quartz Composer.* Figure 9 depicts the contents of a 'macro patch'. In *Quartz Composer*, a macro patch contains sub-patches that normally take incoming data, here image sources[19] , process that data and finally *publish* the resulting data. Making several patches into a macro is an organisational convenience and encapsulates re-usable functionality. Figure 9 uses some annotation and layout niceties available in Mac OS 10.5 (Leopard), that help to describe the data flow: in language: the sources images *provide* dimension data to math patches that perform calculations that are, in turn, passed to an 'image transform' patch to resize the background image to match the size and aspect ratio of the foreground image. The resized background images, the foreground image and two other values, a colour – called *keyColor* – and a number – called *sensitivity* – are passed into a 'Core Image Filter' patch. The 'Core Image Filter' executes a per-pixel routine on incoming source images written in *Open-GL Shader Language* (*GLSL*). The *GLSL* code embedded in the 'Core Image Filter' patch is reproduced below.

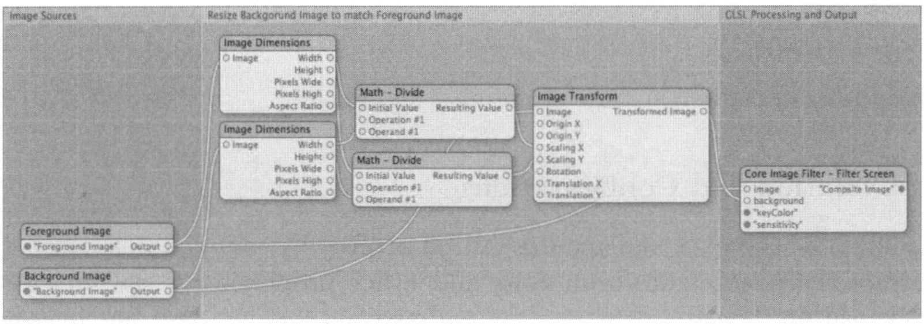


**Fig. 9.** Data processing in the chroma-keying sub-patch

---

[18] A garbage matte is a mask that crops out unwanted elements in a video image.

[19] An image can be a single still or each frame from a video sequence.

*Quartz Composer Core Image Kernel – Subset of GLSL*

```
const float pi = 3.141592654;

float distColorR(vec4 pix, vec4 color)
  {
    float diff = abs(pix.r - color.r);
    diff = diff > 3. ? 6. - diff : diff;
    return diff;
  }

vec4 RGBtoHSV(vec4 rgb)
  {
    float V = max(rgb.r, max(rgb.g, rgb.b));
    V = max(V, 0.0001); // V = 0.0 causes problems later

    float minC = min(rgb.r, min(rgb.g, rgb.b));
    float delta = V - minC;

    float S = delta / V;
    S = S > 1.0 ? 1.0 : S;

    float f = (rgb.r == minC) ? rgb.g - rgb.b : ((rgb.g == minC) ?
      rgb.b - rgb.r : rgb.r - rgb.g);
    float i = (rgb.r == minC) ? 3.0 :
      ((rgb.g == minC) ? 5.0 : 1.0);
    float H = i - f / (V - minC);

    return vec4(H, S, V, 1.0);
  }

kernel vec4 returnCompImage(sampler image, sampler background,
  __color keyColor, float sensitivity)
  {
    vec4 pix = sample(image, samplerCoord(image));
    vec4 backpix = sample(background, samplerCoord(background));
    vec4 color2 = unpremultiply(keyColor);
    vec4 hsv = RGBtoHSV(pix);

    float colorDist = distColorR(hsv,RGBtoHSV(color2));
    float diff = colorDist - 1./sensitivity;

    diff = hsv.b < 0.05 ? 1.0 : diff;

    pix = compare(vec4(diff,diff,diff,1.0), backpix, pix);
    pix.a = 1.0;
    return pix;
  }
```

(Chroma Keying Example GLSL Code adapted from Sam Kass)[20]

### 3.7 Evolution and Configurations

The images of the eyes and mouth can be arbitrarily mapped onto any object or surface. Different transformations and other properties of the images, e.g. hue, saturation, transparency, can be mapped onto sliders and buttons on the Behringer MIDI controller[21] and adjusted as needed during the performance. In figures 10–11 and in the visual documentation, a few different configurations can

[20] Sam Kass. Source: http://www.samkass.com/blog/

[21] Behringer Controller Desk: http://www.behringer.com/BCF2000/index.cfm

be seen. Compare figure 10 with the avatar in other figures: we achieve expressivity with simple translations of the image elements controlled by the *Wii-Remote*. In figure 10 the eyes are mapped onto spheres. MIDI sliders control the color saturation (here deep red) and scale of the objects. The *Wii-Remote* controls rotation, object position and zoom of the figure. In figure 11, we control position, scaling, rotation and the visibility of other elements to make a spontaneous composition.

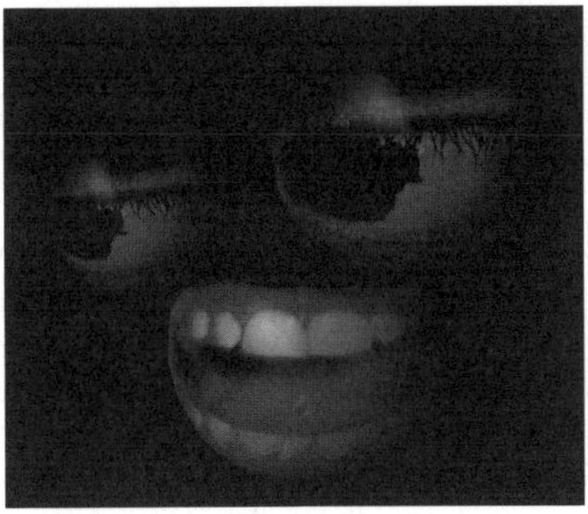

**Fig. 10.** The avatar in performance

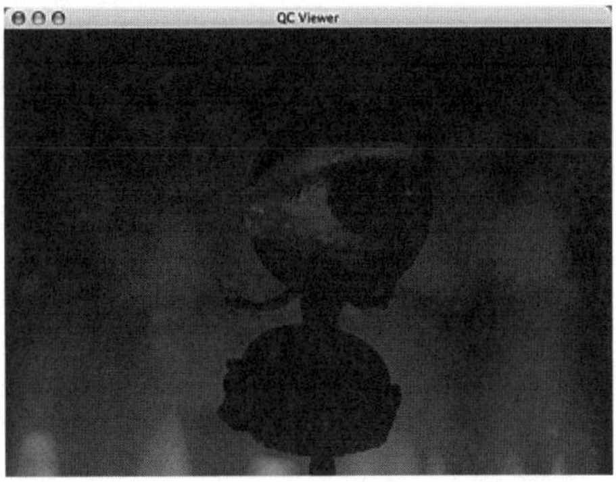

**Fig. 11.** Improvisational avatar control – mouth and other eye turned off

# 4 Visual Documentation with Commentary

## 4.1 Content Creation

To generate the scenographic material, I considered the lyrics of *Minnie the Moocher*[22] and watched ten hours of cartoons by the Fleischer studios. Most of the animations are now in the public domain, allowing mash-ups and remixing. Particularly, I looked at the work containing Cab Calloway and featuring the character *Betty Boop*. I was scouting for figures, objects, scenes and backgrounds. The basic process was to collect the video sequence or frame-grab visuals I wished to use as inspiration for scenes and objects in the performance design.

To give a sense of the available scenographic elements, how they were designed, used and how they are 'dynamic', there follows a scene-by-scene documentation and commentary.

**Figure 12:** The movie title text has an animated blur and is designed to look like poor tele-cined old film. The theatre frame is from a public domain cartoon. The animated smoke effect (hard to see in the still) is generated in *Quartz Composer* and applied in real-time. The title text is dynamic and can be edited in the application preferences, again in real-time – no re-rendering is necessary.

[22] *Minnie the Moocher* (Mills-Calloway): http://www.heptune.com/minnieth.html

**Figure 13:** This is an example of the live video mouth and pre-recorded eyes being composited into a final animated image. Here the video puppet is a fixed scene element. The easel image can be rotated in 3D space and faded in/out using the midi controllers sliders.

**Figure 14:** These are dynamic elements and can appear when-ever and where-ever the operator wishes. The iris can be used for scene transitions or to visually frame the scene providing aesthetic focus. A real-time flame effect can be saturated or de-saturated at will, allowing a careful use of colour within the largely monochrome environment. Currently the silhouette subtly moves at the hip, but is not fully articulated. The 2D shadow-graph/shadow puppet theatre look is flexible and allows simple perspective and depth effects to work.

**Figure 15 and 17** illustrate a multi-planer, theatrical perspective constructed from four flat layers, with transparency. This scene can be rotated using the MIDI sliders in *Open-GL* 3D space] – some may call it – *2-and-a-half-D.* I was particularly looking for source scenes that contained clear receding perspective with single or multiple vanishing points. I could use these scenes to explore an idea I had to set up a multi-plane version of the frame in *Open-GL* 3D space (in *Quartz Composer*). The process involved painting mattes, masking elements and exporting transparent PNGs. I masked the foreground and background characters – isolating them from the background, and exporting them as separate PNGs. I then re-painted the missing background on the back image, using *Photoshop* and a *Wacom* Tablet. The separate PNG (each with alpha transparency) were then layered in 3D space in *Quartz Composer*. I applied blur filters to each element where the 'radius' of the blur was controllable by the MIDI faders – allowing a fake 'depth of field' effect to be created and, as I discovered with play, a 'rack focus' or 'pulling focus' effect. Additionally, the whole environment could be rotated in 3D space across all axis. This created nice parallax movement effects and enabled a transition between the empty ballroom and the scene populated with characters.

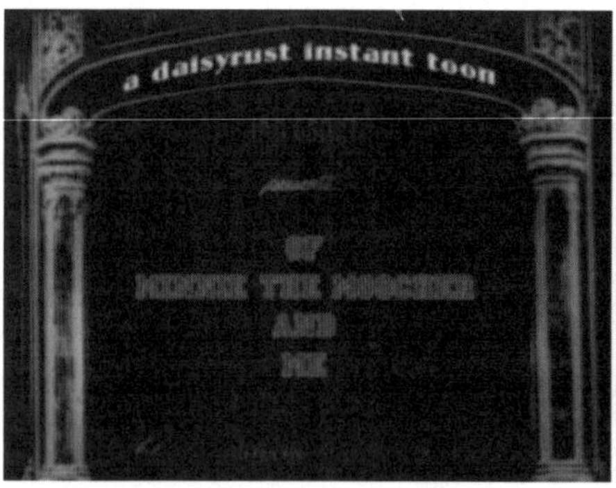


**Fig. 12.** Full title (with iris)

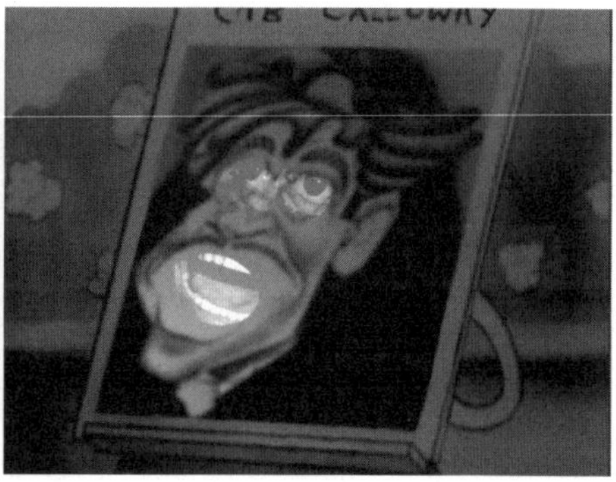

**Fig. 13.** Easel with video composite

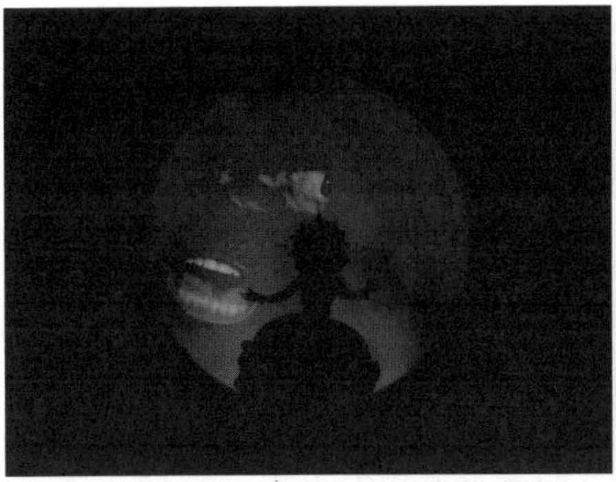

**Fig. 14.** Recorded eyes and live mouth

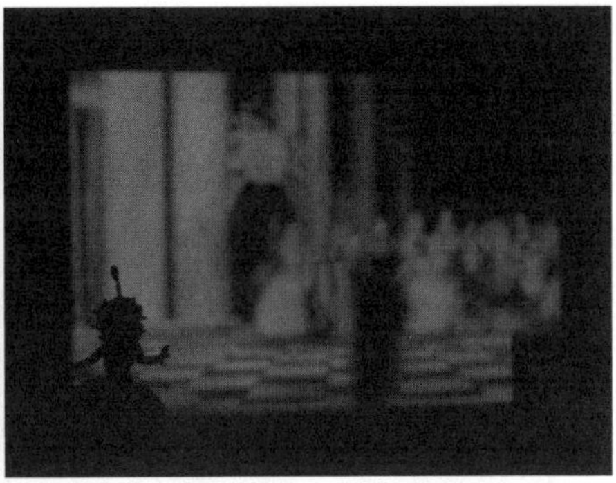

**Fig. 15.** Minnie and the King of Sweden

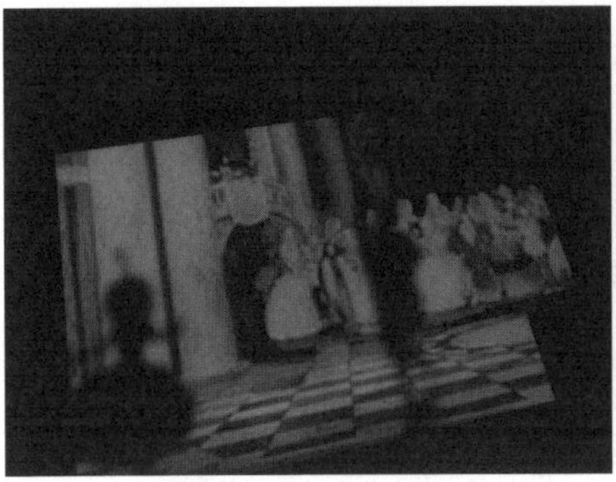

**Fig. 16.** 3D multi-plane and perspective

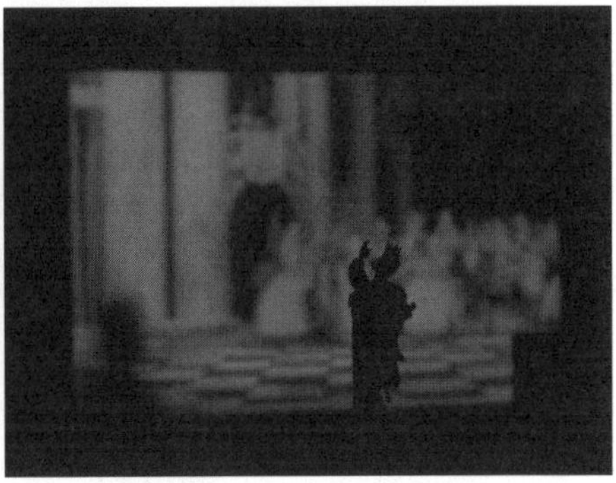

**Fig. 17.** Rack focus and depth of field

## 5 Artistic Insights

Accident, improvisation and deviation from planning are important. The exercise of and desire to assert control leads to a dialectic when designing an 'open', improvisational structure for performance. The haptic wireless controller leads to a great sense of playfulness and with further development will yield significant control over numerous properties of the on-screen objects.

A couple of lovely moments of playful, serendipitous discovery: (i) Duplicate eye movies playing back slightly out of sync made gains in general expressivity, (ii) Silhouetting characters for copyright reasons introduced a wonderful resonance of a different puppetry tradition – shadow theatre, particularly the amazing shadow films of Lotte Reiniger.

It was quite an accident that some of the frames from the sequence resembled the visual style of Reiniger's shadow puppet films. The *Minnie* character in performance animates quite subtly, pivoting at the waist. I wish to expand the control over these elements, with multiple *Wii-Remote* controllers, introducing a game-like collaborative control over the performance space and objects.

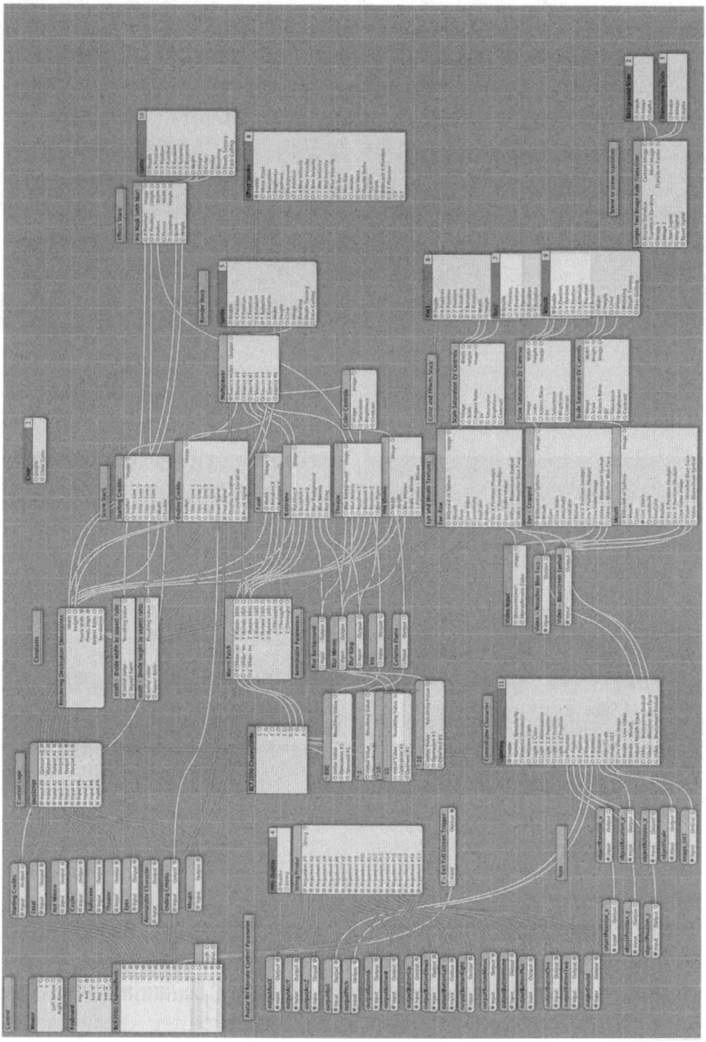

**Fig. 18.** A screen shot of the top level of the main *Quartz Composer* patch

I wish to refine the control system and expand the visual repertoire. A key to success in performance is, I feel, the availability of a large number of scenographic elements and character objects that can be re-configured by an improvising operator on-the-fly. Rehearsal is necessary to overcome the simple linear sequence of pre-defined story-elements. The operator should be knowledgeable about the content of the system in order to be able to improvise and play. The act of performance with such a system needs time and practice in order to achieve spontaneity through control.

## Acknowledgments

Many thanks to the open source project *Darwiin Remote* initiated by Hiroaki for the *Wii-remote* connection framework and Jasen Jacobsen for advice and sample code on how to 'smooth' the *Wii-Remote* values for use in animation. Thanks to Sam Kass for sharing great *Quartz Composer GLSL* code. A big thank you to Stefan Müller Arisona and the DAW07 team in Zurich.

## References

1. Faulkner, M. (ed.): VJ: Audio-Visual Art and VJ Culture (with DVD), London, Laurence King (2006)
2. Wikipedia Community. Augmented Reality. retrieved 10/3/2007 (2007), `http://en.wikipedia.org/wiki/Augmented_reality`
3. Han, J.: Multi-Touch Interaction Research (2006), retrieved 1/1/2008, `http://cs.nyu.edu/~jhan/ftirtouch/index.html`
4. Sieger cited Gere, Charlie: Art, Time and Technology, Oxford, Berg, p. 26 (2006)
5. Gere. Ibid. p.26
6. Apple Computer. Quartz Composer User Guide (2008), retrieved 1/1/2008, from `http://developer.apple.com/documentation/GraphicsImaging/Conceptual/QuartzComposerUserGuide/qc_intro/chapter_1_section_1.html`
7. Latour, P.-O.: PixelShox Studio (2006), retrieved 1/1/2008, `http://www.pol-online.net/pixelshox_technology/index.php`

# Formalized and Non-formalized Expression in Musical Interfaces

Cornelius Poepel[1,2]

[1] Fachhochschule Ansbach, University of Applied Sciences, Residenzstrasse 8, D-91522 Ansbach, Germany
[2] Music Department, The University of Birmingham, Edgbaston, Birmingham B15 2TT, United Kingdom
cornelius.poepel@fh-ansbach.de

**Abstract.** Many musical interfaces are designed to enable musical expression. In this process it is the task of the interface to generate data transmitting the expressivity of the performer's gestures to the synthesis engine. The instrument has to be open or transparent to the performers actions. Building interfaces with this kind of openness may be seen as a problem in interface development because the actions of the performer have to be translated from a phenomenological level to a formal level. This paper investigates the idea to create openness by leaving essentials non-formalized. Examples of implementations in the fields of musical instruments and computer games using this method are presented. The tasks of openness, transparency and flexibility for the users intentions are discussed.

## 1 Introduction

In order to play computer based musical instruments, adequate interfaces are necessary. The construction and use of new controllers has become a wide field of research exemplified by the NIME conference (New Interfaces for Musical Expression) [1]. A primary goal is the creation of new interfaces with high potential for musical expression.

This paper investigates two basic approaches found in interface design. One approach tries to model the performer and to build interfaces that measure all essential playing parameters in order to provide explicit data of the performer's actions. Therefore the input given by the performer to the system has to be formalized. The other approach is based on an architecture that makes use of an instrument's raw and non-analyzed audio signal, a stream which includes implicit data of the performer's actions. This reduces the necessity to formalize all essential playing parameters because they can be perceived in the output signal as long as they are not disrupted in the synthesis algorithm.

The investigation of both mentioned approaches is done by using a set of necessities in the construction process and by applying these necessities to the example of a computer-based instrument for string players. We then point to

R. Adams, S. Gibson, and S. Müller Arisona (Eds.): DAW/IF 2006/2007, CCIS 7, pp. 358–373, 2008.

problems arriving in this process. The paper does not aim to present new technology, instead, the paper focuses on a contribution to the research field of computer music by presenting an increased and more differentiated view on sound synthesis, arrived at by leaving essentials non-formalised.

Musicians often describe their instruments and playing methods by referring to the phenomena they perceive during playing. In order to take those descriptions into account when modeling the performer and constructing the interface, phenomenological described actions of the performer have to be transformed to formal descriptions. Sections 3 and 4 focus on that process. The approach to use implicit data and thus to leave essentials non-formalized is described in section 5. An example of an instrument based on a traditional viola is presented. Besides musical performance, the question of what the player does or might want to do, is also important in computer game design. The current research in musical interfaces uses methods of control where essential playing parameters are investigated and then formalized in computer applications. Facing this fact our proposal to build interactive systems using the construction principle of leaving essentials non-formalized raises the question whether this method is found in other domains of computer interaction. Therefore section 6 provides examples of computer game architectures that make use of the approach to keep essentials non-formalized. In section 7 the possible qualities and impact, which presented construction principles may have on musical interfaces, are discussed.

The digital instruments addressed here cater to traditional musicians seeking to expand their repertoire of sounds or timbre. The interfaces of such instruments are designed to make use of existing skills. Ideally one would examine different types of traditional instruments, however, this is beyond the scope of this paper. While it may be possible to use the proposed methods for different types of instruments, practical examples are mainly relate to bowed stringed instruments.

## 2 Background

Research in musical interfaces often examines construction principles as a means to achieve musical goals. What we are focusing on here is the goal of musical expression and the construction principles found

### 2.1 Expression

The question of what can be understood by the term ‘expressivity’ in this context was addressed by Dobiran and Koppelman [6]. They distinguish between expression in composition and expression in performance. Focusing on performance-interfaces, they see the origin of expression in the performer. The interface should transmit the musical information the performer puts into the interface, or better still, amplify it. A precondition for the construction of such an interface is a detailed consideration of “how the performer will provide musical expression.”

### 2.2 Measure Performer's Inputs

It is a commonly found conviction that an electronic measurement process could, in principle, capture all constitutive actions of the performer. An example may be seen in the description of the hypercello [11] where Paradiso states that "The hypercello sensors measured the player's inputs to the instrument and used them to control a range of sound sources. The goal of the sensing was to unobtrusively and responsively detect the player's actions as he followed notated music."

### 2.3 Mapping

Fels, Gadd and Mulder focus on questions regarding the transparency of a new instrument [7]. They assume an interface will measure essentials in the playing process. They further assume that an adequate mapping method can solve the problem of accurately reflecting and communicating the expressive intent of the performer to the audience. Concerning their idea of transparency they point to the role of the listeners, stating that "The expressivity of an instrument is dependent on the transparency of the mapping for both the player and the audience." The transparency of an instrument can thus be influenced crucially by the perceptual abilities of the listeners.

### 2.4 Select Measurements

In the Digital Stradivarius Project, Schoner [21] uses the synthesis method of Cluster Weighted Modeling to simulate the sound of a Stradivari violin as well as the sound of other instruments or singing voices. Similar to physical modeling, this synthesis method is constructed to be driven directly by the measurement output tracking the actions of the performer. While this approach does not need to focus on questions of mapping, it still has to ask how the performer will create a musical input to the system and thus, which physical measurements of the musical input are necessary. Schoner mentiones that "Defining and carefully executing these measurements was assumed crucial for the success of the model." Criteria to identify these measurements according to Schoner are: hierarchy of input parameters, the physical and technical possibility of measuring these parameters, and signal to noise ratio of the measurement process. It is the task of the developer to investigate and determine the hierarchy of input parameters and to develop appropriate measurement methods.

### 2.5 Formalize Measurements

Prem [16] analyses the process of measurement in control systems for robots. Regarding the question of how the measurement process can be formalized, Prem expresses the following conviction:"It was already John von Neumann who pointed out that results of measurements, choices of observables, the construction of measurement devices and the measurement process itself cannot in principle be formalized [25], [26]. The reason lies in the fact that the process of measurement is not of a purely formal nature." Due to the fact that two dynamical systems interact the measurement process provides an "inherently dynamic nature." An example can be seen in the measurement of electrons. It is obvious that the electrons of a measurement device will influence the behaviour of the electrons to be measured. In seeking to formalize measurement parameters of musical interfaces as control inputs for music making, the problem of measurement validity could also be a factor in musical performance systems. It is important therefore to ask for the conditions under which this factor influences musical expression.

### 2.6 Levels in Expression to Convey

With the development of the Conductors Jacket, a device to analyze the process of conducting in order to control a virtual orchestra, Marrin has investigated the important factors in expressive music [9]. Expression is seen here as the creation of emotion.

When discussing "Interpretative variation as the key to emotion in music" Marrin distinguishes between variations on a macrostructural level (such as the tempo) and variations on a microstructural level. Such slight variations may be done in for example phrasing, timbre, or articulation. Laying on a microstructural level however, they have a significant effect on a specific expression, sometimes more significant than those on the macrostructural level. Beyond these two levels Marrin mentions the dimension of "the magical, deeply felt, emotional (some might call it spiritual) aspect that touches the core of our humanity." She reports that "many dedicated musicians believe that this aspect is not quantifiable."

While Marrin states that the technology we have so far is not "for the most part, able to convey this aspect" she is also convinced that future developments will offer solutions. Looking at the instruments built from wood and metal she mentions "there is no reason that we can't do the same with silicon and electrons." However, it is a task of the future to figure out how to do that. Time is a luxury from which acoustic instruments have benefitted greatly.

## 3 The Performer's Actions

If we accept that the instrument has to be open or transparent to the performer's actions, the questions come up what the performer's actions are and what is meant with the terms 'open' and 'transparent'.

### 3.1 Open and Transparent

The openness that is strived for here is understood as the principal possibility to influence the sound result with all actions that might be meaningful for the performer in the performer-instrument interaction. It would for example not be open if the performer plays different dynamics and the interface had no ability to transmit these changes.

Transparency in this paper is understood as the possibility for the performer to generate a result that is similar to what the performer expects according to the knowledge and skills the performer already has (as long as the instrument is relying on these already existing skills). The results can differ slightly from what is expected, however, they have to lie within an expected range. In the case of a piano interface, transparency would not be achieved if the keystroke the performer uses to generate a sound did not result in a similar ability to form the sound the performer is used to from the acoustic piano. This means that openness and transparency are dependent on the interface as well as on the performer's subjective experience concerning which actions are thought to be meaningful and the range of similarity that is defined by the performer.

### 3.2 Fields of Analysis

In order to clarify the performer-instrument relationship one must seek to understand both, the performers' actions and their expectations regarding the musical instrument. What are the performer's actions? There are five fields that may be seen as important resources to answer this question:

- Individual performers and their actions: One can simply ask them: "What are you doing when you play?"
- Instrumental pedagogy: This is important, because the questions of how to play the instrument or what to do when playing the instrument are addressed.
- Musicians rehearsing together: One can study what musicians achieve and how musicians explain to each other what to do.
- The luthier's workshop: Musicians talk about instrumental requirements when their instrument has to be adjusted or when they seek to buy a new instrument.
- Physical analysis: Measurement of playing parameters for individual performers.

Research in musical instruments is merely focused on physical analysis. It should be asked why other fields are little regarded.

### 3.3 Levels of Reality

Quantifiable data can be gained through the measurement of playing parameters. This data addresses the performer-instrument interaction related to a physical level of description.

In contrast, looking at the literature of instrumental pedagogy, or asking individual performers, will provide descriptions that can be classified on a phenomenological level. Performers as well as teachers will describe the performer-instrument-interaction usually on the basis of perceived phenomena and not on physical measurement results. It may be seen as an open question whether "the reality" about instrumental playing or what "in fact" happens when a performer performs is better described on the phenomenological level or on the physical level.

Interfaces will ultimately succeed or fail in addressing the concerns of users. Therefore, one might argue that phenomenological descriptions are from the user's perspective of what matters in fact, and that descriptions on the physical level should be viewed as abstractions of the player's actions for our purposes here.

### 3.4 Examples of Performer's Actions

As section 3 asks for the actions of a performer, we provide some concrete examples of what a string player's actions can be:
- Playing with different pitches, dynamics, bowings (for example martelé, detaché, spiccatto), finger pressure, bow speed, bow pressure, bow position, bow angle, vibratos, articulations, timbre, muscle tensions.
- Playing vowel and consonant notes, more or less open or full tones, more or less lively, morendo, aggressive, delightful.
- Leaning into the sound, pulling the tone, crushing the tone, making the note bigger or smaller, labored, penetrating.

This list is of course not complete. It would have to include relevant actions that could be gathered in the fields mentioned in section 3.2.

## 4 Phenomenological and Formalized Level

The process of translation from a phenomenological to a formalized level is a problem to be solved in the construction of many computer-based instruments. Since this domain is important here but hardly regarded in the present literature on musical interfaces the following sections will describe this process.

### 4.1 Requirements

In answering the question of what the interface and resulting instrument has to be open and transparent to, one will get a list of requirements. It is common in software engineering to define a requirements document for a system that has to be developed [22].

According to our list of string players' actions in section 4, one might find the following in a requirements document of a string synthesizer:
- The instrument should react adequately to different pitches, dynamics, bowings, finger pressure, bow speed, bow pressure, bow position, bow angle, vibratos, articulations, timbre, muscle tensions.
- It should be possible to play vowel and consonant notes, more or less open or full tones, more or less lively, morendo, aggressive, delightful.
- It should provide the possibility to lean into the sound, pull the tone, crush the tone, make the note more or less big, labored and penetrating.

### 4.2 Formal Specification

Similar to our requirements such documents contain user needs and user descriptions in natural language and will have to be translated into a more detailed software requirements specification. The process of arriving at a formal specification that can be fully translated into code in a programming language, must include the transformation from a non-formal to a formal specification. This process is called formalization and is understood here as the transfer of a procedure or an object into a form where it can be described completely and definitivly (i.e. it will be non-interpretable) by a finite algorithm. Formalization can be seen as a problem, because answers to the question of what the performer does when playing

- are described in natural language and thus may be interpreted in different ways,
- may include descriptions that cannot be expressed in non-interpretable terms because performers may wish to play in an undefined grey zone in specific moments,
- may be different from person to person (playing style) and thus be incomplete from a general point of view,
- may not offer a known physical relation in order to be measurable (at present),
- may include needs - and thus necessary tracking methods - of an unlimited ability to create slightly different but new playing methods (and micro playing parameters) according to situations that come up in a new playing context.

An example concerning the mentioned requirements: It is possible to track playing parameters like pitch, bow speed or muscle tensions due to the obvious physical relations. But it is not yet possible to track how much a performer leans into the tone due to the missing physical relation. According to the physicist and violinmaker Schleske [20] there is no available physical description of 'leaning into the tone'.

### 4.3 Abstraction

It is a common conviction in software engineering that formalization of descriptions in a requirements document can be done by making them more detailed and more precise until the formal level is reached. This is an operation that involves the process of abstraction.

Abstraction will free objects or processes from inessentials and reduce their descriptions to essentials. Winograd and Flores [28] describe a problem coming with such a deliverance. Citing Heideggers concept of objects that are"ready-at-hand" when they are new and get "present-at-hand" when we start to treat those by "analyzing it in terms of objects and their properties," they conclude that abstraction, in general, generates a blindness due to the limited view as "to what can be expressed in the terms we have adopted."

In the case of a musical interface one might say that the system specification was not complete. However, one may ask whether it is in fact possible to get a 100% complete software specification. According to the experiences of Sommerville [22] one would have to say that it is not possible. An important question would then be whether the blindness of the interface bothers the performer and if so, how much.

A general problem occurs if a need on the requirement document contains an open ended explorability of the instrument. Often musicians say that they have to newly adapt or re-learn again their instrument every day, and that it is in fact interesting to explore it and adapt to it again and again and again. An example may be found in the cellist Pablo Casals [5]. If the requirements document specifies a requirement to have a part of the interface and instrument "ready-to-hand" it would be impossible to find a fitting abstraction. This process would already make it "present-at-hand".

### 4.4 Performer's Focus Move

As pointed out in section 2.5, formalization of the measuring process may be a problem because two dynamic systems interact. Measuring the playing parameters in order to get data on the performer's actions would be disruptive and therefore inaccurate if the measuring process causes the performer to do other actions than intended.

According to the author's experience one may find a move of focus when playing systems that mainly use measurement values to control the sound [12]. In a bowed stringed instrument the focus moves from the response of string to the response of the tracking system because the tracking systems can cause values that were not intended. A participant in a study [13] mentioned: "With this instrument one has to play extremely correct. Otherwise I get bubbling sounds I don't want to have. I feel musically restricted." This problem was caused by pitch tracking values that started to wobble when the audio signal of the string had a specific amount of noise. However, using some kind of noisy and knocking sounds is necessary for a string player in order to generate consonant sounds [8] necessary for articulation.

In this case one can say that the formalization of the measuring process has been done. However, it was not done correctly because the measurement disturbingly influences the object that has to be measured. One may conclude that the problem to formalize the process of measurement described in section 2.5 can play a crucial role in musical interfaces. Where the measurement changes the behaviour of the performer, the formalization has failed.

## 5 Leaving Essentials Non-formalized

As mentioned in the introduction the common approach to drive sound synthesis is based on a fixed set of discrete input parameters and follows the idea to formalize essentials.

### 5.1 Parameter Based Approach

Focusing on practical aspects in the design of new computer based instruments, the problems researchers are dealing with often lie in two fields:

1. Physical measurement one would want to do is not possible because of missing or not available methods of measuring.
2. The translation from the phenomenological level to the level of physical descriptions is not possible due to a lack of physical models forming the basis to explain the addressed phenomena.

Therefore a lot of research has been done into the development of required methods of measurement and the search for physical models that may form the base to understand selected phenomena. For example the physical rules of traditional instruments have been studied [29], the performer-instrument-interaction has been investigated [18] [2] or the gestures in playing and their relation to the produced sound have been examined[27].

A general idea behind this research may be found in the aim to gain knowledge of where the expressive potential of traditional instruments comes from and to arrive at an adequate abstraction of tasks in the requirements document in order to have computer based instruments that are open, transparent, and expressive. With this knowledge, essential coherences could be described physically and essential playing parameters could be defined. With these abstractions the formal specification becomes possible because essentials could be formalized. It is of great importance to continue this approach, however, it is possible that other approaches would be equally rewarding and as such raises the question whether alternatives are available.

### 5.2 Audio Signal Based Approach

An approach from a different direction can be seen as an alternative. This approach tries to create openness by leaving essentials non-formalized [23]. An implementation for a synthesizer-viola making use of this approach has been described [12]. Additions for a synthesizer-trumpet were presented [15], and an overview on the philosophy, implementations and user experiences with audio signal driven methods have been illustrated [14]. The basic system architecture that is common in musical interface research uses playing parameters as the base to control the synthesized sound. In contrast, the approach outlined above uses the raw and unanalyzed audio signal as the basis to drive the synthesis algorithm. Therefore it is called "Audio Signal Driven Sound Synthesis" (ASDSS). Where necessary - it depends on the synthesis method used - the synthesized sound is modified indirectly by parameters extracted from the audio signal. The basic principle is presented in figure 1.

### 5.3 Advantages and Drawbacks

If we adopt the audio signal based approach, we need to ask how the resulting instruments relate to the previously mentioned tasks in requirement documents. Assuming the possibility to bring the personal expression of a performer to the audio signal of the string of a bodiless violin the openness will be given because all the actions of a string player affect the sound of the string. It is not necessary to transform natural language descriptions from a non-formal to a formal level

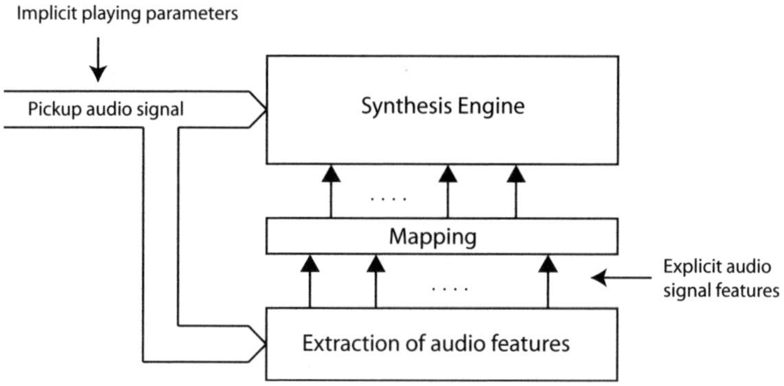


**Fig. 1.** Basic principle of Audio Signal Driven Sound Synthesis

reasoning in the performer's essential actions which are implicit in the resulting audio signal. Since the audio signal mainly drives the synthesized sound an explicit representation of all essential performer actions is not necessary. The audio signal contains essential parameters of the performer already. The two research fields mentioned in the beginning of section 5.1 can thus be seen as secondary due to the ability of this architecture to utilize parameters or nuances that are not modeled and measured. However, transparency is still an issue. In this approach it is the task of the algorithm to be transparent.

An example where transparency is disrupted may be found in modified Subtractive Synthesis (see figure 2) [14]. The timbre of the sound will change significantly as long as the filter frequency is not modified by measurement values of a pitch tracker. In this case the algorithm has to be made transparent by influencing it with measurement data of the input signal. As soon as the transparency is re-established, the performer can still make use of playing parameters or methods from the requirements list, which are not formalized and coupled with a measurement.

One has to say clearly that this method has an important drawback. The common requirement of an interface to drive any kind of parameter driven sound synthesis is not met. Known methods of sound synthesis have to be modified in order to be driven with the audio signal.

## 6 Openness in Computer Games

The alternative to the common approach in sound synthesis (see section 5.2) may be seen as a weak alternative due to its minimal use in commercial synthesizers and the low number of ASDSS-based implementations discussed in research so far. Due to the mentioned advantages it is interesting to see whether basic principles of this approach are found in other domains of computer applications as well. Parallels can be found in the construction of computer games and will described

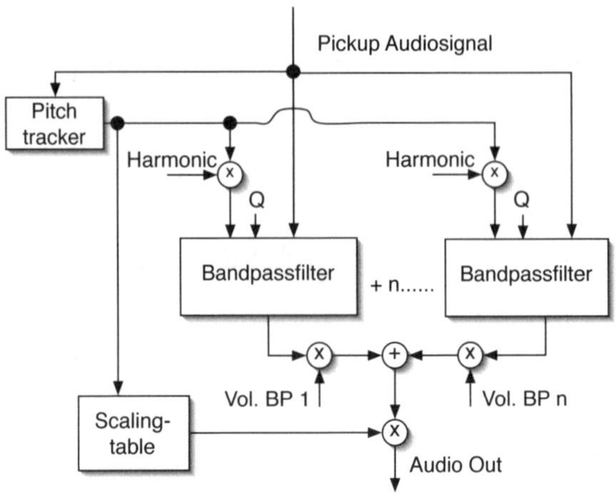


**Fig. 2.** Modified Subtractive Synthesis

below. The principles presented here allow the argument that a non-formalized approach to sound synthesis has potential for further investigation.

Similar to the requirements document for computer based musical instruments computer games are usually built with the help of a game design document. This document tries to describe the complete game in order to give the developers the information necessary to implement the game. It includes descriptions about the general idea and goals of the game as well as detailed ideas about e.g. game characters, user interfaces, weapons, sounds, world layout etc. In order to provide a satisfying interaction, the designers will consider the question of how a player might want to interact inside of the game.

### 6.1 The Problem of Anticipation

Trogemann [23] mentions a problem arising from anticipation in designing computer games. As games increased in complexity, a point was passed beyond which developers were unable to anticipate all the possible actions of a player. According to Trogemann the solution game developers are using recently is to develop systems where this detailed anticipative process is no longer necessary. These systems build a framework where all states occur as implicit natural states within the system and not as explicit implemented features about what exactly the player is doing at present. One might say that in this approach the essentials of what the player does in detail are not formalized. The code does not "know" or analyze what the player does in a specific moment. However, the framework in which all the actions happen are of course formalized.

### 6.2 Examples

Examples may be found in many recent computer games. Half Life 2 [24], one of the most sold games in 2004, offers features where the physical behavior of elements is modeled while the states the player has to reach and the possible ways in which this might be done (anticipation) are not explicitly formalized [19].

An example from Half Live 2: the player has to get onto a wall in order to proceed. In front of the wall a seesaw as well as some bricks are found. If the side of the seesaw that is pointing to the wall is up one might be able to jump from this side onto the wall. Placing the bricks on the other side of the seesaw enables the player to run over it and to jump upon the wall. However, it is also possible to put some bricks closer to the middle of the seesaw and to jump on it. The seesaw starts to swing. By running and jumping in the right moment the player will be able to jump onto the wall. Perhaps one could build stairs with the bricks in front of the wall and walk over it. Perhaps one could fetch objects from other places to build a way in order to get onto the wall. Different solutions are possible and can be found in several game related websites.

The user can recognize the mentioned states, however, using a physical engine it is not longer necessary to formalize these explicitly. The openness is achieved by leaving such essentials non-formalized. It is not necessary for the developer to explicitly implement the state 'whipping seesaw' or 'stairs in front of wall' or any other possibility that would allow the player to jump onto the wall. These options are implemented implicitly by using the physical engine. Using this basic principle in computer games, the user might find methods to solve problems that were not even thought of by the developers.

A precedent of such physical engines, and thus the approach not to anticipate every action a player might want to do, may be found in earlier games like Lemmings [17]. There it is possible to place workers with specific tasks, the so called lemmings, on different places influencing the movement of the lemming community. It is obvious that situations might arrive that the developers did not anticipate when designing the game. This openness might be an important reason for the success of this game.

However, since the physical engine and the presentation in Half Life 2 tries to be "realistic" the user does not need to adapt to the game as much as an adaptation in Lemmings is necessary. In other words, the goal to use existing knowledge in order to deal with game problems may be reached more easily when using a highly developed physical engine.

More sophisticated gaming concepts, which we find for example in the game Oblivion [4] even leave the player in an open concept concerning the general goal or history of the game. While there is a main story, it can always be left and it is possible to define personal goals that have nothing to do with the presupposed goals of the game. It depends on the fun-parameters of the player to define what actions to do when playing this game.

### 6.3 Restricted Openness

A problem in this kind of open systems may occur due to the fact that any game will have to have somehow an anticipative approach in order to answer the question: Why should this game be interesting for a player? One might conclude that the anticipation will never be complete. Oblivion's precedent the game Morrowind [3] for example enables a player by several tricky combinations to mix a drink that makes the player so strong that she or he can beat all enemies easily [19]. In case several of such possibilities are found in the game this may be estimated as a "killer-criteria for its success. In order to minimize such problems the principal openness a game could have, is often restricted. While it is important to give the player the feeling that in this game a lot of existing knowledge can be used to master challenges, the number of possibilities in a concrete situation is often kept much smaller than the basic principle of software construction would allow.

## 7 Discussion

As pointed out earlier, musical interfaces that use a fixed set of defined input-parameters are limited in their openness. Concerning flexibility the user will be restricted. It is not possible to focus playing methods and thus parameters that were estimated to be not important and have therefore not been implemented. The flexibility a performer might have, is therefore fixed into a set of actions predefined by the construction of the interface. This inflexibility goes along with the inflexibility of the computer game Lemmings described in section 6.2.

One might say that a cello, a drum, or a piano is not flexible due to the fact that a cello always sounds like a cello and cannot switch or morph to other sounds. This is of course a true limitation. With respect to the flexibility and potential for expression the performer has within a specific sound, one can say that new interfaces based on the idea of traditional instruments have not yet been - except the keyboard - tremendously successful. Due to this reason research on traditional instruments and the comparison of newly developed instruments to traditional ones is still found often in musical interface publications [7].

### 7.1 Performer's Estimations

According to the author's experience, derived from discussions and an empirical study [13] involving digital bowed stringed instruments and traditional instrumentalists, the loss of openness, transparency and flexibility compared with the possible advantages in sound variations often leads to a rejection of new instruments. Marrin [9] shows similar experiences when she writes "There are good reasons why most musicians have not yet traded in their guitars, violins, or conducting batons for new technologies." She is convinced "that these technologies do not yet convey the most deeply meaningful aspects of human expression."

On the other hand one may say, that the world of traditional musicians is a slowly decreasing one, while lots of wonderful and fascinating art work has been done in the area of digital arts. This is an increasing field with innumerable and highly skilled artists. After discussions with students in the field of media arts, the author came to the conclusion that media musicians may have absolutely no problem with interfaces using a limited fixed set of parameters.

As Moog pointed out [10] also the theremin with only two parameter inputs (frequency and amplitude) has a high potential for expression. So, why should it be important to distinguish between formalized and non-formalized aspects in musical interfaces and to focus this field?

### 7.2 Different Qualities

An answer may be found in the estimation, that the difference between formalized and non-formalized approaches may be of use because it offers different possibilities as to how qualities can be produced. The success of digital arts provides evidence, that formal methods may produce numerous new qualities. The remaining question, why and how traditional instruments can offer the assumed potential for musical expression, provides evidence that non-formal methods may produce many qualities. It is an open question whether such non-formal qualities are not yet formalized or cannot, in principle, be completely formalized.

Anyhow, one will only produce music with the present possibilities. Therefore qualities produced by non-formalized (or not yet formalized) expression may be of use. In addition, as long as the potential for expression is combined with a necessity to keep elements that are ready-to-hand and thus are not formalizable, it seems to be important not to lose the knowledge of its potential.

### 7.3 Impact of Formalisms

Assuming that many input parameters that might have been estimated to be important in the requirements document cannot be implemented due to missing measuring methods or because they are not yet physically understood, one may ask what impact it will have on musicians who grow up in the digital domain of music. Do we have to expect that the blindness of computer based applications and thus instruments Winograd and Flores are referring to [28], will create a similar reflection in their users?

Given the condition that performed and perceived music lies in the digital domain and given the condition that musical experience will form the sensitivities of musicians, it may be likely that an experience-specific sensitivity and unreceivability might occur. In this case a digital artist might lose an area of quality if music is understood mainly from a physical descriptive point of view that allows the formalization of all essentials in music.

According to the experience of the author, digital artists often start by doing personal research on what can be done with the one or the other application, device, programming language, interface, sensor technology or microcontroller. The artistic question, the artistic problem and resulting the requirements evolve out of this process including the personal interests of the artist. One may estimate that descriptions of reality found on a formal level will influence the artist's idea of what is possible and what is crucially of interest.

The composer Hans Zender writes: "Strictly speaking, it is not possible to translate musical thinking into language." [31]. While Iannis Xenakis took a major step ahead with his book "Formalized Music" [30], it would be interesting to have a book focusing on occurrence and on meaning of non-fornmalized aspects in music.

## 8 Conclusions

In summary the opposite poles of formalized versus non-formalized, explicit versus implicit, parameter based versus audio signal based and physical descriptions versus phenomenological descriptions have been addressed. It has been discussed what implications their use on the construction of computer based musical instruments might have. Important differences between the two poles were found in the question of what kind of openness, transparency and flexibility can be generated by using construction principles that tend to one or the opposite pole.

An interesting question concerning digital arts might be, whether the old opposite terms, digital versus analog, might be supplemented by the poles formalized versus non-formalized. Computer based arts show formalisms everywhere. However, formalisms do not necessarily fall into the digital domain because analog computers use also formal programming languages. If formalisms are estimated to have an important impact in contemporary art, it might be interesting to do research on how this impact takes place and what consequences it has.

## Acknowledgments

The author would like to thank Georg Trogemann, Scott D. Wilson, Stefan Grünvogel, Leif Rumbke, Garth Paine, Carter Williams and Lasse Scherffig for the discussions on the topic of the paper.

## References

1. http://www.nime.org, (2001)
2. Askenfelt, A.: Measurement of the bowing parameters in violin playing. ii: Bow-bridge distance, dynamic range, and limits of bow force. Journal of the Acoustical Society of America 86(2), 503–516 (1989)
3. Bethesda, S.: Morrowind. Ubisoft, Paris, France (2002)
4. Bethesda, S.: Oblivion, March 2006. 2K Games, New York, USA (2006)
5. Casals, P.: Licht und Schatten auf einem langen Weg, December 1983. Fischer Taschenbuch Verlag, Frankfurt am Main (1983)
6. Dobrian, C., Koppelman, D.: The 'e' in nime: Musical expression with new computer interfaces. In: Proceedings of the 2006 Conference on New Interfaces for Musical Expression, Paris, France, pp. 277–282 (2006)
7. Fels, S., Gadd, A., Mulder, A.: Mapping transparency through metaphor: towards more expressive musical instruments. Organised Sound 7(2), 109–126 (2002)
8. Galamian, I.: Grundlagen und Methoden des Violinspiels, 2nd edn. Edition Sven Erik Bergh, Frankfurt/M, Berlin (1988)
9. Marrin, T.: Inside the Conductor's Jacket. PhD thesis, Massachusetts Institut of Technology (2000)
10. Moog, R.: personal communication (2004)
11. Paradiso, J.A.: Electronic music: New ways to play. IEEE Spectrum, 18–30 (December 1997)

12. Poepel, C.: Synthesized strings for string-players. In: Proceedings of the 2004 Conference on New Interfaces for Musical Expression, Hamamatsu, Japan, pp. 150–153 (2004)
13. Poepel, C.: On interface expressivity: A player-based study. In: Proceedings of the 2005 Conference on New Interfaces for Musical Expression, Vancouver, Canada, pp. 228–231 (2005)
14. Poepel, C.: Interactive Multimedia Music Technologies. In: chapter Driving Sound Synthesis with a Live Audio Signal, Idea Group Inc. (to appear, 2008)
15. Poepel, C., Dannenberg, R.B.: Audio signal driven sound synthesis. In: Proceedings of the 2005 International Computer Music Conference, Barcelona, Spain, pp. 391–394 (2005)
16. Prem, E.: Epistemic autonomy in models of living systems. In: Husbands, P., Harvey, I. (eds.) Proceedings Fourth European Conference on Artificial Life, Brighton, Great Britain, pp. 2–9 (1997)
17. Psygnosis, G.D.: Lemmings. Psygnosis, Liverpool, UK (1991)
18. Rasamimanana, N., Fléty, E., Bevilacqua, F.: Gesture in Human-Computer Interaction and Simulation: 6th International Gesture Workshop. In: GW 2005. chapter Gesture Analysis of Violin Bow Strokes, Berder Island, France, May 2005. LNCS, vol. 3881, pp. 145–155. Springer, Berlin, Heidelberg (2006)
19. Scherffig, L.: personal communication (2006)
20. Schleske, M.: Report on violin adjustment. In: Talk, RAD-Tagung (February 2005)
21. Schoner, B.: Probabilistic Characterization and Synthesis of Complex Driven Systems. PhD thesis, Massachusetts Institute of Technology (September 2000)
22. Sommerville, I.: Software Engineering, 7th edn., June 2004. Addison-Wesley, Reading (2004)
23. Trogemann, G., Viehoff, J.: Code@Art, Eine elementare Einführung in die Programmierung als künstlerische Praktik. Springer-Verlag, Wien, New York (2005)
24. Valve, G.D.: Half Live 2, November 2004. Vivendi Universal, Paris, France (2004)
25. von Neumann, J.: Mathematical Foundations of Quantum Mechanics. Princeton University Press, Princeton, NJ (1955)
26. von Neumann, J.: The Theory of Selfreproducing Automata. University of Illinois Press, Urbana IL (1966)
27. Wanderley, M.M., Vines, B., Middleton, N., McKay, C., Hatch, W.: The musical significance of clarinetists' ancillary gestures: An exploration of the field. Journal of New Music Research 34(1), 97–113 (2005)
28. Winograd, T., Flores, F.: Understanding computers and cognition. Ablex Publishing Company, Norwood, NJ (1986)
29. Woodhouse, J.: On the playability of violins. II minimum bowforce and transients. Acustica 78(3), 137–153 (1993)
30. Xenakis, I.: Formalized Music: Thought and Mathematics in Music, revised edn. Pendragon Pr, Hillsdayle NY (1992)
31. Zender, H.: Happy New Ears. Verlag Herder, Freiburg im Breisgau (1991)

# Part V

# Digital Space: Design, Movement, and Robotics

# Interactive Spaces

Jeffrey Huang[1] and Muriel Waldvogel[2]

[1] Media and Design Lab, Swiss Federal Institute of Technology (EPFL), BC104-Station 14, 1015 Lausanne, Switzerland
jeffrey.huang@epfl.ch
[2] Convergeo, Avenue des Tilleuls 6, 1006 Lausanne, Switzerland
waldvogelm@convergeo.com

**Abstract.** How do conceptions of space change with the infiltration of new elements of interactivity into our surroundings? What are the effects of digitalization on typological, tectonic and ornamental changes in contemporary architecture and cities? What are the new functional and aesthetic potentials that become available to us? Where are the opportunities and dangers? This article explores such questions at the intersection of the physical and virtual realm through recent examples, built and unbuilt.

**Keywords:** interactivity, architecture, design, prototypes, cities, media, art, wallpaper, ubiquitous computing, pervasive computing, urban screens

## 1 Introduction

What happens when our lives become inundated with information? How is the body to resurface? How can architecture come to the rescue?

At the turn of the 21st century, technologists painted pictures of a disembodied future in which people would shed their skins and live on-line, turning from citizens into "netizens." According to their depiction, people would learn in web-based classrooms, visit virtual museums, shop in online stores, heal in tele-operated beds, and fall in love in chatrooms.

While the virtual world is profoundly changing the way we perform some of our most basic everyday activities -- shopping, learning, working, praying, courting, healing - it is not rendering the physical world obsolete or even less important. People enjoy and need social and sensual contact; they don't want to be disembodied.

But even if the virtual world is not supplanting the physical one, the Internet is becoming an essential conduit, a new kind of space, an "inhabitable media" for many everyday activities. Few elements of physical architecture will be left unaffected. As networking infrastructures become increasingly part our cities and built environments, virtual and physical elements will merge in many ways, leading to new typologies in architecture and new experiences of the city [1]. What happens when websites become inhabitable, and buildings turn into large human-computer interfaces? What happens when physical spaces expand seamlessly to remote places with different time zones, dialects and rituals?

R. Adams, S. Gibson, and S. Müller Arisona (Eds.): DAW/IF 2006/2007, CCIS 7, pp. 377–391, 2008.

Our architectural work explores these questions at the intersection of physical and digital media through the critical investigation of typological changes in architecture and the building of real prototypes that operate in everyday life.

Of particular concern to us is the relationship between architecture and emerging forms of digital media. Traditionally, architects have viewed and deployed digital media as a tool, a better mayline, a faster pencil, and perhaps a more obedient never-tiring model-making robot. This view is changing. Recently, architects are beginning to embrace digital media as a space to be designed, rather than merely as a tool, and explore the potential stakes of digital architecture as a new design territory in the wild west of the 21$^{st}$ century.

In our context, we view digital media as assuming many roles simultaneously: they are communication linkages, windows to the world, connecting people in the space to the larger society; they are sources for endless streams of information; they form metaphorical structures onto which real-time information is mapped; they are sensors that condition the physiology of spaces for our comfort: mechanisms that domesticate the temper of climate and light conditions. And finally, they also play a darker autonomous role, that of "a friend," waiting in the shadow, remembering events, tailoring appearances, conforming to the needs of each of us.

## 2 Premise

The basic premise for our investigation is a profound belief that the massive proliferation of communication networks in our worlds will radically change how we perform some of our most basic everyday activities. There is a shift of the locus where typical everyday activities are performed from the physical to the virtual. This shift is epitomized by phenomena such as instant messaging, elearning, telecommuting, Internet shopping, and googling.

To support these virtual activities (and their fulfillment), a number of completely new architectural typologies is emerging. Some of these new typologies operate quietly at the back-end, out of sight: mega-warehhouses, server farms, telco hotels, call centers, and fulfillment centers. A curious example is the mega-fulfillment center of Amazon in Fernley, in the Nevadan deserts. The gigantic building features several intertwined rotating carousel systems, processes more than 100,000 orders a day, and warehouses over 150,000 SKUs (the equivalent of 54 supermarkets) with a staff of 1,500 human operators (the equivalent of less than 1/4 of 54 supermarkets). It is an ugly, functional building, however, the lack of any visible effort for decoration makes it interesting and offers a preview of a 21st century version of neo-functional aesthetics.

Other new typologies operate at the front-end. More prominent, they take center stage in the urban fabric. E*trade stores, Apple stores, or the Yahoo store in New York City, a physical portal to Yahoo's information space, are good examples. Even though their main right for existence is to act as a physical portal to a deeper virtual space, they appear to blend in seamlessly next to the haute couture boutiques and the chic coffee shops. They operate in the mainstream, mediating between the intangible cyberworld and the vicinity of physical life in the city.

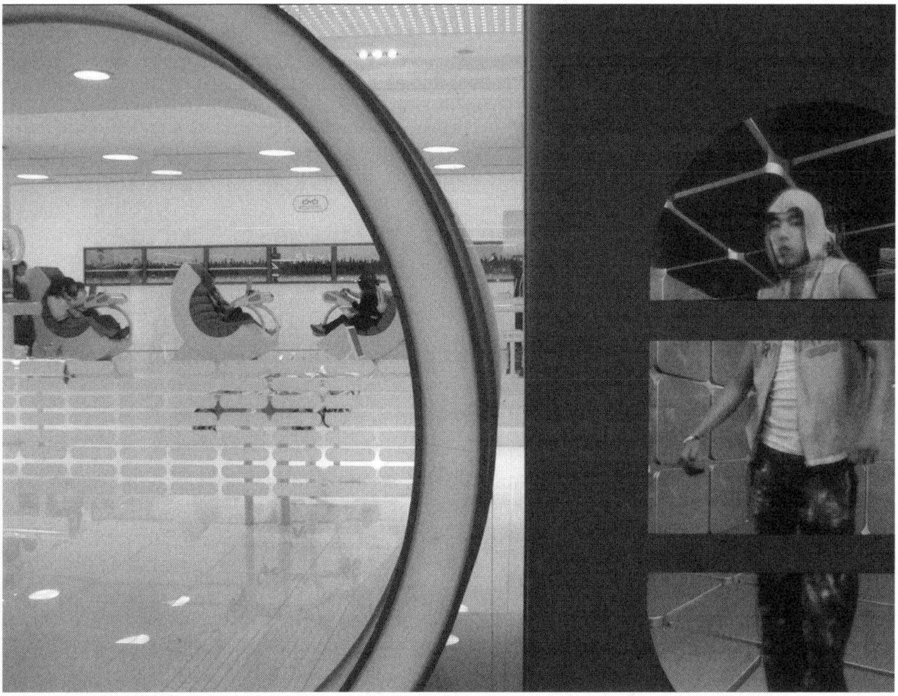

**Fig. 1.** M*zone in Seoul: Example of new typologies that operate at the front-end.

Beyond being new typologies, the architectures, both at the back-end and front-end, intrigue by the way their locations are chosen. Because of their reliance on heavy information flows, the buildings follow different rules when it comes to site selection.

In addition to the traditional locational affordances such as accessibility, visibility, traffic flow and topography, a new invisible layer, that of communication networks and bandwidth, fiber routes and gateways, plays an important, if not most important, role. The stores, fulfillment centers, call centers, server farms, telco hotels, mega-warehouses follow rules defined by fiber routes and access nodes: they grow in close proximity to fiber access nodes. By determining the locations of information intensive architectures, this new invisible layer of communication networks will increasingly play an influence on the positioning of buildings in the city and the morphology of our evolving cities.

## 3 Everyday Activities

Understanding the changing architecture of buildings and the city requires some insights into what is driving the changes. Our investigation therefore does not begin with the architecture itself, but starts with an analysis of the underlying activities: a verb by verb analysis of how the practice of everyday activities is changing and what architectural responses - both physical and virtual - are due [2].

We see verbs, and how the verbs are changing, as the driving force behind the necessity for new spaces.

The table below shows a sample list of basic activities that are being transformed by the digitalization of our everyday lives.

| | |
|---|---|
| learn | classroom vs. e-learning environment |
| work | workplace vs. virtual office |
| shop | physical retail store vs. e-commerce |
| pray | church vs. online religious community |
| play | playground vs. game environment |
| exhibit | museum vs. digital gallery |
| punish | prison vs. electronic surveillance |
| judge | court house vs. virtual juries |

When looking closely at the currently available architectures supporting these verbs, a striking dichotomy between physical and virtual architectures becomes apparent. We have an either-or situation, a purely virtual architecture or traditional physical architecture, but rarely anything in-between. For example, for the verbs listed above, the physical architectures supporting these verbs (the classroom, workplace, retail store, church, playground, museum, prison and courthouse) are seen as completely separate from their virtual counterparts (elearning environments, virtual offices, ecommerce sites, online religious communities, game environments, digital galleries, electronic surveillance and virtual juries), making it impossible for physical architecture to react to or even anticipate any changes happening in the virtual realm.

We are interested in what could be in-between, the possible convergence of physical and virtual components. This convergence can be approached from either the physical or virtual side.

Looking at convergence from the physical side, it seems possible to discover how traditional typologies are being transformed. At the larger scale, a complete redistribution of building mass can be observed: a shift from centralized typologies to radically decentralized, networked architectures.

A good example is the University of Phoenix, a networked university with an online learning space and 151 connected campuses around the country. This is radical departure from the traditional one-campus university typology, epitomized by the typical American campus such as Thomas Jefferson's University of Virginia. The networked typology allows Phoenix University to grow at multiple ends, and consequently extremely fast. Currently, as of the writing of this text, it is adding approximately 1,000 students every week across its decentralized campuses. With over

250,000 students, Phoenix University is already by far the largest private university in the US, approximately six times larger than the second largest private university in the States, New York University (NYU).

What does the virtualization and decentralization of verbs then mean for architecture at the individual building level? What are the potential for new architectural typologies that combine physical and virtual technologies? To what extent can architecture, and architectural elements in which we live, such as walls, ceilings, floors, doors and furniture, act as an interface between virtual and physical everyday activities?

To explore these questions, we have, in parallel to our theoretical investigations, started with the development of several working prototypes and buildings blocks that operate in the real (physical) world in an attempt to test the possibilities of merging physical architectures with digital media into new types of architectures: the conception of interactive spaces at various scales.

## 4 The Swisshouse

Our first example is the Swisshouse. Officially called the Swiss Consulate for Science and Technology, the Swisshouse is a prototype of a physical and virtual consulate for knowledge diplomacy [3].

The project started in 1999 as a response to a problem identified by the Swiss Government as "the brain drain problem." By that the Swiss meant the problem referring to the thousands of researchers and scientists whom they sponsor every year to spend time abroad, typically through a grant from the Swiss National Science Foundation, and who end up not returning back to the mother country, because they find other opportunities in the host country. There is a drain of intelligence from Switzerland to other countries, especially to the US, UK and increasingly also Asia, and this diaspora of Swiss intelligence is growing every year. Over the years, the Swiss officials have tried to contravene brain drain in all sorts of ways. They instituted policies, such as the J1 exchange visa, obligating the young researchers to return after two years of stay in the foreign country. But of course, since these young researchers are typically fairly brilliant people, they usually find ways around it. Finally, after much drainage, the Swiss authorities began to realize that the only effect that most of these policies had was not regaining but alienating their own researchers.

In 1999, we proposed an alternative. The fundamental idea was to create a new kind of diplomatic space that combines physical and virtual technologies into an inhabitable media. It would do two things: First, it would foster the creation of a virtual community for the Swiss scientists and researchers, enabling them to get to know each other, network, and feel a sense of belonging to something greater. And second, it would provide a network of physical nodes in strategic places that the dispersed communities of scientists could visit and use to virtually transfer their knowledge back ("reverse brain drain") without having to physically leave the country. Each node therefore was conceived as an inhabitable media interface where researchers could physically walk in and turn it into a portal or gateway to exchange knowledge and collaborate with people and places in Switzerland and scientists located in other nodes.

The proposed location for the nodes was determined by the present concentration of Swiss scientists in specific geographic locations (such as Boston) and anticipated future exchange between a location and Switzerland (such as Beijing). The initial list of proposed network nodes included Boston, San Francisco, Chicago, Singapore, London, Paris, Hong Kong, Seoul, Beijing, Shanghai, Johannesburg, Sidney, Bangalore, Taipei, Sao Paolo, Kairo.

The proposal received positive reactions from Bern (the Swiss capital), and the Swiss accepted to sponsor the building of a first prototype node in Boston, Massachusetts, where some of the major attractors of brains were located.

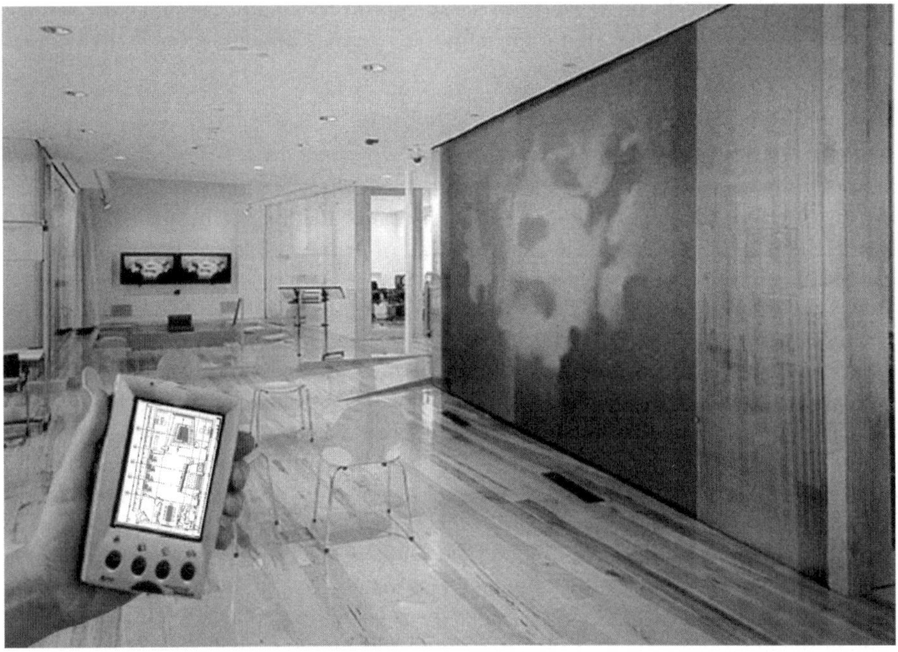

**Fig. 2.** Swisshouse: View of the interior interactive space

We conceived the Swisshouse as a large, inhabitable interface. Traditional architectural elements, such as walls, ceilings and furniture are turned into communication media. A basic shell acts as a giant, inhabitable motherboard containing the basic infrastructure and connectivity (16x16 matrix switch, CAT5 output grid, powergrid) into which various plug and play modules can be inserted, such as "digital walls", "knowledge cafes", "kinetic arenas", "nomadic workspaces" and "guest book walls".

The space is an open, wired loft, defined by ½ inch thick tampered, specially coated glass walls that run from floor to ceiling. The glass is structural and self-supporting; it is clipped in the floor behind the wooden planks and in the ceiling behind the gypsum board. Without any visible framing structure, the glass floats in space. The special coating allows each glass wall to become a high-resolution floor-to-ceiling screen for rear or front projection. When projected upon, the glass loses its materiality and the spatial boundaries are blurred by the projected images. Communication media instead of physical walls begin to define the space. Different places, virtual worlds, artificial environments appear on the surrounding glass transforming the boundaries, program and ambience of the space.

Architecturally, the space features richly textured wooden planks and large amounts of natural light, counteracting the coldness of the glass and technology, and fostering an energetic and creative atmosphere. The glass walls are positioned at a slightly off-orthogonal angle to give the loft space a continuous flow and maximize viewing at any given spot in the building [4].

As of today, the Swisshouse node in Boston has been in operation for 48 months, attracting many visitors from the Swiss diaspora and outside. Typical activities that happen at the Swisshouse include virtual cocktail parties, scientists happy hours, remote lectures, multi-party conferences, brainstorming sessions, virtual career desk, cultural exhibitions, and visits of scientists and researchers. The three planned next nodes will be in San Francisco, Singapore and Shanghai.

The Swisshouse is an early example of an interior "interactive space" deployed in the context of knowledge diplomacy, brain drain and a geographically scattered diaspora. People visiting the Swisshouse experience different levels of presence and embodiment as they virtually and physically interact with the space. Some members of the community will be physically present and visible, others may be physically in the space but invisible, hiding behind translucent walls. A third group may be only virtually present, and only to a certain degree: now and then we may see glimpses of their digital selves wandering about from node to node shifting their attention to us and then, to something else.

Interactive Spaces expands the notion of physical space, provoking new experiences of community, closeness, and proximity. It creates different qualities of presence in the space, connecting local spaces with distant places, and collapsing geographic distance by collocating different dialects, time-zones and rituals in one space.

## 5 Interactive Wallpapers

While the Swisshouse project focused mainly on the hardware components, their configuration, embodiment and media integration, questions about the nature of the media (the content and software) arise. What media supports interactive spaces? What should be on the wall, the ceiling, the floor, the door?

Over the last five years, we experimented with the idea of digital wallpapers in our design studios to explore this concrete question [5]. We were in particular interested to explore how the tectonic and psychological effect of our surroundings can be augmented, subverted, and estranged by animating wallpapers and introducing an interactive, possibly darker dimension. What happens when traditionally static and innocent wallpapers become alive, get a sense of memory, spatiality, connectivity and randomness, and become part of our everyday life?

### 5.1 Word Map

"Word Map" is an example for this kind of interactive wallpaper. We created the piece in 2003 for an installation at the Carpenter Center in Cambridge, Massachusetts.

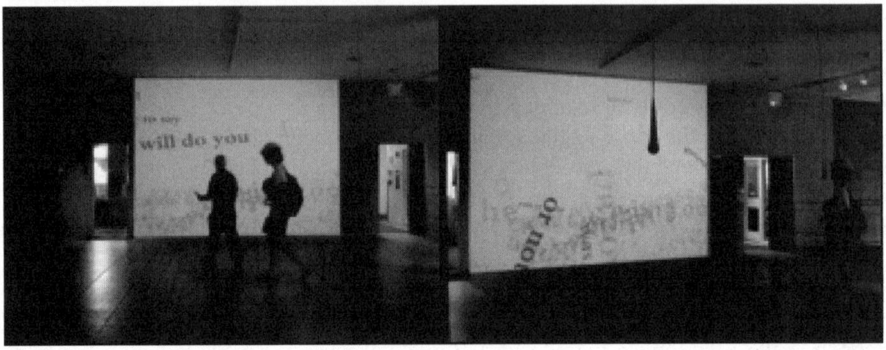


**Fig. 3.** Word map. The walls of the Carpenter Center become a memory container of the common cultural heritage of the Carpenter Center.

Located in the main foyer of the Carpenter Center, the wallpaper remembers conversations happening in the space and on websites connected to this space. Microphones capture snippets of conversations and turn them into floating text that appears on the interactive wallpaper. The text swirls on the surface of the wall, and sinks, fades and scales gradually to become sediments of thoughts on the floor, indicating the presence and traces of human interaction over time. As visitors approach the memory sediment, the individual words sense the warmth of human presence; and the words move slowly towards the visitors, curiously attracted by their bodily activities.

The wallpaper is simultaneously co-constructed at a distance. Visitors can interact with the wallpaper via the Internet by typing in words that appear on the projected wall. The hall transforms itself into an archive space, it becomes the memory of the moods and thoughts of the day. At the end of each day, the ensemble of words can be printed out as daily poems that are the memory of the intellectual discourse happening in this place, physically and virtually.

The piece shows how simultaneously recordings in the space, expressions from the web and interpretations and misinterpretations from the computer combine to create a spatial composition of words that reflect upon the various kinds of information inputs that co-exist in everyday life. The interface devices - microphones, webcam sensors, projectors - are visibly exposed to make the presence of the machines known. The machines are not spying, or secretly recording conversations and intruding privacies, but rather are conversational partners actively listening to visitors.

### 5.2 William Morris

Another example is the "fruit and flower" wallpaper based on an original arts and crafts design by William Morris. The fruit and flower wallpaper decorates the walls of spacious salons and halls. Light yellow lemons and red blossoming flowers hang on the branches of a tree. Green leaves provide a colorful backdrop for the unfolding scene.

This magnificent wallpaper reminds us of a time of siestas and endless meals, when we imagined a thousand stories while looking at the wallpaper. The rich ornaments suggest a hidden life behind the wallpaper. The lemons lightly balance on the branches. Some lemons appear to be more mature than others, and the branches seem to be shaking subtly. A lemon falls to the ground, probably overripe. Minutes pass, hours pass, and the wallpaper changes, telling its story and also speaking of the seasonal and weather condition outside and the passing time.

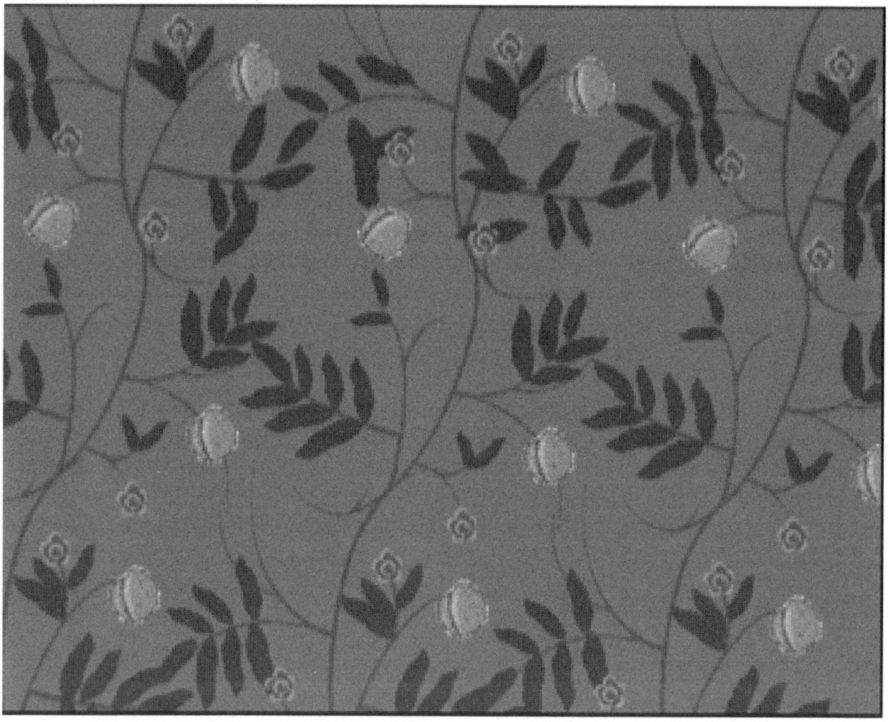

**Fig. 4.** William Morris Interactive Wallpaper (student: Grace Catenaccio)

The William Morris wallpaper estranges the room it inhabits. Based on a daily timeline, the wallpaper changes background color from day to night, from light blue to dark blue. Also at different hours, the flowers open up, the lemon become ripe and start falling. The William Morris wallpaper exhibits an Alice in Wonderland quality. Did it happen or not? Did the flowers become larger? Did the leaves jitter slightly?

### 5.3 Digital Tape

A different idea informed a series of other wallpapers that we explored in our workshops at Harvard: interactive wallpapers that go beyond the visual and acoustic. Overwhelmed by a world of images, text and sound and the domination of the visual over the other senses, this series started with a desire to confront the body's loss of sensibility in front of the screen. How can the tactile and olfactory sense be integrated to enrich visual and auditory perception? How can other senses be evoked to open up a powerful world of more unconscious and visceral responses, of feelings and emotions? How can we create inhabitable media that make us be afraid, exult, feel pleasure and suffering? Such emotions are felt by the body; they can be evoked directly by the choreography of the different senses or associatively by tapping into our tactile memory.

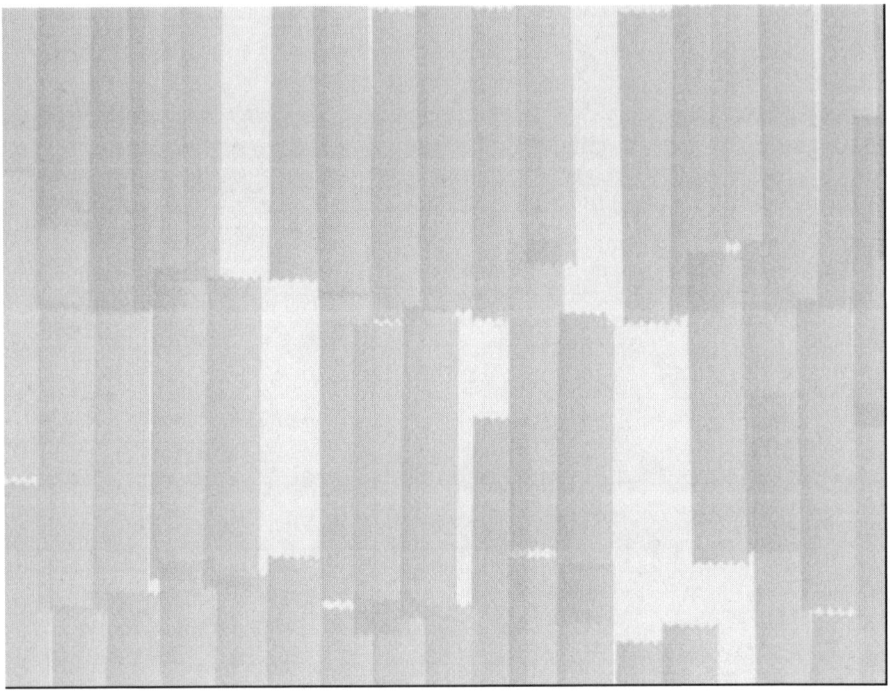

**Fig. 5.** Digital Tape. The haptic wallpaper encompasses all our senses of perception.

"Digital Tape" by Han Yu, one of our sophomore students with a concentration in studio arts, is the example we would like to show to illustrate this kind of wallpaper. The interactive wallpaper taps into our tactile memory. In this piece, the wall is a projection of fragments of semi-transparent adhesive tapes.

The tapes appear to hide behind its translucent veil something precious. In order to go beyond the surface, however, it is necessary to remove the adhesive tapes. The interactivity is not symbolic here, there are no iconic buttons inviting us to participate. Our engagement comes spontaneously from our tactile understanding of the wallpaper. We automatically feel compelled to scratch the surface with certain gestures. We begin with one corner and scratch that corner slightly with our fingers and fingernails in order to remove the adhesive tape. This knowledge of the right gestures (the "scratch" movements) is innate in us, impregnated in our memory through time, since childhood. We all have once scratched an adhesive tape, and our tactile memory has registered these gestures. Incorporating the body in our interaction with the strong and rational computer, makes our media experience sensual and natural.

### 5.4 Digital Shadows

Finally, the shadows piece is a collection of remembered interactions between two people. The interaction is frozen in time and the frozen statues become temporary traces of people on the walls of the room. Similar to an antique freeze illustrating the sentences and gestures of protagonists and antagonists, the silhouettes recounts the brief stories of heroes and encounters. The set of shadows slowly fade away after a few hours.

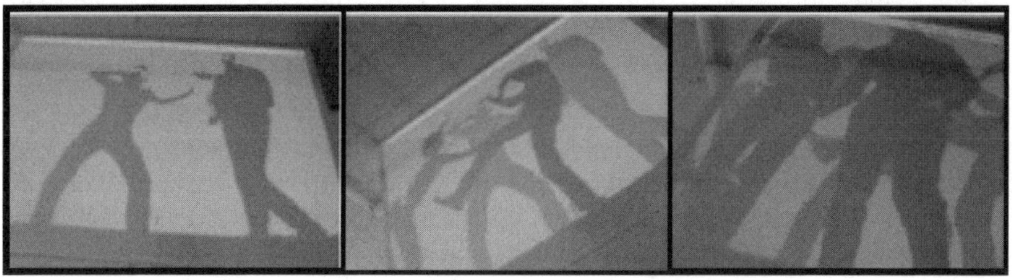

**Fig. 6.** Digital Shadows wallpaper. The shadows of our interactions and encounters through time.

When two or more people have an intense discussion, a sensor detects their strong movement and gesticulation, and a camera takes a snapshot. The picture of the snapshot is transformed into a gray scale image which reveals the beauty of the movement. However, the faces and identities of the actors remain difficult to discern, thus not violating the private realm.

As one enters the room of shadows, the shadows of recent encounters are superimposed and provide a backdrop to actual activities. The various shades of grey create a living memory of body interactions in space.

## 6 Beyond Surface: Skin Deep

"Skin Deep," takes the tactile dimension, started in the interactive wallpapers series such as in the Digital Tape example, one step further. Skin Deep projects go beyond the screen: when media is no longer projected onto a material surface, but the material surface itself becomes animated.

In a time when computer chips, sensors and actuators have become increasingly smaller and inexpensive, it is inevitable that there will be more and more informational devices surrounding us, infiltrating our daily lives.

What should these new elements of our everyday environments be? Will they have a life on their own? Do we want them to have a life? Who or what controls them? How are they changing the way we practice our daily activities? Are they reflecting, subverting, or enriching the way we act in the various contexts? How are they estranging our feeling of intimacy and closeness?

Skin Deep explores such questions by taking elements of the built environment and giving them a certain "depth" and an interactive potential. The selection is taken from student propositions in our workshop at Harvard.

a. Affectionate Velour by Noah Feehan. The affectionate velour is an interactive material that develops a relationship with its user over time. The velour reacts to caresses by emitting unfamiliar noises. It remembers the type of caresses and may ask for more. An inanimate object, the velour takes here a life of its own.

b. The Water Wall by Susan McGregor. The Water Wall prototype uses falling water as an architectural barrier by forming a thin water curtain and by the sound the water makes. Sensor technology allows users to pass through the wall in certain instances without getting wet; at other times, users can interact with the water but cannot pass through without getting soaked. The water wall introduces fear, evoking the displeasure of getting wet. The body is involved.

c. Interactive Fabric by Bea Camacho. The interactive fabric uses traditional crocketing techniques to interweave angora hair with electroluminescent wires (elwires) and embedded touch sensors. Soft and inviting to the touch, it is also connected, electric, responsive. The interactive fabric lights up gradually when you touch it, and fades down over time. The blanket makes it seem as if a person is warming it as opposed to it warming a person. Rather than bringing warmth and security, this blanket emits an unsettling electric light and sound.

d. Lightwall by Anna Ludwig. The Lightwall was developed as a subversive alternative to two architectural details: the light switch and the wall. When viewed as a freestanding piece, the outside world is visible, though filtered through layers of screens, wires, fabric and light. The light wall can be turned on by tracing with the hand the area to be illuminated. This intuitive one-to-one correspondence is shaken when the same area is approached again.

## 7 Public Interfaces

Interactive wallpapers and skin deep can be seen as building blocks for the construction of larger media-buildings and interactive spaces, such as the Swisshouse project. The last project presented here, Madrid Olympic Commuter, takes the idea of interactive spaces to yet another scale, into the public domain.

Madrid Olympic Commuter is a project for the creation of a large inhabitable interface that is public and in the open space, part of the city tissue. It connects distinct areas of the city together, turning the city into a huge interface. Employing similar convergent technologies as discussed in the previous projects, the Madrid Olympic Commuter project originated as a studio project and proposal to support Madrid's bid to hold the Olympic games 2012 in the city; the project is the result of a collaboration of some our students at the Graduate School of Design: Bryan Young, Peter Braun-Himmerich, Anuraj Shah and David Chun.

The project addresses a critical problem that Olympic cities often face, namely that of traffic between scattered Olympic events in a city. The proposed solution attempted to mitigate the downtime problems by channeling information flows into the flow of traffic. The strategic areas of proposed intervention were the central nodes of traffic interchange, subway and commuter railways stations, where most of the traffic congestion was likely to happen. The idea was to leverage the downtime of passengers in

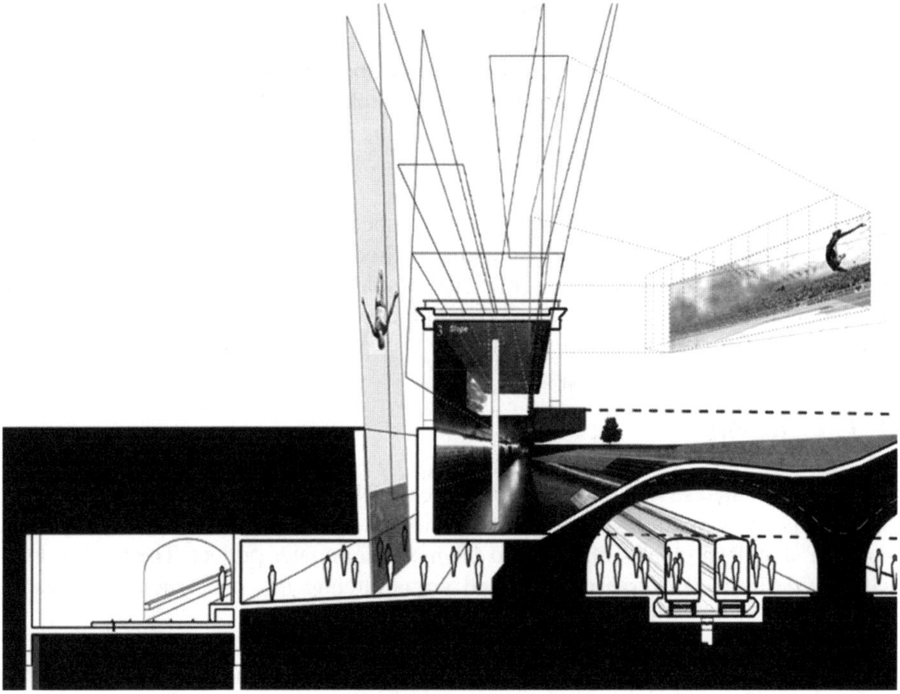

**Fig. 7.** Madrid Commuter Station: interactive spaces in the public realm

these areas, and give them access to the views of the Olympic games while they are waiting for a train, bus or for the circulation to flow.

The project started with a rigorous analysis of the perceived downtimes of typical passengers traveling through the major stations in Madrid. "Speed diagrams" mapped the various speeds at which passengers walk, drive, or ride through the stations, and uncovered the areas of overlapping downtimes. Slower areas such as the waiting areas appeared as dense, dark-colored areas. They were singled out on the map and carefully analyzed in tour visits with regards to their spatial potential. The intention was to correlate downtime areas with "underutilized" architectural surfaces, such as large areas of blank, badly lit concrete surfaces in the subway stations.

The possibility of using virtual projections to activate and inform these underutilized surfaces was then explored. The idea was to give passengers, athletes and general commuters the opportunity to see in real time and in real scale streaming of the Olympic games as they unfolded, adjusted to the average speed of passengers through the use of computer based filters. The streamed spaces were evenly distributed and carved throughout the subterranean circulation systems of the subway, altering the existing condition as well as the daily procession of the commuters. Real scale streaming (in addition to real time) was an important component in the overall choreography of the event broadcasting. In order to accommodate real scale streaming, certain sacrifices were necessary regarding the flexibility of the locality where events were streamed to. For example, sport events that required extreme vertical or horizontal views, such as pole vault, 10m platform diving, or triple jumps, predetermined the location and surfaces where they could be streamed by their sheer dimension and proportions. The real scale component gives events a particular locality within the traffic network, facilitating the ad-hoc creation of instant communities. Informed of such instances on their wireless mobile devices, crowds can momentarily gather and watch and cheer together.

The Madrid Olympic Commuter project is a speculative project. It attempted to allow viewers to reestablish a physical and scaled connection with athletes and events in olympic cities. Passengers in the city would encounter the Olympic games throughout the city with a renewed physical perception, enabled through a convergent physical and virtual architecture.

## 8 Conclusion

We have presented several built and unbuilt examples of interactive spaces developed over the last few years: the Swisshouse project, a series of interactive wallpapers, a series of skin deep objects, the Madrid Olympic Commuter project. The work started with the desire to converge physical and virtual architecture and articulate potential directions for media when it is no longer flat.

Clearly, the cases presented here are still early examples of what could be; we are only beginning to understand what the real opportunities and challenges of interactive spaces are, in the domain of architecture, but the examples seem to be already indicative of the directions where this could be going.

A common pattern that links the examples together is the way we view the relationship between architecture/space on one hand and digital media and computers on the other hand: computers are no longer stand-alone word processors, browsers, drafting machines and number crunchers only, computers are seen as a *social* and *spatial* device [6] [7].

It is important to stress this social and spatial aspect of digital media, in the context of architecture. First, the computer is no longer our grandparents' mainframe or our parents' desktop calculator, it is a social device, a window to other places and to other people, an inhabitable place for creating communities based on shared affinities. And secondly, it is a spatial device. The computer is emancipating and liberating itself from the beige, plastic (or translucent) box and becoming part of our everyday environment, augmenting, possibly subverting familiar everyday objects surroundings.

With this shift and view of the computer as a social and spatial device, architecture can no longer remain an impatient, yet passive place where computing happens, but must raise to the occasion and become an active communicative vector, an inhabitable media itself, an entryway to virtual space: an inhabitable interface that not only connects to other places, filters and orchestrates information flows, but also fulfills its traditional role as a shelter (by its sheer physical mass), protecting habitants from data overload and information misuse, and perhaps carving out moments of privacy.

## References

1. Huang, J.: Future Space: A Blueprint for a New Business Architecture. Harvard Business Review 79(4), 149–161 (2001)
2. Huang, J.: Internet and architecture. Interactions 9(4), 22–24 (2002)
3. Huang, J., Waldvogel, M.: The Swisshouse: an inhabitable interface for connecting nations. In: Proceedings of DIS04: Designing Interactive Systems: Processes, Practices, Methods, & Techniques, pp. 195–204 (2004)
4. Architectural Record: Swisshouse for Advanced Research and Education, Building Types, http://archrecord.construction.com/projects/bts/archives/offices/SwissHouse/overview.asp
5. Huang, J., Waldvogel, M.: Interactive Wallpaper. In: SIGGRAPH Electronic Arts and Animation Catalog (EAAC), SIGGRAPH 2005, Los Angeles (2005)
6. Weiser, M.: The Computer for the 21st Century. Scientific American, 1991 265(3), 94–104 (1991)
7. Brown, J.S., Duguid, P.: The Social Life of Information. Harvard Business School Press, Boston (2000)

# From Electric Devices to Electronic Behaviour

Stijn Ossevoort

SOS Design
Carrer d'Arimon 29, 08022 Barcelona, Spain
stijn.ossevoort@alumni.ethz.ch

**Abstract.** In this paper I give a brief overview of the role electronic devices have played in our daily lives. A century ago electric devices where hailed as a curiosity, soon they became an everyday object, now they have become submerged as embedded devices. In the present day and certainly in the future the ongoing integration of electronic devices will have a profound effect on human-product relationships.In order to guide directions in the future we need to know more about the way we relate to our products. Through my project, "Wearable Dreams", I will illustrate how we can reveal our existing user-product relationships and how these can be used to create unique electronic devices. This line of thinking paves the way for electronic products to become user-inclusive in which the users are an essential part or co-producer of the meaning of an object.

**Keywords:** ubiquitous computing, design, emotion, embedded technology, electronic behaviour, wearable computing.

## 1 Introduction

Electronic devices have come a long way, beginning with the physical phenomenon of electricity which was said to cure the human body, to micro electronic devices which can collect, store and process an increasing amount of information.

### 1.1 A Short History

About 200 years ago electric devices were still a scientific curiosity which was shrouded in mystique and disbelief [1]. In 1797 J. Tholen said, in an inaugural talk about the influence of science on our society and the human ingenuity [2]:

*"If physicists had not spent a long time experimenting with Electricity and would just have deceived the human eye, we would not have been able to secure houses nor boats from the destructive power of lightning.*

*We would not have been able to administer an excellent remedy in case of illness or suffering or thought about applying such a remedy if the accidental discovery of the Leyden Jar[1] would not have directed the physicists into believing that Electricity could have an influence on the human body...."*

[1] An early device for storing electric charge, invented in 1745.

R. Adams, S. Gibson, and S. Müller Arisona (Eds.): DAW/IF 2006/2007, CCIS 7, pp. 392–402, 2008.

Tholen gave his talk about 40 years after Benjamin Franklyn invented the lightning conductor [3]. However the scientific knowledge regarding the phenomenon of electricity was still in its infancy. It was not until Alessandro Volta developed the electric battery in 1800 [4] that scientists could start outright experiments with electricity which resulted in further comprehension and eventually lead to practical applications.

The mystery behind the invisible electric force was especially attractive within the medical profession. Most early applications of electricity can therefore be found in the medical field. However it would take another 50 years before one could truly understand the physics behind electricity; from then onwards the world would soon become electrified.

### 1.2 Electric Devices

At the end of the 19th century the ingenuity of the human mind seemed to be limitless. An enormous amount of electric devices were developed. Through tales of convenience, health and safety salesmen convinced people to purchase electric versions of many familiar products such as cookers, sewing machines, heaters, lights and irons [5].

If a product was to be introduced for the first time it would be designed as a metaphor to facilitate its acceptance and use. A good example of this use of metaphor is the earliest available electric light switch (Fig. 1) which by design and functionality directly derived from, in those days, familiar, taps for gas lights. Once the light switch became accepted it gained its own design language and extended functionality.

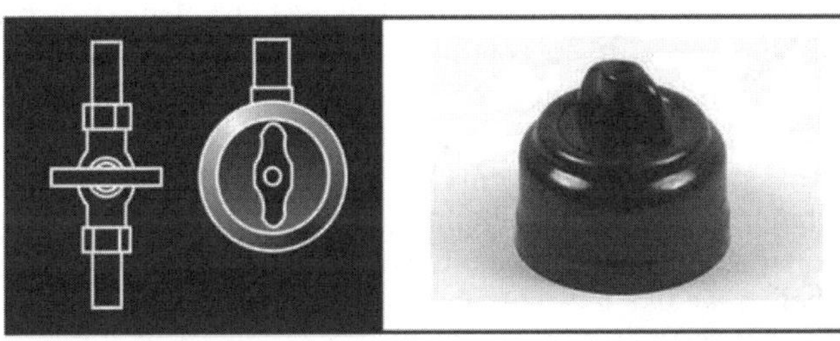

**Fig. 1.** In the drawing on the left a traditional gas-tap, alongside one of the first electric light switches, also shown in the photo on the right

### 1.3 Electronic Devices

During the 20th century the electronic technology advanced to such an extent that totally new devices were developed which had no prior plane of reference. We now purchase these devices mainly for their functionality and performance (generally people do not buy a television or fridge for the desire of the physical object itself).

During the eighties, designers have tried to add implicit meanings to objects. They used semiotics and semantics as a framework to communicate the meaning of a product through its shape. However, applying semiotics has its weaknesses, as it tends to limit the consumer's interpretation of an object and makes it harder to sustain his/her interest in the product [6].

It is not strange, therefore, to witness that electronic devices have tended to become less tangible; their software becomes more important than their hardware [ 7].

## 2 Electronic Behaviour

### 2.1 Ubiquitous Computing

Electronic devices have not only become less tangible; in the last decade ongoing miniaturisation has paved the way to add electronic intelligence and connectivity to any object imaginable [8].

It started when shops introduced electronic article surveillance tags (EAS tags) on their products to prevent theft. These tags do not contain any information besides a unique way to detect their presence.

This changed when RFID tags where introduced. These can contain up to 1kbyte of information about the product and are able to release this data on demand. RFID tags are useful to provide the producer/consumers with information about the product such as batch number, order number, ingredients or contact information [9].

The latest developments are smart sensors, tags with integrated sensors, primarily used to control the damage which may occur during transport of delicate products. In the near future these tags may become a functional part of the product, controlling the use of the product, recording data about its (ab)use or disable the product if it is stolen.

All these developments precede the development of ubiquitous computing systems in which information processing is shared amongst ordinary objects that surround us. Introducing smart sensors into ordinary objects is just one element. A complete ubiquitous computing system needs a continuous network that connects all objects together. Such a network is the biggest challenge in ubiquitous computing. Within an invisible as well as an extensive network, it becomes difficult to say what is controlling what, if the system functions normally or whether a device is broken or works fine in case of failure. Maintaining simplicity and control simultaneously is still one of the major open questions facing ubiquitous computing research [10].

However, whether we like it or not, ubiquitous computing devices are on their way since many powerful institutions have shown a major interest in this emerging area which presents an appealing technical challenge [11]. Again we see that virtual aspects are gaining a foothold in product design as more and more electronics are embedded into ordinary products [12].

### 2.2 Ambient Interaction

Once ubiquitous computing has made its appearance, we will interact less with the actual product but more with(in) its environment. The environment will gradually become the interface; product interaction will become ambient interaction. As a result we will deal more with the context, rather than the content of an electronic device [13].

It is very natural for us to deal with contextual information. During a normal day we encounter such an abundance of information that it is in our interest to be able to distil the most relevant aspects. Our body and mind are very well adapted to blocking irrelevant information.

Our optimal visual area, for example is limited to a visual angle of 30 degrees which we do not consider as a physical limitation but a way to become increasingly alert for changes in our peripheral vision [14].

We also have an astounding cognitive ability when it comes to selective attention. We are able to listen to one conversation whilst ignoring others, we can multitask and many people have a dichotic listening ability [15].

Altogether humans are capable of withdrawing specific elements in their environment in order to deal effectively with others. Our future challenge, as I see it, is to design information elements in our environment which are latent yet available when you need them. Similarly Mark Weiser introduced the term "Calm technology"; technology which engages both the centre and the periphery of our attention and in fact moves back and forth between the two [16].

### 2.3 Intelligent Devices

For a long time designers have tried to make sense of the intangible insides of electronic devices by creating interfaces based on electronic functionality. Now the time has come to abandon the invisible world of electronics and concentrate on developing a parallel visible world based on the context of a product.

The latest developments in sensor technology and real-time information processing allow devices to gain a sense of awareness (context recognition). This allows devices to make an instant "decision" and is referred to by the term "intelligent devices".

With "intelligent devices" we often make the mistake of thinking that the best way to interact with a complex electronic product is via a simulated human-human interaction. However a device one needs to talk to, give commands to, or have a relationship with, is a device which demands too much attention to be of much use [17].

It would be better to view intelligent devices like Chris Schwand from MIT does; he envisions that intelligent devices should know about the user and their preferences and therefore know how they can avoid becoming an annoyance [18]. Unfortunately it is extremely difficult to predict user behaviour, and therefore it will be just as difficult to avoid causing annoyances.

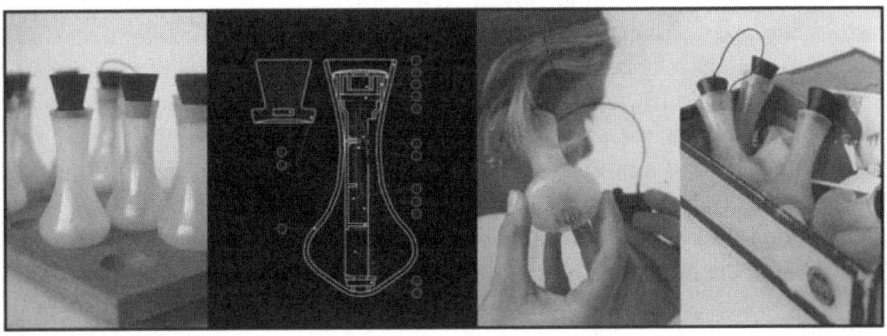

**Fig. 2.** "Message in a Bottle", each bottle contains a small electronic circuit which can capture a telephone message (via RF) or an audio message from the user (via hidden microphone inside). A small diode light array inside each bottle provides feedback whether a message is stored, recorded or played back.

A better way to achieve user satisfaction is by creating a context around the product in which the user can play an active role. In Fig. 2, I depicted an example of this approach. It is answer phone called "Message in a Bottle" which I developed in 2000 as part of my Masters degree during my graduation at the Royal College of Art in London.

The answer phone consists of twelve bottles on a tray which can receive, store and play messages. Any message left is visible through a "whispering" light which "evaporates" when played and can be "emptied" by tilting the bottle. I created a working prototype so people can experience how open, but not necessary shallow, the interaction with the product can be.

As Rob van Kranenburg says: "The design challenge lies in confronting the move from interaction as a key term to resonance as an interpretative framework. Resonance refers most aptly to the way we relate to things, people and ideas in a connected environment" [19].

## 3 User-Product Relationships

Designers need to think holistically when it comes to providing the right context to support user interaction. As in holistic science they need to "observe the specimen within its ecosystem first before breaking it down to study the parts". In such an approach the user cannot be taken out of the equation.

In the past designers were mainly shaping *objects*. Nowadays the role of the designer includes defining, intensifying and shaping the *relationship* between the users and their products. To proceed designers need to know more about user-product relationships.

### 3.1 The Importance of User-Product Relationships

For a long time products were directly designed according to their functionality. Designers considered the relationship between users and their products to be primarily based on its use.

During the sixties some designers started to criticise this point of view [5]. By adding non-functional features or impulsive graphics onto products, they demonstrated that the user-product relationship goes beyond the primary function of the product.

Gradually functionality has become less important and is not considered to be the only matter that relates users to their products. While functionality is closely related to the process of using a product entirely and efficiently, people care as much about the meaning of products. Without a special meaning, products would not be carried into completion. In a sense users are also producers; they create the true meaning of a product through the intimate relationship they establish with the product [20, 21].

### 3.2 Wearable Products: A Special Case

When it comes to user-product relationships the area of wearable products offers the highest challenge since the relationships are more personal. People tend to associate themselves with what they wear which suits the fluid character of electronic technology.

Many recent projects mistakenly urge to develop future clothing which is programmable allowing the user to change the cultural appearance of their clothing as a function of mood or situation. However we should not forget that we often wear our clothes to disguise the mood we are in; they provide us with a certain amount of privacy, status, identification, self-adornment and self-expression [22].

Therefore any future possibilities should not be dictated by technology but by the preferences of the user. Clothing is an essential part of our identity; we have an important relationship with what we wear which is something that should be considered in any future design of wearable products.

## 4 Wearable Dreams

As an example to show the importance of user-product relationships I will briefly discuss a research project called "Wearable Dreams" which I conducted at the Interaction Design Institute Ivrea in 2004 [23].

The project goal was to intensify the personal relationship between users and their wearable products through emerging technologies. I decided to identify existing relationships between consumers and their products which, I assumed, would provide me with enough insight to create wearable electronic objects that support new and intimate "bonds" between consumers and their objects.

### 4.1 Revealing User-Product Relationships through Stories

Stories are useful way to describe the variety of relations between consumers and their objects. For some products, particularly those in the fashion world, stories are even more important than the function or quality of the product itself. With the help of stories, consumers can identify with their products and justify the appearance of the product to other people [24]. There are many types of stories of which the least visible is probably the most important to generating new product ideas, mementos [25].

Mementos are individual stories based on personal memories from the past. They describe the very personal relationships between users and their product. For wearable items this personal aspect is of vital importance, because we identify ourselves primarily by the clothes we wear.

### 4.2 Gathering Stories

I asked a group of 16 subjects to fill in a creative questionnaire which would explore their user-product relationships. The group was selected to be as diverse as possible which was only possible by selecting the subjects via distant friends or relatives. In order to find out if cultural and geographical background had any major influence on the results I decided to select eight subjects from the UK and eight from the Netherlands.

Because most subjects would have had no idea how to write a story (in general people think they lack the creativity to do so) it was important to provide a detailed guide. I decided to create a questionnaire that would inspire creative thinking using images from magazines, analogies and what-if questions.

**Questionnaire.** The questionnaire was divided in three sections. In the first section, respondents were asked both personal questions and questions about their shopping habits. The personal questions were directly relevant to the research; they revealed information about each person's background and profession. The other questions were used to focus the person's attention onto the subject of wearable objects.

In the second part of the research each respondent had to read through a fashion magazine that had been supplied with the questionnaire. They were asked to take cut out any item they liked and place it in front of them. These were to be used for making two collages, one to represent the way they would like to see them selves, the other to represent the way they would dress for a certain occasion (Fig. 3).

In the third section each respondent was asked to give a description of his/her favourite wearable item: "What if your favourite item were a person…could you give a detailed description of this person?" All respondents were asked to create a character that would represent their favourite item.

In a final question the respondents were asked to think about a situation they would not like to see themselves in. For example one of the respondents described a situation in which she lost her most precious possession. They were then instructed to write a story in which the character was trapped in this particular situation. Within character they had to describe how to deal with the problematic situation.

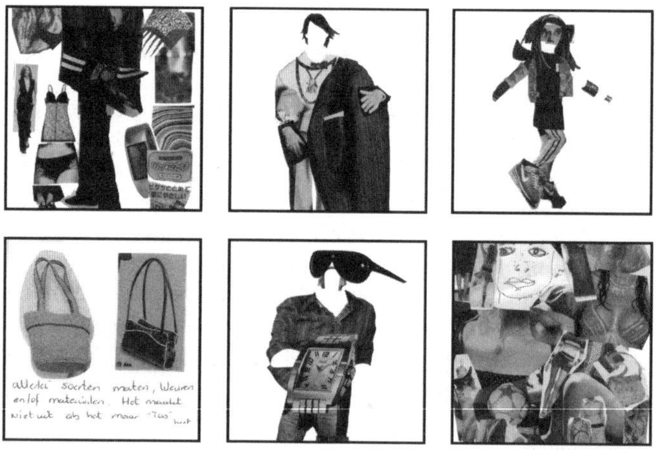

**Fig. 3.** Some of the collages made by the subjects which depict the way they would like to dress themselves. The exercises were given to the subjects to create a clothing focussed mindset.

## 4.3 Outcome

The diversity between the stories was enormous. Some subjects described a dream situation, others a realistic situation with a strange twist. To the purpose of the research it was not necessary to analyse each story individually. The aim of the questionnaire was to reveal a variety of user-product relationships on wearable items. For most respondents their favourite item proved to be a reflection of themselves. It illustrates that wearable items are of great importance to the way we like to identify ourselves. I felt it would be best to maintain these individual variations by selecting two very different, "gendered" stories to be developed into a product.

**Compass Coat.** One of the stories that caught my attention is about a builder, named Colin, who is lost in a forest where every tree looks the same and is planted in regular rows:

*"There is a strong smell of pine. It's getting dark. The temperature is falling below zero. Colin knows how to use the side of each trunk on which moss grows to find north. He heads in one direction. As night falls, he builds a shelter from sticks and branches. He lights a fire using flint and straw. He follows tracks of deer to find water. He sets a snare to catch a rabbit, skins it with tools he makes himself and roasts it on a spit of wood.By the day he uses the sun and his wristwatch as a compass. He finds his way to a village where he tells his story in the local bar to villagers... "*

This story, written by a subject, inspired me to develop a Compass Coat (Fig. 4).

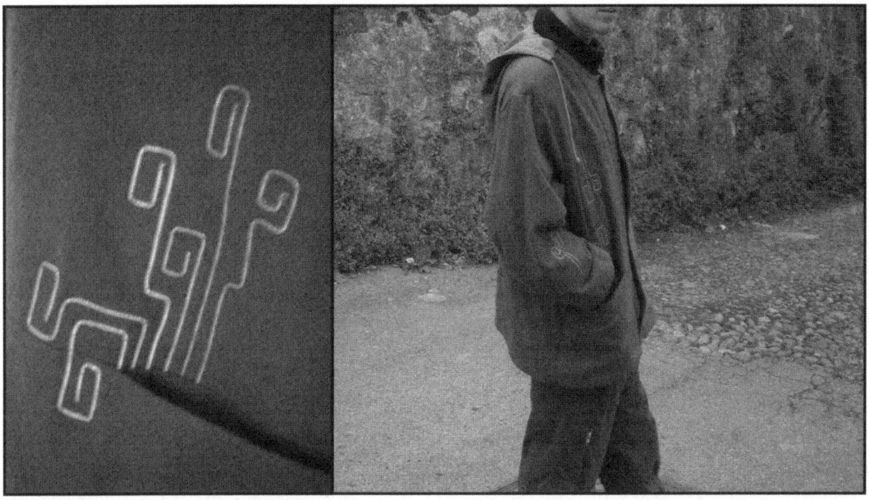

**Fig. 4.** the Compass Coat; on the left a detail of the Electroluminescent wire on the pocket

The Compass Coat is covered with 24 pieces of Electroluminescent wire (Fig. 5), which provide a sense of direction. North becomes visible through a glow of light in the right direction. This coat grows plants to the side it faces north, comparable with a lonely tree on which moss grows to the main wind direction.

**Perfume Jewellery Pieces.** Another story that caught my attention is about a character described as a delicate person, silent, confident and flirty with the characteristics of an angel:

*Heavy, loud rain, chill in the air, distant ringing of a bell, windy chaotic direction, lonely, calm and cold.*

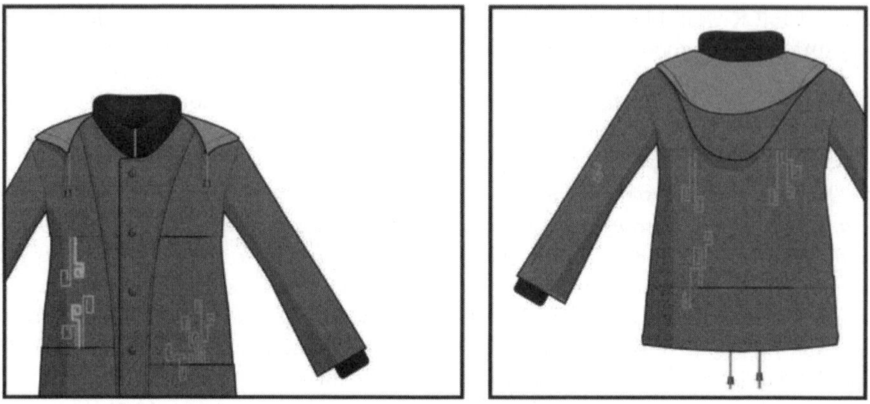

**Fig. 5.** Drawing of the front and back in which the electroluminescent wires are visible

*To get out of this situation she was able to send a message to her lover via her thoughts. Alone in his small warm room with a view on the ocean he begins to smell a faint hint of Jasmine. This reminds him of his lover's neck, just behind the ear. The smell gets stronger, surrounds him. He has an intense itch on his inner thigh; he begins to feel what seem to be his lover's hands in his own, gently pulling him to the window; he is overpowered by her message.*

Inspired by this story, I decided to create an object that enables two lovers to exchange each other's thoughts of affection by means of smell. Since jewellery pieces are a common way to symbolise a relationship, I decided to create two connected perfume jewellery pieces (Fig. 6).

The ring and the necklace are equipped with a small perfume bottle (Fig. 7), filled with the individual perfumes of each person. At the point when someone blows

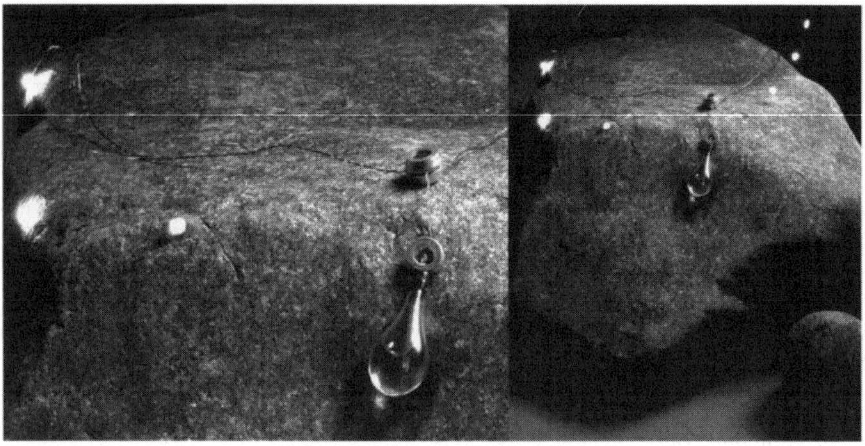

**Fig. 6.** The perfume necklace

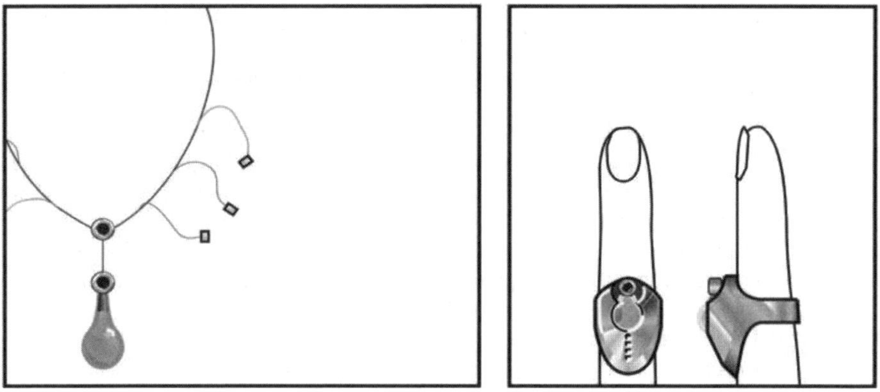

**Fig. 7.** A drawing of the necklace and ring in which the perfume bottles are visible

against one of the jewellery pieces it will respond with sparkling lights. At the same moment it will transmit a signal via both an integrated RF transceiver and the owner's mobile phone to connect over a long distance. Once the signal reaches the other piece it releases a gentle smell signifying the owner's thoughts.

## 5 Conclusion

The research concludes that stories generated by the end user are a helpful tool to reveal the complex relationship between user and their clothes. Once these distinctive relationships are revealed they can be used to inspire new pieces of clothing enhanced with embedded technology.

No need for the final consumer to understand the implicit meaning of the piece of clothing, it is more important to create a narrative space around the piece of clothing which allows the consumer to be a protagonist or co-producer of a narrative experience instead of a passive consumer of clothing's functionality. Technological possibilities could support these views, which can lead to new objects that support a stronger personal relationship between consumers and their objects.

## References

1. Tholen, J.P.: Redevoering; over den invloed van de beoeffening der wijsbegeerte op de menschelijke maatschappij en onze verstandelijke vermogens. Univ. of Franeker (1797)
2. Krider, P.E.: Benjamin Franklin and Lightning Rods. Physics Today 59, 42 (2006)
3. Pancaldi, G.: Volta: Science and culture in the age of enlightenment. Princeton University Press, Princeton (2003)
4. Baudet, M.: een vertrouwde wereld: 100 jaar innovatie in Nederland. uitgeverij Bert Bakker, Amsterdam (1986)
5. Dunne, A.: Hertzian Tales, Electronic Products, Aesthetic Experience and Critical Design. Royal College of Art, London (1999)

6. Djajadiningrat, J.P., Overbeeke, C.J., Wensveen, S.A.G.: Augmenting Fun and Beauty: A Pamphlet, ACM Trans. Program, pp. 131–134 (April 2000)
7. Thackara, J.: The Design Challenge of Pervasive Computing. In: Doors of Perception, Amsterdam (April 2000)
8. Electronic Tagging, RFID and EAS, CRR, report on, Centre for Retail Research, Nottingham (2007), `http://www.retailresearch.org`
9. Weiser, M., Gold, R., Brown, J.S.: The origins of ubiquitous computing research at PARC in the late 1980s. IBM SYSTEMS JOURNAL 38(4) (1999)
10. Greenfield, A.: All watched over by machines of loving grace: Some ethical guidelines for user experience in ubiquitous computing settings, Essay on the threat and promise of ubicomp (2004), `http://www.boxesandarrows.com`
11. Wall Mart RFID labeling system, http://www.rfidtoday.co.uk
12. van Kranenburg, R.: Real Rules of Innovation for the 21st century (Part 3), Inspiration Materials, `http://www.noemalab.org`
13. Lange, W.: Kleine ergonomische Datensammlung. Verlag TÜV Rheinland, Köln (1993)
14. James, W.: The Principles of Psychology, vol. 1, pp. 403–404. Henry Holt, New York (1890)
15. Weiser, M., Brown, J.S.: Designing Calm Technology, Xerox PARC (December 21, 1995), `http://www.ubiq.com/hypertext/weiser/calmtech/calmtech.htm`
16. Weiser, M., Klein, E.: Why should a computer be anything like a human being? I3 magazine. Human Communication Research Centre, p. 30. University of Edinburgh (2003)
17. Fried, L.: Social defence Mechanisms: Tools for Reclaiming our Personal Space. Department of Electrical Engineering and Computer Science, Massachusetts. MIT, Cambridge (2005)
18. van Kranenburg, R.: Mapping territory, `http://www.noemalab.org`
19. Ossevoort, S.H.W.: Wearable Dreams: a research project about clothing that suits personal fantasy. Research Thesis, Interaction Design Institute Ivrea, Ivrea (2002)
20. Falk, P.: The Consuming Body. SAGE Publications, London (1994)
21. Koskijoki, M.: visions on product endurance. In: Hinte van, E. (ed.) eternally yours, pp. 135–143. 010 publishers, Rotterdam (1997)
22. Lyle, D.S., Brinkley, J.: Contemporary Clothing. Bennett and McKnight Publishing Co., Chicago Illinois (1983)
23. Ossevoort, S.H.W.: Wearable Dreams: A research project about clothing that suits personal fantasy. Project report, Interaction Design Institute Ivrea (1988)
24. Wilson, E.: Adorned in Dreams, fashion and modernity. University of California press, Berkely (1985)
25. Hafkamp, W.: visions on product endurance. In: Hinte van, E. (ed.) eternally yours, p. 53. 010 publishers, Rotterdam (1997)

# Scentsory Design®: Scent Whisper and Fashion Fluidics

Jennifer Tillotson

Central Saint Martins College of Art & Design
The Innovation Centre, Southampton Row, London, WC1B 4AP, Great Britain
j.tillotson@csm.arts.ac.uk

**Abstract.** This paper examines a new experience focusing on smell and how it might expand our sensory repertoire; or maximise our sense of wellbeing through fashion. It explores **Scentsory Design®,** a multidisciplinery project that changes the experience of fragrance to a more intimate communication of identity, by employing emerging technologies with the ancient art of perfumery. **Scentsory Design®** specialises in the research and development of wearable wireless sensor networks and microfluidic devices for fragrance delivery and therapeutic applications in *'emotional fashion'*. Intelligent fabrics are discussed which are engineered for pleasure, education, protection and psychological end-benefits, by offering social and therapeutic value in a desirable fashion context. The fabrics incorporate sensors and microfluidics to initiate fragrance delivery of beneficial aromas released in controlled ways responding to personal needs. The paper concludes by suggesting clothes that mimic the olfaction system via electronic nose sensors that emulate a dog's sense of smell.

**Keywords:** Scent, well-being, microfluidics, emotional fashion, electronic nose sensors.

## 1 Introduction

This paper outlines the **Scentsory Design®** research initiative based at the Innovation Centre at Central Saint Martins, University of the Arts London. The first project called *'Scent Whisper'*, describes digital fragrance and wireless sensor networks in jewellery which was designed in collaboration with Professor Andreas Manz, a pioneer of 'lab-on-a-chip' technology and Head of the Institute for Analytical Sciences. Further projects describe *'Fashion Fluidics'*: microfluidics and microtubes constructed to form a digital membrane that 'pulses' different fragrances around responsive fabrics for various applications. The paper concludes by summarising a range of intelligent clothing for a further research project, which will include the embodiment of electronic nose sensors within the structure of clothing.

Scentsory Design® explores *Emotional fashion* and olfaction science through the inclusion of lab-on-a-chip microfluidic devices embedded in wearable items that sense and respond to psychological and environmental changes. Inspired by the human body's nervous system and defense mechanism in bombardier beetles, responsive garments and jewellery produce an intimate, tailor-made *'scent bubble'* around the user, by pulsing beneficial aromas in controlled ways, responding to personal needs, as illustrated in Figure 1.

R. Adams, S. Gibson, and S. M\"{u}ller Arisona (Eds.): DAW/IF 2006/2007, CCIS 7, pp. 403–417, 2008.

Scentsory Design® creates an intelligent multiple scent-output system, targeting specific aroma molecules to precise locations on the body. As a result, digitally controlled scent recipes offering emotional support, are integrated into one sensitive system, so that the user has access to an assortment of scents to enhance different moods, feelings, emotional states and occasions of the day.

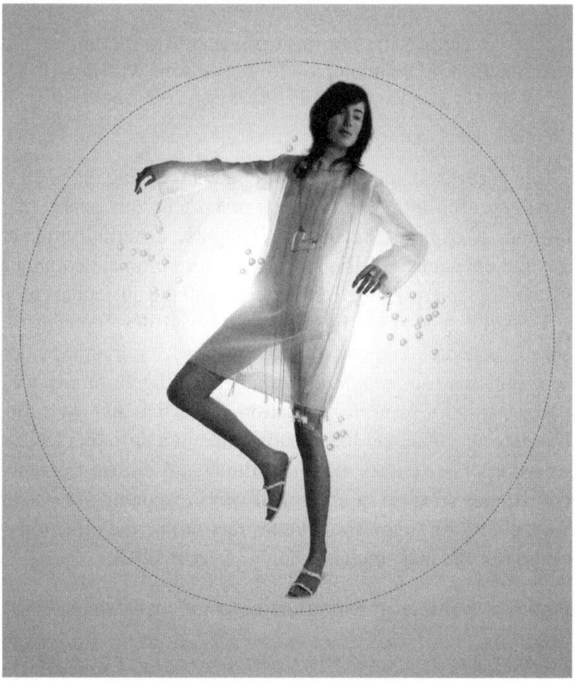

**Fig. 1.** The photograph shows a tailor-made *'scent bubble'*, produced from the mechanics of the *'Smart Second Skin'* dress and developed as a creative garment prototype to illustrate intelligent fabrics interacting with human emotions whereby the aroma dimension is an integral part of the wearer's sensory experience. The dress was constructed from organza silk with micro-tubes containing liquid that demonstrates 'wellbeing' fragrances *'pulsed'* around the body depending on the emotion or mood of the wearer. Photograph by Guy Hills, illustration by Wendy Latham.

## 2 Background

Evolving from the authors PhD work on *'Smart Second Skin'* [1], at the Royal College of Art and BA Fashion work on multi-sensorial surfaces at Central Saint Martins in 1991, the background behind this research describes a multi-sensorial approach to biomedical designs, recognising that all senses interact. In this context a *'Smart Second Skin'* fabric is a membrane of micro-tubes fused with microelectronics, yarns and microfluidics embedded in clothing elements, to create a 'wellbeing' scent delivery system that adds function to fashion and textile design, and was demonstrated by an interactive installation of a fluidic fabric illustrated in Figure 2.

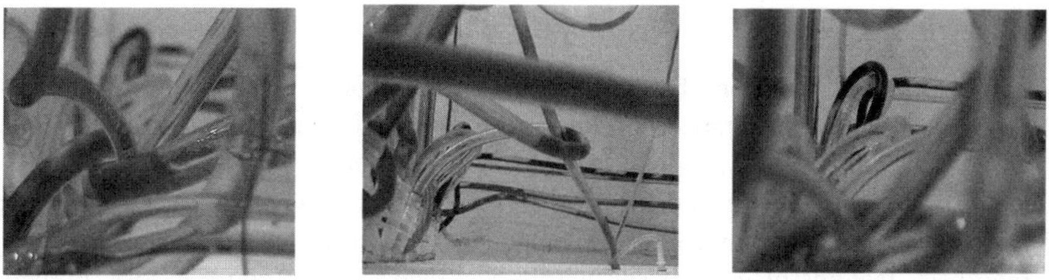

**Fig. 2.** *'Fluidic Fabric'* at Jenny Tillotson's Phd Textile exhibition at the Royal College Of Art 1997. Photograph Jenny Tillotson.

The installation pulsed coloured liquid around a specific area to illustrate 'colodours': colour therapeutic scent delivery for different emotions and moods. The membrane is analogous to the body and human skin thus facilitating interaction between the two membranes, using the blood signals and bodily fluids of the human system. Clothing becomes almost living, as an internal pump represents the heart of the fabric and the tubing as the nervous and respiratory system.

## 2.1 Human Olfactory System and the Digital Arts

Our sense of smell is rarely used as a tool to convey information in the Digital Arts, despite strong evidence to suggest that exploring the link between emotion, and smell might be a more productive area of development in this field (given its significant role in the triggering of emotional responses). Up until recently, computerized scent-output systems have been unreliable as scent is difficult to control. Secondly, as more is being discovered about PsychoNeuroImmunology (PNI) [1], the new interdisciplinary approach of medicine that explores 'positive psychology', and the interactions among behavioral, neural and endocrine, and immunologic processes of adaptation [2], alongside the physiological and psychological mechanisms that govern our relationship with odours; artists and designers are beginning to experiment with new technologies that deliver scent in significant ways, since this evocative sense gives rise to a powerful medium of expression. For Scientists, smell is finally gaining recognition as an important part of life, especially after the recent scientific breakthrough in olfaction and the discovery of odorant receptors and the organization of the human olfactory system [3]. As a result, it is anticipated that this research could not only contribute the Digital Arts arena, but also towards a new age of perfumery that could have a radical impact on health.

Smells engender emotional responses and the raw materials used to create many of them have mood-enhancing effects. This is because fragrances have the power to evoke emotions, since the olfactory sense impacts directly with the limbic system, increasing an individual's wellbeing. Special aroma molecules act powerfully on the brain to change human behaviour in a subtle and acceptable way.

---

[1] Coined by Robert Adler, Department of Psychiatry, University Of Rochester Medical Centre in 1975, interlacing psychology, neuroscience, immunology, physiology, pharmacology, psychiatry, behavioral medicine, infectious diseases, endocrinology and rheumatology.

### 2.2 Emotional Fashion

The properties of Scentsory Design® fashion items could therefore be a source of different aromas to maintain cheerful moods, remember tasks and convey digital information. *Emotional fashion* will be good for all that choose to wear it but of special value to people susceptible to depression and anxiety. Depression is a common mental disorder that presents with depressed mood, loss of interest or pleasure, anxiety or nervousness, feelings of guilt or self-worth, disturbed sleep or appetite, loss of energy and poor concentration. These problems can become recurrent and lead to impairments in an individual's ability to take care of his or her everyday responsibilities. At its worst, depression can lead to suicide, a tragic fatality associated with the loss of about 850,000 thousand lives every year, and it is predicted that by 2020, depression will be a major problem, second to heart disease [4].

Recent research proves that the benefits of fragrance include the balancing of the nervous system, improving concentration, promoting a positive mood, reducing blood pressure that rises during stressful events, reducing heart rate, muscle stiffness, startle reflex, fear and the stress of unpleasant medical procedures e.g. MRI scans [5]. The claims also suggest that certain scents significantly benefit people who suffer from insomnia, bronchitis and indigestion.

### 2.3 Digital Fragrance Technology

This paper describes the development of wearable technology that mimics biological functions such as pulsing bodily fluids. By fusing fashion together with microfluidics, sensors and scent capsule(s), it is possible to create devices that pulse airborne nano-litre sized droplets of scent as an atomized mist, into the air and directed towards the nose, neck and wrists so that the effect is immediate. The devices pick up on the body's vital physical signs to demonstrate a possible change in 'mood' i.e. via sensors for galvanic skin response, perspiration, heart rate, temperature, brain activity etc.

Microfluidics is a new technology, which involves the design and production of devices that deal with extremely small volumes of fluids. These devices can combine electrical and mechanical components down to a characteristic length scale of 1 micron. Microfluidics is the generic technology of manipulating fluids on a chip, including the integration of pumps, valves, mixers and reaction chambers that enable the fabrication of micro reactors and lab-on-a-chip devices.

There is little evidence of similar digital fragrance technology to be found on a micro-scale, which seeks to remedy the limitations of current work on scent-output devices suitable for custom control applications. Recent digital fragrance research has been developed at The Institute for Creative Technologies & AnthroTronics, Inc who have created the 'Scent Collar' which dispenses scent for Virtual Reality computer games, ScentAir have developed the 'ScentKiosk Scent Dispenser' which focuses on retail ambient odors; Trisenex has created the 'ScentDome' with 20 different scents in its scent cartridge, Proctor & Gamble have marketed 'ScentStories', a scent dispensing CD player; Aromajet has a kiosk system that lets users create custom scents and DigiScents developed the 'iSmell' device; but the company dissolved in 2001.

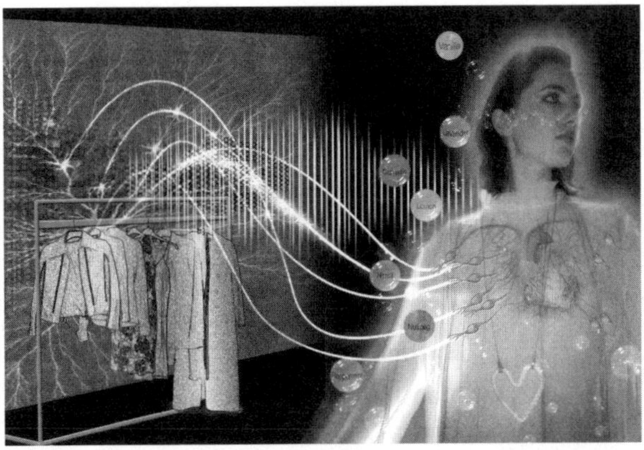

**Fig. 3.** Approaching a wireless *'Perfume-free-zone'*. Scent-output can be increased when required or switched off altogether. Photograph by Guy Hills, illustration by Wendy Latham.

Dispensing fragrance in response to a personal sensor network allows more intelligent and efficient release of fragrance compared with the traditional method of direct application on the skin (i.e. using a perfume bottle). Direct application on the skin relies on evaporation to distribute the scent using the wearer's body heat to vaporise scent, which is typically made more volatile with the addition of ethanol. It is thus impossible to control scent output after application leading to situations where unwanted scent is needlessly released or scent output is insufficient.

There is increasing concern over allergies triggered by scent pollution as well as the offence some people take to being subjected to the over-application of other people's perfumes. Such problems become more acute in confined public spaces such as public transport. Scentsory Design® aims to reduce 'odour annoyance' by using microfluidic inkjet technology to distribute scent directly into the immediate vicinity of the wearer rather, than over the skin. As well as avoiding possible allergic skin reactions on the wearer (the designs are intended to replace astringents that burn sensitive skin since the key advantage of the delivery system is that the fragrance contains a low or zero percentage of alcohol), the technology also allows much greater control over scent output simply by regulating the amount dispensed by the device according to the response of various sensors.

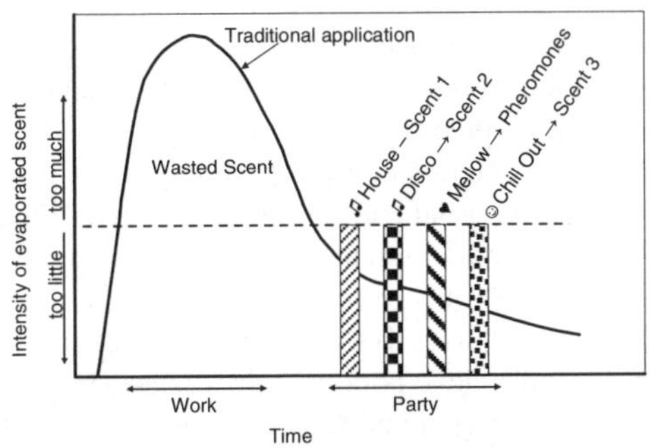


**Fig. 4.** Traditional application verses Scentsory Design® method of fragrance delivery

A *'perfume-free-zone'* scenario, as shown in Figure 3 suggests that an individual's allergy to specific fragrance components could be communicated via clothing to others; in order to inhibit the release of certain fragrances should an individual approach the zone.

A schematic illustrated in Figure 4 shows the comparison of a traditional skin based application from a perfume bottle with that of a device which is configured to release different scents at different stages of a party, depending on the genre of music being played [6]. Using the traditional method, perfume is applied in the morning leading to high levels of scent immediately after application, which lingers during day. The scent is thus largely wasted during work hours, possibly causing annoyance to co-workers and members of the public. By the time of the party in the evening however, when the scent is most desired, the scent wears off.

In contrast, using a sensor-based system a device may be configured to emit various different scents in response to certain genres of music. Different fragrances are released whilst house music and disco tracks are played and pheromones may be released during mellow mood music. A more relaxing scent could then be released during the chill-out phase towards the end. Although music is used in this example, many other sensor mechanisms, such as those previously described may be employed.

## 3 Scent Whisper: A User-Worn Scent Dispenser Where the Frequency and Type of Fragrance Delivery Is Flexible and Determined by the User

The 'Scent Whisper' project focuses on spiders and the defense mechanism in bombardier beetles that squirt predators with a high-pressure jet of liquid in a rapid-fire action. The devices were designed by fusing micro nozzles; reservoirs and power source with wireless components and microfluidics that link a remote sensor with a liquid-dispensing unit to create two items of jewellery that constitute the wireless web. A message is *'scent by a wireless web'* from a spider to a beetle brooch, which sprays a minute sample of fragrance (or something that smells or reacts in an unpleasant manner). The aerial which was wrapped around the abdomen of each jewellery piece and consisted of a copper loop to enable the transmission and receipt of data, allowed the devices to be oriented in many different positions and can be seen in Figure 5.

The microfluidics which have been fabricated in this project, to some extent replicates the firing chambers that bombardier beetles facilitate in their own communities, as they mix their deadly poison in their on-board munitions factory and pulse chemical warfare at immense speed from their tail pipes [7].

The primarily goal is for a fragrance in the jewellery to be released onto a localised area, enabling the user to act on visual cues or detect aromatic signals as 'coded' signals. This allows for immediate information that can be healing (e.g. neroli to reduce anxiety, lavender to promote sleep, eucalyptus to reduce the symptoms of a cold, peppermint to increase athletic performance), protective (e.g. insect repellent, poison, pepper spray, acid) seductive (e.g. pheromones, love potions, aphrodisiacs, fragrance chemicals) or as a preventative for a specific warning signal (e.g. leaking gas, burnt toast, blocked toilets, dead bodies etc).

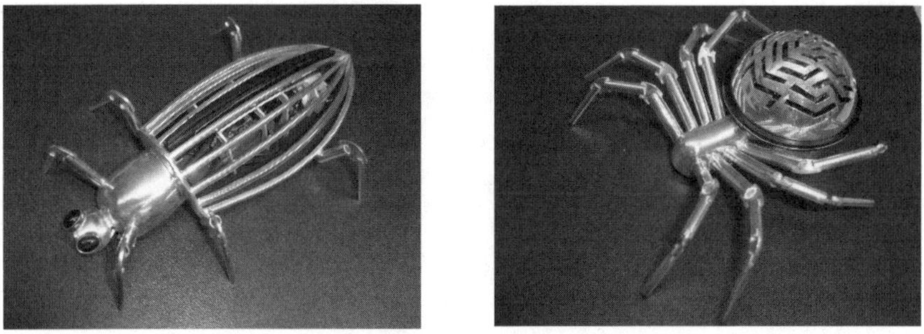

**Fig. 5.** The photographs shows a Bombardier Beetle brooch including inbuilt scent dispenser, and Spider brooch with inbuilt humidity sensor, which measures the humidity of the user's breath as a message is whispered into the abdomen. Photograph by Gareth Jenkins.

Achieving the odourant results required and the process of transporting smell, is more complex than focusing on the mechanics and electronics of pulsating delivery systems would suggest. There are always difficulties with chemical issues, and the compatibility of art and design materials, microfluidic components and threshold timing. The primary ethical concerns relate to the potential for odour pollution and the pulsing of chemicals onto a localized area. However, the advantage is that microfluidic technology allows for the targeted delivery of minute droplets of scent that is more efficient and economic in use, focusing on intimate and personal use rather than generalized and higher volume use, creating a personal scent environment for the user alone.

# 4 Fashion Fluidics and Innovative Applications in Clothing

The next stage of the project is to create a 'scentsory membrane', as an emotional 'living tissue', by incorporating systems of ultra-miniature tubing with microfluidics and sensors that emulate the human nervous and circulation system, heart and scent glands. The network of micro-tubes embedded in the membrane will resemble the body's own capillaries, pulsing droplets of fragrance across the body. Clothing will pick up on vital signs and other aspects of the bodies functioning that can be measured, allowing the user automatic access to a wider range of favorite scents, for example a subtle hint of lemon to boost brain activity in the office, or peppermint to improve performance in sustained attention tasks, or lavender to simply relax.

Examples of digital fragrance applications include sportswear that improves the level of competitive athletes, through the delivery of peppermint odour molecules which has been proven to enhance sports performance [8], or convey 'coded' aroma notes or information through the delivery of specific 'aroma chimes' that correspond with the time as shown in Figure 6.

An aromatic wearable system could assist as a tool to navigate soldiers around battlefields or the sensory disabled around built environments, by delivering an 'aroma rainbow' of scents to substitute the auditory and visual senses, as illustration in Figure 7. *'Scent tones'* could be employed as an alternative to audio tones in mobile phones, or a personal finance system could communicate abstract information by emitting certain scents when changes in banking information occurs, or if there is a change in the status of the stock market should the market go up or down, as demonstrated by the ambient media 'Dollars & Scent' project at the Massachusetts Institute of Technology Media Lab [9].

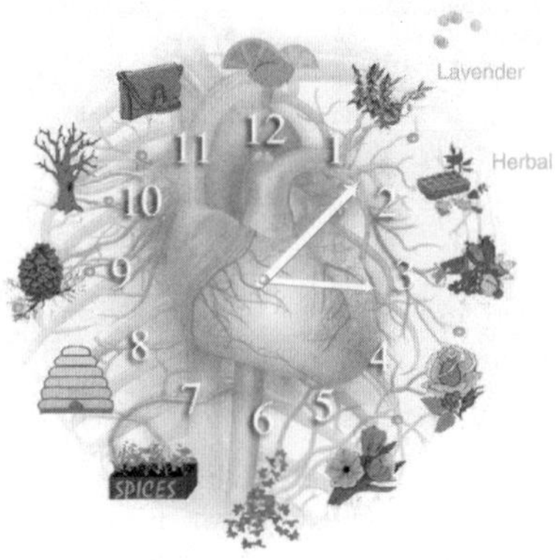


**Fig. 6.** The Electronic Age of Perfumery: An Aromatic Clock with the capacity to choose from an entire palette of scents changing over time. Illustration by Wendy Latham.

Other examples could be clothes worn for education purposes to maximize affectivity in learning situations. This is because there is recent evidence to suggest that aromas given during a learning task can improve consolidation of the memory of that task if 'pulsed' during 'slow-wave sleep' [10].

Figure 8 illustrates a student who is memorising learning situations by wearing Scentsory school uniform that retrieves specific odours in seconds, such as smelling an apple aroma to remember Einstein's famous relationship for energy equation, or an orange aroma to memorize Japanese script. By changing into Scentsory pyjamas which are worn at night whilst sleeping, it is potentially possible for the student to remember the learning task, once the aromas are delivered during the 'slow-wave-sleep' period.

The *'scent bubble'* could also be shared between different individuals or groups of people as illustrated in Figure 9, whereby sensors in garments could detect someone whose pheromone profile is of interest to the user and sends a sample of pheromones. Clothes could also emit 'modulator pheromones' from human sweat, particularly from a male partners underarm which appears to alter the mood of females [11], or alternatively maternal lactation odours and pheromones could be sent to calm newborn babies and anxious school children who are separated from their parents.

A further example could be clothes that offer the ultimate *scratch and sniff*[2] experience by enhancing the multisensory environment in nightclubs, so that all the senses are stimulated to [re]energize the user. Pulsations of ambient aroma molecules could be emitted from clothing to complement sound and vision (colour). Different roles of responsive clothes worn in club communities could harness the power of smell to fulfill the role of fantasy and expand the DJ and VJ[3] dimension.

---

[2] 'Scratch and sniff' is a treated surface with a microencapsulation coating which releases an odour when scratched. 'Scratching' is also a DJ-ing technique which produces distinctive sounds by moving a vinyl record back and forth on a turntable.

[3] VJ or *Video Jockey* is a play on the word *Disc Jockey*. VJ's are performance artists who create moving visual art on displays at clubs in conjunction with live multimedia performance that includes music and video.

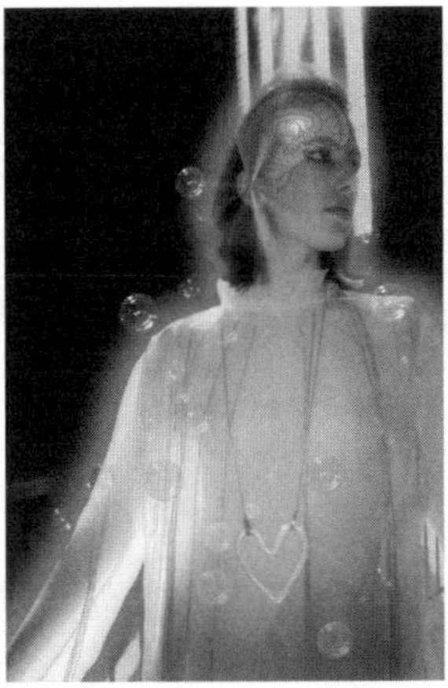

Scentsory Sound

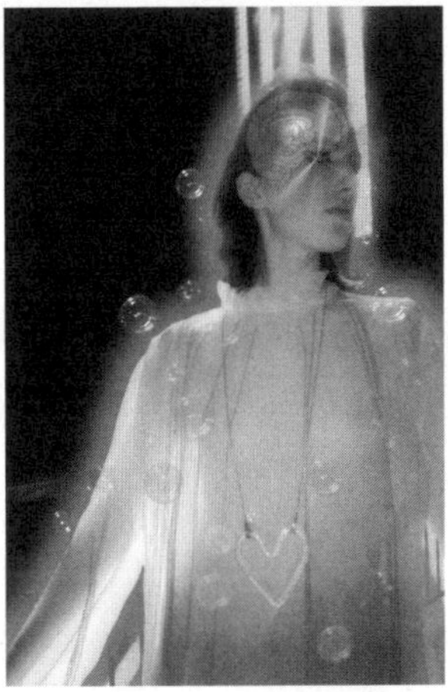

Scentsory Sight

**Fig. 7.** *'Scentsory Communication'* aroma-rainbow coded messages to convey information and substitute sight and sounds. Photograph by Guy Hills, Illustration by Wendy Latham.

The olfactory sense would introduce the 'PJ' (Perfume Jockey) into the equation, by acting as a third party which would control the delivery of a scent symphony, wirelessly from the users clothing, to complement the work of the DJ and VJ, as illustrated in Figure 10. As one of the last sensory frontiers to be explored in wearable technology, these clothes would seek to offer novel olfactory experiences as a new *'scentsory'* appeal in clubwear that adopts wider waves of feeling (and fantasy) in [re]active environments, without invading fellow clubbers personal space [12].

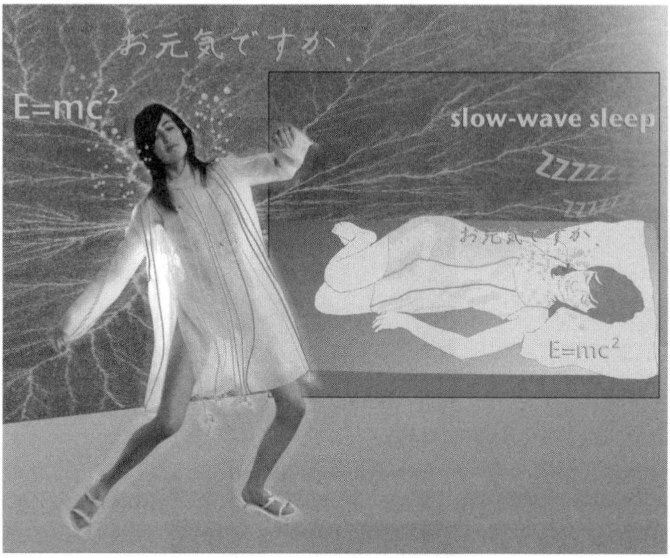


**Fig. 8.** An illustration to show sleep facilitating memory consolidation. The aroma dimension is employed to increase learning ability, concentration and boost creative enhancement, or contextually inappropriate smells could be used to help memorization. Photograph by Guy Hills, Illustrations by Wendy Latham.

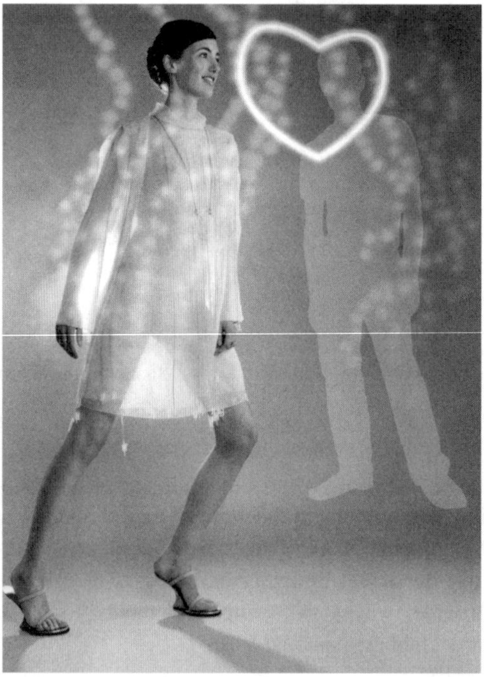

**Fig. 9.** Wearable Technology worn close to the body with embedded pheromones for romance and mood-enhancement. Photography by Guy Hills, illustration by Wendy Latham.

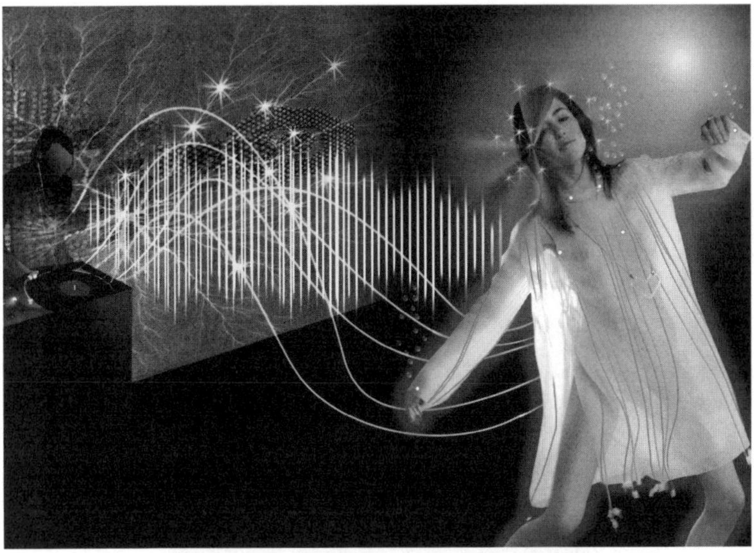

**Fig. 10.** Enhancing sensual landscapes in nightclubs by introducing the Perfume Jockey to complement the work of a Disc / Visual Jockey and augment emotional experiences so that an imaginary world of wonder emerges. Photograph by Guy Hills, illustration by Wendy Latham.

## 5 Conclusion and Further Development

Vision, hearing, smell, taste, and the tactile senses serve as bridges between the external world and our brains. Micro-sensors detect chemical, physical, or biomedical signals that, in turn, can be processed on a computer. The miniaturisation of most sensors has already been achieved, but the 'electronic nose', the sensor that mimics the sense of smell, is only starting to gain recognition. An electronic nose produces unique 'fingerprints' for distinct odours, consisting of olfactory sensors and a suitable signal processing unit, which is able to detect and distinguish odours precisely and at low cost. This makes the sensors very useful for a variety of applications in the food and pharmaceutical industries, environmental control and dental field [13].

The embodiment of electronic noses (or artifical noses) in fashion garments could detect and monitor pollutant chemicals in the air. The interface to nose sensors could be seen as the 'scentreface', and set the basis for revolutionary Scentsory Design® work in the diagnostic area, taking into account the role that olfaction plays in many traditional medicines [14]. By Fusing Electronic noses with Fashion, it would allow clothing the ability to detect diseases similarly to dogs. Clothes could emulate a dog's sense of smell by detecting the early stages of breast cancer, through artificial nose sensors embedded deep within the structure of the material worn on the chest, as illustrated in Figure 11.

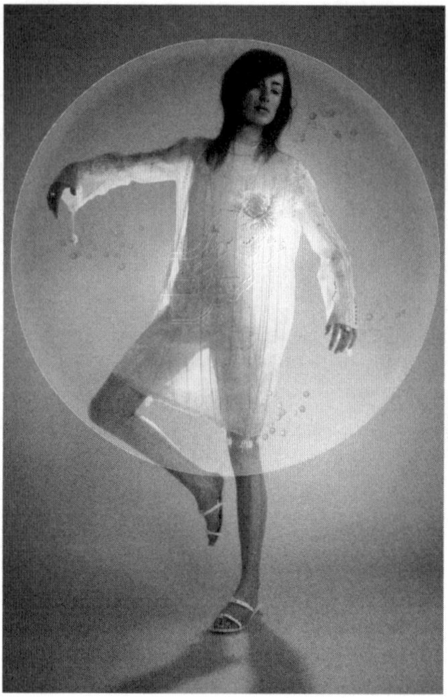

**Fig. 11.** Holistic, responsive fashion showing a garment inspired by the mechanics of a dogs olfactory system to sniff out disease, offering preventative and therapeutic value in a desirable fashion context. Photograph by Guy Hills, illustration by Wendy Latham.

Dogs have long been able to sniff out explosives and narcotics, and more recently 'canine scent detection', research has proved that dogs are capable of smelling early stages of breast cancer with an accurate success rate [15]. The Pine Street Foundation in San Anselmo California, have developed the first state-of-the-art device (Gas Chromatography/Fourier Transform Ion Cyclotron Resonance Mass Spectrometry equipped with a Preconcentrator and a Cryofocuser) to acquire breath fingerprints to help identify biomarkers for the early detection of certain diseases.

Should this technology ever reach the apparel market, such clothing might have the potential to save lives. At the very least, it could help improve the well-being of patients, by assisting those in recovery to feel safe, and achieve 'inner strength' to fight cancer; not to mention offering first-hand personal comfort, through the delivery of medicinal molecules for psychological end-benefits that reduce stress, and alleviate insomnia and depression.

Another example illustrated in Figure 12, shows a dress using similar technology, which not only detects lung cancer, but also pinpoints ovulation in women, based on current research that studies female cattle signalling with odours to a bull that they are fertile and ready to ovulate. An electronic nose offers the potential to successfully detect oestrus non-invasively in female cattle, consisting of conducting polymer sensors, a system for sampling, humidity management (known as the olfactory lens) and pre-processing of data [16]. Such technology could therefore potentially be integrated into birth-control clothing, or boost the chances of fertility in women.

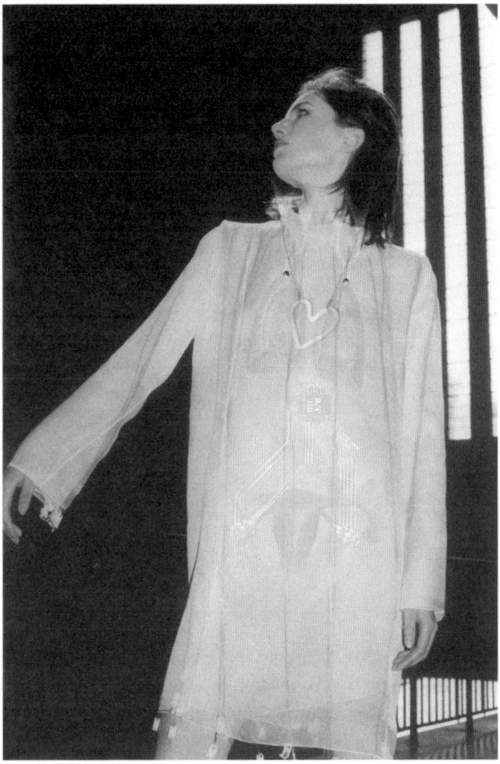

**Fig. 12.** An illustration of a double-purpose, novel method of data analysis in smart clothing with integrated *artificial noses,* for non-invasive detection and diagnosis of lung cancer and ovulation detection. Electronic nose sensors are used to detect chemical compounds in the exhaled air of a patient's breath. Photograph by Guy Hills, illustration by Wendy Latham.

## 5.1 Colodours and 'Coded' Aroma Messages

This study provides the foundation for the future development of clothes that change with emotion by advancing knowledge and understanding of fragrance and its ingredients and their impact on mental health. The clothes will have the positive psychological benefits of manipulating moods by stimulating the adrenal cortex. This will be achieved by exploring the relationship between colour and scent to create a *'colodours'* holistic platform as illustrated in Figure 13.

This paper has demonstrated how it is possible to envisage new modes of interaction with scent-producing devices. These range from digital objects that exploit the performative component of scent applications, to the creation of a personal *'scent-bubble',* around the user that is based on information needs and requests, and can be modified according to mood, environment or occasion, or the numerous design implications in fashion, textiles, responsive environments, diagnostics, healthcare, and other digital systems that use smell to convey. Scent (whether it is for a positive or a negative affect), will become a user-friendlier medium, as technology allows the user to learn 'coded' aroma messages for wellbeing, communication, sex, education, navigation or simply having fun.

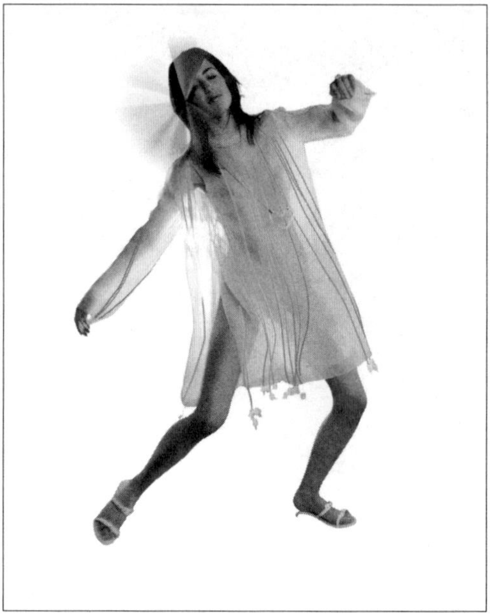

**Fig. 13.** Illustration showing *Colodours* displaying a tranquilising lavender aroma/purple colour effect or confidence boosting neroli aroma/orange colour effect depending on the degree of olfactory and visual intensity. Photograph by Guy Hills, illustration by Wendy Latham.

## Acknowledgements

The author would like to thank Central Saint Martins, The Research Centre for Fashion, The Body and Material Cultures at the University of the Arts London and the Arts and Humanities Research Council. Further thanks should also be extended to Dr Gareth Jenkins, Wendy Latham, Don Baxendale, Adeline Andre, Professor Andreas Manz, Guy Hills, John Ayres and George Dodd.

## References

1. Tillotson, J.R.: Interactive Olfactory Surfaces: The Wellness Collection – A Science Fashion Story, Royal College of Art PhD Thesis, British Library, London, UK (1997)
2. Bonneau, R., Padgett, D.A., Sheridan, J. (eds.): Twenty years of Psychoneuroimmunology and viral infections in Brain, Behavior, and Immunity, vol. 21, pp. 273–280. Elsevier, Amsterdam (2006)
3. Buck, L., Axel, R.: A Novel Multigene family encode odourant receptors: a molecular basis for odour recognition. Cell 65, 175–187 (1991)
4. World Health Organization. Burden of mental and behavioural disorders: depression disorders in The World Health Report, ch. 2, World Health Organization, Geneva (2005)
5. Warrenburg, S., Christensen, C., Wilson, C., et al.: Fragrance Research: Measuring the Emotional Power of Fragrances, March 16-18. ESMOR meeting, Amsterdam (2003)

6. Tillotson, J.R., Jenkins, G.: Scent Whisper. In: Proceedings of the IET Seminar on MEMS Sensors & Actuators (April 2006)
7. Agosta, W.: Bombardier Beetles And Fever Trees, A Close-up Look At Chemical warfare and Signals In Animals And Plants, p. 38. Addison Wesley, Reading (1996)
8. Raudenbush, B., Zoladz, P.: Cognitive enhancement through stimulation of the chemical senses. North American Journal of Psychology 7(1), 125–140 (2005)
9. Kaye, J.: Symbolic Olfactory Display. Master's thesis, Institute of Technology Media Laboratory Boston, Massachusetts, 2001 (2006)
10. Rasch, B., Büchel, C., Gais, S., Born, J.: Odor Cues During Slow-Wave Sleep Prompt Declarative Memory Consolidation. Science 315(5817), 1426–1429 (2007)
11. Preti, G., Charles, J., Wysocki, J., Kurt, T., Sondheimer, J., Leyden, J.: Male Axillary Extracts Contain Pheromones that affect pulsatile secretion of luteininizing and mood in women recipients. Biology of Reproduction 68, 2107–2113 (2003)
12. Tillotson, J.: Scentsory Wave [re]Actor: The First International Conference on Digital Live Art (September 2006), `http://www.digitalliveart.com/archive/2006/index06.htm`
13. Gardner, J.W.: Electronic Noses and Olfaction 2000. In: Proceedings of the 7th International Symposium on Olfaction and Electronic Noses, Brighton UK (July 2000)
14. Di Natale, C., Pennazza, G., Martinelli, E., Santonico, M., Macagnano, A., Paolesse, R., D'Amico, A.: Medical Diagnosis With Electronic Noses. The Journal of the Argentine Chemical Society, J. Argent. Chem. Soc. 93(1-3) Buenos Aires ene (June 2005)
15. McCulloch, M., Jezierski, T., Broffman, M., Hubbard, A., Turner, K., Janecki, K.: Diagnostic Accuracy of Canine Scent Detection in Early- and Late-Stage Lung and Breast Cancers. Integrative Cancer Therapies 5(1) (March 2006)
16. Lane, A.J.P., Wales, D.C.: An Electronic Nose to Detect Change. Perinneal Odours Associated with Estrus in The Cow. Journal of Dairy Science (1998)

# Advances in Expressive Animation in the Interactive Performance of a Butoh Dance

Jürg Gutknecht[1], Irena Kulka[1], Paul Lukowicz[2], and Tom Stricker[1]

[1] ETH Zürich, Clausiusstrasse 59, CH-8092 Zürich
[2] Universität Passau, IT Zentrum, Innstrasse 43, D-94032 Passau
gutknecht@inf.ethz.ch, irena.kulka@gmx.net,
paul.lukowicz@uni-passau.de, tomstr@acm.org

**Abstract.** In our project we are able to track and analyze the abstract-expressive, "emotional" contents of a Butoh dance performance. From the data delivered by a wearable body sensor network we extract semantic information in order to control a variety of visual effects and thus gain an explicit command over expressivity. On the basis of numerous performances we have evaluated and refined the artistic perspective of visual feedback and narrative structures in interactive improvisation. The best results were achieved with an artistic concept based on a notion of force field that is commonly sensed by a Butoh dancer. We have put a particular emphasis on exploring the choreographic challenge caused by the confrontation of intuitive improvisation with a rather rigidly structured visual biofeedback.

**Keywords:** Motion Tracking, Gesture Recognition, Emotion Space, Qualia, Expressivity, Pattern Matching, HMM, Viterbi, Butoh, Interactive Dance.

## 1 Introduction

The use of interactive feedback machines for playfully enhancing artistic performances is often considered interesting as an artistic-technical exploration per se. However, it is generally desirable to enhance a performance in terms of aesthetics and contents on deeper levels of human perception and association. For example, the experience of a meditative dance performance would greatly benefit from feedback that continuously relates to the dancer's actual state of abstract and emotional feeling. We pursued this idea in the case of Butoh dance. The resulting system comprises a motion pattern analyzer, a state recognizer, and a visualization engine.

In addition to our artistic interest, we look at this endeavor as a first step in using simple wearable devices for correlating abstract characteristics of human motion with moods, emotions and aesthetic perception. This research into the abstract expressivity of dance and music is part of the much broader field of gestural expressivity of emotions. Our work distinguishes itself from existing studies in several ways. First, comparatively few studies are targeted at the semantics of expressive movement [1]. [5], [13]. Second, most studies restrict their analysis to the small group of psychological emotions such as happiness, fear, anger etc., while our work opens up a field of applications in need of expressive languages of a more differentiated character.

R. Adams, S. Gibson, and S. Müller Arisona (Eds.): DAW/IF 2006/2007, CCIS 7, pp. 418–433, 2008.

We have implemented a complete system as depicted in Figure 1 and have used it for live performance on stage at several occasions, and we have carried out a systematic study of the accuracy of the recognition technology including an evaluation of recognition during the dance performance.

In the following, we shall first mention some related work and present the project from an artist's perspective. We then continue by explaining the visualization concept and the biofeedback system in some technical detail. Finally, we conclude with a report on the experiences made with the system at several performances.

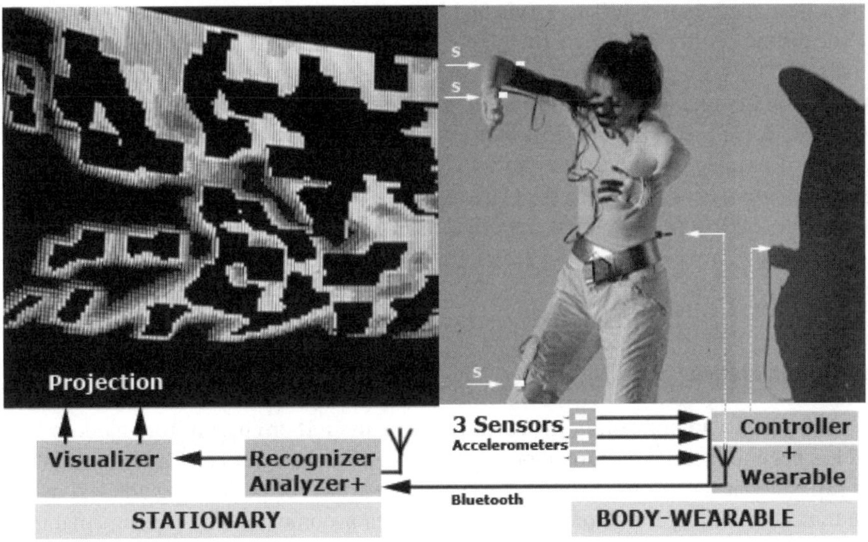


**Fig. 1.** Overview of the animation system including mobile sensors, wearable computer and the stationary visualization engine

## 2 Related work

The topic of expressive motion analysis is not new. In his *Theory of Movement* Laban describes expressive classes of movement in terms of their perceptive quality, see [6]. Recent theoretical contributions in the area come from the fields of psychology [11], motor control and cognitive science.

Motion analysis has mostly been applied so far to two areas: activity and context recognition (for example [3] and [20]) and medically oriented biomechanical analysis ([29]). The development of reliable sensor systems and of general gesture recognition frameworks is subject to ongoing research, see [15], [17], [18], [19] and [26]. The majority of work on emotion recognition has been done in the context of *affective computing*, predominantly using physiological parameters such as galvanic skin response [9]. To the best of our knowledge, acceleration sensors have not been used for emotional analysis yet. In the area of multimedia, the work on emotional analysis primarily aims at the extraction of emotions from sound and optically tracked gesture, see [1] and [4]. Inventive concepts of gestural control for audio and visualization systems have been developed by audio visual performance artists over the past decades ([24], [25], [27]). Further examples of gesture-controlled visualization systems, based on optical tracking, with an emphasis on spatial localization are given in [2]. Artists have developed specific techniques to combine dance gestures with the control of complex instruments. The authors of [14], [15], [16], [21], [22] and [23] present sensor-based interactive dance systems, with [15] and [21] focusing on motion pattern analysis but without emotional interpretation. Acceleration sensors and various other sensor technologies are used for disembodied interaction with sculptural costumes, tangible objects and mobile devices in audiovisual space settings and mobile contexts in [12], where an obvious coupling of gesture parameters to effects is applied. In the work of Levin and Lieberman, generative graphics are controlled by vocal sound patterns, thereby merging constructive rules with intuitive "synaesthetic" perception. Of particular interest to our work is an effort towards extracting emotional information from patterns of movement in dance performances using video signals as it is exhibited in [1], [7], [11] and [5]. However, these studies exploit only a very limited amount of psychic emotions that are related with a "naive" body language (happiness, anger, fear etc.), contrasting our own efforts that are targeted explicitly at differentiating a much wider variety of expressive emotional categories and abstract aesthetic "qualia".

## 3 Artistic Concepts

### 3.1 Butoh Dance

Butoh dance is a contemporary improvisational method. It originated from modern Japan and has been influential on contemporary Western dance, performance and dance theatre, see [8]. Butoh is a mixture of free-form dance improvisation, performing arts and meditative trance technique. Butoh performances are often accompanied by experimental music and visual effects, adding associative dimensions to the abstract and surreal dance. Emphasizing the exploration of inner and mystical worlds, some Butoh dancers today experiment with the "magic" of various digital media in their performances, including technologies such as musical interfaces, visuals, brain-machines and robots.

Movement in Butoh is not regarded as explicitly repeated patterns but as continuously evolving, amorphous shapes that retain some typical expressive qualities. Without any cover of standardized forms, elements of expressivity appear more purely, revealing the human sense of aesthetic abstraction in terms of movement patterns. The resulting patterns feature typical variations and similarities at specific levels of movement. It is this abstraction that makes Butoh a specifically interesting case study and a challenging problem for motion pattern recognition. The relevant patterns are isolated from:

- "Visible" patterns of body movement
- "Invisible" higher level patterns (thereby referring to the idealized model below)
- "Imaginary" external force patterns.

With our choice of a statistical pattern analysis approach described in Chapter 4 below, we capture some information from the different levels still using a relatively simple analytical framework. The higher level of abstraction might be accessible practically through sophisticated physical and motor-physiological simulations of force field effects on joint movement patterns.

Butoh dancers often sense an external field of force that controls the movement of each and every particle of their body. An appropriate model of Butoh would be the body as a swarm of points moved by spatially distributed patterns of external forces. These points mimic uncoupled behavior though in fact they are coupled within the constraints of the physical body.

Butoh dance is based on balancing some inner imagery (the proprioceptive and energetic perceptions are visualized and felt as if in space) with sensitive changes in body shape. This yields a state of continuous mental feedback between imagery and improvised movement, a trait that inspired us to develop a biofeedback system that extends the mental loop consisting of expressive impulses by external interactions with images. It is worth noting that this situation is very different from one of a naive user of interactive settings, whose gestures may have less pronounced expressive content and might be either functional such as pointing, or arbitrarily unrelated to the user's mental engagement.

### 3.2 Artistic Idea of the System or "The Body Is the Instrument"

Our vision was a system that uses gesture-controlled visuals to automatically generate and maintain a continuous semantic balance with the expressivity of improvised dance. Instead of explicitly playing an instrument (manipulating single composition elements) or composing a dance from control gestures, the performer in our case implicitly "plays visuals" through his/her intuitive body-instrument while dancing... However, in principle, the dancer can still exert control on the visual animation by intentionally "playing" his/her instrument, and much of the excitement in the use of the system is caused by the strange duality of looking at body movement as dancing on one hand and playing an instrument on the other hand. A completely new artistic challenge arises for the Butoh dancer: exploring new modes of instinctive manipulation through gestural interfaces.

### 3.3 Generating Visual Feedback as a Concept of Composition

The sensor front-end of our system recognizes different aesthetic patterns of human motion, interprets them in terms of an aesthetic feeling, and translates the "semantics" into machine-generated visual effects. The back-end, the visualization and animation engine, controls the visuals according to the following flow information:

- An abstract discrete *motion space* and a corresponding motion state recognizer
- An abstract discrete *emotion space* and a mapping from the motion space into the emotion space.
- For each emotional state a corresponding basic animation that reflects its ambience is provided.

### 3.4 The Motion Space

We chose to start from a subjective description of the dancer's mental model of motion (imagery). Initially, this lead to an extensive hierarchical system of 50 differentiated hierarchical "dimensions". The three most important ones are (a) space and field aspects, (b) relative trajectorial aspects and (c) global motoric aspects.

We distinguish between (1) space (direction and orientation of an imagined force field), (2) kinesphere (volume of action and center of imagined forces), (3) main symmetries (of force field and of action), (4) typical form of trajectory (relative directionality, fragmentation, shape), (5) texture of trajectory, fine articulation, (6) typical motor condition (muscle tension, velocity, dynamics, rhythmic aspects), (7) posture. For practical reasons, we restricted the system to the most common "dimensions" and omitted the analysis of complex postural aspects, focusing on the dynamic contributions to expressivity in movement. Figure 2 depicts the resulting three-dimensional discrete motion space.

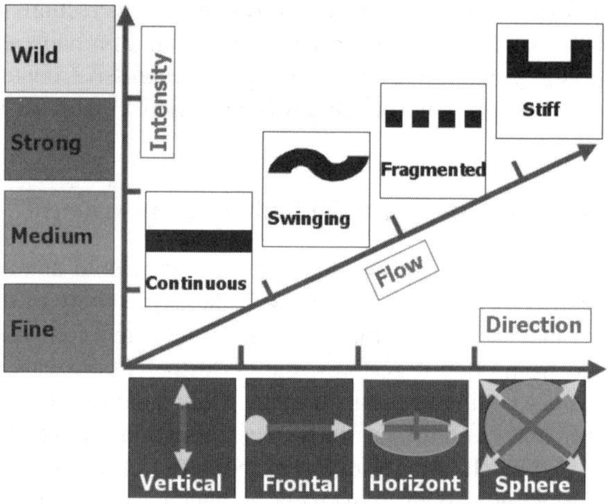


**Fig. 2.** Three-dimensional motion space corresponding to three expressive criteria: *intensity*, *flow* and *direction*, each of them featuring four distinguishable states

For the purpose of better identification we defined a set of characteristic features for each dimension that is directly derived from the tracked data (acceleration sensors mounted on wrist, upper arm and upper leg respectively).

***Dimension of Intensity:*** (1) *Fine* (extremely weak), (2) *Medium* (average, normal, relaxed, weak), (3) *Strong* (forceful), (4) *Wild* (violent, extremely strong).

***Dimension of Direction (given by a mentally sensed force field):*** (1) *Frontal* force field, (2) *Horizontal* radial force field, (3) *Vertical* force field, (4) *Spherical* force field.

***Dimension of Flow:*** (1) *Rigid* (hard, resistant), (2) *Continuous* (smooth, fluent, calm), (3) *Swinging* (dynamic, flexible), (4) *Fragmented* (staccato, discontinuous).

### 3.5 The Space of Emotions as Our Narrative Structure

Rather than aiming at merely imitating emotional human behavior, our goal remains to invent artificial structures that have an inspiring mental effect on the observer. We basically adapted the *circumplex model* [10] to the Butoh case and arranged the emotions in segments of a circular plane spanned by two orthogonal dimensions representing "pleasantness" (horizontal, from negative, painful dark to positive, bright) and "activation" (vertical, from introvert to extrovert) as depicted in Figure 3. States along radiuses vary in intensity but are of a rather similar emotional quality. A third dimension was later added to the emotion-space to enable altered narrative levels and different styles of scenery. Roughly stated, an animation sequence is now a path in the emotion-space that may or may not jump to different levels, depending on the expressive states traveled.

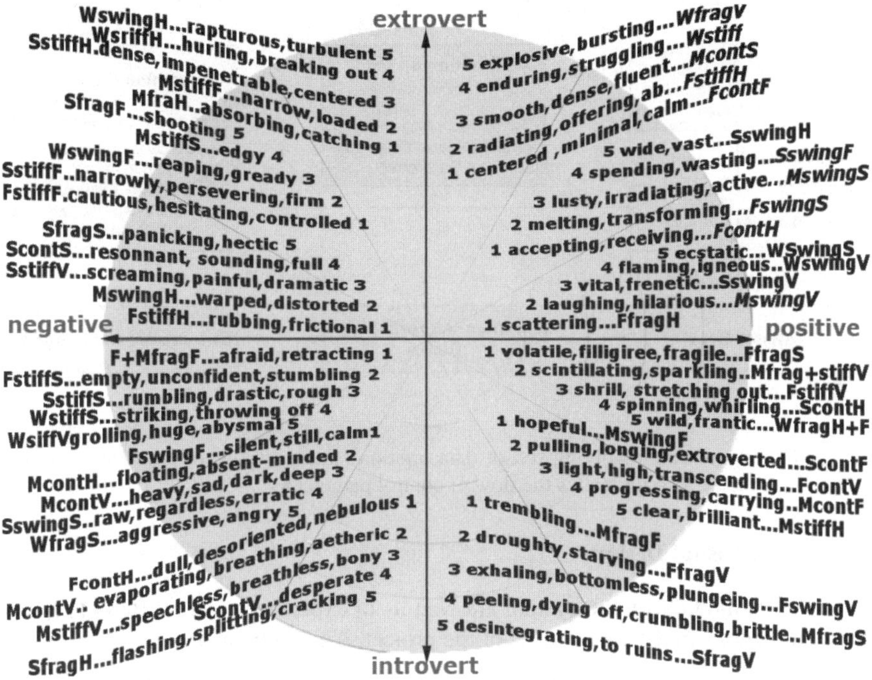


**Fig. 3.** The space of emotions in polar coordinates. Abbreviations refer to the dimensions of the motion space in Figure 2. For example, **WswingH** stands for intensity = **W**ild, flow = **swing**, and direction = **H**orizontal.

### 3.6 Mapping Motion to Emotion

The major purpose of the notions of motion space and emotion space provides a properly abstracted framework for the mapping between the physical level and the semantic level. Taking an artistic perspective, we addressed the problem of relating states of motion to states of emotion in three steps: (1) find a set of aesthetically and expressively relevant criteria that fully define the space of abstract motion states (2) construct a systematically organized scheme of emotions, (3) find an intuitive connection between any specific state of motion and a corresponding emotional state. It should be mentioned that there are many ambiguities in such a mapping [13], and sophisticated psychological methods would have to be used to resolve them.

The corresponding animations in a dance performance are parameterized variants of basic animations reflecting the various emotional states, where the parameters are derived from some continuously sensed expressive features of the movement. A wide spectrum of aesthetic articulation in animations is ranging from basic pictures of ambience to continuous feature-driven effects in real time. Figure 4 summarizes the entire animation logic in schematic form.

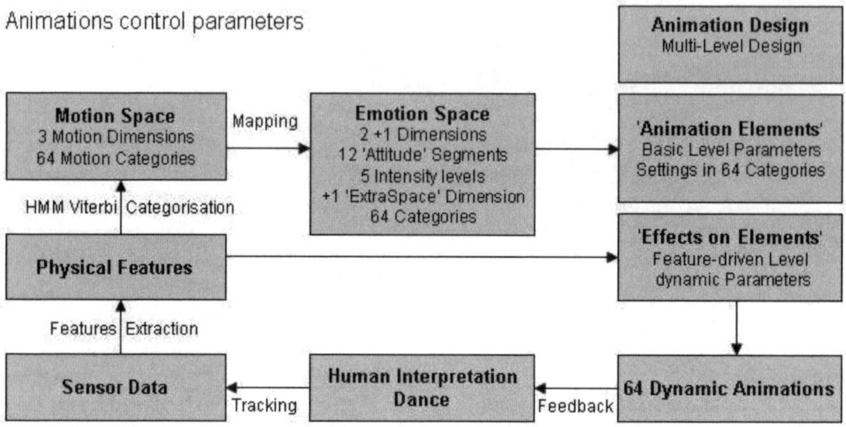


**Fig. 4.** Mapping scheme involving sensor data, motion patterns, space of emotions and visual effects. The scheme also illustrates the flow of control parameters.

### 3.7 Artistic Visual Design

Thanks to its modularity the system allowed us to experiment with different types of visual animations in different stages of the project. Among them are

- Interactively composed abstract visual 'textures' (Figure 9) corresponding to mental imagery in abstract dancing
- Photographic collages with symbolic elements. This class of elements made our performance "Transitions" based on the idea of re-visiting and traveling through a "Space of Memories" and imaginations (Figure 10)
- For the first performances of "Instant Gain in Grace", we used abstract symbols on a photographic background. In the current version of "Instant Gain in Grace" we employ a layered system of vector fields and collections of moving particles as described in Chapter 6. With this concept, we achieved sufficient diversity to animate more than 100 different expressive 'moods'.

## 4 The Recognition Engine

The problem of recognizing the different classes of motion states in a dance performance was a key scientific challenge in the original project. Unlike many other approaches to motion tracking, our method does not rely on optical recognition techniques or on kinematical computations. Instead, the recognition problem is solved as a pure *pattern recognition* problem, where the patterns are generated by a set of cheap, body-mounted acceleration sensors worn by the dancers (see Chapter 5).

Roughly speaking, the basic steps of the recognition algorithm are the following:

- Each body-mounted sensor delivers three *signals*, that is three clocked streams of numerical data $a_x$, $a_y$, $a_z$, each of them reflecting the magnitude of the acceleration relative to one of the sensor's coordinate axes.
- Using a standard sliding window mechanism as depicted in Figures 5 and 6 below, several *features* ("observables") are extracted from the signals, and three Hidden Markov Models (HMM) in combination with a Viterbi algorithm are applied to compute the (most probable) sequence of motion states just passed.
- From the computed sequence of motion states, the *dominant motion state* is determined on the basis of a simple majority criterion.

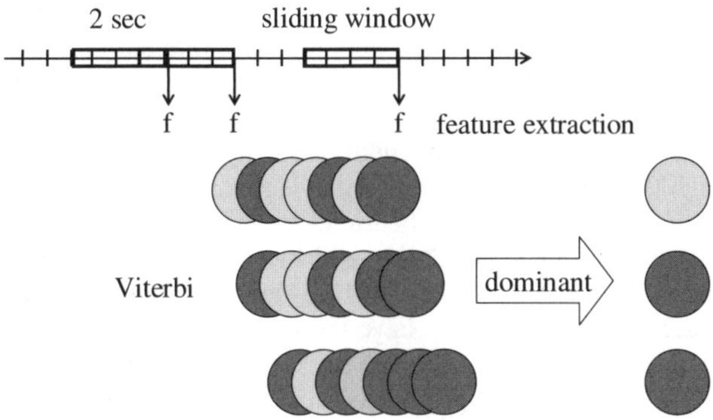


**Fig. 5.** Schematic description of the HMM-based recognition engine

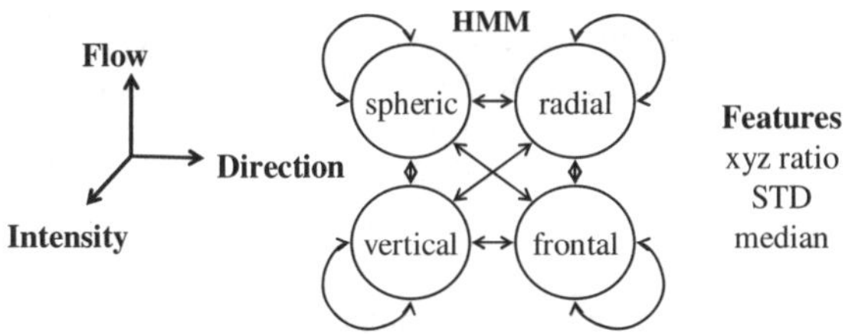


**Fig. 6.** HMM engine corresponding to the *Direction* dimension

The success rate of the recognition algorithm crucially depends on a variety of parameters including the placement of the sensors, the kind of features, the size of the sliding window, and the quality of the transition parameters in the HMM. Thanks to a careful choice of all parameters, based on physical considerations, on an extensive training phase, and on numerous systematic tests, a very good success rate reaching almost 90% could finally be achieved. The optimal placement of the sensors is shown in Figure 1, while all other details of the choice of parameters and of the recognition engine in general are given in [13].

# 5 System Architecture

Figure 1 also shows the overall biofeedback system architecture that comprises three physical subsystems: the *sensor body network*, the *wearable computer*, and the *stationary system*.

## 5.1 The Sensor Body Network

The sensor nodes used are provided by the Pad'Net (Physical Activity Detection Network) wearable sensor network developed at the ETH and described in detail in [3]. It consists of multiple sensor nodes interconnected in a hierarchical network. The purpose of a sensor node is to provide a physical interface for different sensor types, to read out the corresponding sensor signal, to provide certain computation power for signal preprocessing and to enable communication between the other sensor nodes in the network. For the experiments three 3D-accelerometers (ADXL202E from Analog Devices) were used. The analog signals from the sensor were low-pass filtered ($f_{cutoff}$=50Hz), converted from analog to digital with 12Bit resolution using a sampling rate of 100Hz.

Close analysis of a number of dance sequences and interviews with the performer have revealed that the key information about dance style can be found in the motion of the arm. Although the performer has argued that leg motions are irrelevant, signals from the upper legs have been also found to be useful for the separation of some classes. This is due to the fact that leg movements are used mostly to compensate for arm-motions allowing the dancer to keep her balance. Thus they are correlated with style.

As a consequence of the above we have decided to use sensors placed on the wrist, the upper arm and the upper leg. Since, with respect to the dance style, there is no difference between right and left arm/leg, sensors were placed only on the right upper arm, wrist and leg.

## 5.2 The Mobile System (Wearable Computer)

The choice of a wearable computer depends on the amount of processing that it needs to do. In the simplest case it just needs to collect the raw signals from the sensors and send them the visualization system. For this case the top-level node of the Pad'Net hierarchy was connected to a Bluetooth module.

In general however, it is desirable to perform parts or the entire pattern classification task on the wearable system. There are two reasons for this. The first one is technical: transmitting raw data from all sensors to a stationary machine over a wireless network requires more energy than doing the classification locally and transmitting selected events. The second one is conceptual; different performers might want to have their personal mapping of motions to classes and visualization events. Thus it makes sense for the recognition to be done by a personal device, which is fully controlled by the user.

In the more recent performances a wearable computer is used that, in offline mode, can be used to simply record motion patterns.

## 5.3 The Stationary System

The stationary system comprises two functional components: the *recognition- and analyzer-module* and the *visualization engine*. An event-oriented programming interface connects the two functional components through UDP/TCP/IP protocols (see Figure 7 & 8). While the recognition/analyzer module is implemented in *Matlab*, the visualization engine has been designed from the ground up just for this project. The development is based on a super-efficient custom runtime kernel called *Aos* [28] and on its graphics shell *Bluebottle*.

While the first version in 2004 used one single compact PC (Shuttle) to run both the recognition/analyzer module and the visualization engine a more advanced version of the stationary system spreads the work over multiple computers. Synchronizing the multiple visualization engines turned out to be a major challenge. The most consistent results were achieved with a master-slave architecture, where the master computer periodically waits for the slave computers to visualize its part of the next scenery before passing over a new set of feature parameters.

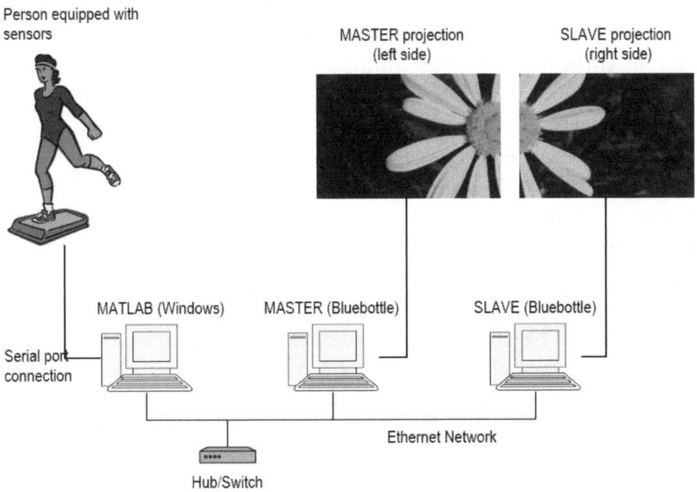


**Fig. 7.** A version of the stationary system using a dual display screen

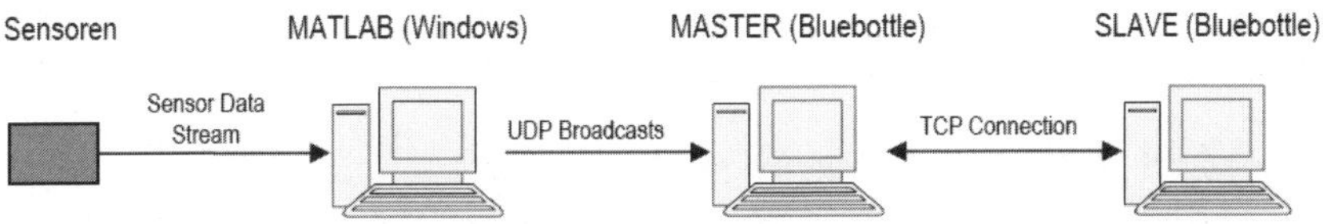


**Fig. 8.** Communication between the different components of the stationary system

## 6 The Visualization Engine

Matching the silent nature of Butoh dance, we decided in favor of a visual approach to feedback, in contrast to the more common audio-oriented systems. After extensive discussions, we agreed on a *two level* event-based animation policy. Basically, first level events are used to select the animation scenery corresponding to the current *expressive category*, while second level events reflect *motion features* such as root mean square or number of peaks and control animation parameters within the current scenery, for example the size and color of actor objects (particles) their density and frequency, the direction and speed of the vector field and thus of the particles. The benefit of the two-level visual system is the option of creating interesting overlays of direct kinematic feedback and less direct effects based on a coarse-grained expressive design of the animation categories.

The animation scenarios supported by our system are *dynamic systems* expressed as vector fields. Figure 9 shows two snapshots. While a suitable type of a dynamic system is statically associated with each expressive category, parameters like flow direction and speed, shape, size and color of moving particles, as well as their appearance are controlled dynamically via motion features. More precisely, the animated dynamics are based on repetitively dropping particles into the corresponding vector field and iteratively visualizing their position while they move along their trajectory. In addition, some enhancing effects are supported such as particle fillings, arbitrary background picture, overlaying clouds, and diffusing and fading of the moving particles. Technically, an object of the following kind is created for each expressive category (corresponding to a "state of emotion") at system start, where the dynamic system controller that orchestrates the animation calls the *Iterate* method repetitively.

```
object Emotion;
  procedure Iterate (img: Raster.Image);
  begin
    dropper.Do(grid); (* Drop elements into the grid *)
    vf.Proceed(grid); (* Move the particles *)
    renderer.Clouds(grid); (* render clouds *)
    diffuser.Do(grid); (* diffuse grid *)
    renderer.Do(grid, img); (* render image *)
  end Iterate;
end Emotion;
```

The system supports a flexible parameterization scheme based on XML configuration scripts. For each expressive category, its name and type are specified as attributes of a describing XML element, while the parameters for dropper, field equation, diffuser and renderer are child elements:

```
<Emotion Name = " " Type = "">
    <Diffusion ExampleValue = "value"/>
    <VectorField/>
    <Render/>
    <Drop/>
</Emotion>
```

It is worth noting that the dancer, who also defined the basic expressive design components of each animation offline, and mapped the corresponding expressive animations to each category of motion expressivity, could easily adjust the parameters. Thanks to the clearly defined event interface, the custom animation engine can easily be replaced by any other. In particular, we recently experimented with Max/MSP as an alternative visualization back-end.

## 7 Artistic Evaluation by Live Performances

Figures 9 and 10 give an impression of the different styles of visual feedback used in a series of five performances in the years 2005 and 2006 in front of a larger audience. Our experience can be summarized as follows. A substantial part of the audience perceived the visual effects spontaneously as correlated with the Butoh dance and enhancing the performance – even without any prior knowledge of the concepts behind our system. Some spectators were disturbed by the simultaneous perception of the dancer and the moving patterns of animation. Establishing true aesthetic harmony usually requires additional artistic steps and some stylistic reduction.

The dancer felt that the interaction with the system added dramaturgic tension to the performance, and the need to simultaneously interact with the image and the audience was quite challenging. The improvising dancer can cope with artifacts such as an inherent delay and intermittent quality of the recognition system. As a matter of fact, the delay creates a sense of a dialogue of alternating action and response between two parties and it thereby fits well our original idea of a continuous dialogue (with some autonomous behavior of the machine) rather than immediate one-way-feedback. The optimal temporal distance and the optimal aesthetic confluence between 'response' and 'answer' (including the sense of aesthetic unity of actor and environment) are still subject to further research.

Some inherent deficiencies of the system require strategic counter measures. For example, delayed or incorrect recognition of motion patterns can partly be overcome by graphical effects that are generated - independently of the classification - from feature data streams to provide a simple aesthetic linking between unmatched categories. Other strategic adaptations are conscious repetitions of some of the trained motion patterns (in addition to the more unintentional, less predictable, typical slow-motion Butoh mode) and artificially extended phases of the dance to achieve congruence with the animated category. In this sense, the machine could also be used as a challenging coach.

Our experience from many performances show that the visual language used for the purpose of enhancement must be relatively simple, aesthetically readable and intuitively interpretable, so that the audience can immediately grasp the essence of the interaction. From this perspective, the use of the vector field metaphor was a big progress. In the future, we will definitely explore additional choreographic possibilities.

Another challenge is continuity across changes of the emotional category. Many spectators perceived transitions from the animation of one emotional category to another one as a 'hard cut'. Again, a more prominent use of graphical effects that are generated directly from feature data streams are a promising approach – besides of the choice of a more minimalist style in the aesthetic design

Future research will not be able to ignore the perception of harmony as a law of tension, reduction and density (minimal amount of differences, near-similarity and redundancy of patterns). Reduction and aesthetic condensation of elements such as colors shapes etc… was a method to achieve a closer aesthetic relationship. Paradoxically, some very small aesthetic variations of sensibilities of the system can lead to a much improved readability and comprehensibility and significantly facilitate the differentiated control by the dancer.

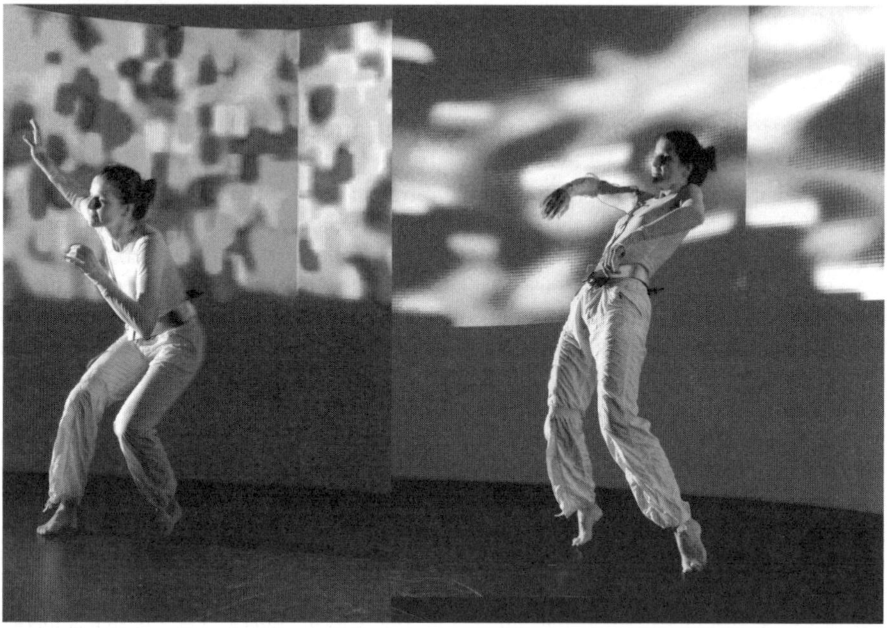

**Fig. 9.** Visually enhanced Butoh dance performance using vector field animations, as presented at the 150-year anniversary celebration of ETH Zurich and at the Digital Art Weeks DAW Zürich in 2005

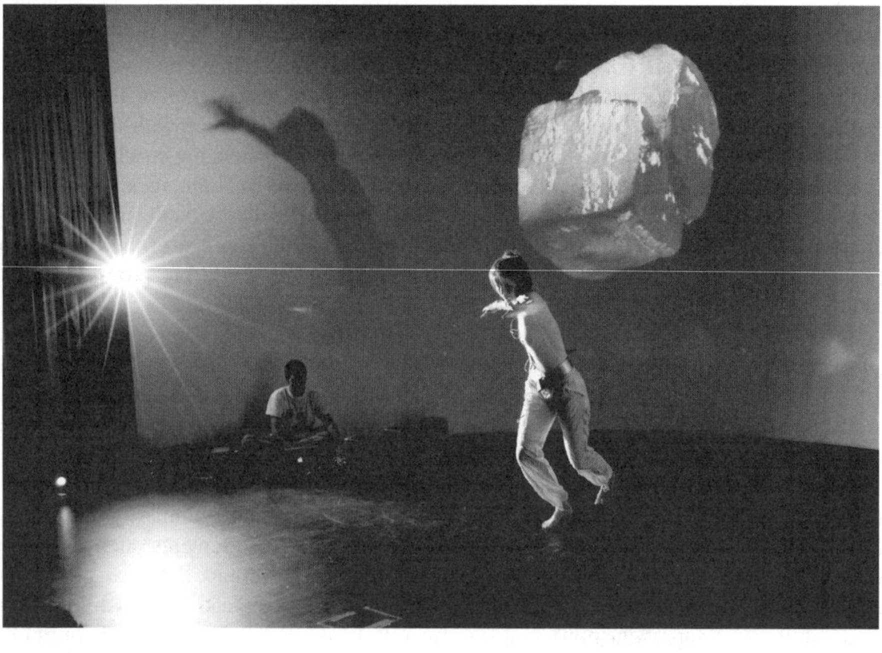

**Fig. 10.** Example of photographic collages used in a performance

## 8 Conclusions and Future Work

Our refined concept of visual animations based on the emotion classification can be used in an artistic performance in such a way that is perceived as enrichment by the artist and the audience. In particular we were able to make a connection between dance and visualization by using the force field sensed by the Butoh dancer to drive the dynamics of the visualization.

The technical system was extended to comprise multiple CPU mapping the streams of sensor and pattern data to an ensemble of different computers running different operating systems. With a master/slave setting we can run an arbitrary number of displays permitting a more immersive experience to a larger audience.

At the conceptual level our artistic project provides technology applicable to a wider scope of applications. For example, future plans include an audio version of biofeedback. Also, there are still limitations to our system at several levels of abstraction, for example concerning the structure of the motion space, the structure of the emotion space, and the mapping between the two.

Still our categories seem to be pronounced enough to perform a quality test of the recognition and most of the classes are consciously created and reproducibly recognized. We achieve a recognition rate of approximately 90 percent while re-recognizing the isolated patterns of the training set itself. The recognition rate during a dance performance might be considerably lower, but the performance experience shows that it is enough give some significant biofeedback to the dancer and the sense of visual enhancement and a great experience to the audience.

**Acknowledgments.** This project grew out of a diploma thesis at the Hyperwerk FHBB in Basel and a first performance took place in 2004. Without the highly dedicated work of many contributors, this interdisciplinary project would not have come to reality. We particularly gratefully acknowledge the valuable contributions of the following persons and institutions: Art Clay (DAW Management), Thomas Frey (Graphics API), Martin Gernss (1st Version Visualization Software), Michael Barry (Recognition Engine), Holger Junker (PadNet SensorSystem), Fabian Nart (2nd Version of the Animations Software), Sven Stauber (Optimization of the communication system and synchronization of the dual screens), and Christine Bärlocher (Photographs).

## References

1. Camurri, A., Mazzarino, B., Ricchetti, M., Timmers, V.G.: Multimodal Analysis of Expressive Gesture in Music and Dance Performances. In: Camurri, A., Volpe, G. (eds.) GW 2003. LNCS (LNAI), vol. 2915, pp. 20–39. Springer, Heidelberg (2004)
2. Horace, H., Ip, S., Hay, Y., Tang, A.C.C.: Body-brush: A body-driven interface for visual aesthetics. In: Proceedings of the 10th ACM intl conf. on Multimedia (Multimedia 2002), pp. 664–665. ACM Press, New York (2002)
3. Junker, H., Lukowicz, P., Tröster, G.: Padnet: Wearable physical activity detection network. In: Proceedings of the 7th International Symposium on Wearable Computers, New York, USA, October 2003, pp. 244–245 (2003)

4. Kang, H.-B.: Affective content detection using hmms. In: Proceedings of the eleventh ACM international conference on Multimedia, pp. 259–262. ACM Press, New York (2003)
5. MacFarlane, L.I., Kulka, I., Pollick, F.E.: The representation of affect revealed by Butoh dance, vol. 47 (2004)
6. Laban, R., Lawrence, F.C.: Effort. Macdonald and Evans, London (1947)
7. Suzuki, R., Iwadate, Y., Inoue, M., Woontack, W.: Midas: Mic interactive dance system. In: Proceedings of the, 2000 IEEE International Conference on Systems, Man and Cybernetics, vol. 2, pp. 751–756 (2000)
8. Nanako, K.T., Hijikata, T.: The words of Butoh. The Drama Review 44, 12–28 (2000)
9. Picard, R.W., Vyzas, E., Healey, J.: Toward machine emotional intelligence: Analysis of affective physiological state. IEEE Trans. Pattern Anal. and Mach. Intel l. 23(10), 1175–1191 (2001)
10. Plutchik, R.H., Conte, H.: Circumplex Models of Personality and Emotions. APA Books, Washington (1996)
11. Pollick, F.E.: The features people use to recognize human movement style. In: Proceedings of the 5th Workshop on Guesture and Sign Language base HCI, Genova (2003)
12. Sha, X.W., Serita, Y., Fantauzza, J., Dow, S., Iachello, G., Fiano, V., Berzowska, J., Caravia, Y., Nain, D., Reitberger, W., Fistre, J.: Demonstrations of expressive softwear and ambient media. In: Proc.of UbiComp 2003 (2003)
13. Barry, M., Gutknecht, J., Kulka, I., Lukowicz, P., Stricker, T.: From Motion To Emotion: A Wearable System for the Multimedial Enrichment of a Butoh Dance Performance. Journal of Mobile Multimedia 1(2), 112–132 (2005)
14. Wechsler, R., et al.: EyeCon - A motion sensing tool for creating interactive dance, music, and video projections. In: Proc. of the SSAISB Convention, Leeds, England (2004), `http://www.palindrome.de`
15. Lovell, S.D.: A system for real-time gesture recognition and classification of coordinated motion. Master's thesis, MIT EECS (January 2005), `https://www.media.mit.edu/resenv/pubs/theses/LovellMEngThesis.pdf`
16. Downie, M.: Choreographing the Extended Agent: Performance Graphics for Dance Theater.m PhD thesis, MIT Media Laboratory (September 2005), `http://www.openendedgroup.com/index.php/publications/thesis-downie/`, `http://www.artificial.dk/articles/downie.htm`
17. Kwon, D.Y.: A Design Framework for 3D Spatial Gesture Interfaces. Dissertation ETH Zürich, Switzerland (2007)
18. Barry, M.K.: Limitations of low-cost wearable sensor systems, and strategies to overcome them, Dissertation University for Health Sciences Mediacl Informatics and Technology, Hall, Tyrol, Austria (2008)
19. Junker, H.: Human Activity Recognition and Gesture Spotting with Body-Worn Sensors.PhD thesis, Swiss Federal Institute of Technology, ETH, Zürich (2005)
20. Junker, H., Lukowicz, P., Tröster, G.: Continuous recognition from activities with body-worn inertial sensors. In: 8th International Symposiumon Wearable Computers (ISWC 2004), Arlington,VA, USA, October 31– November 3, 2004, pp. 188–189 (2004)
21. Aylward, R., Paradiso, J.A.: A compact, high-speed, wearable sensor network for biomotion capture and interactive media. In: Information Processing In Sensor Networks. In: Proceedings of the 6th international conference on Information processing in sensor networks, pp. 380–389 (2007)

22. Qian, G., Guo, F., Ingalls, T., Olson, L., James, J., Rikakis, T.: A gesture driven multimodal interactive dance system. In: Proceedings of the International Conf. on Multimedia and Expo (2004), `http://ame2.asu.edu/faculty/qian/Publications/icme04-ame.pdf`
23. Coniglio, M.: The MidiDancer system, `http://www.troikaranch.org/mididancer.html`
24. Tanaka, A., Babiole, C., Dailleau, L.: Sensors Sonics Sights, `http://www.xmira.com/sss/`
25. Tanaka, A.: Musical Performance Practice on Sensor-based Instruments. In: Wanderley, M., Battier, M. (eds.) Trends in Gestural Control of Music, pp. 389–405. IRCAM, Paris (2000)
26. Kunze, K., Barry, M., Heinz, E., Lukowicz, P., Majoe, D., Gutknecht, J.: Towards recognizing tai chi - an initial experiment. In: Proceedings of the Third International Forum on Applied Wearable Computing, pp. 183–191 (2006)
27. Borchers, J.O., Lee, E., Samminger, W., Mühlhauser, M.: Personal orchestra: a real-time audio/video system for interactive conducting. Multimedia Systems 9(5) (2004)
28. Muller, P.: A multiprocessor kernel for active object-based systems. In: Weck, W., Gutknecht, J. (eds.) JMLC 2000. LNCS, vol. 1897, pp. 263–277. Springer, Heidelberg (2000)
29. Gellersen, M., Sloman, O., Wells, P., Needham, N., Peters, A., Darzi, C., Toumazou, G., Yang, Z.: Medical healthcare monitoring with wearable and implantable sensors. In: International Workshop on Ubiquitous Computing for Pervasive Healthcare Applications (UbiHealth) (2004)

# Anthropocentrism and the Staging of Robots

Louis-Philippe Demers[1] and Jana Horakova[2]

[1] Interaction and Entertainment Research Centre, 50 Nanyang Dr., Research Techno Plaza, Nanyang Technological University, Singapore 637553
lpdemers@ntu.edu.sg
[2] Masaryk University, Faculty of Arts, Department of Musicology/Interactive Media Studies, A.Novaka 1, Brno, Czech Republic
horakova@phil.mu.cz

**Abstract.** By investigating the representations of the human throughout history of the robots, we analyze robotic performances from a theatrical audience *pragmatic* point of view. Hence, this interpretation of robots as performers, or staged robots, involves an act of *suspension of disbelief* as a first and constitutive condition of *theatrical reality*. As an early analysis of *robotic performances* and *robots as performers*, this paper focuses on the notions of *anthropomorphism* and *anthropopathy*.

**Keywords:** Robotic art, kinetic art, acting, puppetry, artificial intelligence, artificial life, theatre, stage, semiotic, ontology.

## 1 Introduction

What is it that we see on a theatrical stage? It is said that it happens here and now but is it real? Or is it just an illusion? Theatre theory and practice no longer look upon stage production and theatrical performances as being more or less realistic, naturalistic, stylized or having the form of an artificial (virtual) reality. Theatrical reality has statute of an illusion or a fiction that indicates, evokes and suggests something, but does not strictly embody it. From a semiotics perspective, theatrical performance is considered as a means to transform 'reality' into sign-systems[1] and/or into a play [2, 34, 38]. This leads towards a formulation of theatre as a laboratory of sign productions and their interpretations. Consequently, robotic theatrical performances deal with the dynamic processes of the sign-robotic creation of significance and interpretations of meanings, within specific cultural and historical contexts. Deleuze positions the mechanical realm within its context: „The machines don't explain anything, you have to analyze the collective arrangements of which machines are just one component." [8] Mumford equally analyzes that machines are a mythical construction, which are not solely a complex tool (apparatus) but also a social apparatus. They are not only constituted of material parts but also of immaterial elements, of a mentality and a belief into a goal or an effect. [29].

[1] In the body of this text, we will refer to sign-systems by the doublet *sign-signifier*, for example *sign-action*.

R. Adams, S. Gibson, and S. Müller Arisona (Eds.): DAW/IF 2006/2007, CCIS 7, pp. 434–450, 2008.

This paper will focus on an understanding of robotic performances and robots as performers from the audience perspective by questioning the human ability and need to identify, empathize and project him/herself into performers, either objects or humans, on the stage.

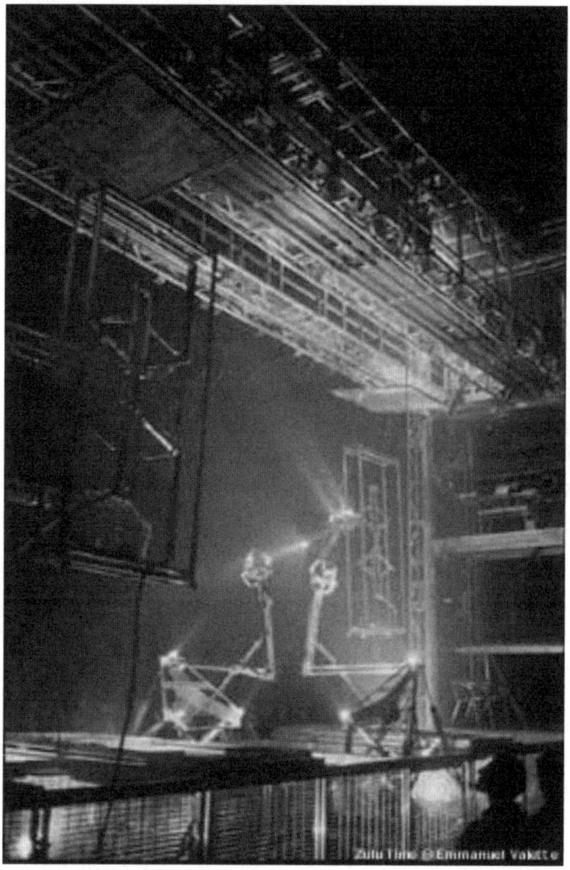

**Fig. 1.** Robot characters from *Le Procès* (1999)

The robotic characters depicted in Figure 1 are the main protagonists of the machinic performance adaptation of Le Procès a novel by Franz Kafka (Kafka 1925, Demers 1999). These robots are deliberately part zoomorphic (an arm, a hand), part mechanomorphic (the lower body is a simulation platform structure); a sign-design that comprises both inert and living connotations about the performing objects. In parallel to human performers, we can ask, whether and how are these robot performers able to carry an alternate set of sign-systems of their bodies (shape, material) and their behaviors (actions).

The semiotic system of theatre is based on theatrical convention as well as on automatisms of (human) semiological communication and understanding. Dennett refers to one of these automatisms when he sustains, that intents are attributed to outside agents that act upon the physical world [13]. This raises questions about the level of anthropomorphism needed in robots to attribute intent onto their behavior [15, 26]. It also raises discussions in relation to the act of projecting intent, questioning if this is an inevitable reflex or not [16].

## 2 Robots – A History of Lures

The history of representations, models and simulations of the living by means of mechanical objects is around two millennia old. This history is driven by the ongoing quest for a true genesis and the deeper understanding of the inner self or the universe. It is significant that outcomes of this effort, embodied in different robots/machines, are typically exploiting theatrical means [20, 36]. The theatrical stage allows, by it's ambiguous ontological character, the arrangement of mise-en-scènes that resonate with the paradoxical status of the quasi-living entities.

### 2.1 Artificial Humans – An Early Quest

In recent artificial intelligence (AI) research, so-called social robots have mainly embraced the humanoid form with friendly behaviors as the privileged mode of intercommunication [17]. The urge for humanoid form/appearance of robots, in the contemporary sense of the word, connects them with a long history written in myths, legends and even in real experiments. This demand includes in itself two motives: on one hand it is the human dream to create an artificial human being. We can analyze this as an attempt to imitate a 'Creator', to make a creature in our own image or even to discover the secret of life. On the other hand it is an entirely practical ambition to make optimal or perfect servants of man (this motif is often connected with utopian projections of an ideally ordered social system). Aristotle in his fundamental work Politics wrote: "For if every instrument could accomplish its own work, obeying or anticipating the will of others, like the statue of Daedalus, or the tripods of Hephaestus, which, says the poet, 'of their own accord entered the assembly of the Gods'; if, in like manner, the shuttle would weave and the plectrum touch the lyre without a hand to guide them, chief workman would not want servants, nor master slaves." [1]

Robotic art emerged in 1960's (see section 2.5), around the same time as Robotics and Artificial Intelligence - scientific and engineering disciplines that have developed from assumptions established by Cybernetics. However, robotic art has deeper roots and a rich cultural history. It refers to modern science-fiction as much as to artificial creatures (either real or imaginary) from ancient artificial maidservants, mediaeval Golem and Homunculus of Renaissance to Enlightenment androids.

Tomas writes about historical modifications of human-machine relationship as the "machine-based history of western body" [39]. Tomas often refers to Cybernetics discourse, particularly to Norbert Wiener's writing on a history of mirroring of human body in machine. Wiener (1948) [40] traced parallel history of machine and human body when he presented a history of automata that was divided into four stages that generated four models of the human body: a mythic Golemic age that refers to the body as a malleable, magical, clay figure; the age of clocks (17th and 18th centuries) that sees the body as a clockwork mechanism; the age of steam (19th century) that brought the body as a " glorified heat engine, burning some combustible fuel instead of the glycerin of human muscles"; finally the age of communication and control (the age of cybernetics), an age marked by a shift from power engineering to information and communication engineering, from "economy of energy" to the economy based on "the accurate reproduction of signal" that understand body as an electronic system.

### 2.2 Čapek's Robots

It is impossible to interpret and understand robot and robotic art out of its cultural context and history, or outside the different connotations and associations connected with the word robot.[2] The word robot appeared for the first time in a play R. U. R., Rossum Universal Robots (National Theatre in Prague, 1921) by the Czech writer Karel Čapek.[3] Figure 2 (left) shows the robot embodiment in the first official stage production of the play, whereas the right image shows the robot as a puppet/apparatus in a later production (Paris, 1924). The variation between mechanized man on the left and the humanoid machine on the right side indicates an interpretative shift towards the conceptualization of the robot during the 20th century [23, 24].

Karel Čapek wrote about concepts/ideas that stand behind his decision to write 'play about Robots'. It shows Čapek's understanding of his Robot/s as an embodiment of the image of man of his time, formed by industrial serial mass production (see machine-based history of human body [39]). "Robots were a result of my travelling by tram.... People were stuffed inside as well as on stairs, not as sheep but as machines. I started to think about humans not as individuals but as machines and on my way home I was thinking about an expression that would refer to humans capable of work but not of thinking. This idea is expressed by a Czech word robot."[4] Čapek connected his Robots with the history of artificial creatures. Specifically with Prague Golem legend, when he said: "R.U.R. is in fact a transformation of the Golem legend into a modern form.... Robots are factory mass-produced Golems".

A further understanding of the origins of the Robot character is to be derived from the many other artificial creatures of the Čapek brothers. The short story Systém (System) (1908/18) is often mentioned as an earlier version of R. U. R. plot. The story is based on the idea of "culturally reformed" workers adjusted for manual work exclusively. In the Instructive Story (1908) and L´eventail (1908/16) the brothers brought into their fiction the figure of Jacquet-Droz (see next section) as a real character along with his fictitious mechanical androids (see fig. 3).

The theme of mechanical humanoid machines is present in separate work by Josef Čapek, the real author of the word, as well. One instance appeared as "mechanical alter-ego" constructed by an engineer in his short story Opilec (The Drunkard) included in collection Lelio (1917). However, the mechanical double is called simply "mechanism", not a Robot in the story. The artistic essay Homo Artefactus (1924) by Josef Čapek is both a recapitulation and a satirical commentary on the theme of the artificial man that appeared in the beginning of the 20th century as a notion of a ´new man´.

---

[2] The word robot is a neologism derived etymologically from the archaic Czech word robota. *Robota* means drudgery or an obligatory work in Czech language.

[3] *R.U.R.* is interpreted as a comedy of confusion in which we are not able to distinguish between man and Robot in [22].

[4] Čapek, K. Evening Standard (June 2, 1924). In Čapek, K. R.U.R. Halík, M. (ed.) Československý spisovatel, Praha, 1966.

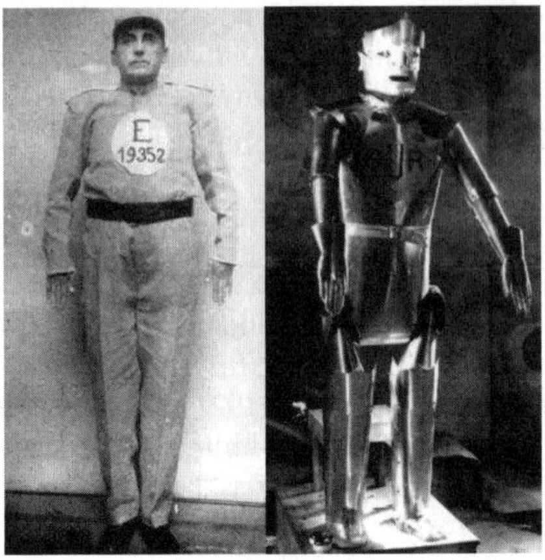


**Fig. 2.** Robot character from *RUR*. Left, first night in Prague. Right, later in Paris.

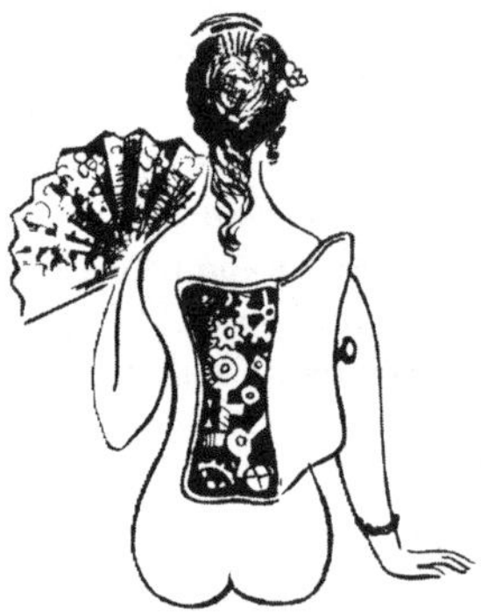

**Fig. 3.** *L'eventail* - Lady with a fan that is able to say only "si" or "no". Illustration from J. Čapek´s *Homo Artefactus* (1924).

### 2.3 Androids

The swindle or trick of the Robot can be found in the ambiguous status of an artificial human-like (android) creature's existence. It is present not only in the case of fictitious artificial creatures but also in the case of 'real' mechanic puppets or androids. As Sussman argues, thaumaturgical strategies often further intensify this trick during their public performances. Sussman started from assumption that "Certain pre-technological performances… can give us some insight into the tense metaphoric operations and interconnections of faith and skepticism, or belief and disbelief, in the staging of new technologies…."[36] In his analysis of staging of Chess Player automaton by Wolfgang von Kempelen from Bratislava, Sussman came to the conclusion, which can be extended to the context of androids/automatons in general: "The automatic thinking machine that concealed, in reality, a human person, can be seen as a model for how a spectator might reify, and deify, the hidden power at work in a new form of intelligent machinery…. The visual proof was, first, the demonstration of control at a distance; and, second, the transmission of human intelligence into inanimate body of the object; the performing object that animates both demystification and reenchantment."[36]

Androids/automata are often connected with the effort of their designers to show their own (human) competence and workmanship. We can find references to designers of anthropomorphic automatons since antiquity (Architás from Tarent, Hérón Alexandricos called Mechanicos). Ample references to androids and their creators in the periods of the Rococo and Neoclassicism (Enlightenment, 18th century) denote the high popularity of mechanical dolls in these periods. Swiss mechanists and clock workers, father and son Pierre and Henri Louis Jacquet-Droz (1721-1790,1752-1791) constructed The Writer, The Draftsman and The Musician (a lady playing the piano). Arguably Jacquet-Droz might have programmed his automaton to write the sentence "Cogito ergo sum" in order to make a play of words on Descartes contemporary theories. This play reflects the undecidable (in logic systems, neither true or false) status of the artificial being; a similar logical problem found in the recursive statement "I am a liar."

The ambiguous existence of androids/automata was enhanced not only by the way they were staged [36], but also by their appearance. Wood takes notice that in the Age of Enlightenment androids/automata were frequently designed in the image of children: "some inventors intended their objects to be artificial forms of an eighteen-century ideal - the child as a blank slate, the purest being."[42] Moreover, Jacquet-Droz's barefoot writing automaton, with its schoolboy appearance, represents the conviction of the period that children would learn more freely if unhampered by shoes [42]. A child-like appearance served as a trick that would manipulate audiences' evaluation and impressions from the performance as well: "their creators wanted them to look young so that the mistakes resulting from their early efforts (as a prototypes) would be forgiven."[42] The android's child-like appearance functioned as a sign of perfection (innocent beings) and suggestion of automatons' ability to learn as well as a trick that change audience's attitude towards (possible) unexpected failures of automatons.

The ontology of these automatons was masked/camouflaged[5] and interpreted as an ambiguous fluctuation between the mechanic and organic, between living and non-living. "When Pierre Jacquet-Droz exhibited his writing automaton in Spain, he was accused of heresy; both the man and the machine were imprisoned for a time by the Spanish Inquisition."[42] A journalist that experienced one performance of „Musical Lady" reports acceptance of the android's liveliness. The android was advertised on poster as a "vestal virgin with a heart of steel", but the journalist gave us a different impression when he wrote: "she is apparently agitated with an anxiety and diffidence not always felt in real life."[42] The android seems to him to be more alive than life commonly manifests itself.

### 2.4 Puppets: Inert Performers

Robotic performers and puppets share two essential characteristics: they are inert entities further "animated" and are called upon to perform in the front of an audience. In addition, puppets' morphologies, as for robotic performers, vary widely from virtual disembodied shadows or abstract objects to strong human representations. Tellis[38] states that puppets that attempt to imitate human often create a superficial sense of realism. The illusion

[5] There are examples of ideas of Androids that bleeds 'real' blood or covered with 'real' skin [42].

of life derived by movements exclusive to their morphology can more easily encourage the audience to accept the living existence of an otherwise inanimate object.

Tellis argues that the puppet takes on its metaphorical connotation because it inherently provokes the process of double-vision, creating doubt as its ontological status. On the other hand it is an example of theatrical suspension of disbelief and projection of audience psychological movements into the actor/character, because "anxiety and diffidence" is a typical human reaction to an artificial double. Sigmund Freud calls it "the Uncanny" [18]. Based on Freud, the robotics engineer Mori coined the expression "Uncanny Valley", an area of repulsive response aroused by a robot with its appearance and movements perceived as between "barely-human" and "fully human." [28]

## 2.5 Puppets as Actors / Actors as Puppets

Čapek wrote his 'play about Robots' in the beginning of the 20th century and this owes its inspiration in machine aesthetics: the 'rational' avant-garde artistic movements of Futurism, Constructivism or Bauhaus. Even in Surrealism we can find the principle of creativity based on an autonomous mechanism (automatism) of the dream. Avant-garde artists' attitudes toward the machine is widely varied from the Futuristic and Constructivist adoration of machine to the fear and skepticism connected with confrontation of man with individual transcending non-human machinist systems (e.g. Expressionism).

Filippo Tommaso Marinetti, the founder of Italian Futurism, wrote in his manifesto Multiplicated Man and Empire of Machine that: "Engines… are really mysterious... They have their moods, unexpected bugs. It seems that they have personality, soul, will. It is necessary to stroke them and behave with respect to them…" [35] This quotation illustrates an anthropomorphic and anthropopathic understanding of the machine by the Futurists, in sense of a system complementary or analogical with a human. From this understanding springs the concept of an ideal member of modern society – the 'man-machine' – a fusion arisen from their harmonization and mutual resonance. The ideal of modern human as an individual equipped with machinist qualities as speed, dynamics, or ambiguous moral attitudes.

We can find similarly positive relationship to the machine in Russian Constructivism. In opposition to Italian Futurism, Russian Constructivism is about more complex understanding of technology and at the same time about collective understanding of the human. Significant example of Constructivist aesthetics is Mejerchold's theatrical Biomechanics – a series of exercises for actors that purport to give them the ability to control their bodies as instruments or as machines. Mejerchold himself said about his method: "According to the given study of the human organism, biomechanics try to raise a man that would examine mechanism of his construction, he would perfectly control and complete it. Contemporary man lives in an age of mechanization that can't ignore mechanization of his organism's kinetic system. Thanks to Biomechanics we will establish principles of exactly analyzed and performed motions…. Contemporary actors have to behave as a modern automobile on a stage."[32] According to Constructivism, the stage becomes a place where human mechanisms as regulated by directors – their designers and mechanics - are presented.

The Futurists suggest the concept of the man as an unloving automaton when they dream about the super-man of the future. While the Constructivist stage production is seen to be a mega-machine constituted of human components, in other words: human group performance is understood as a mega-machine production. This discourse leads towards a conceptual mechanization of man and the anthropomorphisation of the machine. In both cases we can talk about mirroring of man in machine and machine in man.

Part of this relatively early-completed evolutionary line of theatrical experiments inspired by machinist aesthetics, are theatrical performances on the Bauhaus stage. Schlemmer's theatrical experiments were a search for "elements of movement and space." [19] His inspiration by visual art is reflected in his understanding of dancers on the stage as objects and in his performances that evoked the mechanical effect reminding one of puppet theatre. We can read in Schlemmer's diary (1971): "Might not the dancers be real puppets, moved by strings, or better still, self-propelled by means of practice mechanism, almost free of human intervention, at most directed by remote control?" [33]. From 1923, puppets, mechanical figures, masks and geometrical costumes became a characteristic feature of many theatrical performances of the Bauhaus. Another Bauhaus member, Moholy-Nagy (1924) goes even further in the The Mechanized Eccentric (Die mechanische Exzentrik):

"Man, who no longer should be permitted to represent himself as a phenomenon of spirit and mind…. His organism permits him at best only a certain range of action, dependent entirely on his natural body mechanism…. The effect of this body mechanism (Korpermechanik) arises essentially from the spectator's astonishment…. This is a subjective effect. Here the human body is the sole medium of configuration (Gestaltung). For the purposes of an objective Gestaltung of movement this medium is limited, the more so since it has constant reference to sensible and perceptive (i.e., again literary) elements. The inadequacy of human Exzentrik led to the demand for a precise and fully controlled organization of form and motion, intended to be a synthesis of dynamically contrasting phenomena (space, form, motion, sound, and light). This is the Mechanized Eccentric." [30]

Schlemmer's dream about ideal stage representation of man as a puppet, as well as Futurists' dreams about man-machine or Mejerchold´s Biomechanics resonates with the developed vision of modern theatre. A New Theatre as an independent and fully-fledged artistic medium, represented by Craig's vision in which actors are replaced by super-puppets, entirely controlled by the stage director: "An actor has to be removed and at his place, will appear an unloving figure, super-puppet, as we will call it until it will get better name."[6] This utopian theatre of objects has its roots not only in the aesthetics of symbolist theatre but even deeper within Romanticism.

We can find the essence of romantic understanding of puppets in Henry von Kleist´s essay Über das Marionettentheater (1810/11). Paul de Man in his essay Aesthetic formalisation: Kleist´s Über das Marionettentheater (1984) [9] confronts Kleist's text with Schillers' concept of humankind's education through aesthetics and shows that in case of Kleist's essay we are dealing with embodiment of principles of aesthetical formalization: "Each puppet has a focal point in movement, a center of gravity, and when this center is moved, the limbs follow without additional handling. The limbs are pendulums, echoing automatically the movement of the center. Every time the center of gravity is guided in a straight line, the limbs describe curves that complement and extend the basically simple movement."[27]

### 2.6 Robotic Art: An Anti-mimetic Shift?

On the Bauhaus stage we could see abstract images of the human bodies reduced to geometrical shapes that refer to an urge to depict an essence of man not in its individual uniqueness, but in its general sense and universal validity. In the case of the Bauhaus, we can still speak about these machine-like or puppet-like bodies as (generalizing) mirrors of a man.

However, the appearance of robotic art in the midst of the 1960's cybernetic discourse is connected with an anti-mimetic shift in the history of humanlike-machines. As Tomas argues: "The cybernetic automaton's mirroring of the human body was not established on the basis of conventional mimicry, as in the case of androids and their internal parts, so much as on a common understanding of the similarities that existed between the control mechanisms and communicational organizations of machine systems and living organisms."[39]

The anti-mimetic shift tends towards cancellation of borders between field of art and reality (artifact and nature), between mimesis, representation and life itself.[6] From landmark works of robotic art from the 60s, we can derive different aesthetical problems that have formed the development and history of this field: Robot K-456 (1964) by Nam June Paik and Shuya Abe deals with a concept of a remote control; Squat (1966) by Tom Shannon represents cybernetics entities and The Senster (1969-1970) by Edwarda Ihnatowitcz is an instance of autonomous behavior in art. [25]

Contemporary robotic art brings a new aesthetic dimension that prefers modeling of behavior over a representative form or a mimetic static object. In other words, robotic art creates not only forms but also actions and reactions of the robot according to outer or inner stimuli.

## 3 Staged Robots

The following discussion of staging robots is based on samples from the artistic work of one of the author's of this paper.[7] These robotic installations and performances investigate limits and degrees of anthropocentrism. By means of staging robots in a typical human analogies and situations, these performances exploit the robots as the medium of expression. In the works, examples of machines from the very abstract mechanomorphic to the very representative zoomorphic shapes can be found.

### 3.1 Sign-Body: Weak Anthropomorphism

Kinetic art, physical artworks with the element of real-time, can be seen as a one of the historical predecessors of robotic art as well as a broader interpretative context of this field of art. Kinetic art is usually mechanomorphic and feeds on the continuous transformation

[6] Burnham described it as a history of both figurative sculpture according to mechanistic automatons of 17th century and robotic sculptures (Cyborg art in his text). He concludes that: "Suddenly, art history naturally assimilates history of life creation as well as an evolution of machine."[4]

[7] Please refer to www.processing-plant.com for a comprehensive description of the robotic works in this section.

and participation of the viewer. The movement (or perceptible change of state) of an object can be seen in part as its objective nature, while its perception can be its subjective counterpart. Consequently, a rather abstract inert shape can become, from an audience perspective, fluid, organic and eventually anthropomorphic, solely by means of contextualization and movement perception/reception.

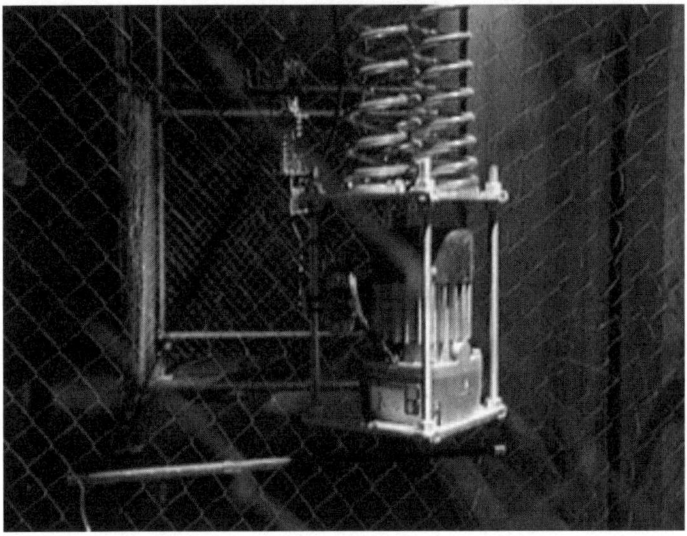

**Fig. 4.** Untamed machine (*La Cour des Miracles* 1998)

For example, in Figure 4 the Untamed Machine is a simple motor mounted on spring coils and this assemblage creates a rich range of chaotic and unpredictable movements. Aligned with the anti-mimetic shift reported in the recent robotic art and also with the swindle of the Chess player [36], the behavior is delivered without an immense degree of computation (as in bottom-up AI [31, 5]).

Staging this object in a cage results on the viewers' anthropomorphisation of its nature by means of an interpretation of the whole situation as a captive untamed and miserable entity in La Cour des Miracles [10,11,12]. The interpreted behavior emanates out of the juxtaposition of this social mise-en-scène and the inherent out of control motion of a complex dynamic and chaotic system in action.

An equal approach was undertaken with the Organic cubes (Figure 5) in which shapes were created by a set of discrete manipulators [37]. These geometries evoke the Deus ex machina of the Greek theatre during the dance performance called Devolution [10]. Beyond the aesthetics of the hypnotic organic movements of these machines, audiences readily address the intent. The uncanny manifestation and cognitive dissonance of these heavy and large floating objects do not push the viewer to retract from the dialogue but rather induce a fascination to understand its stage presence and character. In this scenario, the signs-design (squares, abstract, rigid, cold metal) and the signs-action (fluid and soft, chaotic, organic quality) are in conflict. It is distant to the androids of the Enlightenment era where signs-design (human body) and signs-action (human gestures) are aligned: the

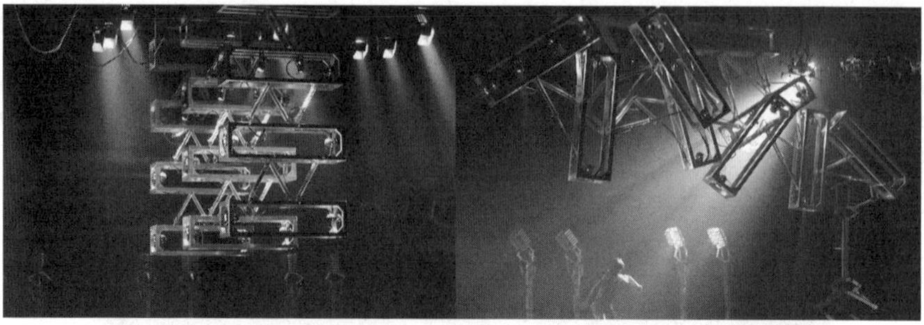

**Fig. 5.** Organic cubes (*Devolution* 2006). Left: Neutral Position. Right: Unfolded and floating.

goal being to achieve greater mimesis. The weak anthropomorphism here is an advantage as it frees the sign from the signified. Therefore, it enables a multiplicity of readings from a simple starting shape: an array of cubes as an incarnation of super/non human elements/forces.

### 3.2 Sign-Action: Anthropopathy

To explore the acceptance of artificial behaviors, theatre can provide fictitious environments to stimulate a suspension of disbelief. Stage performers share similarities with the social robots and the puppets in that they both utilize gesture, body and physical action to incarnate behaviors. Even without an anthropomorphic body, the sign-action of the performing objects can nevertheless find foundations in human acting methods to trigger empathic responses in the audience.

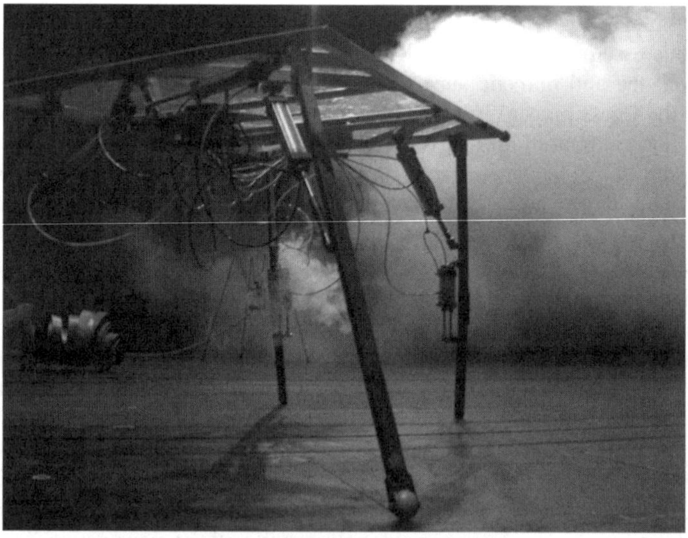

**Fig. 6.** A Walking Table *(Shockheaded Peter 2000).*

Acting methods may call for psychophysical unity where behavior is inherently physically grounded [21]. This unity finds a resonance in Kleist's essay (1810/11) when it comes to the mechanical performer. For instance, the Walking Table during the junk opera Shockheaded Peter (Figure 6) manages to ambulate and properly navigate even under an inflicted and deliberate handicapped gait. The behavior, a tedious stumbling object desperately moving to its destination, is a collaboration of the unstable equilibrium of the construction and the staging. The introduction of a latent failure in the gait not only creates a poetic moment but also gives a supplementary spark of life to the object. In a similar way, it is suggested to add Perlin Noise to robot motions with the introduction of slight erratic, incoherent or random movements in order to enhance the life-likeness of the social robots [15]. Such technique was already reported in the case of Musician Lady (see section 2.3).

Acting methods also propose that opposite stances, presence or absence, can be taken by actors during performance. The presence calls upon the performer's experience to dwell on his/her experience to deliver the character (and refers rather to Performance art and quality of an authentic presence of theatrical production). The absence requires an abnegation of the self to produce a pure rendering of the director's directives and scripts (and refers in its ultimate form to stage production as a re-presentation or sign system, a formal physical rendering of play-writer's text or director's ideas).

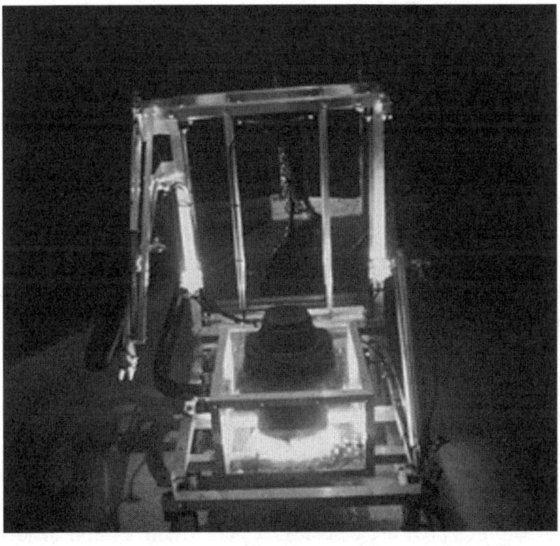

**Fig. 7.** A begging machine - *La Cour des Miracles (1998)*

The Beggar of Figure 7 had neither experience of misery nor of being pitiable. Its shape was a square box (symbol of a chest) that could rock over a hinge connoting the body language of imploring. The beggar performer is rooted towards absence while the table is ingrained in presence via the physicality of its gait.

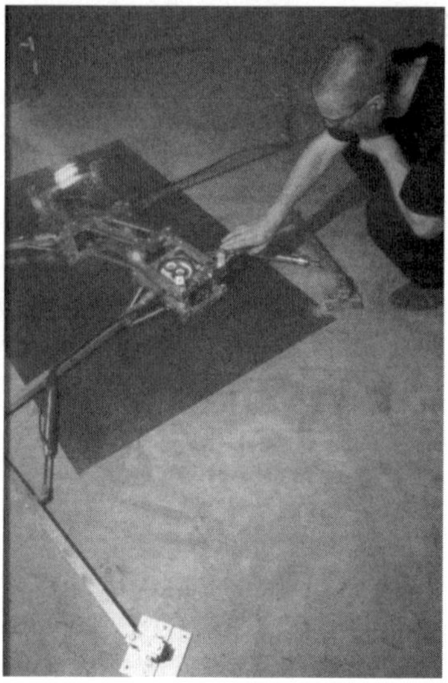

**Fig. 8.** A machine under convulsion – *La Cour des Miracles (1998)*

In La Cour des Miracles, all the robotic performers play the role of miserable machines (begging, convulsing, trapped, limping and crawling) using the above-mentioned acting methods. The convulsive machine of Figure 8 is staggered on the floor, helplessly shivering with spasms. The structure of this robot is derived in such way that the actual mechanisms are under a supreme physical stress and tension. This tension percolates into a perceived psychological stress, enhancing the psychophysical unity of this machine. In fact the malfunctions are so carefully "planned" that they become functional dysfunctional entities. Furthermore, these deviant machines are shaped upon hypothetical functional machines, which never even existed. The perceived behaviors manifested by these robotic agents are then neither real nor strictly faked (as no evidence of robot pain has been proved) but yet they are undoubtedly material and visible. They produce illusive behaviors created by our tendency towards empathy and anthropopathy; models that implode within the hyperreal staging of robotic characters.

### 3.3 Sign-Design: Mechanomorphism

Reflecting on Aristotle's Politics and the analysis of what could be a robot body on the theatre stage, The Colonies [10] are a series of performances and installations where the robot shapes are solely derived from an assemblage of pre-existing mechanism found in assembly lines and industrial manipulators/robots. The initial intents of these robots shapes are purely functional and furthermore, these structures are mostly unknown to the average audience. Thus, the sign-design of the machine is not directly conveying nor commenting on any anthropomorphic entities. The perceived behaviors of these shapes are then primarily rooted in the sign-actions rather than the sign-design of their morphologies or representations (again as opposed to the Androids of the mid 18th century).

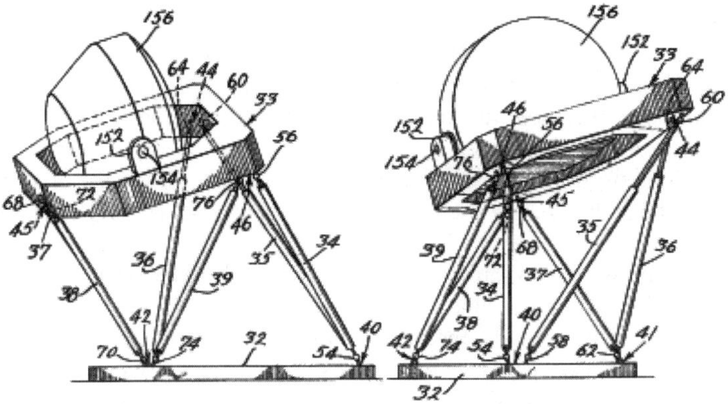

**Fig. 9.** Flight simulation Platform Mechanism

Figure 9 shows the patent drawings of a simulation platform used as part of the body of the robotic performers of Le Procès (Fig. 1). Utilizing existing mechanisms to construct life-like objects brings us back to the paradox of the quasi-living objects of the robot history (see section 2).

# 4 Ontologies Disorder

The theatrical play of signs can happen owing to a "double" quality of the space - that is physical (theatrical) stage and (dramatic) scene at the same time. Every-thing and everybody that is brought on this double-space room is transformed into its double-existence. It means itself and something else at the same time: man can mean thing and thing can mean man. Actions can get their intrinsic philosophical sense, and Hamlet's hesitation (that can be seen as a kind of movement without effect) could be felt as a dramatic action.

Presence and absence, the two mentioned stances of dramatic art/acting are usually parts of actors´ performance in which they dynamically alter each other. They fluctuate between illusive re-presentation of the dramatic character (absence) and actors' pure actions in front of audience (presence). The theatrical "play of signs" leaves open the question if what we see on the stage is real/natural or artificial. As Denis Diderot asked in his famous Paradoxe sur le comédien (Actor's Paradox) [14]: Who is crying on the stage? An actor or the character he re-presents? But does he/she only represent the figure when he/she acts in front of us? This old question wasn't answered yet. In recent science-fiction as well as in R.U.R, robots are often playing their own roles, anthropomorphized by human theatrical codes. So who is acting? The robot itself, is it a robot-role character? Or, the meta-robot? As in the case of examples from section 3, mechanomorphic entities/copies do not represent any originals in "reality" but rather, constitute their own hyper-reality.

What can happen with our understanding/interpretation of robot when it is placed on the stage? We can say that "robot" is originally a dramatic character because it appeared for the first time in a play (see K.Čapek). It was made to "function" on a theatrical stage but then it has escaped its fictional existence and became real. Machines have functioned in a field of art and theatre traditionally as re-presentations and mirrors of human being (see androids above). Does this direction channel the potential of the robot behaviors linking those solely to humanoids shapes and activities? The bottom-up approaches in AI now strongly argue that the body shapes the intelligence [31, 41]: recent researches on intelligent machine behaviors are based upon robot morphologies that bear no direct resemblance to zoomorphic entities. Inspired from the long history of puppetry, we argue that the robotic performer, as a stage character embraced with the act of suspension of disbelief from the audience, can potentially take any shape and form. (See examples from section 3)

We could associate Baudrillard's [3] symbolic orders with the degrees or stages of anthropomorphisation of the machine: it is the reflection of a basic reality, it masks and perverts a basic reality, it marks the absence of a basic reality and finally, it bares no relation to reality whatsoever. The first three call upon anthropomorphic incarnations of the robot while the last is pure simulacra. The Puppet, as Tellis argues, leads the audience to ultimately grapple with matters of being and ontology. The Puppet-Stage and the world-stage both present figures where we have to comprehend and arbitrate on the nature of being.

These artistic explorations of robotic performances and robots as performers/actors (see section 3) fuel themselves in the growing blurred division between the man and the machine and demonstrate the paradox of artificial life - stuck between the real and the artificial, the flesh and the metal, the sign and the signified. The anthropomorphisation of the robot suffers from Multiple Ontologies Disorder, a high-level manifestation of human-robot schizophrenia [12]. Since the principal of artificial reproduction favors the human form and the human existence as construct, is anthropocentrism at the center of this disorder.

## Acknowledgements

The authors wish to thank the producers of the several robotic performances: Canada Arts Council, The Conseil des Arts et des Lettres du Québec, Montreal Contemporary Arts Museum, Ex-Machina, DFAIT Canada, Ars Electronica, Australian Dance Theatre, The Australian Council. The research presented in this paper is partly supported by grant No. LC544 "Research on technology functions in a process of Art work creation and production" (Cultural Ministry of Czech Republic).

## References

1. Aristotle: The Basic Works of Aristotle. In: McKeon, R. (ed.). Book 2, ch. 4, Random House, New York (1941)
2. Aston, E., Savona, G.: Theatre as Sign-System. Routledge, New York (1991)
3. Baudrillard, J.: Simulacra and Simulation. Tr. Sheila Faria Glaser. Ann Arbor. University of Michigan, Ann Arbour, MI (1994)
4. Burnham, J.: Beyond the Modern Sculpture, the effects of science and technology on the sculpture of this century. Georg Braziller, New York (1967)
5. Brooks, R.: New Approaches to Robotics. Science 253 (1991)
6. Craig, E.G.: On the Art of the Theatre. Heinemann, London (1911)
7. Čapek, J.: Homo Artefactus. In: Čapek, J. Ledacos, Dauphin, Praha, p. 196 (1924)

8. Deleuze, G.: Negotations, pp. 1972–1990. Columbia University Press, New York (1995)
9. De Man, P.: Aesthetic formalisation: Kleist´s Über das Marionettentheater. Columbia University Press, New York (1984)
10. Demers, L.-P.: Le Procès/Devolution/La Cour de Miracles/The Colonies (2006), `http://www.processing-plant.com`
11. Demers, L.-P., Vorn, B.: La Cour des Miracles. Museum of Contemporary Arts, QC, Canada (1998)
12. Demers, L.-P., Vorn, B.: Schizoid Ontologies of Cybernetic Lures, Flesh Eating Technologies. In: Diamond, S., Lotringer, S. (eds.) Banff Centre, Canada (1998)
13. Dennett, D.: The Intentional Stance. The MIT Press, Cambridge (1987)
14. Diderot, D.: Paradoxe sur le comédien (Actor´s Paradox). 1769 (?), Mille et une nuits (1999)
15. Duffy, B.R.: Anthropomorphism and The Social Robot. Special Issue on Socially Interactive Robots, Robotics and Autonomous Systems, vol. 42(3-4), pp. 170–190 (March 31, 2003)
16. Duffy, B.R., Joue, G.: The Paradox of Social Robotics: A Discussion. In: AAAI Fall 2005 Symposium on Machine Ethics, Hyatt Regency, November 3-6 (2005)
17. Fong, T., et al.: A Survey of socially interactive robots, Robotics and Autonomous Systems, vol. 42, pp. 143–166. Crystal City, Arlington (2003)
18. Freud, S.: The Uncanny. In: Writings on Art and Literature, Stanford University Press, Stanford (1997)
19. Goldberg, R.L.: Performance art: From Futurism to the Present. C.S. Graphic, Singapur (1996)
20. Gorman, M.J.: Between the Demonic and the Miraculous: Athanasius Kircher and the Baroque culture of machines. In: Stolzenberg, D. (ed.) Encyclopedia of Athanasius Kircher, pp. 59–70. Stanford U. Libraries, Stanford (2001)
21. Hoffmann, G.: HRI: Four Lessons from Acting Method. In: proc. of 50th AI Summit, Switzerland (2006)
22. Horáková, J.: RUR – Comedy about Robots. DISK selections from Czech journal for the study of dramatic arts I, 86–103 (2005)
23. Horáková, J., Kelemen, J.: From Golem To Cyborg: On the Cultural Evolution of Concept of Robot. In: Abbate, F. (ed.) Interdisciplinary Aspects of Human-machine Co-existence and Co-operation. Czech-Argentine Biennale Workshop e-Golems, Czech Technical University in Prague, Prague (2005)
24. Horáková, J.: Staging Robots: Cyborg Culture as a Context of Robots Emancipation. In: Cybernetics and System Research. Austrian Society of Cybernetics Studies, pp. 312–317. University of Vienna, Vienna (2006)
25. Kac, E.: Foudation and Development of Robotic Art. Art Journal 56(3), 60–67 (1997)
26. Kennedy, J.S.: The New Anthropomorphism. Cambridge Press (1992)
27. Kleist, H.: Über das Marionettentheater. Berliner Abenblätter (1810/11). In: Constantine, D. (ed.) Puppet Theatre in Selected Writings, Hackett Publishing Company (2004)
28. Mori, M.: Bukimi no tani The uncanny valley (K. In: MacDorman, K.F., Minato, T., Trans.) Energy, vol. 7(4), pp. 33–35. Originally in Japanese (1970)
29. Mumford, L.: The Myth of the Machine: technics and human development. HBJ. NYC, New York (1967)
30. Moholy-Nagy, L.: Theater, Circus, Variety, from Theater of the Bauhaus (1924)
31. Pfiefer, R., Bongard, J.: How the body shapes the way we think. The MIT Press, Cambridge (2007)
32. Rudnickij, K.L.: Režissjor Mejerchold, Moskva (1969)

33. Schlemmer, O.: The Letters and Diaries of Oskar Schlemmer. Midletown, Conn (1971)
34. Sechner, R.: Performance Theory. Routledge, New York (1988)
35. Schmidt-Bergmann, H.: Futurismus - Geschichte, Ästhetik, Dokumente. Reinbek bei Hamburg, pp. 107–108 (1993)
36. Sussman, M.: Performing the Intelligent machines: Deception and Enchantment in the Life of the Automaton Chess Player. In: The Drama Revue. Fall 1999, vol. 43(3), pp. 81–96 (1999)
37. Suthakorn, J., Chirikjian, G.S.: Design and Implementation of a New Discretely-Actuated Manipulator. In: Proc. of ISER 2000, Hawaii (2000)
38. Tellis, S.: Toward an Aesthetics of the Puppet: Puppetry as a Theatrical Art. Greenwood Press, New York (1992)
39. Tomas, D.: Feedback and Cybernetics: Reimaging the Body in the Age of Cybernetics. In: Featherstone, M., Burrows, R. (eds.) Cyberspace/Cyberbodies/Cyberpunk Cultures of Technological Embodiment, pp. 21–43. SAGE Publications, London – Thousand Oaks – New Delhi (1995)
40. Wiener, N.: Cybernetics: or Control and Communication in the Animal and the Machine. John Wiley, Chichester (1948)
41. Wilson, F.: The Hand: How its Shapes the Brain, Language, and Human Culture. Pantheon Books, NYC, NY (1998)
42. Wood, G.: Edison's Eve. A Magic History of the Quest for Mechanical Life. Anchor Books, New York (2002)

# Part VI

# Digital Performance in Urban Spaces

# Imaging Place: Globalization and Immersive Media

John Craig Freeman

Emerson College
120 Boylston Street
Boston, MA 02116-4624
John_Craig_Freeman@emerson.edu

**Abstract.** "Imaging Place," is a place-based, virtual reality art project. It takes the form of a user navigated, interactive computer program that combines panoramic photography, digital video, and three-dimensional technologies to investigate and document situations where the forces of globalization are impacting the lives of individuals in local communities. The goal of the project is to develop the technologies, the methodology and the content for truly immersive and navigable narrative, based in real places. Activated by the click of a mouse button, the interface leads the user from global satellite images to virtual reality scenes on the ground. Users can then navigate an immersive virtual space. Rather than the linear structure of traditional documentary cinema, "Imaging Place" allows stories to unfold through non-linear database navigation and multilayered spatial exploration.

**Keywords:** Virtual Reality, Immersive Media, Electracy, Choragraphy.

## 1 Introduction

"Imaging Place," is a place-based, virtual reality art project that combines panoramic photography, digital video, and three-dimensional technologies to investigate and document situations where the forces of globalization are impacting the lives of individuals in local communities. The goal of the project is to develop the technologies, the methodology and the content for truly immersive and navigable narrative, from real places. The interface leads the user from global satellite images to virtual reality scenes on the ground. Users can then navigate an immersive virtual space.

The project has been under development since 1997 and includes work from around the world including Sao Paulo Brazil, Kamloops BC Canada, Warsaw Poland, the U.S./Mexico Border, Fort Point MA, Lowell MA, the Miami River, Kaliningrad Russia, Haverhill MA, Niagara, New England, Appalachia, and Florida. Although the method borrows freely from the traditions of documentary still photography and filmmaking, it departs from those traditions by using nonlinear narrative structures made possible by computer technologies and telecommunications networks. The work is projected up to nine by twelve feet in a darkened space with a pedestal and a mouse placed in the center of the installation enabling the audience to interact with it. Activated by the click of a mouse button, the interface leads the user from global satellite images to virtual reality scenes on the ground. Users can then navigate an immersive virtual space. Rather than

R. Adams, S. Gibson, and S. Müller Arisona (Eds.): DAW/IF 2006/2007, CCIS 7, pp. 453–466, 2008.

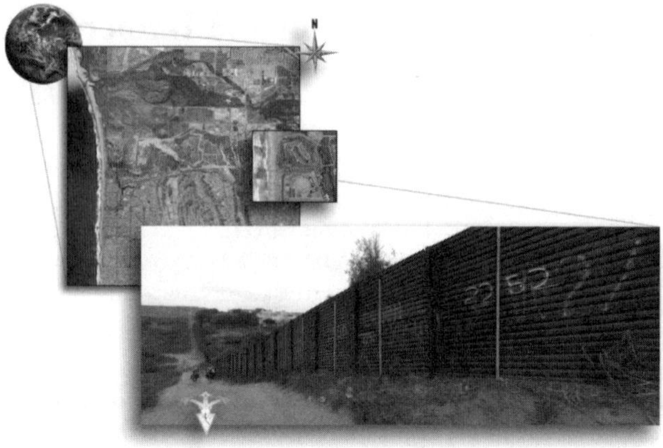

**Fig. 1.** Composite still from "Imaging Place"

the linear structure of traditional documentary cinema, "Imaging Place" allows stories to unfold through non-linear database navigation and multilayered spatial exploration. "Imaging Place" is therefore experienced as a process of navigation and excavation, allowing the user to uncover many layers of history and meaning. "Imaging Place" documents sites of cultural significance that for political, social, economic, or environmental reasons are contested, undergoing substantial changes, or are at risk of destruction. This includes historic sites as well as sites of living culture that are being displaced by globalization. The project also seeks to expand the notion of documentary by exploring how place is internalized, mapping place as a state of mind.

Much of the "Imaging Place" project was developed and produced in collaboration with Greg Ulmer and the Florida Research Ensemble in an attempt to develop a form of Choramancy [1]

Chora is the organizing space through which rhetoric relates living memory to artificial memory. It is the relation of region to place. Chora gathers multiple topics associated with a geographical region into a scene whose coherence is provided by an atmosphere. This atmosphere or mood is an emergent quality resulting in an unforeseeable way from the combination of topics interfering and interacting with one another. Choramancy is the practice of identifying and documenting Chora.

"Imaging Place" is designed to accommodate interdisciplinary collaboration conducted across institutions and over distances. It uses new technology to bring disparate bodies of knowledge together in a single hybrid form. The method attempts to bridge the gaps in understanding that exist between esoteric disciplines that have developed as a result of academic and industrial specialization. The technological tools are now available for bringing the work of experts and stories of local denizens together without sacrificing the depth and dimension of specialized knowledge and to connect the abstraction of highly specialized thinking with the visceral experiences of people on the ground. In addition to providing a form for the generation, dissemination and accumulation of interdisciplinary research and artistic production, "Imaging Place" is designed as a model strategy for collaboration.

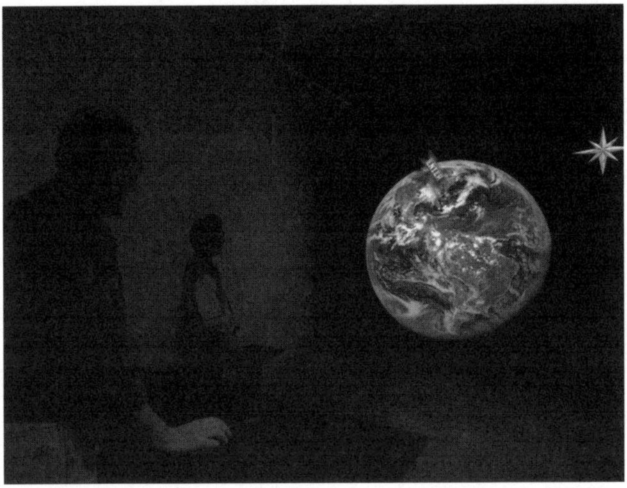

**Fig. 2.** Installation view from "Imaging Place"

This paper examines three recent "Imaging Place" projects from Sao Paulo Brazil, Kamloops BC Canada, and the U.S./Mexico Border.

## 2 Imaging Sào Paulo

In December of 2005, I was invited by Museu de Art ContemporÂnea (Museum of Contemporary Art) da Universidade de Sao Paulo (University of Sao Paulo) to participate in "Acta Media In Signo Sao Paulo (International Symposium of Media Art and Digital Culture)" and to produce an "Imaging Place" project in the city of Sao Paulo, Brazil. On December 10, I delivered a public lecture titled "Realidade Virtual para Representar Lugares (Virtual Reality Represent Places)". This lecture was translated into Portuguese. On December 12 and 13, I conducted a two-day workshop titled "Oficina De Tecnologia Digital E Geografia Imersiva (Workshop of Digital Technology and Immersive Geography)" at the Museum and assembled a team of local collaborators.

The work focuses on a small historic building in the city's center known as the "Castelinho da rua Apa (the Little Castle of Apa Street)." In 1937, the castelinho was the site of a gruesome multiple murder and suicide. The details of what happened the night of May 12th that year remain unclear, as everyone involved died. The story survives as a kind of mysterious urban legend.

It goes something like this: Elza Lengfelder, the cook of the wealthy European family who owned the place, heard shots in the interior of the castelinho. She ran to the streets to call the police. When they arrived, the policeman found three bodies. They were the brothers Alvaro and Armando Reis, and their mother, Maria Candida Guimaraes Dos Reis. Dubbed "o crime do castelinho da rua Apa", the incident gained instant notoriety in the Sao Paulo press. It was assumed that Alvaro, a 43-year-old lawyer, threatened his brother with his 9mm German Mauser pistol during a dispute over a risky business deal involving a plan to start a casino. When the mother tried to intervene both the mother and brother were shot and Alvaro then turned the gun on himself. This explanation never quite fit the facts in the case and rumors circulated for over 70 years.

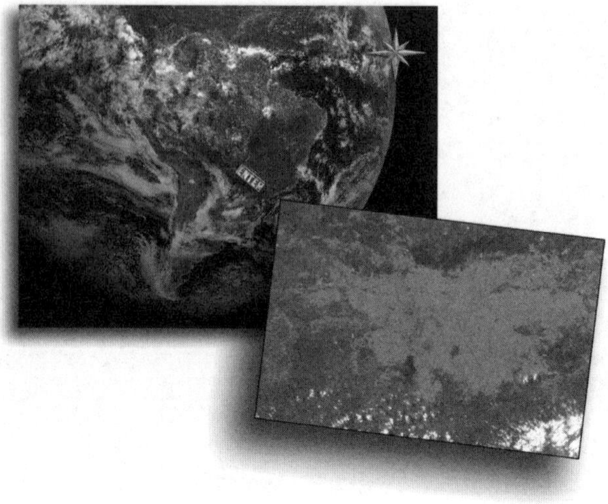


**Fig. 3.** Interface composite from

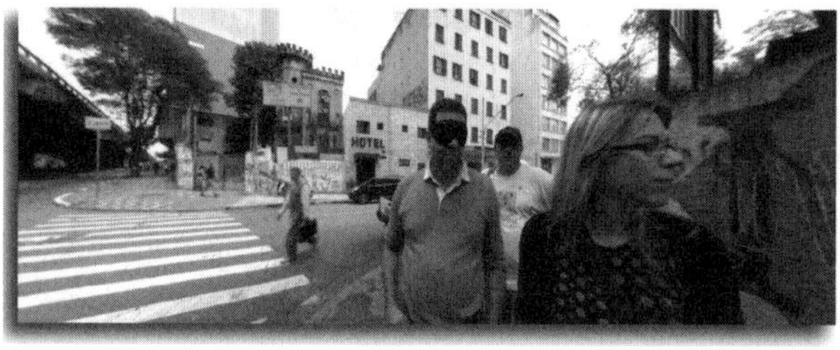


**Fig. 4.** Panoramic still with Artur Matuck and Egle Spinelli from "Imaging Sao Paulo"

After the crime, the castelinho fell into disrepair and became something of a squatter's shelter and crack house. Today the castelinho is being resurrected by the "Clube de Maes do Brasil (Club of Mothers of Brazil)." Founded by Maria Eulina. Without any support from the government, the organization helps the area's large homeless population acquire work skills, and feeds and educates the neighborhood children.

In "Imaging Sao Paulo: Castelinho da rua Apa", the audience will be led thru the virtual space by Sao Paulo denizens and project collaborators Artur Matuck and Egle Spinelli, from the social drama unfolding in the streets thru the wreckage of the castelinho.

Blindfolded, Matuck conducts a performative tribute to the city's homeless children in both English and Portuguese. The performance is based on newspaper articles where homeless children were photographed blindfolded to protect their identities. The blindfold becomes a metaphor for how the society has closed its eyes to the plight of these children. Spinelli helps Matuck - who has no eyes - thru the danger of streets and helps the virtual 'other' - who has no body - to navigate the scene.

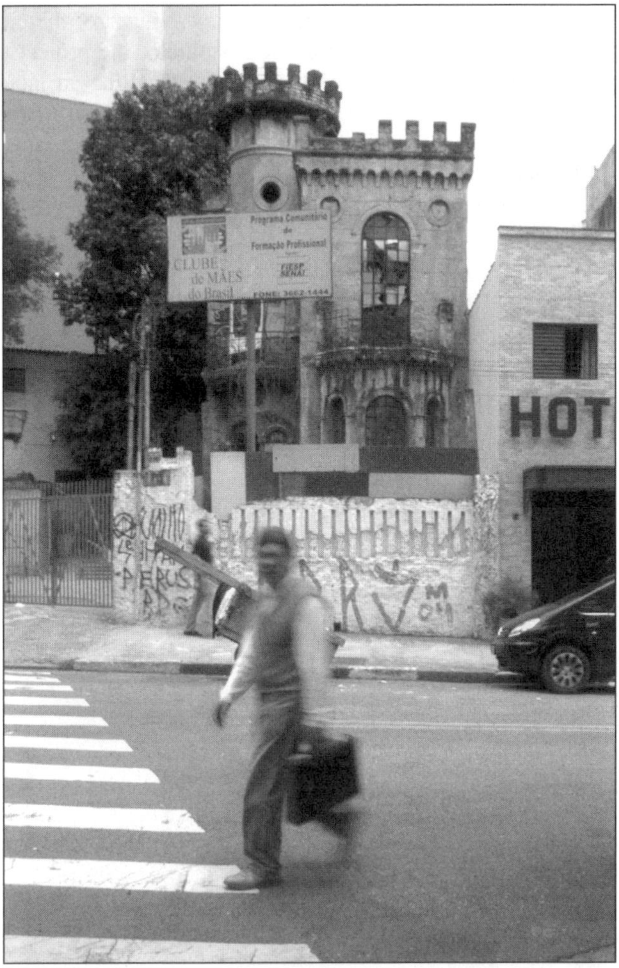


**Fig. 5.** Detail of the "Castelinho da rua Apa" from "Imaging Sao Paulo"

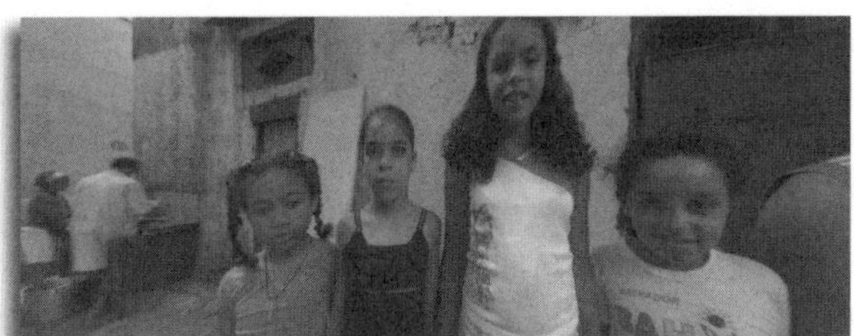

**Fig. 6.** Panoramic still with the children of Clube de Maes do Brasil from "Imaging Sao Paulo"

As the audience makes their way from the noise and chaos of the city streets into the relative quite, yet disturbing interior of the castelinho, the project takes a rather dark and deeply psychological turn as Matuck begins recalling an incident after the recent death of a close friend. He wanted to create a memorial performance where he would wear his late friend's pants. That night he had horrible dreams of the pants growing eyes in the tears around the knees. The next day he returned the pants to the family and said, "I cannot wear these pants." To which thy replied "Of course, we didn't think you should."

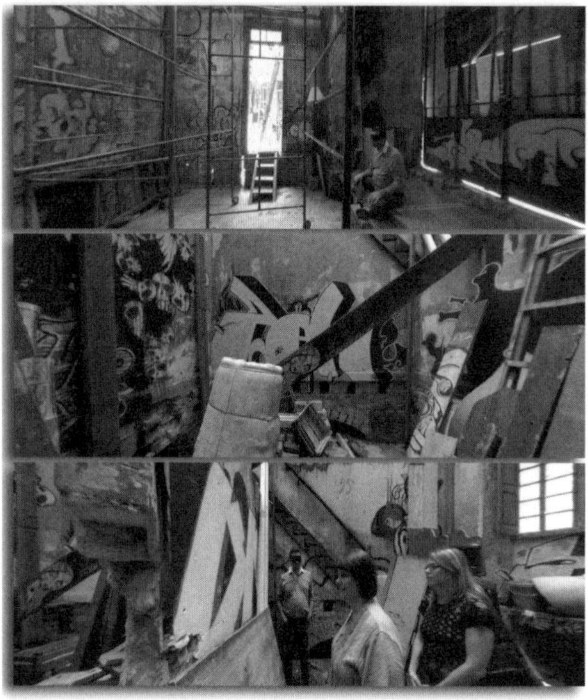

**Fig. 7.** Panoramic still with Artur Matuck, Christina Matuck and Egle Spinelli at the Castelinho da rua Apa from "Imaging Sao Paulo"

The journey takes the audience from the very real political situation created by the mass migration of Brazil's rural peoples to the psychological subconscious represented by Matuck's account of his dreams and the graffiti on the walls of the "Castelinho da rua Apa."

The project also addresses the Minhocao, a local nickname for the elevated roadway across from the Castelinho. In the nineteenth century, many sightings surfaced from South America of a creature called the minhocao. An article by the French naturalist Auguste de Saint-Hilaire (1779-1853) in the American Journal of Science was the first published reference to this illusive creature of southern Brazil. Its name, he said was derived from the Portuguese word minhoca, meaning earthworm. Sainte-Hilaire recorded several instances, usually at fords of rivers, where livestock were captured by one of these creatures and dragged under the water. The minhocao is described as a giant burrowing worm-like animal up to 75 feet long, with black scaly skin and two horn-like tentacle structures protruding from it's head, capable of digging enormous subterranean trenches. Although no credible accounts of sightings have been recorded since the late ninetieth century, the minhocao is commonly blamed for houses and roads collapsing into the earth.

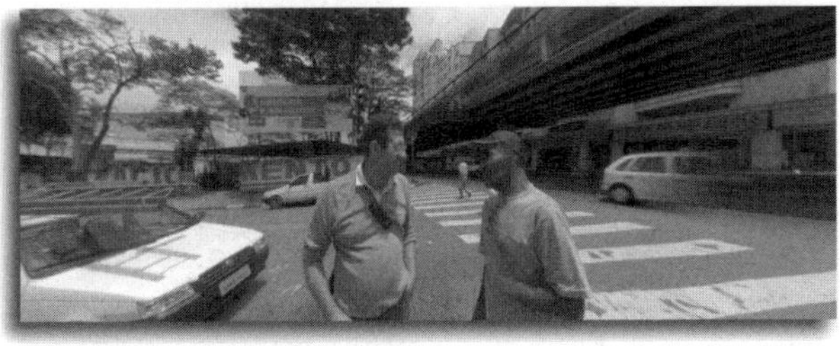

**Fig. 8.** Panoramic still with Artur Matuck and beneath the Minhocao from "Imaging Sao Paulo"

Completed in 1972, the Minhocao roadway runs alternately as tunnels and viaducts as it winds through Sao Paulo, splitting the city and creating an abject space that attracts one of the largest homeless populations in the world.

## 3 Imaging British Columbia: Weyerhaeuser Pulp Mill

In November 2005, I was invited to participate in the "Artist Statement: Artistic Inquiry and the Role of the Artist in Academe" workshop/symposium co-organized by Will Garrett-Petts and Rachel Nash of Thompson Rivers University in Kamloops BC, Canada. The "Artist Statement" workshop/symposium was part a five-year research program supported by a Community-University Research Alliance (CURA) grant from the Social Sciences and Humanities Research Council of Canada. The program focused on how the "artists-as-researchers" model extends and complicates the practice of interdisciplinary research and collaborative practices. On November 26, I delivered a presentation titled "Imaging Place; an artistic Inquiry", and spent November 27 producing the initial fieldwork media for the "Imaging British Columbia" project.

The fist phase of "Imaging British Columbia" focuses on the Soft Wood Lumber Treaty between the U.S. and Canada. In 2001 the U.S. government decided to prop up it's own inefficient timber industry by imposing a large punitive tariff on Canadian softwood lumber imports.[3] Since Canada and the U.S. both signed the North American Free Trade Agreement, the Canadian government went to the World Trade Organization and filed a complaint. What followed was three years of panels and arbitrators looking at the case, finding the U.S. actions illegal under NAFTA. The U.S. position remains that it won't accept any decision that rejects U.S. claims, and if Canada wants to end this dispute they have to agree to U.S. terms. Hundreds of miles from any border, issues of globalization dominate the landscape.

With Weyerhaeuser, a U.S. softwood lumber plant, as a backdrop, Michael Jarrett and other "Artists Statement" participants move through various plant operations drawing correlations between wood pulp and the history of writing.

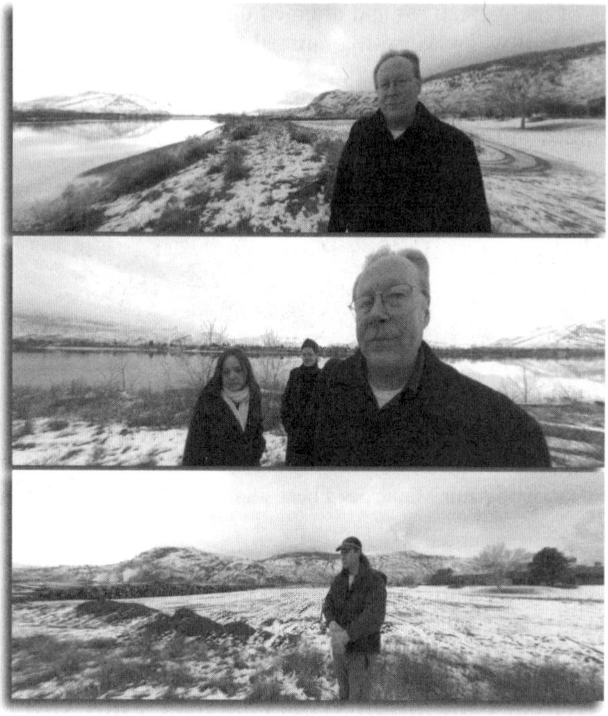

**Fig. 9.** Panoramic still with Michael Jarrett, Danyel Ferrari, Georgia Kotretsos, and Shawn Berney from "Imaging British Columbia: Weyerhaeuser Pulp Mill"

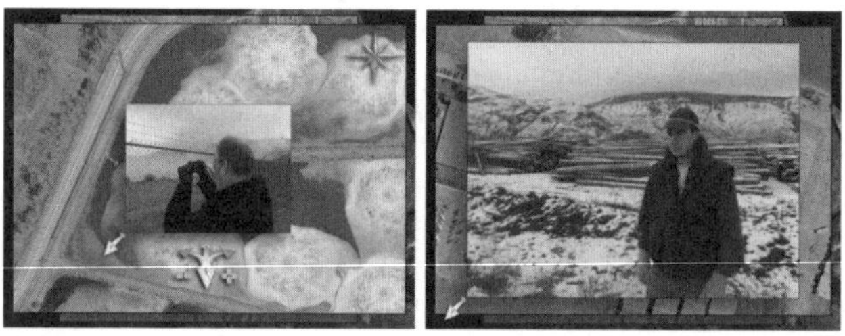

**Fig. 10.** Interface stills from "Imaging British Columbia: Weyerhaeuser Pulp Mill"

# 4 Imaging British Columbia: Kamloops Indian Residential School

In the spring of 2006, Will Garrett-Petts invited me back to Kamloops to deliver a public lecture, conduct a workshop sessions with CURA researchers and to further develop the "Imaging British Columbia" project as a pilot project for CURA.

During this stay in Kamloops, I worked with the local Secwepemc (Shuswap) people to produce a new phase of the "Imaging British Columbia" project that focuses on the stories of the Kamloops Indian Residential School.

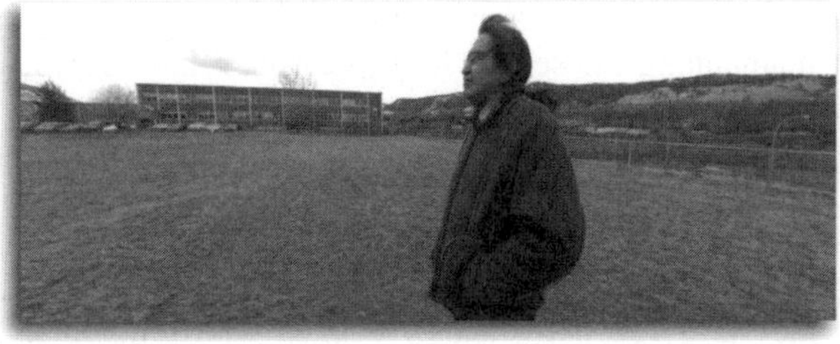

**Fig. 11.** Panoramic still with Don Seymour from "Imaging British Columbia: Kamloops Indian Residential School"

The school was created in 1893 by the Canadian government in cooperation with Roman and Protestant churches. The school building, which stands today, was built in 1923 and operated as the Kamloops Indian Residential School until 1978. For most of its existence, little education took place at the school. Instead, the school was used to colonize and assimilate the Secwepemc.[4]

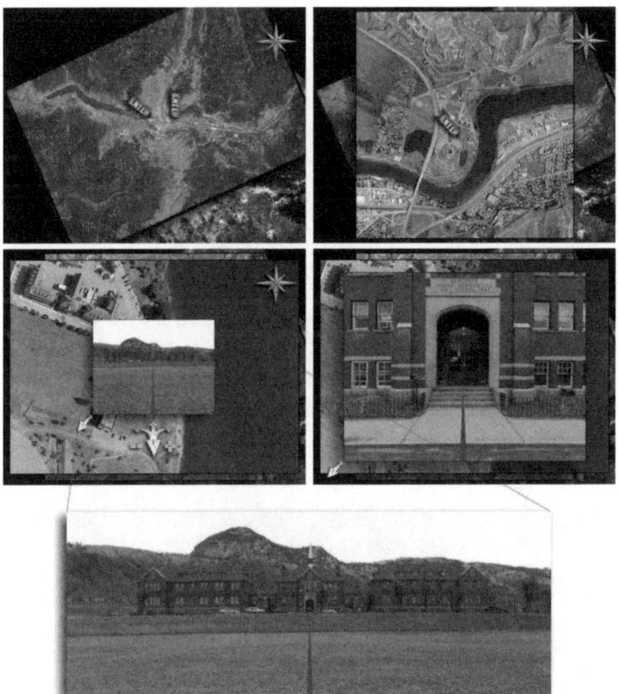

**Fig. 12.** Interface composite from "Imaging British Columbia: Kamloops Indian Residential School"

Students were taught menial farming and homemaking skills, but most of their time was spent maintaining the school itself. Canadian law mandated attendance at the school and parents could be sent to prison if they refused.

Over four generation of Secwepemc children were taken from their parents and forced to attend the School. These children were isolated from their traditional culture and indoctrinated in Catholic religious teachings. Although many of the children did not speak English, they were forbidden to speak Secwpemctsin and were severely punished when they did. The individuals I worked with referred to this practice as strapping, where the children would be hit across the forearms, or elsewhere, with large leather straps. The children themselves were forced to make the straps. The legacy of the Kamloops Indian Residential School has been devastating for the Secwepemc. Shame of the Secwepemc culture and language was deeply instilled in the children. The effects include all manner of personal, social, cultural, and spiritual dysfunction. The Secwpemctsin language was nearly lost.

In "Imaging British Columbia: Kamloops Indian Residential School", users can navigate through this imposing building where they will encounter several generations of former students recounting their experiences at the school.

Since 1978 the Kamloops Indian Band has run the facility, which now houses a variety of Band organization. The word Kamloops is the English translation of the Secwepemc word Tk'emlups, meaning 'confluence,' and for centuries has been a center of the Secwepemc culture. Bands of first nations people from across British Columbia are once again turning to the Secwepemc for leadership. They conduct a well-established project to preserve and restore the Secwpemctsin language and the school they run is one of the best in the province.

At one time the Secwepemc people occupied one large traditional territory covering approximately 145,000 square kilometers. The Kamloops Reserve land base was established in 1862 under the direction of then Governor James Douglas. It included an area approximately 26 miles east of the North Thompson River by 26 miles north of the South Thompson River, adjacent to the City of Kamloops. Although the Secwepemc never signed away their rights to this land, in subsequent years the reserve was reduced in size to around 7 by 7 miles today. In 1988 the Kamloops Indian Band filed a claim to the original Douglas Reserve. In 2001 the Canadian Government rejected the claim. The Kamloops Indian Band is currently preparing to file a new claim under the Douglas Reserve Initiative at Residential School.

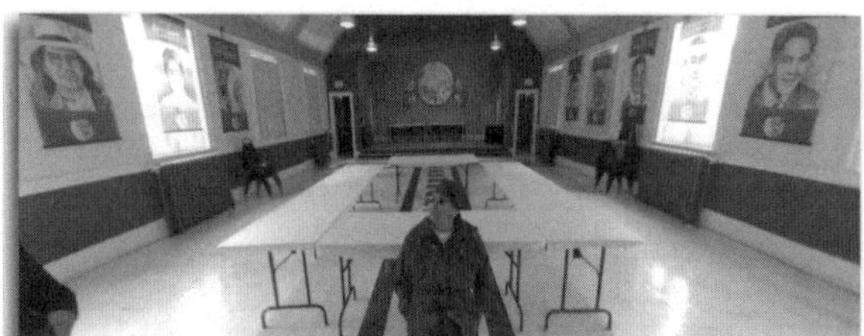

**Fig. 13.** Panoramic still with Loretta Seymour from "Imaging British Columbia: Kamloops Indian Residential School"

## 5 Imaging the U.S./Mexico Border

In August 2005, I traveled to U.S./Mexico Border region at Tijuana and San Ysidro where I began work on the "Imaging the U.S./Mexico Border" project.

Increasingly, I am being drawn to those places where the forces of globalization are affecting the lives of local communities, places like borders and ports, walls and fences, the edges of public policy.

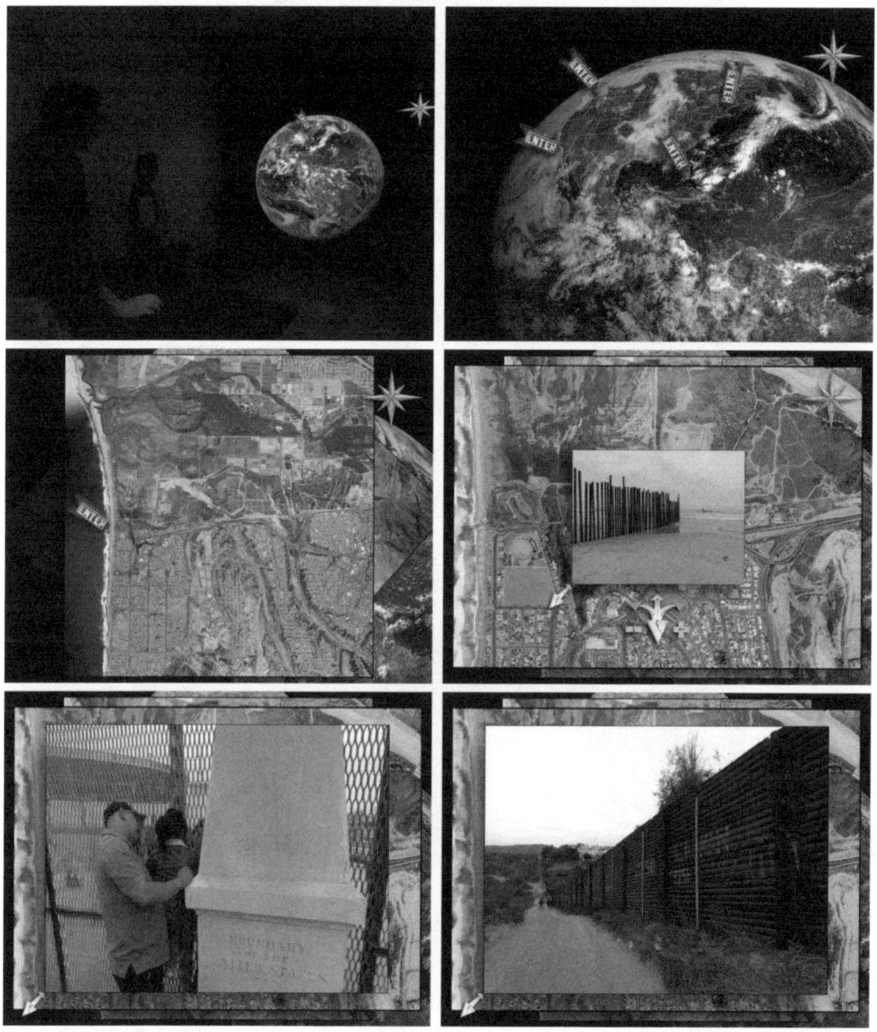


**Fig. 14.** Interface sequence from "Imaging The U.S./Mexico Border"

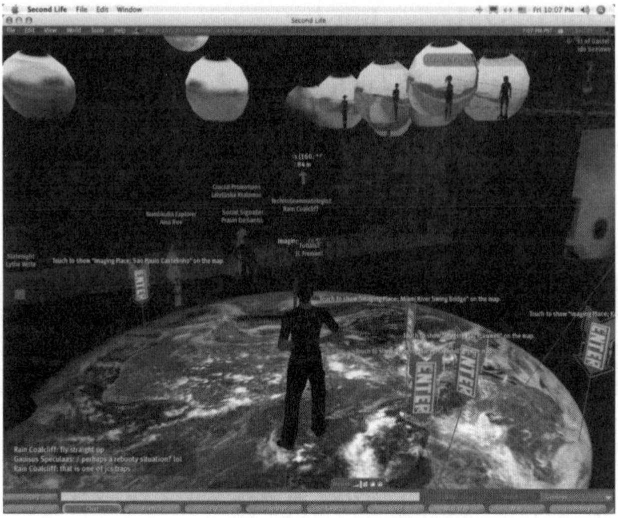


**Fig. 15.** Still image of navigation interface from "Imaging Place SL"

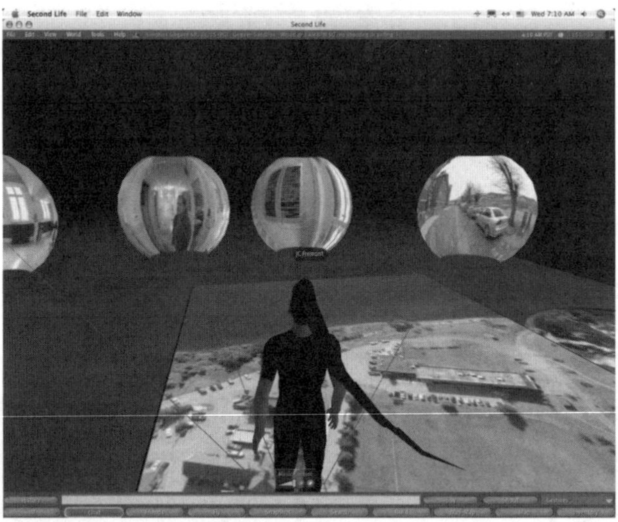


**Fig. 16.** Still image from "Imaging Place SL: Kamloops"

Beginning on the western shore, where the fence terminates in the Pacific Ocean, I plan to work my way east along this contentious border. There are three issues I am exploring with the "Imaging The U.S./Mexico Border" project. First is the contradictions and bigotry of U.S. Immigration policy toward Latin America. Second is the labor and environmental exploitations of North American Free Trade Agreement, and the third is global human trafficking, indentured labor, and the sex slave industry.

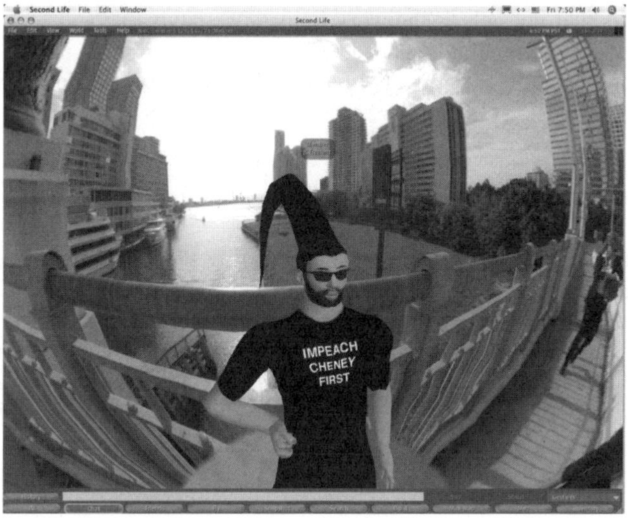


**Fig. 17.** Still image from "Imaging Place SL: Miami"

## 6 Conclusions and Future Work

Since the fall of 2006, I have been implementing the "Imaging Place" project in Second Life, an avatar-based, virtual world that currently has over 1.5 million users.

In her article for SLATEnight, "Art and Aporia: Imaging Place," [5] Lythe Witte (aka Christy Dena) writes, "The mode of interaction, ala Lev Manovich's "Soft Cinema," [6] facilitates a place-based navigation where memory, location and hyperlink imbue a moment with the illusion of control over personal time and space gateways."

The entire body of "Imaging Place" project includes an archive of hundreds of locations and hours of narrative. I currently have seven scenes from this archive constructed in various locations around the Second Life world, or grid.

When a denizen of Second Life first arrives at an "Imaging Place SL" scene he, she or it sees a large black and white satellite picture of the full disk of the Earth, the same one used in earlier versions of the project.

The avatar can then walk over the Earth to a thin red line which leads to an adjacent higher level platform made of a high resolution aerial photographs of specific location from around the world. Mapped to the aerial images are networks of nodes constructed of primitive spherical geometry with panoramic photographs texture mapped to the interior.

The avatar can walk to the center at one of these nodes and use a first person perspective to view the image, giving the user the sensation of being immersed in the location.

Streaming audio is localized to individual nodes providing narrative content for the scene. This content includes stories told by people who appear in the images, theory, humanities scholarship and ambient sound. When the avatar returns to the Earth platform, several rotating enter signs provide teleports to other "Imaging Place" scenes located at other places within the world of Second Life.

The result is that not only is the work immersive, navigable and accessible to multiple users at the same time, it is indeed, inhabitable.

For more information or to access Imaging Place in Second Life please visit ImagingPlace.net.

## Acknowledgments

Gregory L. Ulmer provides theory for the "Imaging Place" project. Funding support from Emerson College, the Social Sciences and Humanities Research Council of Canada and the Small Cities Community-University Research Alliance, and the Museu de Art ContemporÂnea da Universidade de Sao Paulo. The Satellite and Aerial imagery was provided by NASA-GSFC, with data from NOAA GOES, GlobeXplorer, DigitalGlobe, and the City of Kamloops. All other imagery by John Craig Freeman.

## References

[1] Ulmer, G.L.: Choramancy: A User's Guide. Mind Factory. In: Armand, L. (ed.), pp. 200--259. Litteraria Pragensia, Prague (2005)

[2] De Saint-Hilaire, A.: On the Minhocão of the Goyanes. American Journal of Science, Yale University, CT, 2--4 (1847)

[3] The Export and Import Controls Bureau of Canada, Foreign Affairs and International Trade
`http://www.dfait-maeci.gc.ca/eicb/softwood/background-en.asp`

[4] Segerholm, C., Nilsson, I.: Schooling as genocide. Residential schools for First Nations in Canada 1900-1980. In: European Conference on Educational Research, University of Hamburg, September 17-20 (2003)

[5] Witte, L. (aka Dena, Christy). Art and Aporia: Imaging Place. SLATEnight (January 2007)

[6] Manovich, L.: Soft Cinema: Navigating the Database. DVD-video with 40 page color booklet. MIT Press, Cambridge (2005)

# About... Software, Surveillance, Scariness, Subjectivity (and SVEN)

Amy Alexander

Department of Visual Arts,
University of California, San Diego
9500 Gilman Dr. #0084
La Jolla, CA 92093-0084 USA

**Abstract.** The text discusses cultural and political implications of the subjective aspects of software and the SVEN project.[1] SVEN (Surveillance Video Entertainment Network) is a public space software art project that uses custom computer vision software to detect pedestrians who in some way *look like* rock stars. The text introduces general audiences to SVEN's approach to software subjectivity—in this case, concerning computer vision surveillance software. It also presents examples of software bias in contemporary culture and proposes software literacy as a public educational goal.

**Keywords:** surveillance, software art, digital street performance, sousveillance, computer vision, software literacy.

## 1 Introduction

SVEN (Surveillance Video Entertainment Network) is a project developed by Amy Alexander, Wojciech Kosma, and Vincent Rabaud with Jesse Gilbert, Nikhil Rasiwasia, and Marilia Maschion. The following text focuses on SVEN's approach to and issues surrounding computer vision. Cinematography, and its relationship to both software and surveillance video, is also important to SVEN, but it's a topic for a different text. (Art is of course of particular importance to SVEN—but that should go without saying.)

SVEN is a piece of tactical software art. Tactical software art comes out of traditions of tactical media and software art. It's a logical mix: tactical media is a response to the way mainstream media influences culture; software art is a response to the ways mainstream software influences culture. Tactical media often involves a combination of digital actions and meatspace—or street—actions. In SVEN, these are one and the same—digital actions that take place on the street (just off the curb in this case).

SVEN is a self-contained computer vision-based surveillance system that is designed to detect likely "rock stars." In its street performance context, the system is

[1] More info on SVEN can be found on its website, http://deprogramming.us/sven

R. Adams, S. Gibson, and S. Müller Arisona (Eds.): DAW/IF 2006/2007, CCIS 7, pp. 467–475, 2008.

installed in a cargo van that parks along a sidewalk with pedestrian traffic.[2] A video camera is mounted on the roof of the van, pointed at pedestrians half a block or more away. A video monitor sits in the van window displaying what appears to be surveillance video. As pedestrians pass through the camera's view, SVEN matches certain of their physical characteristics against those of rock stars as they appear in selected music videos. The selection of characteristics to match range from facial expression to clothing and hair color to body position. These characteristics are deliberately unorthodox, as though the surveillance system had become bored and longed to catch a person of interest and so grasped at any excuse it could for a match—algorithmic wishful thinking. Thus, when SVEN detects what it believes is a rock star, the normally boring surveillance video on SVEN's monitor erupts into a music video (with corresponding audio). This music video is generated in real time from the live video and stars the unsuspecting pedestrian. Along with the music video, the monitor displays two smaller images illustrating the match between the pedestrian and the rock star. The multi-view effect is similar to the arrangement of large and small monitors in a CCTV control room, where a large monitor shows the main view on which the staff are to focus their attention, and smaller monitors keep track of the activity taking place in front of individual cameras.

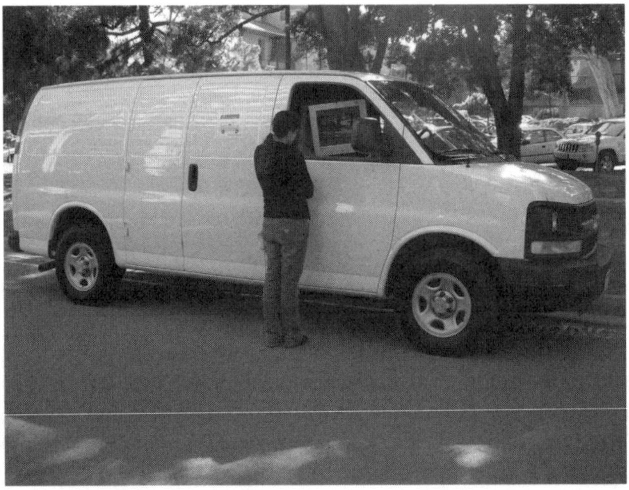

**Fig. 1.** SVEN in its van configuration—aka *SVAN*. A camera with telephoto lens is mounted on the front of the SVAN roof and points at unsuspecting pedestrians up to 150 meters away. The monitor in the window displays video to other pedestrians as they pass the van. Speakers just inside the van window play corresponding music when the system is generating a music video.

[2] Besides its van-based street performances, SVEN has also been installed in storefronts and in public areas of a museum. While it's more common to concern ourselves with surveillance on the street, surveillance inside public places can be just as insidious.

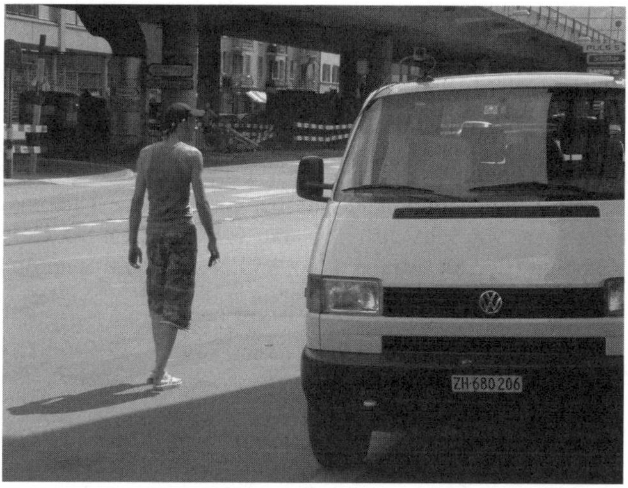


**Fig. 2.** A passerby encounters SVEN in Zürich. The camera on top of the van is pointed at pedestrians approximately 100 meters down the street.

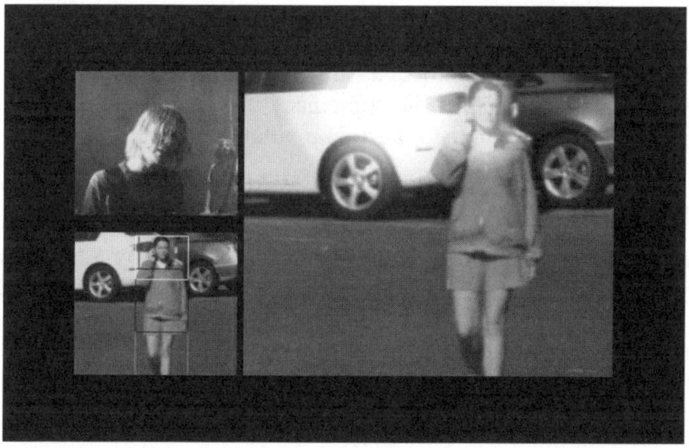

**Fig. 3.** Screenshot of SVEN display in music video mode. On the lower left is the live camera image showing the pedestrian tracked and her body segmented into head, head and shoulders, shirt, and legs. This segmentation data is used by the system both for matching characteristics of rock stars and for positioning effects and cinematographic framing (close-ups, etc.) On the upper left is the actual rock star and music video matched. The large frame on the right shows the result of SVEN's self-deluding algorithms: the live scene is transformed in real-time into the matched music video, featuring the tracked pedestrian as the rock star.

## 2 Surveillance Is Already Scary

Sure, surveillance is scary—but you've probably heard that before. We're being watched all the time, and we don't know by whom, or what they're doing with the images and other data they're gathering. Scared? You bet—there's a bogeyman under the bed, so we'd better not look. But remember, we're supposed to be scared—people are trying to scare us. Foucault pointed out that not knowing when the bogeyman is watching you can scare you into changing your behavior. But not knowing *how* the bogeyman is watching you can scare you too. SVEN's purpose is not to point out that surveillance is scary. People are scared enough as it is.

## 3 Software Shouldn't Be Scary

Technology functioning as a big "black box" often scares people into not looking at it. It's all-powerful and incomprehensible. So, people often don't question how it works. Although the significance of this state of affairs is often-overlooked, it's by no means a recent development. In 1987, William Bowles wrote about the risk of the loss of transparency from the likes of the Macintosh computer:

> … many people have raised serious objections to the "black box" approach used by machines such as the Macintosh, arguing that by making the machine into a closed system it not only reduces the range of choices open to the user, but perhaps more importantly it encourages a particular attitude towards machines in general by mystifying the processes involved, which in turn leads to a state of unquestioning acceptance of the supremacy of technology. This is of course a process which began with the industrial revolution. [1]

A more recent example—an article from WikiWikiWeb entitled "Hermetically Sealed Stuff Is Magic"—reads:

> This is a principle of human nature pointed out to me by ScottAdams and his PointyHairedBoss. There is a Dilbert strip where the PointyHairedBoss works out a schedule for Dilbert, and bases it on the assumption that anything he cannot understand is easy (magic). Thus, he commands the poor drone to build a worldwide networking system in six minutes.
>
> If you can understand something, you can reasonably evaluate it. If you can't understand it (either it is beyond your comprehension, or someone has "hermetically sealed" it so you can't see), you can't reasonably evaluate it. [2]

That might sound at first like a geek-elitist position, implying that everyone should be a programmer and that those who don't program are (lazy/stupid/inferior). I can't speak for the authors of that wiki article, but my point here is not to suggest that everyone learn to program, but rather that perhaps everyone should learn *about* programming: software literacy. Think of software literacy as an extension of media literacy. People are (hopefully) taught how to detect bias in newspapers and television—even if they don't know how to produce a newspaper or television program themselves. Now that software is a mass medium—one that influences people's lives at both consumer and institutional levels—might not it be useful if people learned to detect software's biases?

## 4 How Is Software Subjective?

Some real world examples may be useful in illustrating the subjectivity of software. Example 1: Google, whose search results significantly influence the information people access, touts the objectivity of their PageRank technology:

> PageRank relies on the uniquely democratic nature of the web by using its vast link structure as an indicator of an individual page's value. In essence, Google interprets a link from page A to page B as a vote, by page A, for page B. But, Google looks at more than the sheer volume of votes, or links a page receives; it also analyzes the page that casts the vote. Votes cast by pages that are themselves "important" weigh more heavily and help to make other pages "important. [3]"

I'd argue that the algorithm described isn't "democratic" but is actually rather similar to becoming popular in high school. If the popular kids like you then you can easily become popular. But what if you're not part of the in-crowd? What if you're a dissenter—or just not trendy? According to the algorithm described above, it's difficult to get noticed. Google apparently refines the PageRank algorithm on a regular basis, and they keep its exact workings a secret. (If they didn't, it's likely we'd all see even more ads than we do for products that begin with a "V" and end with an "a.") But at least we can begin to critically question how PageRank influences the information we read. And even though Google assures us that "Google's complex, automated methods make human tampering with our results extremely difficult," (Google) we can keep in mind that humans determined the automated methods in the first place.

Example 2: The United States Internal Revenue Service was recently criticized for freezing the tax refunds of many poor taxpayers by targeting their returns as likely to be fraudulent—even though most were not. An article in *The New York Times* reported that "a computer program selected the returns as part of the questionable refund program run by the criminal investigation division of the Internal Revenue Service. [4]"

The article doesn't tell us any more than that about the computer program, but obviously someone programmed it with rules for finding a "questionable" return. Clearly, those rules were subjective, and they seem suspiciously like they may have been politically motivated. The fact that the deed itself was done by computer doesn't make the decision mechanical, blind or objective. In a software-literate culture, the journalist who wrote the article might be expected to press for details on how the program worked, or at least discuss his inability to obtain this information from his sources. But at present, it seems largely culturally acceptable to shrug such things off: "The computer did it."

## 5 On Algorithms and Data; Verbs and Nouns; Parts and Wholes

Of course, algorithms can't operate without data. A simplistic analogy for thinking about a software process would be to say that data are nouns and algorithms are verbs. I've discussed algorithms above—so, what about data? The idea that we live in a "database culture" is a familiar one: from playing computer games to shopping to going to the doctor, we face one database after another in our daily lives. And just as we worry about our physical bodies being subject to visual surveillance, we also worry that our data bodies are subject to virtual surveillance. Are "they" watching my search habits, my browsing habits, my online purchasing habits? Naturally, we want to know *what* information about us is being used (nouns). But again, we need to look also at what *actions* (verbs) are being performed on or with the data. Consider the situation of registering for an account on a social networking site such as MySpace or Facebook. One is inevitably asked for age, gender, marital status, and various more personal questions. One may or may not find these questions individually inappropriate or prying, but what's less obvious is how one may feel about the ways in which the responses to these questions are put together. As Aileen Derieg wrote on the Furtherfield Blog:

> In the end, I found myself defined—seemingly voluntarily—over and over as a female over 40, married with children. By itself, this information is wholly devoid of any content, although it might well serve as a surface for myriad projections. Some anonymous stranger might read that as a description: traditional, conventional, conservative, maybe interested in cooking and gardening and parenting issues ... Or it might suggest a bored housewife potentially up for all kinds of illicit naughtiness, following a well established narrative from spam. As entirely inane and irrelevant as this is, however, what concerns me is how my goal of exploring possibilities of exchange and connections within the framework of "terms of use" and "privacy policies" defined by the respective corporate owners was initially deflected from the start through the rigid constraints of constructing an identity through the process of "registration. [5]"

As with many things, the whole can be quite different than the sum of its parts. And seemingly benign, objective computer algorithms such as the display of fields from a database can turn into something quite different when combined with such subjective human "algorithms" as interpretation.[3]

## 6 I'm Not Myself Today…

If we say someone "matches" a terrorist (or anything else)—what does it really mean? Some characteristics of that person's appearance have been determined to be significant—they match some terrorist's photo more closely than others in the database. This raises the question – what are these "significant" characteristics?

In "Face Recognition Using Eigenfaces,"[4] images document the results of researchers' attempt to use computer vision algorithms to match photographs of individuals with those in a database. The second grid of photographs from the top of the web page shows the results of an attempt to use computer vision algorithms to match black and white photos of test subjects with photos of the same subjects in a database. We see that the algorithm detected the correct person from the database in a large

[3] As of this writing (December 2007), semantic web technologies—those that allow objects on the web to be located by combining arbitrary user-defined criteria—are still in the early stages. Assuming these evolve and become widely used, I suspect there will be a lot more discussion on this topic.

[4] Accessible online at http://www.cs.princeton.edu/~cdecoro/eigenfaces

percentage of cases. [6] However, the few incorrect cases are interesting. The software attempted to detect similarity between photographs and faces—and it did so—according to *some* characteristics. Not, in these cases, the characteristics that would have given the "right" answer and identified the same person. But the wrong answers may not be what we expected – or feared. Instead of confusing people of the same race, for example, the software will sometimes confuse two people with a smug expression on their face. Maybe in some ways smug people have more in common than people of the same race. Maybe, on days when you're not yourself, you're really more like someone else. In any case, attitude profiling may turn out to be a greater risk of technology than racial profiling.

But profiling concerns aren't limited to race. If the computer vision bogeyman were used to identify "undesirables," what would those undesirables look like? Presumably, everyone could envision their own profile of an "undesirable." And in fact, such profiling could be programmed into a computer vision system. But—the profiles would need to be quantified for the computer. It turns out, computers are subject to the same sorts of stereotyping as humans are – only more so. For example, say you're on the lookout for troublemaking emo kids. You could tell a human, "Watch out for emo[5] kids," and this would be asking the human to stereotype. But you'd have to tell the software, "Detect people wearing all black, with pale skin and very black hair." This is more extreme stereotyping than the human might do, at least consciously. But of course, humans chose those characteristics.

So—one of SVEN's aims is to reflect on the human subjectivity inherent in technology. Because this subjectivity must be reduced to objective rules, such implementations obviously have limitations in mimicking the way humans would perform the

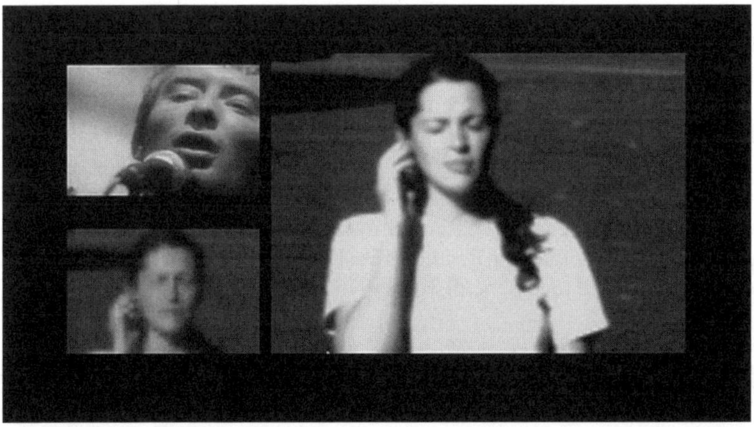

**Fig. 4.** Screenshot of SVEN detecting the resemblance between a contemplative pedestrian and Thom Yorke of Radiohead

[5] The term "emo" is used here to describe the stereotypical appearance of teenagers who have adopted the so-called emo fashion. This fashion involves, among other things, dyed black hair, and skin that appears pale (perhaps in contrast to their artificially darkened hair.)

intended task. However, the implementations and their results can, through these limitations and exaggerations, reveal less obvious things about how their human creators "see" things—and about humans in general. Technological development expects machines to think like humans and humans to think like machines – under this stress both give something about themselves away.

## 7 Technology and the Way It's Used Aren't the Same Thing

This might seem an obvious point, but the opportunities it presents for tactical software might easily be overlooked. Take for example, computer vision surveillance technology. It conjures up depressing connotations, and our gut reaction is to respond to it by resisting. That's because we're used to it being used to find when someone looks, in someone else's judgment, well, bad. But that's not necessarily the case. Why limit ourselves to defensive positions against "scary" technologies? Why not take some offensive ones? If computer vision can determine when we look bad, we can develop some computer vision technology that can figure out when we look good. And who looks better than... rock stars?

## 8 Coda: Keeping Things in Perspective

It's tempting to think of "sousveillance"[6] projects as empowering—but it can be a mistake. Although timidity in the face of surveillance is a risk, taking an active position presents the risk that we fool ourselves into thinking we've somehow changed the status quo. SVEN does nothing to disrupt authoritarian surveillance systems. But funny, even ridiculous examples can sometimes help break the ice and provide a way in to discussion of subjects that might otherwise seem dry, inaccessible—and scary. The author hopes that SVEN can help provoke rational discussion and understanding of the cultural and technical matters it addresses. Talk doesn't change anything either, but it can contribute toward a larger, mainstream shift in public perception—a shift in which the mainstream public doesn't see concerns about surveillance as limited to fringe activists, malcontents and other "scary" people. Similarly, tactical media projects with mainstream sensibilities could eventually make Big Brother resistance as popularly acceptable as the Big Brother TV show. Only through shifts in mainstream perception can we hope to see the disruption of scary status quos.

## References

1. Bowles, W.: The Macintosh Computer – Archetypal Capitalist Machine (1987), `http://www.williambowles.info/sa/maccrit.html`
2. Hermetically Sealed Stuff is Magic. In: WikiWikiWeb, `http://c2.com/cgi/wiki?HermeticallySealedStuffIsMagic`

---

[6] *Sousveillance*, a term originally coined by Steve Mann, refers to community-generated surveillance activity: surveillance from underneath (sous) rather than from overhead (sur). [7]

3. Our Search: Google Technology. In: Google, http://www.google.com/technology/index.html
4. Johnston, D.C.: I.R.S. Limited Tax Refunds of Poor, Congress Is Told. In: New York Times (2006), http://www.nytimes.com/2006/01/10/business/10cnd-tax.html
5. Derieg, A.: Exploring Limited Spaces. In: Furtherfield Blog (2007), http://blog.furtherfield.org/?q=node/134
6. DeCoro, C.: Face Recognition using Eigenfaces (2004), http://www.cs.princeton.edu/~cdecoro/eigenfaces
7. Mann, S.: Sousveillance (2002), http://wearcam.org/sousveillance.htm

# The NOVA Display System

Simon Schubiger-Banz[1] and Martina Eberle[2]

[1] Computer Systems Institute, ETH Zurich, Clausiusstrasse 59, 8092 Zurich, Switzerland
simon.schubiger@inf.ethz.ch
[2] Horao GmbH, Giessereistrasse 5, 8005 Zurich, Switzerland
martina.eberle@horao.biz

**Abstract.** NOVA is a volumetric LED object that creates fascinating visual effects by arranging LED voxels in a three-dimensional matrix. The NOVA is animated by user defined video- or graphics sequences that are viewable at an angle of 360° and across multiple layers of LEDs. 2D and 3D assets can be visualized, and depending on the viewer perspective, perceived as concrete or imaginative pictures creating a totally new perception of visual content in physical space. The volumetric content creation is realized by unique software developed at ETH Zurich (Swiss Federal Institute of Technology) exclusively for the NOVA system. The LED modules, equipped with voxel strings of variable length, offer the opportunity to create a wide range of user-defined physical objects that in combination with a boundless variety of content options invite the creative community in architecture, interior design and communications to explore the visual properties and possibilities of this new medium. This paper discusses the design principles and concepts together with the software and hardware behind the NOVA display. In this regard, the installation at Zurich's main station serves as an example how the NOVA display is integrated in public space and interacts with the audience. Furthermore, the paper covers the lessons learned from operating the system as well as the continuous development of its hardware, software and content over the past 18 months.

**Keywords:** NOVA, 3D display, voxel, LED screen, media, voxel content.

## 1 Introduction

NOVA ends the era of flat rectangular screens: NOVA is the first "real 3D" LED object that can create fascinating visual effects by colored LED voxels in a three-dimensional regular grid. The 100mm spaced voxels can be individually addressed and work at a refresh rate of 25 Hz, a voxel diameter of 40mm and a color-depth of 16 millions colors, thus enabling the presentation of high quality content combined with an emotional dimension achieved by a low-resolution, soft and imaginative image. The real 3D LED object is animated by user defined video- or graphics sequences that can be presented at an angle of 360° and across multiple layers of LEDs in both directions, horizontally and vertically.

2D and 3D assets can be visualized and depending on the viewer perspective, be perceived as concrete or imaginative pictures, creating a totally new perception of visual content in physical space.

R. Adams, S. Gibson, and S. Müller Arisona (Eds.): DAW/IF 2006/2007, CCIS 7, pp. 476–487, 2008.

The representation of content in three dimensions is made possible by unique software, developed at ETH. NOVA LED modules equipped with voxel strings of variable length, offer the opportunity to create an infinite amount of user-defined physical objects that in combination with the variety of content options invite the creative community in architecture, interior design and communications to explore the visual properties and possibilities of this new medium.

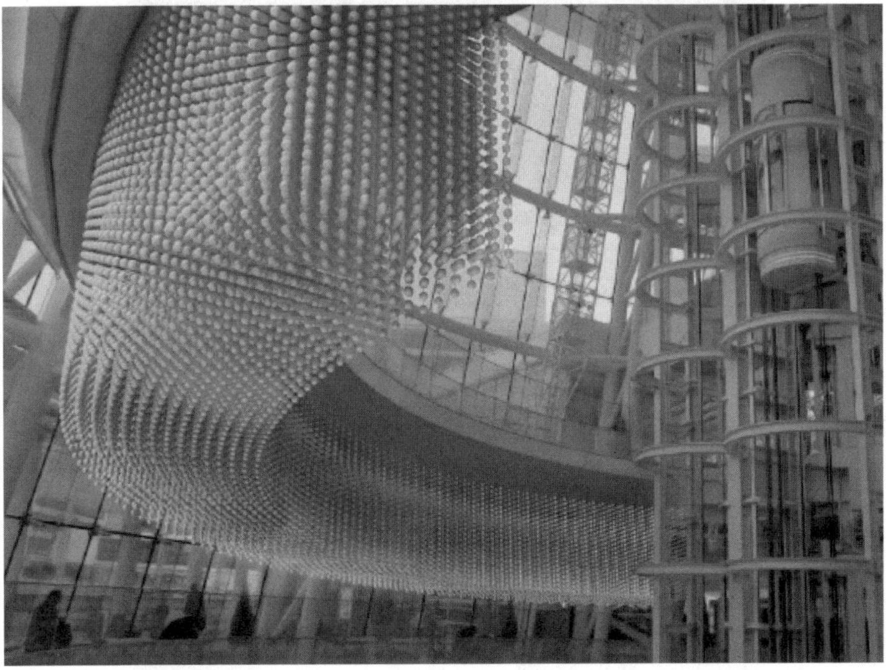

**Fig. 1.** A possible NOVA physical configuration used as an architectural element

## 2 Background

NOVA is a project that can be associated with the term "Third Culture" as it has been used by Kevin Kelly, Senior Editor of the magazine "Wired", in an article he published in the magazine "Science" [1]. He used the term "Third Culture" to describe a pop-art-based culture, based in technology for technology; a culture where new tools offer insights to everyone through novel experiences – favoring the irrational if it brings options and possibilities, "because new experiences trump rational proof" [1]. In this concept, modern culture evolves around technology facilitating mutual exchange among groups of people from various backgrounds beyond anything theoretical digressions have achieved in the past. This vision can be traced back to an essay published by C.P. Snow [2], where he formulated the idea of a world without rupture where literary intellectuals converse directly with scientists. In 1952, a collection of interviews was published by the "Edge" Foundation by John Brockman [3], where natural scientists address topics in a way that can be understood by the broad public.

In this tradition, NOVA aims at communicating science in way that can be understood and appreciated by anybody and inspire an audience independent of educational background, professional activity, gender or age making John Brockmann's statement alive: "Technology is simply more relevant than footnotes" [3].

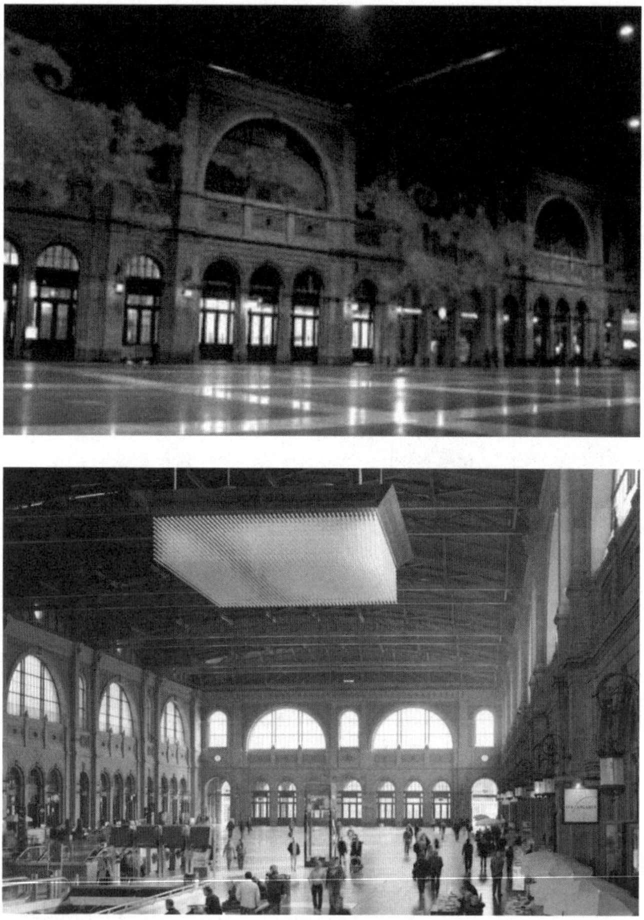

**Fig. 2.** On the top, one of several ideas explored. On the bottom, the finally realized voxel display at Zurich's main station

NOVA was one of many projects that were developed for the 125th anniversary of ETH Zurich. The goal was to bridge the gap between science and the public, to make science visible and tangible in an unprecedented way – showing the actual results obtained in scientific experiments and the abstract beauty that lies behind the data that describes them. Although the scientific data sets originated from different sources, their renderings appear to have a common visual ground. This results from the generic nature of mathematics that are used to describe the phenomena of nature and man-made environments.

The initial vision that drove the development of NOVA was the desire to visualize algorithms in three dimensions. Several technologies were explored – projections on a variety of media including fog as well as holograms were considered. However, none of the solutions that were available at the time provided the desired effect within the constraints of a public space exposed to several factors such as sunlight, dust from the train tracks, extreme heat and cold, wind and last but not least building regulations all of which limited the choices of a technical solution. As a result, the idea for a three-dimensional matrix was born which enables visualization in actual three dimensions.

The NOVA system built for the 125th anniversary at Zurich's main station was entirely financed by sponsors. The NOVA technology is now further developed and has been commercialized by Horao GmbH and extended towards stage and show environments, leaving behind its roots of scientific visualization.

## 3 Related Work

Due to the superior technical parameters of LEDs (brightness, lifespan, power consumption, etc.) compared to traditional projection- or light-systems combined with falling prices, a general trend towards LED based displays can be observed.

To our knowledge, no commercial product manufactured in large quantities is using an analogous concept of arranging voxels in a 3D grid with the purpose of 3D imaging in the manner of NOVA. However, the new media arts have created several volumetric visualizations with similar properties – but none of them have used/achieved the capability of displaying interpretable imagery based on photographic or video input for a variety of reasons:

- Use of single color LEDs only
- Refresh rate of LEDs too low
- Spacing, size, and arrangement of voxels not optimized for "interpretable" imaging
- Choice/lack of diffuser
- Lack/limitations of 3D-imaging/voxel-based content creation and player software

The next paragraphs give a brief overview of the most prominent examples that were available, installed or on view between 2005 and 2007.

### 3.1 MiSPHERE (Barco)

Barco has developed a 360° LED module in the size of a tennis ball in 2005, called MiSPHERE [4], which consists of individual pixels arranged in a 2D plane: individual MiSPHEREs are daisy-chained into a string, with several strings forming a curtain. Each MiSPHERE acts as a pixel within the curtain, making it possible to display images and simulate lighting effects across the entire curtain, while achieving a "look-through" effect and multiple-angle-viewing for the audience around the scene.

The major differences in comparison to NOVA are: the system is used in 2D settings (curtains) only; the size of the individual pixel and the pitch are rather large which limits the imaging capabilities unless the system is used as a huge backdrop; the technical concept of the individual voxel as well as the processing is significantly different.

### 3.2 3D Display Cube, White (James Clar&Associates)

James Clar's Cube [5] has been exhibited widely in 2005 and 2006. Individual monochrome LEDs are mounted on a sturdy orthogonal grid. The cube comes in a size of 10 x 10 x 10 voxels. As with NOVA Studio, stills and video can be imported and displayed on the screen using software that has been specifically developed for the hardware.

The major differences in comparison to the NOVA system are NOVA's color capability and higher refresh rates which allow showing "interpretable" imagery. Furthermore, NOVA is equipped with diffusers hiding the individual LEDs.

### 3.3 Pixel Cloud (Jason Bruges Studio)

In a London office building of a law firm designed by Foster and Partners, Jason Bruges studio has installed a pixel cloud [6] matching the grid of the architecture. What is unique about this solution is the concept of the individual voxel measuring 120mm and consisting of 24 LEDs. The concept has been developed by Jason Bruges Studio together with Ledon Lighting, a subsidiary of Zumtobel.

Similar to James Clar's White Cube and Networks Wizards' Cubatron [7], the pitch has been designed pretty wide which prevents displaying interpretable photographic or video imagery which NOVA can.

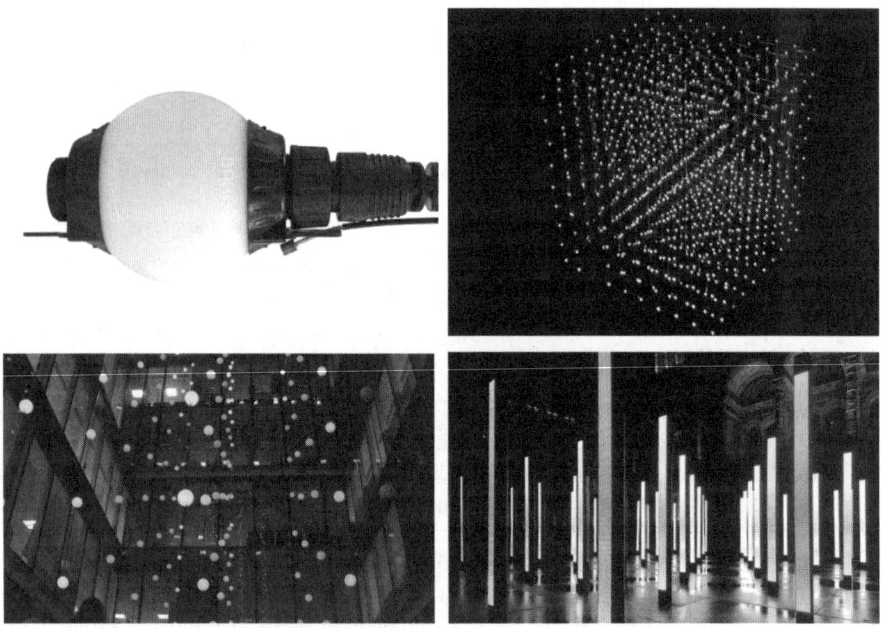

**Fig. 3.** A single Barco MiSPHERE pixel (top left), 3D Display Cube by James Clar (top right), Pixel Cloud by Jason Bruges (bottom left), Volume at the Victoria and Albert Museum by UVA

### 3.4 Volume at the V&A (United Visual Artists)

UVA has developed an installation for the atrium of the Victoria and Albert Museum using a standard Barco LED product to create a three-dimensional imaging space [8]. Graphical patterns are shown across the pylons arranged throughout space.

The concept of the player software that UVA has been using for the V&A installation seems to be similar to the NOVA player software.

## 4 NOVA System Overview

The NOVA System is a combination of software and hardware that allows the modular design of a physical configuration as well as content creation within different software environments. All components were developed from scratch with long-running, fixed installations (e.g. Zurich's main stations) as well as event-like installations (e.g. exhibitions, rock-concerts) in mind. Several design ideas were explored during development and the resulting hardware and software is presented in the following paragraphs.

### 4.1 Hardware

In order to allow a wide range of physical configurations, the NOVA hardware is composed of several configurable elements. The NOVA hardware consists of top-plates with a size of 50 x 50 x 12 $cm^3$. Each top-plate can be equipped with 5 x 5 = 25 strings of variable length. The strings consist of 1 up to 32 voxels that can be mixed with spacers to create arbitrary physical configurations. The spherical voxels have a diameter of 40mm, are placed at a regular distance of 100mm and act as a diffuser for the LEDs. Four LEDs for each primary color (red, green, and blue) are combined to cover a full 360° angle resulting in 12 LEDs for each voxel capable of more than 16 million RGB colors (see figure 6). The top-plates take their input data either over an Ethernet interface or a DVI (Digital Visual Interface) that is daisy-chained to all top-plates. The input data is then split by each top-plate into the respective string data and sent over a high-speed serial link to the strings. Each voxel picks its corresponding color information from this high-speed link and drives the LEDs accordingly. At Zurich's main station, a configuration of 50 x 50 x 10 = 25'000 voxels is used resulting in a "box" like shape of 5 x 5 x 1 $m^3$ (see figure 2, bottom).

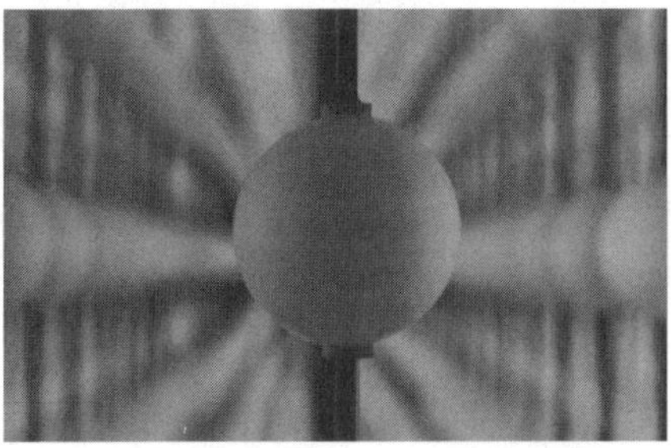

**Fig. 4.** Close-up of a NOVA voxel. The diameter of each voxel is 40mm and each voxel contains control electronics and 12 LEDs for full-color RGB.

## 4.2 Content Creation

Well-engineered hardware is pointless without appropriate content that exploits its possibilities. Unfortunately, volumetric data is handled only by specialized software packages (e.g. found in medical applications or geology). Therefore, content creation tools had to be developed for various audiences in order to get content on the display. In terms of content, we broadly distinguish three classes:

1. Offline content stored as voxel movies in a proprietary file format (3DD)
2. Procedural content that renders voxel frames in real-time but has no interactive interface
3. Interactive content that renders voxel frames in real-time and provides a graphical user interface for interaction.

For the first content class, a voxel content creation suite was developed called NOVA Studio. NOVA Studio is modeled after well known video editing applications and has been extended towards voxel based content. NOVA Studio offers a media browser, where 2D stills (JPG, BMP, TIFF, PNG, and GIF), 2D movies and animations (QuickTime, animated GIF) and voxel movies (3DD) can be accessed. These elements are then placed on a timeline as in any other video editing software.

Elements can be extruded, rotated, scaled, and translated to multiple voxel layers as well as combined (stacked) in NOVA Studio to create voxel animations.

3D content can be imported for example by using a 3D content creation package such as Maya, SoftImage or 3D Studio Max, where 3D animations can be easily created. 3D animations have to be rendered in these packages as multiple slices into individual 2D movies by placing appropriate clipping planes and camera positions. These "movie slices" are then recombined (stacked) in NOVA Studio in order to yield a true voxel movie.

NOVA Studio provides some basic effects and animation capabilities directly on the timeline and enables simple creation of volumetric content starting from existing 2D assets. For example a company logo can be very easily extruded and animated inside NOVA Studio without resorting to a 3D animation application (see figure 5).

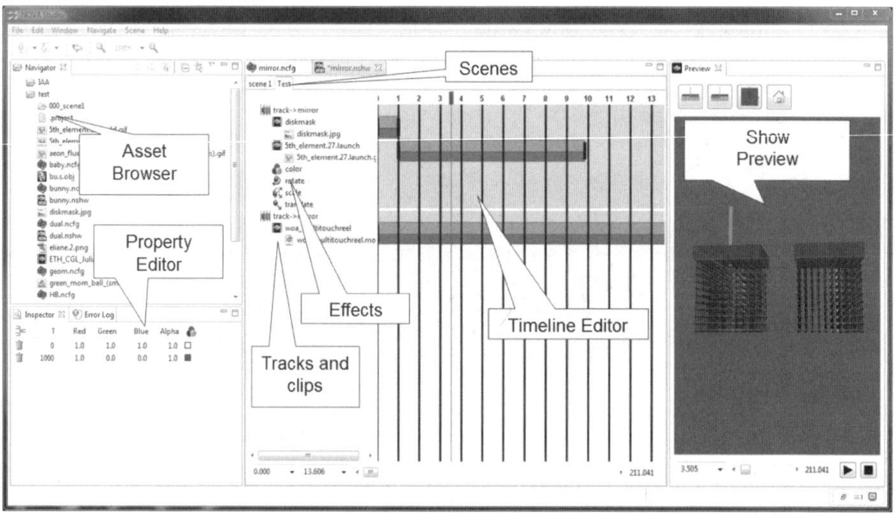


**Fig. 5.** Content creation with the NOVA Studio software

Due to the flexible physical configuration options of the NOVA hardware, content is closely related to an actual configuration. For that reason, physical configuration is also handled by the NOVA Studio software. Inside NOVA Studio, a voxelizer creates physical configurations from existing CAD or other 3D models (see figure 6).

Whereas offline content creation targets more the classic video-oriented user base, *procedural content* creation (which we earlier referred to as the second class of content) attracts new media artists. Procedural or generative art is based on algorithms usually expressed in a programming language which manifests itself in the physical world through sound, images etc. For the NOVA system, this translates to rendering voxel frames for a specific physical configuration in real-time. For that purpose, we provide the creation of physical configurations through NOVA Studio and a simulator application that renders real-time voxel content. The simulator can be attached to various programming environments and behaves exactly as a real NOVA system. We currently support C++ [9], Java [10], Python [11], and Processing [12] as development environments. For each programming environment an appropriate integration of the NOVA system was implemented. For example in Processing, specific parts of the applet window are mapped to slices which are then composed by the NOVA system into voxel frames. There is only one additional line of code needed to turn any Processing applet into an applet that simultaneously outputs to the NOVA system.

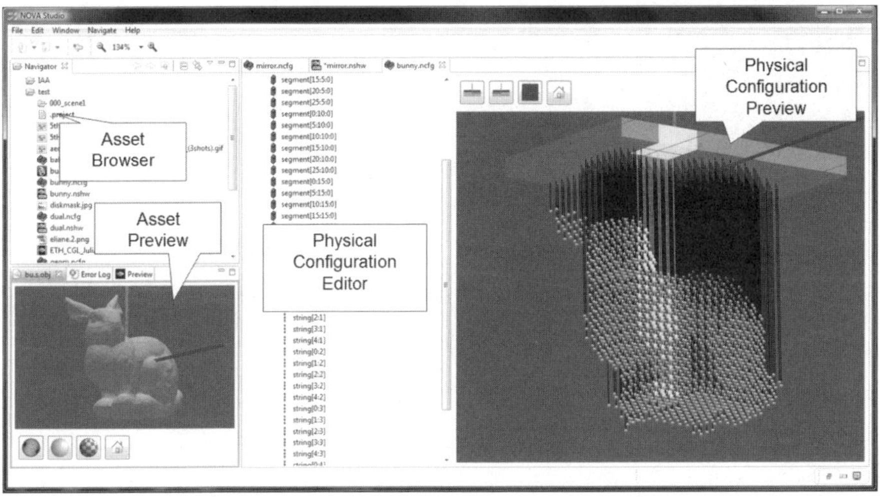


**Fig. 6.** The result of voxelizing a 3D model in NOVA Studio is a physical NOVA configuration consisting of appropriately placed spacers and bulbs. A single 5 x 5 top plate and its attached strings are highlighted on the right hand side (physical configuration preview).

The most demanding class in terms of complexity is *interactive content* (which we earlier referred to as the third class of content). Currently we support Java/Eclipse [13] based development of interactive applications for a touch-screen with and a proprietary OpenGL [14] based widget toolkit together with the same Java interface also used for procedural content. Currently there are four interactive applications available at the main station in Zurich and it is planned to largely extend that set during the next year.

### 4.3 Interaction

The interactive console located at the group meeting point in Zurich's main station is the result of making the NOVA more tangible to the passers-by as well as offering a platform to the sponsors to present their logos. It consists of a standard PC, a HoloPro [15] projection surface, and a touch-screen integrated in a glass/steel structure of 1.5 x 1.5 x 4.5 $m^3$.

A custom widget toolkit renders the GUI that was specially designed for the NOVA system. Besides being very simple and intuitive, the GUI picks up design elements found elsewhere in the NOVA system (e.g. spheres and circles) and thus enhances the visual link between the software and the hardware.

One of the main reasons for using a transparent HoloPro projection surface was that the user can simultaneously look at the NOVA through the HoloPro and interact with the system (see figure 7). Thus most of the GUI is rendered transparent which gives the interface the same light, high-tech look also found in the hardware.

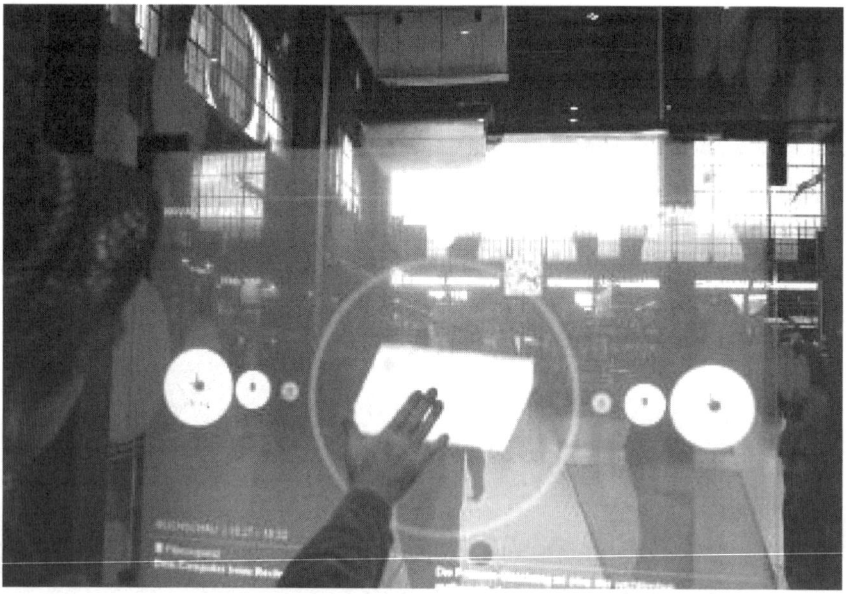

**Fig. 7.** The transparent user interface in action

The GUI has a very simple, three screen interface: a welcome screen that mirrors the current content and invites passers-by to touch the screen, a browser screen that allows the user to activate content (voxel movie, procedural, or interactive), and a help/information screen (see figure 8).

To further enhance the user experience, the console is currently being extended by directional speakers from Sennheiser, facilitating the integration of audio.

For the event market, the NOVA system can also be controlled by Art-Net/DMX512 thus opening a wide range of interaction possibilities with existing stage equipment and show control systems.

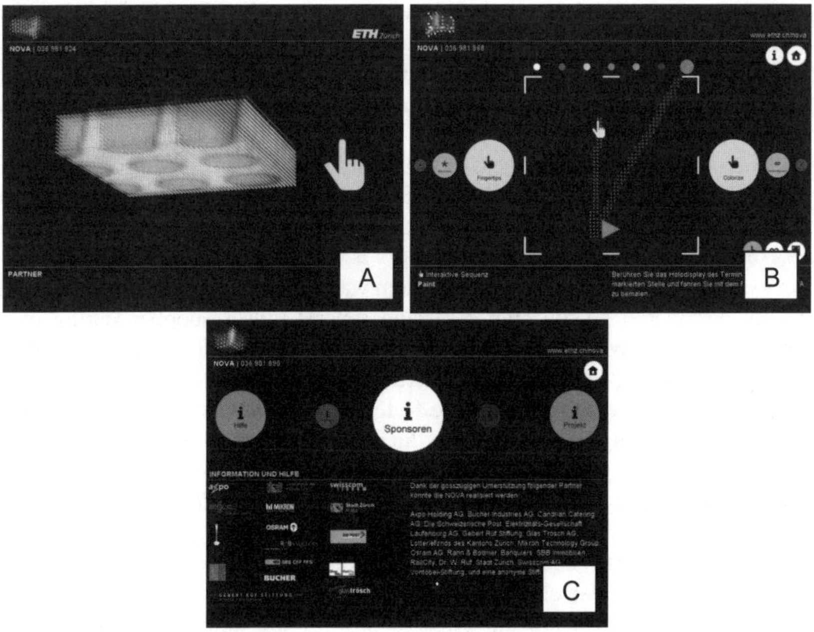


**Fig. 8.** The welcome screen [A], the browser screen (with the interactive paint application activated) [B], and the help/information screen [C]

## 5 Results and Discussion

Creating content for the NOVA display is still one of the main research topics we are working on. Today, creating great hardware is not sufficient – scientists, artist and other creative communities expect a broad software support to realize their ideas with tools they already know. For that reason, we had to learn what tools are used in these communities and methodically introduce appropriate bridges and supporting tools for them in order to open and exploit the possibilities of the NOVA system. This resulted in the creation of the NOVA Studio software, and the various bridges to programming environments such as C++, Java, Python, and Processing.

Even though we are now offering a significantly enlarged palette of tools in comparison to 18 months, the adoption of voxel content creation tools takes a lot longer than anticipated. We learnt that more than the technical hurdles of linking proprietary software format with existing software, the lack of imagination of the individual designer in regard to voxel imaging actually presents the toughest challenge. Apparently, the thinking of the visual community is very much driven by what tools are broadly available and used today, whereas the impact of new solutions on visual concepts beyond the familiar are minimal. New solutions which will be potentially driving tomorrow's imaging opportunities face a lot of resistance and unfortunately until now only a very small community of pioneers could be attracted to explore its potential. Furthermore, the unique visual properties of the medium seem to present an inviting playground to some, whereas others perceive them as imposing factors that not only define the technical dimension of a project but also the conceptual, contextual and formal ones to an extent which can be interpreted as a loss of artistic control.

Although it was clear form the beginning that placing a prototype system in public space has its risks, we clearly underestimated the impact of dust and heat and in turn the amount of maintenance the system requires. Maintenance in a public location tends to be expensive due to the available timeframes (e.g. in Zurich's main station the system can only be accessed during night hours when the station is closed) as well as the involved personnel and equipment (e.g. we need to rent a crane each time we access the NOVA because it can not be fully lowered to the ground).

An example of a typical prototype problem was a design flaw in the power supply that was only discovered on-site after replacing several power supplies during expensive maintenance cycles. What clearly helped in this case was a tight monitoring of the system operating parameters, an appropriate alerting system as well as using programmable hardware (FPGAs, Field Programmable Gate Arrays) where possible. For example, the power supply problem was fixed entirely "in software" by re-programming the hardware.

Dust is still the key problem the hardware is struggling with, despite several successful modifications to the ventilation system. For example, at the interactive console, a two-stage air filter increased the life-span of the projector lamp from a couple of weeks to four months and in turn reduced considerably the number of maintenance cycles. Currently, regular cleaning and filter replacement keep the system within its operating parameters but are the price to pay for the amount of dust present in a highly frequented, open, public location.

Also related to dust was the decision to have a very smooth voxel surface. At the beginning of the project, an integrated voxel cleaning system was discussed (e.g. by spraying water on the voxels) but it turned out that a smooth surface combined with a carefully engineered airflow effectively prevents accumulation of dust on the voxels.

On the interactive side, the first design of the console was a combination of keyboard, trackball and screen in order to have a standard physical appearance and use standard software tools to design the graphical user interface. The evaluation of various installations in public space lead to the conclusion that mechanical interfaces are almost impossible to realize in a sturdy and reliable way while sustaining hundreds of users per day. The next design was based on a multi-touch table, similar to the Microsoft Surface [16]. During discussions and some testing it turned out that horizontal surfaces are impractical in public space because not only will dust accumulate on it but also all sorts of garbage (e.g. beer cans). Furthermore, people tend to (ab)use it as opportunity to sit on. Therefore, a vertical design was the only option that made gravity work in the correct sense while simultaneously preventing most of the inadvertent use.

Another point of concern was the all-glass design of the interactive console that many people considered as invitation to break, scratch and scribble-on. After more than 20 months of operation, the glass was never broken, we can find no scratches on it and very few tags and scribbles have been found and these have been easily erased.

To conclude, although every new installation in public space includes some risks, most of them can be eliminated by proper testing, talking to people working on a day-to-day basis at the location (especially cleaning personal and maintenance staff) and proper monitoring of the system that allows taking countermeasures when necessary. The NOVA system now runs flawlessly with very few exceptional interventions in a public location having more than 300'000 by-passers and approximately 10'000 interactions at the console per day.

**Acknowledgments.** We would like to thank Horao GmbH for supporting this paper as well as the computer systems department of ETH Zurich as well as all sponsors that made the NOVA project possible.

## References

1. Kelly, K.: The Third Culture. Science 279(5353), 992–993 (1998)
2. Snow, C.P.: The Two Cultures and the Scientific Revolution. Cambridge Univ. Press, New York (1959)
3. Brockman, J.: The Third Culture (1996), http://www.edge.org/3rd_culture/index.html
4. MiSPHERE, http://www.barco.com/projection_systems/downloads/BR_MiSPHERE_oct05+.pdf
5. 3D Display Cube, http://www.jamesclar.com/product/2005/3dcubewhite/pic1.html
6. Pixel Cloud, http://www.jasonbruges.com/
7. Cubatron, http://www.nw.com/nw/projects/cubatron/
8. UVA Volume, http://www.uva.co.uk/archives/49
9. Stroustrup, B.: The C++ Programming Language, 2nd edn. Addison-Wesley, Reading (1992)
10. Gosling, J., Joy, B., Steele, G.: The Java Language Specification. Addison-Wesley, Reading (1996)
11. van Rossum, G., Drake, F.L.: The Python Language Reference Manual. Network Theory Ltd. (2003)
12. Reas, C., Fry, B.: Processing: A Programming Handbook for Visual Designers and Artists. MIT Press, Cambridge (2007)
13. Holzner, S.: Eclipse. O'Reilly & Associates (2004)
14. Schreiner, D.: OpenGL Reference Manual: The Official Reference Document to OpenGL, Version 1.2. Addison-Wesley Longman, Amsterdam (1999)
15. HoloPro projection surface, http://www.holopro.de/index.php?id=6&L=1
16. Microsoft Surface Computing, http://www.surface.com

# Four Wheel Drift

Petra Watson[1] and Julie Andreyev[2]

[1] 603 - 1260 Bidwell St., Vancouver, BC, Canada, V6G 2L2
[2] 1490 Adanac St, Vancouver, BC, Canada, V5L 2C3
watsonpr@telus.net, julie@fourwheeldrift.com

**Abstract.** This paper describes *FWDrift* [remix] and *VJFleet* [redux], both performative mobile artworks that fall under the Vancouver-based artist Julie Andreyev's practice *Four Wheel Drift*. In these works customized cars equipped with audio, visual, and interactive technologies cruise the city, serving as hybrid forms seeking engagement with the urban environment. These works take up influences from popular culture. VJ / DJ cultural effects contribute as interventionist strategies that use the city as a canvas to identify and explore contemporary urban landscape through the use of a fleet of cars as mobile, interactive, and experimental platforms.

**Keywords:** VJ / DJ platforms, urban culture, cityscape, car culture, local knowledge, hybridity, interactive technologies, collaborative performance, space, mapping, Situationists.

## 1 Introduction

As an interdisciplinary, technologically mediated and interactive *practice Four-Wheel Drift* maps site-responsive images and sounds taken from cars travelling through the urban landscape. By combining the mobility of the car with audio / visual and interactive components, the private space of the car connects with public space, and serves as a vehicle for critical commentary about the city, its urban controls, systems and environments, and its use. This essay begins by describing the conceptual approaches that informs this practice, and then turns to examine the specifics of *FWDrift* [remix] and *VJFleet* [redux]

This site-specific approach is reliant on the selection of place, space, and location read through a collaborative process. Local participants contribute to the involvement of the *Four-Wheel Drift* team to propose and plan routes that engage the space of the city. This becomes a matrix where local knowledge is situated between technological mediation and urban interaction.

The performances that take place within the urban landscape lead to creative outcomes in which central elements are mobile and details are left to chance. Exploring the everyday, space and culture are the means of negotiating through the urban environment. The performances create an interpretive record and commentary by generating visual forms pertaining to the cityscape as a physical space and diverse social and cultural structure. The process and technological mediation is therefore transformative.

R. Adams, S. Gibson, and S. Müller Arisona (Eds.): DAW/IF 2006/2007, CCIS 7, pp. 488–500, 2008.

## 2 Four Wheel Drift and the Space of the City

Traversing the cityscape is dependent on concrete circumstances and abstract phenomena, and when combined these are plotted through mobility, or terms of exchange, where the city is a place of altered structures, ambiences, and feelings. The performance is then realized as a matrix of images and sounds that allow for both arbitrary and schematic forms. Between the car and its technologies a creative productive process is realized; this outcome introduces an exchange between high and low cultures, between demarcating place and realizing urban situations. This leads to recognizing hybrid forms within notions of transforming images as a statement of diversity, raising notions of fusion within terms of reception, or a discursive approach to modulation and formation, representation and audience. Rather like the space of the city itself.

Taking this concept of performance as cultural practice—characterized as *drift*—local knowledge and technological adaptation determines a visual mapping of the city where topographical and vernacular elements characterize location and place. The essence of the performances characterized as drift leads to site-responsive images and sounds. These are performed as a spatial reading of the city, enabling a broad field of observation taking place through the use of cars, characterized as cultural mobile forms and dispensed of utilitarian functions, except their ability to move through city streets gathering data and mediating visual forms. While this mapping gives emphasis to topographical elements, it investigates a mobile relationship between the city's structures and uses, and between space and cognition.

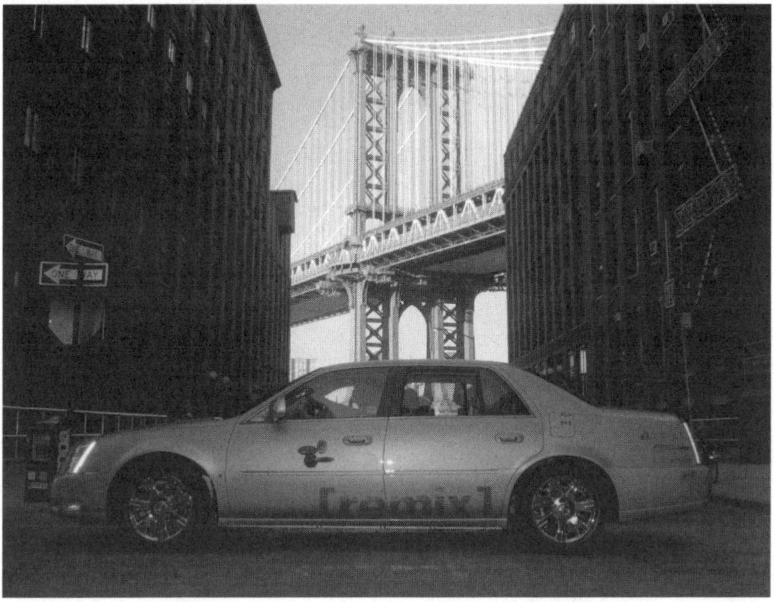


**Fig. 1.** *FWDrift* [remix] data gathering for performance at Pace Digital Gallery, New York, 2005. Photo courtesy of Daniel Mirer.

This bringing together of ideas and practice in the formulation of *Four-Wheel Drift* elicits a form of mediation within material, social, cultural and metaphorical space to map out and address issues of social identity and cultural belonging. This is investigated by extending beyond any formative recognition of fixed capital, secured boundaries or known patterns identified in established maps or topographical schemes. Rather it is an inquiry drawn from subcultures, human practices, communities and cultural identities that permeate private and public space, media, technology, representation, and perception. Taking the concept of space as formed by the circulation and flows of the city, and images and sound captured within the city through time-space compression form a record of the urban landscape. This becomes the viewing matrix and the circulatory fragments of a larger whole.

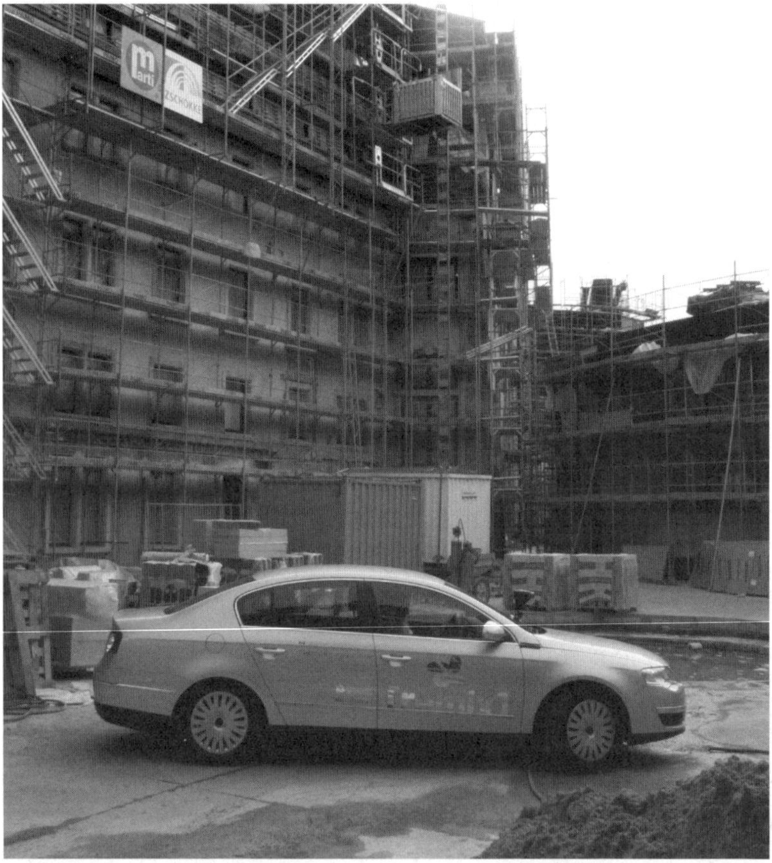

**Fig. 2.** *FWDrift* [remix] data gathering for performance at Digital Art Weeks, Zurich, 2005. Photo courtesy of Anna Kanai.

# 3 Conceptual Approaches

## 3.1 Drift as Metaphor

The notion of drift arises from two sources. The first is linked to car culture and terminology applied to an advanced technique and illegal skill of driving, which produces conditions of experimentation, perception and fantasy that make up a greater subculture. Drift is taken from drifting a racing strategy in which the driver puts the car into a controlled sideways slide to maintain high speed around a corner. Drifting is a racing manoeuvre, a competitive practice, and a sub-cultural activity associated with a popular auto-sport in Japan where drivers challenge each other along curved mountain roads. Drifting competitions, or battle drifts, are also localized judged events that examine the performer's speed, angle and style. The notion of drift also comes from the French term dérive, referring to a tactic formulated by the interventionist Parisian movement, Situationist International (1957-1972). Dérive entails spatial encounters with the urban landscape as a type of liberation, or breaking out of fixed perceptions of the cityscape, and the economies of capital and exploitation. It speaks to flow, and to circulation without fixed controls, leading to passing through and composing real or fictitious forms. This leads to the concept of critical drift that involves techniques of transient passage through varied urban ambiences, in other words, a breaking-out, a phrase applicable within the nomadic desires of car culture.

These two interpretive directions of drift are connected to an interest in everyday life, space, and culture. For the Situationists exploring and interpreting urban Paris during the mid-twentieth century, the concept of drift was tied to a nexus for creating a framework of direct intervention in the urban environment tied to a more human geography. Dérive translates as drift. Situationist artists saw cities as centers of "possibilities and meanings," or as Guy Debord, a prominent member of the group and its self-appointed leader, wrote: "We wanted to break off conditioning, in quest of another use of the urban landscape, in quest of new passions" to be found in urban experiences." [1]

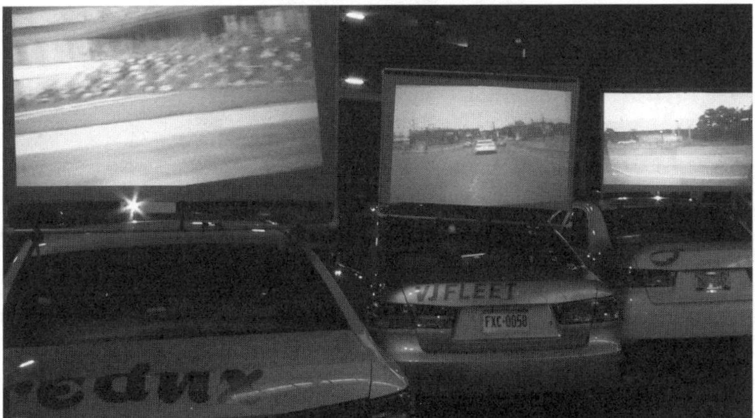


**Fig. 3.** *VJFleet* [redux] performance at SIGGRAPH, Boston, 2006. Photo courtesy of Liana Schmidt.

Chiefly this was described through terms of *psychogeography*, *détournement*, and *unitary urbanism*. These are forms of mapping space and heightened awareness of the social structures of the city, of the complex ways in which cities are divided into distinct quarters based on economic, social and cultural boundaries. For the Situationists these terms were conceptualized through a leisurely walking, or drift, that connected cultural passageways as a thrill of moving into the unknown, or relative space. Andreyev has taken this cultural reading of re-recording and re-conceptualizing conditions of urbanism, and has placed these concepts within interpretative configurations of twentieth century car culture.

### 3.2 Car Cultures as Hybrid Forms in Motion

The project takes its motivation and interactive media from popular culture, specifically custom car and club sub-cultures. Car cultures are present through the selection of specific cars in the performance host city.

The car cultures at the core of this process can be seen as part historical traces of styles, ethnicity and economies, and part acknowledgment of contemporary culture ranging from activities of consumption, social symbols, lifestyles, social identity, cultural memory, and the considerations of urban life and the changes brought by the automobile during the last century. This sense of recent history continues with conditional economic and environmental factors challenging transportation systems, their use and viability, their visibility and metaphors of status and exchange. Like the notion of drift there are aspects of a guerrilla mentality, dispatching metaphorical space that influences perception and consciousness, and emphasizes collective ambiences and impressions. And within the process carried forth through these works this is a transformative remaking of the city through images and sounds.

**Fig. 4.** *VJFleet* [redux] logo. Design by Sandra Hanson.

The performance aspect of the project is informed through an intermingling of *high* and *low* cultures. This is a working process connected to contemporary, interdisciplinary art practices, such as performance art, video projection and interactive reception.

In popular car cultures, cars are customized in ways that may have little to do with practical utility or function. For example, in Vancouver, the diverse population of Asian residents is visually present in *rice-rocket* subcultures. Recent models of Japanese cars are customized, sometimes to an extreme degree, to identify an *elite* owner. This is revealed in micro details; cars are *shaved* of any trim, *nosed* and *decked* to remove any logos. However, to this elite the removal of logos does not make the branding less recognizable, but serves to visually signify the concept of colonization of the car's body

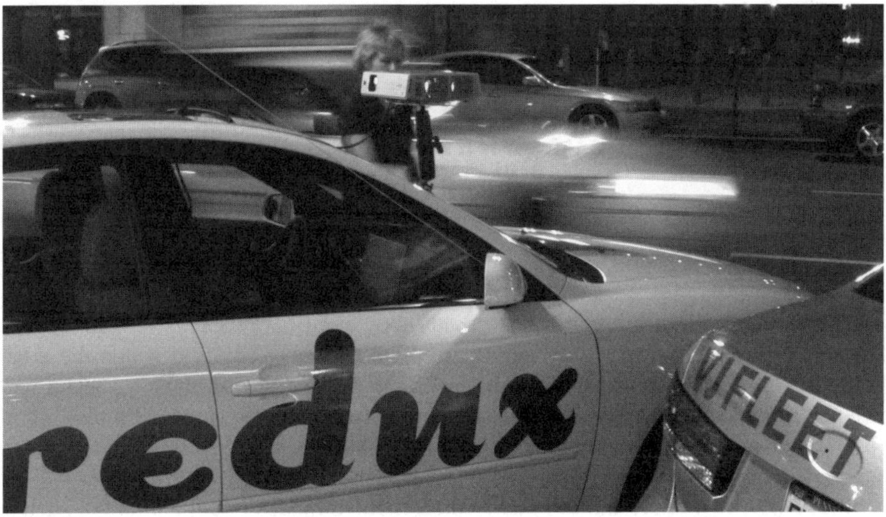


**Fig. 5.** *VJFleet* [redux] performance at SIGGRAPH, Boston, 2006. Photo courtesy of Liana Schmidt.

by the owner. In the roots of U.S. Latino low-rider culture, the car can be seen as a socio-political reference responding to Che Guevara's car (a Chevy Impala). In this low-rider culture, the Impala is seen to represent a form of classicism.

### 3.3 Collaboration at the Centre of Performance

The work as described is a collaborative activity concerned with creating a nuanced and compelling place, reliant on chance, community exchange, yet always displaying the weight of physical sensations against the weightlessness of drift. In responding to images and music, and encounters of familiar and unfamiliar cities, these conditions suggest that the ambiences of a city are both a perceived unity and fragmentation of existence mediated by space and time, and now represented through the terms of the project including community dialogue and technological mediation. These are all complex conditions of encounter and thinking through space, culture and everyday life.

The project is collaborative by design and process with artist Julie Andreyev joining up with: Simon Overstall contributing tactical research and software; Sean Arden tactical research and hardware specialization; Hyuma Frankowski hardware design; and Sandra Hanson graphic design. What arises is a shared space of production and reception, and this results in an interactive temporal space of representation comparative to that which envelops and surrounds us as we go about our daily lives.

The works themselves are collaborative in their making, with the way they interface with the city relying on local participants who come on board as navigators bringing local knowledge, and contributing in this way to the city as a situation meeting up with new encounters, interpretation and audience. For example, within the performance unit of *VJFleet* [redux] gathering data is carried out by three cars, which are brought together as team "players"—or wheels in motion—and forming a collaborative unit, working

**Fig. 6.** *FWDrift* [remix] logo. Design by Sandra Hanson.

separately, yet realized as contributing jointly they contribute their performative tasks. The cars map the cityscape as dynamic perception and recording, and within the urban landscape it is genres of subcultures that offer the possibilities of making contact with different voices and situations now realized through the strategic spaces of transit—both physical and cultural—between image and sound seduction and reflection where both are interpreted, but left unresolved.

Both *FWDrift* [remix] and *VJFleet* [redux] involve modes of collaboration, such as those between the car and driver, between the production team and local participants, and between the performers as they describe the route through the city. The teamwork gives realization to the audio and video archive of the performance. Local knowledge determines the specific approach to visually mapping the city and its vernacular highlights. As the cars are staged as a fleet of performative producers they cruise the city, and conversations, the choice of music played on the cars' stereo, directions from the local participants, and the team's responses are recorded.

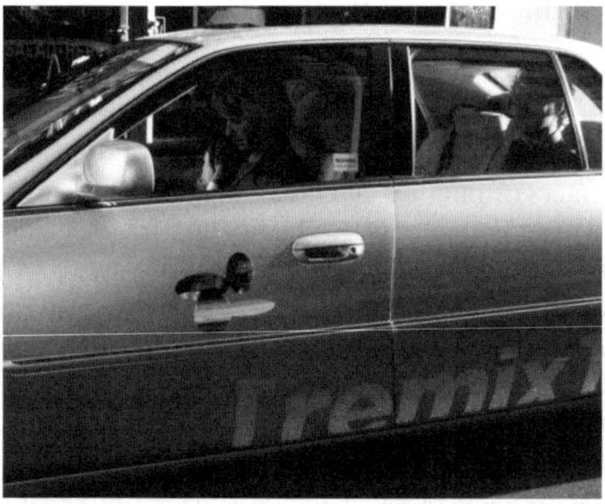

**Fig. 7.** *FWDrift* [remix] data gathering for performance at Pace Digital Gallery, New York, 2005. Photo courtesy of Daniel Mirer.

Each performance begins with a preparatory drive through the city. Yet each time the work is performed, the interpretation of city space is localized and unique through ways that consider the collaborative connections to the local community. A local participant acts as a guide during the passage through the city. Their directions and knowledge of the city contribute not only to the source of mapping the space traveled, but their voice becomes part of the recordings of the travel itself, along with the sounds taken from the cityscape.

Cameras provide video imagery of the city manipulated by the interaction of the cars and drivers using VJ techniques. The movement of the cars, interpreted by sensors and software, create effects on the video images reflecting the choices made during the drive. While their performance capacities have comparisons, each final presentation is quite varied. Creation takes place on-the-fly in a public setting rather than in the isolation of the studio. This studio space is mobile and site-responsive.

As a highly collaborative process the images and sound are produced or performed through interactive strategies defining the work as taking place within a live setting. This interactive inquiry becomes a way to bring together, remix, reduce, and screen, and this is a process of aesthetic formulation, interpretation, and reception of the cityscape and local culture. These are realized as hybrid forms, as fragments dissolved from overall schematic renderings, of known systems and traditional recognition of how the city is not only seen but functions.

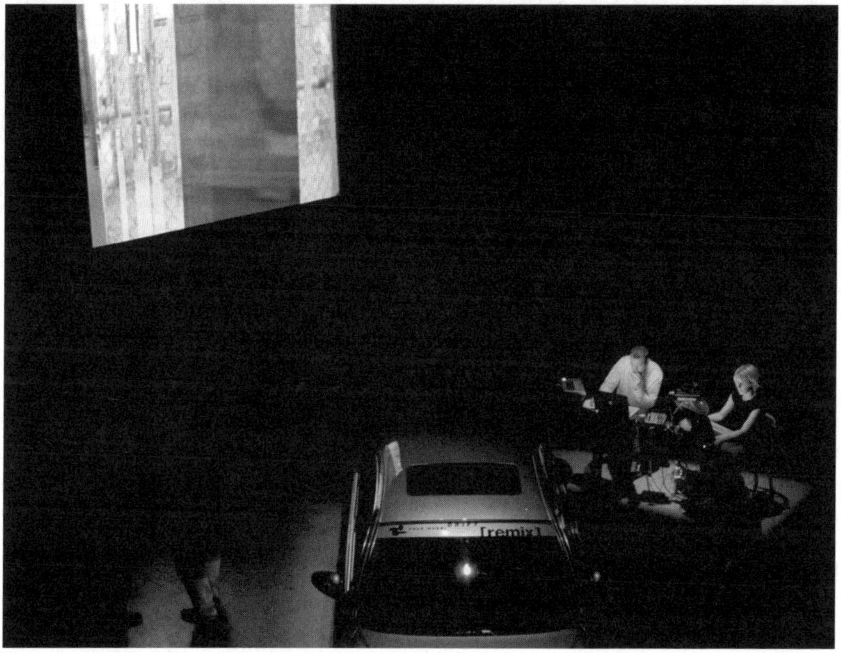


**Fig. 8.** *FWDrift* [remix] performance for Elektra, Montreal, 2005. Photo courtesy of Liana Schmidt.

### 3.4 Psychogeography or the Remaking of Representation

As the cars cruise the urban landscape and map the topography of the city within a critical geography and interventionist practice this performance is associated with the activities of the Situationist. Influential to this work is dérive that entails a spatial

**Fig. 9.** *VJFleet* [redux] performance at SIGGRAPH, Boston, 2006. Photo courtesy of Liana Schmidt.

encounter of urban landscape as a type of free-form through varied urban geographies, urban signs, and ambiences. Drift as a concept offers an innovative surveying of urban landscape, and a new way of representing space to explore the lived environment, and express a relationship of moving through and perceiving space and place that extends beyond the city street map to a diversity localized by the lived everyday. Imminent to the work is an urban navigational system that operates independently of any planned network, or pattern of circulation. Rather it presents a psychogeography of information picking up fragments, and freeing up a space of thinking about the city and its permutations that define an urban consciousness and mode of living. Drifting leads to bypassing urban spectacle by taking up activity and sensation, and reformulating the city as a hybrid discourse, and as a lived space of everyday interpretation.

Comparatively, in Julie Andreyev's work local knowledge of the cityscape and its elements of geography and culture are brought into dialogue through art. By using the car as a platform for experimentation, a rethinking of the artist's studio space occurs, as does the involvement of art in a non-traditional space. Local knowledge taken from genres of popular culture, public space, and the private space of the car are reconsidered and reconnected through a technological interactive grid.

# 4 *VJFleet* [redux] and *FWDrift* [remix] Technical Overview and Performance

## 4.1 *VJFleet* [redux]

*VJFleet* [redux] is a work reliant on interactive and audio/visual technologies to produce a performance-based work that sets out to explore the city as a mobile tableau. Subcultures are exposed and explored to become strategies to negotiate through the city. These are systems of collaborative networking that draw from local sources such as DJ and VJ culture, and these cultures then move into this application of new media practice.

While driving through city streets, the cars remain independent within the fleet that contributes to the performance. The cars are fitted with sensors that read acceleration, braking, turning, and weight-shifting, a video camera that provides a view out the front or side window, a microphone placed in the engine compartment and in the passenger area to send input to a digital audio recorder, a video projector and screen on the rear windshield, custom-cut removable vinyl decals to style or custom mark the cars, and laptops to process information.

In this work, digital information is a record of the driver's actions, and is then processed by a Max/Jitter software patch that manipulates the video feed from the camera. The passengers and crew's conversation and local music are recorded via the interior microphone. The audio within both the car and the exterior environment is recorded via the microphone in the engine compartment.

When the cars are stopped for a performance, the video is then projected on screens and the team uses a custom Max/MSP patch to sample and manipulate the audio clips and send them to the car's sound system. Software syncs the three channels of video clips and plays them on the screens.

Software is used to remix the audio and video recordings based on the sensor data of the drive (i.e. acceleration, braking and turning). The DJ uses audio software informed by well-developed granulation techniques to transform the audio recordings of the drive into discrete, musical micro-units that are then arranged by the sensor data into new sound. In this way, the physical experience of driving in the city is the decisive factor in the eventual manipulations of the materials during the performance. Each time the project is performed the interpretation of city space is unique, and elements of perception are localized to each site. Normally in a car environment, the driver singularly consumes music. But now each car in the fleet has a specific role to play in the collaborative role of music making.

These terms of embracing space can be compared to those found in the image of a panorama, a type of seeing signified by taking everything in at a glance. But the images of the work itself aspires to remain fragmentary, and does so in both representation, and the process taking place. The soundscape is more readily encompassing in gathering and presentation. The city is a multidimensional space of recording, presentation and viewing, and the data gathered is displayed to the audience within public space itself, rather than a specified viewing location such as a club or gallery.

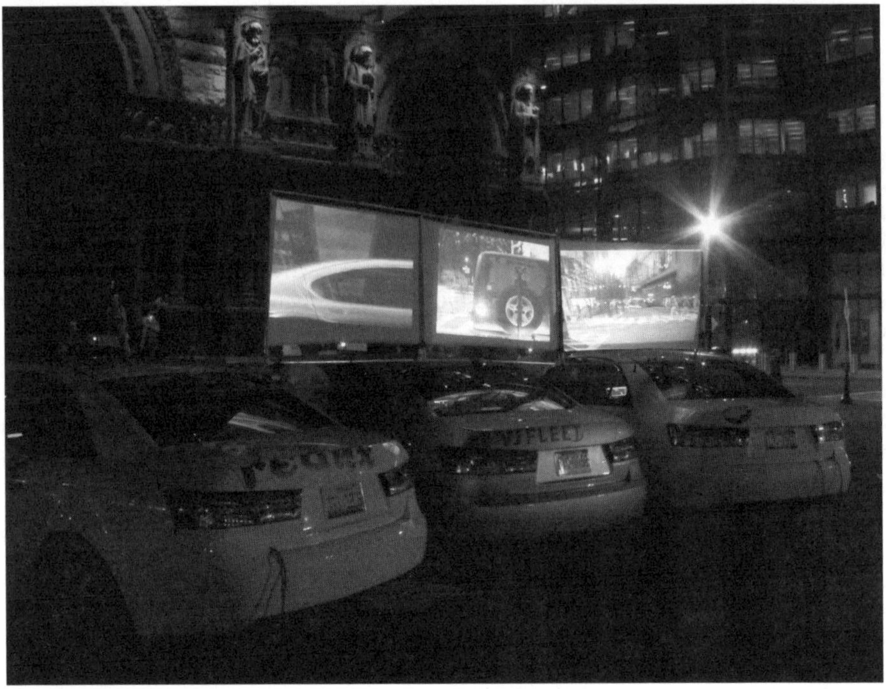

**Fig. 10.** *VJFleet* [redux] performance at SIGGRAPH, Boston, 2006. Photo courtesy of Liana Schmidt.

### 4.2 *FWDrift* [remix]

In *FWDrift* [remix] the installation / performance presents an audio archive captured by a drive through the urban landscape, and is treated via software and a DJ to create a live soundscape. In the *FWDrift* [remix] performance, the DJ manipulates the recordings in the audio playlist for the creation of new musical arrangements. Each sound source has a particular role: the engine sounds are used to create the baseline, conversations between the local participant and other passengers create the vocals. As the soundscape plays, the VJ uses software to mix and project a video panorama. Many video tracks can be selected and played, and certain areas of each video track can be selected to be played. In this sense the video mix can be seen as a moving collage, and as a panorama, or as an overview, representing varying locations of the city within one presentation.

This image / sound exploration is a place of movement and transformation; nothing stands still. This is a reflection of modern spectacles of entertainment, especially characterized in the work by international club cultures, terms of private and public space, and gallery viewing situations.

Drift links up with *remix* to conceptualize these ideas of seeking out a matrix of representation and strategies of intervention. Remix refers to producing a different version of an existing song or cultural material. It is a term used to describe the

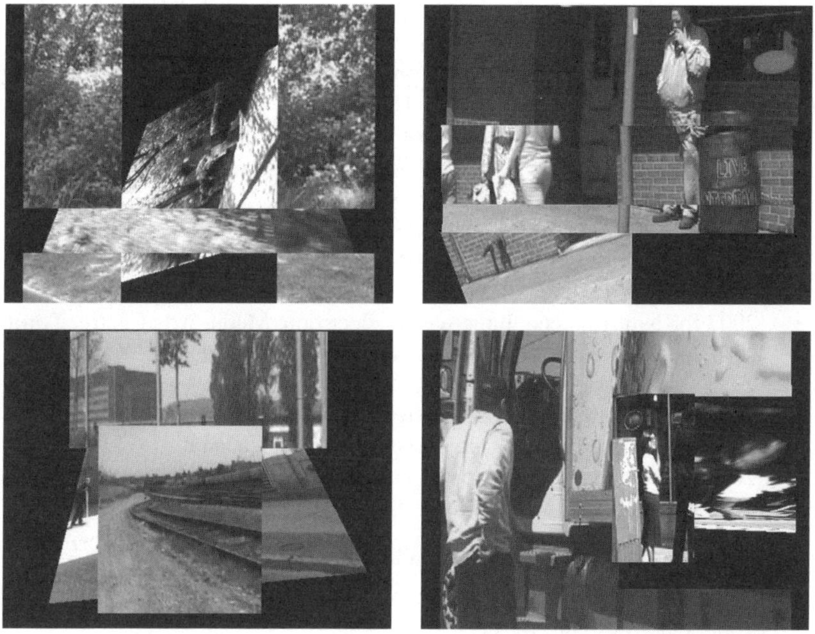

**Fig. 11.** Video stills from a *FWDrift* [remix] performance

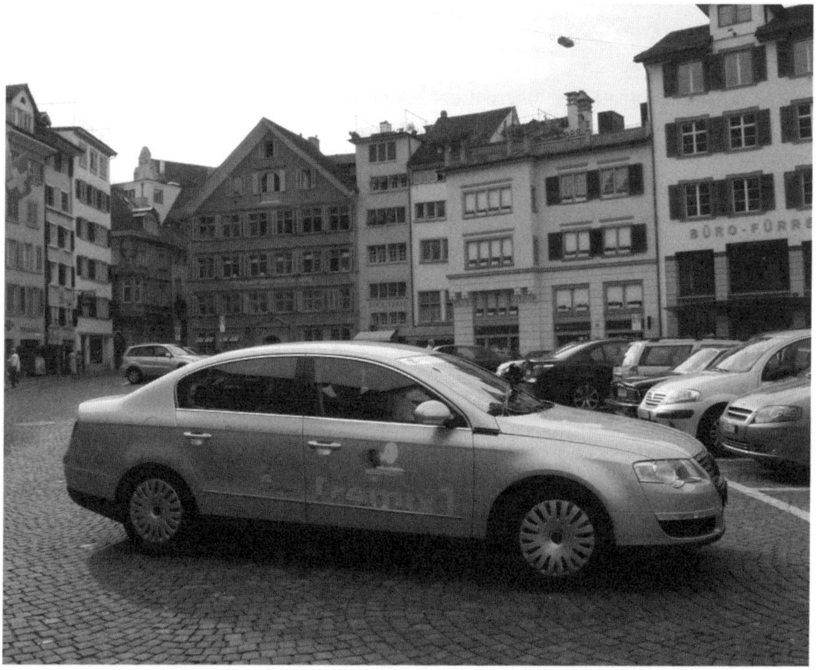

**Fig. 12.** *FWDrift* [remix] data gathering for performance at Digital Art Weeks, Zurich, 2005. Photo courtesy of Anna Kanai.

reformatting or fusion of music taken from various genres. Therefore a piece of existing recorded music is transposed usually with the melodic line removed and added special effects, and this type of processing exemplifies the reformatting or remixing of music, or image and sound. This melding of form, the mixing of sound can also include adding text, audio or music to a film, recording or broadcast.

## 5 Works Performed

*FWDrift* [remix] performances have taken place in:

- 2007 for Nuit Blanche, InterAccess Electronic Media Arts Centre, Toronto;
- 2007 Interactive Futures Conference, Victoria, Canada;
- 2006 Digital Art Weeks, Zurich;
- 2006 Computational Poetics Conference, Vancouver;
- 2006 Interactive Futures Conference, Victoria, Canada;
- 2005 Pace Digital Gallery, New York;
- 2005 Elektra Festival, Montreal.

*VJFleet* [redux] performances have taken place in:

- 2006 SIGGRAPH 2006, Boston;
- 2005 Viper Festival, Basel;
- 2003 New Forms Festival, Vancouver.

## References

1. Knabb, K. (ed.): Situationist International Anthology. Bureau of Public Secrets, Berkeley (1981)
2. Oettermann, S.: The Panorama: History of a Mass Medium. Zone Books, New York (1997)
3. Sussman, E. (ed.): On the Passage of a few people through a rather brief moment in time: the Situationist International 1957 - 1972, pp. 1957–1972. The MIT Press, Cambridge (1989)

# Author Index

Printing: Mercedes-Druck, Berlin
Binding: Stein+Lehmann, Berlin